ALASTAIR S
SPECIAL PLACES

KT-147-770

ALASTAIR SAWDAY'S
SPECIAL PLACES TO STAY

BRITISH
HOTELS, INNS
& OTHER PLACES

Opinionated, honest, useful, handsome – and popular!

EDITED BY TOM BELL

£14.99/$23.95

ALASTAIR SAWDAY'S
SPECIAL PLACES TO STAY

BRITISH
BED &
BREAKFAST

Sleeker, smarter, and more interesting – B&Bs
just get better and better.

EDITED BY NICOLA CROSSE

£14.99/$23.95

ALASTAIR SAWDAY'S
SPECIAL PLACES TO STAY

BRITISH
BED & BREAKFAST FOR
**GARDEN
LOVERS**

Discover gorgeous B&Bs with outstanding gardens –
and owners who want to share both with you.

EDITED BY NICOLA CROSSE

£14.99/$23.95

ALASTAIR SAWDAY'S
SPECIAL PLACES TO STAY

IRELAND

Come to rediscover your easy, human self among
the most hospitable people in Ireland.

EDITED BY ANN COOKE YARBOROUGH

£12.99/$23.95

Credit card orders (free p&p) 01275 395431
www.specialplacestostay.com

In US: credit card orders (800) 243-0495, 9am-5pm EST,
24-hour fax (800) 820-2329 www.globepequot.com

Fourth edition
Copyright © 2007
Alastair Sawday Publishing Co. Ltd

Published in 2007
Alastair Sawday Publishing,
The Old Farmyard,
Yanley Lane, Long Ashton
Bristol BS41 9LR
Tel: +44 (0)1275 395430
Fax: +44 (0)1275 393388
Email: info@specialplacestostay.com
Web: www.specialplacestostay.com

A catalogue record for this book is
available from the British Library.

Design:
Caroline King

Maps & Mapping:
Maidenhead Cartographic Services Ltd

Printing:
Butler & Tanner, Frome, UK

UK Distribution:
Penguin UK, 80 Strand, London

ISBN-13: 978-1-901970-89-0

Paper and Printing: We have sought the lowest
possible ecological 'footprint' from the production
of this book, using super-efficient machinery,
vegetable inks and high environmental standards.
Our printer is ISO 14001-registered.

The publishers have made every effort to
ensure the accuracy of the information
in this book at the time of going to
press. However, they cannot accept
any responsibility for any loss, injury
or inconvenience resulting from the
use of information contained therein.

ALASTAIR SAWDAY'S
SPECIAL PLACES

PUBS & INNS
OF ENGLAND & WALES

Contents

Alastair Sawday Publishing

Our main aim is to publish beautiful guidebooks but, for us, the question of who we are is also important. For who we are shapes the books, the books shape your holidays, and thus are shaped the lives of people who own these 'special places'. So we are trying to be a little more than 'just a publishing company'.

New eco offices

In January 2006 we moved into our new eco offices. With super-insulation, underfloor heating, a wood-pellet boiler, solar panels and a rainwater tank, we have a working environment benign to ourselves and to the environment. Lighting is low-energy, dark corners are lit by sun-pipes and one building is of green oak. Carpet tiles are from Herdwick sheep in the Lake District.

Environmental & ethical policies

We make many other gestures: company cars run on gas or recycled cooking oil; kitchen waste is composted and other waste recycled; cycling and car-sharing are encouraged; the company only buys organic or local food; we don't accept web links with companies we consider unethical; we bank with the ethical Triodos Bank.

We have used recycled paper for some books but have settled on selecting paper and printing for their low energy use. Our printer is British and ISO14001-certified and together we will work to reduce our environmental impact.

In 2005 we won a Business Commitment to the Environment Award and in April 2006 we won a Queen's Award for Enterprise in the Sustainable Development category. All this has boosted our resolve to promote our green policies. Our flagship gesture, however, is carbon offsetting; we calculate our carbon emissions and plant trees to compensate and support projects overseas that plant trees or reduce carbon use.

Carbon offset

SCAD in South India, supports the poorest of the poor. The money we send to offset our carbon emissions will be used to encourage village tree planting and, eventurally, low-carbon technologies. Why India? Because the money goes a long way and admin costs are very low.
www.salt-of-the-earth.org.uk

Ethics

But why, you may ask, take these things so seriously? You are just a little publishing company, for heaven's sake! Well, is there any good argument for not taking them seriously? The world, by the admission of the vast majority of scientists, is in trouble. If we do not change our ways urgently we will doom the planet and all its creatures – whether innocent or not – to a variety of possible catastrophes. To maintain the status quo is unacceptable. Business does much of the damage and should undo it, and provide new models.

Pressure on companies to produce Corporate Social Responsibility policies is mounting. We are trying to keep ahead of it all, yet still to be as informal and human as possible – the antithesis of 'corporate'.

The books – and a dilemma

So, we have created fine books that do good work. They promote authenticity, individuality and good local and organic food – a far cry from corporate culture. Rural economies, pubs, small farms, villages and hamlets all benefit. However, people use fossil fuel to get there. Should we aim to get our readers to offset their own carbon emissions, and the B&B and hotel owners too?

We are gradually introducing green ideas into the books: the Fine Breakfast scheme that highlights British and Irish B&B owners who use local and organic food; celebrating those who make an extra environmental effort; gently encouraging the use of public transport, cycling and walking. Last year we published *Green Places to Stay* focusing on responsible travel and eco-properties around the globe.

Our Fragile Earth series

The 'hard' side of our environmental publishing is the Fragile Earth series: *The Little Earth Book*, *The Little Food Book* and *The Little Money Book*. They consist of bite-sized essays, polemical, hard-hitting and well researched. They are a 'must have' for anyone who seeks clarity about some of the key issues of our time. Last year we have also published *One Planet Living*.

Lastly – what is special?

The notion of 'special' is at the heart of what we do, and highly subjective. We discuss this in the introduction. We take huge pleasure from finding people and places that do their own thing – brilliantly; places that are unusual and follow no trends; places of peace and beauty; people who are kind and interesting – and genuine.

We seem to have touched a nerve with thousands of readers; they obviously want to stay in special places rather than the dull corporate monstrosities that have disfigured so many of our cities and towns. Life is too short to be wasted in the wrong places. A night in a special place can be a transforming experience.

Alastair Sawday

Acknowledgements

David Hancock is the reason why this is such a fine book. He knows virtually every pub in it. I have yet to mention a pub to him that he doesn't already know. It is a near-encyclopedic knowledge, and his enthusiasm is boundless. He loves the sort of pubs that all of us in this office consider special, and he has introduced us to hundreds more.

David has marshalled a platoon of brilliant and devoted 'inspectors'. That mechanistic and limited word fails to tell us what they do. They carry David's enthusiasms with them and have co-created this book. We also owe much to: Maria, for her data-base wizardry and attention to detail, Julia and her production team, for their careful completion of a complex project and Jo, for her sensitive writing and text-tweaking.

Alastair Sawday

Series Editor Alastair Sawday

Editor David Hancock

Editorial Director Annie Shillito

Writing David Hancock, David Ashby, Jo Boissevain, Elizabeth Carter, Charles Edmondson-Jones, Philip Moss, Mark Taylor, Mandy Wragg

Inspections David Hancock, David Ashby, Elizabeth Carter, Colin Cheyne, Rebecca Harris, Charles Edmondson-Jones, Philip Moss, Aideen Reid, Mark Taylor, Jenny White, Glyn Williams, Mandy Wraggs

Accounts Bridget Bishop, Jessica Britton, Christine Buxton, Sandra Hassell, Sally Ranahan

Editorial Jackie King, Jo Boissevain, Maria Serrano

Production Julia Richardson, Rachel Coe, Tom Germain, Rebecca Thomas

Sales & Marketing & PR Andreea Petre Goncalves, Sarah Bolton

Web & IT Russell Wilkinson, Chris Banks, Isabelle Deakin, Joe Green, Brian Kimberling

A word from Alastair Sawday

Like a lady's dress, an introduction should be long enough to cover the subject and short enough to be interesting. Is that possible in this case? Pubs are a noble subject, and here we have another fine book, its pages filled to overflowing with good news, good brews, good people, good ideas and hope for the future.

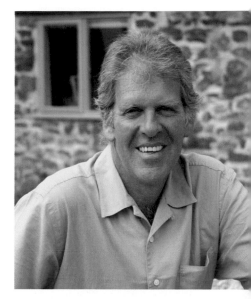

For example, there is news here of a pub in Suffolk that has been bought, and saved, by the community and now performs the role of shop, community centre, post office and boozer. That must be the way forward – pubs rescuing rural life by redefining themselves. It is inspiring and timely. Never before has the British village, and the best of our traditions that go with it, been so threatened by the malign forces of market capitalism. Vast and unaccountable economic forces prey on them, circle them and engulf them. What the economic system fails completely to destroy, the supermarkets finish off. They do a brilliant job of preparing the ground for the final assaults. They rarely lose. But the goal posts are moving; once villagers become aware that they are citizens first and foremost, rather than consumers, there is little that they cannot achieve.

The increase in the number of local breweries, too, is a fine story. David Hancock, in his opening passages here, tells us that there are now over 400 of them. In the US this revolution is even more exciting, with micro-breweries flourishing as never before. So there is hope – lots of it. All that is needed is for people to wake up, climb out of their boxes and engage with their fellows. Banging off letters on the computer isn't enough. Let's 'get political' – albeit with a small 'p'.

This pub guide is now one of Britain's favourites, and it is racing up the ladder of popularity edition by edition. The secret? We have strong opinions and are not afraid to express them. We really like these pubs.

Alastair Sawday

PUBS AND INNS THAT STAND OUT FROM THE CROWD

hospitable and the little known. We look for a genuine welcome from hands-on licensees, good local, seasonal or organic food, happy staff and a easy charm. Sometimes it's hard to put your finger on what exactly it is that draws people back, but it could be a memorable meal or a cosy drink by a log fire, a bedroom with a beautiful view or a sloping riverside garden. The result is 650 pubs and inns so engaging that they merit a half or full-page entry, and a further 250 in our Worth a Visit section at the back.

Our quest to keep pace with the fascinating and ever-evolving pub scene continues and we bring you an even bigger and better Edition 4. Within these pages are pubs and inns that stand out from the crowd, 900 of the very best in England and Wales, about 100 of which are new to this edition, inspected and selected because we believe them to be special and think you will too.

Alastair Sawday's *Special Places* guides are about individuality, and our inspectors have trawled England and Wales in search of the quirky, the unusual, the hugely

How we go about it
We have visited every entry in this guide to check on atmosphere, style and warmth of welcome. Reader feedback and re-inspections have seen some pubs fall from grace; others have been nudged into 'Worth a Visit' (see below) as landlords change and chefs move on; these await re-inspection. We pick up those details that cannot be gleaned over the internet or the phone, and we write the descriptions ourselves, avoiding cliché. If a pub is in, we think it's special, and the write-up should tell you if it's your sort of special.

Photo left, britainonview.com/Adrian Houston
Photo right The Thomas Cubitt, entry 302

Introduction

Our 'Best For...' choices listed at the back are pubs that stand out as the best of their type. Among them are country locals whose owners are passionate about everything organic, and that includes the beers. You'll find a city pub with a fascinating literary past, a Yorkshire tavern whose gas lamps hiss, and an inn with saltmarsh views and stylishly simple rooms. The Worth a Visit section includes those pubs that didn't make a full entry this time but are still well worth seeking out. In this section, too, you will find excellent pubs that have recently changed hands and foodie pubs that we believe to be on the up. These pubs also appear on our maps, so you can see where they are.

Photo The Wildebeest Arms, entry 341

Feedback, please

Things evolve at an astonishing pace in the world of pubs and inns . So let us know whether your experience at any of the places in this book has been a success or a disappointment or a bit of both. Or if you hear that a pub has changed hands, or if you think a pub listed under 'Worth a Visit' deserves upgrading. Your input is always appreciated. Tell us, too, about any new pubs you have found and think deserves to be in our guide. There is a form at the back of the book – or go to www.specialplacestostay.com and click on 'contact'.

Trends – the changing pub scene

Rural pubs have had to change, and, in some cases, diversify in order to meet social change and the demands of today's pub-goer. Dotted across the country, in decreasing numbers, are Britain's gems, unspoilt and refreshingly plain, many in the family for decades (centuries even). With the closure of village shops and halls, some pubs have become the very hub of the community, and a few are even owned by consortiums of villagers. A growing number also operate as the local shop and post office.

But the key to the survival of Britain's rural pub is the provision of good food – and, increasingly, the added appeal of a few cosy bedrooms. Pubs are now seen as places to eat, drink or sleep. And, with the nation's spiralling interest in a healthier lifestyle, people have come to expect food that is fresh and vital, not tired, microwaved or frozen.

Smoking ban

The single most important challenge facing pubs in 2007 is the smoking ban. It came into force in Wales on 2nd April and extends into England on 1st July. A good number of the top food pubs listed in this guide went smoke-free last year and have seen trade increase because of it. Community pubs, where food is not integral to the business, may at first suffer a drop in trade. However, many pubs will be upgrading their outdoor areas, providing heaters and shelter for steadfast smokers.

Pubs with rooms ⊨

A growing number of pubs and inns combine a relaxing, informal atmosphere with fantastic food and bedrooms to match – and at lower prices than many hotels. It's true that some pubs are virtually indistinguishable from hotels, but a lively bar serving real beer as well as food should put them into the classic inn category. And you can ask for a room at the back or a room away from the pub if you are worried about noise at weekends. Other pubs with rooms are more humble village affairs where the enthusiasm to get things right in the bar extends

upstairs. So the next time you take a weekend or business break, dismiss those roadside lodges and impersonal hotels in favour of a friendly country inn. Our Pubs with Rooms section has almost doubled in number from the last edition to 111, with the Olive Branch in Rutland, the Punch Bowl in Cumbria and the Inn at Grinshill in Shropshire joining our award winners.

Room inspections

We are known for our *Special Places to Stay* books. Each entry is inspected and included only if we like it. We are not interested in 'tick' boxes or grading systems as they are incapable of accounting for the things we hold dear: character, style, warmth of welcome. Owners pay for their bedrooms to be mentioned in our books but it is not possible for anyone to buy their way in; the fee goes towards the cost of the inspection process and a web site presence www.specialplacestostay.com. So look for the room symbol ⊨, the coloured entry flag on the map, or view our special 'rooms' pages (pp. 30-57.)

Gastropubs

A term born in London and embraced by the rest of the country. In London, basic backstreet boozers continue to be transformed into thriving food pubs where restaurant quality food is served in casual but contemporary surroundings. The

Introduction

ripple-effect out of the capital has been impressive, and the trend for young entrepreneurs and talented chefs to buy failing pubs and re-invent them as pub-bistros continues to gather pace. Now pubs are becoming a serious challenge to restaurants as a wave of casual dining envelops the nation.

Pub or restaurant – a fine line
Too many gastropubs are losing sight of their pubby roots as cash tills tot up meals rather than pints of beer. High rents dictated by owner pub companies and big breweries, combined with a steady decline in beer sales and stricter drink-driving laws, has seen food begin to dominate the rural scene, to the extent that villagers are losing their 'local' in favour of high food revenues.

Photo left Fleece on the Green, entry 398
Photo right The Punch Bowl Inn, entry 91

If 90% of the tables are prepared for dining and covered in 'reserved' signs, if you are greeted with a menu and "have you booked a table, sir", and if the pristine bar is virtually devoid of real ale handpumps, then you can be pretty sure your once-treasured boozer has metamorphosed into a restaurant.

The best food pubs in England and Wales are listed within these pages and all strike a good balance between being a restaurant/bistro and a pub. A pub is a pub when you find three or more (often local) real ales, a genuine welcome for those popping in for a pint, and an easy-going, convivial atmosphere.

Wines – an improving picture
The rise and rise of the pub-bistro has not only seen a transformation in the quality of food being served. Walk into any foodie pub and you are likely to find chalked-up wines lists that reflect the landlord's personal tastes, with wines often sourced from a range of small merchants, even individual vineyards, and chosen to match the style of food served up in the kitchen.

Some pubs may only have a dozen or so wines on their lists but they're likely to have been chosen with care and blend the New World with the Old. And there are pubs that take their wine so seriously they have

Introduction

Three Crowns in Ullingswick, Herefordshire and the Talbot Inn at Knightwick, Worcestershire becoming venues for monthly farmers' markets, while others have created farm shops on the premises. These include the Spotted Dog in Penshurst, Kent, 'Victoria's Plums' at the Sun Inn in Dedham, Essex, and The Parrot at Forest Green in Surrey, where Charles and Linda Gotto have created a farm shop inside the pub, with meats supplied from their own farm. On a smaller scale, it is not uncommon to find deli counters by the bar filled with an array of goodies prepared in the pub kitchen. It's a definite trend!

impressive lists that can easily match the best restaurants. Landlords are also investing in wine stopper preservation systems that allow them to offer a raft of wines by the glass, often up to ten and sometimes as many as 20.

Local food champions

These chefs are champions of local produce and believers that gastronomy is rooted in the soil. The ingredients they use are fresh, mostly seasonal and come from the best regional suppliers. We applaud those pubs that are banishing laminated menus listing deep-frozen foods in favour of fresh, homemade meals.

The passion for local foods and small suppliers has seen pubs like the

Timeless gems

Often family-owned and unchanged down the years, in historic or unusual buildings, or buried down a city backstreet or a country lane, these belong to Britain's diminishing breed of traditional pubs. We have unearthed an interesting crop. At some, expect few frills and modern-day intrusions, just basic parlour rooms, lively banter, ale tapped from the cask and, if you're lucky, soup and sandwiches. Others offer more in the way of food and facilities but remain genuinely unspoilt examples of the great British pub, and include our award winners, the Harrow at Steep, Hampshire, the Bridge at Topsham, Devon, and the Black Bull in Frosterly, Durham.

Photo, The Bridge Inn, entry 144

Pub as hub – community pubs

A well-loved pub with a big welcome, a crackling fire and the landlord's personality etched into the very fabric of the building lifts the spirits. Add tasty food and fine beer and you're in pub heaven. A village pub like this draws the community together and meeting in it knock meeting in a soulless village hall into a cocked hat. Our award winning Community Pubs – the White Hart in Otley, Suffolk, the Old Poets' Corner at Ashover, Derbyshire, and the Duke of York in Iddesleigh, Devon – are a pleasure to visit.

Such pubs may even encourage folk to settle in the area. They generally have thriving darts, pool and football teams and are often the first venue for raffles, carol singing, farmers' markets and polling stations. A growing number are taking on an even wider community role, becoming part-time post offices, shops and delicatessens as village stores are forced to close.

It sounds too good to be true. Yet the reality is that 26 pubs close each month across Britain. Why? High rents and falling sales are forcing publicans out. Rocketing property prices make bricks and mortar more valuable that the business itself, so the pub becomes ripe for conversion – or sale – for residential use. And many villages are becoming

dormitory settlements whose villagers take little active involvement in the community. However, some pubs threatened with closure have been bought by village consortiums, with locals chipping in cash and becoming shareholders. With the right landlord at the helm such a pub can thrive.

Seasonal, local and organic food

The competitive global marketplace has driven our eating habits for too long, fobbed us off with cheap food and deprived us of the ebb and flow of the seasons. In 2001 there was the salutary wake-up call of a foot and mouth epidemic, followed by more recent scares such as the cancer risk associated with farmed

Introduction

salmon. Now the message is filtering through: mass production comes at a cost. And, as a happy antidote to this, and a reaction to it, the number of farmers' markets continues to rise, re-introducing us to real food and the joys of seasonal and artisanal produce. 'Local', 'seasonal' and 'organic' have become the buzz words.

Many pubs trumpet regional and seasonal food – Cumbrian ham in Cumbria, fish from the nearest coast, asparagus in season and partridge from the local shoot. On such menus lamb is not just lamb, it's Lancastrian and heather-reared. Cheeses are west country. Beef is Herefordshire. Smoked salmon is

Photo left, Black Bull Inn, entry 157
Photo right, Greene Oak, entry 18

Irish – and, increasingly, wild. The emphasis on regionality and authenticity, so deep-rooted in Italy, France and Spain, is gaining momentum here.

Paradoxes exist. We may raise our eyebrows at the prospect of Kenyan beans in February and Peruvian asparagus in October yet insist on freshly squeezed orange juice at breakfast. Most of us appreciate lamb all year round. And who can say whether a factory-farmed tomato is better or worse than air-freighted organic? The real battle is to persuade producers to move away from artificially grown, extended-shelf-life, textbook-perfect produce, and to rear (and slaughter) livestock humanely so that the meat is full of texture and taste.

What is 'Modern British' food?
Modern British cooking, first defined in 1987, puts the best British produce in the spotlight, demands a freshness of approach (let the ingredients do the talking) and shows a respect for seasonal bounty. Increasingly, 'Mod Brit' has also come to mean a nod to Mediterranean and oriental shores – hence linguine with roasted peppers and squid with lime and chilli.

'British rustic' cooking
Lately, in some of the more adventurous gastro-kitchens, an

Introduction

unexpected element has come into play. A number of chefs are moving away from the Mediterranean and 'fusion' fixation of the past decade and placing an emphasis on British tradition. Hence the welcome revival of British dishes of low or 'rustic' origin, from Lancashire hot pot to ginger parkin.

So, food that was once confined to below stairs turns out to be the trendiest thing on your plate. These British-rustic delicacies tend to have simple, strong flavours and go rather well with a pint. Look out for:

- Bath chap – pig's cheek, as delicious as a trotter
- faggots – meat balls that developed as a way of using up all the unwanted bits of pig, served with mushy peas
- black pudding – a large sausage made of pig's blood, suet, bread crumbs and oatmeal, sautéed and served with mash
- champ – of Irish descent: potatoes mashed, mixed with onions, lashings of butter, and served with sausages
- sausages – voguishly served with onion marmalade (also known as 'confit') and created from venison, wild boar or Cumberland pork (provenance is all)
- fish and chips, served with 'minted' mushy peas and hand-cut chips
- oxtail and kidney pudding; smoked eel on bread; potted ham with chutney; herring and potato salad
- bubble and squeak – a tasty way of using up yesterday's mashed potatoes and cooked cabbage, fried until crunchy. Originally, the dish included chopped boiled beef

Whatever happened to duck à l'orange?

Gastropubs Sweeping the land, the new bistros of Britain are blurring the distinction between casual-chic restaurants and old-fashioned drinking dens.

Slow Food Anti fast-food movement founded in Italy, inching its way into Britain and most conspicuous in Ludlow. Based on the philosophy that food tastes better when grown organically, harvested locally and eaten in season. The movement champions artisan-producers.

- Pan-fried steak, sea bass etc are in; 'fried' is out. 'Deep-fried' is acceptable if it's calamari or cod.
- Trio of chops – on every modish menu. Look out for trio of fish, trio of ice cream, trio of crème brulée.
- Jus A concentrated reduction made from meat juices and wine: gravy without the flour.
- Coulis A pretty puddle of fruit or vegetable purée. May disappear from menus as ultra-plain garnish gains momentum.
- Triple-booked chips Heston

Blumenthal's trademark (viz. the Hind's Head, Bray). Expect to see these popping up on others' menus in 2007.

- Baguette is out, ciabatta in. And sandwiches are called panini.
- Bruschetta – toasted Italian sourdough bread rubbed with garlic and drizzled with oil; sometimes served with melting mozzarella.
- Polenta – the cornmeal cooked in a similar manner to porridge is still in fashion, eaten hot with a little butter or cooled until firm, cut into squares and fried in olive oil. Often mixed with cheese.
- Pancetta Italian bacon, cured with salt and spices but not smoked. Good with scallops.
- Carpaccio Thin shavings of raw beef fillet, drizzled with olive oil and lemon juice or served with a mayonnaise or mustard sauce.
- Duck confit – salted duck poached slowly in fat to preserve it; rich, gamey and meltingly tender.
- Braised lamb shank Slow-cooked front leg – a ubiquitous dish on the bistro-pub menu.
- Venison – roast, casseroled, 'sausaged' or 'terrined'. Free-ranging game and rabbit are becoming popular alternatives to livestock reared in dubious conditions.
- Pommes dauphinoises – Britain's favourite dish? Layers of thin slices cooked in a creamy, cheesy, garlicy sauce. Sometimes known as Pommes Gratin.

Photo Carnarvon Arms, entry 220

- Salad is out, 'leaves' are in and rocket rules.
- Old-fashioned root vegetables – very now. Beetroot is everywhere, roasted or in relish; suede, parsnip and celeriac make brilliant mash.
- Pumpkin and squash Another must-have – roasted or puréed.
- Wilted spinach – on many a fashionable menu.
- Wild mushrooms, garnered from the homeland's rich but neglected natural larder, these fungi fulfil every foodie's dream. Good in risotto.
- Nursery puddings have been restored to their rightful place, to be joined by lighter English desserts. Look out for walnut tart, quince tart, treacle tart, lemon posset, poached pears, fruit crumble ('Bramley' or 'plum and armagnac').
- Panna cotta 'Cooked cream' is an egg custard, divinely silken, served cold and accompanied by fruit.
- Crème fraîche – the stylish alternative to cream, adding a tangy note to sweet tarts and fruits.

Introduction

imbue them with character, the Belgian trappist beers being an appealing example.

In the 1960s and early 1970s the big breweries flooded the market with keg beers and lager. Then, in 1971, CAMRA (The Campaign for Real Ale) was founded. Its success in inspiring the real ale revival has been a dramatic example of a consumer group in action, forcing the brewing industry to rethink its strategy and produce real ales. The new century has seen a flowering of craft breweries across the country, with beer being brewed on farms, on industrial estates and in sheds behind pubs. The Progressive Beer Duty was introduced in 2002 to give micro-brewers a further boost; now there are over 400 independent breweries in Britain.

What is a real ale?

Cask or keg ale – what's the difference? One's a living organism, the other isn't. After the brewing process, cask-conditioned green beer ('real ale') is put into barrels to allow a secondary fermentation, producing a unique flavour and bubbles that are natural. Mass-produced fizz, on the other hand, has been filtered and sterilised and, like lager, is dead – until the gas is pumped back to give the distinguishing bubbles. Stored in sealed containers, it tastes more like bottled beers – and is put through the same process. Their advantage? They have a longer shelf life, and are easier to dispense. However, some bottled beers still contain the life-giving yeast(s) that

Finding the right place for you

At the back of the book (pp.441-450) we highlight pubs that stand out for a special reason. We list the best:

- Pubs for real ale
- Pubs that brew their own beer
- Pubs for local/organic food
- Pubs for seafood
- Pubs for cheese
- Authentic pubs
- Pubs with views
- Pubs with waterside settings
- Pubs for real fires
- Pubs for summer gardens

Photo left The Cherry Tree Inn, entry 387
Photo right Amberley Inn, entry 176

Introduction

Quick reference indices

At the back of the book (pp. 458-461) we list those pubs with

- special bedrooms
- wheelchair-accessible bars & wcs
- live music
- and those that are open all day

How to use this book
Opening times

We asked owners to give the days/sessions their pub is open and closed. We list the varying hours they are closed during the afternoon and if they are closed during particular lunchtimes and evenings. We state if the pub is 'open all day', or 'open weekends', or 'open Friday-Sunday'. We do advise that you check before setting out, especially in winter.

Meals and meal prices

We give the times meals are served and the approximate cost of main courses – in the bar and/or restaurant. Note that some pubs charge extra for side dishes, which significantly increases the main course price. Where set menus are mentioned, assume these are for three courses. Note that many pubs do fixed price Sunday lunches, and that prices may change. Check when booking.

Map and directions

The map pages at the front of the book show the position, with an entry number, for each of our pubs and inns. Mauve map flags indicate pubs with rooms, brown flags the award winners, blue flags the Worth a Visit pubs. Our maps are for guidance only; use a detailed road map or you may get lost down a tangle of lanes! The map and entry numbers are given at the foot of the separate guide entries. The directions given are, again, for guidance.

Bedrooms, bathrooms and breakfasts

If you're thinking of staying the night in a simple pub or inn do bear in mind that an early night may not be possible if folk are carousing below. Some bedrooms do not have en suite bathrooms; if this is important, check before booking. Breakfasts are generally included in the room price, but check. Most places serve breakfast between 8am and 10am.

Bedroom prices

Prices are per room for two people sharing. If a price range is given, then the lowest price is usually for the least expensive double room in low season and the highest for the most expensive room in high season. These may change during the year. The single room rate (or the single occupancy of a double room) generally follows. Occasionally, prices are for half board, ie. they include dinner, bed and breakfast.

Symbols

On the inside back cover we explain our symbols. Use them as a guide, not as a statement of fact, and double-check anything that is particularly important to you.

Real Ale 🍺 identifies those pubs with a real passion for beer. It is given to pubs serving four or more real ales, including local microbrewery beers.

Wine 🍷 As food improves in pubs so' generally, does the wine quality and the selection of wines available by the glass. In many top food pubs wine sales far exceed beer sales. We give this symbol to pubs that serve eight or more wines by the glass.

Bed The 🛏 symbol is given to pubs/inns that have had their rooms inspected and that we consider special. (See Room Inspections p. 13.)

Children The 🧍 symbol is given to places that accept children of any age. That doesn't mean that they can go everywhere in the pub, nor that highchairs and special menus (or small portions) are provided. Nor does it mean that children should be anything less than well-monitored! Call to check details such as separate family rooms, whether children are allowed in the dining room and whether there is play equipment in the garden.

Dogs The 🐕 symbol is given to

places where your dog can go into some part of the pub – generally the bar and garden. It is unlikely to include restaurant areas.

Dogs in rooms The 🐕 symbol is for pubs with rooms that allow your dog to sleep in the room but not on the bed.

Payment 💳 All our pubs and inns take cash and cheques with a cheque card. If they also take credit cards, we have given them the appropriate symbol. Check that your credit card is acceptable. Visa and MasterCard are generally fine. American Express is sometimes accepted; Diners Club hardly ever. Debit cards are widely accepted.

Wheelchair ♿ We use this symbol

where we've been told those in wheelchairs can access the bar and loos. The symbol does not apply to accommodation.

Walking ⇨ This symbol indicates where a pub has walking information (ie. leaflets and guides) and, perhaps, maps on display for customers to peruse.

Bookings

At weekends, food pubs are often full and it is best to book a table well in advance. At other times, only tables in the dining rooms may be reserved; tables in the bar may operate on a first-come, first-served basis. Always phone to check meal times. Some of the best gastropubs do not take reservations at all, wanting to hold on to their pubby origins. Arrive early and pick your table! Most pubs and inns will ask for a credit card number and a contact phone number when you telephone to book a room for the night.

Tipping

It is not obligatory but it is appreciated, particularly in pubs with restaurants.

Internet

www.specialplacestostay.com has online pages for all the pubs with bedrooms listed here and from all our other books – around 4,500 places in total. There's a searchable

Photo Black Swan, entry 474

database, a snippet from the write-up and colour photos. We also have a dedicated UK holiday home web site, www.special-escapes.co.uk

Disclaimer

We make no claims to pure objectivity in choosing our Special Places. They are here because we like them. Our opinions and tastes are ours alone and this book is a statement of them; we hope that you will share them. We have done our utmost to get our facts right but apologise unreservedly for any mistakes that may have crept in.

We do not check such things as fire alarms, kitchen hygiene or any other regulation with which owners of properties in this guide should comply, for that is their responsibility.

And finally

Feedback from you is invaluable. With your help and our own inspections we can maintain our reputation for dependability.

Thank you to all those who have taken the time to share your opinions with us. You have helped make this edition of the book even better than the last. Please let us have your comments; there is a report form at the back of this book. Or email us at info@sawdays.co.uk

David Hancock

Pub awards

Local, Seasonal & Organic Produce Award

Hearts soar when our inspectors come across a chalkboard menu promoting seasonal produce, perhaps farm meats, village-baked bread, locally shot game, fish and shellfish from local boats, organic wines and local brewery ale. We have seen a marked improvement in pubs actively sourcing seasonal foods from high-quality suppliers. So much so that we have introduced an award for our champions of local, seasonal and organic produce.

The Sun Inn
Dedham, Essex
entry 170

The Wellington
Wellington, Herefordshire
entry 234

The Parrot
Forest Green, Surrey
entry 476

Authentic Pub Award

We have visited dozens of simple, unadulterated pubs and a host of authentic rural watering holes and those that we found to be very special have a half-page entry – many more are listed in our Worth a Visit section. The cream of the crop, all with a full-page entry, are:

The Bridge Inn
Topsham, Devon
entry 144

Black Bull Inn,
Frosterley, Durham
entry 157

Harrow Inn,
Steep, Hampshire
entry 223

Pub with Rooms Award

For Edition 4 our inspectors visited an eclectic bunch of bedrooms, from swish country suites sporting flat-screen TVs to fresh, simple bedrooms overlooking the sea. For a complete list and photographs of our pubs with special rooms see pages 30-57.

The Punch Bowl
Kendal, Cumbria
entry 91

The Olive Branch
Clipsham, Rutland
entry 409

The Inn at Grinshill
Grinshill, Shropshire
entry 412

Community Pub Award

Within these pages you will find some cracking rural locals run by enterprising, hard-working landlords who have succeeded in making their pub the hub of the community. Our shining examples are:

Old Poets' Corner
Ashover, Derbyshire
entry 112

Duke of York
Iddesleigh, Devon
entry 139

White Hart
Otley, Suffolk
entry 463

Pubs with rooms

Berkshire
Crown and Garter – entry 9
Bedrooms, in a single-storey building around a garden, have painted floorboards, blended voiles, brass or wooden beds and super little bathrooms.
Rooms: 8: 6 doubles, 2 twins £90. Singles £59.50.
Great Common, Inkpen, Hungerford
Tel 01488 668325   www.crownandgarter.com

Buckinghamshire
The Dinton Hermit – entry 28
You have a garden for summer and rooms for the night: charming four-posters and 'Regency' bedrooms in the old, wonky-floored part, stylish modern rooms in the converted barn.
Rooms: 13: 12 doubles, 1 twin £80-£125. Singles from £80.
Water Lane, Ford Village, Aylesbury
Tel 01296 747473   www.dinton-hermit.com

Three Horseshoes Inn – entry 31
There are four super bedrooms up in the eaves. Named after local shoots, with Farrow & Ball colours, bold fabrics, flat-screen TVs and cosy extras, they are quirky and fun, one with an unusual claw-foot hip bath.
Rooms: 4 doubles £85-£95. Singles £65.
Bennett End, Radnage, High Wycombe
Tel 01494 483273   www.thethreehorseshoes.net

Cambridgeshire
The Anchor Inn – entry 42
Spotless rooms above fit the mood exactly – not posh but supremely comfy – and have trim carpets, wicker chairs, crisp duvets and Indian cotton throws.
Rooms: 4: 1 double, 1 twin, 2 suites £65-£149.50. Singles from £55.
Bury Lane, Sutton Gault, Ely
Tel 01353 778537   www.anchorsuttongault.co.uk

Cheshire
Albion Inn – entry 49
The bedrooms at the top (separate entrance) are compact and comfortable, with some good antiques. A nostalgic city pub with an eccentric streak.
Rooms: 2: 1 double, 1 twin £75. Singles £65.
Park Street, Chester
Tel 01244 340345   www.albioninnchester.co.uk

Cornwall
The Gurnard's Head – entry 67
Bedrooms upstairs are warm and cosy, simple and spotless, with Vi sprung mattresses, crisp white linen and throws over armchairs.
Rooms: 7: 5 doubles, 2 twins/doubles £62.50-£82.50.
Treen, Zennor, St Ives
Tel: 01736 796928   www.gurnardshead.co.uk

Halzephron – entry 70
Return to cosy, cottage-style bedrooms with deep-sprung beds, patchwork quilts, fresh fruit, real coffee and rolling farmyard views.
Rooms: 2 doubles from £84. Singles from £48.
Gunwalloe, Helston
Tel: 01326 240406   www.halzephron-inn.co.uk

The Mill House Inn – entry 82
The pub's contemporary bedrooms vary in size and have a stylish Cape Cod feel, in sympathy with the setting. Views reach across the valleys or the gardens.
Rooms: 9 twins/doubles £80-£120. Singles £50.
Trebarwith, Tintagel
Tel: 01840 770200   www.themillhouseinn.co.uk

Pubs with rooms

The Bay View Inn – entry 83
Stay all night: stylish, upbeat bedrooms have a beachy feel,
many with great sea views. Throw open the windows and
breathe in the fresh sea air.
Rooms: 6: 3 doubles, 2 family, 1 single £38–£110.
Marine Drive, Widemouth, Bude
Tel: 01288 361273   www.bayviewinn.co.uk

Cumbria
The Mason's Arms – entry 89
Attractive, contemporary suites have beds on the mezzanine and
kitchenettes; cottages are stylish; hamper breakfasts (full English
if required) are provided. And the views are stunning.
Rooms: 3 suites £55–£105. 2 cottages: 1 for 6, 1 for 4, £105–£175.
Strawberry Bank, Cartmel Fell
Tel: 01539 568486   www.strawberrybank.com

The Punch Bowl Inn – entry 91
Withdraw gracefully to fabulous rooms with bold fabrics, king-
size beds, flat-screen TVs and bathrooms with heated floors; the
amazing suite has double baths and views down the valley.
Rooms: 9: 8 doubles, 1 suite £110–£280.
Singles £82.50–£108.75.
Crosthwaite, Kendal
Tel: 015395 68237   www.the-punchbowl.co.uk

Drunken Duck Inn – entry 95
Bedrooms are dreamy: those in the main house snug in the
eaves, those across the courtyard crisply uncluttered and
indulgent. Some have terraces, several have walls of glass to
frame the mountains, all have peaty water straight off the fell.
Rooms: 16: 14 doubles, 2 twins £95–£225. Singles from £71.25.
Barngates, Ambleside
Tel 01539 436347   www.drunkenduckinn.co.uk

The Pheasant – entry 98

Cosseting bedrooms, warm in yellow, come with pretty pine beds, thick fabrics, Roberts radios, flat-screen TVs, and robes in spotless bathrooms. Most are in the main house, two are in a nearby garden lodge.

Rooms: 15: 11 twins/doubles, 1 single, 3 suites, £70-£185.
Bassenthwaite Lake, Cockermouth
Tel: 01768 776234 www.the-pheasant.co.uk

Derbyshire

Devonshire Arms – entry 110

The Duchess of Devonshire had a hand in the revamp, so rooms are vibrant, contemporary and lavish, with Emma Tennant art works and Neal's Yard cosmetics.

Rooms: 4: 3 doubles, 1 suite £125-£165.
Beeley, Matlock
Tel 01629 733259 www.devonshirebeeley.co.uk

Devon

Old Chapel Inn – entry 122

Whatever they turn their hands to, they do to perfection, and that includes the bedrooms across the courtyard, with their hand-made, new-medieval beds, snowy duvets and velvety covers .

Rooms: 4: 3 doubles, 1 twin £85-£115. Singles £50.
St Ann's Chapel, Bigbury-on-Sea
Tel: 01548 810241 www.oldchapelinn.com

The Dartmoor Inn – entry 137

And so to bed... new mattresses on antique beds, soft lights and sofas, beautiful fabrics and perhaps a mini chandelier: absolutely gorgeous.

Rooms: 3 doubles £95-£125.
Lydford, Okehampton
Tel: 01822 820221 www.dartmoorinn.com

Pubs with rooms

Sandy Park Inn – entry 140
Bedrooms above the kitchen are simple, crisp, comfortable and quiet. Some overlook thatched roofs to fields, one opens to the garden – another delight – beds are big and bathrooms smart.
Rooms: 5: 4 doubles, 1 twin £92. Singles £55.
Sandy Park, Chagford
Tel: 01647 433267   www.sandyparkinn.co.uk

Culm Valley Inn – entry 150
Bedrooms are simple and cheerful, with white bed linen and vibrant walls, and share two spotless bathrooms.
Rooms: 3: 1 double, 1 twin, 1 family room from £55.
Singles £30.
Culmstock, Cullompton
Tel: 01884 840354

Dorset
Stapleton Arms – entry 153
Stay the night: you get big beds and Egyptian cotton, traditional furnishings, flat-screen TVs, super mosaic-tiled bathrooms and fabulous breakfasts.
Rooms: 4 doubles £90–£120. Singles £72–£96.
Church Hill, Buckhorn Weston, Gillingham
Tel: 01963 370396   www.thestapletonarms.com

Durham
The Victoria Inn – entry 158
Upstairs bedrooms are traditionally furnished and good value, breakfasts are generous and there's off-street parking and garaging. Original, timeless, welcoming.
Rooms:5: 3 doubles, 1 twin, 1 family £60–£65.
86 Hallgarth Street, Durham
Tel: 0191 386 5269   www.victoriainn-durhamcity.co.uk

Rose and Crown – entry 159

Bedrooms are lovely; those in the converted barn tumble with colour, those in the main house come with antique pine, padded window seats and warm country colours.

Rooms: 12: 6 doubles, 4 twins, 2 suites £126-£166.
Singles from £70.
Romaldkirk, Barnard Castle
Tel: 01833 650213   www.rose-and-crown.co.uk

Essex

The Bell Inn & Hill House – entry 167

Come for warmth and gregariousness and, if you're staying, go for a suite: cosy, traditional, individual, rather wonderful.

Rooms: 16: 7 doubles, 3 twins, 6 suites £50-£85;
1 family from £105.
High Road, Horndon-on-the-Hill
Tel: 01375 642463   www.bell-inn.co.uk

The Sun Inn – entry 170

Gorgeous, luxurious bedrooms have panelled walls or madly sloping ceilings, antique wardrobes or stylish mirrors. Next door, Pier's wife runs Victoria's Plums, a tiny shop selling locally grown fruit and veg.

Rooms: 5 doubles £70-£130. Singles £60-£130.
High Street, Dedham, Colchester
Tel: 01206 323351   www.thesuninndedham.com

The Mistley Thorn – entry 171

Bedrooms are calm with big beds, pale green paintwork, spotless bathroooms; some have watery views. A confidently-run family operation with a great weekend buzz.

Rooms: 5 twins/doubles £70-£95. Singles £60-£80.
High Street, Mistley, Colchester
Tel: 01206 392821   www.mistleythorn.co.uk

Gloucestershire
Bathurst Arms – entry 179
Smartened-up bedrooms provide a homely base for exploring the Cotswolds: they are clean, comfortable, freshly painted and well-equipped.
Rooms: 6 twins/doubles £75. Singles £55.
North Cerney, Cirencester
Tel: 01285-831281   www.bathurstarms.com

The Red Hart Inn at Awre – entry 181
Open fires, hearty meals, real ales and a lovely welcome. Do stay: a private (steepish) staircase to the second floor leads to fresh, comfortable, carpeted bedrooms with pretty views.
Rooms: 2 doubles £80. Singles £50.
Awre, Newnham on Severn
Tel: 01594 510220

Puesdown Inn – entry 186
The light, shuttered brasserie is a favourite, as are the three compact but beautifully, globally themed bedrooms, all with 'storm' showers.
Rooms: 3 doubles £85-£90. Singles £50-£60.
Compton Abdale, Northleach
Tel: 01451 860262   www.puesdown.cotswoldinns.com

Horse and Groom – entry 197
Bedrooms are nicely plush – smart but uncluttered; the red room is huge and comes with a sofa, while another, at the back, has doors opening to the terrace.
Rooms: 5 doubles £90-£115. Singles from £65.
Bourton-on-the-Hill, Moreton-in-Marsh
Tel: 01386 700413   www.horseandgroom.info

Hampshire
The Peat Spade – entry 204
The six new bedrooms – big beds, sumptuous fabrics, flat-screen TVs, WiFi and bathrooms with Longbarn toiletries – are proving popular. Foodies and fishermen love this pub.
Rooms: 6 doubles £110.
Longstock, Stockbridge
Tel: 01264 810612   www.peatspadeinn.co.uk

The Greyhound – entry 205
Smart bedrooms sport spotlights, auction antiques, flat-screen TVs, classy bathrooms and cosseting extras. A small garden overlooks the Test: rest here with a glass of chilled chablis or cast a line.
Rooms: 8: 3 doubles, 4 twins, 1 single £70-£100.
31 High Street, Stockbridge
Tel: 01264 810833   www.thegreyhound.info

Carnarvon Arms – entry 220
Bedrooms are equally smart, with soft blankets on crisp white linen, plasma screens, internet access and posh bathrooms with toiletries.
Rooms: 12: 8 doubles, 3 twins, 1 single £59.95-£89.95.
Winchester Road, Whitway, Burghclere, Newbury
Tel 01635 278222   www.carnarvonarms.com

Herefordshire
The Hawkley Inn – entry 222
Big sleigh beds, Italian cotton sheets, goose down duvets, flat-screen TV, WiFi broadband and bathrooms with power showers and Molton Brown treats; bedrooms are firmly 21st century.
Rooms: 5: 4 doubles, 1 suite £75-£90. Singles £65-£80.
Pococks Lane, Hawkley, Liss
Tel: 01730 827205   www.hawkleyinn.co.uk

The Cottage of Content – entry 237
Small, beamy bedrooms are carpeted and cottagey, and bathrooms fresh and new. Good value, and wonderful food in the little restaurant below.
Rooms: 5: 3 doubles, 2 twins £56–£60.
Carey, Hereford
Tel: 01432 840242   www.cottageofcontent.co.uk

The Saracens Head – entry 242
Make a night of it: upstairs, and in the boathouse, is a flurry of new oak-floored bedrooms, stylishly furnished, beautifully cared for and with great river views.
Rooms: 10: 8 doubles, 1 twin, 1 family £70–£130.
Singles from £48.50.
Symonds Yat East, Ross-on-Wye
Tel: 01600 890435   www.saracensheadinn.co.uk

Lancashire
Sun Hotel & Bar – entry 265
Super bedrooms, spread over three floors, have chic leather headboards, piles of pillows and cafetières for fresh coffee.
Rooms: 15: 13 doubles, 2 twins, 1 suite £65–£125.
Singles £55–£85.
63-65 Church Street, Lancaster
Tel: 01524 66006   www.thesunhotelandbar.co.uk

Leicestershire
The Queen's Head – entry 278
A cool, relaxed drinkers' bar, a bistro with an open fire...Add bedrooms that have a similarly stylish feel and you have a well-nigh perfect coaching inn.
Rooms: 6: 4 doubles, 2 twins £70–£100. Singles £65.
2 Long Street, Belton
Tel: 01530 222359   www.thequeenshead.org

Lincolnshire

Brownlow Arms – entry 286

The mood of baronial elegance continues into four superb
bedrooms above, immaculate, traditional and replete with DVDs
and flat screen TVs.

Rooms: 4 doubles £96. Singles £65.
High Road, Hough-on-the-Hill, Grantham
Tel: 01400 250234 www.thebrownlowarms.com

Houblon Inn – entry 287

Cosy, well-equipped rooms await in a converted barn across the
courtyard. In the heart of a conservation village, the Houblon Inn
is honest, unaffected and intelligently run.

Rooms: 4: 3 doubles, 1 twin £60-£70. Singles £40-£45.
Oasby, Grantham
Tel: 01529 455215 www.houblon-inn.co.uk

The Manners Arms – entry 289

The pristine bedrooms, each with its own décor, are smartly
feminine, each named after family members past and present,
from the Flying Duke to Violet the Soul.

Rooms: 10: 8 doubles, 2 singles £55-£80.
Croxton Road, Knipton, Grantham
Tel: 01476 879222 www.mannersarms.com

Collyweston Slater – entry 290

With a spacious, open-plan and uncluttered interior and fresh
tasteful bedrooms above, the transformation from rundown
village boozer into relaxed country inn is a resounding success.

Rooms: 5: 3 doubles, 1 family, 1 single £60-£120.
87-89 Main Road, Collyweston, Stamford
Tel: 01780 444288 www.collywestonslater.co.uk

Pubs with rooms

London

Portobello Gold – entry 293

Redecorated bedrooms have good beds, 'wet' rooms and flat-screen TVs, and the roof terrace apartment comes with a foldaway four-poster and small putting green!
Rooms: 8: 6 twin/doubles, 1 suite, 1 apartment £60–£180.
95-97 Portobello Road, Notting Hill
Tel: 020 7460 4910   www.portobellogold.com

Norfolk

Saracens Head – entry 343

Bedrooms have bold colours, sisal floors and linen curtains – top stuff. The whole mood is of quirky, committed individuality, in the middle of nowhere.
Rooms:6: 5 doubles, 1 twin £90. Singles £50.
Wolterton, Erpingham
Tel: 01263 768909   www.saracenshead-norfolk.co.uk

The Globe Inn – entry 348

The bedrooms are as fresh and as un-traditional as can be, gleaming with oak floors, white walls and Venetian blinds, powerful showers and digital TVs – warmly contemporary
Rooms: 7: 5 doubles, 2 twins £65–£130.
The Buttlands, Wells-next-the-Sea
Tel: 01328 710206   www.globeatwells.co.uk

The Victoria at Holkham – entry 350

There are serene bedrooms upstairs, some with views to marsh and sea, and three luscious self-catering lodges in the grounds.
Rooms: 10 + 3: 9 doubles, 1 suite £120–£225.
Singles £100–£130. 3 lodges £120–£275 (max. 4).
Min. stay 2 nights weekend.
Park Road, Wells-next-the-Sea
Tel: 01328 711008   www.victoriaatholkham.co.uk

The White Horse – entry 351

Bedrooms in a wavy extension facing the tidal marshes and North Norfolk Coastal Path have generous proportions and a patio each. Huge sunsets, fine food, big breakfasts, and a welcome for children and dogs.

Rooms: 15: 9 doubles, 6 twins £100–£120.
Main Road, Brancaster Staithe
Tel: 01485 210262   www.whitehorsebrancaster.co.uk

The Kings Head Hotel – entry 354

The bedrooms are swish – enormous beds, flat-screen TVs, a decanter of port as well as a mini-bar, and a welcome-you-in plate of home-baked biscuits.

Rooms: 12 doubles £125–£225. Singles from £69.50.
Great Bircham
Tel: 01485 578265 www.the-kings-head-bircham.co.uk

The Rose and Crown – entry 355

Inside, a warren of rooms filled with old beams and log fires, a family-friendly garden room, and a flurry of delightfully stylish bedrooms. Brilliant.

Rooms: 16 twins/doubles £85–£95. Singles £50–£65.
Old Church Road, Snettisham
Tel: 01485 541382   www.roseandcrownsnettisham.co.uk

Northumberland

The Pheasant Inn – 369

Bedrooms next door in the hay barn are fresh, simple, compact and cosy. You are in the glorious Northumberland National Park, so no traffic jams, no rush.

Rooms: 8: 4 doubles, 3 twins, 1 family £80–£85. Singles £45–£50.
Stannersburn, Kielder Water
Tel: 01434 240382 www.thepheasantinn.com

Pubs with rooms

Battlesteads Hotel – entry 370
All the bedrooms are carpeted, well-equipped – toiletries, TVs, broadband – and a good size. The newest, with wheelchair access, are on the ground floor, and the housekeeping is exemplary.
Rooms: 17 twins/doubles £80. Singles £45.
Wark, Hexham
Tel: 01434 230209   www.battlesteads.com

Oxfordshire
Miller of Mansfield – entry 381
There are cow-hide rugs on white wooden floors and colours in pink, orange and electric green. Bathrooms tend towards the extravagant with monsoon showers or claw-foot baths.
Rooms: 10: 7 doubles, 1 twin, 2 suites £90–£175. Singles £90–£110.
High Street, Goring-on-Thames
Tel: 01491 872829   www.millerofmansfield.com

The Cherry Tree Inn – entry 387
In keeping with the minimalist bar's good looks, bedrooms in the barn are contemporary and stylish, with flat-screen TVs, king-size beds and feather pillows.
Rooms: 4 doubles £95.
Stoke Row, Henley-on-Thames
Tel: 01491 680430   www.thecherrytreeinn.com

The Boar's Head – entry 391
Rooms are unmistakably smart, with good beds, crisp linen and piles of cushions. The small double has a beamed ceiling, the big double comes with a claw-foot bath, the suite has a sofa for kids.
Rooms: 3: 2 doubles, 1 suite £85–£130. Singles £75–£95.
Church Street, Ardington, Wantage
Tel: 01235 833254   www.boarsheadardington.co.uk

The Trout at Tadpole Bridge – entry 396

Sleep tight in one of six redecorated rooms, neatly kitted out with Farrow & Ball paints, flat-screen TVs, bateau or brass beds, tasteful antiques and views across fields. Bliss!

Rooms: 6: 4 doubles, 1 twin, 1 suite £100–£130.
Min. 2 nights weekends May–Sep.
Buckland Marsh, Faringdon
Tel: 01367 870382   www.troutinn.co.uk

Fleece on the Green – entry 398

In a Georgian pub overlooking Witney's green, delightful bedrooms are big enough to hold an armchair or two.

Rooms: 10: 1 twin/double, 8 doubles, 1 single, £80–£90.
11 Church Green, Witney
Tel: 01993 892270   www.fleecewitney.co.uk

The Kings Head Inn – entry 402

The bedrooms look fabulous: all are different, most have a stunning view, some family furniture mixed in with 'bits', painted wood, great colours and lush fabrics.

Rooms. 12: 10 doubles, 2 twins £70–£125. Singles £55.
The Green, Bledington
Tel: 01608 658365   www.kingsheadinn.net

Falkland Arms – entry 405

Bedrooms are cosy, some verging on snug; the attic room is wonderfully private. Brass beds and four-posters, old oak and an uneven floor; you'll sleep well. It's all blissfully free of modern trappings.

Rooms: 5 doubles £80–£120.
Great Tew, Chipping Norton
Tel: 01608 683653   www.falklandarms.org.uk

Pubs with rooms

Rutland

The Olive Branch – entry 409
Stay the night in Beech House across the lane. Stylish, individual rooms ooze comfort – goose down duvets, flat-screen TVs, Roberts radios, lavish bathrooms, real coffee. Superb.
Rooms: 6: 5 doubles, 1 family £80–£160. Singles from £65.
Main Street, Clipsham
Tel: 01780 410355   www.theolivebranchpub.com

The Old Pheasant – entry 411
The bedroom extension has been done up with a good eye: attractive wallpapers, a restful feel, and bathrooms sporting Gilchrist & Soames.
Rooms: 9 twins/doubles £75–£100. Singles £50–£60.
Main Road, Glaston, Uppingham
Tel: 01572 822326   www.theoldpheasant.co.uk

Shropshire

Riverside Inn – entry 414
Upstairs, well-proportioned Georgian bedrooms are in excellent order, and the service, as in every good pub, is both relaxed and efficient.
Rooms: 7: 6 doubles, 1 twin £60–£70. Singles £45.
Cressage, Shrewsbury
Tel: 01952 510900   www.theriversideinn.net

The Inn at Grinshill – entry 412
Bedrooms, understatedly elegant, come with piles of pillows, crisp white linen, wispy mohair blankets or shiny quilted eiderdowns, and technology hidden behind mirrors.
Rooms: 6: 3 doubles, 2 twins, 1 single £50–£120.
High Street, Grinshill, Shrewsbury
Tel: 01939 220410   www.theinnatgrinshill.co.uk

The Crown Inn – entry 424

Lavish bedrooms are divided between the inn and three new cottages, all with drinks trays and excellent power showers.
Rooms: 18: 15 doubles, 3 twins £95-£115. Singles £59.50.
Hopton Wafers, Cleobury Mortimer
Tel: 01299 270372 www.crownathopton.co.uk

Somerset

Royal Oak at Luxborough – entry 427

For those lucky enough to stay, bedrooms ramble around the first floor (one below has a private terrace) and are individual, peaceful, homely and great value.
Rooms: 11: 8 doubles, 2 twins, 1 single £55-£85.
Luxborough, Dunster
Tel: 01984 640319 www.theroyaloakinnluxborough.co.uk

Carew Arms – entry 429

Recently decorated bedrooms are upstairs: new pine, good linen, creaking floorboards. Well-behaved dogs are welcome, and extra beds are available for children.
Rooms:6: 3 doubles, 3 twins £65-£84.
Crowcombe, Taunton
Tel: 01984 618631 www.thecarewarms.co.uk

Farmer's Inn – entry 433

Stay the night in off-beat but elegant and big rooms with distinctive beds (all antique) and expansive, gleaming wooden floors. Bathrooms are shiny and chic, with power showers or claw-foot baths. And the grounds have great views.
Rooms: 5 doubles £80-£110. Singles £60-£90.
Slough Green, West Hatch, Taunton
Tel: 01823 480480 www.farmersinnwesthatch.co.uk

Pubs with rooms

Lord Poulett Arms – entry 435
Contemporary wallpapers set the tone for super bedrooms
upstairs – along with open-stone walls, brass bedsteads and
seagrass floors; Roberts radios add a fun touch. Good value,
friendly to dogs.
Rooms: 4 twins/doubles £88. Singles £59.
High Street, Hinton St George, Crewekerne
Tel: 01460 73149   www.lordpoulettarms.com

Devonshire Arms Hotel – entry 437
Outside are a new patio and sunny walled garden; upstairs,
a flurry of large, light and absolutely fabulous bedrooms.
This hotel-inn is an engaging place to drink, eat and stay.
Rooms: 9: 8 doubles, 1 family room £70-£130.
Singles from £60.
Long Sutton, Langport
Tel: 01458 241271   www.thedevonshirearms.com

The Manor House Inn – entry 440
After, totter out to the single-storey building where smart and
generous bedrooms await; beds are hugely comfortable, shower
rooms a treat. In the morning, discover a picture-perfect village
amid gently rolling hills.
Rooms: 3: 2 doubles, 1 twin £90. Singles £50.
Ditcheat, Shepton Mallet
Tel: 01749 860276   www.manorhouseinn.co.uk

The Three Horseshoes – entry 441
There's a super bedroom in the eaves with church views, and
two more on the same level, equally good. Perfect peace at the
end of a country lane in Somerset.
Rooms: 3 doubles £75. Singles £50.
Batcombe, Shepton Mallet
Tel: 01749 850359   www.three-horseshoes.co.uk

Bear & Swan – entry 446

Retire to airy and spacious bedrooms; there are charming antiques, stylish bathroom suites and an open-plan living area, with a kitchen, to share.

Rooms: 2 doubles £80. Singles £50.
13 South Parade, Chew Magna
Tel: 01275 331100   www.bearandswan.co.uk

The Queen's Arms – entry 451

Bedrooms are stunning with fresh checks or sumptuous silks, perfect bath and shower rooms, posh smellies and breathtaking views – book the French room! A friendly labrador, Butcombe on tap, comfort and authenticity.

Rooms: 5 twins/doubles £75-£120.
Corton Denham
Tel 01963 220317   www.thequeensarms.com

Suffolk

Old Cannon Brewery – entry 457

A cobbled courtyard beyond the old coach arch has swish tables and chairs for summer sipping, in the former brewery building are five light, cheerful and airy bedrooms.

Rooms: 5: 4 doubles, 1 twin £69. Singles £55.
86 Cannon Street, Bury St Edmunds
01284 768769   www.oldcannonbrewery.co.uk

The Crown and Castle – entry 464

Rooms in the main house come in pastels, those at the back have long river views, and garden rooms are big and airy, with crisp white linen and seagrass matting.

Rooms: 18: 16 doubles, 2 twins £90-£145; family £110-£160.
Orford
Tel: 01394 450205 www.crownandcastle.co.uk

The Westleton Crown – entry 466
Bedrooms vary in size and are hugely stylish, some with four-posters, all with goose down duvets and flat-screen TVs, and those in the stables and the cottage have umbrellas so you'll arrive at breakfast exquisitely dry. Chic bathrooms are a further (huge) treat.
Rooms: 25 twins/doubles £110–£170. Singles £85–£95.
The Street, Westleton, Southwold
Tel: 01728 648777   www.westletoncrown.co.uk

The Anchor – entry 467
A pity not to stay; there's one big bedroom above the pub, and more in the annexe chalets, set around a charming pebble and sea plant garden.
Rooms: 7: 4 doubles, 3 twins, 1 family room £90. Singles £75.
Main Street, Walberswick, Southwold
Tel: 01502 722112   www.anchoratwalberswick.com

Surrey
The Swan Inn and Restaurant – entry 478
Contemporary rooms have a minimalist feel, with muted earthy colours, flat-screen TVs and trendy bathrooms with power showers and posh toiletries.
Rooms: 11: 9 doubles, 2 suites £70–£140.
Petworth Road, Chiddingfold, Guildford
Tel: 01428 682073   www.theswaninn.biz

Sussex
Halfway Bridge Inn – entry 483
The old stables have been converted into excellent rooms where deep beds, leather chairs, plasma screens and PlayStations "for the boys" sit beautifully with old beams and rustic brickwork.
Rooms: 6: 2 doubles £90–£110, 4 suites £120–£150. Singles from £65.
Halfway Bridge, Midhurst
Tel: 01798 861281 www.thesussexpub.co.uk

The White Horse – entry 487

Good, fresh bedrooms in a detached annexe have CD players, snowy bathrobes and continental hamper breakfasts. What's more, this is a Green Tourism gold award-winner, committed to sourcing local and organic wherever possible.

Rooms: 9 twins/doubles £95–£160. Singles £65–£120.
Chilgrove, Chichester
Tel: 01243 535219   www.whitehorsechilgrove.co.uk

The Royal Oak Inn – entry 488

Bedrooms are divided between three cottages, a nearby barn and upstairs at the back; all have DVD and CD players and plasma screens, brown leather chairs and big comfy beds.

Rooms: 8: 4 doubles, 1 twin, 3 cottages £80–£160.
Singles £60–£70.
Pook Lane, East Lavant, Chichester
Tel: 01243 527434   www.thesussexpub.co.uk

The Foresters – entry 492

Bedrooms are small and simple with good linen, trim carpets and chunky beds and the price includes an excellent continental breakfast hamper.

Rooms: 2 doubles £70–£80. Singles £45–£55.
The Street, Graffham
Tel: 01798 867202   www.foresters-arms.com

The Griffin Inn – entry 495

Bedrooms have an uncluttered country-inn elegance: uneven floors, country furniture, soft coloured walls, free-standing baths, huge shower heads, crisp linen. Those in the coach house are quieter; swish new rooms in next-door Griffin House are quieter still.

Rooms: 13: 1 twin, 12 doubles £80–£130.
Singles £60–£80 (not w'ends).
Fletching, Uckfield Tel: 01825 722890 www.thegriffininn.co.uk

Pubs with rooms

The Bull – entry 500
Return to white bed linen in gorgeous rooms where new and old blend as beautifully as below. Expect bold silks, walk-in rain showers and fresh lilies.
Rooms: 4 doubles £80-£100.
2 High Street, Ditchling, Burgess Hill
Tel: 01273 843147   www.thebullditchling.com

Warwickshire
The Fox and Goose – entry 513
The fun spills over into the bedrooms upstairs, eccentrically dressed à la Cluedo – Plum, Scarlet, Peacock, Mustard. Bathrooms have luxurious claw-foot tubs with candleholders and Lady Godiva lotions. And there's a big elegant garden.
Rooms: 4 doubles £85-£120. Armscote, Stratford-upon-Avon
Tel: 01608 682293   www.foxandgoose.co.uk

The Howard Arms – entry 514
Gorgeous bedrooms are set discreetly apart, mixing period style and modern luxury; the double oozes old world charm, the twin is more folksy, the half-tester is almost a suite.
Rooms: 3: 2 doubles, 1 twin £120-£138. Singles £85.
Lower Green, Ilmington, Stratford-upon-Avon
Tel: 01608 682226   www.howardarms.com

College Arms – entry 515
Bedrooms are cosy and comfortable, one with low beams and a romantic sleigh bed, and the price includes a continental breakfast spread.
Rooms: 4 twins/doubles £65-£75.
Lower Quinton, Stratford-upon-Avon
Tel: 01789 720342   www.collegearms.co.uk

The Rose and Crown – entry 521
Lovely contemporary bedrooms upstairs have large bath and shower rooms and overlook the square. It's young and fun and Warwick has history in spades. Good value.
Rooms: 5: 2 doubles, 3 triples £65-£75.
30 Market Place, Warwick
Tel: 01865 249796   www.roseandcrownwarwick.co.uk

Wiltshire
The Pear Tree Inn – entry 531
Exquisite bedrooms, up in the eaves or out in the old barn, are painted Lime White and have suede bedheads, Bang & Olufsen TVs and funky rugs for colour. Fabulous.
Rooms: 8: 6 doubles, 2 family £105-£140. Singles £75.
Top Lane, Whitley, Melksham
Tel: 01225 709131   www.thepeartreeinn.com

The Tollgate Inn – entry 532
Bedrooms are in excellent order: oak beams, good antiques and smart linen. Two overlook the Westbury White Horse, two the village green.
Rooms: 4 doubles from £75. Singles £50.
Ham Green, Holt, Bradford on Avon
Tel: 01225 782326   www.tollgateholt.co.uk

Spread Eagle Inn – entry 539
The higgledy-piggledy stairs are great if you're nimble and the bedrooms peaceful – muted colours, white linen, original fireplaces, delightful views. Bathrooms are perfectly plain – and spotless.
Rooms: 5 twins/doubles £70-£90. Singles £50-£60.
Stourton, Warminster
Tel: 01747 840587   www.spreadeagleinn.com

The Compasses Inn – entry 543
Bedrooms are at the top of stone stairs outside the front door and have the same effortless charm: walls are thick, windows are wonky, bathrooms are new.
Rooms: 4 + 1: 2 doubles, 2 twins/doubles. Cottage for 3, £75-£90.
Lower Chicksgrove, Tisbury
Tel: 01722 714318   www.thecompassesinn.com

The Bath Arms – entry 540
Bedrooms are a treat, some in the main house, others in the converted barn, and there's a romantic two-bedroom lodge overlooking Longleat House. Expect lots of colour, big wallpapers, beds dressed in Eygyptian cotton.
Rooms: 14: 10 doubles, 2 twins, 2 singles £70-£130.
Longleat Estate, Horningsham, Warminster
Tel: 01985 844308   www.batharms.co.uk

Worcestershire
The Fleece – entry 550
The one timbered bedroom is small but perfectly formed with seagrass flooring, an antique mahogany bed and a picture window view of the church and village square.
Rooms: 1 double £85.
The Cross, Bretforton, Evesham
Tel: 01386 831173   www.thefleeceinn.co.uk

Yorkshire
Shibden Mill Inn – entry 559
Bedrooms, some to be renovated this year, are carpeted, comfortable and individual; the suite, its large armchairs upholstered in dark purple velvet, is huge fun.
Rooms: 11 doubles/singles/suites £90-£136.
Shibden, Halifax
Tel: 01422 365840   www.shibdenmillinn.com

The Tempest Arms – entry 564

Rooms include swish new suites with private terraces and hot tubs or balconies overlooking a babbling stream; all have hand-crafted furniture and bathrooms sporting Molton Brown toiletries; a dozen are on the ground floor.

Rooms: 21: 9 twins/doubles, 12 suites, £74.95–£99. Singles £59.95–£74.95.

Elslack, Skipton Tel: 01282 842450 www.tempestarms.co.uk

The Lister Arms Hotel – entry 565

Super bedrooms are a steal: some are small and newly decorated (exposed stone walls, cast-iron beds, pretty fabrics); other big but not as up-to-date (flock wallpaper, wicker chairs, good showers). Stay a week and you can take their gorgeous cottage next door.

Rooms: 9 + 1: 5 doubles, 3 family, 1 twin £60–£70. Singles £50–£55. Cottage for 8, £275–£1,200 p.w.

Malham, Skipton   Tel: 01729 830330   www.listerarms.co.uk

Foresters Arms – entry 571

The bedrooms are either sweet and old-fashioned or the best of contemporary; two are ensuite and there's homemade marmalade for breakfast. Characterful and worth a detour

Rooms: 3: 2 doubles, 1 twin £79.

Carlton-in-Coverdale, Leyburn

Tel: 01969 640272 www.forestersarms-carlton.co.uk

Golden Lion – entry 577

Walk the coast-to-coast path by day, return to a flickering fire and retire to fresh new bedrooms with appealing colours, good materials and super slate-floored showers.

Rooms: 3 twins/doubles £80. Singles £60.

6 West End, Osmotherley

Tel: 01609 883526 www.goldenlionosmotherley.co.uk

Pubs with rooms

The Boar's Head Hotel – entry 582

Up the pretty staircase to very comfy bedrooms, with sherry and truffles in the best. (Twenty more rooms lie in outbuildings across the street.) Visit the castle gardens and the National Hyacinth Collection as a guest of the hotel.

Rooms: 25 twins/doubles £125-£150. Singles £105-£125.
Ripley Castle Estate, Ripley, Harrogate
Tel: 01423 771888   www.boarsheadripley.co.uk

The General Tarleton – entry 583

Retire to comfortable rooms in a purpose-built extension, the newest flaunting the best of contemporary. And breakfasts are delicious.

Rooms: 14 doubles £97-£120. Singles £85-£108.
Boroughbridge Road, Ferrensby, Knaresborough
01423 340284   www.generaltarleton.co.uk

Blackwell Ox Inn – entry 584

After a rustic French dinner in a soft-lit dining room, retire to handsome bedrooms, two with pretty views, all with generous bathrooms and every hotel comfort.

Rooms: 5 twins/doubles £95-£110.
Huby Road, Sutton-on-the-Forest, York
Tel: 01347 810328   www.blackwelloxinn.co.uk

The Abbey Inn – entry 586

Traditional bedrooms are spacious and special with bathrobes, aromatherapy oils, fruit, homemade biscuits and a 'treasure chest' of wine.

Rooms: 3 doubles £95-£155.
Byland Abbey, Coxwold
Tel: 01347 868204   www.bylandabbeyinn.com

Fairfax Arms – entry 594

Upstairs are seven simple, sunny bedrooms, some overlooking the village street, with modern bathrooms and snowy towels. The suites are very good value.

Rooms: 10: 8 twins/doubles, 2 family suites £70-£100. Singles £50.
Main Street, Gilling East, Malton
Tel: 01439 788212 www.fairfaxarms.co.uk

The White Swan Inn – entry 597

The bedrooms are luxurious (antique beds, smart magazines, Penhaligon smellies). Stay awhile – for beach walks, the moors and a ride on the steam railway.

Rooms: 21 doubles/twins/suites £129-£229. Singles from £89.
Market Place, Pickering
Tel: 01751 472288 www.white-swan.co.uk

Wales
Ceredigion

Harbourmaster Hotel – entry 611

The bedrooms – cosy, characterful, contemporary – are a pleasure to return to, with their sea views, white Frette bed linen and fluffy white towels.

Rooms: 9: 7 doubles, 2 singles £55-£140.
Pen Cei, Aberaeron
Tel: 01545 570755 www.harbour-master.com

Conwy

The Queen's Head – entry 613

Complete the treat by booking a night in the sweet parish storehouse across the road, recently converted into a charming self-catering cottage for two.

Cottage for 2, £100-£125.
Glanwydden, Llandudno Junction
Tel: 01492 546570 www.queensheadglanwydden.co.uk

The Kinmel Arms – entry 615
You're a hop from Snowdonia and that stunning coast – walks start from the door – so treat yourself to one of the four dreamy suites, each with French windows to a decked seating area.
Rooms: 4 suites £135–£175.
The Village, St George, Abergele
Tel: 01745 832207   www.thekinmelarms.co.uk

Monmouthshire
The Bell at Skenfrith – entry 626
Bedrooms are country smart with Farrow & Ball colours and beds dressed in cotton piqué and Welsh wool; plus homemade biscuits, Cath Collins toiletries and a hi-tech console by the bed.
Rooms: 8: 5 doubles, 3 suites £100–£180.
Singles £70–£110 (not weekends).
Skenfrith   Tel: 01600 750235   www.skenfrith.co.uk

Beaufort Arms – entry 631
Bedrooms – the best in the main house – are as pleasing as all the rest: fresh, spotless and new. Try to get one with a church view and you'll feel like the cat who got the cream.
Rooms: 15: 7 doubles, 7 twins, 1 single £55–£95.
High Street, Raglan, Usk
Tel: 01291 690412   www.beaufortraglan.co.uk

Black Bear – entry 633
Recover from your over-indulgence in one the two basic but comfortable bedrooms in the converted stables. In deepest Monmouthshire, the Black Bear is worth negotiating the several country lanes it takes to get here.
Rooms: 2 twins/doubles £60–£75. Singles £30–£35.
Bettws Newydd, Usk   Tel: 01873 880701

The Newbridge Inn – entry 635

If you can stay over, do. Comfortable bedrooms are purpose-built, just across the car park and rustically styled with solid oak furniture and lovely bathrooms. Go up a level for a four-poster and a view.

Rooms: 6: 4 doubles, 2 twins/doubles £95–£120. Singles from £80.
Tredunnock, Usk
Tel: 01633 451000   www.thenewbridge.co.uk

Pembrokeshire

The Old Point House Inn – entry 636

After a seafood dinner, no need to rush home. Three simple white and blue bedrooms await upstairs; ask for the quiet twin with the stunning bay view.

3 twins/doubles £60. Singles £30.
Angle, Pembroke
Tel: 01646 641205

Powys

The Felin Fach Griffin – entry 646

Bedrooms are fresh, warm and simple with a few designer touches: tulips in a vase, check curtains, snowy white towels and linen. Charles, Edmund and Julie are a great team.

Rooms: 7 twins/doubles £97.50–£125. Singles from £67.50.
Felin Fach, Brecon
Tel: 01874 620111   www.felinfachgriffin.co.uk

London map

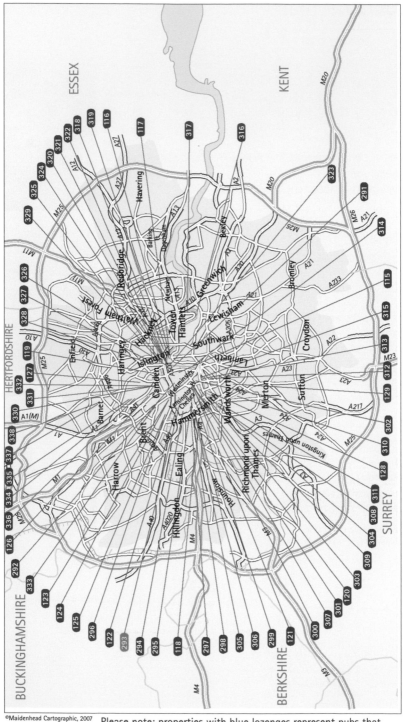

Please note: properties with blue lozenges represent pubs that are Worth a Visit. See pages 409–439

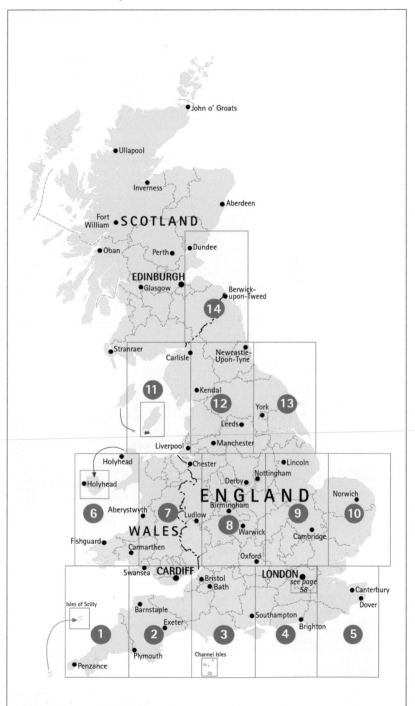

©Maidenhead Cartographic, 2007

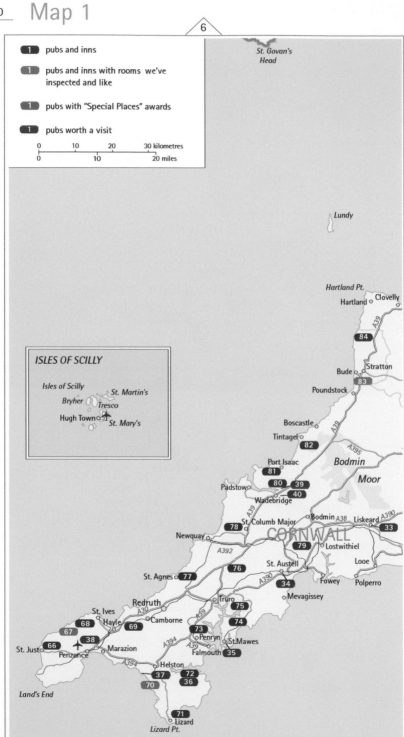

6

pubs and inns

pubs and inns with rooms we've inspected and like

pubs with "Special Places" awards

pubs worth a visit

| 0 | 10 | 20 | 30 kilometres |
| 0 | | 10 | 20 miles |

St. Govan's Head

Lundy

Hartland Pt.   Clovelly
Hartland

84

Stratton
Bude
Poundstock

ISLES OF SCILLY

Isles of Scilly   St. Martin's
Bryher   Tresco
Hugh Town   St. Mary's

83

Boscastle
Tintagel
82

Port Isaac
81
Padstow   80   39
Wadebridge   40

Bodmin   CORNWALL
St. Columb Major   Bodmin A38 Liskeard A390
78
Newquay   79   Lostwithiel   33
A392   Looe
St. Agnes   77   76   St. Austell
34   Fowey   Polperro
Mevagissey
Redruth   Truro
St. Ives   75
68   Hayle   69   Camborne   74
67   38   73
St. Just   66   Penryn   St. Mawes
Penzance   Marazion   Falmouth   35
Helston
37   72
70   36

71
Lizard
Lizard Pt.

Land's End

Bodmin Moor

A39
A395
A39
A30
A39
A394
A394
A390
A39

Please note: properties with blue lozenges represent pubs that are Worth a Visit. See pages 409–439

Map 2

61

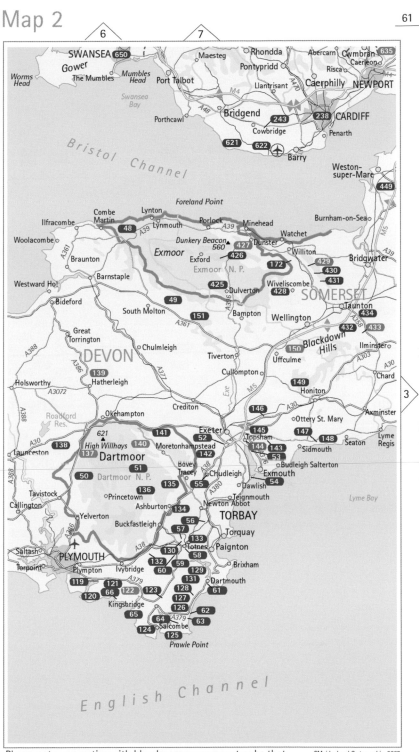

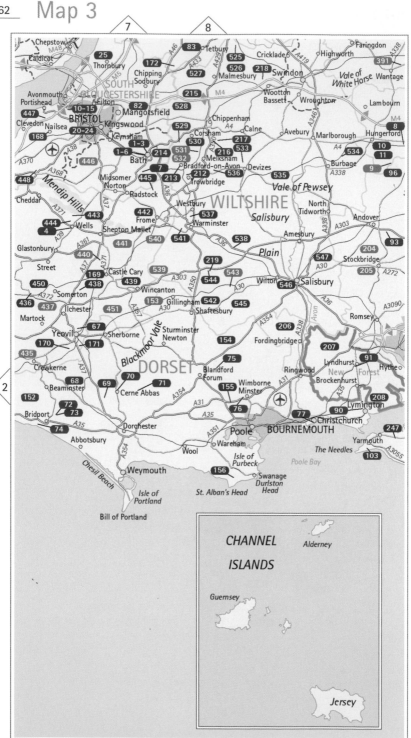

Please note: properties with blue lozenges represent pubs that are Worth a Visit. See pages 409-439

Map 4

63

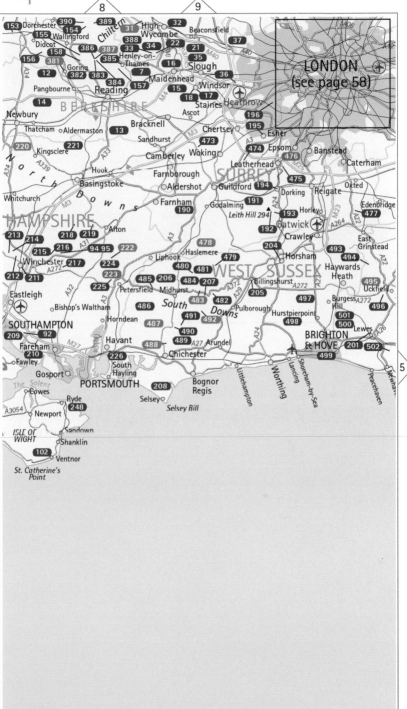

9 10

Foulness Pt.
Foulness I.

Brentwood
Wickford
Rayleigh
Basildon
Southend-on-Sea
Coryton
Canvey Is.
Shoebury Ness
167
Grays
Tilbury
Thames Estuary
Gravesend
Grain
Sheerness
A2
Dartford
Swanley
Rochester
MEDWAY TNS
Isle of
Sheppey
Herne Bay
Margate
North Foreland
Gillingham
Chatham
Sittingbourne
249 250
Whitstable
106
Broadstairs
M20
Wrotham
North Downs
M2
A2
Faversham
251
Ramsgate
Sandwich
Sevenoaks
258
257
Maidstone
Chilham
Canterbury
252
253
Deal
104
KENT
A28
254
Tonbridge
Vale of Kent
Staplehurst
Ashford
Wye
255
South Foreland
259
260
Royal
Tunbridge
Wells
263
256
A2070
105
A20
Dover
Channel Tunnel Terminal
261
262
A265
Cranbrook
264
Tenterden
Romney
Marsh
Hythe
Folkestone
199
200
509
A265
197
Rye
198
A259
New Romney
EAST SUSSEX
Heathfield
508
Battle
Winchelsea
Lydd
Dungeness
Strait of Dover
Cap
Gris-Nez
A22
203
507
Hailsham
506
A259
Hastings
505
Polegate
Bexhill
4
202
504
A27
Seaford
503
Eastbourne
Beachy Head

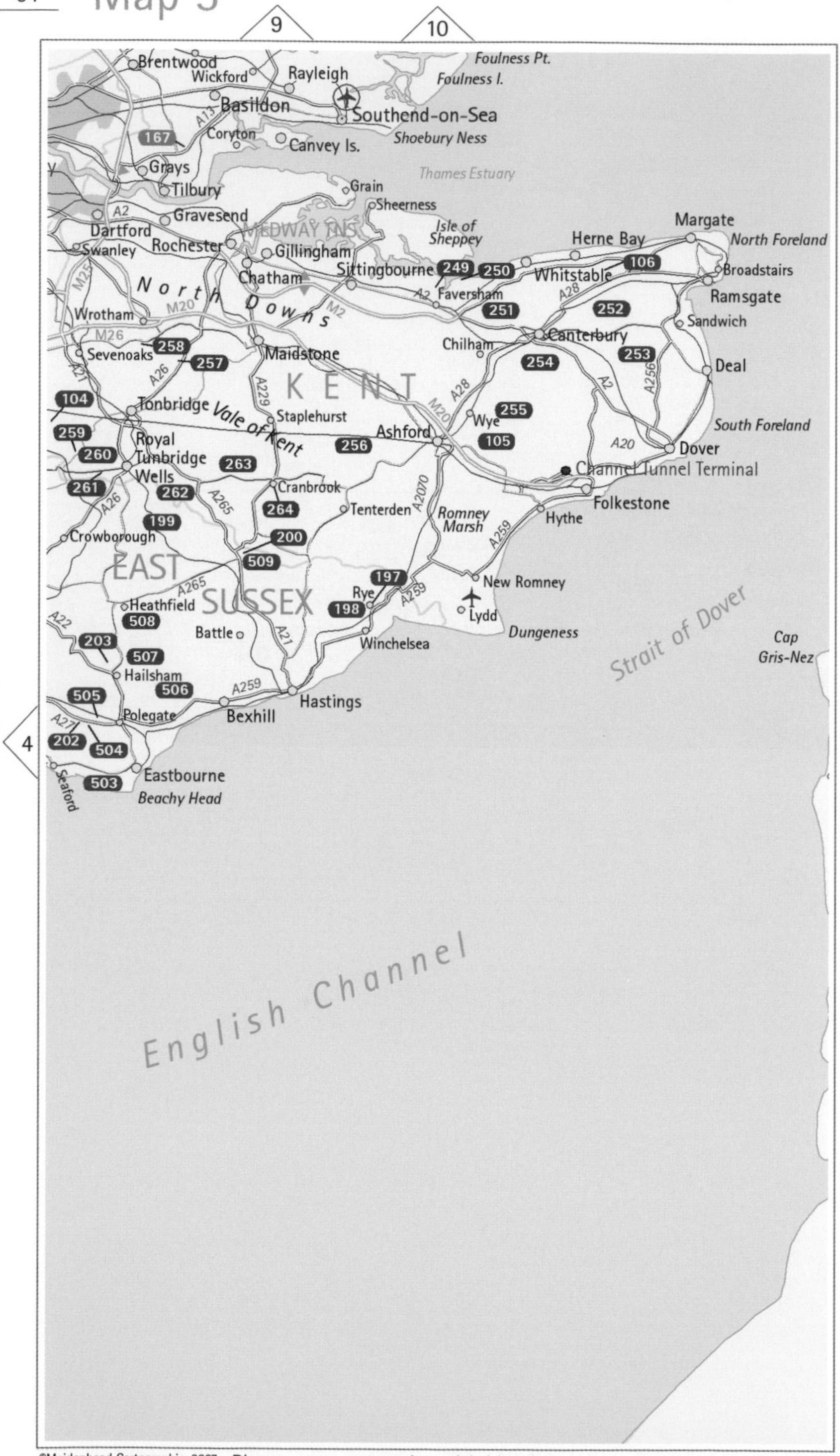

English Channel

Map 6

65

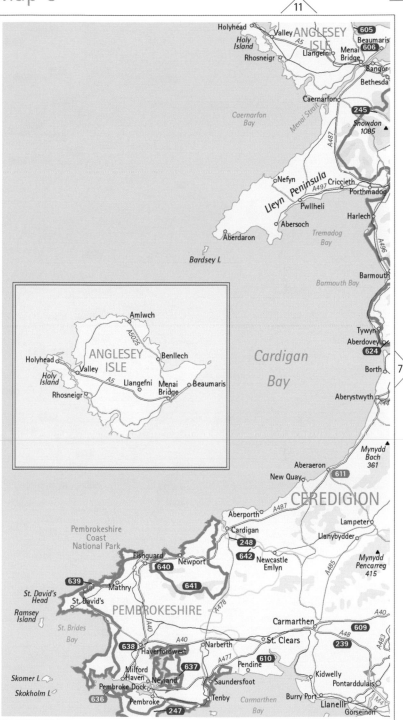

Please note: properties with blue lozenges represent pubs that
are Worth a Visit. See pages 409-439

©Maidenhead Cartographic, 2007

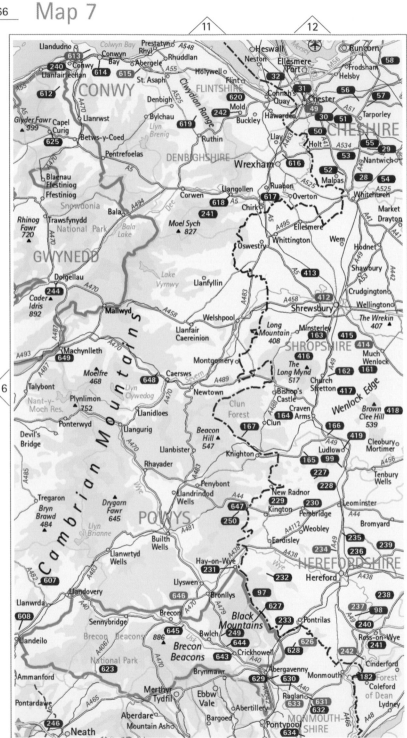

Map 8

67

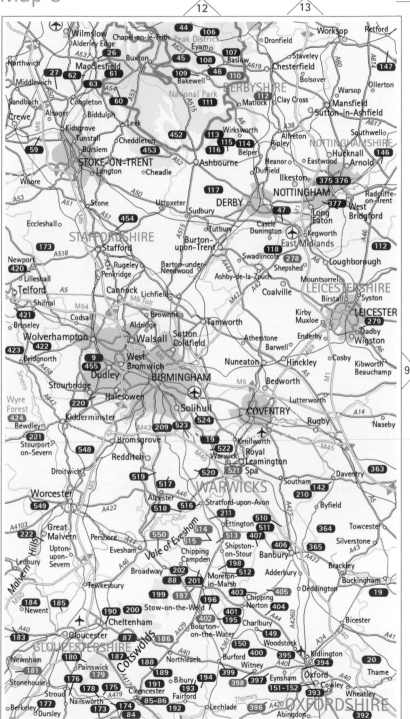

Please note: properties with blue lozenges represent pubs that are Worth a Visit. See pages 409-439

©Maidenhead Cartographic, 2007

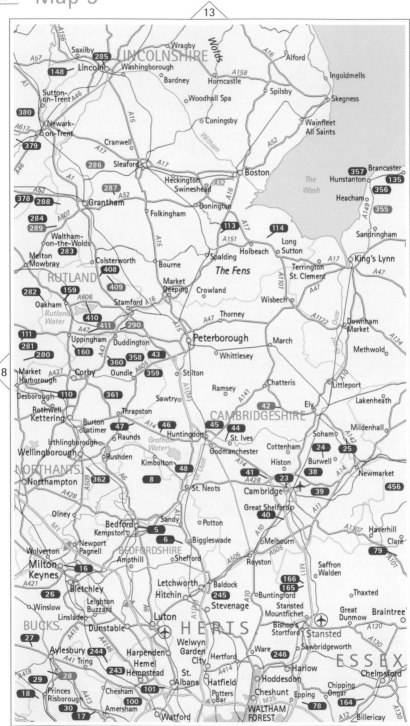

Please note: properties with blue lozenges represent pubs that are Worth a Visit. See pages 409–439

Map 10

69

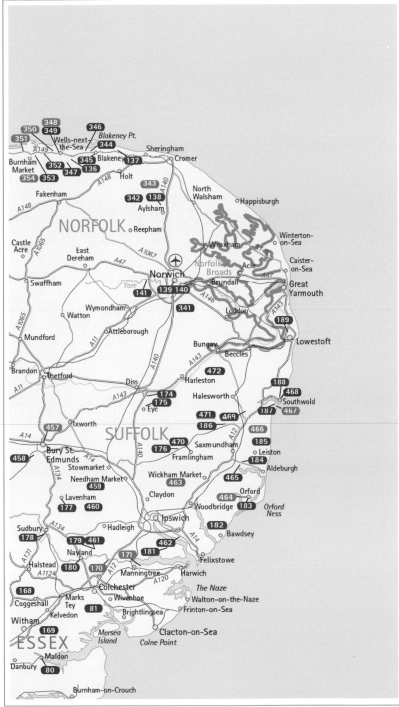

Please note: properties with blue lozenges represent pubs that
are Worth a Visit. See pages 409–439

©Maidenhead Cartographic, 2007

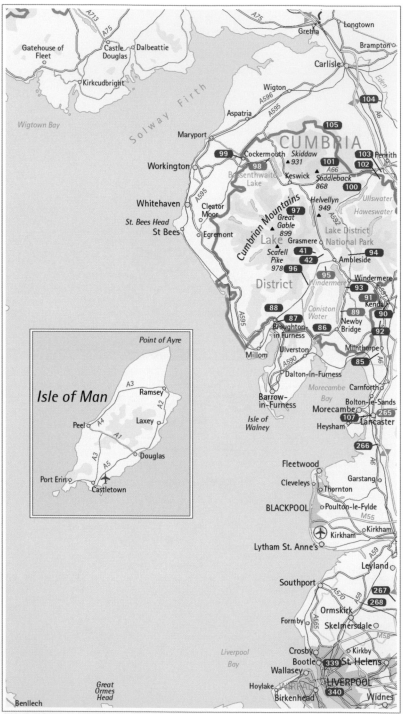

Gatehouse of Fleet
Castle Douglas
Dalbeattie
Kirkcudbright
Wigtown Bay
A713
A75
A75
Gretna
Longtown
Brampton
Carlisle
Eden
A6
Wigton
A596
A595
Aspatria
Solway Firth
Maryport
104
105
C U M B R I A
Cockermouth
Skiddaw
▲ *931*
99
98
Workington
101
103 Penrith
102
A66
Keswick
Saddleback
868
100
Bassenthwaite Lake
A595
Whitehaven
Cleator Moor
St. Bees Head
St Bees
Egremont
Cumbrian Mountains
Great Gable
▲ *899*
97
Helvellyn
▲ *949*
Ullswater
Haweswater
A592
Lake District National Park
Lake
Scafell Pike
978
Grasmere
41
42
96
Ambleside
94
District
95
Windermere
Windermere
93
91
Kendal
88
Coniston Water
87
86
Newby Bridge
89
90
92
A595
Broughton in Furness
Millom
Ulverston
A590
Milnthorpe
85
A6
Dalton-in-Furness
Morecambe Bay
Carnforth
Barrow-in-Furness
Isle of Walney
Bolton-le-Sands
Morecambe
107
265
Heysham
Lancaster
266
A6
Fleetwood
Garstang
Cleveleys
Thornton
BLACKPOOL
Poulton-le-Fylde
M55
Kirkham
Kirkham
Lytham St. Anne's
A59
Leyland
Southport
A570
A59
267
268
Ormskirk
Formby
A565
Skelmersdale
M58
Liverpool Bay
Crosby
Kirkby
Bootle
339 St. Helens
Wallasey
Hoylake
LIVERPOOL
Birkenhead
340
Widnes
Great Ormes Head
Benllech

Point of Ayre
Isle of Man
A3
Ramsey
A2
Peel
A4
Laxey
A1
A3
A5
Douglas
Port Erin
Castletown

Please note: properties with blue lozenges represent pubs that are Worth a Visit. See pages 409-439

Map 12   71

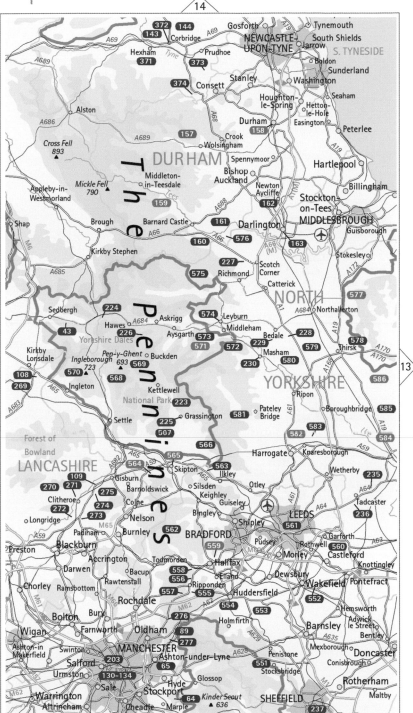

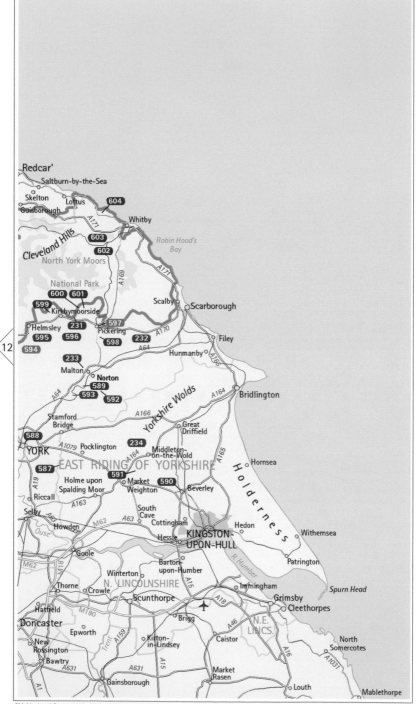

Please note: properties with blue lozenges represent pubs that are Worth a Visit. See pages 409–439

Map 14

73

Please note: properties with blue lozenges represent pubs that
are Worth a Visit. See pages 409-439

©Maidenhead Cartographic, 2007

England

Bath & N.E. Somerset

Garricks Head
Bath

The famous pub by the Theatre Royal has become a second success story for the proprietors of the King William. Built in 1720, the pub was once the home of dandy Beau Nash, uncrowned 'king' of Bath. It's been a refuge for theatre goers and actors ever since. The drinking side of things is important still but the food is something special. Chef Charlie used to work at the gutsy Anchor & Hope in Waterloo and it shows: the style is rustic-heritage English. Top produce and seasonality are paramount and the dishes pay a debt to Fergus Henderson of London's St John's; hard not to love the roast rib of beef for two with goose fat chips followed by rhubarb jelly and custard. The beers change all the time with the emphasis on small West Country breweries (Milk Street, Uley), while draught cider comes from the venerable Julian Temperley at Burrow Hill. Prices are fair, given the setting.

directions	5-minute walk from Bath railway & bus stations, opposite Bath Theatre Royal.
meals	12pm-3pm; 6pm-10.30pm. No food Sun eve. Main course £8.50-£15.
closed	Open all day.

Charlie & Amanda Digney
Garricks Head,
8 St John's Place,
Bath BA1 1ET
tel 01225 318368
web www.thegarricksheadpub.com

map: 3 entry: 1

Bath & N.E. Somerset

Gascoyne Place
Bath

"Functional yet ornate" is how Marty Grant and Wayne Taylor hoped Gascoyne Place would be – and so it is. Bang opposite the Theatre Royal, the place is steeped in history. The old city wall intrudes – beautifully – on the lower floor, there's a Georgian hoist near the main staircase and an Edwardian match-board ceiling. This sympathetic and striking restoration includes green hand-glazed tiles over the chimney breast, a Victorian mahogany bar from an East End pub and 1930s opaline lights. There are five seating areas in all: a snug, a public bar, a mezzanine area and two fine-dining rooms. Food is simple, British and based around produce sourced from local farms. Pluck a pint of Black Sheep to accompany your Rainbow Wood Farm braised shin of beef stew, or one of 65 delicious wines. A contemporary pub that feels like it's been around for years.

directions	5-minute walk from Bath railway & bus stations, next to Bath Theatre Royal.
meals	12pm-5pm (4pm Sun); 5.30pm-9.30pm. No food Sun eve. Main courses £5.50-£19.95; bar meals up to £9.95.
closed	Open all day.

Marty Grant & Wayne Taylor
Gascoyne Place,
1 Sawclose,
Bath BA1 1EY
tel 01225 445854
web www.gascoyneplace.co.uk

map: 3 entry: 2

The Old Green Tree
Bath

Right in the centre, the tiny dark pub, whose staff are fanatical about ale (at least six guest beers chalked up on the board outside), hums with life even before midday. Deep in conversation, old regulars clutch pint jars to their chests as you squeeze through the narrow wooden-floored bar into a cabin-like room. Undecorated since the panelling was installed in 1928, the pub is part of our heritage and has no intention of changing – Tim and Nick refuse any form of modernisation. In three little, low-ceilinged rooms, dog-eared banknotes from across the world and a mosaic of foreign coins are stuck up with yellowing sellotape behind the bar – along with artists' work in spring and summer. The menu is far from traditional, however, with adventurous twists on old English dishes. They have a devoted following, young and old, and drink is not limited to beer: there are malts, wines, Pimms and hot toddies. Easily a place to fall into idle chat with a stranger.

directions	Green Street, off Milsom Street. Bath city centre.
meals	12pm-3pm. Main courses £5.50-£8.50.
closed	Open all day.

Mr T Bethune & M F N Luke
The Old Green Tree,
12 Green Street,
Bath BA1 2JZ
tel   01225 448259

map: 3 entry: 3

The Salamander
Bath

The main bar, like a Victorian apothecary, is stacked with bottles on a Welsh dresser, hand pumps gleam under the glass fluted lights and looking up is hoppy heaven. The narrow room stretches its wooden self from the Parisian café-style front window to the moody orange recesses of the back. Bath Ales dominate, though the bottled beer list is eclectic (Leffe and Erdinger, for example), and there are the usual oddities such as an old beer tap collection; the Salamander has become one of the most popular – and friendly – boozers in Bath. Up a set of creaky stairs hides the 'dining room', which has recently had a refit. From an open kitchen flow dishes both traditional and with a global slant, from cheddar and jalapeno soup to Spa Ale battered haddock with chips. A fine pub without the spittle, and live folk sessions take place every other night.

directions	Behind Jollys in Bath city centre, off Milsom Street.
meals	12pm-2.30 (3pm Sun); 6.30-9.30 (12pm-3pm Sun). No food Sun eve. Main courses £8.95-£16.95; bar meals £3.95-£7.50.
closed	Open all day.

Robert Kinsella
The Salamander,
3 John Street,
Bath BA1 2JL
tel   01225 428889
web   www.bathales.com

map: 3 entry: 4

King William
Bath

The scruffy little corner pub has been transformed. Named after the king who was on the throne when the Duke of Wellington passed his Beer Act (in a bid to wean people off nasty foreign spirits, anyone with two guineas could open a beerhouse), the King Billy near Walcot Street has a chilled café/bar feel and a terrific range of wines and beers. They get into gastropub gear at lunch; the food's so popular Charlie and Amanda have created extra space in the intimate dining room upstairs (booking advised). Ingredients are locally sourced and largely organic, dishes are simple and modern – terrine of pigeon and rabbit, wild bass with roast fennel, local unpasteurised cheeses. Bare boards, village hall furniture, gold flock velvet curtains and background reggae and soul pull in an art-funky crowd. And the staff couldn't be nicer.

The Star Inn
Bath

A sepia-tinted drinkers' pub oozing history. Listed on the National Inventory of Historic Pubs, it's serious boozer and museum piece wrapped into one. A pub since 1760, refitted in the 19th century, the Star is partitioned off into three numbered rooms, each with rough planks, panelled walls, ancient settles and opaque toplights. A real coal fire pumps out the heat in one room and you can still get a free pinch of snuff from the tins on the ledge above the wall… you can almost imagine the wrinkled Victorian regulars pressing their lips to their pewter tankards. To this day Bass is served in four-pint jugs which you can take away for a small deposit. There are no meals, just the odd bap from a basket on the bar – no fuss. What counts is the beer, so much so that Alan has started brewing his own Abbey Ales and has since scaled the heady heights of the real ale world to win several awards for his Bellringer tipple. A jewel.

directions	Short walk from Walcot Street, off London Road.
meals	12pm-2.30pm; 6.30pm-10.30pm. No food Sun eve. Main courses £9-£15; bar meals £5-£14.
closed	3pm-5pm. Open all day Sat & Sun.

directions	On A4 (London Road) in Bath.
meals	Fresh rolls served all day. Rolls from £1.80.
closed	2.30pm-5.30pm. Open all day Sat & Sun.

Charlie & Amanda Digney
King William,
36 Thomas Street,
Bath BA1 5NN
tel 01225 318368
web www.kingwilliampub.com

map: 3 entry: 5

Alan Morgan
The Star Inn,
23 Vineyards, The Paragon,
Bath BA1 5NA
tel 01225 425072
web www.star-inn-bath.co.uk

map: 3 entry: 6

Bath & N.E. Somerset

The Wheatsheaf Inn
Combe Hay

Ian and Adele Barton have worked miracles on this majestic 16th-century inn, a 15-minute drive, or a two-mile hike across fields, from Bath. Overlooking the pretty village of Combe Hay, the Wheatsheaf is a long, clotted-cream stone building that trumpets original dovecotes and a fabulous garden. In summer, sit outside and soak up the views, along with a pint of Thatchers and a superior steak sandwich. (Ham, egg and chips, too, is simple but perfect.) In the darker months, settle by a crackling log fire with a glass of wine; then be ushered into the lovely dining room, all calm contemporary colours, Lloyd Loom chairs and solid oak tables. Husband and wife team Nick and Jess Brodie, ex Bath Priory, concoct stunning dishes such as rabbit cooked in Thai spices and coconut, breast of Gressingham duck and five-spice pear tart.

directions	From A367 south of Bath take left turn at Park & Ride for Combe Hay; pub 1 mile on left.
meals	12pm-2pm; 6pm-9.30pm (10pm Fri & Sat). Main courses £16.50-£20; bar meals £5-£9.
closed	3pm-6pm & Mon all day.

Ian & Adele Barton
The Wheatsheaf Inn,
Combe Hay,
Bath BA2 7EG

tel	01225 833504
web	www.wheatsheafcombehay.com

map: 3 entry: 7

Bedfordshire

The Plough at Bolnhurst
Bolnhurst

The pub equivalent of a phoenix from the ashes. A tavern has stood here since the 1400s, but 15 years ago the last one burnt down; tradition lives on in this happy reincarnation. The Plough subtly holds on to its heritage, employing reclaimed blackened beams and cast-iron chimney, yet overlaying this is a modern touch – stripped boards, hewn-wood bar and crisp white walls. Food is equally sophisticated. Chef-patron Martin Lee and his wife Jane have had a string of successes, and his grounding was with Raymond Blanc. Braised pork belly with black pudding mash, roast pumpkin tart... 'gutsy flavours but restrained formulation' are the order of the day, and, going by the heaving crowd of happy foodies, they've got it right. Come to dine rather than pop in for a swift pint – the wine list is impressive, though the well-kept Village Bike bitter also slips down a treat. Great staff, great feel, great food.

directions	On B660 north of Bedford; pub in village centre.
meals	12pm-2pm (2.30pm Sun); 6pm-9.30pm (6pm-10pm Fri & Sat). Main courses £9.95-£17; bar meals £3.95-£11.50
closed	3pm-6.30pm, Sun eve & Mon all day.

Martin & Jayne Lee
& Michael Moscrop
The Plough, Kimbolton Rd,
Bolnhurst, St Neots MK44 2EX

tel	01234 376274
web	www.bolnhurst.com

map: 9 entry: 8

Crown and Garter
Inkpen

Quiet lanes dip through fields and woodland, past cottages draped in honeysuckle – this is England at its most fairytale-ish and you can walk from the front door. The oldest part of the building is the wooden floored bar area with an inglenook and the ceilings are criss-crossed by ancient beams and beers served include local Good Old Boy and Mr Chubbs. Gill, ex-university lecturer, had a complete lifestyle change to take over here. Tuck into some hearty food – Thai curries, venison and cranberry sausages, lamb shank – in the bar, restaurant or garden, under a huge oak. Bedrooms, in a single-storey building around a garden, have painted floorboards, blended voiles, brass or wooden beds and super little bathrooms.

directions	M4 junc. 13; A4 for Speen & Winchester; left to Kintbury; left at village store; 2 miles, on left.
meals	12pm-2pm (2.30pm Sun); 6.30pm-9.30pm. No food Sun eve. Main courses £9.95-£17.95; Sun roast £10.95.
rooms	8: 6 doubles, 2 twins £90. Singles £59.50.
closed	3pm-5.30pm (5pm-7pm Sun), Mon & Tues lunch.

See pp 30-57 for full list of pubs with rooms

	Gill Hern
	Crown and Garter,
	Great Common, Inkpen,
	Hungerford RG17 9QR
tel	01488 668325
web	www.crownandgarter.com

map: 3 entry: 9

Pheasant Inn
Shefford Woodlands

It may look like it's seen better days but don't be put off: this is a cracking place with a reputation among the horse-racing set. This may explain the certain shabby gentility (rustic tiling, blood red walls, big mirrors, pine tables, heavy drapes) and certainly explains the TV tuned into the racing – often drowned out by the hubbub of jockeys and trainers. Butt's Jester, Loddon Hoppit and Wadworth 6X help charge the atmosphere, backed up by half a dozen wines by the glass. As for food, good ingredients are used in comfortingly familiar ways. Nothing is forced or pretentious and prices are reasonable. A short menu delivers simple but careful home cooking: carrot and coriander soup, lamb stew with herbed potatoes, excellent meaty burgers; for dinner, grilled fillet of turbot with rosemary roast potatoes, asparagus, ginger and shellfish sauce. It's the best M4 pit-stop for miles.

directions	M4 exit 14; A338 towards Wantage; 1st left onto B4000 for Lambourn; pub on right.
meals	12-2.30pm (12.30-2.30pm Sun); 7pm-9.30pm (9pm Mon & Sun; 7.30pm-10pm Sat & Sun). Main courses £9.95-£20.50.
closed	Open all day.

	John Ferrand
	Pheasant Inn,
	Ermin Street, Shefford Woodlands,
	Hungerford RG17 7AA
tel	01488 648284
web	www.thepheasantinnlambourn.co.uk

map: 3 entry: 10

Berkshire

The Dundas Arms
Kintbury

The Dalzell-Pipers have run this delightfully old-fashioned inn since the 1960s. At the junction of river and canal, dabbling ducks entertain diners while narrowboats glide by and the summer crowds gather on the waterside patio. All year round people come for the food; the carpeted small bar and the restaurant room at the back are both a stage for some fine country cooking. Using fresh ingredients, notably estate game and prime meats from local dealers, David's short, swift-changing menus highlight crab au gratin, crispy duck salad, honey-roast ham hock with mustard sauce, and old favourites like steak and kidney pie and bread and butter pudding. There's a great wine list, and ale drinkers will not be disappointed with Adnams Bitter and West Berkshire's beers – try a pint of the hoppy Mr Chubb's Lunchtime Bitter.

Berkshire

The Bell Inn
Aldworth

Once a medieval hall house, The Bell has the style of village pubs long gone and has been in the Macaulay family for 200 years. Plain benches, varnished tables, venerable dark-wood panelling, settles and an outside gents: it's an unspoilt place to which folk flock. There's an old wood-burning stove in one small room, a more impressive hearth in the public bar, and early evening drinkers cluster around a glass hatch. Fifty years ago the regulars were agricultural workers; today piped music and mobile phones are fervently opposed. The food fits the image and they keep it simple: choose from crusty rolls filled with thick slices of home-baked ham, salt beef or crab, good puds and winter soups of the day. Drink prices are another draw; the ales come from the local Arkell's and West Berkshire breweries and the house wines are well-priced. There's also a great big garden next to the cricket ground for summer.

directions	1 mile off A4 between Newbury & Hungerford.
meals	12pm-2pm; 7pm-9pm. No food Mon eve or Sun all day. Main courses £13.50-£16; bar meals £4.50-£16.
closed	2.30pm-6pm & Sun eve.

David Dalzell-Piper
The Dundas Arms,
53 Station Road,
Kintbury RG17 9UT

tel	01488 658263
web	www.dundasarms.co.uk

map: 3 entry: 11

directions	Off B4009, 3 miles W of Streatley.
meals	11am-2.30pm (12pm-3pm Sun); 6pm-9.30pm (7pm-9.30pm Sun). Bar meals £2.50-£3.25.
closed	3pm-6pm (7pm Sun) & Mon (except bank hols).

H E Macaulay
The Bell Inn,
Aldworth,
Reading RG8 9SE

tel	01635 578272

map: 4 entry: 12

George & Dragon
Swallowfield

You'd slay a dragon to reach the George & Dragon's unassuming door. Though very much food-orientated, the place hasn't compromised its pubby roots and gives an open-hearted welcome to all: enjoy Fuller's London Pride, Flowers IPA and good wines. There's oodles of character in flagstones, stripped beams and timbers, exposed bricks and a winter fire in the big inglenook. Walls are warm terracotta strung with country prints; over the bar is a collection of old woodworkers' planes and blue and white crockery. It's cosy and inviting, with newspapers to browse, country furniture in the bar, and a series of connecting rooms set up for the serious business of dining. An enterprising menu raids the globe for inspiration while respecting British classics, and is supplemented by daily blackboard specials; try pan-fried red snapper, five-cheese tortellini, treacle sponge. In summer, a pretty garden for you and your (well-behaved) children.

The Pot Kiln
Frilsham

TV chef Mike Robinson drank his very first pint in this remote and determinedly old-fashioned ale house – and jumped at the chance to buy it. A sprucing up of the dining room has not altered the faded character one jot, and you still find thirsty agricultural workers crowding the tiny, basic bar (bare tables, dartboard, doorstep sandwiches) with foaming pints of Brick Kiln Bitter from the brewery across the field. Perfectly lovely in summer – the garden looks onto fields – it's also wonderful in winter, when log fires and a menu strong on game come into their own. In the restaurant expect "European country cooking". That means rich pumpkin soup with fontina cheese fondue, warm salad of wood pigeon, gnocchi with wild mushrooms and truffle, daube of slow-cooked oxtail, hot treacle tart. The wine list is serious and affordable, the smell of baking bread drifts through the bar and the service is everything it should be.

directions	M4 junc. 11; A33; turn for Swallowfield.
meals	12pm-2.30pm (3pm Sun); 7pm-10pm (9pm Sun). Main courses £9.95-£16.95; bar meals £5.95-£7.95.
closed	Open all day.

Paul Dailey
George & Dragon,
Church Road,
Swallowfield, Reading RG7 1TJ
tel   0118 988 4432
web   www.georgeanddragonswallowfield.co.uk

map: 4 entry: 13

directions	In Yattendon, turn opp. church for Frilsham. Cross motorway; on for Bucklebury; on right after 0.5 miles.
meals	12pm-2pm; 7pm-9pm. Main courses £13-£15. Set lunch £12.50 & £14.95 (weekdays only).
closed	3pm-6pm. Open all day Sat & Sun.

Mike & Katie Robinson
The Pot Kiln,
Frilsham,
Yattendon RG18 0XX
tel   01635 201366
web   www.potkiln.co.uk

map: 4 entry: 14

The Royal Oak
Maidenhead

Modest at first glance, it has star quality inside. Nick Parkinson (son of showbiz dad Michael) may have given this small inn a contemporary and stylish lift, but he has cleverly managed to keep lots of the traditional character. There are scrubbed wooden floors and stripped beams, timbers and panelling, and a collection of cricketing mementos... along with photographs of star personalities and Dad's interviewees: Mohamed Ali, Victoria Beckham, Sting. The bar is cosy and inviting, with solid wooden furniture, an open fire and a couple of armchairs. Beyond, dining tables are laid with white linen on gingham undercloths. Filled baguettes are available at lunchtime, while the dining room's food is modern and classy, with a very good choice of wines by the glass. The Royal Oak is friendly and well run, opening its door to drinkers and diners with equal enthusiasm.

Hind's Head Hotel
Bray

When the Tudor tavern across the road from Heston Blumenthal's Fat Duck came on the market, the triple-Michelin-starred chef snapped it up. Two years on, the old Hind's Head is once again the most genuine of village pubs (polished panelling, open fires) with one striking difference: terrific food. Expect a short slate of British classics... pea and ham soup, potted shrimps with watercress salad, oxtail and kidney pudding, roast cod with champ and parsley sauce, Heston's trademark triple-cooked chips, treacle tart. Dominic Chapman, virtuoso Fat Duck-trained chef, heads the kitchen and never loses the focus: to maximise the taste of the finest and freshest materials. (Note that side dishes are extra.) Heston's interest in food history, together with the involvement of food historians at Hampton Court Palace, may put historical English recipes on the menu. You are advised to book if you wish to sit in the restaurant end.

directions	On B3024 west of Paley Street, between A330 south of Maidenhead & Twyford.
meals	12pm-2.30pm (3pm Sun); 6.30pm-10pm. Main courses £9.50-£14.50.
closed	3pm-6pm & Sun eve.

Nick Parkinson
The Royal Oak,
Paley Street,
Maidenhead SL6 3JN

tel	01628 620541
web	www.theroyaloakpaleystreet.com

map: 4 entry: 15

directions	On B3028 in Bray.
meals	12pm-2.30pm (4pm Sun); 6.30pm-9pm. No food Sun eve. Main courses £12-£18.50; bar meals £1.50-£10.95.
closed	Open all day.

Heston Blumenthal
Hind's Head Hotel,
High Street, Bray,
Maidenhead SL6 2AB

tel	01628 626151
web	www.hindsheadhotel.co.uk

map: 4 entry: 16

Two Brewers
Windsor

A locals' secret revealed. In the royal town, next to the Home Park gates and the famous Long Walk, small rooms meander around a tiny panelled bar and come quaintly decked with dark beams, wooden floors and scrubbed-wood tables. One room with big shared tables reveals dark red walls and matching ceilings; the other two have more intimate seating areas. There are winter fires, magazines to dip into and walls crammed with posters, press-cuttings, pictures and mirrors. On a blackboard above the fire, anecdotes commemorating each day are chalked up in preference to menu specials. If you reserve a table you won't go hungry: the compact menu follows a steady pub line, with four daily specials, roasts on Sundays, homely puddings and informal tapas on Friday and Saturday evenings. Beer, champagne, cigars… and a sprinkling of pavement tables to tempt you after the rigours of The Big Tour. *No under-18s.*

Greene Oak
Oakley Green

With a background in London gastropubbery, Henry and Katherine Cripps could hardly fail at their first solo venture, a swishly renovated dining pub close to Windsor, Ascot, Sunningdale and foodie hot-spot Bray. Enter a warm-coloured interior of wood and slate floors and soft green hues, period features, antique French light fittings and big country mirrors. Most people come to eat and the style is traditional with a contemporary twist, a mix of British classic dishes and fashionable modern. Lunch may include pheasant and pistachio terrine with chilli jam and Caesar salad, or homemade beefburger with tomato and chilli relish. In the evening, potted crab and brown shrimp perhaps, roast belly pork with wok-fried Asian greens, fillet steak with béarnaise – polished off by a Valrhona chocolate pot with mascarpone. Service, wines and beers are as elegant as all the rest.

directions	Off High Street, next to Mews.
meals	12pm-2.30pm (4pm Sat & Sun); 6.30pm-10pm (tapas menu only Fri & Sat eve). Main courses £8-£13.50. Sunday roast £10-£12.
closed	Open all day.

Robert Gillespie
Two Brewers,
34 Park Street,
Windsor SL4 1LB

tel	01753 855426

map: 4 entry: 17

directions	On B3383 south of A308, 2 miles west of Windsor.
meals	12pm-3pm (3.30pm Sun); 6.30pm-9.30pm. No food Sun eve. Main courses £7.90-£16.90.
closed	Open all day.

Henry & Katherine Cripps
Greene Oak,
Oakley Green,
Windsor SL4 5UW

tel	01753 864294
web	www.thegreeneoak.co.uk

map: 4 entry: 18

Birmingham

The Orange Tree
Chadwick End

The flagship dining pub of the Classic Country Pubs group has a striking interior. Be seduced by earthy colours, lime-washed low beams, open log fires, big lamps, deep sofas around low tables and chunky lightwood furnishings in airy eating rooms. A gorgeous Italian-style deli counter shows off breads, cheeses and vintage oils. This tastefully rustic-Mediterranean décor with oriental touches is matched by an ambitious, Italian-inspired menu, and diners with deep pockets descend in their droves for authentic wood-fired pizzas and robust, full-flavoured meat dishes cooked on an in-view rotisserie spit, perhaps Moroccan lamb or rib-eye steak. There are also homemade pasta meals such as linguine with prawns, coriander, chilli and coconut, delicious warm salads and fishy specials. Great wines by the bottle or glass, Greene King ales, a heated patio dotted with stylish teak tables and all-day opening hours.

directions	On A4141 between Warwick & Solihull. On edge of village, 5 miles south of M42 junc. 5.
meals	12pm-2.30pm (4.30pm Sun); 6pm-9.30pm. No food Sun eve. Main courses £8.95-£18.95.
closed	Open all day.

	Paul Hales
	The Orange Tree,
	Warwick Road,
	Chadwick End B93 0BN
tel	01564 785364
web	www.theorangetreepub.co.uk

map: 8 entry: 19

Bristol

Star and Dove
Bristol

In a funky, hilly suburb of Bristol, this once unloved boozer has been joyfully revived. And its young owner carries a history: Eamon Fullalove used to be a top chef at the celebrated Fifteen, Jamie Oliver's London restaurant. His first solo venture since leaving the Jamie stable is this – a red-brick, early 20th-century neighbourhood pub with parquet floors and fireplaces intact. Walls are painted green and red, there are battered leather armchairs, rickety village hall chairs and a 'cor blimey' piano in the left-hand bar – a laid-back shabby chic. In spite of Eamon's cheffy credentials, food in the bar is restricted to pork pies, cheeses and charcuterie (the best, naturally); upstairs, the restaurant flaunts an Italian and French-inspired menu with bistro classics such as steak and frites, steaming bowls of mussels and generous platefuls of pasta.

directions	10-min walk from Bristol Temple Meads station. From York Road, left into St Luke's Road, past Victoria Park.
meals	12-3pm (4pm Sat & Sun); 6pm-10pm. Main courses £3-£15.
closed	Open all day.

	Eamon Fullalove
	& Christiane Jones
	Star and Dove,
	75 St Luke's Road,
	Totterdown, Bristol BS3 4RY
tel	0117 300 3712

map: 3 entry: 20

The Albion
Bristol

Clifton village is Georgian to the core: Bath without tourists. Boutiques, restaurants and delis abound but no-one had, until summer 2005, quite mastered the gastropub idea. Step forward Messrs Johnson, Rayner and George who have given the back alley student boozer the classiest of makeovers with a summer patio, a long bar serving Butcombe and monthly guest ales, a winter log fire and a discreet wooden staircase leading to a restaurant that feels like a private room. They may have installed a pair of chefs with noteworthy pedigrees and packed the open bar with Clifton's loudest and proudest but the Albion is still a pub, its menu available at every table. There are light bites at lunch and weekend brunch (artisan and home-cured charcuterie; skirt steak, chips and béarnaise) and posh nosh at dinner (parsnip and pear soup; Cornish brill, boulangère potatoes, cockles and butter sauce). Service comes with a young smile.

Bag o'Nails
Bristol

A five-minute walk from the harbourside and centre, this is a one-room drinkers' pub with a big reputation. Gas lamps, a tiled Victorian bar, a bare-boarded floor with three 'portholes' surveying the cellar, the odd game of draughts... it's that rare thing, a traditional boozer. And the sight of nine shiny handpumps offering real ales from across the UK makes it a honeypot for CAMRA types (take a pint home). A blackboard of 'coming soon' beers whets the appetite for future visits, there's a fabulous selection of bottled beers and ciders from independent breweries at good prices and a formidable range of ports. Dispensers for draught lager are camouflaged on the wall, the food menu stops at filled rolls for £1, and there's no jukebox, simply the landlord's radio in the background. A serious temple for all things malt and hops, but with just five tables, get there early or expect to stand at the bar.

directions	In centre of Clifton village. (Tricky) on-street parking.
meals	12pm-3pm; 7pm-10pm. No food Sun eve. Main courses £12-£18.50; bar meals £6-£10.
closed	Open all day.

Camilla Dunsterville
The Albion,
Boyces Avenue,
Clifton, Bristol BS8 4AA
tel   0117 973 3522
web   www.thealbionclifton.co.uk

map: 3 entry: 21

directions	Right on Hotwells roundabout, opp. SS Great Britain.
meals	Rolls only (all day).
closed	2.15pm-5.30pm (3pm-5pm Fri) & Mon lunch. Open all day Sat & Sun.

James Dean
Bag o'Nails,
141 St Georges Road,
Hotwells,
Bristol BS1 5UW
tel   0117 940 6776

map: 3 entry: 22

Bristol

Cornubia
Bristol

Hidden behind the head offices of the Soil Association is one of central Bristol's best-kept secrets. This characterful inn used to be two Georgian houses; now, after several changes of ownership in recent years, it has been rescued by Wiltshire's Hidden Brewery and given a new lease of life. Out goes the brown paintwork and the notoriously threadbare and sticky carpet, in comes a fresh a lick of paint and a new function room upstairs. Surrounded by modern office blocks, this is a drinkers' pub at heart with up to eight real ales available at any one time; stout's on draught and there are always a couple of west country ciders on tap. Food is basic – pies, baguettes, sandwiches – but with so many local beers to chose from, the Cornubia is driven more by conversation than gastronomy. A boozer with soul – and popular with office workers and *Evening Post* scribes.

Bristol

The Hare on the Hill
Bristol

Not much to encourage you from the outside, but step through the swing doors and you feel that you're in a pub that knows its business. Bath Ales took on this down-at-heel street corner boozer in 1998 for complete renovation – yet it feels as if it's been like this for a hundred years. Wooden floors, simple furniture and fuss-free décor lend a certain masculinity and the cosmopolitan/student crowd clearly appreciates the changes and enjoy what the landlord prides himself on: good beer and conversation. No games machines, and the TV in the corner, provided for occasional sport, barely makes an impact. The place is full of nooks and crannies so you can easily find a quiet spot for a chat and a cracking pint of Bath Gem. Homemade soups, Spanish chicken and roasts on Sundays are prepared and cooked on the spot, and it was CAMRA Pub of the Year the moment Bath Ales moved in.

directions	5-min walk from Temple Meads station. From Victoria St, right into The Countershop, right again into Temple St.
meals	12pm-8pm Mon-Fri. Main courses £4-£7.
closed	Sat & Sun lunch. Open all day Mon-Fri.

Ross Nicol & Karen Beesley
Cornubia,
142 Temple Street,
Bristol BS1 6EN
tel   0117 925 4415

map: 3 entry: 23

directions	At top of Nine Tree Hill overlooking Stokes Croft.
meals	12pm-2pm (4pm Sun); 6pm-9pm. Main courses from £5.45. Bar meals from £1.95.
closed	2.30pm-5pm. Open all day Fri-Sun.

Paul & Dee Tanner
The Hare on the Hill,
Dove Street,
Kingsdown, Bristol BS2 8LX
tel   0117 908 1982
web   www.bathales.com

map: 3 entry: 24

Bristol

White Hart
Littleton upon Severn

Park at the back but go in at the front: it's worth it for the door alone. Step into a panelled vestibule with a wonderful turned staircase; marvel at huge fireplaces in big, rambling, ex-farmhouse rooms. Hops hang from main bar beams, tables, chairs and cushioned settles are scattered across flagged floors, and it's packed on Sundays. At this 16th-century pub the beers are good and the kitchen ingredients carefully sourced. Outside, a sheltered terrace and a splendid front garden for summer revels and peaceful views. No music, just vintage billiards in the back bar, shelves of books and a good family room. Greg is the man in the kitchen, and our butter-fried, corn-fed chicken with creamed wild mushrooms and rocket salad was generous and full of flavour. The ploughman's, the baguettes and the nursery puds look equally good. Very nice staff, too.

directions	From old Severn Bridge for Avonmouth, then Thornbury. 1st left at Elberton.
meals	12pm–2pm (2.30pm Sat); 6.30pm–9.30pm (12pm–9.30pm Sun). Main courses £7.95–£14.95. Sunday roast £8.50.
closed	2.30pm–6pm. Open all day Sun.

Greg Bailey
White Hart,
Littleton-on-Severn,
Thornbury BS35 1NR
tel 01454 412275

map: 3 entry: 25

Buckinghamshire

The Crooked Billet
Newton Longville

The twin talents of a former Sommelier of the Year, John Gilchrist, and head chef Emma have put the 16th-century pub on the county's culinary map. With innovative menus and a 400-bin wine list (all, astonishingly, available by the glass), you may imagine it's more restaurant than pub but it's an exemplary local with a great bar, weekly-changing ales, a log-fired inglenook and a great pubby atmosphere. Munch sandwiches, salads or steak and chips in the beamed bar at lunch; or crayfish Caesar salad, crispy pork belly with mustard mash, cabbage and bacon, and treacle and ginger parkin in the restaurant – inviting with its deep red walls, candles and country prints. Delicious cheeses come with fig and walnut cake and Emma's seasonal menus make full use of produce from first-class suppliers, villagers included.

directions	From Milton Keynes A421 for Buckingham, left for N. Longville.
meals	7pm–10pm (12.30pm–3pm Sun); bar meals 12pm–2pm Tues-Sat. No food Sun eve. Main courses £12.50–£22.50; bar meals £5.75–£10; tasting menu £55.
closed	2.30pm–5.30pm; Mon lunch.

John & Emma Gilchrist
The Crooked Billet,
2 Westbrook End, Newton Longville,
Milton Keynes MK17 0DF
tel 01908 373936
web www.thebillet.co.uk

map: 9 entry: 26

Buckinghamshire

Five Arrows Hotel
Waddesdon

Live like a lord at this inn-hotel yards from the A41. Inside: woven carpets, antique furnishings and unusual paintings from Lord Rothschild's collection. It is part of the model village built in 1887 by Baron Rothschild – along with Waddesdon Manor and its Versailles-like gardens. The recent Pugin-style refurbishment creates an indulgent mood in perfect keeping with the lofty ceilings and open fires. From a cosy chair in the bar, enjoy a pint of Fuller's London Pride or a glass of champagne as you browse the papers. In the dining room, carefully sourced produce is subtly transformed into escalope of pork with cream and wild mushroom sauce, roasted sea bass with fennel and parmesan crisps, and honeycomb ice cream, while the magnificent wine list focuses on Rothschild interests around the world. There's a peaceful sheltered garden too, and the service is impeccable.

directions	6 miles west of Aylesbury on A41.
meals	12pm-2.15pm; 7pm-9.15pm (12pm-7pm Sun). Main courses from £15.50; bar meals from £6.50.
closed	Open all day.

Simon Offen
Five Arrows Hotel,
Waddesdon,
Aylesbury HP18 0JE
tel 01296 651727
web www.waddesdon.org.uk

map: 9 entry: 27

Buckinghamshire Pub with rooms

The Dinton Hermit
Ford

With a bright fire, friendly proprietors, freshly-prepared food and rural views, this 15th-century pub-hotel – named after the man who signed Charles II's death warrant – has been transformed in three short years. The old part is listed, the rest is the best of new, and small pretty windows overlook wide fields. Dine on roast beef sandwiches and local Wychert ale in the cosy bar with its inglenook and vast cushioned settle – or book a table in the stone-walled restaurant. On seasonal menus are king prawn and avocado salad with balsamic dressing, rack of lamb served with cassoulet beans, and fabulous wines, brandies and hand-rolled cigars. You have a garden for summer and rooms for the night: charming four-posters and 'Regency' bedrooms in the old, wonky-floored part, stylish modern rooms in the converted barn.

directions	Off A418 between Thame & Aylesbury.
meals	12-2pm; 7-9pm (12-7pm Sun). Main courses £6.95-£16.95; bar meals £5.50-£10.50.
rooms	13: 12 doubles, 1 twin £80-£125. Singles from £80.
closed	Open all day.

See pp 30-57 for full list of pubs with rooms

John & Debbie Collinswood
The Dinton Hermit,
Water Lane, Ford Village,
Aylesbury HP17 8XH
tel 01296 747473
web www.dinton-hermit.com

map: 9 entry: 28

The Green Dragon
Haddenham

In what was once a manorial courthouse by Haddenham's pretty green, Paul Berry creates fabulous modern food. In the attractive, open-plan bar, kitted out with a laid-back medley of furniture and an open fire, relax over a pint of village-brewed Notley Ale or one of several good wines by the glass. Graze on a decent lunchtime sandwich or a platter of organic cheeses, or settle down to something more substantial. The imaginative menu never stays still and set lunch (Monday to Thursday) is a snip at £11.50. Look forward to canon of lamb with spring greens, white beans and basil dressing, or halibut with creamed bacon, lettuce and peas (they have 18 different ways with fish). Sweet tooths will be happy with a pretty plateful of peach tart tatin or a cappuccino crème brûlée. Families come for Sunday lunch served by bright, informed staff – and there's a sheltered courtyard for al fresco meals.

directions	2 miles from Thame; follow signs for Haddenham & Thame Parkway station.
meals	12pm-2pm, 7pm-9.30pm. Main courses £9.95-£18.00; set menu £11.50 & £14.95 (Mon-Thur); Sunday lunch £19.95.
closed	3pm-6.30pm & Sun from 4pm.

Paul Berry & Peter Moffat
The Green Dragon,
8 Churchway,
Haddenham HP17 8AA
tel 01844 291403
web www.eatatthedragon.co.uk

map: 9 entry: 29

The Polecat Inn
Prestwood

A quirky place, fun and packed with character. Chintzy curtains, low lighting and beams, button-backed chairs, cosy corners, stuffed animals, antique clocks, rugs and a fireplace stacked with logs make the yellow-painted 17th-century Polecat Inn feel more home than pub. The unusual flint bar serves several real ales, including Morland Old Speckled Hen and Marstons Pedigree, and there is an impressive selection of malts, and 16 wines by the glass. Among ticking clocks and happy banter, walkers and families tuck into tempting dishes such as steak and kidney pie, seafood hotpot, or roast duck with orange and cognac sauce. A roulade of date and pecan with butterscotch cream might just finish you off, so take one of the walking maps thoughtfully provided by John and work off any over-indulgence in the Chiltern Hills. It's a beautifully run place, and has a gorgeous garden.

directions	On A4128 between Great Missenden & High Wycombe.
meals	12pm-2pm; 6.30pm-9pm. Main courses £9.20-£14; bar meals £3.70-£5.50.
closed	2.30pm-6pm & Sun from 3pm.

John Gamble
The Polecat Inn,
170 Wycombe Road,
Prestwood HP16 0HJ
tel 01494 862253

map: 9 entry: 30

Buckinghamshire Pub with rooms

Three Horseshoes Inn
Radnage

It's a year ago that chef Simon Crawshaw swapped Le Gavroche and Chez Nico for the remotest pub in the Chilterns. His enthusiasm for this sweet 18th-century brick cottage, lost down a leafy lane, remains undimmed; now there are four super bedrooms up in the eaves. Named after local shoots, with Farrow & Ball colours, bold fabrics, flat-screen TVs and cosy extras, they are quirky and fun, one with an unusual claw-foot hip bath. Pints of Rebellion can be quaffed by the log fire in the tiny flagstoned bar, while Simon's imaginative food – scallops with chorizo and cauliflower fritter, lamb rump with aubergine caviar and black olive jus, lemon cheesecake with confit pineapple – will be satisfying the foodies next door. And there are excellent lunchtime sandwiches for passing walkers. The garden overlooks tranquil hills .

directions	M40 junc. 5 to Stokenchurch, left to Radnage; 2 miles; 1st left into Bennett End; sharp bend to right, pub on hill on left.
meals	12pm-2.30pm; 6.30pm-9.30pm. Main courses £10.50-£15.50; bar meals (lunch) £3.75-£13.50.
rooms	4 doubles £85-£95. Singles £65.
closed	3pm-6pm & Mon. Open all day Sun till 8pm.

See pp 30-57 for full list of pubs with rooms

	Simon Crawshaw Three Horseshoes Inn, Bennett End, Radnage, High Wycombe HP14 4EB
tel	01494 483273
web	www.thethreehorseshoes.net

map: 4 entry: 31

Buckinghamshire

Old Queen's Head
Penn

David and Becky Salisbury's mini-empire has expanded with the inspired acquisition of this pub by the green. Dating from 1666 it has character and charm while inside, old beams and timbers in the rambling bar and dining areas blend perfectly with a stylish and contemporary décor – rug-strewn flags, warm colour-washed walls, polished boards, classic fabrics, lovely old oak. Food follows the successful formula of the Alford Arms, Frithsden, The Swan at Denham and the Royal Oak at Marlow, innovative seasonal menus and chalkboard specials mixing classic pub recipes with modern British flair. Choices range from 'small plates' – eg. rustic breads with roast garlic and pan-fried pigeon on roast beetroot with crispy shallots – to big dishes of creamy fish pie or sea bass with saffron potatoes and red pepper confit. Great puddings too, 17 wines by the glass and a glorious summer garden.

directions	From High Wycombe (M40 junc. 4), A40 towards Beaconsfield, then left for 1.5 miles into Hammersley Lane; pub on left, opposite church.
meals	12pm-2.30pm (4pm Sun); 7pm-10pm. Main courses £10.25-£16,
closed	Open all day.

	David & Becky Salisbury Old Queen's Head, Hammersley Lane, Penn, High Wycombe HP10 8EY
tel	01494 813371
web	www.oldqueensheadpenn.co.uk

map: 4 entry: 32

Buckinghamshire

Hand and Flowers
Marlow

Tipped as 'the next Ludlow', Marlow is on the up and chef Tom Kerridge is leading the way. When he and Beth took over, the old slot machines were generating more money than the refreshments – how things have changed! Informal and charming, with low beams, newspapers and the odd vibrant sofa, this is reputed to be a favourite haunt of über-chef Heston Blumenthal (a Marlow resident). Foodies travel far to sample Tom's cooking. Sausages are from pigs that munch windfalls in the orchards of a Suffolk estate, grass-fed fillet steak is from Denham Vale, oysters from County Louth. There can't be many pubs where you can choose between homemade pork scratchings and a pint of perfect Greene King IPA, or an impeccably cooked fillet of sea bream with salsify, cockles and parsley sauce. Booking is advised.

directions	Head west out of Marlow town centre; pub on right in 0.25 mile.
meals	12pm-2.30pm; 7pm-9.30pm. Main courses £12.50-£21; bar lunch from £7.50.
closed	3pm-6pm & Sun eve.

Tom & Beth Kerridge
Hand and Flowers,
126 West Street,
Marlow SL7 2BP
tel   01628 482277
web   www.thehandandflowers.co.uk

map: 4 entry: 33

Buckinghamshire

Royal Oak
Marlow

A mile yet a world away from Marlow's bustle, the old whitewashed cottage stands in a hamlet on the edge of the common. It's one of a thriving quartet of dining pubs owned by David and Becky Salisbury (the Alford Arms, Hertfordshire; the Swan and the Old Queens Head, Buckinghamshire) and the relaxed but professional staff make it special. Beyond the rosemary-edged terrace is a stylish, open-plan bar, cheerful with terracotta walls, rug-strewn boards, scrubbed tables, cushioned pews and crackling log fires. Order a pint of local Rebellion ale or one of the 17 wines available by the glass and check out the daily chalkboard or printed menu. Innovative pub grub comes in the form of 'small plates' (salt and pepper squid on cannelini bean salad) and main meals (pan-roast lamb rump on pancetta with braised cos lettuce): fresh and delicious. Sprawling summer gardens are filled with fragrant herbs and there's a sunny terrace with teak tables and smart brollies.

directions	From Marlow A4155; ight signed Bovingdon Green.
meals	12pm-2.30pm (4pm Sun); 7pm-10pm. Main courses £10.75-£15.25.
closed	Open all day.

Ms Trasna Rice-Giff
Royal Oak,
Frieth Road, Bovingdon Green,
Marlow SL7 2JF
tel   01628 488611
web   www.royaloakmarlow.co.uk

map: 4 entry: 34

Buckinghamshire

King of Prussia
Farnham Royal

Two year's on and the King of Prussia remains a hugely popular pub. It's the sort of place where you wish you'd ordered absolutely everything that goes by. Spicy cauliflower stew with king prawns and Thai curried mussels may be considered pub classics these days, but canon of Welsh lamb with dauphinoise and rosemary and broad bean sauce, and rib-eye steak with chunky chips and peppercorn sauce have a timeless appeal. Puddings get the respect they deserve and include such enticements as apple crumble with vanilla custard and winter berry brulée. The décor – much of it wood – is simple and understated and there's a delightful informality about the whole operation, helped along by friendly, well-drilled service. It's a great little place for drinkers: a small, revamped bar area sports leather seats and dispenses real ales alongside the daily papers and magazines.

directions	A355 towards Slough; 3.5 miles; right into Cherry Tree Road; right into Blackpond Lane.
meals	12pm-2.15pm (4pm Sun); 6pm-9.15pm. Main courses £9.95-£19.50.
closed	3pm-6pm & Sun eve.

Chris Boot & David Gibbs
King of Prussia,
Blackpond Lane,
Farnham Royal, Slough SL2 3EG
tel 01753 643006
web www.thekingofprussia.com

map: 4 entry: 35

Buckinghamshire

The Ostrich
Colnbrook

The Ostrich is an ancient, rambling place, within a mile of the motorways. New owners Cross Oak Inns must have balked at the prospect of refurbishment, but a new Ostrich has emerged, and one that vibrantly blends the old with the new. The wonky timbered façade remains, but step through the huge glass doors that span the old entrance and you enter another world. There's a glittering scarlet and steel bar that picks up the colour in the original stained glass, while the floors are slate-tiled and the furniture chunky. Then there are massive, sand-blasted beams, original standing timbers and, in the atmospheric dining room, lovely, bowed, putty-coloured walls. Food is modern British and the menu wide ranging, so pitch up for salads and sandwiches, ham hock terrine, herb-crusted lamb rump with red wine jus, and chocolate chilli parfait with mango compote. Take a peek upstairs at the lofty, tightly raftered function room – amazing.

directions	Colnbrook is signed off M4 (junc. 5) & A4 east of Slough.
meals	12pm-2.15pm; 6pm-9.15pm (7pm-9.45pm Sat; 8.45pm Sun). Main courses £8.75-£18.50; sandwiches from £4.95.
closed	3pm-6pm. Open all day Fri-Sun.

Lee Mitchell
The Ostrich,
High Street, Colnbrook,
Slough SL3 0JZ
tel 01753 682628
web www.theostrichcolnbrook.co.uk

map: 4 entry: 36

Buckinghamshire

The Swan Inn
Denham

Swap the bland and everyday for the picture-book perfection of Denham village and the stylish Swan. Georgian, double-fronted, swathed in wisteria, the building has had a makeover by David and Becky Salisbury (of the Alford Arms, the Queen's Head and the Royal Oak). It, too, has been transformed by rug-strewn boards, modishly chunky tables, cushioned settles, big mirrors, a log fire and a fabulous terrace and garden for outdoor meals. Food is modern British. If pressed for time, choose from the 'small plates' list – seared spiced squid with chorizo cream or pickled mushrooms with parmesan and griddled bread. If you've nothing to rush for, linger over free-range pork and oregano sausages and mash with red onion gravy, accompanied by a pint of Courage Best or one of 17 wines by the glass. The owners have thought of everything, and the gardens are large enough to lose the kids in.

directions	From A412 (M25 junc. 17 or M40 junc. 1) follow signs for Denham.
meals	12pm-2.30pm (4pm Sun); 7pm-10pm. Main courses £10.75-£14.75.
closed	Open all day.

David & Becky Salisbury
The Swan Inn,
Village Road,
Denham UB9 5BH
tel   01895 832085
web   www.swaninndenham.co.uk

map: 4 entry: 37

Cambridgeshire

Crown and Punchbowl
Horningsea

The second of Oliver Thain and Richard Bradley's pubs (the other's The Cock at Hemingford Grey) combines the traditional with contemporary zing. This large, homely set-up (two buildings, one 17th century, the other Victorian, backing onto the church and graveyard) is actually run as a restaurant; there is no bar as such – only one real ale is served – but the menu has many old-fashioned delights. Try the signature dish, their sausages with a choice of flavoured mash and sauces; or rabbit and apple salad with hazelnut vinaigrette, confit duck leg with chorizo and shallot dauphine, wilted greens and braised red cabbage or aubergine tart with fennel and wild mushrooms. For pudding there's hot chocolate fondant with ginger ice cream. With the food so tasty and the staff so charming, it's hard not to like such a place.

directions	Off A14, 2 miles north west of Cambridge.
meals	12pm-2.30pm; 6.30pm-9pm (9.30pm Fri & Sat). Main courses £9.95-£15.95; set lunch £9.95 & £12.95; Sunday roast £12.95.
closed	2.30pm-6.30pm & Sun eve.

Oliver Thain
Crown and Punchbowl,
The High Street,
Horningsea CB5 9JG
tel   01223 860643
web   www.cambscuisine.com

map: 9 entry: 38

Hole in the Wall
Little Wilbraham

Hiding down a hundred lanes, the Hole in the Wall was just another pretty country pub. In the hands of veteran chef Stephen Bull it has been transformed, with Jenny Chapman perfect front of house. It's clear it's well-loved; regulars drop by for a swift half in the big timbered bar, and gather for lunch in the newer, country-style restaurant at the back. In the bar are horse brasses and country prints, junk-shop find tables and several winter log fires. In contrast to this old-fashioned rusticity the food is decidedly modern: ingredients are as local and as organic as can be and the blackboard specials change regularly. Chris Leeton's cooking embraces many ideas, from classic chargrilled rump steaks with hand-cut chips and brandy sauce to panzanella salad with chorizo, or butternut squash and tomato strudel. The setting is lovely and, on summery days, the front garden is glorious.

The Queen's Head
Newton

It is charming and unspoilt outside and in. David and Juliet Short have run the Queen's Head for a quarter of a century and are now joined by son Robert who shares their commitment. There's a timeless appeal in the bare, almost spartan main bar where clattering floorboards, plain wooden tables, benches, aged paintings and a splendid winter fire are watched over by a fine old clock that keeps the beat. A tiny carpeted lounge with deep red walls, dark beams and well-worn, almost rickety furniture is a cosier alternative when the fire is blazing. The whole interior is unusual and utterly unspoilt, a proper background for shove-ha'penny, cribbage and beef dripping on toast. Yes, the food is simple, but deliciously so: rare roast beef sliced wafer-thin, ham on the bone, a mug of rich brown soup, locally baked bread — dispensed with slow deliberation and perfect accompaniments to Adnams ales tapped from the cask. Real-pub-lovers come from far and wide.

directions	Take Stow cum Quy turn off A14, then A1303 Newmarket road & follow signs to Little Wilbraham.
meals	12pm-2.30pm (2pm Sun); 7pm-9.30pm Main courses £10.50-£17.50; bar meals £3.75-£8.
closed	3pm-6.30pm, Sun eve & Mon.

directions	M11 junc. 11; A10 for Royston; left on B1368.
meals	12pm-2.15pm; 7pm-9.30pm. Bar meals £3-£5.
closed	2.30pm-6pm (3pm-7pm Sun).

	Stephen Bull Hole in the Wall, 2 High Street, Little Wilbraham, Cambridge CB1 5JY
tel	01223 812282
web	www.the-holeinthewall.com

	David & Juliet Short The Queen's Head, Newton, Cambridge CB2 5PG
tel	01223 870436

map: 9 entry: 39

map: 9 entry: 40

Cambridgeshire

Three Horseshoes
Madingley

From the outside, the thatched pub looks old-worldy; push the door and you embrace the new century. Here is a simple, stylish, open feel in pale wooden floors and furniture, soft sage and cream paintwork, modern prints; there is space and light yet the familiar features of the old pub remain. The bar has local ales such as Cambridge Boathouse Bitter, a modern open log fire and a blackboard menu packed with Italian country dishes and imaginative combinations. Chef-patron Richard Stokes has run this classy gastropub (part of the Huntsbridge Group – see the Falcon at Oundle and the Pheasant at Keyston) for over 14 years and he serves some of the best food in the region. Excellent service matches the laid-back atmosphere of the busy bar while formality and white linen come together in the conservatory dining room, popular with business lunchers. In either room the choice of wines is superb – pity the designated driver.

directions	Off A1303, 2 miles west of Cambridge.
meals	12pm–2pm (2.30pm Sat & Sun); 6.30pm–9.30pm (8.30pm Sun). Main courses £14.95–£24.95; bar meals £7.95–£10.95.
closed	3pm–6pm.

Richard Stokes
Three Horseshoes,
High Street, Madingley,
Cambridge CB3 8AB
tel 01954 210221
web www.huntsbridge.com

map: 9 entry: 41

Cambridgeshire   Pub with rooms

The Anchor Inn
Sutton Gault

Wedged between the bridge and the raised dyke, the little inn was built in 1650 to bed and board the men conscripted to tame the vast watery tracts of swamp and scrub. Whether you sit under the huge Fenland sky on the terrace and take in the miles of peace and quiet, or blow in with the winter winds and hunker down in front of one of three open fires, you'll relish this independent country inn. Rooms are understated and stylish, filled with scrubbed pine tables and antique settles, lit by gas and candles, and the cooking is a major draw – light, imaginative and surprising; try roast guinea fowl with wild mushroom and tarragon cream sauce, or smoked haddock brandade with braised fennel. Spotless rooms above fit the mood exactly – not posh but supremely comfy – and have trim carpets, wicker chairs, crisp duvets and Indian cotton throws.

directions	6 miles west of Ely, off B1381.
meals	12pm–2pm (2.30pm Sun); 7pm–9pm (6.30pm–9.30pm Sat). Main courses £12.50–£16.95; Sunday lunch £17 & £21.
rooms	4: 1 double, 1 twin, 2 suites £65–£149.50. Singles from £55.
closed	3pm–7pm (6.30pm Sat).

See pp 30–57 for full list of pubs with rooms

Adam Pickup & Carlene Bunten
The Anchor Inn,
Bury Lane, Sutton Gault,
Ely CB6 2DB
tel 01353 778537
web www.anchorsuttongault.co.uk

map: 9 entry: 42

Cambridgeshire

Crown Inn
Elton

Conkers, hundreds of them, harden to a deep russet brown in the late summer sun by the front door and under the chestnut tree. The ancient sandstone inn looks across the green of this Wolds village that harbours the equally beautiful Elton Hall. Flagstoned and beamed, the bar beckons with a selection of real ales including the highly prized Woodforde's Wherry. While light meals are offered here, there is a small dining room furnished, in keeping, with simple period tables and chairs. Seated by the big log fire on a wintery day, be comforted by lamb shank, glazed root vegetables and rosemary, or a vegetarian risotto of gorgonzola, rocket, spinach and peas. The main dining is in the octagonal conservatory, a relatively new addition, sitting under its local Collyweston slate. Nestling at the bottom of Duck Street, this is an inn for all seasons and occasions.

directions	Village signed off A605, 6 miles south west of Peterborough. Pub on village green on Nassington Rd.
meals	12pm-2.30pm; 6.30pm-9pm. No food Sun eve or Mon all day. Main courses £7.50-16; bar meals £3.95-£16; Sunday lunch £14-£16.95.
closed	3pm-6pm & Mon lunch. Open all day Sun.

Marcus & Rosalind Lamb
Crown Inn,
8 Duck Street, Elton,
Peterborough PE8 6RQ
tel   01832 280232

map: 9 entry: 43

Cambridgeshire

The Cock
Hemingford Grey

The young, enterprising licensees have stripped the lovely 17th-century village pub back to its original simplicity. Step directly into an attractive bare-boarded bar, cosy with low beams, log burner and traditional benches and settles at which you may sup award-winning East Anglian ales: Woodforde's Wherry and a monthly guest beer from Nethergate Ales. For food, move into the airy restaurant where buttermilk walls and modern prints sit beautifully with wooden floors and tables. The menu is strong on pub classics and the chef makes his own sausages, served with a choice of mash with horseradish or spring onions, and wonderful sauces (wild mushroom, wholegrain mustard). Duck parcel with sweet and sour cucumber is a favourite starter and the white chocolate and pistachio cheesecake very popular; fish and game dishes reveal a refreshing, modern view. The British and Irish farmhouse cheeses should not be missed.

directions	From A14 south for Hemingford Grey; 2 miles S of Huntingdon.
meals	12pm-2.30pm; 6.30pm-9pm (9.30pm Fri & Sat, 8.30pm Sun). Main courses £9.95-£19.95; light lunch £6.95-£12.95.
closed	3pm-6pm (4pm-6.30pm Sun).

Oliver Thain & Richard Bradley
The Cock,
47 High Street, Hemingford Grey,
Huntingdon PE28 9BJ
tel   01480 463609
web   www.cambscuisine.com

map: 9 entry: 44

The Crown
Broughton

The pub sits in the shadow of the church where jackdaws spiral in the breeze to be top bird on the steeple. There's been a pub cum saddler's shop in this peaceful hamlet since medieval times; villagers saved the Crown from residential conversion in 2001 and now you find one of Cambridgeshire's best gastropubs. Inside: huge terracotta floor slabs; a long lightwood bar aimed at drinkers; white wines under ice in a vast brass trough bucket. Round the side of the chimney breast is a dining room with fresh blooms, tall woodburner and orange check curtains – impressively 21st-century. If the rich and chunky confit duck terrine and red onion ragout is anything to go by, Simon Cadge's food, refined and unshowy, is worth travelling the distance for. Happy helpful young staff are clad in black and welcome all; children have capacious lawns to play on in summer, and conkers from majestic chestnuts to plunder.

The George Inn
Spaldwick

The rambling, buttermilk building dates from the 1500s and overlooks the village green – a quintessentially English scene. The interior is equally pleasing. Walls are aubergine and hung with contemporary art, leather sofas and chunky wood tables speak 'modern brasserie', old timbers are exposed, log fires crackle, and floors are bare boards. The cool, uncluttered styling blends beautifully with the history of the place. Modern variations on traditional dishes fit the bill – black pudding and seared scallops with chive and tomato butter sauce, calves' liver with red wine jus, and warm Valrhona chocolate mousse with pistachio ice cream. This is simple, robust, hugely appealing food based on first-rate ingredients. The relaxed feel extends to the several eating areas in the rambling bar and the magnificent high raftered restaurant, and to drink there's Adnams Broadside or Greene King IPA. Or one of a slate of 24 wines by the glass.

directions	Broughton is signed off A141 north east of Huntingdon.
meals	12pm-2pm; 6.30pm-9pm (9.30pm Sat); 12pm-4pm, 7pm-9pm Sun. Main courses £9.50-£17; bar meals £9.50-£16.
closed	3pm-6pm; Mon & Tues. Open all day Sun.

directions	Beside A141, junc. 18 of the A14, 5 miles west of Huntingdon.
meals	12pm-2.30pm; 6pm-9.30pm. Main courses £5.95-£15.95.
closed	Open all day.

	Simon Cadge The Crown, Bridge Road, Broughton, Huntingdon PE28 3AY
tel	01487 824428
web	www.thecrownbroughton.co.uk

	Nick Thoday & Louise Smith The George Inn, High Street, Spaldwick, Huntingdon PE28 0TD
tel	01480 890293

Cambridgeshire

The Pheasant
Keyston

The Huntsbridge group is known for injecting urban chic into rural hideaways. Here you have one remarkably self-assured chef (Jay Scrimshaw), a menu that looks to the Mediterranean and points beyond, and a classic thatched exterior. Add an enterprising list of wines and expertly kept ales and you have the Pheasant to a T. This text-book country pub does beams, open fires and comfy sofas better than anyone, and the cooking is as restorative as the surroundings, with the likes of confit garlic, thyme and almond risotto, roast mallard with braised puy lentils, quince and sautéed foie gras, and treacle sponge and custard. The light lunch and early supper menu is tremendous value, and if you don't want a full-blown meal, there's bar food and beautiful unpasteurised British cheeses. The Pheasant never forgets it's a pub and Adnams ales, together with two or three guest ales, are always on handpump.

directions	Keyston off A14, halfway between Huntingdon & Kettering.
meals	12pm–2.15pm (2.30pm Sun); 6.30pm–9.30pm (9pm Sun). Main courses £12.95–£19.95; bar meals £8.95–£10.95; Sunday lunch £18.50 & £22.50.
closed	3pm–6pm.

Taffeta & Jay Scrimshaw
The Pheasant,
Village Loop Road, Keyston,
Huntingdon PE28 0RE

tel	01832 710241
web	www.huntsbridge.com

♿ 🧍 🐟 🍺

map: 9 entry: 47

Cambridgeshire

Tavern on the Green
Great Staughton

Clive Dixon of the Snooty Fox in Northamptonshire is edging closer to his former employer's Huntsbridge Group territory with his outpost near Grafham Water. Both the aim (to serve British dishes from fine produce) and the style (lime-washed beams, wood-burning stove) are close to the Lowick original, although this is an unassuming village pub with an intimate feel. Menus are short and to the point: steak and kidney pie and sausage and mash chalked up on a board in the bar; Cornish lamb fillets with cavalo nero, or pan-fried pollack with garlic butter on the dinner menu. As at the Snooty Fox, steaks from rib-eye to fillet are on display, cut to order, priced accordingly and served with garlic butter or peppercorn sauce. And chips. Clive's business partner David Hannigan is in charge, service is smartly dressed and friendly, Greene King IPA and Old Speckled Hen are on tap, and there are decent wines by the glass.

directions	On B645 west of A1 & St Neots.
meals	12pm–2pm; 6pm–9.30pm. Main courses £6.95–£16.
closed	Open all day.

Clive Dixon & David Hennigan
Tavern on the Green,
12 The Green,
Great Staughton,

tel	01480 860336
web	www.snootyinns.com/tavern/

♿ 🧍 📖 🐟 🍺 🍷

map: 9 entry: 48

Albion Inn
Chester

It's an unprepossessing pub near the Chester almshouses, but enter! Bucket-loads of WW1 memorabilia, sepia photographs, flocked wallpaper, soft glowing lamps, leather sofas, and a 1928 Steck Duo Art Player piano which gives occasional performances. Mike Mercer insists on old-fashioned good behaviour so leave little ones at home. There are four cask ales, a flurry of malts and a decent selection of New World wines. 'Trench Rations' come in un-trench-like portions: corned beef hash with pickled red cabbage, Staffordshire oatcake filled with black pudding, brandy-apricot ice cream. There's even hot chocolate on the menu – Green & Black's organic. The bedrooms at the top (separate entrance) are compact and comfortable, with some good antiques. A nostalgic city pub with an eccentric streak.

directions	Opp. city walls between The Newgate & River Dee.
meals	12pm-2pm; 5pm-8pm (6pm-8.30 Sat). No food Sun eve. Main courses from £6.50-£7.80; bar meals £4.75-£4.90
rooms	2: 1 double, 1 twin £75. Singles £65.
closed	3pm-5pm (6pm Sat; 7pm Sun). Open all day Fri.

See pp 30–57 for full list of pubs with rooms

	Michael Mercer Albion Inn, Park Street, Chester CH1 1RN
tel	01244 340345
web	www.albioninnchester.co.uk

map: 7 entry: 49

The Grosvenor Arms
Aldford

Pretty Aldford, part of the vast Grosvenor Estate, is all prim cottages and farms with barleysugar-twist chimneys and chequerboard brickwork. Not far from the old church and castle is the imposing brick and Victorian half-timber village local rejuvenated by Brunning & Price as their flagship pub. Something for everyone here in this most relaxing and classy pastiche: a traditional taproom and snug with log fire, tiled floor and a wonderful old photo of drunks in the stocks, an imposing part-panelled Library Room and a verdant conservatory. There are prints and pictures, bottles and plates, sales bills and Victorian cartoons, acres of refectory and rustic kitchen tables on boards, tiles and rugs, a panoply of seating choices and a dark-wood bar groaning beneath handpumps dispensing local beers. The ever-reliable B&P menu carries something for everyone and you can eat in summer on huge tree-shaded lawns next to the village cricket pitch.

directions	6 miles south of Chester on B5130 to Farndon & Holt.
meals	12pm-10pm (9pm Sun). Man courses £7.95-£18.95.
closed	Open all day.

	Gary Kidd The Grosvenor Arms, Chester Road, Aldford, Chester CH3 6HJ
tel	01244 620228
web	www.grosvenorarms-aldford.co.uk

map: 7 entry: 50

The Pheasant Inn
Chester

After a hike along the Sandstone Trail, come and stand before the largest fireplace in Cheshire with a pint of Weetwood Old Dog. Or sit out on the terrace and gaze across the Cheshire Plain all the way to North Wales. Gloriously positioned up in the Peckforton Hills, the Pheasant has been stylishly re-vamped inside. The old laid-back feel has survived the smartening up of the big, beamed and wooden-floored bars, and food is informally served in both bar and restaurant. Seared scallops with lime and dill dressing, beef fillet with red wine sauce, smoked haddock and salmon fishcakes, lambs' liver, smoked bacon and onion gravy, and sticky toffee pudding with toffee sauce should satisfy the most ravenous walker, while lunchtime's hot beef sandwiches are equally hearty. There are four ales and 12 wines by the glass but it's the views that you'll come back for.

Blue Bell Inn
Tushingham

Mossy-tiled and wonkily beamed, it was rebuilt in 1667. There are ghosts (a phantom duck walled up in a bottle), a medieval spiral staircase, a Cavalier's hat found behind the inglenook, and Derek, the pub's pet sheep, who grazes the meadow where kids are free to roam. There's a beautifully lived-in, old-fashioned feel nurtured by the friendly owners. The snug behind the bar makes a superb family room; the taproom has wall benches, armchairs and huge inglenook; there are maps, old prints, horse brasses, timeworn carpets and faded patterned wallpapers. Settle down to a pint of Shropshire Gold from a Salopian brewery, served from the hatch. Food is nothing fancy but portions are generous and the meat and game come from local suppliers – lamb shank, pork with apple and calvados sauce. The garden is peaceful, the views verdant; anyone yearning for a charismatic village pub will love the Bell.

directions	A534 for Wrexham; right opp. Copper Mine pub; right for Burwardsley after 1 mile. At post office, right & follow signs.
meals	12pm-9.30 (10pm Fri & Sat; 8.30 Sun). No food 3pm-6pm Mon. Main courses £8.50-£18.95; bar meals £3.95-£8.50.
closed	Open all day.

directions	Off A41, 3 miles north of Whitchurch. Signed.
meals	12pm-2pm; 6pm-9pm (from 7pm Sun). Bar meals £7.25-£10.50.
closed	Mon (except bank hols).

Andrew Nelson
The Pheasant Inn,
Higher Burwardsley,
Tattenhall, Chester CH3 9PF

tel 01829 770434
web www.thepheasantinn.co.uk

map: 7 entry: 51

Jerry & Ginette Ward
Blue Bell Inn,
Bell o' th' Hill,
Tushingham,
Whitchurch SY13 4QS

tel 01948 662172

map: 7 entry: 52

The Cholmondeley Arms
Cholmondeley

The gabled Victorian schoolhouse, with its unusual, octagonal bell tower, stands virtually opposite Cholmondeley Castle and Gardens. It conveniently metamorphosed into a pub when the school closed in 1982 but is still part of the Viscount's estate and keeps that airy 'schoolroom' feel with its raftered, vaulted ceilings, large windows and huge radiators. Today the rooms are nicely furnished with an auction lot of tables, pews and chairs, good colours, subtle lights, characterful old prints and a blazing log fire. Educational relics in the form of old school desks, blackboards and easels fill a gallery above the bar and antique blackboards have been put to good use – of course; one is chalked up with the daily-changing choice of first-class bar food, the other lists seven wines by the glass. Popular with suits, Barbours and a smattering of farmers.

Bhurtpore Inn
Aston

The problem with this extended old Cheshire-brick village farmhouse is just where to start. Should it be the 11 real ales? The countless bottled continental beers and the 100 malts? The farmhouse ciders and perry? Or is it best to salivate at the marvellous, ever-changing blackboard menu? There again, time could be spent simply lapping up the fascinating décor. The pub was named after an Indian city besieged by a local army commander, and multitudinous maps, paintings and ephemera spread through the warren of rooms vividly recall this deed. Low beams sag beneath myriad water jugs, and open fires crackle in the cosy lounge, where a mongrel-mix of furniture and seating, settles, a longcase clock and absorbing local bric-a-brac add tremendous character. The home-cooked food is top quality, with local fodder to the fore, the portions generous, the choice vast, and there are curries – galore!

directions	On A49, 6 miles north of Whitchurch.	
meals	12pm-2.30pm; 6.30pm-10pm. Main courses £8.75-£16.75; bar meals £4.95-£7.95.	
closed	3pm-7pm (6.30pm Sat).	

Carolyn Ross-Lowe
The Cholmondeley Arms,
Cholmondely,
Malpas SY14 8BT
tel 01829 720300
web www.cholmondeleyarms.co.uk

map: 7 entry: 53

directions	Off A530, 5 miles SW of Nantwich. Follow signs for Wrenbury from turn in Aston near pottery.	
meals	12pm-2pm (2.30pm Sat); 6.45pm-9.30pm (12pm-9pm Sun). Main courses £7.95-£13.	
closed	2.30pm-6.30pm. Open all day Sun.	

Simon George
Bhurtpore Inn,
Wrenbury Road, Aston,
Nantwich CW5 8DQ
tel 01270 780917
web www.bhurtpore.co.uk

map: 7 entry: 54

Cheshire

The Dysart Arms
Bunbury

It is one of those rare places – all things to all people. With separate areas clustered round a central bar, it feels open and cosy at the same time. There's an inglenook packed with logs, a dining area in a library, the staff are lovely, the food is special, the beers and wines superb. Once a farm on the Dysart estate, this 18th-century brick building by the church protects a listed interior. The refreshingly airy rooms have scrubbed floorboards, yellow walls, good solid tables and chairs, pictures, prints and plants, and French windows opening to the terrace and garden. Two walls are lined with books. They're proud of their food here and rightly so: game casserole with herb dumplings, salmon and smoked haddock fishcakes with tartare sauce, roast plum and almond tart... the cheeses are taken as seriously as the cask ales (try the local Weetwood Bitter), and the wines are thoughtfully chosen. Warm, intimate, friendly... the place appears to run on well-oiled wheels.

directions	Off A49, 3.5 miles from Tarporley.
meals	12pm-9.30pm (9pm Sun). Main courses £8.50-£14.50.
closed	Open all day.

Darren & Elizabeth Snell
The Dysart Arms,
Bowes Gate Road, Bunbury,
Tarporley CW6 9PH
tel 01829 260183
web www.dysartarms-bunbury.co.uk

map: 7 entry: 55

Cheshire

The Boot Inn
Willington

Strewn with ivy and pyracantha, a country cottage turned pub. Set against wooded hills in the middle of fruit farming country ('Little Switzerland'), the village local looks west towards the Welsh Hills and south over the Cheshire plain. It's a gorgeous, sheltered spot with walks nearby. Inside, the pub has been opened up with the bar at the hub, though you still get the flavour of individual rooms. Old quarry tiles, some panelling, characterful beams and a log-burning stove pull the walkers and talkers in. And there are donkeys, dog and cats to keep children entertained. The stone-flagged dining room opens onto a garden you can spill into on warm days and there's a log fire in winter. Popular food ranges from sandwiches, baguettes and panini at the bar to local lamb with roast vegetables and sea bass deep-fried in sesame batter. Local Weetwood Ales are on draught, and there are a number of wines.

directions	Chester-Manchester A54; right for Willington; 2 miles, left at T-junc. for Boothsdale.
meals	11am-2.30pm; 6pm-9.30pm. Main courses £8.50-£12.95.
closed	3pm-6pm. Open all day Sat & Sun.

Mike Gollings
The Boot Inn,
Boothsdale,
Willington,
Tarporley CW6 0NH
tel 01829 751375

map: 7 entry: 56

The Fox & Barrel
Cotebrook

So called because a former landlord let a persued fox escape to the cellar, this busy, roadside dining pub throngs with drinkers and diners in equal measure. Inside, a comfortable mix of tables and chairs, snug corners, interesting ornaments, pictures and prints on bay-windowed walls, a large open brick fire stacked with logs, and quarry tiles covered with traditional patterned rugs. All is spotless and welcoming. There's also a large and pleasant dining room in cream; tables are candlelit and easy on the eye, the background music is gentle on the ear. There are several cask ales, good wines and enjoyable food generously served: goat's cheese terrine with apple chutney, lamb rump with cranberry and redcurrant jus, steak and kidney pie, bouillabaisse – homemade, of course. Service is exemplary and the staff are attentive, whether you're here for a swift half or a slap-up meal.

directions	On A49 near Oulton Park.
meals	12pm-2.30pm; 6pm-9.30pm (12pm-8pm Sun). No bar meals Fri & Sat eves & Sun. Main courses £8.95-£16.15; bar snacks from £6.95; set menu, 2 courses, £11.75; Sunday lunch £12.50 & £14.50.
closed	3pm-5.30pm. Open all day Sat & Sun.

	Chris Crossley The Fox & Barrel, Forest Road, Cotebrook, Tarporley CW6 9DZ
tel	01829 760529
web	www.thefoxandbarrel.com

map: 7 entry: 57

Chetwode Arms
Lower Whitley

The 400-year-old, Cheshire-brick roadside inn hides a warren of small rooms and passageways. There's the bar room itself, tiny, with an open coal fire, and four more; the snuggest may be used as a private dining room. Expect low ceilings, exposed brick and beams, fresh flowers and mirrors, oodles of atmosphere and tasty food. In the dining room – opening onto a terrace that overlooks the pub's own bowling green – contented locals tuck into local game pie, beef Wellington with wild mushroom sauce, salmon fishcakes with homemade chips and herb mayonnaise, and steaks cooked on hot rocks. There are lunchtime sandwiches, salads and ploughman's, four changing guest ales on tap and the wine list favours some top vineyards from Richard's home country – South Africa. Great for judicious drinkers of wine and beer, and a super dining pub.

directions	On A49 2 miles from M56 junc. 10.
meals	12pm-2.30pm; 6pm-9.30pm (10pm Sat; 12pm-7pm Sun). Main courses £10.75-£17.95.
closed	3.30pm-6pm & Mon all day.

	Richard Starnok Chetwode Arms, Saint Lane, Lower Whitley, Warrington WA4 4EN
tel	01925 730203
web	www.chetwodearms.com

map: 7 entry: 58

The White Lion
Barthomley

An inn since 1614 and a siege site in the Civil War, the character-oozing White Lion – all wonky black and white timbers and thick thatched roof – stands beside a cobbled cart track close to the fine sandstone church. Step in to three gloriously unspoilt rooms, all woodsmoke and charm, wizened oak beams, ancient benches and twisted walls, tiny latticed windows and quarry-tiled floors. No music or electronic games, just the crackling of log fires and the hum of conversation from hikers and locals. Lunchtime food is listed on a printed menu, with occasional specials. At scrubbed wooden tables on ancient settles, accompany sausages and mash, hot ham and pineapple, hearty ploughman's or daily roast with a well-kept pint of Cheshire-brewed Burtonwood Top Hat – or opt for the regularly changing guest ale. Summer seating is at picnic benches on the cobbles, with pretty views onto the village. Gorgeous!

The Ship Inn
Wincle

The red sandstone building – one of Cheshire's oldest – houses a small and well-loved local. Its two little taprooms are utterly simple, one with half barrels as ends for its counter, the other with a stone-flagged floor and a cast-iron range. Food is taken seriously in the new dining room extension, ingredients are local and booking is essential at weekends. Dishes include beer battered haddock, canon of lamb with date and herb crust and rosemary jus, turbot and sea bass on crab linguine and roasted tomato sauce, and lunchtime sandwiches. The Ship is also known for its beers – usually four on handpump plus a traditional cider or perry – and its fruit wines. Giles is full of enthusiasm and know what makes a pub tick. The little country garden by the car park has tables and chairs shaded by mature trees – you're on the edge of the Peaks and fine walks stretch in every direction.

directions	From Congleton A54 for Buxton for 7 miles; right at Clulow Cross for Wincle, 1.5 miles.
meals	12pm-2.30pm (4pm Sat & Sun); 6pm-10pm. Main courses £10.95-£16.95; sandwiches from £4.95.
closed	3pm-6.30pm Tues-Thurs & Mon all day (except bank hols). Open all day Sat & Sun.

directions	M6 junc. 16; 3rd exit for Alsager; left for Barthomley.
meals	12pm-2pm (2.30pm Sun). No food in the eve. Main courses £3.50-£5.95.
closed	Open all day.

Laura Condliffe
The White Lion,
Barthomley,
Crewe CW2 5PG

tel 01270 882242

Giles Meadows
The Ship Inn,
Wincle,
Macclesfield SK11 0QE

tel 01260 227217

map: 8 entry: 59

map: 8 entry: 60

Hanging Gate
Sutton

High above Macclesfield, the high heather moors of the Dark Peak fracture into steep, finger-like ridges; this very old pub hangs from the western slope. A staircase of tiny rooms drops sharply from a sublime little tap room via brass, copper and watercolour-dressed snugs to the 'View Room', where picture windows unveil an inspiring panorama that stretches to the West Pennine Moors. Several open fires add to the timeless atmosphere created by the wizened beams, flagged and carpeted floors and cosy corners where beers from Hydes' of Manchester complement the splendid home-cooked food. Game from local estates, meat and fowl from nearby farms and fish from Manchester's Smithfield Market are crafted into unfussy, fulfilling meals with a strong local following. It's popular, too, with ramblers from the nearby Gritstone Trail and Macclesfield Forest, pausing on the compact terrace or lawns.

Harrington Arms
Gawsworth

You'd barely know it was a pub. The creeper-covered, red-brick building started life as a farmhouse in 1663 and still looks as if it could be part of a working farm. The outside may have grown but the inside has barely changed; it wasn't long ago that they were serving beer here just from the cask. Off the passageway are a bar and a quarry-tiled snug, big enough for a settle chair, a table and an open fire. Then two more public rooms: the traditionally furnished Top Parlour, and the Tap Room, a red and black quarry-tiled room with simple scrub-top tables where Friday's folk club sessions take place. The Wightmans took over in November 2006 and, other than a lick of paint and opening up another timeless lounge, plan to change little, and that includes the quality of the ale; it's said that you won't get a finer pint of Robinsons than at the Harrington. Snacks are of the traditional pork pie, ploughman's and slab-sandwich variety – simple and good.

directions	From A54 follow signs to Langley at Fairway Motel.
meals	12pm-2.30pm (Sat 3pm); Sun 12pm-5pm, 7pm-9.30pm. Main courses £7.50-£17.50.
closed	3pm-7pm Mon-Fri.

Ian Rottenbury
Hanging Gate,
Meg Lane, Sutton,
Macclesfield SK11 0NG
tel   01260 252238
web   www.thegatetinyworld.co.uk

map: 8 entry: 61

directions	On A536, 2.5 miles from Macclesfield.
meals	12pm-2.30pm; 5pm-8pm. Sandwiches & pies only.
closed	3pm-5pm.

Andy & Caroline Wightman
Harrington Arms,
Church Lane,
Gawsworth,
Macclesfield SK11 9RR
tel   01260 223325

map: 8 entry: 62

The Plough
Eaton

The food at the Plough is fields ahead of much of the competition – but that's not all. This attractive red-brick building on a busy stretch of road has been serving up ales since the 17th century, when it started out as a coaching inn. Today, the hospitality is as welcome. Eat or drink in rooms arranged around a central bar area; all are smart and comfortable, with antiques, prints and a convivial air. Then there's the Old Barn Restaurant – all rustic beams and centuries-old atmosphere – which was brought, in pieces, from Wales, and painstakingly reconstructed here. Outside is a lawned raised garden. Specials might include asparagus brûlée topped with goat's cheese and caramelized onions, grilled sardines in a garlic tomato sauce, and roast pheasant with cognac, wild mushroom and bacon sauce and coarse-grain mustard mash. Puddings are a homemade treat to be squeezed in after generous portions.

directions	Beside A536, 2.5 miles north west of Congleton.
meals	12pm-2.30pm; 6pm-9.30pm (12pm-8pm Sun). Main courses £7.95-£16.75.
closed	Open all day.

Mujdat Karatas
The Plough,
Macclesfield Road,
Eaton,
Congleton CW12 2NH
tel   01260 280207

♿ ♈ ▤ ◫ ▾

map: 8 entry: 63

Oddfellows Arms
Mellor

Amid a strand of pretty cottages on a steep, narrow lane up to the moors, this mellow, three-storey gritstone pub revels in a reputation for food and ales. Folk travel from miles around and ramblers tumble down footpaths from the tops to indulge in the eclectic offerings on the modern, well-priced menu that features a strong seafood hand, inventive vegetarian options, a huge starters-and-snacks choice and great spicy dishes. Warm up beside log-burner and open fires, watching woodsmoke curl across the low-beamed ceilings past light-streamed, lead-latticed windows. Charming Victorian photos of bucolic country folk, mirrors aplenty and unusual frames of keys adorn the walls amid pews, lived in seating and smart oak tables. Upstairs is a modern, airy restaurant. Well-kept beers are from local craft breweries.

directions	M60 junc. 1 to Marple A626. After 6 miles, to Marple Bridge & Mellor; for 2 miles.
meals	12pm-2pm (4pm Sun); 6.30pm-9.30pm. Main courses £9.50-£15.95; bar meals £4-£7.
closed	3pm-5.30pm & Mon all day.

Phil McCartney
Oddfellows Arms,
73 Moor End Road,
Mellor,
Stockport SK6 5PT
tel   0161 449 7826

♈ ▤ ◀ ◫ ▾ 👟

map: 12 entry: 64

Cheshire

The Buffet Bar
Stalybridge

Only a handful of these charming Victorian establishments survive. Basic, clean and timeless, this extraordinary, narrow little bar opened in 1885 as an integral part of the busy Stalybridge Station; access is still from Platform One, served by trans-Pennine trains. Its original features include coloured glass windows, a grand, black-leaded fireplace and a moulded-wood, marble-topped old bar groaning with handpumps. Parts of the former station-master's house and ladies' waiting room add much-needed space, as does a venerable old wooden conservatory tagged on to one end. Stringing the place together is a huge collection of railway bric-a-brac: shed plates and numberplates, nameplates and lamps, totems, plans and paintings. Quirky this may be, but it's double anorak heaven here, as the Bar is renowned for its real ales: over 6,000 different beers over the past seven years and usually eight on tap. Don't miss, either, their black peas, pies and puddings.

directions	8 miles east of Manchester. On the trans-Pennine line to Leeds/York.
meals	Food available most hours. Bar meals £3.50-£5.50.
closed	Open all day.

John Hesketh & Sylvia Wood
The Buffet Bar,
Stalybridge Station,
Stalybridge SK15 1RF
tel 0161 303 0007
web www.buffetbar.freewebspace.com

map: 12 entry: 65

Cornwall

The Star Inn
St Just

Entrenched in the wild landscape close to Land's End is the 'last proper pub in Cornwall'. This 18th-century gem, owned by the ex-mayor of St Just and its oldest and most authentic inn, proudly shirks the trappings of tourism and remains a drinkers' den. Bands of locals sink pints of Tinners Ale in the low-beamed, spick-and-span bar, old pub games thrive and the place is the hub of the local folk scene, with live music at least ten nights a month, singalongs and joke-telling all part of the Monday evening entertainment. The dimly-lit bar is jam-packed with interest and walls are littered with seafaring and mining artefacts; coals glow in the grate on wild winter days. Come for St Austell ale and the 'craic', and simple, home produced food using locally sourced produce – no chips or microwaves. A free juke box, mulled wine in winter and that pub rarity: a great family room.

directions	A3071 from Penzance. On right-hand side of square in centre.
meals	12pm-5pm. Bar meals from £2.50.
closed	Open all day.

Johnny McFadden
The Star Inn,
Fore Street,
St Just,
Penzance TR19 7LL
tel 01736 788767

map: 1 entry: 66

Cornwall — Pub with rooms

The Gurnard's Head
Zennor

The coastline here is magical and the walk up to St Ives is hard to beat. Secret beaches appear at low tide, cliffs tumble down to the water and wild flowers streak the land pink in summer. As for the inn, it's earthy, warm, stylish and friendly, with airy interiors, colourwashed walls, stripped wooden floors and log fires at both ends of the bar. Super food, all homemade, can be eaten wherever you want: in the bar, in the restaurant or out in the garden in good weather. Snack on rustic delights – pork pies, crab claws, half a pint of Atlantic prawns – or tuck into more substantial treats, maybe fresh asparagus with a hollandaise sauce, fish stew with new potatoes, rhubarb crème brûlée. Wines are generously priced, local ales are on tap and picnics are easily arranged. Bedrooms upstairs are warm and cosy, simple and spotless, with Vi-sprung mattresses, crisp white linen, throws over armchairs.

directions	On B3306 between St Ives & Land's End.
meals	12.30pm-2.30pm; 6pm-9.30pm. Main courses £4.50–£10.95 (lunch); £4.50–£14 (dinner).
rooms	7: 5 doubles, 2 twins/doubles £62.50–£82.50; .
closed	Open all day.

See pp 30–57 for full list of pubs with rooms

Charles & Edmund Inkin
The Gurnard's Head
Treen, Zennor,
St Ives TR26 3DE
tel 01736 796928
web www.gurnardshead.co.uk

map: 1 entry: 67

Cornwall

Tinner's Arms
Zennor

Under landlords Grahame and Richard, one of Cornwall's most historic pubs has been given a welcome shot in the arm. Close to the church in the bleak, windswept, coastal hamlet of Zennor, the 13th-century inn is pretty unspoilt with its flagstone floors, whitewashed walls, old tables and fabulously long, well-stocked bar. Cornishman Grahame spent many years in London running the ultra-fashionable Kensington Place, so the food and drink have moved sharply up a gear – Newlyn crab, local cheeses, ales from St Austell, Sharp's and Skinners, Burrow Hill ciders from Somerset. Still, the Tinners Arms remains a proper inn bursting with character and open log fires and will always be a popular stop for walkers heading for the nearby coastal paths. Windswept Zennor is worth the visit alone; D H Lawrence was inspired to write *Women In Love* here. It's packed in summer, but you could be alone in the bar in off-season – just you and the dog.

directions	Off B3306 St Ives-St Just road, 4 miles west of St Ives.
meals	12pm-2.30pm; 6pm-9pm. Main courses £6.50–£14.50.
closed	Open all day.

Grahame Edwards & Richard Motley
Tinner's Arms,
Zennor, St Ives TR26 3BY
tel 01736 796927
web www.tinnersarms.com

map: 1 entry: 68

Angarrack Inn
Angarrack

Personality alone would earn the Angarrack a place in this guide. It starts with David, the landord, and ends with to a bizarre assortment of paraphernalia - bagpipes, a clarinet, plates, photos, horns... to list all would risk incredulity. The pub is exquisitely cosy, with small spaces, sometimes squashed – a snug around a coal fire, a couple of small dining areas separated by a screen, dark walls and ceilings – it feels not unlike a 1970s French bistro. The food is cheap, cheerful, generous – 'school dinner' of the best kind, with the addition of an excellent game paté for a touch of sophistication. Ingredients are locally grown, there is a sound emphasis on local beers and the cider, from local apples, is strong and delicious. Plonked beneath a massive Victorian railway viaduct the pub has an unusual site, while David and Jackie's enthusiasm for doing things honestly and without pretence is a tonic.

Halzephron
Gunwalloe

An opera singer running a remote smuggler's inn – irresistible! Looking out across the bay, the whitewashed inn has been taking in guests (and smugglers: there's an underground passage) for 500 years. It reopened in 1958 as the Halzephron, old Cornish for 'cliffs of hell' and testament to the numerous ships dashed onto this stunning but treacherous coastline. Angela, exuberant and charming, has created numerous cosy eating areas around the bar, and a patio with a huge sea view. Food is freshly cooked and carefully presented: seafood chowder, smoked duck and wild mushroom risotto, crab salad platter, roast monkfish with saffron mussels, raspberry pavlova. Blow away the cobwebs on the cliff-top walk to Gunwalloe's 13th-century church beside the sand. Return to cosy bedrooms with deep-sprung beds, patchwork quilts, fresh fruit, real coffee and farmyard views.

directions	A3083 from Helston for The Lizard; right for Gunwalloe; 2 miles to pub.
meals	12pm-2pm; 7pm-9pm. Main courses £8.95-£17.50; bar meals from £4.50.
rooms	2 doubles from £84. Singles from £48.
closed	2.30pm-6pm.

See pp 30–57 for full list of pubs with rooms

directions	In village centre, 1/2 mile from A30 north of Hayle.
meals	12pm-2pm; 6.30pm-9pm. Main courses £6.50-£14.95; sandwiches from £2.95; Sunday roast £7.50.
closed	3pm-6pm (7pm Sun).

David & Jackie Peake
Angarrack Inn,
12 Steamers Hill,
Angarrack,
Hayle TR27 5JB
tel   01736 752380

Angela Thomas
Halzephron,
Gunwalloe,
Helston TR12 7QB
tel   01326 240406
web   www.halzephron-inn.co.uk

map: 1 entry: 69

map: 1 entry: 70

Cadgwith Cove Inn
Ruan Minor

Smack on the Cornish coastal path, in a thatched fishing hamlet on the Lizard Peninsula sits this 300-year-old smugglers' inn. The two dimly-lit little bars with two open fires, furnished simply and decked with mementos of seafaring days, have five ales on draught and pub grub from printed menus. For fresh and fishy daily specials, perhaps pan-fried sea bass with bacon and garlic or poached hake Florentine, look to the chalkboard. Mullet, sea bass, lobster and crab for delicious soup and sandwiches is landed on the beach below. Or try the plump mussels served with chunks of crusty bread – perfect after a cliff-path stroll to beautiful Church Cove and accompanied by a malty pint of Sharps Doom Bar. On Friday nights there is traditional Cornish singing: the rafters resonate to the refrain of a male voice choir. In summer, lap up the views across Cadgwith's tiny working cove from the sunny front terrace.

The Shipwright's Arms
Helford

Helford straggles beside a tidal creek on the wood-fringed waters of the river. Reachable only by foot (park in the car park and walk down), the pretty thatched pub has a gorgeous terraced garden of flowers and palms, with picnic benches on the water's edge. It was built in 1795 as a farmhouse – the shipwright connections came later – and as a summer pub is exceptionally popular... certainly on summer evenings, once the barbecue has got going. The interior is special, staunchly traditional, with simple country furnishings and open fires, full of nautical bits and pieces. Yachtsmen tie up outside and there's always a buzz. The black panelled bar dispenses Sharps Doom Bar Bitter and buffet lunches. Walk off your ploughman's on the long distance coastal path that passes the front door – or the shorter circular walk via Frenchman's Creek, a smuggler's hideaway made famous by Daphne du Maurier, thrilling at high tide.

directions	Off A3083 between Helston & The Lizard.
meals	12pm-2pm; 7pm-9pm. No food Wed eve. Main courses £7-£11; bar meals £3.50-£7..
closed	3pm-6.30pm. Open all day Fri-Sun.

directions	On south side of Helford river & via Helston on The Lizard peninsula.
meals	12pm-2pm; 7pm-9pm. Main courses £11.70-£14.95; bar meals £3.90-£8.05
closed	2.30pm-6pm, Sun & Mon eve in winter.

	David & Lynda Trivett Cadgwith Cove Inn, Cadgwith, Ruan Minor, Helston TR12 7JX
tel	01326 290513
web	www.cadgwithcoveinn.com

	Maria & Charles Herbert The Shipwright's Arms, Helford, Helston village TR12 6JX
tel	01326 231235

map: 1 entry: 71

map: 1 entry: 72

The Pandora Inn
Mylor Bridge

Yachtsmen moor at the end of the pontoon that reaches into the creek. The building, too, is special: thatched and 13th-century. Originally The Passage House, it was renamed in memory of the *Pandora*, a naval ship sent to Tahiti to capture the mutineers of Captain Bligh's *Bounty*. The pub keeps the traditional layout on several levels, along with some panelled walls, polished flagged floors, snug alcoves, three log fires, loads of maritime mementos – and amazingly low wooden ceilings. But it's not only the position, patio and pontoon that makes this one of Cornwall's best-loved inns; the bar food has something to please everyone, with fresh seafood dominating the 'specials' board. Arrive early in summer – by car or by boat; the place gets packed and parking is tricky. On winter weekdays it's blissfully peaceful, and the postprandial walking along wooded creekside paths easy.

directions	A39 from Truro; B3292 for Penryn & Mylor Bridge; descend steeply to Restronguet.
meals	12pm-3pm; 6.30pm-9pm (9.30pm Fri & Sat). Main courses £8.50-£14.95; bar meals £4.75-£14.95.
closed	Open all day.

John Milan
The Pandora Inn,
Restronguet Creek, Mylor Bridge,
Falmouth TR11 5ST
tel   01326 372678
web   www.pandorainn.com

map: 1 entry: 73

The Roseland Inn
Philleigh

Beside a peaceful parish church, two miles from the King Harry Ferry, a cob-built Cornish treasure. The front courtyard is bright with blossom in spring, climbing roses in summer. Indoors: old settles with scatter cushions, worn slate floors, low black beams and winter log fires. Local photographs, gig-racing memorabilia and a corner dedicated to rugby trophies scatter the walls. The place is spotlessly kept and run with panache by father and son team, William and Douglas Richards, and attracts locals and visitors in search of real ale and good food such as local farm meats and fish landed at St Mawes. Menu and blackboard dishes range from decent sandwiches to game terrine, scallops wrapped in bacon, shoulder of lamb, fillet steak and whole sea bass. Staff are full of smiles – even when the pub doubles as the Roseland Rugby Club clubhouse and the lads down pints of Sharps Doom Bar on winter Saturday nights.

directions	Off A3078 St Mawes road or via King Harry Ferry from Truro (Feock) to Philleigh.
meals	12pm-2.30pm (3pm Sun); 6pm-9.30pm (7pm-9pm Sun). Main courses £11-£16; sandwiches from £4; Sunday roast £7.
closed	3pm-6pm.

William & Douglas Richards
The Roseland Inn,
Philleigh,
Truro TR2 5NB
tel   01872 580254
web   www.roselandinn.co.uk

map: 1 entry: 74

Cornwall

Kings Head
Ruan Lanihorne

A pub with a heart. Niki and Andrew are warm, friendly and love what they do. Children are welcome in each of the dining rooms, dogs snooze in the bar. Find pine-backed stools, a comfy old sofa, a real fire. An impressive collection of tea cups hangs from the ceiling, a window sparkles with a display of multi-hued bottles and all is quirky and fun. Off the main bar are a second room with maps and woodburner and a homely, carpeted dining room with gleaming tables and Windsor chairs. Ales are from Skinners in Truro, fish from St Mawes, milk and cream from an organic Jersey herd. Tuck into venison casserole with parsley mash and finish with lemon posset, or come on Sunday for the magnificent roast beef platter. The quiet little village on the old coach road from Penzance to London has a church with a Norman font and a creek that is a haven for waders and waterfowl... behind is the Roseland countryside.

directions	Village signed off A3078 Tregony-St Mawes road.
meals	12pm-2pm; 6pm-9pm. Main courses £8.95-£16.15.
closed	2.30pm-6pm. Mon all day Nov-Mar.

	Andrew & Niki Law
	Kings Head,
	Ruan Lanihorne,
	Truro TR2 5NX
tel	01872 501263

map: 1 entry: 75

Cornwall

The Plume of Feathers
Mitchell

A sanctuary off a lonely stretch of carriageway. It was an inspired move to transform the old 16th-century coaching inn where John Wesley once preached into a warm and stylish pub-restaurant with rooms. The imaginative cooking draws an appreciative crowd and, in summer, food is available all day. Low stripped beams, half-panelled walls hung with modern art, fresh flowers, candle-studded pine tables and soothing lighting make this place a pleasure to walk into; it feels novel and fun. Delightful staff serve Scottish beef and local vegetables and fish at sensible prices – take roasted whole sea bass with crispy fennel and basil salad and grilled Dover sole with lemon butter, thick steak sandwiches at lunch and delicious puddings, perhaps chilled vanilla rice pudding with spiced pineapple. The central bar is lively with TV, piped music and Sharps Doom Bar on tap.

directions	Off junction of A30 & A3076.
meals	12pm-10pm. Main courses £7.50-£14.95.
closed	Open all day.

	Vicky Powell
	The Plume of Feathers,
	Mitchell,
	Truro TR8 5AX
tel	01872 510387
web	www.theplume.info

map: 1 entry: 76

The Driftwood Spars Hotel
St Agnes

You find the best of old and new
Cornwall here: a great old Cornish
pub with a bar as authentic as they come,
and a crisp modern restaurant alongside.
In a small hamlet, yards from sandy,
sheltered Trevaunance Cove, is this solid
17th-century inn – saunter in to a big
traditional bar with open stone walls,
roaring log fires, imaginative barrel
seating and plain wooden tables and
chairs. Most remarkable of all, great dark
ceiling beams, the timbers pillaged from
ships wrecked centuries ago in the
breakers below. The family room has a
pool table, a woodburner and its own
bar. Things get lighter and brighter in the
restaurant where fish, fresh from the
slab, is served: saffron-infused moules,
black tiger gambas, monkfish marinated
in fresh chillies and Moroccan spices. The
wines are delicious, the homebrewed
Driftwood Cuckoo Ale is tasty and from
the pretty gardens you can just glimpse
the sea.

directions	From A30 to St Agnes, through village to mini r'bout, signs to Trevaunance Cove. Pub on right.
meals	12pm-2.30; 6.30-9.30 (restaurant 7pm-9.30 only). Main courses £8.95-£16.95; bar meals £6.20-£11.60.
closed	Open all day

Jill & Gordon Treleaven
The Driftwood Spars Hotel,
Trevaunance Cove,
St Agnes TR5 0RT

tel	01872 552428/553323
web	www.driftwoodspars.com

map: 1 entry: 77

The Falcon Inn
St Mawgan

Traditional pubs are an endangered breed
in Holiday Land; the Falcon is one of
them, a pub-lover's delight. In an
attractive village, in the Vale of Lanherne,
a stone's throw from its tiny stream, this
16th-century wisteria-draped inn is
utterly unspoilt and a summer haven for
those escaping the bucket-and-spade
beach. The game-free main bar is neatly
arranged with pine farmhouse tables and
chairs. Andy and Jan Marshall source
local meats, fish and seafood from
Newlyn (fresh cod in beer batter and
Fowey mussels in cider and cream), and
seasonal fruits and vegetables for decent
pub dishes – speciality sausages, seafood
and broccoli mornay. The dining room
has a rug-strewn flagged floor, a pine
dresser and French windows leading out
into the cobbled courtyard. Beyond the
rose-covered arch is a splendid terraced
garden, ideal for summer quaffing.

directions	A30 for Newquay airport; right for St Mawgan. At bottom of hill by church.
meals	12pm-2pm; 6pm-9pm (from 7pm Sun); 12pm-2.30pm; 6pm-9.30pm in summer. Main courses £5.95-£15; Sunday roast £7.25.
closed	3pm-6pm. Open all day Sun & daily in summer.

Jan & Andy Marshall
The Falcon Inn,
St Mawgan,
Newquay TR8 4EP

tel	01637 860225
web	www.thefalconinn-newquay.co.uk

map: 1 entry: 78

Cornwall

The Crown Inn
Lanlivery

You are on the bucolic Saint's Way, along which Irish drovers used to 'fat walk' their cattle from Padstow to Fowey before setting sail for France. Walkers still stop by for sustenance and a bed. Most of the 12th-century longhouse's flagged floors have been carpeted in red and blue, but the deep granite-lined clome oven remains and a country mood prevails – the Crown is the hub of the village. Five areas ramble: the largest for dining, the conservatory for the sun, and three small bars. Tasty food comes courtesy of fine Cornish produce, and is cooked to order: crayfish cocktail, seared scallops with lemon and garlic butter, creamy steak and ale pie, lamb shoulder with red wine and rosemary gravy, Cornish rump steak with all the trimmings. There's a decent wine list, and hand-pumped ales include one brewed specially for the pub, Crown Inn Glory. Outside is a pretty garden with a view of the church tower.

directions	Signed off A390 between Lostwithiel & St Blazey. Pub opp. church.
meals	12pm-2.30pm; 6pm-9.15pm. Main courses £5.95-£15.95; bar meals £3.95-£7.95.
closed	Open all day in summer.

	Andy Brotheridge The Crown Inn, Lanlivery, Bodmin PL30 5BT
tel	01208 872707
web	www.wagtailinns.com

ﺡ ﺡ ﺡ ﺡ

map: 1 entry: 79

Cornwall

St Kew Inn
St Kew Churchtown

Lost down a maze of lanes in a secluded wooded valley, the St Kew is a grand old inn that stands next to the parish church. Though its stone walls go back 600 years – it was built for the masons working on the church – it has been welcoming visitors for a mere 200. Reputedly haunted by a Victorian village girl discovered buried beneath the main bar, it is an irresistibly friendly, chatty place with a huge range and a warming fire, a dark slate floor, winged settles and a terrific unspoilt atmosphere – no pub paraphernalia here. Meat hooks hang from a high ceiling, earthenware flagons embellish the mantelpiece, fresh flowers brighten the bar. Local St Austell ales are served in the traditional way, straight from the barrel, and the famous St Kew Inn steaks are delicious. In summer, the big streamside garden is the place to be.

directions	From Wadebridge for Bude on A39 for 4 miles; left after golf club. 1 mile to St Kew Churchtown.
meals	12pm-2pm; 7pm-9.30pm. Main courses £7.25-£13.95.
closed	2.30pm-5.30pm (3pm-6pm Sun).

	Justin & Sarah Mason St Kew Inn, St Kew Churchtown, Bodmin PL30 3HB
tel	01208 841259

ﺡ ﺡ ﺡ ﺡ

map: 1 entry: 80

Cornwall

The Port Gaverne Hotel
Port Gaverne

Once an ordinary seaside hotel, now a stylish little inn. The food, cooked fresh in a modern English style – sweet pepper soup, mussels, baked wing of skate – has come on in leaps and bounds since the Sylvesters took over. The 17th-century inn is set back from rocky, funnel-shaped Port Gaverne near the pretty fishing village of Port Isaac where people come for the sea and quiet relaxation, and there's a sheltered swimming cove within seconds of the door. In the warren-like bar, snug cubby-holes warmed by a woodburner are ideal for recuperating with a pint after a hike along the coast. A wonderful stained-glass picture of a rigger leads to the formal restaurant, where an emphasis is placed on locally sourced beef, lamb and fish and fresh garden produce. And there's a choice of roasts on Sundays.

directions	From Wadebridge B3314; B3267 to Port Isaac. There to Port Gaverne. Inn up lane from cove on left.
meals	12pm-2pm; 6.30pm-9pm. Main course £17; bar meals £4–£14.
closed	Open all day.

Graham & Annabelle Sylvester
The Port Gaverne Hotel,
Port Gaverne,
Port Isaac PL29 3SQ

tel	01208 880244
web	www.chycor.co.uk/hotels/port-gaverne-inn

map: 1 entry: 81

Cornwall   Pub with rooms

The Mill House Inn
Trebarwith

You coast down a steep winding lane to the 1760s mill house in its pretty woodland setting. The bar is the best of old and new Cornish: big flagged floor, whitewashed beams, wooden tables, chapel chairs, two leather sofas by a wood-burning stove. The dining room over the mill stream has light, elegance and a bistro feel: sea blues, white linen. Settle down to baked local mushrooms stuffed with spinach and sun-dried tomatoes and topped with Tesyn cheese, Cornish haddock with crayfish risotto, Michaelstow beef on a bed of roast vegetables; the locally sourced dishes are updated daily. Trebarwith beach, all surf and sand, is five minutes away, while coastal trails lead to Tintagel, official home of the Arthurian legends... stay a while. The pub's contemporary bedrooms vary in size and have a stylish Cape Cod feel, in sympathy with the setting.

directions	From Tintagel, B3263 south, to Trebarwith Strand.
meals	12pm-2.30pm (3pm Sun); 6.30pm-8.30pm (9pm Fri & Sat). Main courses £12-£17; bar meals £4-£12.
rooms	9 twins/doubles £80-£120. Singles £50.
closed	Open all day.

See pp 30–57 for full list of pubs with rooms

Mark & Kep Forbes
The Mill House Inn,
Trebarwith,
Tintagel PL34 0HD

tel	01840 770200
web	www.themillhouseinn.co.uk

map: 1 entry: 82

Cornwall — Pub with rooms

The Bay View Inn
Widemouth Bay

Surfers, sunsets and Sharp's Ale – all can be savoured from the large deck that faces the foaming Atlantic, while a barbecue sizzles with temptations. This family-friendly pub has a play area to the side, often with a bouncy castle slide, and accepts the sandiest of children and adults. Inside; soft leather sofas and chunky wooden coffee tables, a Cape Cod inspired dining area with sea views, more space for families, and a photo gallery of local surfing heroes, secret spots and shipwrecks. Skinners Ale, Addlestone's Cider and 20 wines by the glass complement an ever-changing modern Cornish menu. Try the sea bass on pesto mash with coriander salsa for a fishy treat; finish with New York style cheesecake for a taste of the Big Apple. Stay all night: stylish, upbeat bedrooms have a beachy feel, many with great sea views.

directions	From Bude along coast road; on left just before Widemouth Bay Beach.
meals	12pm-2.30pm (3pm Sun); 6.30pm-9.30pm (6pm-9pm Sun); sandwiches 2.30pm-6.30pm. Main courses £9-£14; bar meals £7-£11
rooms	6: 3 doubles, 2 family, 1 single £38-£110.
closed	Open all day.

See pp 30–57 for full list of pubs with rooms

Clive Mansell & Alison Carter
The Bay View Inn,
Marine Drive, Widemouth,
Bude EX23 0AW
tel   01288 361273
web   www.bayviewinn.co.uk

map: 1 entry: 83

Cornwall

The Bush Inn
Morwenstow

After a blowy walk along the cliffs – where the eccentric 19th-century local vicar and poet, Robert Hawker, contemplated the sea and the greater questions – the Bush Inn, a genuinely ancient pub, makes the perfect resting place. Local farmer Rob Tape took over in 2005 and has carefully updated the place, one of England's oldest pub buildings. Once a monastic rest-house, it dates back in part to AD950, and a Celtic piscina carved from serpentine is set in one wall. Slate-flagged floors, a huge stone fireplace and lovely old wooden furnishings in the bar preserve the timeless character of this immutable tavern. Visitors will find two new dining areas and all day food that takes in local mussels, beef and lamb from neighbouring farms, fish from Widemouth Bay, and crispy duck confit with sautéed potatoes and red wine sauce. Weary walkers will find excellent beer and hearty snacks. There's seating on the front lawn, and a view out to sea.

directions	Follow signs for Morwenstow off A39, 9 miles north of Bude.
meals	12pm-9pm (9.30pm summer). Main courses £5.50-£16.
closed	Open all day.

Rob & Edwina Tape
The Bush Inn,
Crosstown, Morwenstow,
Bude EX23 9SR
tel   01288 331242
web   www.bushinn-morwenstow.co.uk

map: 1 entry: 84

The Wheatsheaf
Beetham

A timeless air pervades the village of Beetham. The Wheatsheaf traces its origins back to the 16th century: witness the leaded windows, dark wood panelling, fine mouldings and wide open stairs. Comfortable furnishings, pictures and flowers lend a restful air. Beyond the cocooning bar is a classic tap room with a big open fire and old prints while the first-floor dining rooms have a country-house feel. Lunchtime bar food ranges from generous sandwiches to dishes like Thai-spiced crab and salmon fishcakes or Cumberland sausages with creamy mash. Marinated leg of lamb steak with honey roast vegetables and red wine gravy, and pheasant with wild mushroom and tarragon sauce appear in the evening; cask ales from Jennings and Tirril breweries keep drinkers happy.

directions	Off A6, 1 mile south of Milnthorpe.
meals	12pm-2pm; 6pm-9pm; 6.30pm-8.30pm Sun. Main courses £8.95-£16.95; Sunday lunch £11.95 & £13.95.
closed	Open all day.

Mark & Kath Chambers
The Wheatsheaf,
Beetham,
Milnthorpe LA7 7AL
tel   015395 62123
web   www.wheatsheafbeetham.com

map: 11 entry: 85

White Hart Inn
Bouth

The main bar has a counter dripping with brass, jugs, hops and beer pumps; walls and shelves are strewn with clay pipes, old photos, washboards, taxidermy, tankards and mugs. It's a friendly, sleepy-village local, where regulars mingle with visitors over pints of Black Sheep, Jennings Cumberland and Hawkshead Bitter. There are loads of malts, too, and a no-nonsense menu that includes rare-breed meat from nearby Abbots Reading farm, local lamb cooked in fresh thyme and red wine, and wild mallard and pheasant from the shooting parties that congregate in the pub car park on winter Saturdays. They source locally, and offer small portions to children. An age-polished, sloping flagged floor reflects the light from the window; grand fires at both ends are log-fuelled in cold weather. The walking's marvellous and pub and village fit snugly into the ancient landscape of wooded valleys and tight little roads.

directions	Village signed off A590 Barrow road after Lakeside & Haverthwaite Steam Railway.
meals	12pm-2pm; 6pm-8.45pm. Main courses £7.25-£11.95.
closed	2pm-6pm, Mon all day (except bank hols) & Tues lunch. Open all day Sat & Sun.

Nigel & Kath Barton
White Hart Inn,
Bouth,
Ulverston LA12 8JB
tel   01229 861229
web   www.bed-and-breakfast-cumbria.co.uk

map: 11 entry: 86

Manor Arms
Broughton-in-Furness

Unspoilt, grey-stoned Broughton-in-Furness — complete with village stocks — is a market town that feels like a village. In a corner of its Georgian square stands the 18th-century Manor Arms, a modest inn that has been in the Varty family for 17 years. This is not a foodie's pub, though snacks are on tap all day — hot and cold rolls, homemade soup and the like. Its main fascination lies in its traditional bar and its eight handpumped ales; try Yates, Hawkshead, Roosters, and more in the cellar. In their unpretentious quest for perfection, David Varty and son Scott go to some lengths to ensure the beers are in top-class condition. Cosy up on the bay window seat with children's books and games — little ones are welcome here. Logs burn in a rare 'basket' fireplace into whose oak mantel drinkers have scored their names down the centuries.

Blacksmiths Arms
Broughton Mills

An utterly unspoilt little local — there are few this good in the north of England. In the land of rugged hills and wooded valleys, you approach down a winding lane between high hedges; once you are round the final bend, the low-slung farmhouse-inn comes into view. Inside are four small, slate-floored rooms with beams and low ceilings, long settles, big old tables and several log fires. It couldn't be more 'homely' with its ornaments, dominoes and darts. The bar is strictly for drinking — indeed, there's not much room for anything else; there are three cask ales (two local, one guest) and traditional cider in summer. Across the passage, a room serving proper fresh food, snacks or full meals, and two further dining rooms that sparkle with glass and cutlery. The blackboard advertises dishes with a contemporary slant plus beef and Herdwick lamb reared in the valley. The food is seriously good, so it gets busy; in summer you can spill onto the flowery terrace.

directions	On A593, 10 miles south west of Coniston.
meals	Bar snacks 12pm-10pm (9pm Sun). Bar snacks only.
closed	Open all day.

David & Scott Varty
Manor Arms,
The Square,
Broughton in Furness LA20 6HY
tel 01229 716286

directions	Off A593, Broughton to Coniston.
meals	12pm-2pm; 6pm-9pm. Main courses £6.95-£14.95. Bar meals from £2.95.
closed	2.30-5pm Tues-Fri (winter only) & Mon lunch. Open all day Sat & Sun.

Michael & Sophie Lane
Blacksmiths Arms,
Broughton Mills,
Broughton-in-Furness LA20 6AX
tel 01229 716824
web www.theblacksmithsarms.com

map: 11 entry: 87

map: 11 entry: 88

Cumbria Pub with rooms

Cumbria

The Mason's Arms
Strawberry Bank

Slake your thirst with damson beer. Or
gin: the Lyth valley is known for its fruit.
The countryside is gentle and the pub
sits high on a steep wooded hillside; from
the terrace you can see for glorious
miles. Getting here may test your map
reading skills but persevere – this is no
ordinary local. Three score bottled beers
are on sale – continental beer engines
gleam next to ebony handpumps – with
a range from nearby Hawkshead Brewery
plus others. There's charm too, in open
fires, old flag floors, black beams,
Jacobean panelling and a family parlour.
Dishes range from warm Cumbrian duck
sausage salad to beef and beer cobbler,
fish and chips and rib-eye steak.
Attractive, contemporary suites have
beds on the mezzanine and kitchenettes;
cottages are stylish; hamper breakfasts
(full English if required) are provided.
And the views are stunning.

The Watermill Inn
Ings

Fifteen years and several extensions on,
the converted bobbin mill is Tardis-like
outside. Inside: beams, open stonework,
open fires and lots of traditional pubby
stuff to give the idea they've been
serving beer for centuries. Everyone
loves the Watermill: locals, tourists,
walkers, dogs. They come for the 50
malt whiskies, the heady farm ciders and
the mind-boggling range of 16 real ales
served in award-winning condition,
including cracking beers brewed next
door. There's a sunny front bar good for
families, a dimly-lit drinkers' bar and
several eating areas that overlook the
rushing stream. Tuck into tasty pub food
locally supplied: fish and chips, chicken
with mustard and rosemary, ale pie,
cheddar platter. The pub is on the edge
of good walking country and handy for
Windermere, Taffy the Storyteller drops
by on the first Tuesday of the month, and
a late night bus back to Kendal is the
icing on the cake.

directions	A5074 for Bowness; 6 miles; signs to Bowland Bridge; just beyond village.
meals	12pm-2pm; 6pm-9pm (12pm-9pm Sat & Sun). Main courses £9.95-£14.95.
rooms	3 suites £55-£105. 2 cottages: 1 for 6, 1 for 4, £105-£175.
closed	Open all day.

directions	Just off A591 in Ings, midway between Kendal & Windermere.
meals	12pm-4.30pm; 5pm-9pm. Main courses £7-£14.
closed	Open all day.

John & Diane Taylor
The Mason's Arms,
Strawberry Bank,
Cartmel Fell LA11 6NW
tel   01539 568486
web   www.strawberrybank.com

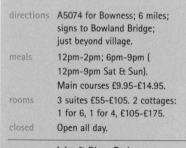

map: 11 entry: 89

Brian Coulthwaite
The Watermill Inn,
Ings,
Kendal LA8 9PY
tel   01539 821309
web   www.watermillinn.co.uk

map: 11 entry: 90

The Punch Bowl Inn
Crosthwaite

A reassuring old inn in a gentle setting, overlooking the valley. The Punchbowl has gone from strength to strength since being restyled by the owners of the famous Drunken Duck, but the old rafters are intact and the dining room keeps its intimate corners. The long bar is stylishly slate-topped, a fitting accompaniment to flagged floors, polished dressers and immaculately chalked boards; relax over a pint of Barngates beer and a posh ploughman's. Outside is a sheltered area overlooking the church; in the restaurant are gleaming dark oak boards, swish leather chairs, white cloths and a fine 18th-century stone fireplace. The man in the kitchen is Matt Waddington, whose popular dishes employ the best local ingredients: try mussel, salmon, shrimp and monkfish broth, Tag Lag ale stew with thyme

dumplings, and café crème parfait to finish. Withdraw gracefully to fabulous rooms with bold fabrics, king-size beds, flat-screen TVs and bathrooms with heated floors; the amazing suite has double baths and views down the valley.

directions	For Kendal on A591; 1st exit Barrow; onto A5074 & towards Bowness; after 2 miles, at sharp bend, right for Crosthwaite. Inn next to church.
meals	12pm-3pm; 6pm-9pm. Main courses £12-£24.
rooms	9: 8 doubles, 1 suite £110-£280. Singles £82.50-£108.75.
closed	Open all day.

SPECIAL AWARD see pages 28-29

Jenny Sisson
The Punch Bowl Inn,
Crosthwaite,
Kendal LA8 8HR
tel   015395 68237
web   www.the-punchbowl.co.uk

map: 11 entry: 91

Strickland Arms
Sizergh

Locked, barred and bolted for eight years, the National Trust-owned pub finally opened its doors in 2005 following a highly unusual and locally approved arrangement between the Trust and Martin Ainscough, pub entrepreneur. Right beside the gates to Sizergh Castle, a medieval pile with stunning gardens, this pub was desperate for attention. Now, behind the stark stone exterior, are two civilised rooms decked out in Trust style, with earthy Farrow & Ball colours, rugs on slate and wooden floors and an eclectic mix of antiques. Order a pint of Coniston Bluebird, pick a seat by a glowing coal fire, and peruse the daily papers or the grand oils that line the walls. Then tuck into some hearty and traditional pub food made from local and organic ingredients – steak, ale and black pudding pie, chump of lamb with port and shallot sauce. And there's a fine, flagged front terrace with pretty views.

directions	Just off A590 north of Kendal, by Sizergh Castle gates.
meals	12pm-2pm; 6pm-9pm; 12pm-8.30pm Sun. Main courses £9.95-£14.50; bar lunch £5-£8.95.
closed	3pm-6pm. Open all day Sat & Sun.

Martin Ainscough
Strickland Arms,
Sizergh,
Kendal LA8 8DZ

tel 01257 462297

map: 11 entry: 92

Hole in t'Wall
Bowness

Known in 1612 as the New Inn, the name was later changed – thanks to the landlord's habit of passing beer though the wall to the blacksmith's next door. It's a good, old-fashioned tavern, not plain but not plush, packed with tourists in season, popular with walkers all year round. The slate flagstones and fireplace have been uncovered and restored to their former glory, the black beams are hung with hops, chamber pots and pretty plates, and the flagged front terrace is a cheerful suntrap in summer. You get two bars downstairs, one long and narrow with that characterful log fire, the other small and snug with an old range, and a third room up. Food is straightforward, from prawn platter to curry of the day; there are jacket potatoes (oven-baked, not microwaved), sandwiches, chicken nuggets, real ale and mulled wine. Lake Windermere, with jetty and boat trips, is a three-minute walk.

directions	From Windermere A592; fork off right onto Fallbarrow Rd for Lowside before A592 joins A5074.
meals	12pm-2.30pm; 6pm-8.30pm. 12pm-7pm Fri & Sat. No food Sun eve. Main courses £6.25-£9.95.
closed	Open all day.

Susan Burnet
Hole in t'Wall,
Lowside,
Bowness-on-Windermere LA23 3DH

tel 015394 43488

map: 11 entry: 93

Queens Head Hotel
Troutbeck

The Queen's Head crouches at the foot of the Kirkstone pass, with sweeping views over moor and valley. Inside is a warren of fascinating rooms. The flagged bar is built around a magnificently carved Elizabethan four-poster, old instruments hang above beams, stuffed birds and beasts gaze down from mantelpiece and alcove. In the bar there's a carved giant's chair, and blazing logs in the large open fireplace are a pull on chilly days. Food is taken seriously, and there's masses of choice: homemade bread and soup or a plate of local cheeses for a quick lunch, or roast lamb with saffron risotto, garlic confit and lamb jus, roast duck with beetroot syrup, and sticky toffee pudding with toffee sauce. There's even real food for children. The bar appeals just as much to those in search merely of a drink, with its fine cask beers (some local), and a wide choice of wines by the glass.

directions	A590/A591 through Windermere. Right at mini r'bout for Troutbeck; 0.75 miles past church.
meals	12pm-2pm; 5pm-8.45pm; bar snacks 2pm-5pm. Main courses £12.95-£16.95; set menu £18.50.
closed	Open all day.

Mark Stewardson
& Joanna Sherratt
Queens Head Hotel, Townhead,
Troutbeck, Windermere LA23 1PW
tel   015394 32174
web   www.queensheadhotel.com

map: 11 entry: 94

Drunken Duck Inn
Barngates

You're up on the hill, away from the crowds, cradled by woods and highland fell — views from the terrace shoot off for miles to towering Lakeland peaks. As for the Duck, she may be old but she sure is pretty, so step into a world of airy interiors, open fires, grandfather clocks, rugs on the floor, exquisite art, stripped floors in the beamed bar and timber-framed walls in the restaurant. They brew their own beer, have nine bitters on tap and the food is utterly delicious: venison with chestnut polenta and caramelised figs; halibut with wild mushroom risotto. The chips are the best and all suppliers are listed. Bedrooms are dreamy: those in the main house snug in the eaves, those across the courtyard crisply uncluttered and indulgent. Some have terraces, several have walls of glass to frame the mountains, all have peaty water straight off the fell. And the staff are brilliant.

directions	Ambleside B5286 for Hawkshead for 2.5 miles. Signed on right, up Duck Hill to crossroads.
meals	12pm-2.15; 6pm-9pm. Main courses £15.95-£24.95. Bar meals £4.25-£7.95.
rooms	16: 14 doubles, 2 twins £95-£225. Singles from £71.25.
closed	Open all day.

See pp 30–57 for full list of pubs with rooms

Stephanie Barton
Drunken Duck Inn,
Barngates,
Ambleside LA22 0NG
tel   01539 436347
web   www.drunkenduckinn.co.uk

map: 11 entry: 95

The Sun Hotel & Inn
Coniston

Coniston skirts the edge of Coniston Water — famous for Donald Campbell's world water-speed trials in *Bluebird*. Off its busy hub sits the Sun. At the front is the hotel with its Edwardian façade, at the back, the old inn. Inside, stone flags, open-stone walls, settles and a 19th-century range. It's a no-nonsense little pub, the ideal place in which to quaff a fine selection of local ales from the cask. Wines too are well-chosen with at least six by the glass. Wooden agricultural implements add to the old-fashioned Cumbrian feel, as do the stools at the bar, the dartboard and the blackboard of tasty dishes, nothing too fancy — steak and kidney cobbler, that sort of thing. For summer there's seating outside on a flagged area, and a tree-sheltered garden in front of the hotel's conservatory restaurant, with views.

The Langstrath Country Inn
Borrowdale

A magnet for walkers: just a track up the Lang Strath to the Lakes' highest peaks (note, parking can be tricky). Mike and Sarah Hodgson are settling in well; planned changes include repositioning the dining area. Vertical timbers create cosy stable-like corners, carpeting and a crackling fire add warmth, and there are fascinating old photos of local characters and scenes to peer at over your pint. The slate-topped bar with its polished brass rail sports four hand-pulls for Jennings, Black Sheep, Hesket Newmarket and Coniston; good wines are available by the glass and a couple of dozen malts enliven the varnished rack. The changing dinner menu indicates an enthusiasm for local produce — Rosthwaite Herdwick lamb, Cumbrian Galloway steak, Morecambe Bay shrimps (potted); lunch is a soup and sandwich affair. A popular refuelling stop on the Coast to Coast path and the Cumbrian Way.

directions	100 yds up hill from bridge in centre, off A593 Ambleside road.
meals	12pm-2.30pm; 6pm-9pm. Main courses £8.50-£18.50; bar meals £3-£7.50.
closed	Open all day.

Alan Piper
The Sun Hotel & Inn,
Coniston LA21 8HQ
tel   015394 41248
web   www.thesunconiston.com

directions	From Keswick B5289 to Borrowdale. Stonethwaite on left between Rosthwaite & Seatoller.
meals	12.30pm-2.30pm; 6.30pm-8.30pm. Main courses £8.95-£13.95; bar lunch from £4.50.
closed	Open all day. Check opening times in winter.

Mike & Sarah Hodgson
The Langstrath Country Inn,
Stonethwaite, Borrowdale,
Keswick CA12 5XG
tel   01768 777239
web   www.thelangstrath.com

map: 11 entry: 96

map: 11 entry: 97

Cumbria — Pub with rooms

The Pheasant
Cockermouth

An English country-cottage garden (apple blossom, climbing roses, the trimmest lawn) looks to Sale Fell and is for guests only, so grab a deckchair on the lawn and settle in for an early evening drink. Interiors are no less spoiling; this is a comfortable country-house inn, with open fires in elegant sitting rooms and a low beamed ceiling in a bright and breezy dining room. The snug bar has a ceiling coloured by 300 years of tobacco smoke and polish, 40 malts, and a couple of Thompson sketches hanging on the wall (he exchanged them for drink). Cosseting bedrooms, warm in yellow, come with pretty pine beds, thick fabrics, Roberts radios, flat-screen TVs, and robes in spotless bathrooms. Most are in the main house, two are in a nearby garden lodge. Wander the corridors and meet Housekeeping armed with feather dusters.

directions	From Keswick, A66 for 7 miles. On left, signed.
meals	12pm-2pm (bar); 12pm-1.15pm; 7pm-8.30pm (restaurant). Main courses (bar) £6-£14.50; set dinner £30.95 & £34.75.
rooms	15: 11 twins/doubles, 1 single, 3 suites, £70-£185.
closed	2.30pm-5.30pm.

See pp 30-57 for full list of pubs with rooms

	Matthew Wylie
	The Pheasant,
	Bassenthwaite Lake,
	Cockermouth CA13 9YE
tel	01768 776234
web	www.the-pheasant.co.uk

map: 11 entry: 98

Cumbria

Kirkstile Inn
Loweswater

Hard to imagine a more glorious setting than that of the Kirkstile Inn, tucked in among the fells, next to an old church and a stream, a half mile from the lakes of Loweswater and Crummock. Roger Humphreys is well up to the job of hosting this legendary bar. There's a peaceful old farmhouse feel to the several low-beamed rooms, and no shortage of space. The whole place is authentic, traditional, well looked after: whitewashed walls, cosy carpeting, solid polished tables, cushioned settles, a well-stoked fire, plants, flowers and the odd horse harness to remind you of the past. Settle down with an unforgettable pint of Coniston Bluebird Bitter or their own excellent Melbreak Bitter. Five chefs deliver unfussy traditional dishes such as steak and ale pie, chicken breast stuffed with Cumberland sausage with onion and red wine sauce, and sticky toffee pudding.

directions	Lorton road from Cockermouth; follow signs to Loweswater.
meals	12pm-2pm; 6pm-9pm. Main courses £7.50-£13; bar snacks £4-£6.
closed	Open all day.

	Mr Roger Humphreys
	Kirkstile Inn,
	Loweswater,
	Cockermouth CA13 0RV
tel	01900 85219
web	www.kirkstile.com

map: 11 entry: 99

Brackenrigg Inn
Ullswater

The terrace and bay windows of this 18th-century inn have breathtaking views across the water to the fells. Attention to detail is noticeable here, and the service is swift and friendly. The part-panelled bar with polished old boards, darts and open fire has a homely feel, as does the carpeted lounge-dining room where families are welcome. Black Sheep and local beers are on tap, and there's a good long wine list. Menus have a modern British slant. In the bar, try mussels cooked in white wine, garlic and cream sauce, or superb Cumberland sausages with mash and onion gravy; in the restaurant, spicy fish soup, sea bass with pea purée and basil oil, and guinea fowl stuffed with black pudding and thyme, served with bubble and squeak and a redcurrant sauce. Sunday lunch is brilliant value, and the treacle toffee pudding sensational.

directions	M6 junc. 40 A66 for Keswick; A592 for Ullswater; Watermillock 3 miles.
meals	12pm-2.30pm; 5pm-9pm. Main courses £11.95-£18.95; bar meals £3.95-£12.95; Sunday lunch £9.95 & £12.95.
closed	Open all day.

Michael Evans
Brackenrigg Inn,
Ullswater,
Penrith CA11 0LP
tel   01768 486206
web   www.brackenrigginn.co.uk

map: 11 entry: 100

Mill Inn
Mungrisdale

By a tumbling burn at the foothills of Blencathra... the setting could not be more idyllic. The village inn has a solid northern feel and is there to provide a down-to-earth yet comfortable welcome. The neat, simple bar has a warming fire and a wooden counter that dispenses Jennings ales to locals and walkers. A light and airy room at the back doubles for games and families and there's a riverside garden for summer. Since their arrival a few years ago, Jim and Margaret Hodge have built up a reputation for home-cooked country dishes; they even organise an annual pie festival. Evening specials may include Blencathra pie (beef in Cumberland ale with shortcrust pastry topping), local Cumberland sausage, rack of Herdwick lamb with whisky cream sauce, or pan-fried venison with roast garlic mash and red wine sauce – and there are homemade scones for tea.

directions	From M6 junc. 40, A66 for Keswick for 10 miles; right for Mungrisdale; 1.5 miles to inn.
meals	12pm-2.30pm; 6pm-8.30pm; 5.30pm-9pm weekends in summer. Main courses £8.25-£15.25; bar meals £6.95-£7.95.
closed	Open all day.

Jim & Margaret Hodge
Mill Inn,
Mungrisdale,
Penrith CA11 0XR
tel   01768 779632
web   www.the-millinn.co.uk

map: 11 entry: 101

The Queen's Head Inn
Tirril

William Wordsworth and his brother sold the inn in the early 1800s to a Mr Bewsher after whom one of Tirril Brewery's ales is named. Chris Tomlinson brewed here before expanding operations at nearby Brougham Hall, but the whitewashed village inn is still the 'brewery tap' and hosts the Cumbrian Beer & Sausage Festival each August. Inside, oodles of charm: low beams, wooden settles and several open fires including a vast inglenook – logs smoulder, even, occasionally, in June. At the back is a lively bar and games room. Sit down to some well-priced food in the bar or the cosy, carpeted restaurant, where peppered lamb shoulder with rich apricot jus or steamed steak and ale suet pudding with Tirril ale gravy will set you up for a day on England's highest peaks. Other chalkboard specials may include local fish and fresh pasta. Only three miles from the M6 at Penrith – or Ullswater and its grand scenery.

The Gate
Yanwath

It was built as a toll gate in 1683 – hence the name. Known to locals as the Yat, the old pub is gaining a reputation for its food – locally sourced and served in hearty portions. The place is immaculate, the young staff are attentive and the landlord remains loyal to the pub's roots, so you may eat anywhere, as well as on the sunny shetered patio at the back. Walk in to a characterful, carpeted, dimly-lit bar, all cosy corners and roaring fire, background music and happy chatter. Beyond is a light, airy and raftered dining room, with crisply laid tables and Windsor chairs. The menu depends on fresh deliveries every day including Cumbrian meat and plenty of fish, and there's real food for children, with pizzas, beefburgers and fishcakes homemade. Wines come from an excellent wine merchant's in Kendal, beers include the fruity and full-flavoured Doris's 90th Birthday Ale.

directions	On B5320, 3 miles south of Penrith.
meals	12pm-2pm; 6pm-9.30pm (8.30pm Sun). Main courses £8.95-£15.95; baguettes from £4.95.
closed	Open all day.

directions	On B5320 south-west of A6 & Penrith; pub 2.5 miles from M6 junc. 40.
meals	12pm-2.30pm; 6pm-9pm. Main courses £5-£24.
closed	Open all day.

Chris Tomlinson
The Queen's Head Inn,
Tirril,
Penrith CA10 2JF
tel 01768 863219
web www.queensheadinn.co.uk

map: 11 entry: 102

Matt Edwards
The Gate,
Yanwath,
Penrith CA10 2LF
tel 01768 862386
web www.yanwathgate.com

map: 11 entry: 103

Highland Drove
Great Salkeld

Yards from the Norman church with its keep-like tower (protection against marauding Scots), the timber porch leads into a flagged bar – cosy, warm, civilised. Now there's a new bar-dining area with easy leather chairs and pine tables, and a popular games room with pool table. With open log fires, tartan, brick and timber, this is a spruce, 21st-century inn that pleases drinkers, diners and walkers. The popular Newton family have turned it into a great local and a successful restaurant. Named after the waters ('kyloes') that the cattle drovers' crossed on their way to Scottish market, the dining room has a Highland lodge feel, its great windows gazing to the lush Pennines. Tuck into rack of lamb, pan-fried Nile perch, chargrilled beef fillet with port and thyme reduction, and toffee and banana crumble. Beers are from the cask, wines are well-chosen. Or keep things simple with ham, egg and chips, or a fresh baguette in the bar.

Old Crown
Hesket Newmarket

The old pub is owned by a cooperative of one hundred souls and is run by Lou and Linda Hogg. Its tiny front room with bar, settles, glowing coals, thumbed books, pictures and folk music (the first Sunday of the month) squeezes in a dozen; a second room houses darts and pool; a third and fourth are dining rooms. Not only is this the only pub where you can sample all of Hesket Newmarket's beers brewed in the barn at the back – Blencathra Bitter, Helvellyn Gold – but it is the focal point of the community, even supporting the post office whose postmistress repays in puddings and pies. The Old Crown is also known for its bangers and mash, ham and eggs, fine curries and Sunday roasts. Its authenticity draws people from miles around – even Prince Charles, who dropped by to launch the *Saving Your Village Pub* guide. Walkers come to explore the Caldbeck Fells. Ask about brewery tours.

directions	Just off B6412 in Great Salkeld.
meals	12pm-2pm;
	6.15-7.45 (5.45-7.15 Sat).
	Restaurant 6.30-9pm only.
	Main courses £6.25-£10.95 (bar);
	£9.95-£18.50 (dinner).
closed	2.30-6pm. Mon lunch (except bank
	hol). Open all day Sat & Sun.

directions	M6 junc. 41 for Wigton on B5305.
	6.5 miles turn for H. Newmarket.
meals	12pm-2pm; 6.30pm-9pm.
	No food all day Mon or Sun eve.
	Main courses £6-£13;
	bar meals £2.50-£6.50.
closed	3pm-5.30pm (7pm Sun),
	Mon & Tues lunch.

Donald & Paul Newton
Highland Drove,
Great Salkeld,
Penrith CA11 9NA
tel   01768 898349
web   www.highland-drove.co.uk

Lewis Hogg
Old Crown,
Hesket Newmarket,
Carlisle CA7 8JG
tel   01697 478288
web   www.theoldcrownpub.co.uk

map: 11 entry: 104

map: 11 entry: 105

Derbyshire

The Plough
Leadmill Bridge

Expect a big welcome from Bob and Cynthia and their team at their 16th-century free house, once a corn mill, on the banks of the river. Acres of grounds and a riverside garden high in the National Park are the perfect backdrop to a perfect inn. The atmosphere is convivial in the cosy, carpeted, split-level bar; settle down to log fires, exposed beams and stone walls, good solid furniture and, beyond, a plush country restaurant. With over 40 dishes to choose from, this is very much a diners' pub; tasty dishes, from lamb sweetbreads with pancetta to lemon sole with papardelle, are the order of the day, there's a good range of hand-pulled ales and wines for connoisseurs. You're on a main road but the large sloping gardens are lovely, and have pretty valley views.

directions	On B6001, 1 mile south from Hathersage towards Bakewell.
meals	11.30am-2.30pm; 6.30pm-9.30pm (Sat 11.30am-9.30pm, Sun 12pm-9pm). Main courses £9.50-£18.95; bar meals £8.95-£9.95.
closed	Open all day.

Bob & Cynthia Emery
The Plough,
Leadmill Bridge,
Hathersage S32 1BA
tel   01433 650319
web   www.theploughinn-hathersage.co.uk

map: 8 entry: 106

Derbyshire

The Chequers Inn
Hope Valley, Calver

The setting is almost alpine in its loveliness – impossible to pass this pub by. Once four stone-built cottages going back to the 16th century, Jonathan and Joanne Tindall's ancient whitewashed inn has been sympathetically modernised, recently refurbished, and is full of homely touches. Wooden floorboards, pine and country prints, cottage furniture and interesting objets give character to rooms that radiate off a stone-walled, timber-ceilinged bar. While blackboards promise modern bistro-style dishes – crab and pea linguine, pan-fried calves' liver with celeriac purée and red pepper sauce – the standard menu lists doorstep sandwiches and traditional casseroles and pies. From the raised garden behind, a path leads straight up through woods to stunning Froggatt Edge; the walking is marvellous.

directions	On A625 8 miles northwest of Chesterfield, 9 miles southwest of Sheffield.
meals	12pm-2pm; 6pm-9.30pm; 12pm-9.30pm Sat (9pm Sun). Main courses £8.50-£15.95.
closed	2.30pm-6pm. Open all day Sat & Sun.

Jonathan & Joanne Tindall
The Chequers Inn,
Froggatt Edge, Hope Valley,
Calver S32 3ZJ
tel   01433 630231
web   www.chequers-froggatt.com

map: 8 entry: 107

Three Stags Heads
Wardlow Mires

Traverse the moor slowly… you don't want to miss this modest collection of cottages that house a pub and a pottery run by Geoff and Pat Fuller – one thrown and the other pulled! It's a gem inside, and couldn't be plainer: just two small rooms, one heated by a fire, the other by a coal-burning kitchen range, perfect for drying out waterproofs and dogs (of which there are a few). So settle into a pint of Abbeydale's Black Lurcher, the house bitter with an 8% ABV, named in memory of one of the dogs. The menu really is a case of what is available from the surrounding countryside and features a lot of game; it has been known for squirrel to have gone into the pot. Opening times are restricted depending on whether you're here for some saltglaze pottery or a pint and a plate of something hot and wholesome from the chalked board. Pat and Geoff have a splendidly relaxed attitude and a great sense of fun.

directions	At junction of A623 & B6465 south east of Tideswell.
meals	12.30pm-3.30pm; 7pm-9pm. Main courses £6.50-£10.50.
closed	Mon-Thur all day & Fri until 7pm. Open all day weekends & bank holidays.

Geoff & Pat Fuller
Three Stags Heads,
Wardlow Mires,
Tideswell SK17 8RW
tel   01298 872268

map: 8 entry: 108

The Bull's Head
Ashford-in-the-Water

Lovely carved settles, cushions, clocks and country prints – this is pub heaven. There are newspapers and magazines to read, light jazz hums in the background, coals glow in the grate. The busy Bull's Head has been in Debbie Shaw's family for half a century and she and Carl have been at the helm for the past seven. Carl cooks, proudly serving "bistro food, not a laminated menu"; even the bread and the cheese biscuits are homemade. With a strong emphasis on local and seasonal produce, there could be courgette and lemon soup, steak and Old Stockport pie with braised red cabbage, pan-fried calves' liver with bubble-and-squeak and red wine gravy, sticky toffee pudding with black treacle sauce. Service is swift and friendly and, this being a Robinson's pub, Unicorn Best Bitter, Old Stockport and Wards are on handpump. Roses round the door, tables round the back, and a pretty village with a bridge from which to throw bread to the ducks. A brilliant place.

directions	Off A6, 2 miles north of Bakewell. 5 miles from Chatsworth.
meals	12pm-2pm; 6.30pm-9pm (7pm-9pm Sun). Main courses £9-£16.50.
closed	3pm-6pm (7pm Sun).

Debbie Shaw
The Bull's Head,
Church Street,
Ashford-in-the-Water,
Bakewell DE45 1QB
tel   01629 812931

map: 8 entry: 109

Derbyshire — Pub with rooms

Devonshire Arms
Beeley

Classic Peak District scenery surrounds Beeley's stone cottages and this handsome public house. Converted from three cottages in 1747, it became a coaching inn once visited by Edward VII and is popular now because of its proximity to Chatsworth House. In 2006 it was taken over by the Duchess. Always a civilised lunch spot for well-heeled locals, it now verges on the opulent – in a stylish and understated way. Along with the beams, log fires and settles are candy-stripe tub chairs in vibrant hues and cushions tucked into cosy crannies. In a room where floor-to-ceiling windows overlook the beck are snazzy bar stools – and more enticing colours. Bar and brasserie serve traditional and modern food and meat from the estate, the wine list reaches the dizzy heights of Château Petrus and, in a stone-flagged tap room, walkers are refreshed with expertly kept ales. Bedrooms are equally vibrant, contemporary and lavish.

directions	Follow signs for Chatsworth off A6 at Rowsley Bridge.
meals	12pm-9.30pm. Main courses £8.95-£16.95; bar meals £4.95-£9.95.
rooms	4: 3 doubles, 1 suite £125-£165.
closed	Open all day.

See pp 30–57 for full list of pubs with rooms

Richard Palmer
Devonshire Arms,
Beeley,
Matlock DE4 2NR
tel   01629 733259
web   www.devonshirebeeley.co.uk

map: 8 entry: 110

Derbyshire

Druid Inn
Birchover

A strange, enticing countryside of tors, crags, wooded knolls and stone circle-strewn moors erupts high above Matlock. In the midst of this morphological mayhem stands the Druid Inn, its mellow stone exterior disguising an ultra-chic gastropub and a menu drawing on traditional British and the best of European; chicken liver parfait with homemade chutney, soft shell crab with pea and mint risotto, rump of lamb with confit Mediterranean vegetables and basil pesto mash. Shadows of the old village local remain: a quarry-tiled snug with open fire, antique seats and beers brewed by the Leatherbritches brewery – but the general atmosphere is that of bistro-in-the-country, with blond wood to the fore, designer seating in the split-level restaurant rooms and a minimalist décor. Suntrap patios among a colourful flood of planters and shrubs promise village views, and ramblers rub shoulders with epicures.

directions	From A6; B5056; signs for Birchover.
meals	12pm-2.30pm (3pm Sun); 6pm-9pm. Main courses £9-£16; sandwiches from £6.
closed	Open all day.

Chris King
Druid Inn,
Main Street, Birchover DE4 2BL
tel   01629 650302
web   www.thedruidinn.co.uk

map: 8 entry: 111

Old Poets' Corner
Ashover

Old Poets' Corner has something for every one, and it has been achieved with effortless style. Inside this mock-Tudor village-centre inn, ideally placed for forays into the Peaks and Dales, is a whirlwind of activity that pulls together live music, eight real ales, one perry, an ever-changing range of five ciders, good stout food and an Edwardian Arts and Crafts interior. And, living up to its name, there's a regular poets' night for local rhymesters. From good hefty farmhouse settles and pine tables, music-loving regulars sup Old Poets ale brewed locally by Leatherbritches and Tower (4.1% alcohol by volume) and ciders such as Broadoak Moonshine (8.4% abv)... And with that in mind the menu is more than substantial, trumpeting chillis, pastas, meat and potato pies, casseroles and a carvery on Sundays. Few pubs can give so much and succeed, but here they do, so sit back, relax, and, as if by accident, be entertained by the energy and good vibes surrounding you.

directions	Village centre; just off B6036 between Kelstedge & Woolley Moor.
meals	12pm-2pm; 6.30pm-9pm; 12pm-3pm Sun. Main courses £4.25-£14; bar meals £.3.25-£9.50; Sunday roast £6.95.
closed	2.30pm-5pm. Open all day Fri-Sun.

SPECIAL AWARD
see pages 28-29

Kim & Jackie Beresford
Old Poets' Corner,
Butts Road,
Chesterfield S45 0EW

tel   01246 590888
web   www.oldpoets.co.uk

map: 8 entry: 112

Derbyshire

Ye Olde Gate Inne
Brassington

One of the most exquisite pubs in Derbyshire, built from timber salvaged from the wrecks of the Armada. Furnishings are plain: ancient settles, rush-seated chairs, polished tables, gleaming copper pans, a clamorous clock, a collection of pewter. In winter a fire blazes in the blackened range that dominates the quarry-tiled main bar. In the dim yet wonderfully atmospheric snug are a glowing range and flickering candlelight. There's a short, changing blackboard menu and traditional tucker: ploughman's, filled baguettes (delicious roast beef with onions and mushrooms), game hotpot, curries, Derbyshire specialities like fidget pie, lemon sponge. Come too for superbly kept Marstons Pedigree on handpump and a number of malts. Mullioned windows look onto a sheltered back garden perfect for the popular evening barbecues that are held from Easter until October.

directions	Midway between Ashbourne & Wirksworth off B5035.
meals	12pm-1.45pm; 7pm-8.45pm. No food Sun eve. Main courses £7.95-£18.95; bar meals £3.85-£10.95.
closed	2.30pm-6pm (7pm Sun); Mon (except bank hols) & Tues lunch.

Paul Burlinson
Ye Olde Gate Inne,
Well Street,
Brassington,
Matlock DE4 4HJ
tel   01629 540448

map: 8 entry: 113

Derbyshire

The Bear Inn
Alderwasley

The best of olde England – the sort of place that Americans travel far to find. (And it is in the back of beyond!). Enter a dressed-stone, bare-boarded, atmospheric warren. Expect a long passageway, a comfy lobby for families chatty with budgies and cockatoos, and a solid old door to a delightful snug – all high-backed settles, old pews and stools, low beams and clutches of farmers and chinwagging locals. Yet more rooms, more alcoves and carved chairs, old brass scales, gilt-framed prints, a dresser packed with porcelain, horsey ephemera, blackened cooking pots, ancient clocks and bottles, candles, stone fireplaces and aromatic log fires. The blackboard menu is long, with up to 30 main courses available all day and great Sunday roasts, there are six handpumps with a changing array of beers, and lots of wines. Great staff make this a well-nigh perfect place – but be sure to book your table for evenings and weekends.

directions	From B5025 east of Wirksworth, turn off at Wirksworth Moor at the Malt Shovel pub. Continue for 1 mile.
meals	12pm-9.30pm (9pm Sun). Main courses £8.95-£17.95; bar meals £3.95-£5.95.
closed	Open all day.

Nicola Fletcher-Musgrave
The Bear Inn,
Alderwasley,
Belper DE56 2RD
tel   01629 822585

map: 8 entry: 114

Derbyshire

The Barley Mow
Kirk Ireton

Sunlight streams through the stone mullioned windows of this Jacobean pub, Outside, its resplendent sundial is dated 1681. So authentic is the Barley Mow that Sir Isaac Newton could be penning the last words of a thesis in the parlour, sitting by the black-leaded range where coals glow in the bow-fronted basket. The worn tiled tap room floor is framed by simple wall benches and dotted with a few old stools; barrels of ale are racked neatly behind the bar; it is austere, dimly lit, addictive. To the side, up a few steps from the front parlours, are adjoining rooms that include the original kitchen with its huge 17th-century working bread oven. A selection of fresh cobs is available at lunchtime while suppers are for residents only – and as you sip your Thatchers cider or Whim Hartington IPA, you will notice the slate topped tables with a missing corner and wonder why? For drinkers, ramblers and historians, a delight.

directions	Signed off B5023 Wirksworth to Duffield road.
meals	Rolls available 12pm–2pm. Rolls 95p.
closed	2pm–7pm.

	Mary Short The Barley Mow, Kirk Ireton, Ashbourne DE6 3JP
tel	01335 370306

map: 8 entry: 115

Derbyshire

The Red Lion Inn
Hognaston

Jason and Jenny took over this endearing and enduring village local and have changed little. The open-plan, L-shaped bar room quakes with quarry tiles and mature floorboards, on which stand a Pandora's box of classic tables, pews, settles and grand and simple chairs overseen by umpteen artefacts, from an HMV-style gramophone to a ship's gimbal hanging from a low-slung beam. The original and imposing wood-panelled bar sweeps between levels warmed by capacious open log fires, dispensing ales from Marston's and some of the raft of craft breweries that have exploded in Derbyshire. Filling fodder, from light bites to hearty creations, includes crab cakes, beef stroganoff, orange and tarragon duck, and lamb dishes that are the signature of the place. This is a fine old pub for the traditionalist – in great walking and shooting country.

directions	Off the B5035 between Ashbourne & Wirksworth.
meals	12pm–3pm; 6.30pm–9.30pm. Main courses from £7.95; bar snacks from £5.95..
closed	3pm–6pm. Open all day Sun.

	Jason & Jenny Waterall The Red Lion Inn, Hognaston, Ashbourne DE6 1PR
tel	01335 370396

map: 8 entry: 116

Derbyshire

The Red Lion Inn
Hollington

When Robin Hunter took over six years ago the inn was in a sorry state. His dedication has paid off: the Red Lion pulls such a crowd at the weekends that you'll need to book in advance. Modernisation has been sensitive to character and bar food keeps the traditional mood going with steak and kidney pie and sticky toffee pudding. But it is on the main daily menu that Robin gets to show off, using fresh, seasonal ingredients; try sesame tiger prawns in teriyaki marinade on gingered Swiss chard, followed by venison on swede mash with shallot and cep marmalade. While the menu revels in being wide-ranging and up-to-date, Robin's style is commendably direct and simple and his staff really make you feel at home. If you are here just for a drink, try Marstons Pedigree on handpump or a guest beer. There's a pretty garden, too.

directions	Off A52 between Derby & Ashbourne.
meals	12pm-2pm (2.30pm Sun); 6.30pm-9pm. No food Mon lunch. Main courses £10.75-£16.95; bar meals £6-£10.
closed	Mon eve. Open all day Sun.

Robin Hunter
The Red Lion Inn,
Main Street,
Hollington DE6 3AG
tel   01335 360241
web   www.redlionhollington.co.uk

map: 8 entry: 117

Derbyshire

Three Horseshoes
Breedon-on-the-Hill

Ian Davison and Jennie Ison are revitalising this listed village pub and have successfully created a relaxed modern atmosphere with a menu to match. Expect painted brickwork, seagrass matting, antique tables and chairs, an eclectic mix of photos and prints and masses of space. Smaller rooms include a simple quarry-tiled bar and an intimate red dining room with three tables, while pride of place goes to a handsome Victorian bar counter picked up years ago and stored in anticipation of the right setting. Dishes are chalked up on boards in the bar and the winning food formula takes in halibut with garlic and prawn sauce, lamb shank with mustard mash, and bread and butter pudding. Marston's Pedigree and Theakstons on hand pump should satisfy those in for a swift half. The ongoing renovation has created a sheltered patio at the back and will eventually see bedrooms in a restored barn.

directions	Follow signs off A42 between Ashby de la Zouch & Castle Donington.
meals	12pm-2pm; 5.30pm-9.15pm (12pm-3pm Sun). Main courses £13.50-£19.50; bar meals £4.95-£7.95.
closed	2.30pm-5.30pm & Sun from 3pm.

Ian Davison & Jennie Ison
Three Horseshoes,
Breedon-on-the-Hill,
Derby DE73 8AN
tel   01332 695129
web   www.thehorseshoes.com

map: 8 entry: 118

Rose & Crown
Yealmpton

Delicious smells tempt you the moment you enter this big, bustling, open-plan pub. People travel miles for the food: the man in the kitchen is Daniel Gillard, who cut his teeth at the Carved Angel. So this rustic-stylish revamp of a former dingy boozer looks set to pay off. Cheerful staff dispatch good-looking dishes to softly-lit tables in one of two dining areas. A step or two down are squashy cow-hide sofas around an open fire, cream-washed open-stone walls and wooden Venetian blinds – perfect simplicity. The best wines represent the best value, and the ales and the menu change monthly. Curried prawn wontons in a clear consommé are just one example of a beautifully executed Pacific Rim menu, but you can have pork and leek sausages too, and roasted skate wing with chestnut mushrooms, and west country cheeses, and poached apple with calvados ice cream. *Seafood restaurant in neightbouring barn.*

The Ship Inn
Noss Mayo

At the head of a tidal inlet, a 16th-century pub remodelled with a nautical twist. While visiting boats can tie up alongside (with permission!), high-tide parking is trickier. When the tide is in, you enter via the back door on the first-floor level; when out, it's a quick stroll over the 'beach' and in at the front. Downstairs are plain boards, a wooden bar, solid wood furniture and walls richly caparisoned with maritime prints. Open fires, books and newspapers add to the easy feel. Upstairs the Galley, Bridge and Library areas have views and a happy, dining buzz. The menu strikes a modern chord and is fish-friendly: fish stew and fresh crab sandwiches alongside Devon lamb and rhubarb and ginger crumble. They have well-kept beers from Devon breweries, many malts and 11 wines by the glass: take your drink to the sunny patio at octagonal tables and relish the watery views. This is a civilised stop-off for walkers on the South Devon coast path.

directions	On A379, 7 miles south-east of Plymouth.
meals	12pm-2pm (3.30pm Sun); 6.30pm-9.30pm (9pm Sun). Main courses £9-£18; set lunch £9.95 & £12.95.
closed	Open all day.

John Stevens
Rose & Crown,
Market Street, Yealmpton,
Plymouth PL8 2EB
tel   01752 880223
web   www.theroseandcrown.co.uk

map: 2 entry: 119

directions	South of Yealmpton, on Yealm estuary.
meals	12pm-9pm. Main courses £8-£16; bar meals £5-£8.
closed	Open all day. Closed Mon in winter.

Bruce & Lesley Brunning
The Ship Inn,
Noss Mayo,
Plymouth PL8 1EW
tel   01752 872387
web   www.nossmayo.com

map: 2 entry: 120

Dartmoor Union
Holbeton

Don't be deceived by the unassuming plaque next to the front door of this former cider press and village union room. Inside is stylish, welcoming and full of surprises. The leather sofas, chopped logs and glossy piles of *Country Living* in the flagstoned bar create a comfortable farmhouse feel, while the burgundy walls of the dining area add a bistro touch. The pub is part of the Wykeham Inns group who also own the Rose & Crown at Yealmpton — so broad and keenly-priced daily menus appeal to all tastes, with some judicious sourcing of ingredients from head chef Ollie Luscombe. Tuck into partridge with spicy lentils and parsnip purée, roast canon of lamb with confit garlic and red wine jus or crab crostini. Another surprise: they have just created a microbrewery in the enclosed, decked and sunny garden, producing two ales from a Kentish blend of Goldings, Brambling Cross and Fuggles hops. Beaches and walks beckon…

directions	Village signed off A379, 10 miles east of Plymouth.
meals	12pm–2pm (3pm Sun); 6.30pm–9.30pm (9pm Sun). Main courses £7.95–£16.95; bar meals £6.95–£12.95.
closed	3pm–5.30pm. Open all day Sun.

John Stevens
Dartmoor Union,
Fore Street, Holbeton,
Plymouth PL8 1NE
tel   01752 830288
web   www.dartmoorunion.co.uk

map: 2 entry: 121

Old Chapel Inn
Bigbury-on-Sea

How steeped in character is it possible for a pub to be? Perched on a 13th-century stone fireplace by a winter fire, surrounded by candles in silver sconces, chablis to hand — you cannot help but love this place, at the heart of which lies a small chapel with a vaulted beamed roof and holy well. There's a welcome for children and dogs but most come for the food — compassionately sourced, cooked with passion by Paul and served in an elegant dining room. Choose between traditional fish and chips or pan-fried chicken supreme marinated with fresh herbs and served with roasted Mediterranean vegetables. Whatever they turn their hands to, they do to perfection, and that includes the bedrooms across the courtyard, with their hand-made, medieval-style beds, snowy duvets and velvety covers — saintly but indulgent at the same time.

directions	On B3392 Modbury to Bigbury.
meals	12pm–2.30pm; 6pm–9.30pm (7pm restaurant). Main courses £11.50–£16.50; bar meals £6.95–£14.95.
rooms	4: 3 doubles, 1 twin £85–£115. Singles £50.
closed	3pm–6pm & Sun eve; Mon in winter.

See pp 30–57 for full list of pubs with rooms

Paul & Britt Clement
Old Chapel Inn,
St Ann's Chapel, Bigbury-on-Sea TQ7 4HQ
tel   01548 810241
web   www.oldchapelinn.com

map: 2 entry: 122

Fortescue Arms
East Allington

Tom and Werner are the 'highlights' here.
Canadian Tom is maitre d' and has looked
after heads of state; Austrian Werner has
cheffed in starred restaurants. The
Fortescue's double doors fling open in
summer and the wine corks pop in the
bar. Your hosts have settled in well,
welcoming both locals and vistors alike, as
well as reinventing pub food – and how!
Portions are generous, quick to arrive,
great value and, if the rabbit and pumpkin
stew is anything to go by, delicious.
Emphasis is on local produce so there's
venison steak with red wine and berry
gravy; pheasant stuffed with chestnuts;
bacon and onion with a port sauce; tuna
with red wine and caper sauce;
apfelstrüdel with crème patissière. The
dark panelled and flagstoned bar is where
Tom and the bar girls hold court, the
restaurant is inviting with terracotta walls
and glowing candles, and the outdoor
decked area is smartly spotlit at night.

Victoria Inn
Salcombe

Separated from the rock pools and the
sea by a modest car park, this fully
revamped and rather civilised inn has
won several awards under chef-
proprietor Andrew Cannon. Local
pictures and nautical *objets* acknowledge
the coastal location and history – as does
the menu, whose range is broad. Pop in
for a swift half and a sandwich and chips
or stay for a daily fish special – codling,
sea bass, trout – served in generous
portions. Young and cheery staff make all
ages welcome and the large three-tiered
garden, with super wooden play area,
makes this an excellent family venue in
summer. Salcombe's yachties and second
home owners mean that star-spotters
may get lucky – though you might be
better off having a nautical natter with
the sea dogs at the bar. Flowers and
white linen in the restaurant, log fires
and malt whiskies in the bar, coastal
walks to make the heart soar.

directions	Village signed off A361 between Totnes & Kingsbridge.
meals	12pm-2pm; 7pm-9.30pm. Main courses £9.95-£17.65; bar meals £6.80-£12.95.
closed	2.30pm-6pm & Mon lunch.

directions	Town centre.
meals	12pm-2.30pm; 6pm-9pm. Main courses £9.95-£17.
closed	Open all day.

	Werner Rott & Tom Kendrick Fortescue Arms, East Allington, Totnes TQ9 7RA
tel	01548 521215
web	www.fortescue-arms.co.uk

	Andrew Cannon Victoria Inn, Fore Street, Salcombe TQ8 8BU
tel	01548 842604
web	www.victoriainnsalcombe.co.uk

map: 2 entry: 123

map: 2 entry: 124

Devon

Pig's Nose Inn
East Prawle

Winding lanes with skyscraper hedges weave from the main road to the edge of the world. There are an awful lot of porcine references round these parts (South Hams, Gammon Head, Piglet Stores) and the Pig's Nose is Devon's most southerly pub. Filled with character, cosy corners and quirky ephemera, it has an atmosphere all of its own. A pie, pint and a paper at lunchtime can give way at night to the entire pub joining in a singalong; Peter's connections entice legendary acts – The Yardbirds, Wishbone Ash – to play in the adjacent fabulous hall. If your teenagers fail to join in, a ready supply of 50p coins will keep them entertained in the pool room. Lifelong friendships may be struck up by the woodburning stove as you tuck into good old pub favourites cooked up by Carlo the chef. Your hosts have a terrific sense of fun and faithful visitors return again and again.

directions	A379 Kingsbridge-Dartmouth; at Frogmore, right over bridge opp. bakery; signs to East Prawle. Pub by green.
meals	12pm-2pm; 6.30pm-9pm (7pm-9pm in winter). Main courses £5.50-£11.
closed	2.30pm-6pm (7pm in winter), Sun eve & Mon all day in winter.

Peter & Lesley Webber
Pig's Nose Inn,
East Prawle,
Kingsbridge TQ7 2BY
tel   01548 511209
web   www.pigsnoseinn.co.uk

map: 2 entry: 125

Devon

Tradesmans Arms
Stokenham

Nick Abbott swapped a thriving Chiltern's dining pub for the good life in the South Hams. His 14th-century, part-thatched pub, formerly a brewhouse with three cottages, stands in a sleepy village inland from Slapton Sands and takes its name from the tradesmen who used to call in for a jug of ale while trekking the coastal bridlepath. You may still find a tradesman or two here today, downing a pint in the main bar. Beamed and attractively rustic, it has an open fire and antique dining tables, while gilt framed pictures fill the Georgian dining room; both have views that reach across the valley. The menu and daily chalkboard specials list some innovative pub food, all created by a local chef. As well as the usual lunchtime sandwiches, the daily-changing and seasonal selection includes fresh Brixham fish, scallops from the bay and game – perhaps venison steak with red wine sauce. You'll find six real ales on handpump, including Brakspear Bitter – Nick's favourite tipple.

directions	1 mile from Slapton Sands & Torcross, off A379.
meals	12pm-2.30pm; 6.45pm-9.30pm. Main courses £7.95-£15.95; bar meals £3.95-£7.95.
closed	3pm-6pm. Open all day Sun.

Nicholas Abington Abbott
Tradesmans Arms,
Stokenham,
Kingsbridge TQ7 2SZ
tel   01548 580313
web   www.thetradesmansarms.com

map: 2 entry: 126

Devon

The Tower Inn
Slapton

Despite the drawbacks of hidden access and tricky parking, this 14th-century inn attracts not just locals but visitors from Slapton Sands. Standing beside the sinister ivy-clad ruins of a chantry tower, and built to house the artisans working on it, the pub is a flower-bedecked classic, and hugely atmospheric inside. Dark and gloomy by day, the low-beamed and stone-walled interior – all rustic dark-wood tables, old pews and fine stone fireplaces – comes into its own by night, when flickering light from candles and fires creates the cosiest possible atmosphere. Choose golden, bitter-sweet St Austell Brewery Tribute from the array of handpumps on the bar, then soak it up with a plateful of crispy fried red mullet with roasted pepper salsa, or local beef, venison and lamb dishes. A lovely, sleepy village setting – and a super landscaped garden at the back with views of the parish church and the eerie tower.

directions	Off A379 between Torcross & Dartmouth. Signed.
meals	12pm–2pm; 7pm–9pm. Main courses £10–£19; bar meals £4.50–£15.
closed	2.30pm–6pm (3pm–7pm Sun).

	Andrew & Annette Hammett
	The Tower Inn,
	Slapton,
	Kingsbridge TQ7 2PN
tel	01548 580216
web	www.thetowerinn.com

map: 2 entry: 127

Devon

Kings Arms
Strete

Tempting to visit on a dark and rainy night – but a shame to miss the glorious views of Start Bay. In three years Rob Dawson has revitalized the Edwardian hotel-turned-pub, bringing a natural warmth to the place *and* a fine menu – much of it fishy. A modest bar and a few tables greet you, then up the pine stair to a mezzanine dining room. Delicious smells waft from the kitchen – of seared scallops with pea mousses and Serrano ham, brill with red wine glaze and garlic confit, poached pears with Devon Blue ice cream and port jelly. Oysters are gathered from the river Dart, lobsters and crabs come from the bay, the cheeses are local and the wines are wide-ranging with an excellent number by the glass – surprising for such a small place. The Kings Arms and its garden fill up at summer weekends as holiday-cottagers get wind of the place, and return – for the food, the friendliness and the views.

directions	Between Dartmouth & Torcross on the A379.
meals	12pm–2pm (3pm Sun); 6.30pm–9pm. Main courses £9.50–£19.95.
closed	2.30pm–6pm (3pm–7pm Sun). Sun eves & Mon all day in winter.

	Rob Dawson
	Kings Arms,
	Dartmouth Road, Strete,
	Dartmouth TQ6 0RW
tel	01803 770377
web	www.kingsarms-dartmouth.co.uk

map: 2 entry: 128

Devon

The Ferry Boat Inn
Dittisham

Little has changed at this waterside pub since it was built three centuries ago. The only inn right on the river Dart, it used to serve the passenger steamers plying between Dartmouth and Totnes – you can still arrive by boat. Inside, big windows show off the view to the wooded banks of the Greenway Estate (once Agatha Christie's home, now owned by the National Trust: shake the bell and catch the ferry). Arrive early to bag the best seats in the rustically charming, unspoilt little bar with its bare boards, crackling log fire, nautical bric-a-brac and unmissable, all-important 'high tides' board; if you happen to have overlooked the village car park, negotiated the steep lane and parked on the 'beach', then check the board before ordering your pint. Similarly, the tide dictates whether or not you can dine outside in summer. Expect a rousing welcome and decent home-cooked pub food. Gents can 'spray and pray' next door in the converted chapel.

directions	Off A3122, 2 miles west of Dartmouth.
meals	12pm-2pm; 7pm-9pm. Main courses £6.95-£12.
closed	Open all day.

Ray Benson
The Ferry Boat Inn,
Manor Street,
Dittisham,
Dartmouth TQ6 0EX
tel 01803 722368

map: 2 entry: 129

Devon

The White Hart Bar
Dartington

Down a long, long drive past farmland and deer, Dartington Hall finally peeps into view: the college, conference centre, arts centre, dairy farm and 14th-century hall built for a half-brother of Richard II. Sneaked away in the corner of the courtyard – dotted with picnic tables in summer – is the White Hart. The bar and restaurant is informally 21st century, with chunky beams, York stone floor, smouldering log fires, round light-oak tables and Windsor chairs. Organic and local produce are the mainstay of the menus, from courgette and almond soup to venison, root vegetable and port stew with orange and thyme dumplings. In the trestled dining hall: Start Bay crab cake; pan-fried duck with orange and ginger glaze; Belgian double chocolate cake. Beers are from Otter Brewery, there are good wines and as many organic juices and ciders as you could wish for. Walk off a very fine lunch with a stroll through sweeping parkland that borders the Dart.

directions	Off A385, 2 miles north west of Totnes.
meals	12pm-2pm; 6pm-9pm. Snacks 2pm-6pm. Main courses £7-£12.95.
closed	Open all day.

John Hazzard
The White Hart Bar,
Dartington Hall,
Dartington, Totnes TQ9 6EL
tel 01803 847111
web www.dartingtonhall.com

map: 2 entry: 130

The Normandy Arms
Dartmouth

The Commercial of the 1850s became The Normandy 90 years later – named after the landings; some of the sailors who died were buried on a farm in this parish. With its charming slate bar and floor, open wood beams, lovely red corner seating and bright, friendly staff, The Normandy is, in spite of its brilliance with food, still a pub. Peter, who cut a dash at the Dorchester and was the previous tenant of the Blue Ball at Triscombe, is chef; Sharon does front of house. Both are splendidly hands-on. People come from Kingsbridge, Totnes, Dartmouth for the food, a further dining room is planned, and the menu changes monthly. Our meal of pigeon breasts with dauphinoise potatoes and red cabbage, followed by warm plum tarte tatin, was a winning blend of restraint and indulgence. West country cheeses come with homemade chutney, fish comes from Brixham and the wine list is long. Spoiling all round.

Turtley Corn Mill
Avonwick

The mill's six acres slope down to a lake, so there's space for a multitude of picnic tables (order your hampers in advance). And, more unusually, boules, croquet, jenga and a ginormous chess set. Inside has been recently revamped to create a series of spacious and appealing inter-connected areas: the bar with its dark slate floors and doors to the garden; the wooden-floored 'library' lined with books; the dining area with scrubbed tables large and small – plus woodburner, prints on pristine white walls and oriental rugs. The food is traditional and homemade, be it crab sandwiches on granary bread or fillet of sea bass served on chorizo mash. Side orders are extra, a paper menu is printed off every day, and wines start at £14.95, plus several by the glass. A cosy pub for a rainy day, and with outdoor space to roam in summer.

directions	Village signed off A3122 5 miles west of Dartmouth.
meals	12pm-2pm; 7pm-9pm. No bar food Fri & Sat eve. Main courses £9.95-£16.95; bar meals £7.50-£13.95.
closed	3pm-7pm, Tues lunch, Sun eve & Mon all day Dec-Feb (except Xmas & New Year).

directions	A38 eastbound, turn for South Brent/Avonwick; 1st right to Avonwick, on B3372. Bear left & rejoin A38 westbound towards Totnes; pub 100m on left.
meals	12pm-9.30pm (9pm Sun). Main courses £7.50-£16.
closed	Open all day.

Peter Alcroft & Sharon Murdoch
The Normandy Arms,
Chapel Street,
Blackawton,
Totnes TQ9 7BN

tel   01803 712884

Bruce & Lesley Brunning
Turtley Corn Mill,
Avonwick,
South Brent TQ10 9ES

tel   01364 646100
web   www.avonwick.net

map: 2 entry: 131

map: 2 entry: 132

Devon

The Church House Inn
Marldon

The old village pub is a civilised place, popular with retired locals and ladies that lunch – indeed, anyone who appreciates a glass of rioja and a naturally reared Exmoor steak. With its welcoming bar, several dining areas and lovely sloping garden, this is a great all-rounder. The feel is one of a well-crafted, rustic elegance – stonework and beams, original bell-shaped windows, paintings in gilt frames, crisp table settings and smiling service. The long central bar has been partitioned into three areas, plus one four-tabled candlelit snug, perfect for a party. The chef has been here 14 years and the diners keep coming; the food is modern British and locally sourced. Some come just for a pint of well-kept Dartmoor Best and a chat by the fire. The pub originally housed the artisans who worked on Marldon Church, and its ancient tower overlooks the hedged garden.

directions	Marldon off Torquay-Brixham ring road. At bottom of village, signed.
meals	12pm-2pm (2.30pm Sun); 6.30pm-9.30pm (9pm Sun). Main courses £5-£16.50.
closed	2.30pm-5pm (3pm-5.30pm Sun).

Julian Cook
The Church House Inn,
Marldon,
Paignton TQ3 1SL
tel 01803 558279

map: 2 entry: 133

Devon

Rising Sun
Woodland

The farmhouse on the edge of Dartmoor was once a tearoom. Now the plushly-furnished open-plan bar, cosy with beams and log fire, delivers Princetown Jail Ale, Luscombe cider and fine wines. Fresh market produce feature prominently on daily menus that list fish from Brixham, game from local estates and smoked meats and fish from Dartmouth's smokehouse. Hearty ploughman's come with a selection of Devon cheeses, or try lemon sole with lemon and dill butter, roast belly pork on garlic and leek mash with apple sauce, perfect flaky pastry pies generously filled with, say, lamb and apricot, and Devon apple cake with clotted cream for pudding. Children have toys and dressing-up clothes in the family room; in the big garden are swings and an old tractor. There are a sunny terrace and rolling South Hams views, too.

directions	Off A38 before Ashburton junction heading west for Plymouth.
meals	12pm-2.15pm (3pm Sun); 6pm-9.15pm (7pm Sun). Main courses £6.95-£14.95; bar meals £4.95-£6.95.
closed	3pm-6pm (3.30pm-7pm Sun).

Simon & Hazel Towle
Rising Sun,
Woodland,
Ashburton TQ13 7JT
tel 01364 652544
web www.risingsunwoodland.co.uk

map: 2 entry: 134

The Rock Inn
Haytor Vale

Originally an ale house for quarrymen and miners, the 300-year-old Rock Inn stands in a tiny village high on Dartmoor's windswept southern slopes. Run by the same family for over 20 years, this civilised haven oozes character; there are polished antique tables and sturdy settles on several levels, a grandfather clock, pretty plates and fresh flowers, cosy corners and at least two fires. Settle down with a pint of Dartmoor Best in the beamed and carpeted bar and peruse the supper menu that highlights local, often organic, produce. All that fresh Dartmoor air will have made you hungry, so tuck into rib-eye steak with black peppercorn and brandy sauce, lusciously followed by chocolate, orange and cointreau tart. Lunchtime meals range from soup, sandwiches and ploughman's to local sausages in onion gravy. There's a pretty beer garden, too.

Rugglestone Inn
Widecombe-in-the-Moor

Beside open moorland within walking distance of the village – and named after the massive Ruggle Stone nearby – is a rustic, 200-year-old stone building whose two tiny rooms lead off a stone-floored passageway. Few of the hordes who descend on this honey-pot village in the middle of Dartmoor make it to this rare gem. Head-ducking beams fill the old-fashioned parlour with its simple furnishings, open woodburner and deep-country feel. Both rooms are free of modern intrusions, the locals preferring time-honoured games such as cribbage, euchre and dominoes. The tiny bar serves local farm cider; Butcombe Bitter and St Austell Dartmoor Best are tapped straight from the cask. From the kitchen come simple bar meals, from ploughman's lunches and homemade soups to hearty casseroles. Across the babbling brook at the front is a lawn with benches and peaceful moorland views. Heaven.

directions	At Drumbridges roundabout A382 for Bovey Tracey; B3387 to Haytor. Left at phone box.
meals	12pm-2pm; 7pm-9pm. Main courses £7.50-£13.95 (lunch); £15.95-£18 (dinner); sandwiches £4.95.
closed	Open all day.

directions	600 yards from centre of Widecombe; signed.
meals	12pm-2pm; 7pm-9pm. Main courses from £6.95-£10.95.
closed	3pm-6pm. Open all day Fri-Sun.

Christopher & Susan Graves
The Rock Inn,
Haytor Vale,
Widecombe TQ13 9XP
tel 01364 661305
web www.rock-inn.co.uk

map: 2 entry: 135

Richard Palmer & Vicki Moore
Rugglestone Inn,
Widecombe-in-the-Moor,
Bovey Tracey TQ13 7TF
tel 01364 621327

map: 2 entry: 136

The Dartmoor Inn
Lydford

Karen and Philip Burgess are self-confessed foodies and their rambling dining pub turns out some serious surprises. In flight-of-fancy rooms are updates on gourmet evenings and seasonal celebrations, a Parisian bistro supper or a Brazilian jazz night. Evening menus match the occasion and are seasonal; locals take advantage of monthly set lunches. (And mobile phones are wisely discouraged!). In November you might start with ham hock terrine with apricot chutney or red mullet with crab, leek and potato broth, then move on to roast partridge with savoy cabbage, bacon and port wine sauce. Walkers and dogs stride in from the moors and squeeze into the bar for Dartmoor Best Bitter, organic bottled cider, fish and chips or a hearty steak sandwich. And so to bed… new mattresses on antique beds, soft lights and sofas: absolutely gorgeous.

directions	On A386 between Okehampton & Tavistock.
meals	12pm-2pm; 6.45pm-9pm. Main courses £9.50-£22.50; bar menu £4.95-£12.95; set menus £13.75 & £16.50.
rooms	3 doubles £95-£125.
closed	2.30pm-6.30pm, Sun eve & Mon all day.

See pp 30-57 for full list of pubs with rooms

Karen & Philip Burgess
The Dartmoor Inn,
Lydford,
Okehampton EX20 4AY
tel   01822 820221
web   www.dartmoorinn.com

map: 2 entry: 137

The Harris Arms
Lewdown

An unusually delightful place where you are welcomed on the way in and thanked on the way out. The passion Andy and Rowena have for food and wine is infectious and the awards they are gathering is proof of their commitment. Expect a long bar, a fire at one end, a patterned carpet, maroon walls and a big strawberry blond cat named Reg. A large new decked area at the back has rich rolling views. The Whitemans are members of the Slow Food movement so real food is their thing: cheeses are the west country's finest, fish, meat, vegetable and dairy produce come from exemplary local suppliers, and wines are chosen from small growers. Flavoursome food is what the Cornish team of chefs delivers and whether it be shoulder of lamb braised in red wine, baked sea bream or roast venison with spiced red cabbage and red wine gravy, it is consistently good. Great value, too.

directions	On old A30 between Lewdown & Lifton; exit A30 at Broadwoodwidger & head south.
meals	12pm-2pm; 6.30pm-9pm (7pm-9pm Sun). Main courses £7.75-£9.50 (lunch), £8.95-£14.50 (dinner).
closed	3pm-6pm (Sun 7pm). Mon all day (except bank hols) & Sun eve in winter.

Andy & Rowena Whiteman
The Harris Arms,
Portgate,
Lewdown EX20 4PZ
tel   01566 783331
web   www.theharrisarms.co.uk

map: 2 entry: 138

Duke of York
Iddesleigh

Built to house the 14th-century stonemasons working on the church next door, the thatched Duke of York is the most genuine of locals: a big-hearted, generous place. It serves comforting food, real ale, Sams Cider from Winkleigh and a great welcome from farmer-pub landlord Jamie Stuart and his wife. Pass a parked tractor on your way in; enter to mingle with farmers, shooters and the odd slaughterman parleying in the single bar over pints of Cotleigh Tawny tapped from the cask. Scrubbed oak tables have fresh flowers and candles, there are village photographs on the walls, bank notes on the beams, rocking chairs by the blazing log fire – it's rustic and enchanting. With fish fresh from Clovelly and Brixham and locally sourced beef, lamb and pork, you tuck into the heartiest home cooking: tureens of homemade soup, steak and kidney pudding, lamb chops with rosemary and garlic gravy, whole baked sea bass with lemon butter, scrummy puddings. And the all-day breakfasts are not for the faint-hearted.

directions	On B3217 between Exbourne & Dolton, 3 miles NE of Hatherleigh.
meals	12pm-10pm (9.30pm Sun) . Set menu, 3 courses, £22; bar meals £4.50-£13.
closed	Open all day.

SPECIAL AWARD
see pages 28-29

Jamie Stuart & Pippa Hutchinson
Duke of York,
Iddesleigh,
Winkleigh EX19 8BG
tel   01837 810253

map: 2 entry: 139

Sandy Park Inn
Chagford

You'll like it the moment you step in. Benched snugs and oriental rugs, worn flagstones and crackling logs, delicious smells and a happy hum. And it gets lively on Friday and Saturday nights. The restaurant is in two parts, cosy like the rest, daily specials are chalked up on a board above the fire and chef Andrew Burkin's food is "creative-brasserie". We chose well: a rich and flavoursome pasta carbonara, a fresh seared tuna steak and a warm treacle tart. Nick has been here just over a year and is extending his list of wines, while ales are Otter, St Austell and two guests. It's so lovely you'd be mad to leave – so stay! Bedrooms above the kitchen are simple, crisp, comfortable and quiet. Some overlook thatched roofs to fields, one opens to the garden – another delight – beds are big and bathrooms smart. Teign Valley makes a lovely walk, Castle Drogo is up the road and the magical moors beckon.

directions	On A382, 5 miles south of A30 & Whiddon Down.
meals	12pm-2.30pm; 6.30pm-9.30pm. Main courses £7.50-£14.
rooms	5: 4 doubles, 1 twin £92. Singles £55.
closed	Open all day.

See pp 30-57 for full list of pubs with rooms

Nick Rout
Sandy Park Inn,
Sandy Park,
Chagford TQ13 8JW
tel 01647 433267
web www.sandyparkinn.co.uk

map: 2 entry: 140

The Drewe Arms
Drewsteignton

Long, low and thatched, in a pretty village square above the wooded slopes of the Teign valley, the Drewe Arms is better known as Auntie Mabel's. Mabel Mudge, once Britain's longest-serving landlady, retired in 1996 aged 99. No longer the time-warp it once was, it does remain an unpretentious and well-loved local. Otter, Princetown and Dartmoor ales straight from the cask are served from two hatchways, one opening to a front room with rustic benches and tables; a second room across the flagged passageway has sturdy old pine tables and a roaring log fire. Mabel's Kitchen, now the dining room, keeps the original dresser and old black cooking range. Home-cooked food using fresh local produce is listed on a daily-changing blackboard menu. Stride off through National Trust woodland to Castle Drogo – the walks are wonderful.

directions	Off A382, 2 miles south of A30, 8 miles west of Exeter.
meals	12pm-2.15pm; 6pm-9pm. Main courses £6.95-£16.95.
closed	Open all day.

Paul Brodsworth
The Drewe Arms,
The Square,
Drewsteignton EX6 6QN
tel 01647 281224
web www.thedrewearms.co.uk

map: 2 entry: 141

Nobody Inn
Doddiscombsleigh

We remember an excellent cheese and wine lunch ten years ago and little has changed... the Otter bitter is still racked on a wooden stillage behind the bar. Nick Borst-Smith also has his own wine company (800 bins), the wines of the moment standing on an uneven counter; pick up a bottle and the others glide into place. Settles and tables are crammed into every corner, horse brasses brighten low beams, there's an inglenook glowing with logs and a part of the bar dates from Tudor times. Choose a tranche of pork and apple pie followed perhaps by white chocolate marquise with raspberry coulis... Sweet and spicy Nobody soup is made from chicken stock, vegetables and local fruit; smoked eel comes from Dartmouth; local quail is stuffed with rice and apricots; there are Devon cheeses and 260 whiskies, and their own Nobody's beer comes in old pint glasses. The village is buried down a maze of lanes but it's not hard to find and worth the detour.

Digger's Rest
Woodbury Salterton

Months of searching led the Rushtons to this 500-year-old, fat-walled former cider house built of stone and cob. It is the quintessential thatched Devon inn. A good looking makeover swiftly followed, the timbered interior was revived: fresh yellow décor, new carpets, an eclectic mix of old dining tables, subtle wall lighting, tasteful prints. Arrive early to bag the sofa by the log fire. In addition to the local Otter and guest ales, the impressive list of wines (ten by the glass) and the relaxing atmosphere, there are organic soft drinks, Italian Gaggia coffee, soothing piped jazz, baby-changing facilities, daily newspapers and a brilliant pub menu that employs the best local produce. Treat yourself to Brixham fish (pan-fried scallops with bacon, on dressed leaves), Devon Ruby Red beef (21-day hung rib-eye with herb butter), and local Kenniford Farm pork, roasted for Sunday lunches. And there's a landscaped patio garden.

directions	Off A38 at Haldon Racecourse exit, then 3 miles.
meals	12pm-2pm; 7pm-10pm. Main courses £10-£14.
closed	2.30pm-6pm (7pm Sun).

directions	Off A3052, 3 miles east of Exeter & 3 miles from M5 junc. 30.
meals	12pm-2.30pm; 6.30-9.30 (Sat 12pm-9.30, Sun 12pm-9pm). Main courses £7.25-£14.95; bar meals £2.95-£14.95.
closed	3pm-6pm. Open all day Sat & Sun.

	Nick Borst-Smith Nobody Inn, Doddiscombsleigh, Exeter EX6 7PS
tel	01647 252394
web	www.nobodyinn.co.uk

	Steve & Sarah Rushton Digger's Rest, Woodbury Salterton, Exeter EX5 1PQ
tel	01395 232375
web	www.diggersrest.co.uk

map: 2 entry: 142

map: 2 entry: 143

The Bridge Inn
Topsham

Cut across the bridge too fast and you miss one of England's last traditional ale houses. Unchanged for most of the century – and in the family for as long – the 16th-century Bridge is a must for ale connoisseurs. And for all who appreciate a genuine pub furnished in the old-style: just high-back settles, ancient floors and simple hatch. (The Queen chose the Bridge for her first official 'visit to a pub'.) Years ago it was a brewery and malthouse; Caroline's great-grandfather was the last publican to brew his own here. No lager and no louts! This is beer-drinker heaven, with up to ten real ales served by gravity from the cask in a timeless setting by the Exe. There's cider and gooseberry wine, too. Cradle your pint to the background din of local chatter in the Inner Sanctum, under a

grandfather clock by a blazing log fire, or out in the garden by the steep river bank. With bread baked at the local farm, home-cooked hams, homemade chutneys and Devon cheeses, the sandwiches and ploughman's are top-hole.

directions	M5 exit 30; A376 to Exmouth; 2 miles, right to Topsham; Elmgrove Road into Bridge Hill.
meals	12pm-1.45pm. Bar meals £2.50-£5.50.
closed	2pm-6pm (7pm Sun).

SPECIAL AWARD
see pages 28-29

Caroline Cheffers-Heard
The Bridge Inn,
Topsham,
Exeter EX3 0QQ

| tel | 01392 873862 |
| web | www.cheffers.co.uk |

map: 2 entry: 144

Devon

The Blue Ball
Sandygate

The Blue Ball is a popular place – though it is more informal eatery than traditional pub. Handy for the motorway, the colourwashed, thatched, roadside inn offers a welcoming respite to any savvy traveller. Brasserie-style food is generous and well presented, while a separate restaurant menu struts its stuff in the evening. There's an earthy pubbiness to the dimly-lit front bar, with its flagstones, low beams, reassuring settles and log fire. Pink walls may add a cosmopolitan touch, but the old handsaws hung around the fire reinforce its essential rusticity. A further bar has a lighter feel with polished floorboards; a contemporary dining room extension brings things bang up to date: an airy atmosphere, blond-wood furniture, cord carpeting and modern art. A great open-hearted village local, and, with a play area in the garden, family-easy too.

directions	M5 exit to Sidmouth. At r'bout on Sidmouth road, double-back towards m'way. Left 200 yards down lane.
meals	12pm–2.30pm; 6pm–9.30pm (7pm–9.30pm Sun). Main courses £9.95–£16.95; bar meals £5.95–£10.95.
closed	3pm–6pm (7pm Sun).

Colin Sparks
The Blue Ball,
Sandygate,
Exeter EX2 7JL
tel   01392 873401

map: 2 entry: 145

Devon

The Jack in the Green
Rockbeare

Bustle and buzz in the dark wood bar, and good local brews on tap – Otter Ale, Cotleigh Tawny, Branscombe Vale Bitter. But this is more restaurant than pub: "For those who live to eat," reads the sign. In a series of smart, brightly lit, blue-motif carpeted rooms, chef Matthew Mason's bar menu goes in for modern and mouthwatering variations of tried and trusted favourites: braised faggot with creamed potato, steamed venison pudding with port and juniper jus… even the ploughman's is impressive. More ambition on display in the restaurant, where seared fillet of salmon with sorrel and hollandaise sauce and roasted Creedy Carver duck breast with griottine cherries make for succulent seasonal choices. For summer there's courtyard seating. Paul Parnell has been at the helm for years and he and his staff do a grand job. Good for company dinners too.

directions	5 miles east of M5 (exit 29) on old A30 just past Exeter Airport.
meals	11.30am–2pm (2.30pm Fri & Sat); 6pm–10pm (9.30pm Mon); 12pm–9.30pm Sun. Main courses from £16.50; bar meals from £7.50.
closed	2.30pm–5.30pm (3pm–5.30pm Fri, 3pm–6pm Sat). Open all day Sun.

Paul Parnell
The Jack in the Green,
Rockbeare,
Exeter EX5 2EE
tel   01404 822240
web   www.jackinthegreen.uk.com

map: 2 entry: 146

Fountain Head
Branscombe

With an ale festival in June, they take their beer seriously here: local and top brew. The food is plentiful too, but not for the small of appetite. There's not much to say about the history, except that the dining room was once a blacksmith's forge, but there is an authentic feel: be charmed by big flagstones, wood-clad walls, dimly-lit corners and a tap room that used to be the cellar. No TV screens, no fruit machines, just local babble and possibly a snoozing dog. (It's great walking country.) The Forge Restaurant is dominated by a vast central chimney and grate; tables are candlelit and horse-shoes hang from beams, along with the landlord's boots. Locals and visitors tuck into honest pub food and plenty of it – half a pint of prawns, beef and Branoc Ale pie, game in season, curry of the day, Sunday barbecues in summer. Beers are brewed in the village, ciders are Green Valley and the staff are great.

Masons Arms
Branscombe

Approach straggling Branscombe down narrow lanes to this creeper-clad inn. The 14th-century bar has a traditional feel with dark ship's timbers, stone walls, slate floor and fireplace that cooks spit-roasts to perfection. Quaff pints of Otter Bitter or Branscombe Vale Brannoc by the fire; on warm days, there's the sun-trap terrace. Nothing is too much trouble for the staff, whose prime aim is for you to unwind. Local produce, including fresh crab and lobster landed on Branscombe's beach, is the focus of the modern British menu. There's smoked Dartmouth duck with red onion marmalade and whole Brixham plaice, local crab ploughman's and spit roast leg of organically reared Branscombe lamb with redcurrant jus. The pebbly beach is a 12-minute stroll across National Trust land and coastal path walks reward the adventurous.

directions	Village signed off A3052 between Seaton & Sidmouth; head for upper village; pub above parish church.
meals	12pm-2pm; 7pm-9pm. Main courses £7.50-£12; bar lunch £3.95-£5.95.
closed	3pm-6pm.

directions	Off A3052 between Sidmouth & Seaton.
meals	12pm-2pm (2.15pm Sat & Sun); 7pm-9pm. Set menu £27.50; bar meals £6.95-£14.95.
closed	3pm-6pm in winter. Open all day Sat & Sun, every day in summer.

Graham William
Fountain Head,
Street,
Branscombe,
Seaton EX12 3BG
tel   01297 680359

Colin & Carol Slaney
Masons Arms,
Main Street,
Branscombe EX12 3DJ
tel   01297 680300
web   www.masonsarms.co.uk

The Drewe Arms
Broadhembury

Nigel Burge runs a relaxed ship – the secret of his long success. The 15th-century thatched Drewe is the cornerstone of a thatched Devon village in a blissful area. By the fire are the day's papers and magazines; on the bar, local Otter ales tapped straight from the cask and wines beyond reproach. It's a captivating little place. Beams are oak-carved, walls plank-panelled, there are country tables, wood carvings, walking sticks, flowers and a log-fired inglenook that crackles in winter. Food is way above average for a country pub, with fish from Brixham and Newlyn. Go for spicy crab soup, whole Dover sole or Lyme Bay lobster. Plenty of classy modern touches, too, in sea bream with orange and chilli, hand-dived scallops seared to perfection, and, for carnivores, roast partridge or beef fillet with Café de Paris butter. All this, and a garden that's as dreamy as a country garden can be.

directions	M5 junc. 28; A373 Honiton to Cullompton.
meals	12pm-2pm; 7pm-9pm. Main courses £10-£20.
closed	3pm-6pm (from 5pm Sun).

Kerstin & Nigel Burge
The Drewe Arms,
Broadhembury,
Honiton EX14 3NF
tel 01404 841267

map: 2 entry: 149

Culm Valley Inn
Culmstock

Don't be put off by the unprepossessing exterior of Richard Hartley's pub by the river Culm. It may not be posh but it's warm, easy and charming: deep pink-washed walls, glowing coals, flickering candles. From ragged bar stools the locals sample microbrewery beers while the gentry drop by for unusually good food. Easy-going chef-patron Richard and his efficient band make this place zing. Look to the chalkboard for south coast seafood, weekend fish specials (monkfish with crispy ginger and garlic noodles), Ruby Red Devon beef from nearby farms, and tapas. From the English elm bar you can order from a fantastic array of rare and curious spirits, French wines from specialist growers and local beers tapped from the cask. Bedrooms are simple and cheerful, with white bed linen and vibrant walls, and share two spotless bathrooms.

directions	On B3391, 2 miles off A38 west of Wellington.
meals	12pm-2pm; 7pm-9.30. No food Sun eve. Main courses £7-£20; bar meals £6-£10.
rooms	3: 1 double, 1 twin, 1 family room from £55. Singles £30.
closed	3pm-7pm winter (except Sat & Sun).

See pp 30–57 for full list of pubs with rooms

Richard Hartley
Culm Valley Inn,
Culmstock,
Cullompton EX15 3JJ
tel 01884 840354

map: 2 entry: 150

Devon

The Masons Arms Inn
Knowstone

Leaving windswept Exmoor behind, arrive through fern or twisting lane. Wood is stacked against the 13th-century walls, you are drawn to enter. The dim, low, flagged bar, with inglenook and elaborate burner, fills with dogs and walkers in wellies, in for a natter and a pint of Cotleigh Tawny ale. But who would imagine, down worn stone steps, a cosy lounge with deep sofas and a restaurant extension complete with mural? Served at candlelit tables is food fit for kings. Mark Dodson spent 18 years working at the celebrated Waterside Inn, 13 of those as head chef. Short menus accompanied by French wines major in classic French and British dishes and are concocted from the finest regional produce; try pan-fried scallops with pear and vanilla, roulade of belly pork with braised red cabbage and apple compote, John Dory with cider cream sauce. And the rear terrace has wonderful views to Exmoor.

directions	M5 junc. 27; A361 for Barnstaple; Knowstone signed after 20 miles. Into village, right at bottom of hill & pub on left.
meals	12pm-2pm; 7pm-9pm. Main courses £12.80-£17.50.
closed	3pm-6pm, Sun eve & Mon all day.

Mark Dodson
The Masons Arms Inn,
Knowstone,
South Molton EX36 4RY

| tel | 01398 341231 |
| web | www.masonsarmsdevon.co.uk |

map: 2 entry: 151

Dorset

The Shave Cross Inn
Marshwood Vale

Fancy a pint of Branoc and a spicy salad of jerk chicken? Once a busy stop-off point for pilgrims and monastic visitors (who had their tonsures trimmed while staying), the cob-and-flint pub now sits dreamily off the beaten track at the end of several tortuously narrow lanes. It was rescued from closure by the Warburtons, back from the Caribbean. Life has stepped up a gear and the old tavern thrives – thanks largely to the exotic and delicious cuisine. Where else in deepest Dorset can you tuck into a zarzuela of fresh fish with a mild coconut curry sauce? There's simple pub grub for less adventurous palates, while surroundings remain strictly traditional: flagged floors, low beams, country furniture, a vast inglenook and the oldest thatched skittle alley in the country. The meandering garden, with goldfish pool, wishing well and play area, is gorgeous.

directions	B3162 for Broadwindsor; left in 2 miles for Broadoak. Follow unclassified road for 3 miles.
meals	11am-3pm; 6pm-9.30pm (7pm-8pm Sun Jun-Aug). Main courses £6-£15; set menus £22.50 & £26.
closed	3pm-6pm & Mon (except bank hols). Open all day Jun-Aug.

Roy & Mel Warburton
The Shave Cross Inn,
Shave Cross, Marshwood Vale,
Bridport DT6 6HW

| tel | 01308 868358 |
| web | www.theshavecrossinn.co.uk |

map: 3 entry: 152

Stapleton Arms
Buckhorn Weston

Rupert and Victoria Reeves of the Queens Arms at Corton Denham set to work on this village local in 2006 and the results are impressive. A country-chic décor combines with modern food and no loss of community spirit. So there's a slate-flagged bar for a pint of Butcombe and a homemade pork pie, and comfy leather sofas and big scrubbed tables. The dining room has a more sophisticated air — well-spaced tables, deep blue walls, a huge mirror — while the food is simple, modern and inventive, the daily menus making serious use of fresh, local and seasonal produce. Try guinea fowl and partidge terrine with spicy tomato chutney, hake with chive mash and tomato hollandaise, or good old ham, egg and chips. Stay the night: you get big beds and Egyptian cotton, traditional furnishings, flat-screen TVs, super mosaic-tiled bathrooms and fabulous breakfasts.

directions	From A303 B3081 south for Gillingham. Right for Cucklington; signs to Buckhorn Weston.
meals	12pm-3pm; 6pm-10pm. Main courses £8.60-£13.50; bar snacks from £4.80; Sunday roast £11.50.
rooms	4 doubles £90-120. Singles £72-£96.
closed	3pm-6pm. Open all day Sat & Sun.

See pp 30-57 for full list of pubs with rooms

Kaveh Javvi
Stapleton Arms,
Church Hill, Buckhorn Weston,
Gillingham SP8 5HS
tel   01963 370396
web   www.thestapletonarms.com

map: 3 entry: 153

The Museum Inn
Farnham

In a village with roses round every door is the Museum Inn, one of the finest in the south of England. Vicky, Mark and their (mostly) Aussie staff have created a blissfully warm and happy place to be: she does bubbly, he does laid-back. The refit of the big 17th-century bar has kept the period feel — all flagstones, inglenook, fresh flowers and fashionably mismatched tables and chairs. It is usually jam-packed with smart country folk and their dogs and is best out of season. Expect cosy alcoves to hide in, a gorgeous, book-filled drawing room to browse and a smart, white-raftered dining room. New chef Clive Jory is Michelin-trained and his sophisticated dishes range from chicken liver and foie gras parfait with toasted pain d'epices to whole grilled lemon sole with saffron potatoes, braised salsify and tomato and chive vièrge. Dark chocolate brownies come with bitter chocolate sauce, hot lime sponge with custard.

directions	From Blandford, A354 for Salisbury for 6.5 miles; left for Farnham.
meals	12pm-2pm (2.30pm Sat & Sun); 7pm-9.30pm (9pm Sun). Main courses £13.95-£19.95.
closed	3pm-6pm (7pm Sun).

Vicky Elliot & Mark Stephenson
The Museum Inn,
Farnham,
Blandford Forum DT11 8DE
tel   01725 516261
web   www.museuminn.co.uk

map: 3 entry: 154

Coventry Arms
Corfe Mullen

A 15th-century riverside pub with its own island, and fishermen for landlords. David's freshly caught trout are sometimes reeled in by customers and may end up on your plate. Fish is a bit of a speciality – turbot with tomato and herb linguine, roast monkfish with baby leeks and herb butter sauce – with the menu focusing on fresh ingredients cooked simply and well. The local butcher provides all the meat, and game comes from the local estates. Ploughman's and salads are equally good. Comfortably rustic rooms ramble around the main bar, a display of antique fishing reels hangs above the beer barrels, and local ales are pulled straight from the cask. There are low beams, logs in the grate, weekly musicians and tables by the stream: John and David's waterside pub is loved by all – and don't miss the annual beer, game and seafood festivals.

The Square & Compass
Worth Matravers

The name honours all those who cut stone from the nearby quarries. Built as a farm in the 17th century, this splendid old pub has been in the family for 100 years and remains gloriously unchanged. A narrow (and rare) drinking corridor leads to two hatches from where young Charlie Newman draws Ringwood and guest ales straight from the cask. With a pint of farmhouse cider and a homemade pastie – that's all the food they sell – you can chat in the flagged corridor or settle in the sunny parlour with its painted wooden panels, old tables, wall seats, local prints and cartoons. The woodburner will warm you on a wild night. The rustic, stone-walled main room has live music; there's cribbage and shove-ha'penny; the family's fossil museum is next door. High on the edge of the village, gazing out across fields to the sea, the pub and its sunny front terrace – dotted, from time to time, with free-ranging hens – is a popular stop for coastal path hikers. A treasure.

directions	A31 between Dorchester & Wimborne; 2 miles W of Wimborne.
meals	12pm-2.30pm; 6pm-9.30pm. All day on Sun. Main courses £10-£17; bar meals £5-£10.
closed	3pm-5.30pm. Open all day Sat & Sun.

directions	B3069 east of Corfe Castle; through Kingston; right for Worth Matravers.
meals	Pasties and pies only. Pasties £2.50.
closed	3pm-6pm. Open all day Sat & Sun & every day July-Sep.

	John Hugo, David Armstrong Reed Coventry Arms, Mill Street, Corfe Mullen, Wimborne BH21 3RH
tel	01258 857284
web	www.coventryarms.co.uk

	Charlie Newman The Square & Compass, Worth Matravers, Swanage BH19 3LF
tel	01929 439229

map: 3 entry: 155

map: 3 entry: 156

Black Bull Inn
Frosterley

Here is an enticing village pub run just as its owners like it. It is atmospherically lit – Duncan Davis was a photographer before the Black Bull came his way – and you'll love the solid tables and high-back settles (cushioned for comfort), the stone flags, the ticking clocks, the glowing ranges, the warmth and good cheer. No lagers, but coffee and scones from 10.30am (truly!), followed by cider from the cask and beers from a few villages away. How about a dark malty porter from Wylam Brewery or a bitter from Allendale? The hop is treated with reverence here, and the inexpensive food is a joy. Rather than devising a menu then searching for suppliers, Diane and Duncan, ever perfectionists, source the produce first: local as much as possible, and in tune with the seasons. A shin of Broomhill Farm beef braised in ale on root vegetables with dumplings and roast potatoes is the sort of thing they do brilliantly. Once a month local musicians play classical, folk or jazz…hey, this place even has its own peel of bells.

directions	Beside A689 in Weardale between Wolsingham and Stanhope.
meals	12pm-2.30pm; 7pm-9pm. No food Sun eve. Main courses up to £10.50. Sunday roast £7.50.
closed	Open all day. Closed Mon eve.

SPECIAL AWARD
see pages 28-29

Duncan & Diane Davis
Black Bull Inn,
Bridge End,
Frosterley DL13 2SL
tel   01388 527784

map: 12 entry: 157

The Victoria Inn
Durham

Imagine an old Victorian public house with small rooms, high ceilings, marble fireplaces, etched and cut glass and a vast collection of Victoriana. Once upon a time, shawled women popped in for a porter or in search of an errant husband, now it's frequented by builders, students, academics. Virtually unaltered since it was built in 1899, the Vic has been in the Webster family for 31 years and has a strong local following. The three traditional rooms are spick and span; above the bar servery is an unusual gallery with shining figurines and ornaments of Queen Victoria and the Prince Consort. Simple snacks are available but it is the Darwins Ghost Ale and other local and Scottish beers, the whiskies and the camaraderie that makes this place enticing. Upstairs bedrooms are traditionally furnished and good value, breakfasts are generous and there's off-street parking and garaging. Original, timeless, welcoming.

directions	5-minute walk over Kingsgate Bridge from cathedral, castle & market place.
meals	12pm-3pm. Toasted sandwiches only.
rooms	5: 3 doubles, 1 twin, 1 family £60-£65.
closed	Open all day.

See pp 30-57 for full list of pubs with rooms

Michael Webster
The Victoria Inn,
86 Hallgarth Street,
Durham DH1 3AS
tel   0191 386 5269
web   www.victoriainn-durhamcity.co.uk

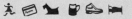

map: 12 entry: 158

Rose and Crown
Romaldkirk

Few country inns match one's expectations as well as the Rose & Crown. Built in the 1750s, this dreamy inn is gently informal, utterly unpretentious and run by easy-going perfectionists. In the small bar, warmed by an open fire while a few trophies peer down, locals sit at settles and browse the *Stockton Times*. A shiny brass door latch reveals more: an elegant lounge where a grandfather clock sets a restful pace, and a panelled dining room for more formal fare. Bedrooms are lovely; those in the converted barn tumble with colour, those in the main house come with antique pine, padded window seats and warm country colours. And the food is scrummy – from scallop, bacon and wild mushroom risotto to steak and kidney pie with Theakston gravy. Outside, a village green, with church and unblemished stone cottages, opens onto countryside as good as any in Britain.

directions	From Barnard Castle, B6277 north; right in village for green; on left.
meals	12pm-1.30pm; 6.30pm-9.30pm (9pm Sun). Main courses £10.50-£14.95.
rooms	12: 6 doubles, 4 twins, 2 suites £126-£166. Singles from £70.
closed	Open all day.

See pp 30-57 for full list of pubs with rooms

Christopher & Alison Davy
Rose and Crown,
Romaldkirk,
Barnard Castle DL12 9EB
tel   01833 650213
web   www.rose-and-crown.co.uk

map: 12 entry: 159

The Morritt Arms Hotel
Greta Bridge

Old-fashioned peace and quiet are the keynotes of the Dickens Bar of this well-loved coaching inn; the novelist stayed here while researching *Nicholas Nickleby*. The imposing building, right by the old stone bridge, invitingly floodlit after dark, has been welcoming travellers on the long road from Scotch Corner over Bowes Moor to Carlisle and Scotland since the 17th century. It's a warm and stylish stopover: the interior is effortlessly homely, polished block floors are graced with colourful rugs and deep chintz armchairs front open log fires in panelled lounges – a cosy spot for afternoon tea and homemade cakes. The Dickens Bar has three local cask ales, views across the lawn to the river, and a wonderful mural painted in 1946 by John Gilroy, who selected well-known local figures and created a Dickensian theme around them. Bar snacks in the bar, elaborate modern dishes in the restaurant and bistro.

Bridgewater Arms
Winston

A Victorian schoolhouse with views rising across fields to distant woods is the slightly quirky setting for this fun and welcoming modern bar and restaurant. The memory of the old school is carefully retained in the bar, with its high ceiling, decorative leaded windows, shelves of books and photos of past pupils. The names of the children that took part in the 1957 production of *Jack and the Beanstalk* are inscribed in big letters above the bar and add charm and a sense of recent history to the room. Adjoining half-panelled dining rooms are warmly decorated and furnished in contemporary style. Blackboards and daily printed menus place firm emphasis on the local, seasonal, fresh and organic, the choice of dishes ranging from traditional Yorkshire with a modern twist to Asian-inspired. Try simply the egg and Parma ham sandwich and a pint of Timmy Taylor's for lunch – exceptional!

directions	Off A66, 10 miles west of Scotch Corner.
meals	12pm-9.30pm. Main courses £10-£19.
closed	Open all day.

	Barbara-Anne Johnson The Morritt Arms Hotel, Greta Bridge, Barnard Castle DL12 9SE
tel	01833 627232
web	www.themorritt.co.uk

map: 12 entry: 160

directions	A67 between Darlington & Barnard Castle. In the village of Winston.
meals	12pm-2pm; 5.30pm-9pm. No food Sun eve. Main courses £9.50-£17.
closed	2.30pm-5.30pm; open all day Sun.

	Claire & Barry Dowson Bridgewater Arms, Winston, Darlington DL2 3FY
tel	01325 730302
web	www.bridgewaterarms.com

map: 12 entry: 161

Durham

The County
Aycliffe

Having won a Raymond Blanc scholarship in 1995, and worked with Gary Rhodes in London, Andrew Brown brought his skills north and restored the fortunes of a once run-down pub overlooking Aycliffe's pretty green. The patterned carpeting and faded walls have gone; in their place are bare boards, fresh walls and a pleasing minimalist feel. The award-winning food draws an eager crowd, while the open-plan bar is still the focal point of the community. Eat here, or in the stylish bistro. There are open sandwiches at lunchtime, and sausages with black pudding mash; in the bistro, crab and prawn risotto with lobster sauce, confit shoulder of lamb with Mediterranean vegetables and mint couscous, grilled tuna with fennel and a tomato ragout. The touch is light, bringing out textures and flavours superbly. Several real ales are on handpump, wines are mostly New World, and service is swift, young and friendly.

Durham

Number Twenty 2
Darlington

It is young, yet it is Darlington's most classic Victorian-style pub. Just off the town centre, the Traditional Alehouse & Canteen looks no different from the neighbouring shopfronts. Inside, a high ceiling and raised areas in the front bays give a vault-like impression; indeed, Number Twenty 2 is licensed for the sale of ales, wines and only a limited range of spirits. The odd cask provides a useful place to rest your glass. There are five changing guest ales alongside eight regular beers, nine continental beers on tap, and a good choice of wines chosen for easy quaffing; it's a civilised place favoured by local business folk. At the back of the long bar is a seating area known as the 'canteen' at lunchtimes. Lunchtime food is good and uncomplicated. Number Twenty 2 is closed on Sundays, but for the rest of the week Darlington has a very fine local.

directions	North of junc. 59 A1 (M), by A167.
meals	12pm-2pm; 6pm-9.15pm (6.45pm-9.15pm Sat). Main courses £12.50-£19.95; bar meals £5-£10.50.
closed	2pm-5.30pm (6.30pm Sat) & Sun all day.

	Andrew Brown The County, 13 The Green, Aycliffe, Darlington DL5 6LX
tel	01325 312273
web	www.the-county.co.uk

map: 12 entry: 162

directions	Just west of Darlington town centre. Coniscliffe Road leads into A67 to Barnard Castle.
meals	12pm-2pm. Main courses £4.95-£9.95.
closed	Open all day. Closed Sun.

	Ralph Wilkinson Number Twenty 2 , 22 Coniscliffe Road, Darlington DL3 7RG
tel	01325 354590
web	www.villagebrewer.co.uk

map: 12 entry: 163

The Viper
Mill Green

Isolated, but not lonely, this little pub is deep in magnificent woodland on an empty road. The snug, neat, open-plan front bar is warm and jolly – the place has been in the family since 1938 and they are determined to keep things simple. Locals will tell you, with a well-placed pride in their traditions, that these two plain simple rooms have stayed unchanged, bar the odd lick of paint, for 60-odd years. One blackboard lists a regularly changing selection of East Anglian real ales, such as Mighty Oak Jake the Snake and Viper Ale brewed by Nethergate, another lists a decent choice of wine. The classic, good-value bar snacks are served at lunchtime only – sandwiches, soup, chilli, ploughman's – with a choice of roast lunches on Sunday. The setting is so quiet you can ignore the nearby road; tables on the lawn overlook a cottage garden, resplendent in summer with flowers and shrubs. Super woodland and common-land walks start from the door.

The Cricketers
Clavering

It achieved fame as the family home and training ground of Jamie Oliver and, as such, draws a few passers-by… but this big 16th-century inn on the edge of Clavering handles its glory with good humour. Trevor and Sally Oliver's pub has low beams, original timbers and a contented, well-cared for air; light floods in, reflected in the highly polished tables and gleaming brass and glass. A serious commitment to seasonal food is obvious the moment you see the printed menu: steamed mussels with white wine and shallots, served with homemade sourdough bread, braised oxtail, venison with celeriac and parsnip puree and port wine jus, halibut with tomato and shellfish bisque. The daily changing blackboards give tempting options including fish, seasonal game and superb steaks. Another blackboard lists good value wines of the month, many served by the glass.

directions	From A12 for Margaretting; left up Ivy Barn Lane; pub at top.
meals	12pm-2pm (3pm Sat & Sun). Main courses £3-£5.95; Sunday roast £7.95.
closed	3pm-6pm. Open all day Sat & Sun.

Donna Torris
The Viper,
The Common,
Mill Green,
Ingatestone CM4 0PT
tel 01277 352010

map: 9 entry: 164

directions	On B1038 between Newport & Buntingford.
meals	12pm-2pm; 7pm-10pm. Main courses £10-£18; set menu £22 & £27.
closed	Open all day.

Trevor & Sally Oliver
The Cricketers,
Clavering,
Saffron Walden CB11 4QT
tel 01799 550442
web www.thecricketers.co.uk

map: 9 entry: 165

Axe & Compasses
Arkesden

At the heart of an absurdly pretty village of thatched cottages with a stream running down its middle, the 400-year-old building resembles the perfect English pub. The rambling interior is a classic too: beamed ceilings, timbered walls, panelling, regiments of horse brasses gleaming in the light from little lamps, open fires, comfy sofas – and that's just the lounge bar. From the well-loved, lived-in feel to the attentive service, the place is nigh-perfect. It's all down to the Christou family, with father Themis at the head, whose pride in his pub over the past 13 years and respect for the traditions of English inn-keeping puts many English landlords to shame. Local Greene King ales are excellent; food is either the best of English – steak and kidney pie, lamb's liver and bacon, chicken supreme, wing of skate – or recognises the family's Greek Cypriot roots, with moussakas and Greek salads. It is all fresh, apparently effortlessly cooked and generous.

directions	On B1038 between Newport & Clavering.
meals	12pm-2pm; 6.45pm-9.30pm. Main courses £11.95-£17.50; bar meals £4.95-£13.95; Sunday lunch £17.
closed	2.30pm-6pm (3pm-7pm Sun).

Themis & Diane Christou
Axe & Compasses,
Arkesden,
Saffron Walden CB11 4EX
tel   01799 550272

map: 9 entry: 166

The Bell Inn & Hill House   🛏
Horndon-on-the-Hill

The flagstoned bar, with oak panelled walls and French wood carvings, bustles at lunchtime. Bare flags or boards covered in rugs, an open fire, a grandfather clock, fine prints, ancient hot-cross buns hanging from beams – all add warmth and gregariousness. In contrast the breakfast room is light and airy, with elegant white table and chair coverings. In the evenings, black-clad waiters serve an interesting array of dishes under the watchful eye of Master Sommelier Joanne. Try rabbit terrine with spiced plum chutney, pot-roasted partridge with black pudding mash and button onion jus, and squeeze in a glazed lemon tart. Fat chips come with balsamic mayonnaise and the food picks up awards, as do Christine's flower arrangements. If you're staying, go for a suite: cosy, traditional, individual, rather wonderful.

directions	M25; A13 for Southend, 3 miles; B1007 to Horndon-on-the-Hill.
meals	12pm-1.45pm (2.30 Sun); 6.30pm-9.45pm (from 7pm Sun). No food bank holiday Mon. Main courses £10.50-£14.95; bar meals £7.50-£10.50.
rooms	16: 7 doubles, 3 twins, 6 suites £50-£85; family from £105.
closed	2.30-5.30pm (3pm Sat; 4-7pm Sun).

See pp 30-57 for full list of pubs with rooms

Christine & John Vereker
The Bell Inn & Hill House,
High Road, Horndon-on-the-
Hill SS17 8LD
tel   01375 642463
web   www.bell-inn.co.uk

map: 5 entry: 167

Compasses at Pattiswick
Pattiswick

Jono and Jane Clark's transformation of the old pub that started life as a row of 18th-century estate workers' cottages is a huge success. Slick and sophisticated bars mix flagstones with floorboards, modern furniture and soft lights with creams and sages. Yet at heart it remains a local, with plenty of space for drinkers in for a pint of Greene King IPA or Abbot Ale. And the food is the major draw, served in the bar or the elegantly beamed and spacious restaurant. Old favourites such as Gloucester Old Spot bangers with mash and onion gravy are founded on well-sourced raw materials, for the kitchen cultivates a network of small local producers. More modish dishes might include chicken breast with creamy goat's cheese, and leek and bacon pasta; and for pudding, who could resist spotted dick with Bird's custard? Outside: a terrace and an adventure play area so children may joyfully romp.

The Swan
Little Totham

In a village of 300 souls with no shop, post office or bus service, the highpoint has to be the pub with the award-winning ales. Little Totham is lucky: Gavin takes his role as publican seriously. He's taken over the running of the Swan from his parents, so you could say it's in the blood, and the pretty, listed, 400-year-old cottage inn is as merry as can be. There are quiz nights, live music events of folk, Irish and contemporary music, a choice of old pub games, and old-fashioned pickled eggs on the bar. Lunchtime food ranges from toad-in-the-hole to scampi and chips to roast on Sundays with all the trimmings. No glamour, no frills, just a lovely, lively local with low beams, open fires, soft lighting and bar room chat. Once you're here it's a job to tear yourself away. There's a splendid dining room too, ideal for family gatherings, and the front beer garden is a lively spot in summer.

directions	Take B1024 towards Coggeshall from A12, then left on A120 towards Braintree & take 2nd right for Pattiswick.
meals	12pm-3pm (4pm Sun); 6pm-10pm. Main courses £9.95-£16.95 (dinner); £6.75-£14.75 (lunch).
closed	Open all day. Closed Sun eve.

directions	Leave A12 at Rivenhall for Great Braxted, right onto B1022, then immed. left into Loamy Hill Road; 2 miles, on right, in village centre.
meals	12pm-2.30pm (3pm Sun). No food eves & Mon. Main courses £4.95-£8.95.
closed	Open all day.

Jono & Jane Clark
Compasses at Pattiswick,
Pattiswick,
Braintree CM77 8BG
tel   01376 561322
web   www.thecompassesatpattiswick.co.uk

Gavin Pascoe & Rebecca Davis
The Swan,
School Road,
Little Totham CM9 8LB
tel   01621 892689
web   www.theswanpublichouse.co.uk

map: 10 entry: 168

map: 10 entry: 169

The Sun Inn
Dedham

The rambling layout, timbered Tudor ceilings, panelled walls, planked floors, log fires in grand grates and board games on old tables take you back centuries. Piers Baker's food, on the other hand, is entirely modern, with produce and seasonality paramount. The Mediterranean is a strong influence, particularly Italy, so among the treats are penne with slow-cooked beef ragu and parmesan, and grilled rib-eye steak with artichokes, borlotti beans, kale, squash and fresh horseradish. Fish (almost) always comes from British waters, beef and pork is reared naturally, there's locally shot game and organic ginger beer from Belvoir. Come for fair prices, real ale (including stout-like Oyster from Kent) and children's portions of whatever takes their fancy. Busy in the tourist season, the Sun is a quiet, warm refuge on a winter's day. Gorgeous,

luxurious bedrooms have panelled walls or madly sloping ceilings, antique wardrobes or stylish mirrors. Next door, Pier's wife runs Victoria's Plums, a tiny shop selling locally grown fruit and veg.

directions	From A12 towards Dedham & Stratford St Mary; pub 2 miles.
meals	12pm-2.30pm (3pm Sat & Sun); 6.30pm-9.30pm (10pm Sat). Main courses £8.50-£16.50; bar meals £4.50-£8.50.
rooms	5 doubles £70-130. Singles £60-£130.
closed	Open all day. Closed Sun from 6pm.

SPECIAL AWARD
see pages 28-29

Piers Baker
The Sun Inn,
High Street, Dedham,
Colchester CO7 6DF
tel   01206 323351
web   www.thesuninndedham.com

map: 10 entry: 170

Essex	Pub with rooms	Gloucestershire

The Mistley Thorn
Mistley

In Constable country: an unexpectedly chi-chi village, its Georgian cottages gathered around the river estuary with bobbing boats and hills beyond. David and Sherri (who has a cookery school next door) run a happy ship: staff are young and on the ball, there are plenty of locals tossed into the mix and some impeccably well-behaved children. The mood is more laid-back city wine bar than country pub, colours are soft and easy, candles flicker, modern art rubs along well with the odd antique and food is taken seriously. Lots of good local fish and seafood – smoked haddock chowder, crab linguine with chilli, garlic and parsley, seared cod with spiced lentils, chunky fishcakes, brilliant chips. Bedrooms are calm with big beds, pale green paintwork, spotless bathroooms; some have watery views. A confidently-run family operation with a great weekend buzz.

The King's Arms Inn
Didmarton

This fine roadside village inn sports slate floors, Cotswold stone lintels, terracotta walls and oak settles in the traditional bar, a separate, cheekily-bright front adorned with lithographs of the area, and a newly done-up dining room with deep red walls, carved panels, chunky wooden tables and high-backed chairs. There's a big old fireplace for winter, darts and dominoes, too, a walled garden and a boules pitch that people travel some way for. For a light lunch are wholemeal sandwiches of Wiltshire ham and coleslaw or crispy bacon, tomato and melted brie. 'Classics' on the menu might include local game or rib-eye steak with grain mustard mash and onion marmalade, while daily dishes may highlight roast guinea fowl. Uley Bitter stands alongside guest ales: 'If they don't serve beer in heaven, then I'm not going', reads the sign behind the bar.

directions	On B1352, off A137 between Colchester & Ipswich.
meals	12pm-2.30; 6.30-9.30; 12pm-4pm; 6pm-9.30 Sat & Sun. Main courses £8.95-£15.95; bar meals £4.25-£8.95.
rooms	5 twins/doubles £70-£95. Singles £60-£80.
closed	3pm-6.30. Open all day Sat & Sun.

See pp 30–57 for full list of pubs with rooms

David McKay & Sherri Singleton
The Mistley Thorn,
High Street, Mistley,
Colchester CO11 1HE
tel 01206 392821
web www.mistleythorn.co.uk

map: 10 entry: 171

directions	On A433 between Tetbury & M4, junc. 18.
meals	12pm-2.30pm; 6pm-9.30pm (12pm-8.45pm Sun). Main courses £8.95-£16.95; bar meals £4.95-£9.95.
closed	3pm-6pm Mon-Thur. Open all day Fri-Sun.

Alastair Sadler
The King's Arms Inn,
The Street, Didmarton,
Badminton GL9 1DT
tel 01454 238245
web www.kingsarmsdidmarton.co.uk

map: 3 entry: 172

Gloucestershire

The Trouble House
Tetbury

Busy road, another pub: but you would miss a Michelin star if you drove past this one. Rhodes-trained chef-patron Michael Bedford is another cook who has swapped the glamour of the city for doing his own thing in a country pub. The food is unfussy, exemplary modern British. For a snack go for foie gras and apple terrine – or fragrant homemade bread and scrumptious cheese. For something more substantial, Hereford rib-eye steak with sensational chips and a melt-in-the-mouth béarnaise… then, perhaps, orange and rosemary syrup cake. The wine list is accessible and serious and the brilliant thing is, you don't have to book. Just get there early and choose a scrubbed pine table in a cosy corner. Everything is done with simplicity and integrity and that includes the interior of bare boards, cream walls and open fires. And the Trouble? The framed news clippings will explain all that.

directions	On A433, 2 miles north-east of Tetbury.
meals	12pm-2pm; 7pm-9.30pm. Main courses £15.99-£18.
closed	3pm-6.30 (7pm in winter), Sun eves & Mon.

Michael & Sarah Bedford
The Trouble House,
Cirencester Road,
Tetbury GL8 8SG
tel 01666 502206
web www.troublehouse.co.uk

map: 8 entry: 173

Gloucestershire

The Tunnel House Inn & Barn
Coates

Follow the bumpy track down from the church, "and don't give up," said the passer-by upon our enquiry. We didn't; the setting is idyllic – one of John Betjeman's favourite places. Emerge via the portico tunnel of the Stroudwater canal to find a sweet Bath stone house in the clearing; it was built in the 1780s to house the canal workers. Its latest conversion has been beautifully considered. Not only are there wheelchair-accessible toilets but a delightfully quirky, bareboarded décor: scrubbed tables and huge sofas in front of a fire, a cacophony of bric-a-brac in the bar (most on the ceiling!), an Ogygian juke box with decent tunes. In the lovely light dining room choose from a seasonal menu: beef and horseradish sandwiches, spiced potted pheasant, rabbit pie, haddock and chips, sticky toffee pudding. Uley Bitter and Hook Norton will keep ale fans happy, and there are several wines. Outside, a big garden with open-field views – great for kids – and a very smart terrace.

directions	Between Coates & Tarlton.
meals	12pm-2.15; 6.45-9.30. Main courses £8-£13.
closed	3pm-6pm. Open all day Fri-Sun.

Andrew Freeland
The Tunnel House Inn & Barn,
Tarlton Road, Coates,
Cirencester GL7 6PW
tel 01285 770280
web www.tunnelhouse.com

map: 8 entry: 174

Gloucestershire

The Bell at Sapperton
Sapperton

This elegant pub attracts wine-lovers, foodies, ramblers and riders: note the tethering rail. Inside is a spacious but intimate décor that spreads itself across several levels – stripped beams and woodburners, modern art on stone walls, old settles and church chairs, fresh flowers and newspapers. Sup on local Cotswold lager or Butcombe ale, dine on fresh local produce and rare breed and organic meats. The monthly menus or daily specials are chalked up above the fireplace and the food is generous in its range: local pigeon and Cotswold crayfish, lamb from Lighthorne, fish from Cornwall, poached plums with crème brulée, a delicious local goat's cheese called Rachel. Not a typical family pub but Sunday roast lunches are hugely popular and the wine list is expertly conservative to match the clientele. Summer eating can be outside on the well-tended terrace and spills over into the sun-trapping courtyard.

directions	Off A419, 6 miles west of Cirencester.
meals	12pm-2pm; 7pm-9.30pm (9pm Sun). Main courses £11.95-£16.95; ploughman's £7.25; Sunday lunch £13.50 & £17.50.
closed	2.30pm-6.30pm (3pm-7pm Sun).

Paul Davidson & Pat Le Jeune
The Bell at Sapperton,
Sapperton,
Cirencester GL7 6LE
tel 01285 760298
web www.foodatthebell.co.uk

map: 8 entry: 175

Gloucestershire

Amberley Inn
Amberley

High on Minchinhampton Common nudged by the odd cow, the baronial building has enchanting views across five valleys. Amberley Inn, Victorian-built, refreshingly unmodernised, feels like a miniature country house, thanks to lofty ceilings, oak floors, mullioned windows, stone fireplaces and elegant staircases. The public bar is workmanlike, the panelled lounge bar, its winter fires crackling, is a delight, the light-flooded dining room is decidedly smart. Food is unashamedly English and ingredients proudly local: pan-fried pigeon breasts with crispy smoked ham and fresh leaves; slow-braised lamb shanks with mustard mash. Ales – Otter, Uley Old Spot, Archers – are excellently kept, wines unexpectedly good for a pub. New co-owner Rupert is hands-on, his staff are attentive and knowledgeable. And they organise the occasional curry night.

directions	Amberley is signed off A46 between Stroud & Nailsworth.
meals	12pm-2.30pm; 7pm-9.15pm. Main courses £7.95-£13.95; bar meals £5.50-£7.50; Sunday lunch £12.95 & £15.95.
closed	Open all day.

Rupert Longsdon
Amberley Inn,
Culver Hill, Amberley,
Stroud GL5 5AF
tel 01453 872565
web www.theamberley.co.uk

map: 8 entry: 176

The Old Spot
Dursley

Nudged by a car park and Dursley's bus station is the old and lovely Old Spot. Built in 1776 as a farm cottage, when Dursley was a cloth-weaving town, the pub has since gained national recognition among ale aficionados, who make pilgrimages to sample the local brews. Indeed, the Old Spot has become something of a showcase for the beers of Uley Brewery, including Pig's Ear and Old Ric, the latter named after a former landlord. Real ciders include Weston's and Ashton Press. For a pub named after a rare-breed pig, it comes as no surprise that there are plenty of figurines and pictures dotted around the place, as well as a fair number of old prints and posters. Food is simple and pubby – BLT sandwiches and home-baked pies with shortcrust pastry lids. Friendly, deeply traditional and one of the must-visits of the county.

White Horse Inn
Frampton Mansell

Wonderful: a quirky-chic bar and restaurant, with good ales and first-class food. Emma and Shaun Davis have filled it with candlelit tables on seagrass floors, modern art on vibrant walls, Indian curios inspired by their travels. Expect an informal atmosphere and a big smile from Emma as she pulls pints of Uley Bitter and oversees the restaurant. Fresh food is the mainstay of Shaun's imaginative modern menus: traceable meats come from Butts Farm down the road, fish from Looe is delivered twice a week. So tuck into duck leg confit with chorizo and orange salad, followed by bream fillet with roasted cherry tomatoes and smoked salmon and dill cream. All this and lobsters, oysters, crabs and clams fresh from the tank and puddings to entice you (orange and Grand Manier cheesecake). It may not be very lovely and it may be next to a petrol station in the middle of nowhere – but what a pity to pass it by.

directions	100 yards from Dursley town centre.
meals	12pm-8pm (12pm-3pm Fri-Sun). Bar meals£2.95-£7; Sunday roast £6.95.
closed	Open all day.

Steve Herbert
The Old Spot,
Hill Road,
Dursley GL11 4JQ
tel   01453 542870
web   www.oldspotinn.co.uk

map: 8 entry: 177

directions	On A419, 6 miles W of Cirencester.
meals	12pm-2.30pm (3pm Sun); 7pm-9.45pm. Main courses £10.95-£15.95; bar meals £3.95-£9.95; set menu, 2-3 courses, £14.25-£15.95.
closed	3pm-6pm & Sun from 4pm.

Shaun & Emma Davis
White Horse Inn,
Cirencester Road,
Frampton Mansell,
Stroud GL6 8HZ
tel   01285 760960

map: 8 entry: 178

Gloucestershire

Pub with rooms

Bathurst Arms
North Cerney

Young James Walker has worked hard in breathing new life into this handsome inn on the Bathurst Estate. Once unloved, the 17th-century building now has warmth and energy as locals, walkers and travellers drop in for pints of Wickwar Cotswold Way and decent pub food. The stone-flagged bar is the hub of the place, warmed by a crackling log fire. Eat here or head next door to James's pride and joy, the revamped restaurant, with open kitchen and a sitting area that displays an organic wine list – choose a bottle from the shelf. Allotment vegetables, Cerney goat's cheese, game from Withington and local farm beef are championed – try the beef and ale pie with suet crust. Smartened-up bedrooms provide a homely base for exploring the Cotswolds: they are clean, comfortable, freshly painted and well-equipped.

directions	Beside A435 Cirencester to Cheltenham road, 4 miles north of Cirencester.
meals	12pm-2pm (2.30pm Fri-Sun); 6-9pm (9.30pm Sat; from 7pm Sun). Main courses £8.95-£15.95; bar meals £3.95-£8.95.
rooms	6 twins/doubles £75. Singles £55.
closed	3pm-6pm (7pm Sun). Open all day Sun in summer.

See pp 30-57 for full list of pubs with rooms

Mr James Walker
Bathurst Arms,
North Cerney,
Cirencester GL7 7BZ
tel   01285-831281
web   www.bathurstarms.com

map: 8 entry: 179

Gloucestershire

The Butcher's Arms
Sheepscombe

Hidden away in the folded hills and valleys of the glorious Cotswolds, the 17th-century Butcher's Arms is not easy to find. But persevere down these twisting, Gloucestershire lanes – it's worth it. A favourite with Laurie Lee, this has everything you would hope for from a village pub: friendly welcome, well-kept beer – Wye Valley, Otter & Moles – and a good choice of traditional and modern pub food. The rustic bar is hung with old banknotes, postcards and brass, and leads into two tiny dining rooms. Try the handmade sausages on a leek and mustard mash with onion gravy, or ham, egg and chips, or a daily special of mixed game braised in cranberries and port. Picnic tables are scattered across the front courtyard and the precipitous garden has superb views over the village. Look out for the unusual pub sign with a carving of a butcher and pig over the Guild of Butchers' coat of arms – and don't set your watch by the clock over the bar.

directions	Off A46 north of Painswick.
meals	12pm-2.30pm; 7pm-9.30 (12pm-9.30 Sun). Main courses £8.50-£15; bar meals £4.50-£7.50.
closed	3pm-6.30pm. Open all day Sun.

Johnny & Hilary Johnston
The Butcher's Arms,
Sheepscombe,
Painswick GL6 7RH
tel   01452 812113
web   www.cotswoldinns.co.uk

map: 8 entry: 180

The Red Hart Inn at Awre

Gloucestershire

Find genuine old-fashioned cheer at the 15th-century freehouse with Georgian additions, beautifully tucked-away in a charming village between the Severn and the Forest of Dean. The Red Hart is rambler-, dog- and child-friendly, has open fires, great food (great value too), real wines, real ales and a lovely welcome. Expect flagstones and carpeted floors, pine tables and chairs, old beams, stone fireplaces, wattle and daub. 'From plough to plate' is the philosophy in the kitchen, and almost all the ingredients come from within five miles. Rabbit and turkey from the village, wild salmon from the Severn – all wash down beautifully with a pint of Wye Valley Butty Bach or a guest ale. Severn Cider is made in the village, there's a beer garden and riverside walks. Do stay: a private staircase to the second floor leads to fresh, comfortable, carpeted bedrooms with pretty views.

directions	Off A48, 3 miles south of Newnham.
meals	12pm-2pm; 6.30pm-9pm. Main courses £7.50-£14; bar meals £7.95-£9.95.
rooms	2 doubles £80. Singles £50.
closed	3pm-6.30pm. Open all day weekends in summer.

See pp 30–57 for full list of pubs with rooms

Marcia Griffiths
The Red Hart Inn at Awre,
Awre,
Newnham on Severn GL14 1EW
tel   01594 510220

map: 8 entry: 181

Gloucestershire

Ostrich Inn

Newland

In the pretty village of Newland, the Ostrich is where the beer drinkers go. Across from All Saints Church, the famous 'Cathedral of the Forest', you'll rub shoulders with all sorts before a log fire; huntsmen and trail bikers pile in for the massive portions of delicious food, from the Newland bread and cheese platter to rib-eye steak with lashings of fresh béarnaise. The nicotine-brown ceiling that looks in danger of imminent collapse is supported by a massive oak pillar in front of the bar where the locals chatter and where 1940s jazz CDs keep the place swinging. The weekly menu, served throughout the pub, takes a step up in class, and is excellent value. Energetic landlady Kathryn and her chef Sue keep the place buzzing. To the back is a walled garden – and the loos, 'just by there', beyond the coal sacks and guarded by the pub pooch Alfie.

directions	Signed on lane linking A466 at Redbrook & at Clearwell between B4228 Coleford & Chepstow road.
meals	12pm-2.30pm; 6.30pm-9.30pm (6pm-9.30pm Sat). Main courses £12.50-£18.50; bar meals £5.50-£9.50.
closed	3pm-6.30pm (6pm Sat).

Kathryn Horton
Ostrich Inn,
Newland GL16 8NP
tel   01594 833260
web   www.theostrichinn.com

map: 7 entry: 182

The Glasshouse Inn
Longhope

If you are an aficionado of Bass and Butcombe, Weston's ciders and all good, nature-blessed produce, you have to come here. Ramshackle tables and open log fires are considered modern at this converted 16th-century brick cottage where glass was once blown in wood-fired ovens and cider pressed in the shed. Guinness adverts, cartoons and horseracing prints decorate the place as do autographed England rugby shirts — and the chiming clock never serves as an invitation to leave. Say landlords Steve and Jill: "We buy the best available produce locally, so our lady cooks can provide our customers with generous portions of tasty, interesting homemade food." There's a lovely calm atmosphere at the Glasshouse Inn, and youngsters under 14 are welcome in the garden during the summer months.

directions	Signed from A40 at Longhope, between Gloucester & Ross-on-Wye.
meals	12pm-2pm; 7pm-9pm. No food Sun eve. Main courses £7.50-£15.
closed	3pm-6.30pm & Sun eve.

Steve & Jill Pugh
The Glasshouse Inn,
May Hill,
Longhope GL17 0NN

tel 01452 830529

map: 8 entry: 183

The Kilcot Inn
Kilcot

The smart blue and sand painted exterior bodes well, then step in to a happy tumble of exposed stone walls, flagged floors, Tudor beams and three quirky 'tree-stump' chairs before a central fire. There's an open feel to this cosy inn, with the large bar dominating the drinking side. Beers include Cats Whiskers, Hobgoblin and Bass on handpump; there are a couple of ciders, including Weston's Old Rose, and decent wines. The restaurant area has deep blue walls, pine furniture, an eclectic mix of chairs, a new tapestry on the wall; it's ideal for romantic suppers and big family do's. And weekly menus make good use of local organic and free-range produce, as seen in prawn and halibut pie, Wye Valley duck with grape and honey sauce, dark chocolate tart with parsnip ice cream, and the hugely popular Sunday roast — rack of Gloucester Old Spot pork. Work it all off with a good walk — and bring the dogs and children.

directions	Kilcot signed off B4421 between Newent & Gorsley.
meals	12pm-2.30pm; 6pm-9.15pm (12pm-9pm Sun). Main courses £8.95-£16.95; bar meals £6.95-£8.95; Sunday roast from £7.95.
closed	3pm-6pm. Open all day Sun & in summer.

Sue Harper
The Kilcot Inn,
Ross Road,
Kilcot,
Newent GL18 1NG

tel 01989 720663

map: 8 entry: 184

The Boat Inn
Ashleworth

This extraordinary, tiny pub has been in the family since Charles II granted them a licence for liquor and ferry – about 400 years! It's a gem – a peaceful, unspoilt red-brick cottage on the banks of the Severn and an ale-lover's paradise. Settle back with a pint of Beowulf, Church End or Archer's in the gleaming front parlour – colourful with fresh garden flowers, huge built-in settle and big scrubbed deal table fronting an old kitchen range – or in the spotless bar. On sunny summer days you can laze by the languid river. Adjectives are inadequate: this place is cherished. Real ale straight from the cask, Weston's farm cider, a bar of chocolate, a packet of crisps… but don't feed Sam, he's on a diet. There's no 'jus' here; lunchtime meals are fresh filled rolls with homemade chutney. Perfect.

directions	On A417 1.5 miles from Hartpury, between Gloucester & Ledbury.
meals	12pm-2pm. Filled rolls (lunchtime only).
closed	2.30pm-7pm (3pm-7pm Sat & Sun), Wed lunch & Mon.

Ron Nicholls
The Boat Inn,
Ashleworth Quay, Ashleworth,
Gloucester GL19 4HZ
tel 01452 700272
web www.boat-inn.co.uk

map: 8 entry: 185

Puesdown Inn
Northleach

Leave the A40 behind and step into this stylish Cotswold inn. Be cheered by log fires, fresh flowers, cosy sofas and magazines in an an upbeat, open-plan interior. The light, shuttered brasserie is a favourite, as are the three compact but beautifully, globally themed bedrooms, all with 'storm' showers. Chef-patron John creates daily menus of modern British dishes based on high quality, often local ingredients: beef from Gloucestershire, game from the local shoots, fish delivered daily from Brixham. Tuck into super-fresh tian of crab and avocado followed by an assiette of Old Spot pork, finish with a remarkably light bread and butter pudding or a tuile basket of seasonal fruits. And there are traditional pub favourites too. The quality of the ingredients shines through, and the wine list is short but well chosen.

directions	Beside A40 15 miles east of Cheltenham.
meals	12pm-3pm; 6pm-10.30pm (6pm-9.30pm Sun). Main courses £9.95-£20; bar meals £6.50-£17; set lunch £16.75 & £19.95.
rooms	3 doubles £85-£90. Singles £50-£60.
closed	3pm-6pm, Sun & Mon eve in winter. Open all day Sat & Sun.

See pp 30-57 for full list of pubs with rooms

John & Maggie Arnmstrong
Puesdown Inn,
Compton Abdale,
Northleach GL54 4DN
tel 01451 860262
web www.puesdown.cotswoldinns.com

map: 8 entry: 186

Gloucestershire

Five Mile House
Cirencester

In 300 years the interior has changed not a jot; Boswell could be scribbling away in a corner. Expect bare wooden floors, open fires, two curving settles, a sunlit lounge bar, newspapers and cribbage. There's a flagstoned 'poop deck' of a snug for locals and a galley a few steps below; a more genteel wardroom – the owners' private parlour for a century or more – stands across the hall. Review here the pick of the day's produce, as it appears in lamb with rosemary jelly or splendidly thick sandwiches of roast beef with horseradish. All is cooked to order by Johann and his team, while young service is nice and old-fashioned. Deserving more consideration than the proverbial swift half, the beer, which includes guests and Taylor's Landlord, is seriously good. You can hardly go wrong here, with serene views from the garden to the valley below. Above is the busy main road – mercifully concealed by a bank and burgeoning hedgerows.

directions	On A417, turn at D. Abbots Services; pub down the road past the petrol station.
meals	12pm-2.30pm, 6pm-9.30pm; 7pm-9pm Sun. Main courses £8.50-£15.50.
closed	3pm-6pm.

Jo & Jon Carrier
Five Mile House,
Lane's End, Old Gloucester Road,
Duntisbourne Abbots,
Cirencester GL7 7JR

tel   01285 821432

map: 8 entry: 187

Gloucestershire

Seven Tuns Inn
Chedworth

As you nudge the brow of the hill and look down on the Seven Tuns, you know you've found a goodie. In 1610, and for few centuries after that, it was a simple snug; then they diverted the river and built the rest. Part-creepered on the outside, it rambles attractively inside, past open fires, aged furniture, antique prints and a skittle alley with darts. After a gentle walk to Chedworth's Roman Villa, buried in the wooded valley nearby, there's no finer place to return to for a pint of Young's Bitter. Mingle with cyclists, walkers and locals in the little lounge or rustic bar. If you're here to eat you can do so overlooking the garden through two gorgeous mullioned windows; a little further, across the road is a raised terrace by a waterwheel and babbling brook. Pub grub is listed on daily menus, from ploughman's to calves liver with bubble-and-squeak. This is still the village hub, just as it should be.

directions	Off A429, north of Cirencester.
meals	12pm-2.30pm (3pm Sun); 6.30pm-9.30pm (9.45pm Fri & Sat, 9pm Sun). Main courses £7.95-£14.95.
closed	3pm-6pm. Open all day Sat & Sun in winter, every day in summer.

Alex Davenport–Jones
Seven Tuns Inn,
Queen Street,
Chedworth,
Cirencester GL54 4AE

tel   01285 720242

map: 8 entry: 188

Inn at Fossebridge
Fossebridge

A vast two-acre lake, hog roasts in summer and Harvey the friendly black labrador – such details set the Inn at Fossebridge apart. Throw in roaring fires, real ales, roast lunches and a family-friendly feel and you have somewhere worth going out of your way for on a Sunday. The Jenkins family run this thriving coaching inn and draw in diners with daily menus of Thai fishcakes, duck leg confit, steak burger and fries, and crayfish and rocket sandwiches. In the stone-walled bars – one with darts board and stag's head – is loads of rustic character; in the dining room, a gentler Georgian feel and dressers guarding antique china. And there's a cosy check-sofa'd sitting room in country-house style. Outside is just as fine: a great decked and fenced terrace to the side and a five-acre garden bordering the river Coln, replete with perch- and carp-filled lake.

The Beehive
Cheltenham

Curious that there are so few pubs of character in Cheltenham. The Beehive shines like a beacon in the bohemian backstreets of Montpellier. Owned by the team in charge of The White Hart in Winchcombe, this is the place to come for lively conversation, well-kept beer and hearty food. And it's popular with the racing crowd during the Gold Cup. Hidden among antique shops and cafés, the Beehive has a pubby bar and two dining areas, the usual scrubbed floors, mismatched wooden tables and the summery bonus of a courtyard at the back. There are three regular real ales on tap – including the locally-brewed Goff's Jouster – and generous portions of gastropub dishes such as Old Spot sausages with mustard mash and gravy, and the more southern-inspired grilled cod with a merguez, chorizo and chickpea stew.

directions	Beside A429 between Cirencester & Northleach.
meals	12pm-3pm; 6.30pm-10pm. Main courses £8.95-£18.50; bar meals £5.95-£8.50; Sunday roast £10.75.
closed	Open all day.

Robert & Liz Jenkins
Inn at Fossebridge,
Fossebridge,
Cheltenham GL54 3JS
tel 01285 720721
web www.fossebridgeinn.co.uk

map: 8 entry: 189

directions	Montpellier Villas is off Suffolk Road.
meals	12pm-2.30pm; 6pm-8.30pm (7pm-10pm Thur-Sat). No food Sun eve. Main courses £8.95-£16; Sunday lunch £13.50 & £15.50.
closed	Open all day.

Matt Walker
The Beehive,
1-3 Montpellier Villas,
Cheltenham GL50 2XE
tel 01242 702270

map: 8 entry: 190

Gloucestershire

The Village Pub
Barnsley

It's the 'jeans and twinset' twin of the Barnsley House hotel opposite: a smart village pub. An old favourite of locals and faithfuls from far and wide, this civilised boozer has it all: seasonal food based on the best local produce, good-quality beers and wines. There's even a service hatch to the heated patio at the back, so you can savour your sauvignon until the sun goes down. Cotswold stone and ancient flags sing the country theme; past bar and open fires, quiet alcoves provide a snug setting that will entice you to stay. On a typical dinner menu there may be potted rabbit with celeriac and mustard, roast cod with salad nicoise, and lamb's sweetbreads with wild mushroom risotto cake. Pudding-lovers will appreciate the rum baba or the chocolate and espresso tart – delicious. With award-winning cooking and such authenticity, who could wish for more?

directions	A419 for Gloucester; right onto B4425 for Bibury; village 2 miles.
meals	12pm-2.30pm (3pm Sat & Sun); 7pm-9.30pm (10pm Fri & Sat). Main courses £10.50-£16; bar meals £4.50-£8.50.
closed	3pm-6pm Mon-Thurs. Open all day Fri-Sun.

Tim Haigh & Rupert Pendered
The Village Pub,
Barnsley,
Cirencester GL7 5EF
tel   01285 740421
web   www.thevillagepub.co.uk

map: 8 entry: 191

Gloucestershire

Falcon Inn
Poulton

Look out for this old cream stone pub as you swing round the bends through the village. Young owner Jeremy Lockley has given wing to this bird's potential – a superb gastropub for Gloucestershire. One eating area faces an open theatre kitchen, creating plenty of room for private dining without spoiling the feel of the traditional village bar and fireside tables at the front. Chef William Abraham does not go in for towering lunches: simplicity is the key to his near-perfect seared scallops with pea purée with crispy prosciutto and mint vinaigrette. Main courses graduate to rare-breed rib-eye steak with a chive and peppercorn butter. Whatever you choose, try the hand-cut real chips dusted with sea salt (children cannot resist them), along with memorable guest beers such as West Berkshire's Good Old Boy, or one of several equally well-chosen wines by the glass.

directions	Beside A417, midway between Ampney Crucis & Fairford, 5 miles east of Cirencester.
meals	12pm-2pm; 7pm-9pm. Main courses £8.95-£16.95; bar meals from £3.50.
closed	3pm-7pm & Sun eve.

Jeremy Lockley
Falcon Inn,
London Road, Poulton,
Cirencester GL7 5HN
tel   01285 850844
web   www.thefalconpoulton.co.uk

map: 8 entry: 192

The Victoria Inn
Eastleach Turville

The golden-stoned Victoria pulls in the locals – whatever their age, whatever the weather. Propping up the bar, welly-clad with dogs or indulging in great home-cooked grub by the log fire, the locals and their laughter suggest a whale of a time is had by all. If frolic you must, this is the place to do it: summer brings river tug-o-war and the village's Frolic Day. (The highlight of which involves a large oak tree, children in sacks and a loaf of treacle-coated bread.) Refreshments are available for all from proprietors Stephen and Susan Richardson who, in spite of opening up the rooms, have kept much of the character and cosiness of the low-ceilinged pub. And who could fail to enjoy warm smoked chicken, steak and mushroom pie and lamb shank on minty mash, accompanied by Arkells on handpump? There are picnic tables out front, from where you can look down onto the pretty stone cottages and the churches of the village below. A lovely spot following a country stroll.

The Swan at Southrop
Southrop

Its fans include Sir Terence Conran and Simon Hopkinson – the handsome Georgian Swan is the jewel in the Cotswolds' crown. Chef James Parkinson trained under Simon Hopkinson at Bibendum and his seasonal, unshowy, British-European menu reads like the index of one of his mentor's classic cookbooks – potted shrimps, grilled entrecôte with béarnaise sauce, pommes frites and green salad, panna cotta with raisins in armagnac, sticky date pudding with clotted cream. An excellent wine list matches a tasty selection of local real ales, accompanied by scrumptious bar 'snacks' such as steak baguette with red onion, rocket and aïoli, and a cheese ploughman's. A roaring log fire, a sober décor, a relaxed mood and a skittle alley for locals – this is the village inn on the village green that everyone dreams of.

directions	Off A361 between Burford & Lechlade.
meals	12pm-2pm; 7pm-9.30pm (9pm Sun). Main courses £7.25-£14.50.
closed	3pm-7pm.

Stephen & Susan Richardson
The Victoria Inn,
Eastleach Turville,
Fairford GL7 3NQ
tel 01367 850277

map: 8 entry: 193

directions	2 miles west off A361 between Burford & Lechlade.
meals	12pm-2.30pm (3pm Sat & Sun); 7pm-10pm. Main courses £12.50-£17.
closed	2.30pm-7pm (3pm-7pm Sat & Sun). Closed from 10pm every day.

Graham Williams
& James Parkinson
The Swan at Southrop,
Southrop, Lechlade GL7 3NU
tel 01367 850205
web www.theswanatsouthrop.co.uk

map: 8 entry: 194

The Horse and Groom
Upper Oddington

Cotswold stone, hanging baskets, hefty beams and flagstone floors, chunky logs around the double fireplace... is this the pub from central casting? Given that it's 500 years old, the publican ought to be a spry old character. Instead, this is a first-pub venture for incomers Simon and Sally Jackson, who have rejuvenated without losing traditional charm. There's a good selection of guest ales, some from nearby microbreweries, including Wye Valley Best, Butty Bach and Hereford Pale Ale, Barley Mole and Banks's Best. The menu takes a Cook's tour of Europe, with a good serving of trad-English: salmon, chablis and shallot fishcake with salsa verde, lamb tagine, rabbit casserole, braised pork belly, game from the Adlestrop Estate. Produce is organic and local whenever possible, breads and puddings are all homemade. No fewer than 25 wines are available by the glass.

The Fox Inn
Lower Oddington

Amid the grandeur of old Cotswold country houses, the Fox evokes a wonderful sense of times past, gently at odds with the fast pace of modern life. Low ceilings, worn flagstones, a log fire in winter, good food and an exemplary host... people love it here. The comfortably stylish bar has scrubbed pine tables topped with fresh flowers and candles; newspapers, magazines and ales are on tap; rag-washed ochre walls date back years; no wonder the locals are happy. Eat here or in the elegant, rose-red dining room, or on the terrace, heated on cool nights, of the pretty cottage garden.Imaginative, sometimes elaborate dishes include wild rocket, olive and parmesan tart, carrot, coriander and ginger soup, lamb tagine, rib-eye steak with mustard butter, dark chocolate torte. Before you leave, explore the honey-stone village and 11th-century church, known for its magnificent frescos.

directions	Village signed off A436 east of Stow-on-the-Wold.
meals	12pm–2pm; 6.30pm–9pm (7pm–9pm Sun). Main courses £12–£19.75.
closed	3pm–5.30pm.

Simon & Sally Jackson
The Horse and Groom,
Upper Oddington ,
Moreton-in-Marsh GL56 0XH

tel	01451 830584
web	www.horseandgroom.uk.com

map: 8 entry: 195

directions	From Stow A436 for 3 miles.
meals	12pm–2pm (3.30pm Sun); 6.30pm–10pm (9.30pm Sun). Main courses £9.50–£14.50.
closed	Open all day.

Ian McKenzie
The Fox Inn,
Lower Oddington,
Moreton-in-Marsh GL56 0UR

tel	01451 870555
web	www.foxinn.net

map: 8 entry: 196

Gloucestershire

Horse and Groom
Bourton-on-the-Hill

Having saved this roadside boozer, Tom and Will Greenstock – whose parents run the Howard Arms at Ilmington – have created a dining pub of note. The charming, listed, Georgian building may be on an A road, but inside, tranquillity reigns. Log fires burn at either end of the bar, while period features, wooden furniture, vintage posters and fresh-faced staff add to the inviting feel. Food, too, surpasses the pub norm, the blackboard-only menu being continually updated. Local produce, including home-grown vegetables, dominates in dishes such as braised sea bream with haricot beans, sage and smoked bacon, and pork chop with red cabbage and mustard cream sauce. Cask ales include such stalwarts as Wye Valley Dorothy Goodbody's and Everard's Tiger. Bedrooms are nicely plush – smart but uncluttered; one is huge with a sofa, another has doors opening to the terrace.

directions	Beside A44, 2 miles west of Moreton-on-Marsh.
meals	12pm-2pm (2.30pm Sun); 7pm-9pm (9.30pm Fri & Sat). Main courses £9.50-£15.50; bar meals £3.50-£7.50.
rooms	5 doubles £90-£115. Singles from £65.
closed	3pm-6pm, Sun eve & Mon lunch.

Tom & Will Greenstock
Horse and Groom,
Bourton-on-the-Hill,
Moreton-in-Marsh GL56 9AQ
tel   01386 700413
web www.horseandgroom.info

map: 8 entry: 197

Gloucestershire

The Farriers Arms
Todenham

A treasure: a couple of tables in front, a private dining room in the 'library', a restaurant for 25, and smart tables in the recently landscaped rear garden, one of several improvements made by Nigel and Louise since their arrival in 2005. It's cosy, cheerful and reassuringly old-fashioned. Polished flagstones, hop-hung beams and an inglenook with a woodburner; add great beers, real cider, 11 wines by the glass, an enjoyable blackboard menu and colouring books for kids and you have one special little pub. The Farriers is jam-packed on Sundays (lunch must be booked), and the draw is the high quality pub food: fresh ingredients with tasty sauces. There are homemade lamb burgers, local sirloin steaks, fresh soups, Baileys crème brûlée. The mellow-stone village is as pretty as the pub.

directions	Signed from Moreton-in-Marsh & from A3400.
meals	12pm-2pm (2.30 Sun); 7pm-9pm (9.30pm Fri & Sat). Main courses £9-£17; bar meals £4-£8; Sunday roast £10.
closed	3pm-6.30pm (7pm Sun).

Nigel & Louise Kirkwood
The Farriers Arms,
Todenham,
Moreton in Marsh GL56 9PF
tel   01608 650901
web www.farriersarms.com

map: 8 entry: 198

Gloucestershire

The Plough Inn
Cheltenham

Horses from the local stables gallop past, local shoots lunch here, race-goers dine. The rustic walls of The Plough are lined with photographs of meetings at nearby Cheltenham: this place is dedicated to country pursuits. Cheltenham week is bedlam, and a marquee is erected in the garden, but – because of the food – every week is busy. The cooking has a loyal following, and the dining room is famous for its asparagus suppers. Aberdeen Angus fillet in a brandy and black peppercorn sauce tastes every bit as good as it looks. There are good local beers, real ciders and well-chosen wines. The building has been an inn since the 16th century, probably dates from the 13th and was once a courthouse, so bars are darkly cosy with low beams, flagstones and smouldering fires. In spite of its success, The Plough still pulls in the locals. Children will make a bee-line for the play fort in the garden.

directions	B4077 between Stow on the Wold & Tewkesbury.
meals	12pm-9pm. Main courses £6.95-£14.95.
closed	Open all day.

Craig & Becky Brown
The Plough Inn,
Ford, Temple Guiting,
Cheltenham GL54 5RU
tel 01386 584215
web www.theploughinnatford.co.uk

map: 8 entry: 199

Gloucestershire

The White Hart Inn
Winchcombe

After a period of Swedish ownership the White Hart has returned to its English coaching inn roots. Gone is the Gustavian furniture and the sisal matting, in comes scrubbed pine, quarry tiles and framed cricket memorabilia – including England wicketkeeper Jack Russell's 1990 Ashes sweater. Peter Austen used to run the successful Clifton Sausage in Bristol and the good old British banger rules the roost here. Although it's been gastrofied, this is still a pub, and whether you're eating in the restaurant or the front bar, you order at the counter. Choose one of three real ales to accompany a succulent Old Spot pork pie with grape chutney – or order from the main menu, awash with local produce and a list of suppliers. The small wine shop means good wines at cost price, plus corkage – a nice touch.

directions	From Cheltenham, B4632 to Winchcombe. Inn on right.
meals	12pm-10pm. Main courses £8.50-£12.50; bar meals £1.50-£6.50.
closed	Open all day.

Peter Austen
The White Hart Inn,
High Street,
Winchcombe GL54 5LJ
tel 01242 602359
web www.the-white-hart-inn.com

map: 8 entry: 200

The Churchill Arms
Paxford

The Churchill is fun. Walk into the bar to a hub of happy chatter. Energetic Leo and Sonya are right to be proud of their creation – one guest described it as "Fulham in the country", and the locals downing their well-kept Hook Norton like it that way. Aunt Sally teams may make good use of the garden in summer, but the food is the real draw; no bookings, so arrive early. Whether it's celery and blue cheese soup, black bream with herb polenta and creamed fennel, assiette of rabbit with madeira (saddle, leg, confit and faggot) or triple chocolate torte with raspberry parfait, you're in for a serious treat. The L-shaped dining room/bar is full of rustic charm – books, prints, cushioned pews, a roaring woodburner in the inglenook. Beams, old radiators and uneven floors: a relaxed and engaging mix.

The Eight Bells
Chipping Campden

It was built to house masons building the nearby church – and to store the bells. Royalty has passed through the door; even, rumour has it, William Shakespeare. The tiny Cotswold stone building holds its history close – 14th-century beams and standing timbers, flagstones, a priest's hole – but the focus today is the food. Walkers in socks by the fire wolf down lunchtime sandwiches, Hook Norton Best and Old Hooky, while the hot menu combines modern and traditional ideas. Local ingredients are used to vibrant effect in thick-cut roasted prime English ham studded with cloves and glazed with honey, or brace of pheasant with wild mushroom, cream and brandy sauce. For veggies there's baked aubergine stuffed with goat's cheese and spinach on tagliatelle. The large, flower filled terraced garden is a sun-trap in summer.

directions	A44 through Bourton-on-Hill; right to Paxford, via Blockley.
meals	12pm-2pm; 7pm-9pm. Main courses £10.50-£13.50.
closed	3pm-5pm.

Leo & Sonya Brooke-Little
The Churchill Arms,
Paxford,
Chipping Campden GL55 6XH
tel   01386 594000
web   www.thechurchillarms.com

map: 8 entry: 201

directions	Just off High Street near church.
meals	Mon-Thu 12pm-2pm; 6.30pm-9pm. Fri-Sun 12pm-2.30pm; 6.30pm-9.30pm (7pm-9.30pm Sun). Main courses £8-£15; bar meals £5-£15.
closed	Open all day.

Neil & Julie Hargreaves
The Eight Bells,
Church Street,
Chipping Campden GL55 6JG
tel   01386 840371
web   www.eightbellsinn.co.uk

map: 8 entry: 202

Greater Manchester

The White Hart
Lydgate

Decay was settling in at this 18th-century ale house overlooking Saddleworth Moor when Charles Brierley took it over 13 years ago. It has since been transformed into a charming restaurant-pub. Relax in the bar with a glass of Timothy Taylors Landlord, toast your toes by the wood-burning stove and admire its colourful lack of clutter, or have your drink in a room lined with Tibetan photographs. Try British cheeses, a platter of oysters, homemade 'Saddleworth' sausages (five, with five different kinds of mash). Or move upstairs to the restaurant, where delicacy combines with robustness in some unusually fine cooking: chilli squid with saffron and garlic mayonnaise, braised lamb with pickled red cabbage, pan-fried cod with tomato compôte. This is a beautiful village where, on a fine day, you can stretch your eyes all the way to the distant Cheshire Plain.

directions	From Oldham E on A669 for 2.5 miles. Before hill right onto A6050; 50 yds on left.
meals	12pm-2.30pm; 6pm-9.30pm (1pm-7.30pm Sun). Main courses £12.50-£17.
closed	Open all day.

Charles Brierley
The White Hart,
51 Stockport Road, Lydgate,
Oldham OL4 4JJ
tel 01457 872566
web www.thewhitehart.co.uk

map: 12 entry: 203

Hampshire

The Peat Spade
Longstock

It's a short drive through the glorious Test Valley to Longstock, a straggling village of thatched cottages with this striking gabled Victorian pub at its heart. Behind the lozenge-paned windows the feel is more private home than country pub, with neatly furnished eating areas around an uncluttered bar. Lucy Townsend and Andy Clark deliver a near-perfect version of country-pub food; working to a short menu and buying from first-class suppliers they offer rabbit rillette with pickled cherries, fish pie, rib-eye steak with béarnaise, salmon fishcakes with tartare sauce. Handpumped beers include the local Ringwood Fortyniner. The six new bedrooms – big beds, sumptuous fabrics, flat-screen TVs, WiFi and bathrooms with Longbarn toiletries – are proving popular with walkers, shooting folk and fishermen. The latter will find an onsite tackle shop; ask about ghillies and private tuition. And there's a secluded rear terrace.

directions	Off A3057, 1 mile north of Stockbridge.
meals	12pm-2pm (4pm Sun); 7pm-9.30pm. No food Sun eve. Main courses £9.50-£16.
rooms	6 doubles £110.
closed	Open all day.

Lucy Townsend & Andy Clarke
The Peat Spade,
Longstock,
Stockbridge SO20 6DR
tel 01264 810612
web www.peatspadeinn.co.uk

map: 3 entry: 204

The Greyhound
Stockbridge

Civilised, one-street Stockbridge is England's fly-fishing capital, and the colour-washed Greyhound draws fishing folk and foodies. This 15th-century coaching inn is a dapper, food-and-wine-centred affair – and of some pedigree; Helene Schoeman produces modern dishes based on impeccable produce. Charming staff serve pan-fried halibut with smoked bacon and spring onion bubble-and-squeak, and and pork tenderloin with black pudding and caramelised apples; lighter bar meals take in eggs Benedict and goat's cheese bruschetta. There's a lounge with low beams, armchairs and a log fire, and an open-plan dining area with stripped floors and big trestle-style tables. Smart bedrooms sport spotlights, auction antiques, flat-screen TVs, classy bathrooms and cosseting extras. A small garden overlooks the Test: rest here with a glass of chilled chablis or cast a line.

directions	On A30, 10 miles west of Winchester.
meals	12pm-2pm (2.30pm Fri-Sun); 7pm-9pm (9.30pm Fri & Sat). Main courses £11.50-£19.95; bar meals £5.50-£15.
rooms	8: 3 doubles, 4 twins, 1 single £70-£100.
closed	3pm-6pm.

Helene Schoeman
The Greyhound,
31 High Street,
Stockbridge SO20 6EY
tel   01264 810833
web   www.thegreyhound.info

map: 3 entry: 205

The Rose & Thistle
Rockbourne

A thatched Hampshire dream with a dovecote and a rose-tumbled garden. Like many rural pubs, it started life as two cottages so the two huge fireplaces come as no surprise. It is a perfect mix of heavy oak beams and timbers, carved benches and flagstoned or tiled floors. Add country-style fabrics, dried flowers, tables strewn with magazines and you have a thoroughly enchanting place to return to after a visit to Rockbourne's Roman villa. Tim Norfolk has built up a good reputation for his steaks and sauces and his ever-changing blackboard specials make use of fresh local produce: estate game in season, south-coast fish. At lunchtime you might find it hard choosing between smoked salmon and scrambled eggs, prawns by the pint and a classic steak and kidney pudding. The more elaborate evening menu favours fish, such as monkfish wrapped in pancetta. The village of Rockbourne is also delightful.

directions	3 miles NW of Fordingbridge, off B3078.
meals	12pm-2.30; 7pm-9.30. Main courses £8.75-£19.50; bar meals from £5.
closed	3pm-6pm (Sun from 8pm Nov-Mar).

Tim Norfolk
The Rose & Thistle,
Rockbourne,
Fordingbridge SP6 3NL
tel   01725 518236
web   www.roseandthistle.co.uk

map: 3 entry: 206

The Royal Oak
Fritham

A small, ancient, thatched, secluded New Forest inn – an ale-lover's retreat. There's no truck with fruit machines or muzak here: the atmosphere is one of quiet, old-fashioned bonhomie. Locals sup pints and exchange stories around the bar; ramblers and dogs are equally welcome. Huge fires glow through the winter and the smell of logs seduces one to linger. Neil and Pauline McCulloch believe in local produce and deliver honest, unpretentious pub lunches: ploughman's with homemade pâté, home-baked pies, soups, quiches, no chips. Though rustically simple, the three small rooms are well turned out, with light floorboards, solid cottagey tables and spindleback chairs, homely touches, darts, dominoes and cribbage. Five local beers are drawn straight from the cask, including Hop Back Summer Lightning and Ringwood Best. Also: a large garden for summer barbecues and a September beer festival.

directions	M27 junc. 1; B3078 to Fordingbridge; turn for Fritham after 2.5 miles. Follow signs.
meals	12pm-2.30pm (3pm Sat & Sun). Main courses £4-£7.50.
closed	3pm-6pm. Open all day Sat & Sun.

Neil & Pauline McCulloch
The Royal Oak,
Fritham,
Lyndhurst SO43 7HJ
tel 023 8081 2606

map: 3 entry: 207

The East End Arms
East End

The name may conjure up images of a Londoner's local, but this is about as far from the average city boozer as you can get. Hidden down narrow New Forest lanes, it's winningly unpretentious; owned by John Illsley of the band Dire Straits, its walls are lined with photographs of the famous. Walkers, wax jackets and the odd gamekeeper congregate in the earthy Foresters Bar – or in the lounge/dining room, carpeted-comfortable with sturdy tables, sofa and log fire. Good, no fuss, value-for-money dishes flow from the kitchen; homemade beef pie or rare beef platter may be chalked up for lunch; in the evening, a printed menu trumpets whole lemon sole with caper and basil sauce, and braised rabbit with grain mustard sauce. In the small garden are picnic benches and a big green brolly. At first glance this plain little pub might not warrant a second; in fact, it's all a pub should be.

directions	Off B3054, 3 miles east of Lymington; follow signs for Isle of Wight ferry & keep going.
meals	12pm-2.30; 7pm-9.30. No food Sun eve & Mon. Main courses £8-£17.50.
closed	3pm-6pm. Open all day Sun.

Joanna Dydak & Jeremy Willcock
The East End Arms,
East End,
Lymington SO41 5SY
tel 01590 626223
web www.eastendarms.co.uk

map: 3 entry: 208

White Star Tavern & Dining Rooms
Southampton

Placing the city on the gastropub map, the former seafarers' hotel has been stylishly revived. Large etched windows carry the White Star logo, while a cluster of lounges round a lofty, dark wood bar are kitted-out with suede banquettes, leather armchairs and retro mirrors. Open fires add warmth. The raised dining room has impressive wooden panelling, an open-to-view kitchen and the original chandeliers; reclaimed wooden dining furniture, black leather banquettes and shipping photographs add to the metropolitan mood. Up-to-the-minute dishes should hit all the right notes — game terrine with beetroot salad, lobster linguine, warm chocolate fondant with pistachio ice cream — while the bar flaunts cocktails, champagnes, wines by the glass and real ales. Pavement tables are just the thing for fine-weather drinking, accompanied by the papers.

The Bugle
Hamble

Hamble's famous pub, celebrated by yachtsmen the world over, was saved in 2005 by the people behind Southampton's White Star. Using traditional materials and methods they have remodelled the Bugle's 16th-century heart — so you find new-oak beams and standing timbers, stripped-back brick fireplaces and open fires, natural flagstone floors and polished boards. The atmosphere is relaxed, the bar throngs with drinkers and diners on sailing days, there's a simply adorned dining area for escaping the bustle and an intimate private room upstairs. Space and a wide-ranging clientele, from yachties to trippers, informs the style of the food. Sit at the bar with a pint of Deuchars and a pork pie, or go the whole hog and order ham, egg and chips or calves' liver with pancetta mash. Or slip off to the super front terrace for views of bobbing boats on the Hamble.

directions	A33 to Southampton city centre & head for Ocean Village & Marina.
meals	12pm-2.30pm (3pm Fri & Sat); 6.30pm-9.30pm (10pm Fri & Sat). 12pm-9pm Sun. Main courses £7.95-£15.95; bar meals £5.
closed	Open all day.

directions	M27 junc. 8; signs to Hamble, right at mini-r'bout & follow cobbled street down to riverside car park.
meals	12pm-2.30pm (3pm Fri); 6.30pm-9.30pm (6pm-10pm Fri). 12pm-10pm Sat (9pm Sun). Main courses £7-£15; bar meals from £4.
closed	Open all day.

Mark Dodd & Matt Boyle
White Star Tavern & Dining Rooms,
28 Oxford Street,
Southampton SO14 3DJ
tel   023 8082 1990
web   www.whitestartavern.co.uk

Matthew Boyle & Mark Dodd
The Bugle,
High Street,
Hamble SO31 4HA
tel   023 8045 3000
web   www.buglehamble.co.uk

The Black Boy
Winchester

Quirky pubs with personality, real ale and fine food are worth tracking down. Winchester's example is best reached on foot – following the riverside path from the National Trust's Winchester Mill. Landlord David Nicholson has filled the various areas of his unassuming tavern with fascinating paraphernaila, from fire buckets and old signs to a 'library' crammed with books. Oddities greet the eye at every turn; this the easiest place in which to while away an hour – or three. Choose a pint of Flower Pots Bitter (one of five handpumped ales) and a cosy corner with a deep sofa and a log fire to relish it in. Lunchtime peckish? Tuck into beer-battered cod, shepherd's pie or sandwiches. In the evening, splash out on something a touch more inventive – like crab bisque, braised beef cheek with parsnip purée, skate wing with saffron mash and nut brown butter. Rather special.

Running Horse
Littleton

Littleton saw its 200-year-old pub close in 2003. A sweeping renovation of the boarded-up boozer followed, and a 2004 opening saw the horse 'up and running', with a slick and sleek new look and a big emphasis on food. Now, in the experienced hands of Richard and Kathryn Crawford – who run the hugely successful Plough in neighbouring Sparsholt – this revitalised local is set to thrive. Pop in for pints of Palmers or Ringwood in the smart bar, all polished boards, leather chairs and subtle uplighting, or head off to the slate-floored restaurant extension for some serious pub food. Look to the chalkboard for the day's choice, perhaps Thai fishcakes with Asian dressing, shoulder of lamb with red wine jus, and sea bass with anchovy, caper and lemon butter. Or settle down to a lunchtime sandwich or a ploughman's in the bar or on the terrace.

directions	Head south out of city along Chesil Street; Wharf Hill 1st road on right; parking off Chesil Street.
meals	12pm–2pm; 7pm–9pm. No food Mon all day, Sun eve, Tues lunch. Main courses £4.50–£8 (lunch); £14 (dinner).
closed	3pm–5pm (7pm Sun).

directions	Village signed off A272 just west of Winchester.
meals	12pm–2pm (4pm Sun); 6.30pm–9.30pm. No food Sun eve. Main courses £11.75–£17.50; sandwiches from £4.95.
closed	3pm–5.30pm. Open all day Sat & Sun.

David Nicholson
The Black Boy,
1 Wharf Hill,
Winchester SO23 9NQ
tel 01962 861754
web www.theblackboypub.com

Richard & Kathryn Crawford
Running Horse,
88 Main Road,
Littleton,
Winchester SO22 6QS
tel 01962 880218

map: 4 entry: 211

map: 4 entry: 212

The Plough Inn
Sparsholt

Children frolic in the flowery garden's wooden chalet and play fort while grown-ups can relax and enjoy the views. The beer's good, too, with Wadworths ales on draught. Walkers come here for a lunchtime snack of beef-and-horseradish sandwiches with relish. Inside, the pub is smart and open-plan, with pine tables, hop-garlanded beams and an open log fire. The 200-year-old cottagey front rooms are particularly cosy places to have dinner and the enthusiastic tenants, Richard and Kathryn Crawford, with a loyal and hard-working team, run this busy pub with good humour. Blackboards proclaim the dishes of the day; favourites, like lamb's liver and bacon, are given a modern twist, and restaurant-style main courses show imagination and flair. Try cod with olives, crushed potato and herb oil, followed by fruits of the forest crumble. Wines are taken seriously and 12 are available by the glass.

The Wykeham Arms
Winchester

The old Wykeham is English to the core, full of its own traditions and neatly hidden away between the cathedral and the city's famous school. Ceilings drip with memorabilia, the walls are packed with pictures, and bow-tied regulars chat, pints in hand. It's grand too, a throwback to the past and brimming with warm colours and atmosphere. There are small red-shaded lamps on graffiti-etched desks (ex-Winchester College), three roaring fires and two dining rooms. At heart it remains a pub, but it's easy to mistake it for something smarter – viz. the Latin prose in the gents. Food is not cheap, but superb, from posh sandwiches and cottage pie at lunch to daily-changing evening dishes, perhaps seared loin of tuna and Gressingham duck. When they tried to take the roasted rack of Hampshire Down lamb off the menu, a small scale rebellion erupted. The Fuller's and Gales ales are good, the wine list is long and the staff young and laid-back.

directions	Off B3149 Winchester to Stockbridge road.
meals	12pm-2pm; 6pm-9pm (9.30 Fri & Sat; 8.30 Sun). Main courses £9.95-£19.95. Bar meals £4.95-£9.95.
closed	3pm-6pm.

Richard & Kathryn Crawford
The Plough Inn,
Sparsholt,
Winchester SO21 2NW
tel   01962 776353

directions	Near Winchester College; call for directions; parking tricky.
meals	12pm-2.30pm (12.15pm-1.45pm); 6.30pm-8.45pm. No food Sun eve. Main courses £10.95-£19.50; bar lunch £5.95-£9.25.
closed	Open all day.

Peter Miller
The Wykeham Arms,
75 Kingsgate Street,
Winchester SO23 9PE
tel   01962 853834

map: 4 entry: 213

map: 4 entry: 214

Chestnut Horse
Easton

In the beautiful Itchen valley, this rather smart 16th-century dining pub has been taken over by Karen Wells. She worked with the previous owner for six years, so we expect standards of food and service to remain high. A decked terrace leads to a warren of snug rooms around a central bar, warmed by log fires and cheered by a vast collection of jugs, teapots and country pictures. At night it is cosy and candlelit; you can eat either in the low beamed Red Room, with its wood-burning stove, cushioned settles and mix of dining tables, or in the panelled and plate-filled Green Room. Try the two-course menu (ham hock terrine, coq au vin, treacle and chocolate brownie — all good value). Or tuck into shellfish risotto, saddle of venison with red wine jus or beer-battered fish and chips. Great local ale from Itchen Valley Brewery and decent wine and champagne by the glass.

directions	1 mile off B3047 (Winchester to Alresford), 4 miles E of Winchester.
meals	12pm-2pm; 6pm-9.30pm (from 7pm Fri & Sat); 12pm-6pm Sun. Main courses £11.95-£17.50; set menu, 2 courses, £10 (lunch & before 7.30); Sunday roast £11.95; sandwiches from £6.95.
closed	3pm-5.30pm. Open all day Sat & Sun.

	Karen Wells Chestnut Horse, Easton, Winchester SO21 1EG
tel	01962 779257

map: 4 entry: 215

Bush Inn
Ovington

Down a meandering lane alongside the clear running waters of the river Itchen, the 17th-century inn is brimful of character — a jewel in the county crown. In winter it's dark and atmospheric, with a roaring log fire (Real-fire Pub of the Year 2001, no less), walls and ceilings are painted dark green and lit by gas lamps and candles on tables. In summer the cottagey garden comes into play, and there's the added bonus of a stroll along an idyllic stretch of the river. Cottage furniture and high-backed pews fill the series of small rooms around the bar, while walls are hung with fishing and country paraphernalia; among these, a stuffed four-pound salmon's head. The atmosphere is calm, cosy and friendly, the clientele well-heeled. The kitchen deals in fresh local produce and presents its appealing modern menu with flair — venison steak, perhaps, with spiced red cabbage and a whisky and sherry vinegar sauce — but there are simpler dishes too.

directions	Off A31 between Winchester & Alresford.
meals	12pm-2.30pm (3pm Sun); 7-9pm (8.30pm Sun). Main courses £9-£16; bar meals £9-£10.
closed	3pm-6pm (7pm Sun).

	Nick & Cathy Young Bush Inn, Ovington, Alresford SO24 0RE
tel	01962 732764

map: 4 entry: 216

The Flower Pots Inn
Cheriton

Ramblers and beer enthusiasts beat a path to Pat and Jo Bartlett's door, where award-winning pints of Flower Pots Bitter and Goodens Gold are brewed in the brewhouse across the car park. Open fires burn in two traditional bars: one a wall-papered parlour, the other a quarry-tiled public bar with scrubbed pine and an illuminated, glass-topped well. Ales are tapped from casks behind the counter hung with hops, and drunk to the accompaniment of happy chat; music and electronic games would be out of place here. In keeping with the simplicity of the place, the menu is short and straightforward: baps with home-cooked ham, sandwiches toasted or plain, home-cooked hotpots, spicy chilli with garlic bread, hearty winter soups. Curry-lovers come on Wednesday evenings for authentic Punjabi dishes; Morris dancers drop by in summer.

The Yew Tree
Lower Wield

Tim Manktelow-Gray arrived from the Masons Arms, Branscombe in 2004 and his experience is revitalising this hard-to-find inn. Once again folk are beating a path to its rather smart door. The re-worked, stone-flagged bar and the fresh dishes daily chalked up on the board are proving a hit with walkers, retired locals and those who lunch. Triple fff Moondance goes down a treat with gargantuan ham and mustard sandwiches, not to mention deep tureens of oven-roasted courgette and tomato soup. Splash out on a good wine to accompany salmon and crab fishcake with tartare sauce, steamed red snapper with fennel, leeks, dill and pernod, or lamb and mint pudding with red wine and rosemary jus. On summer weekends it's especially buzzy and the beer flows as the local cricket team plays on the pitch opposite. If cricket's not your thing, retreat to the peaceful garden with its rolling Hampshire views.

directions	Village signed off A272 east of Winchester; pub off B3046 in village centre.
meals	12pm-2pm; 7pm-9pm (6.30pm-10pm Weds). No food Sun eve & bank hol eves. Main courses £3.50-£7.50.
closed	2.30pm-6pm (3pm-7pm Sun).

Joanna & Patricia Bartlett
The Flower Pots Inn,
Cheriton,
Alresford SO24 0QQ
tel 01962 771318

directions	4.5 miles north of Alresford, off B3046.
meals	12pm-2pm; 6.30pm-9pm (8.30pm Sun). Main courses £8.95-£17.95.
closed	3pm-6pm & all day Mon. Open all day Sun.

Tim Manktelow-Gray
The Yew Tree,
Lower Wield,
Alresford SO24 9RX
tel 01256 389224

map: 4 entry: 217

map: 4 entry: 218

Hampshire

The Sun Inn
Bentworth

Stonehenge Pigswill, Badger Tanglefoot, Brakspears Bitter, Cheriton Pots... a parade of hand pumps pulls the beer boys in. There's charm, too: this friendly, flower-decked local was once a pair of 17th-century cottages. Surprisingly little has changed. On ancient bricks and bare boards is a rustic mix of scrubbed pine tables and oak benches and settles; beams are hung with horse brasses, walls adorned with prints and plates; there are fresh and dried flowers, candelight and smart magazines. Three cosy log-fired inglenooks warm the interlinking bars. Food is mostly perfect English: onion and cider soup, venison cooked in Guinness with pickled walnuts, pheasant braised in black beer and raisin wine, Sunday roasts, wicked puddings. Hidden down a tiny lane on the edge of a village in deepest Hampshire the Sun Inn could scarcely be more rural. There's a garden at the back and footpaths radiate from the door.

directions	Off A339, 2 miles from Alton.
meals	12pm-2pm; 7pm-9.30pm. Main courses £7.95-£14.95. Sunday roast £8.95-£10.95.
closed	3pm-6pm. Open all day Sun.

Mary Holmes
The Sun Inn,
Sun Hill,
Bentworth,
Alton GU34 5JT

tel   01420 562338

map: 4 entry: 219

Hampshire   Pub with rooms

Carnarvon Arms
Whitway

Fears that the beloved old pub would become a mere restaurant have proved to be unfounded. There are still ales on tap, wines by the glass and a bar menu listing steak and ale pie and classic fillet burgers. The renovation of this rambling old coaching inn near the gates of Highclere Castle is a spruce one, so expect fresh natural colours, bare boards, deep sofas in lounges and a stylish yet traditional bar. In the high-vaulted dining room are painted beams, rug-strewn boards, an ornate fireplace and Egyptian motifs inspired by collections at the Castle. Michelin-starred Rob Clayton oversees the menu, the à la carte taking in crab with pasta and lobster sauce, monkfish with tomato and basil risotto, and beef fillet with madeira. Bedrooms are equally smart, with plasma screens, internet access and posh bathrooms.

directions	Leave A34 at Tothill Services south of Newbury; signs to Highclere Castle; pub on right.
meals	12pm-2.30; 6pm-9.30. Main courses £13.95-£18.95; bar meals £4.50-£11.95; Sunday lunch £15 & £20.
rooms	12: 8 doubles, 3 twins, 1 single £59.95-£89.95.
closed	Open all day.

See pp 30–57 for full list of pubs with rooms

Harwood Warrington
Carnarvon Arms,
Winchester Road, Whitway,
Burghclere, Newbury RG20 9LE

tel   01635 278222
web   www.carnarvonarms.com

map: 4   entry: 220

The Wellington Arms
Baughurst

Lost down a web of lanes, the remodelled 'Welly' is drawing foodies from miles. Wonders have been worked at this tiny pub over the past year by Simon Page and Jason King. Cosy, compact and decorated in style – terracotta floor, checked cushions on wall benches, rustic pictures, quirky objets d'art – the single bar-dining room has only eight tables (do book!). Jason's modern British cooking is first-class and inventive, the boards are chalked up daily and the produce is mainly organic, sourced within a five-mile radius. Kick off with crispy fried pumpkin flowers stuffed with ricotta and feta, follow with venison and goose pie or whole plaice with brown butter, finish with apricot and almond tart. A big emphasis on food in such a small pub begs the question, is this really a pub? The answer must be yes: the mood is easy and there's Wadworth 6X on tap. And you can migrate to the huge garden (with rare-breed chickens) for summer meals.

The Hawkley Inn
Hawkley

A chatty mix of locals, farmers and walkers fill this no-frills inn. In a sleepy village at the end of plunging lanes, the Hawkley's front bars remain delightfully scruffy (a 'listed' carpet, nicotine-stained walls, a mad moose head above the log fire). Venture upstairs to another world – of big sleigh beds, Italian cotton sheets, goose down duvets, flat-screen TV, broadband and bathrooms with power showers and Molton Brown treats; bedrooms are firmly 21st century. Back in the bar, bag one of the rustic scrubbed tables, quaff amazing local beers – Ballards Wassail, Dark Star Espresso – and tuck into country food from a spanking new kitchen. Food ranges from soups and ploughman's to Sussex beef stew – and book ahead for Sunday roast beef served 'pink'. Marvellous.

directions	Baughurst is signed off A340 at Tadley, or A339 east of Kingsclere.
meals	12pm-2.30pm; 6.30pm-9.30pm. Main courses £12.50-£18.50; set lunch Weds-Fri £15 & £18.
closed	3pm-6.30pm, Tues lunch, Sun eve & Mon all day.

directions	After A3/B3006, thro' Burgates, right into Hawkley Road & back over A3; 2 miles to hairpin bend; next left is Pococks Lane.
meals	12pm-2pm (3pm Sat & Sun); 7pm-9.30 (9pm Sun). Main courses £7.50-£13.50; bar snacks £5; Sunday roast £9.75.
rooms	5: 4 doubles, 1 suite £75-£90. Singles £65-£80.
closed	3-5.30 (4pm-5.30 Sat, 4-7pm Sun).

See pp 30-57 for full list of pubs with rooms

Jason King & Simon Page
The Wellington Arms,
Baughurst Road,
Baughurst RG26 5LP
tel   0118 982 0110
web   www.thewellingtonarms.com

Jeannie Jamieson
The Hawkley Inn,
Pococks Lane, Hawkley,
Liss GU33 6NE
tel   01730 827205
web   www.hawkleyinn.co.uk

map: 4   entry: 221

map: 4   entry: 222

Harrow Inn
Steep

The 16th-century Harrow is a gem. Unspoilt, brick-and-tiled, it hides down a country lane that dwindles into a footpath by a little stream – not easy to find! Formerly a drovers' stop, it has been in Claire and Nisa McCutcheon's family since 1929 and they keep it very much as it must always have been. Where nicer to spend an hour than within these two small rooms with their timbered walls, brick inglenook fireplace aglow in winter, scrubbed elm tables and benches along the wall? No bar, just a hatch-like serving counter behind which barrels of local ale rest on racks, bundles of drying hops hanging above. There's a small, wild orchard garden, and some weather-worn rustic benches and tables to the front – only the distant hum of the hidden A3 disturbs the bucolic calm. Food is limited to generously-filled sandwiches, a split-pea and ham soup full of fresh vegetables served with great chunks of bread, a ploughman's platter or salad of home-cooked ham, homemade treacle tart – served with a smile. Loos are a quick dash across the lane.

directions	Off A272 at Sheet west of Petersfield, left opp. garage; left at church; cross A3 to reach pub.
meals	12-2pm; 7-9pm. No food Sun eve. Bar meals £4.30-£11.
closed	2.30pm-6pm (3pm-6pm Sat, 3pm-7pm Sun); Sun eve Oct-Apr.

SPECIAL AWARD
see pages 28-29

Claire & Nisa McCutcheon
Harrow Inn,
Steep,
Petersfield GU32 2DA
tel   01730 262685

map: 4 entry: 223

The White Horse Inn
Priors Dean

Locally known as 'The Pub with No Name' – there being no sign in the cradle on the nearby road – this isolated pub is fiendish to find. But worth the effort for it is a wonderful 17th-century farmhouse pub of utterly simple charm. Untouched by modernity, its two splendid bars have open log fires, a motley collection of old tables, old clocks and farming implements and a warm patina on the walls achievable only by age. The ticking of a grandfather clock and the gentle motion of the rocking chairs in front of the fire transport one to an earlier age. First World War poet Edward Thomas used to drink here and the pub inspired his first published work, *Up in the Wind*. The White Horse stands 750 feet up on the top of the Downs, with peaceful views rolling out on every side. Expect up to eight real ales on handpump, a menu listing homemade pies, pan-fried pheasant and beer battered with hand-cut chips, and a decent range of wines.

The Trooper Inn
Petersfield

Any reservations about the slightly awkward exterior of this 17th-century roadside inn melt away on entering the large open bar with its optics and beer handles and polished Hungarian front of house. Choose a table by the crackling log fire in winter or in the sunny, old-fashioned conservatory overlooking fields. European staff mix efficiency with engaging chat as they serve pints of Sharps or Ringwood or deliver unusual, seasonal dishes to your lunch/dinner table – such as starters of fig, feta and Parma ham or homemade confit duck with red onion and cumin. Main courses of wild boar – local, of course – and poached mussels cooked Thai style in coconut, chilli and lemongrass will tickle the most jaded palettes, while traditional puddings of spotted dick or treacle sponge with light custard should keep nanny more than happy. A delight.

directions	Between Petersfield & Alton. 6 miles from Petersfield, beyond Steep.
meals	12pm-2.30pm; 6.30pm-9.30pm (from 7pm in winter) Main courses £8.95-£14.95; sandwiches from £4.95..
closed	2pm-6pm. Open all day Sat & Sun.

directions	From A3 take exit for Winchester (A272); left at r'bout for Petersfield, then 1st exit left at next r'bout for Steep; up hill for 3miles; pub on right.
meals	12pm-2pm (2.30pm Sun); 7pm-9pm (9.30pm Fri & Sat). Main courses £10-£18,
closed	3pm-5pm & Sun eve.

Paul & Georgie Stuart
The White Horse Inn,
Priors Dean,
Petersfield GU32 1DA

tel	01420 588387
web	www.stuartinns.com

Hassan Matini
The Trooper Inn,
Alton Road, Froxfield,
Petersfield GU32 1BD

tel	01730 827293
web	www.trooperinn.com

map: 4 entry: 224

map: 4 entry: 225

Hampshire

The Royal Oak
Langstone

Twitchers regularly beat a path to the door of this wonderful waterside pub. The views across Chichester Harbour are stunning and it's magical on a fine summer's evening to listen to the plaintive call of the curlew across the water. From your bench at the water's edge you can watch the tide ebb and flow and study the waders in the mudflats; at very high tide the water laps the front door. The pub, licenced since 1725, was once a row of 16th-century cottages lived in by workers at Langstone Mill next door; they used to have a 'tidal licence' allowing travellers a drink while waiting for the tide to ebb. These were the days before the bridge to Hayling Island was built. When inclement weather forces you inside and away from the view you'll find rambling rooms with flagstone and pine floors, beams, and open fires. There are four real ales, traditional pub food (go for Sunday lunch) and sandwiches all day.

directions	Beside Chichester harbour, off A3023 before bridge to Hayling Island.
meals	12pm–9pm. Main courses £6.95–£14; bar snacks from £2.95; Sunday roast £7.95.
closed	Open all day.

Chris Ford
The Royal Oak,
19 Langstone High Street,
Langstone,
Havant PO9 1RY
tel   023 9248 3125

map: 4 entry: 226

Herefordshire

The Riverside Inn
Aymestrey

Edward IV had a celebratory noggin here after a decisive incident in the Wars of the Roses. He was declared King soon afterwards. It is much altered, to an easy mix of antiques, fresh flowers, hops and pine. Menus change with the seasons and the seductive dishes include gravadlax of Lugg trout with honey, mustard and dill, lemon sole stuffed with prawn, garlic and herb butter, and roast Ludlow venison. Wander from the bar into linked rooms with log fires; order a pint of Wye Valley Ale from Stoke Lacy or a house wine from Italy, Chile, Spain. And look for the map of the kitchen gardens from which so much of the fruit and vegetables come: an interesting idea which we wish others would copy. The setting is bucolic, tucked back from a stone bridge over the river Lugg, alive with river trout, with waterside seats and a lovely terraced garden. And the Mortimer Trail passes the front door.

directions	On A4110 18 miles north of Hereford.
meals	12pm–2.15pm; 7pm–9pm (6.30–8.30 Sun). Main courses £9.95–£19.95; bar meals £3.75–£10.95.
closed	3pm–6pm (6.30pm Sun).

Richard & Liz Gresko
The Riverside Inn,
Aymestrey,
Leominster HR6 9ST
tel   01568 708440
web www.theriversideinn.org

map: 7 entry: 227

Herefordshire

Bell Inn
Yarpole

The pub car park fills up fast these days. And a peep through the window reveals chefs in pristine whites calling "service" as great-looking dishes are ferried off to tables. The kitchen is in the hands of Mark Jones, whose daily chalked-up menu flourishes fish and chips with mushy peas and ploughman's with robust fillings. Crispy crab cakes rub shoulders with coq au vin, and there's butternut squash and chestnut lasagne for vegetarians. But it's still a village pub where locals meet over a pint of Wye Valley, dogs doze and children play in the large leafy garden. Large and reassuringly traditional, there are plush red benches, patterned carpets, beams, horse brasses and a roaring log fire – and you can eat where you like, in the bar or the gloriously converted barn. Children have mini portions of real food, heavenly homemade petits-fours come with your coffee and the staff are charming.

directions	Yarpole signed off B4361 between Ludlow & Leominster.
meals	12pm-2.30pm (3pm Sun). Main courses £13.50-£14.95; bar meals £5.25-£16.
closed	3pm-6.30pm & Mon.

Claude & Claire Bossi
Bell Inn,
Yarpole,
Leominster HR6 0BD
tel 01568 780359

map: 7 entry: 228

Herefordshire

The Stagg Inn
Titley

It took some courage for Steve Reynolds to take on a tiny village pub in the back of beyond and, defying all odds, become a Herefordshire food hero. What strikes you is the attention to detail on the daily boards: the only thing you're not told is the name of the bird from which your pigeon breast (perfectly served with fig and port sauce) came. And most of the produce is organic. They fully deserve their Michelin star, won in 2003: the first for a British inn. Come for seared scallops on parsnip purée with black pepper oil, traditional roast grouse with game chips and bread sauce, trio of crème brûlée (vanilla, coffee, cardamom) and an ancient Caerphilly that arrives in the mail because the lane leading to the farm where it's made is impassable. The intimate bar is perfect and dog-friendly, there's beer from Hobsons, cider from Dunkerton's and some very classy wines.

directions	On B4355 between Kington & Presteigne.
meals	12pm-2pm; 6.30pm-9pm (9.30pm Fri & Sat). Main courses £13.50-£17.50; bar meals £8.50-£10.90.
closed	3pm-6.30pm, Sun eve & Mon all day.

Steve & Nicola Reynolds
The Stagg Inn,
Titley,
Kington HR5 3RL
tel 01544 230221
web www.thestagg.co.uk

map: 7 entry: 229

The New Inn
Pembridge

Perfect for English heritage lovers with big appetites. The food is generously portioned, the building is as old as can be (1311), and Pembridge is a remarkable survivor; its market hall could be in deepest France. It is a simple but great pleasure to amble in to this ancient inn, order a drink and squeeze into the curved back settle in the flagstoned bar. You could film a period drama in here it's so history-laden, and when the fireplace logs are lit, it's heaven. Yet this is a real local, with photos of village shenanigans up on the wall and a darts board put to good use. Upstairs has floral carpets, books and sofa – a reassuring spot in which to tuck into reassuringly familiar smoked chicken and avocado salad, duck with cranberry and port sauce, seafood stew and haddock and spring onion fishcakes. Jane Melvin is evidently happy doing what she does best.

Old Black Lion
Hay-on-Wye

Heaven for historians, book lovers and foodies in equal measure. Oliver Cromwell lodged here while laying siege to Hay Castle and the main building, Georgian on the front, 13th-century in places, is packed with oak beams, ancient artefacts and conspiratorial nooks and crannies. Dolan Leighton has changed little at this popular dining pub, where cheerful staff pull pints of their own Black Lion bitter. Seasonal bar favourites keep the kitchen working flat out through every session as diners feast on trout grilled with prawns and Morrocan lamb casserole with fig compote. In the evening, pick a table in the cosy 20-seat restaurant and sample some local fallow venison with parsnip purée, or steak and kidney pie with cabbage and smoked bacon. Most bottles on the wine list are under £20 but there's always something competitively priced and a good list of halves. Visit Hereford Cathedral, antique hunt in Leominster or bag a book in the second-hand bookshop capital of Britain.

directions	Just off A44 in Pembridge. In centre next to Market Square.
meals	12pm-2pm; 6.30pm-9pm (7pm-8.30pm Sun). Main courses £6.95-£12; bar meals £4.95-£8.50.
closed	2.30pm-6pm (3pm-6pm Sat, 3pm-7pm Sun).

	Jane Melvin
	The New Inn,
	Market Square,
	Pembridge HR6 9DZ
tel	01544 388427

directions	2-minute walk from centre of Hay.
meals	12pm-2.30pm; 6.30pm-9.30pm. Main courses £10-£18; bar meals from £5; Sunday roast £9.95.
closed	Open all day.

	Dolan Leighton
	Old Black Lion,
	26 Lion Street,
	Hay-on-Wye HR3 5AD
tel	01497 820841
web	www.oldblacklion.co.uk

map: 7 entry: 230

map: 7 entry: 231

The Pandy Inn
Dorstone

Going way back to 1165, a half-timbered, Herefordshire gem – another contender for 'oldest pub in the land'? Inside are heavy beams, a well-worn flagstoned floor, much smoke-stained stone, a vast oak lintel over the old log grate and an intimate dining room beyond the red velvet curtain. This is the county of Dorothy Goodbody and Butty Bach ales, Old Rosie and 'cloudy' scrumpy. On the menu are mussels, big Hereford beef steaks and seasonal British specials, while for hungry walkers there are filled baguettes, hearty vegetable soup and homemade chicken-liver pâté with first-class bread. Families feel welcome here and children may spill into the garden with its picnic tables and play area in summer. You are in the so-called Golden Valley, so set off for Abbey Dore, Arthur's Stone or bookish Hay-on-Wye, just a short drive away.

Carpenter's Arms
Walterstone

A marvellous little chapel-side pub in the middle of nowhere, with great views up to Hay Bluff. Vera has been dispensing Wadworth 6X and Breconshire Golden Valley from behind the corner hatch for 20 years and spoils you rotten; all get a generous welcome, from locals to walkers to babies. Through an ancient oak doorway is a tiny bar with a log-fired range, and a dining area to the side. Floors are Welsh slate, settles polished oak, tables cast iron, walls open stone; it's as cosy and cared for as can be. On the menu are fishcakes and salad, chicken breast stuffed with stilton and wrapped in bacon, syrup and stem ginger pudding – proper homemade food, some organic. Beer is served from the drum, cider and perry from the flagon. In summer you may spill into the grassy garden at the end of the car park and gaze up at the Skirrid, then pull on the hiking boots and climb it. Gentler walks take you along beautiful Offa's Dyke.

directions	Signed from B4348 Hereford to Hay-on-Wye, 5 miles from Hay.	
meals	12pm-3pm; 6pm-9pm. Main courses £5.95-£12.50; Sunday roast £8.95.	
closed	3pm-6pm (6.30pm Sun) & Mon all day in winter. Open all day Sat.	

Bill Gannon
The Pandy Inn,
Dorstone,
Hay-on-Wye HR3 6AN
tel   01981 550273
web   www.pandyinn.co.uk

map: 7 entry: 232

directions	Village signed from Pandy; Pandy signed from A465 from Abergavenny.	
meals	12pm-3pm; 7pm-10pm. Main courses £10.95-£14.95; bar meals from £5.	
closed	Open all day.	

Vera Watkins
Carpenter's Arms,
Walterstone,
Hereford HR2 0DX
tel   01873 890353

map: 7 entry: 233

The Wellington
Wellington

The austere frontage hides a welcoming bar and some memorable food. At comfortable banquettes around the fire, Butty Bach, Landlords and Hobsons ales can be quaffed; beyond the bar is a dining room of exposed brickwork, old beams and lots of hops – very Herefordshire. Settings are simple: some tables clothed, others bare, and smart dining chairs with comfortable rush seating. A list of suppliers is on show, the chef is a stickler for seasonality and visiting celebrities like Franco Taruschio (ex Walnut Tree, now Barnsley House) have left their mark. So pitch up for *vincisgrassi Maceratese* (Parma ham and porcini lasagne finished with truffle oil: a sumptuous starter), Hereford sirloin with hand-cut chips and red onion marmalade, and wild mushroom risotto with parmesan shavings and white truffle oil… there's a notable Italian accent. Puddings might include damson, honey and whisky fool, the cheeses are local and the Sunday roasts magnificent. Be sure to book: Wellington is a big, hungry village.

directions	Village signed off A49, 4 miles north of Hereford.
meals	12pm-2pm (12.30pm-2pm Sun); 7pm-9pm. No food Sun eve.
	Main courses £9.50-£16.75; bar meals £4.95-£7.95; Sunday lunch £12.50 & £17.50.
closed	3pm-6pm (7pm Sun) & Mon lunch.

SPECIAL AWARD
see pages 28-29

Ross & Philippa Williams
The Wellington,
Hereford HR4 8AT
tel   01432 830367
web   www.wellingtonpub.co.uk

map: 7 entry: 234

Herefordshire

Herefordshire

The Railway
Hereford

What a discovery: the railway tavern on the slopes of Dinmore Hill has become a welcoming gastropub. Work up an appetite as you mount the Ziggurat steps from the car park to the top terrace (there are easier routes on the other side!) where sweeping views of the countryside compete with two Victorian railway bridges. Inside: a contemporary mix of old and new, with smooth plaster walls painted in muted tones and original stones. Pull yourself away from the leather sofas to enter a bistro-like dining room with beech-topped tables and bentwood chairs; tuck into locally made breads served with salty Welsh butter before sampling a pretty parcel of Lay & Robson smoked salmon and cream cheese. Follow with a rustic baked duck with root vegetables, or a succulent Gloster (sic) Old Spot chop, carved and fanned across the plate and served with a whole poached pear. Service can be diffident but is always charming.

The Crown & Anchor
Lugwardine

Locals, families, couples, walkers – all sorts gather here, drawn by the happy buzz. Three miles from the centre of Hereford, the old pub is friendly, countrified and atmospheric. Intimate rooms are cosy with red quarry tiles scattered with rugs, solid pine tables, corner settles and comfy sofas in corners. Pastoral prints dot the walls, bookshelves spill with books, bottles and jars. There's a big log fire and a hop-decorated bar from which Butcombe, Worthy Pedigree and Timothy Taylor beers flow; Nick offers malts from Oban and Talisker and a good few wines, and Julie oversees an excellent kitchen. Whether you choose a cheddar sandwich or a fillet of pollock with parsley sauce and mash, it will be fresh and good. There's plenty for vegetarians, too, and bread and butter pudding with custard. The garden, overlooking the car park, is pretty in summer.

directions	On A49 between Leominster & Hereford, 4 miles S of Leominster.
meals	11.30am-2.30pm (12pm-3pm Sun); 7pm-9pm. Main courses £9.50-£19.50; bar meals £2.25-£10.50.
closed	2.30pm-6.30pm, Sun from 3.30pm, Tues lunch & Mon all day.

Gill Morris
The Railway,
Dinmore,
Hereford HR1 3JP
tel 01568 797053

map: 7 entry: 235

directions	From Hereford A438 to Ledbury. In Lugwardine, 1st left into Cotts Lane.
meals	12pm-2pm; 7pm-10pm (9.30pm Sun). Main courses £8.50-£12.
closed	Open all day.

Nick & Julie Squire
The Crown & Anchor,
Cotts Lane,
Lugwardine,
Hereford HR1 4AB
tel 01432 851303

map: 7 entry: 236

The Cottage of Content
Carey

Svenia does friendly 'front of house' and Paul cooks — with imagination. Having worked their socks off for two years, they have put this old pub in the depths of Herefordshire on the map; walkers, families, retired holiday makers, locals with dogs — all beat a path to its door. Décor is pared-down traditional: flagstones in the bar, polished wood beyond, Windsor chairs, pine tables and pews. Beams are hung with horse-and-hop impedimenta, paintings are for sale, light jazz plays and one area merges merrily into another. Vegetables are organic, produce local and the menu is tempting in its simplicity: rack of lamb with chargrilled vegetables and mint pesto, sirloin of beef with tarragon and mustard sauce, warm walnut tart and clotted cream. Small, beamy bedrooms are carpeted and cottagey, and bathrooms fresh and new. Good value.

The Butchers Arms
Woolhope

Martin produces thoroughly reliable food from his fully-modernised kitchen, and there are log fires and smiling Cheryl to settle you in. Surrounded by walking country, opposite Marcle Ridge and close to the Forestry Commission's Haugh Woods, this half-timbered 'magpie' house (once owned by equestrian streaker Lady Godiva) goes back to the 14th century — and the ceiling beams just about reach the level of your nose. Taken over by returning locals it has undergone a restoration that it deserved long ago. From the central bar, cosy with Windsor armchairs and hung with Weston's cider lithos and sepia prints, French windows slide open to a charming terrace with roses and a garden that stretches down to the village brook — eat out here. In the evening, dine by candlelight in the tiny restaurant from a menu that tempts with big salads in summer and, in winter, local game or warming rabbit pie with sage and bacon.

directions	A40 west of Ross-on-Wye, then A49 towards Hereford; signs for Hoarwithy, then Carey.
meals	12pm-1.45pm; 7pm-9pm. Main courses £9.25-£18.50; bar meals from £3.95.
rooms	5: 3 doubles, 2 twins £56-£60.
closed	2.30pm-6.30pm; Sun eve & Mon all day.

See pp 30–57 for full list of pubs with rooms

directions	Off B4224 between Hereford & Ross-on-Wye.
meals	12pm-2pm; 6.30pm-9pm. Main courses £8.95-£19.95; bar snacks (lunch) from £3.95; Sunday roast £9.25.
closed	3pm-6.30pm & Mon lunch in winter.

Svenia Wolf & Paul Franklin
The Cottage of Content,
Carey,
Hereford HR2 6NG
tel 01432 840242
web www.cottageofcontent.co.uk

Martin & Cheryl Baker
The Butchers Arms,
Woolhope,
Hereford HR1 4RF
tel 01432 860281

map: 7 entry: 237

map: 7 entry: 238

Three Crowns Inn
Ullingswick

The Three Crowns is worth any number of missed turns. Hop-strewn beams and settles in the bar, open fires, candles on tables, cribbage – all that you'd expect of an old-fashioned inn. Walk into a flagstoned bar to find the day's set lunch menus or early evening specials chalked up to tempt you; since chef-landlord Brent Castle arrived we've not had a poor meal. And there are some unusual dishes, such as roast woodcock with risotto of its liver and winter vegetables, hake and potato pie, and crispy belly pork with black pudding, red cabbage and mustard mash. Ingredients are likely to be organic and local, extras, like home-baked bread and cafetière coffee, are perfect. With a restaurant extension this may sound more restaurant than pub, but there's always a table set aside for drinkers. The Wye Valley ale is delicious, and there's Hereford cider and the odd bargain wine too. Seek out the monthly farmers' markets.

The Lough Pool Inn
Sellack

The words 'Lough' and 'Pool' are almost synonymous and, perversely, the pool and stream by which the pub once stood, deep in the bosky folds of Herefordshire, have long run dry. David and Janice Birch have maintained the high standards since taking over in 2005 and the pub continues to go from strength to strength. A cosy fire, a glowing bar, head-ducking beams and a refreshingly unshowy dining room – solid tables, comfortable chairs – in which to enjoy daily-changing dishes. Seasonal menus successfully balance comfort food and modern treatments of superb local ingredients, be it ham hock and foie gras terrine with plum compote, game casserole served with homemade bread, or Welsh lamb rump with ratatouille and tarragon jus. Stock-in-trade are good real ales from Wye Valley Brewery, strong draught ciders, wines by the glass of surprising quality; try the French fizz. A relaxed and civilised place to be.

directions	1 mile from A465, north-east of Hereford.
meals	12pm-2.30pm; 7pm-9.30pm. Main courses from £14.25; set lunch £12.95 & £14.95.
closed	3pm-7pm & Mon.

Brent Castle
Three Crowns Inn,
Bleak Acre,
Ullingswick HR1 3JQ
tel   01432 820279
web www.threecrownsinn.com

directions	A49, 3.5 miles north-west of Ross-on-Wye, follow Sellack signs; The Lough Pool Inn signed.
meals	12pm-2pm; 7pm-9pm. Main courses £4.85-£12.95 (lunch & specials), £10.95-£18.95 (dinner).
closed	3pm-6.30pm; Sun eve & Mon lunch Oct, Nov & Jan.

David & Janice Birch
The Lough Pool Inn,
Sellack,
Ross-on-Wye HR9 6LX
tel   01989 730236
web www.loughpoolinn.co.uk

The Mill Race
Walford

A real surprise to push open the 'ecclesiastical' door and find yourself in a boldly stylish space. The central log fire is the focus of the room, a blackboard proudly lists the local suppliers and a stainless steel kitchen glistens beyond the granite-topped bar. Relax in a black bucket chair as you browse the papers, perch at the bar on a chrome and wood stool or gaze on the Herefordshire hills from the terrace. An eclectic choice of music may play in acknowledgement of a mostly young clientele, but foodies of all ages come here for the chef, Aaron Simms, who trained at Le Manoir aux Quatres Saisons. Printed menus change seasonally and nothing is showy – it's the best of modern British pub food. For lunch there are steak burgers with onion marmalade and quiche of the day, for dinner, 'real' prawn cocktail, wild mushroom risotto and Herefordshire steak and kidney pie. It looks great on the plate and it's jolly good value.

directions	Walford is on B4234 3 miles south of Ross-on-Wye.
meals	12pm-2.30pm; 6.30pm-9.30pm. Main courses £5.95-£16.95.
closed	3pm-5pm. Open all day Fri-Sun.

Rebecca Bennett
The Mill Race,
Walford,
Ross-on-Wye HR9 5QS
tel   01989 562891
web   www.millrace.info

map: 7 entry: 241

The Saracens Head
Symonds Yat East

This is an adventure before you've booked in. The bar staff still, obligingly, run the old, hand-cranked ferry across the water. The old riverside inn goes back to the 16th century and became a pub in the 18th, but it has a modern buzz now, thanks to an enthusiastic staff and a lively new brasserie. Locals loiter, Brummies drop by, and dishes are chalked up on the blackboard by the bar: exotic sandwiches and bruschettas, local pheasant terrine, Welsh goat's cheese panna cotta, Hereford fillet with buttered kale, crème brulée. The terraces by the water attract crowds in summer; there's a seaside-holiday feel. In winter, the public bar is a warm haven; pool tables attracts the young and trippers come for Symonds Yat. Make a night of it: upstairs, and in the boathouse, is a flurry of new oak-floored bedrooms, stylishly furnished, beautifully cared for and with great river views.

directions	A449 Ross-on-Wye to Monmouth; exit at Little Chef; signs for Symonds Yat East.
meals	12pm-2.30pm; 6.30pm-9pm. Main courses £8-14.50 (lunch); £10-18 (dinner); bar meals £4.75-8.50.
rooms	10: 8 doubles, 1 twin, 1 family £70-£130. Singles from £48.50.
closed	Open all day.

See pp 30-57 for full list of pubs with rooms

Chris & Peter Rollinson
The Saracens Head,
Symonds Yat East,
Ross-on-Wye HR9 6JL
tel   01600 890435
web   www.saracensheadinn.co.uk

map: 7 entry: 242

The Alford Arms
Frithsden

It isn't easy to find, so be armed with a detailed map or precise directions before you set out – David and Becky Salisbury's gastropub is worth any number of missed turns. It's in a hamlet enfolded by acres of National Trust common land – bring your boots! Inside, two interlinked rooms, bright, airy, with soft colours, fresh flowers, scrubbed pine tables on wooden or tiled floors, and prints on the walls. Food is taken seriously and ingredients are as organic, free-range and delicious as can be. On a menu that divides dishes into small plates and main meals, there are crispy chorizo risotto balls with vine tomato sauce, venison steak and kidney pudding with parsnip mash, raspberry and basil crème brûlée. Wine drinkers have the choice of 17 by the glass, while service is informed, friendly and alert. Arrive early on a warm day to take your pick of the teak tables on the sun-trapping front terrace, shaded by posh brollies.

The Valiant Trooper
Aldbury

A pretty village in a pretty setting. A Roman road – the Ridgeway Path – runs past, and the Saxon name means 'old fort'. Named in honour of the Duke of Wellington, said to have held a meeting here during the Napoleonic wars, the dear little brick and tiled cottage has been a pub since 1752. Now it caters for booted ramblers, diners escaping town and families (there's a little play house in the garden). You'll find dark beams on rough-plaster walls, bare brick, blazing log fires, tiled floors, an old-fashioned feel and a big welcome from landlord Tim O'Gorman, who's been pleasing customers for over 20 years. Walkers can slake a thirst with a decent pint of ale from a chalked-up choice of five and refuel on ciabatta sandwiches. The light and airy stable restaurant groans with lunchers on Sundays. Come for roasts and sound English dishes: peppered mackerel with horseradish relish, and bread and butter pudding.

directions	A4146 Hemel Hempstead to Water End; 2nd left after Red Lion to Frithsden; left after 1 mile at T-junc., then right; on right.
meals	12pm-2.30pm (4pm Sun); 7pm-10pm. Main courses £10.75-£14.75.
closed	Open all day.

directions	North of Berkhamsted off B4506 towards Aldbury Common.
meals	12pm-2.15pm; 6.30pm-9.15pm. No food Sun & Mon eve. Main courses £8-£12; bar meals £5; Sunday roast £8.
closed	Open all day.

David & Becky Salisbury
The Alford Arms,
Frithsden,
Hemel Hempstead HP1 3DD
tel   01442 864480
web   www.alfordarmsfrithsden.co.uk

map: 9 entry: 243

Tim O'Gorman
The Valiant Trooper,
Trooper Road,
Aldbury,
Tring HP23 5RW
tel   01442 851203

map: 9 entry: 244

The Fox
Willian

Willian locals have been making the most of The Fox since it opened. It has good lighting, a solid, comfortable feel and a modern menu that showcases British ingredients and fish from the north Norfolk coast. The Fox could beat many neighbourhood restaurants into a cocked hat but part of its charm is that it is still a place where beer drinkers are welcome (and shares this ethos with Cliff Nye's other pub, the White Horse at Brancaster Staithe in Norfolk). A cool, formal dining room sits astride a relaxed bar, where Cromer crab and smoked salmon sandwiches add glamour to a menu that includes cod, hand-cut chips and pea purée. The restaurant is a mix of French bistro and British pub: foie gras and chicken liver parfait with black cherry compote, grilled lobster with garlic butter, partridge wrapped in bacon with raisin red wine jus. This Fox is one you'd do well to hunt down.

The Fox & Hounds
Hunsdon

London chefs quitting fabulous establishments to set up in rural pubs may be an increasing trend, but few have managed it with the aplomb of James Rix. Witness a comfy laid-back bar with log fire, leather sofas and local ales from Tring Brewery. Then tuck into something simple like a ploughman's, a plate of Spanish charcuterie or a classic calves' liver and mash with bacon and onion gravy. But note also the funky country-house-on-a-shoestring dining room that tosses together polished old tables with a crystal chandelier and deals in peppered venison steaks with beetroot and port sauce, and tagliolini with clams, garlic and chilli — a starter or a main. Whether eating in the bar or dining room, do not miss out on the homemade foccacia — it merely emphasises the attention paid to the smallest detail. A treat to see an old pub in the right hands, and the garden at the back comes into its own in summer. Booking is recommended.

directions	A1 junc 9 for Letchworth; 1st left into Baldock Lane; pub 0.5 miles.
meals	12pm-2pm; 6.45pm-9.15pm. No bar food Sun. Main courses £9.95-£16.95; bar meals £7-£15.95.
closed	Open all day.

Cliff Nye
The Fox,
Baldock Lane, Letchworth,
Willian SG6 2AE
tel 01462 480233
web www.foxatwillian.co.uk

map: 9 entry: 245

directions	Off A414 between Harlow & Hertford on B1004.
meals	12pm-3pm; 6.30pm-10pm. Main courses £9-£22; bar meals £4.95-£16.50.
closed	4pm-6pm, Sun eve & Mon all day.

James Rix
The Fox & Hounds,
2 High Street,
Hunsdon SG12 8NH
tel 01279 843999
web www.foxandhounds-hunsdon.co.uk

map: 9 entry: 246

The New Inn
Shalfleet

Built in 1746 on the site of a church house, this old fishermen's haunt is worth more than a passing nod – especially if you are on the 65-mile coastal path trail. Or have got here by boat and moored at Shalfleet Quay. The place now draws a cheery mix of tourists, walkers and sailors to a spick-and-span bar with 900-year-old flagstones, beams and old fireplaces, and a series of pine-tabled dining rooms decked with nautical bits and bobs. Refreshment includes pints of island-brewed ales and fabulously fresh seafood marked up on the daily-changing chalkboard. The huge platter is a treat; other (cheaper) fish choices might include sea bass cooked with lemon or simply grilled plaice. Mouthwatering fresh crab and lobster are landed at Newtown Quay; the crab sandwiches are memorable, as is the lobster salad. And carnivores are not forgotten, with prime steak, game in season and traditional pub grub.

Seaview Hotel
Seaview

Seaview is an island institution – smart, buzzing, by the sea and full of thirsty sailors. The gaily-parasoled terrace, with its railings, mast and flag, is like the prow of a boat; in the back bar, learn your knots; in the front, brush up your semaphore. When the weather is warm, have a pre-dinner drink in the front garden and watch the sun go down over the Solent – perfect. Then wander past portholes, ships' wheels, lanterns and sails for a plateful of roast monkfish with crab mash and chilli sauce in the restaurant; the food is pricey but praiseworthy. In the bar, order island-brewed Goddard's Special and the famous hot crab ramekin; if you're here on a Sunday, don't miss the roast. Afterwards, retire to a sitting room for binoculars and views of the sea. Ask for details about wine-tasting, cycling and adventure breaks.

directions	On A3054 between Yarmouth & Newport.
meals	12pm-2.30pm; 6pm-9.30pm. Main courses £6-£20.
closed	3pm-6pm.

Martin Bullock
The New Inn,
Main Road, Shalfleet,
Yarmouth PO30 4NS

tel	01983 531314
web	www.thenew-inn.co.uk

map: 3 entry: 247

directions	B3330 from Ryde; left into Puckpool Hill for Seaview.
meals	12pm-2.30pm; 7pm-9.30pm. Main courses £7-£14. Sunday lunch £13.95 & 16.95.
closed	Open all day.

Andrew Morgan
Seaview Hotel ,
High Street,
Seaview PO34 5EX

tel	01983 612711
web	www.seaviewhotel.co.uk

map: 4 entry: 248

Shipwright's Arms
Faversham

It's been called the loneliest pub in the world. Surrounded by salt marshes, the below-sea-level-building and boatyard are protected by a dyke from inundation by the tidal creek above. Its isolation calls for self-sufficiency: water is still drawn from a well and propane gas used for cooking. Plain and simple just about sums up the three tiny bar rooms separated by standing timbers and wooden partitions, all warmed by open fires or stoves and with booths formed by black-panelled settles. Furniture is ancient and there's no shortage of boating paraphernalia. Beers are from Kent brewers Goachers and Hopdaemon and are expertly kept, food sustains sailing folk and walkers on the Saxon Shore Way, and Derek and Ruth are lovely people. Join the summer crowd in the garden and sup a pint on the sea wall.

The Sportsman
Seasalter

Slip off to Seasalter for a meal you won't forget. Brothers Phil and Steven Harris's pub is a gastronomic haven amid wastes of marshland, faded beach huts and caravan sites with the North Sea somewhere behind. In defiance of the pub's bleak surroundings, happy eaters fill the three large, light-filled rooms, spreading across the stripped pine floors, pine wheelback chairs, chunky tables built from reclaimed wood and winter log fire. It's simple, fresh, unprecious: red stools at a cream-boarded bar, neat lighting, modern prints on white walls and a glassed-in front porch, a good place for soaking up the winter sun. The blackboard menu is short and sweet with everything seasonal and with an understandable emphasis on fish. So, fantastic food at reasonable prices, such as Thornback ray with balsamic vinaigrette, new-season lamb with pommes Anna, roast baby pineapple and coconut sorbet... There are good wines by the glass and, on handpump, Shepherd Neame beers.

directions	From A2 for Sittingbourne. Through Ospringe, right at r'bout on to western link road; right at end (T-junc.). Right again opp. school in 0.25 miles. Cross marsh to pub.
meals	12pm-2.30pm; 7pm-9pm. No food Sun eve. Main courses £6.95-£11.95.
closed	3pm-6pm & Mon all day in winter.

Derek & Ruth Cole
Shipwright's Arms,
Hollowshore,
Faversham ME13 7TU

tel 01795 590088

directions	On coast road between Faversham & Whitstable.
meals	1pm-2pm; 7pm-9pm. No food Sun & Mon. Main courses £13.95-£18.30.
closed	3pm-6pm.

Phil Harris
The Sportsman,
Faversham Road,
Seasalter,
Whitstable CT5 4BP

tel 01227 273370

map: 5 entry: 249

map: 5 entry: 250

The Dove
Dargate

In winter, woodsmoke hangs in the air, in summer, it's the heady scent of roses. This is an idyllic rural pub in the gloriously named Plum Pudding Lane. Enter through a series of small rooms with bare-boarded floors, scrubbed wooden tables and plain solid chairs to a hop-garlanded bar and winter fire. Nigel Morris cooks with skill and imagination using the freshest ingredients he can get his hands on. It's not your usual pub grub and raw materials are mostly regional: pheasant and partridge from local shoots, lemon sole, plaice and hake from Hythe. There could be roast shank of lamb, or a smashing confit of duck. Lunchtime snacks include soups, baguettes and a never-off-the-menu marinated chicken with mint. The sheltered, formal garden has tables under fruit trees, a swing for children, a dovecote with doves. Remember to book to eat, especially in the evening. There are Shepherd Neame ales on handpump and a short, good-value wine list.

The Red Lion
Stodmarsh

A genuine country pub reached down rutted lanes that wind through bluebell woods. The tiny, 15th-century rooms have bare boards, log fires, garlands of hops, fresh flowers and candles on every table… and prints, framed menus from France, old wine bottles, milk churns, trugs and baskets, tennis rackets, straw hats and two lazy cats. Then there's Robert Whigham, one of life's characters; the perfect landlord. A basket of freshly-laid eggs (chickens in the garden), locally-made chutney and a sign for the sale of locally-smoked ham add to the rural feel. Greene King IPA and Old Speckled Hen are tapped direct from barrels behind the bar and everyone here is a regular – or looks like one. The blackboard menu changes every couple of weeks depending on what's available from local farms and shoots, food arrives on huge, individually painted plates and the quality is high.

directions	Off A299, 4 miles south west of Whitstable.
meals	12pm-2pm; 7pm-9pm. Main courses £14-£21.
closed	3pm-6pm & Mon all day.

Nigel & Bridget Morris
The Dove,
Plum Pudding Lane,
Dargate,
Canterbury ME13 9HB
tel   01227 751360

map: 5 entry: 251

directions	Off A257 Canterbury to Sandwich road.
meals	12pm-2.30pm (3pm Sun); 6.30pm-9.30pm. No food Sun eve. Main courses £9.95-£15.95.
closed	Open all day.

Robert Whigham
The Red Lion,
High Street, Stodmarsh,
Canterbury CT3 4BA
tel   01227 721339
web   www.red-lion.net

map: 5 entry: 252

The Griffin's Head
Chillenden

Jerry and Karen's hugely attractive Shepherd Neame pub – a Wealden hall house from the 14th century – will charm you. Dominated by a log fire in the tiny, flagstoned, central bar and back-to-back with its doppelganger hearth in the snug, attractive restaurant, this is a superb winter pub. Pale beams and standing timbers are everywhere, ceilings are low and the beams above the bar are a mass of glass beer mugs. Lovers of fizz know they've come to the right place the moment they step in and spot the blackboard listing champagne. Wine is taken seriously too, with a fair choice by the glass – three reds, three whites; you can always try a taster before you commit. Good country cooking is of the creamy garlic mushrooms, steak and kidney pie, roast partridge in cranberry sauce variety, and very delicious it is too. In spring the gorgeous garden is surrounded by wild roses. Popular with the Kent cricketing fraternity.

The Granville
Lower Hardres

From the same stable as the Sportsman in Seasalter, the Granville mirrors its older sibling, comfortably straddling the divide between restaurant and pub. Rugs are strewn, cream walls bear tasteful lithographs, leather sofas fill one corner and there's a big beer garden outside. It's a pleasure to sit in this laid-back place, downing rock oysters with shallot vinegar, with a pint of stout or a well-chosen wine. Overseeing it all is Gabrielle Harris, aided by chef Jim Shave heading an open-to-view kitchen that deals in classically modern, uncontrived dishes. Chalked up on a blackboard in the bar are tried-and-trusted favourites like whole roast wild sea bass with garlic and rosemary. There's lovely homemade bread to dip, and a flourless chocolate cake that will charm those even without wheat allergies: it's divine. Staff are switched on, ingredients are impeccably sourced, and it's great for walkers, foodies, families. And the Channel tunnel.

directions	A2 from Canterbury; left on B2068 for Wingham; Chillenden signed.
meals	12pm-2pm; 7pm-9.30pm. No food Sun eve. Main courses £18–£25.
closed	Open all day.

Jeremy Copestake
The Griffin's Head,
Chillenden,
Canterbury CT3 1PS
tel   01304 840325

map: 5 entry: 253

directions	On B2068 just outside Canterbury.
meals	12pm-2pm (2.30pm Sun); 7pm-9pm. No food Sun eve. Main courses £11.95–£16.95; b ar meals £4.95–£11.95.
closed	Open all day.

Phil & Gabrielle Harris
The Granville,
Street End,
Lower Hardres,
Canterbury CT4 7AL
tel   01227 700402

map: 5 entry: 254

Froggies at the Timber Batts
Bodsham

Winding lanes lead, finally, to Bodsham, with glorious views of the North Downs. Wander into the splendidly rural Timber Batts – built in 1485 – and you are in for a surprise. Along with the bar menu is a slateboard of British and Gallic specialities, chalked up in French, and the Loire house wine comes from the vineyard of the owner-chef's cousin. So sit yourself down at an old pine table and be cheered by platefuls of local game, Rye Bay fish, moules farcis, confit de canard, prime fillet of beef with roquefort, and tarte tatin. In winter, nurse a whisky by one of three fires, in summer enjoy the garden with its lush Kentish views. And make the most of delicious local and French produce at the last-Sunday-of-the-month market in the car park.

directions	B2068 for Canterbury; left for Wye & Bodsham; 1st left fork; 1.5 miles; right for Wye; right for Bodsham; 300 yds up on top of hill.
meals	12pm-2.30pm (12.30pm Sun); 7pm-9.30pm. No food Sun eve. Main courses £14-19; Sunday lunch £16 & £20.
closed	3pm-6.30pm & Mon (Tues if bank hol Mon). Open all day Sat & Sun.

Joel Gross
Froggies at the Timber Batts,
School Lane, Bodsham,
Wye TN25 5JQ

tel	01233 750237
web	www.thetimberbatts.co.uk

map: 5 entry: 255

The Dering Arms
Pluckley

Pluckley is possibly the most haunted village in England (16 ghosts at the last count) and the gothicky Dering Arms contributes its share. The former hunting lodge is hidden down country lanes almost two miles from the village. Owner/chef James Buss has given this civilised place a fantastic reputation for food and drink. Stone floors, blazing logs, old wooden tables and chairs and two bars garlanded with hops, farming implements, guns and prints – feast amid it all on fine produce and fish that will have you hooked: fillets of plaice with crisp Serrano ham and beurre noisette or a whole crab salad. Or dine more formally in the pretty restaurant, candlelit at night. The blackboard also lists seasonal game, pie of the day, confit of duck. Dering Ale on handpump is brewed for the pub by Goachers of Maidstone; wines and whiskies galore.

directions	8 miles west of Ashford (M20 south junc. 8). Signed from Pluckley, by railway station.
meals	12pm-2pm; 7pm-9.30pm. No food Mon. Main courses £9.45-£21.95.
closed	3.30pm-6pm & Sun eve.

James Buss
The Dering Arms,
Station Road,
Pluckley TN27 0RR

tel	01233 840371
web	www.deringarms.com

map: 5 entry: 256

The Swan on the Green
West Peckham

West Peckham may be the back of beyond – albeit a well-heeled beyond – but there's nothing backward about Gordon Milligan's 16th-century pub. People are drawn by its growing reputation for good food and beer that comes from the microbrewery to the rear. The décor is fresh, contemporary and open-plan: blond wood, rush-seated chairs, big flowers, modern black and white photographs. Under the Swan Ales label, half a dozen brews are funnelled from the central bar: Ginger Swan, Swan Mild, Trumpeter Best, Fuggles, Bewick, Cygnet. The printed menus are a compendium of updated pub classics and the likes of haddock, tomato and root vegetable chowder, red mullet with mussel broth, and crispy duck confit with red wine jus. In spite of clear gastropubby leanings, Gordon and his team have created a balanced mix of drinking bar – replete with locals – and dining areas. You may even borrow a rug and eat on the village green.

The Harrow
Ightham Common

The continuing, hands-on approach of John Elton and Claire Butler is reaping rewards. Their Kent ragstone country pub looks the part, with cottage garden flowers outside and old benches, candlelight and a roaring winter fire within. The cooking is based on sound supplies, from local game to wild mushrooms, and the food adds enough spice to provoke interest without being overpowering: mustard and chive sauce with home-baked ham, fillet of chicken with Cajun spices. Some of the starters might make a meal in themselves: spicy vegetable and lentil soup comes with a whole loaf, and tomato and anchovy salad is a heaped pile. A separate restaurant, that spreads into a small conservatory, has a more formal feel to match the starched white cloths on the bookable tables. It's first-come, first-served for tables in the bar – and this is a popular place!

directions	From A26 north, 2nd left off B2016.
meals	12pm-2pm (4pm Sun); 7pm-9pm. No food Sun & Mon eves. Main courses £9.95-£15.95; bar meals £5.65-£12.95.
closed	3-6pm; check Sun eves in winter.

directions	Ightham Common signed off A25.
meals	12pm-2pm (3pm Sun); 6pm-9pm. Main courses £9.50-£17; bar meals £6.50-£17.
closed	3pm-6pm, Sun eve & Mon all day.

	Gordon Milligan The Swan on the Green, The Village Green, West Peckham, Maidstone ME18 5JW
tel	01622 812271
web	www.swan-on-the-green.co.uk

	John Elton & Claire Butler The Harrow, Ightham Common, Sevenoaks TN15 9EB
tel	01732 885912

map: 5 entry: 257

map: 5 entry: 258

Spotted Dog
Smarts Hill

Everyone loves this 16th-century English pub... walkers, babies, grannies, dogs. It is rambling, low-beamed, panelled, nooked and crannied to the hilt. But there's nothing traditional about the short daily-changing menu, a well-priced blending of country dishes with current trends. And it's good – whether a plate of Weald Smokery Parma ham, olive roasted skate with a beurre noisette, game stew with parsley dumplings, or a simple BLT sandwich. Sit back with an expertly kept pint of Larkins or Harveys Best at an ancient settle by an inglenook fire – there are several and one is vast – and admire the tiny doors and the mullioned windows, the rough hewn beams and the ancient panelling; this is a textbook English pub. In summer, stroll into one of the tiered beer gardens at the front and back, then pop into the pub's wonderful farm shop next door. Fun, friendly and charismatic.

George & Dragon
Speldhurst

"We try to buy from people not companies,'" says Julian Leefe-Griffiths – before launching into an exuberant description of the produce he finds in the local woods and the beers that come from microbrewers Westerham. Meat, game and vegetables are local and often organic; cheeses come mostly from Sussex. Julian realises that rescuing one of the oldest inns in southern England from years of mediocrity is no easy task, but he's made a fine start; there are plush new loos, a smart front terrace, a lovely rear garden. It's a characterful old pub, too, worth popping into for its massive flagstones, doors, inglenook and beams. But chef Max Leonard's gutsy food is the biggest treat: crisp, salty sea purslane cooked with creamy soft scallops, wood sorrel with seared local wood pigeon breast, smoked eel on toast with poached duck egg and confit garlic, Valrhona chocolate tart. The atmosphere is easy, the staff friendly, and Chiddinstone Castle and Penshurst Place are delightfully close by.

directions	Off B2188, 1.5 miles from Penshurst.
meals	12pm-2.30pm; 6pm-9.30pm; 12pm-7pm Sun. Main courses £7.95-£12.95; set menu £19.95 & £24.95 Fri & Sat.
closed	3pm-6pm. Open all day Sat & Sun.

directions	In centre of village opposite church.
meals	12pm-3pm (4pm Sun). Main courses £9.50-£15.50; bar meals £5.50-£9.50.
closed	Open all day.

	Pierce Adkin Spotted Dog, Smarts Hill, Penshurst TN11 8EE
tel	01892 870253

	Julian Leefe-Griffiths George & Dragon, Speldhurst Hill, Speldhurst, Tonbridge TN3 0NN
tel	01892 863125
web	www.speldhurst.com

map: 5 entry: 259

map: 5 entry: 260

The Hare
Langton Green

As you negotiate the green and the surrounding roads in the quest for somewhere to park, you'd be forgiven for thinking The Hare is hardly Kent's best-kept secret. Don't be put off. The feel inside is stylish and relaxed and the food among the best in the area. Large, light rooms create marvellous eating areas, with gleaming, well-spaced tables on polished floorboards, and character from old prints, paintings, books – and a collection of chamber pots dangling over broad doorways! The blackboard menu has pub classics such as steak and ale pie with braised cabbage and good sandwiches (crab, avocado and lemon mayonnaise), plus more ambitious dishes like shoulder of lamb with red wine sauce, and slow-roast belly-pork with dauphinoise potato. Cheerful staff dispense Greene King Abbot Ale and guest beers such as Ruddles County and Archers. Wine is taken seriously too; the well-balanced wine list has 17 by the glass.

The Swan at the Vineyard
Lamberhurst

Real ale, real flowers, real food and real English wines – from Lamberhurst, naturally. A complete remodelling in 2005 has made the most of the building's 15th-century origins (low ceilings, beams, worn brick walls, boards and flagstones), added an extra dining room and moved and improved the previously cramped bar area. Vanessa and Sean Arnett have put in a lot of hard work to achieve this mellow look, incorporating slate walls, leather sofas and dining chairs, modern wrought-iron light fittings and lots of church candles. Folk are drawn by the friendly and relaxed atmosphere, the blazing winter fires, the local ales and wines, as well as the adventurous dishes: duo of meatballs with classic beef glaze and sautéed mushrooms; pork medallions with caramelised apple and brandy sauce on dauphinoise. The outside terrace overlooking the children's adventure playground is a summer treat.

directions	On A264 3 miles west of Tunbridge Wells.
meals	12pm-9.30pm (9pm Sun). Main courses £7.50-£19.50.
closed	Open all day.

Chris Little
The Hare,
Langton Green,
Tunbridge Wells TN3 0JA
tel   01892 862419
web   www.brunningandprice.co.uk

map: 5 entry: 261

directions	From A21 in Lamberhurst, B2100 for Wadhurst; right at x-roads.
meals	12pm-2.15pm; 6pm-9pm. Main courses £9-£18; bar meals from £6.
closed	3pm-5.30pm. Open all day Sat & Sun.

Sean & Vanessa Arnett
The Swan at the Vineyard,
The Down,
Lamberhurst TN3 8EU
tel   01892 890170
web   www.theswan.org

map: 5 entry: 262

The Three Chimneys
Biddenden

Ramble through tiny, unspoilt rooms –
all rough panelling, stripped brick, faded
paintwork, old flags, ancient timber and
several smouldering fires. During the
Napoleonic wars French officers
imprisoned nearby were allowed to
wander as far as the point where the
three paths – 'trois chemins' – met
(hence the name)… so, nothing to do
with chimneys at all (of which there are
only two). The cooking is modern, in
contrast to the rest, and tasty; try
parmesan and herb-crusted loin of lamb
followed by chocolate and praline torte
with pistachio ice cream. You may eat in
the bars, apart from the spartan public
one, and in the charming restaurant,
built 20 years ago to look like a barn
from reclaimed wood. In summer, tables
spill out onto a stylish and sheltered
patio. They get the balance just right here
between pub and restaurant – prop up
the bar for as long as you like. There's
farm cider and Adnams Best Bitter drawn
straight from the cask.

George Hotel
Cranbrook

It may look like a brasserie inside but The
George is this town's favourite local.
Relaxed, casual and understated, the
interior reveals pale wood and soft
colours to complement the building's
13th-century origins; magnificent is the
ancient staircase that divides the
brasserie/bar from the stunning beamed
and inglenooked restaurant. While a
network of local producers has been
assiduously encouraged to add a sense of
local identity, it is the consistently high
standards that keep the place afloat. The
kitchen moves deftly through a
repertoire of contemporary dishes such
as slow-roasted pork belly and sea bass
with salsa verde, with the odd pub classic
– beer-battered cod and chips,
homemade burgers – thrown in. Well
kept Harvey's and Adnams make a
matchless accompaniment to a Weald
smokery salmon platter or a thick-cut
sandwich filled with rare roast beef, and
the wines are as good.

directions	On A262 2 miles west of Biddenden.
meals	12pm-2pm (2.30pm Sun); 6.30pm-9.30pm (7pm-9pm Sun). Main courses £11.95-£18.95; bar snacks £3.95-£8.95.
closed	3pm-6pm (3.30pm-7pm Sun).

directions	On the main village street.
meals	12pm-3pm; 7pm-9.30pm. Main courses £8.50-£16.50; bar meals £4.50-£11.50.
closed	Open all day.

	Craig Smith
	The Three Chimneys,
	Hareplain Road,
	Biddenden TN27 8LW
tel	01580 291472

	Mark & Sarah Colley
	George Hotel,
	Stone Street,
	Cranbrook TN17 3HE
tel	01580 713348
web	www.thegeorgehotelkent.co.uk

map: 5 entry: 263

map: 5 entry: 264

Sun Hotel & Bar
Lancaster

The dramatically lit display of spirits tells the story: the old townhouse hotel has had a makeover. The mood is cheerful, the stone walls are rustically exposed, the furniture is new and chunky and the ground floor is spacious. Start the day with a brilliant breakfast: hen or duck eggs, and sausages and bacons cooked freshly to order. Or pop by for a lunchtime pint; the orginal bar carries eight hand-pulls and a superb selection of Lancastrian and Cumbrian beers. Continental beers include Liefman's Frambozen and Konig Ludwig and nearly all the wines are available by the glass. No evening meals other than early-evening cheese platters, but lunch, served by excellent young staff, could be locally smoked fish or tasty lamb stew. Super bedrooms, soundproofed and spread over three floors, have chic leather headboards, piles of pillows and cafetières for fresh coffee.

directions	Town centre; close to the castle.
meals	Breakfast 7.30-10.30 (8-11am Sat; 8.30-11am Sun); 12-3pm (3.30 Sun); cheeseboard 12-9pm (7pm Fri & Sat). Main courses £7-£9; sandwiches £5; cheeseboard from £6.
rooms	15: 13 doubles, 2 twins, 1 suite £65-£125. Singles £55-£85.
closed	Open all day.

See pp 30–57 for full list of pubs with rooms

Matt Jackson
Sun Hotel & Bar,
63-65 Church Street,
Lancaster LA1 1ET

tel	01524 66006
web	www.thesunhotelandbar.co.uk

map: 11 entry: 265

Bay Horse Inn
Forton

The Wilkinsons have been in the saddle for a number of years during which their son Craig has become an accomplished chef. Lancashire produces some marvellous ingredients and Craig takes full advantage of them in his modern British cooking; specialities include fish pie with cheese mash, Lancashire hotpot of Bowland lamb with pickled red cabbage, and roast Lune Valley venison with honey sauce. Although the Bay Horse considers itself to be a gastropub, there's a traditional pubby atmosphere and a range of cask beers. Interconnecting areas are comfortably furnished with a mix of old chairs and cushioned seating in bay windows, the dining room sparkles and the bar is warm and inviting with its low beams, soft lighting and open fire in winter. Gentle background jazz adds to the relaxed mood and the service is friendly and professional. Beware: the inn is easy to miss on the corner of a country lane.

directions	From M6 junc. 33; A6 for Preston, 2nd left; pub on right.
meals	12pm-2pm (3pm Sun); 7pm-9.15pm (6pm-8.30pm Sun). Main courses £12-£21.
closed	3pm-6.30pm & Mon all day.

Craig Wilkinson
Bay Horse Inn,
Forton,
Lancaster LA2 0HR

tel	01524 791204
web	www.bayhorseinn.com

map: 11 entry: 266

Mulberry Tree
Wrightington

The old wheelwright's workshop has become a freehouse and restaurant with a Wrightington-born chef who headed the kitchen at Le Gavroche. A big jewel in Lancashire's crown, it's a vast, rambling place with a fresh, modern look to match the cooking. There's a smart lounge with a long bar, a private dining room and an open-plan eating area – subtly lit, softly hued, warmly carpeted. Whether you order something simple like rump steak with pepper sauce from the bar, or book for a serious meal, you'll be impressed by the presentation and the finesse. Start with Tuscan white bean soup with pesto, move onto breast of wood pigeon with wild mushrooms and rich merlot sauce. Lush puddings include bread and butter pudding with apricot coulis, and rhum baba with chantilly cream. Chef-patron Mark Prescott's verve in the kitchen makes the Mulberry Tree one of the best gastropubs in the north-west.

The Eagle & Child
Bispham Green

There's an old-fashioned pubbiness here *and* a sense of style – an informality touched with zing. The candlelit main bar welcomes you in with rug-strewn flagged floors, well-used tables and chairs, hop-decked beams and open fire, and the other rooms are equally engaging – one hessian-carpeted with burgundy walls, the other cosy, with a cast-iron fireplace. Hand pumps line the bar (with beers from lesser-known brewers like Beartown Brewery), the shelves parade an army of malts, and the wine cellar has some fine offerings, including English fruit wines. The staff seem to enjoy themselves as much as the customers and the food has won awards: Lancashire hotpot, roast suckling pig with apple and cider gravy, cod with roasted garlic and potato cake. The pub's reputation lies, too, with its cask ales, and a weekend beer festival in May packs the place out with beers and beer buffs.

directions	M6 junc. 27; B5250 for Eccleston; 2 miles, on right.
meals	12pm-3pm; 6pm-9.30pm. 12pm-10pm Sat & Sun. Main courses £9.95-£18.50; bar meals £5.50-£14.95; Sunday roast £14.50 & £18.
closed	3pm-6pm. Open all day Sat & Sun.

	Mark Prescott Mulberry Tree, 9 Wrightington Bar, Wrightington, Wigan WN6 9SE
tel	01257 451400

map: 11 entry: 267

directions	From M6 junc. 27, A5209 for Parbold; right along B5246; left for Bispham Green. Pub in 0.5 miles.
meals	12pm-2pm; 5.30pm-8.30pm (9pm Fri & Sat); 12pm-8.30pm Sun. Main courses £10-£16.50; bar meals £3.75-£7.
closed	3pm-5.30pm. Open all day Sun.

	Martin Ainscough The Eagle & Child, Malt Kiln Lane, Bispham Green, Ormskirk L40 3SG
tel	01257 462297
web	www.ainscoughs.co.uk

map: 11 entry: 268

The Lunesdale Arms
Tunstall

A soft, wide, undulating valley, the Pennines its backdrop – this is the setting of The Lunesdale Arms. A traditional pub with a fresh, modern feel: Pimms in the summer, mulled wine in the winter, good ales and good cheer. Comfort is deep: big sofas and wood-burning stoves, cushioned settles, newspapers to browse and oil paintings to consider – even to buy. A big central bar separates drinkers (three local cask ales, whiskies and wines) from diners. Sit down to locally reared produce, home-baked bread and seasonal, often organic, vegetables at tables away from the bar. Chef Richard Price delivers wholesome food full of flavour – clam and mussel marinière with home-baked bread, roast belly pork stuffed with lemon, garlic and thyme with apple mash and caraway cabbage, damson Bakewell tart – and encourages children to have small portions. The Lunesdale is a great local for all ages, with a popular games room.

directions	M6 junc. 34; A683 for Kirkby Lonsdale.
meals	12pm-2pm (2.30pm Sat & Sun); 6pm-9pm. Main courses £8.50-£14.50; bar meals £4-£14.50.
closed	3pm-6pm (3.30pm-6pm Sat) & Mon all day.

Emma Gillibrand
The Lunesdale Arms,
Tunstall,
Kirkby Lonsdale LA6 2QN
tel　01524 274203
web　www.thelunesdale.co.uk

map: 12 entry: 269

The Inn at Whitewell
Whitewell

The owner was advised not to touch this inn with a bargepole... but you'll be hard-pressed to find anywhere better than this. The old deerkeeper's lodge sits just above the river Hodder with views across parkland to rising fells in the distance. Merchants used to stop by and fill up with wine, food and song before heading north through notorious bandit country; the hospitality remains every bit as good today and the most that will hold you up is a stubborn sheep. The long restaurant and an outside terrace drink in the view – which will only increase your enjoyment of venison with blackcurrant jam, Bowland lamb with minted pease pudding and red wine sauce, homemade ice creams and great wines, including their own well-priced Vintner's. In the bar, antiques, bric-a-brac, log fires, old copies of *The Beano*, fish and chips, warm crab cakes and local bangers. Marvellous.

directions	M6 junc. 31a; B6243 east through Longridge; follow signs to Whitewell for 9 miles.
meals	12pm-2pm; 7.30pm-9.30pm. Main courses £8-£13.75 (bar) £14-£23 (restaurant) ; bar meals from £3.65-£8.50.
closed	Open all day.

Charles Bowman
The Inn at Whitewell,
Whitewell,
Clitheroe BB7 3AT
tel　01200 448222
web　www.innatwhitewell.com

map: 12 entry: 270

Craven Heifer
Chaigley

You dream about walking into a place like this on a chilly autumn day after a yomp through damp Lancashire fields and the welcome is a warm as the wood-burning stove in the bar. Take your wellies off in the porch, flop into a battered leather sofa and browse the papers with a pint of Golden Trough brewed up the road. The glowing parquet plundered from a church in Liverpool, the undressed stone walls, the specials chalked up on boards and the jugs of fresh flowers – all create a sense of ease. Nick Warfe trained with Pauls Heathcote and Rankin, and locally sourced ingredients are thoughtfully prepared. Ham and Lancashire cheese risotto with rocket pesto arrives steaming and fragrant, with a good glass of wine from the impressive list. Polish it all off with pan-fried spotted dog with vanilla ice cream and you'll be ready to venture out into the rolling hills outside the door.

directions	M6 exit 31A Longridge; signs for Chipping (Trough of Bowland); before Chipping, right for Chaigley. Right at end, right again; 500 yds.
meals	12pm-2.30; 6pm-9pm (12pm-8pm Sun). Main courses £8.50-£16.50; set menu (Wed-Sat) £11 & £14; Sunday lunch £18.
closed	Mon & Tues. Open all day Sun.

Nick & Ali Wharf
Craven Heifer,
Chipping Road, Chaigley,
Clitheroe BB7 3LX
tel   01254 826215
web   www.cravenheiferchaigley.co.uk

map: 12 entry: 271

The Three Fishes
Mitton

The producers, suppliers and growers are the heroes of this venture, named and proclaimed on the back of every menu. Quite rightly – the region is a hotbed of food artisans. This 17th-century village pub in the lovely Ribble Valley reopened in 2004; under the auspices of Nigel Haworth of Michelin-starred Northcote Manor it is taking gastropubbery to a mouthwatering new level. The long whitewashed public house has been restyled in rustic-smart 21st-century fashion and is vast: up to 130 people inside, a further 60 out. Walls are pale brick, floors stone, furniture sober, lighting subtle and winter logs glow. Wines are gorgeous, local pints and real ciders are served and the food is generous and delicious. Lunchtime prawn sandwiches, buttered crumpet with crumbly Lancashire curd, slow-baked succulent pigs' trotters, hotpot from heather-reared lamb, orange and bitter chocolate pudding.

directions	Into Whalley, then B6246 signed Great Mitton (not Mitton).
meals	12pm-2pm; 6pm-9pm (5.30pm-9.30pm Sat); 12pm-8.30pm Sun. Main courses £8.50-£15.50; bar meals £3.50-£6.75.
closed	Open all day.

Nigel Haworth & Craig Bancroft
The Three Fishes,
Mitton Road, Mitton,
Whalley BB7 8PQ
tel   01254 826888
web   www.thethreefishes.com

map: 12 entry: 272

The Freemasons Arms
Wiswell

Nothing fazes Ian Martin. He cooks brilliantly, serves great ales, vintage cognacs and malt whisky, and must have one of the finest wine lists in the country. All this in a tiny pub in a village in Lancashire. Formerly three small cottages, one of which was a free masons' lodge, its small beamed bars are simply and freshly decorated in green, pink and white with not a flounce in sight – just fresh flowers and modern art. The cooking is equally contemporary, allowing the flavours and textures to speak for themselves. Smoked bacon and lentil soup followed by salmon fishcakes with homemade tartare sauce make for a fantastic value two-course lunch. Potted Goosnargh duck and Bowland ham comes with apple and ale chutney, wild Lune salmon with samphire and sorrel butter sauce. There are fine cheeses and the vintage clarets – some 120 of them – go back 30 years. Extraordinary.

Assheton Arms
Downham

Assheton is the family name of the Lords of Clitheroe and Downham is their village. It has remained splendidly preserved since the 16th century, its stone cottages strung out along a stream; not long ago it remodelled itself as Ormston in the BBC TV series *Born and Bred*. In the best traditions of country life, the pub stands opposite the church – it's the community's hub. The rambling, low-beamed bar bustles more often than not with both village regulars and hikers fresh from a walk up Pendle Hill. Diners drop by for the fresh oysters, the moules and frites, the pan-fried monkfish and Lancashire hotpot, and the rib-sticking puddings. The atmosphere of an old inn has been preserved, right down to the huge stone fireplace and the horse brasses on the walls. Sit at solid oak tables on wing-back settles and bask in the absence of electronic games. In summer the front terrace entices you out to its serene pastoral views.

directions	From A59, 2 miles south of Clitheroe, A671 to Blackburn. After 0.5 miles, 1st left to Wiswell.
meals	12pm-2pm; 6pm-9.30pm (12pm-8pm Sun). Main courses £8.95-£16.95.
closed	3pm-6pm, Mon & Tues all day. Open all day Sun.

directions	Off A59, 3 miles NE of Clitheroe.
meals	12-2pm (2.30pm Sun in winter); 7pm-9.30pm; 12pm-9pm Sun in summer. Main courses £8.50-£15.50.
closed	3pm-7pm. Open all day Sun in summer.

	Ian Martin
	The Freemasons Arms,
	8 Vicarage Fold,
	Wiswell,
	Whalley BB7 9DF
tel	01254 822218

	David Busby
	Assheton Arms,
	Downham,
	Clitheroe BB7 4BJ
tel	01200 441227
web	www.assheton-arms.co.uk

map: 12 entry: 273

map: 12 entry: 274

Lancashire

The Black Bull
Rimington

It looks normal but step inside: traditional rooms are filled with railway models and transport memorabilia. Unusual, yes, but carpeted, wallpapered, polished and comfortable. No jukebox – that would be too modern! – just mellow background music. Pop in for a sandwich and a pint of Theakston's Draught Bitter, or stay for a mustard glazed sirloin of beef; everyone's welcome, and nothing is too much trouble. There are a number of malt whiskies and some very good wines, while blackboards in the cosy, log-fired bar reveal that the food is taken most seriously. Chef Carl Spencer has an inventive approach to the fish that is delivered daily (smoked salmon parcel with scrambled egg and truffle, seared sea bass), his spotted spiced syrup sponge is legendary and there's an Express Lunch if you're in a hurry. No beer garden, but beautiful views at the front to Pendle Hill.

directions	In middle of Rimington village; signed from Chatburn or Gisburn on A59.
meals	12pm-3pm; 6.30pm-9.30pm. Food served all day Sat & Sun. Main courses £6.95-£15.
closed	3pm-6.30pm. Open all day Sat & Sun.

Neil Buckley
The Black Bull,
Rimington,
Clitheroe BB7 4DS
tel   01200 445220

map: 12 entry: 275

Lancashire

The Rams Head Inn
Denshaw

High on the moors between Oldham and Ripponden – you're on the border here – with glorious views, the inn is two miles from the motorway but you'd never know. Unspoilt inside and out, there's a authentic, old-farmhouse feel. The small rooms, cosy with winter log fires, are carpeted, half-panelled and beamed and filled with interesting memorabilia. Until recently beer was served straight from the cask; there's still an old sideboard behind the bar to remind you of former days. Blackboards announce a heart-warming selection of tasty and well-priced food cooked to order: game and venison in season, seafood specialities and great steaks. Even the bread and ice creams are homemade. A wonderfully isolated Lancashire outpost, staffed by people who care, and with a farm shop, deli and tea rooms. Well behaved children are very welcome – but watch the open fires!

directions	M62 junc. 22 for Oldham & Saddleworth; 2 miles on right.
meals	12pm-2.30pm; 6pm-10pm. 12pm-8.30pm Sun. Main courses £8.95-£17.95; set menu, 3 courses, £10.95; sandwiches £3.95-£7.95.
closed	2.30pm-6pm Mon-Sat, Sun from 8.30pm & Mon all day.

Mr G R Haigh
The Rams Head Inn,
Denshaw,
Saddleworth OL3 5UN
tel   01457 874802
web   www.ramsheaddenshaw.co.uk

map: 12 entry: 276

Lancashire

The Church Inn
Uppermill

Next to the church on the way to the moors – it's not easy to find. Julian Taylor brews their own Saddleworth beers and is involved in everything. At the top end of the long curved bar are a grand fire and some window tables; at the other end, a big log burner in an old fireplace, with a heavily framed mirror above. Seating is a mix of padded benches, settles, chairs and a pew named Hobson's Choice. There's a fine atmosphere: lofty beams, leaded windows, lamps on sills, nightlights on tables, brass plates, Staffordshire jugs, fresh flowers. The soft background music is entirely bearable. In the dining room with valley views the food is honest, unpretentious and good value; so are the beers. The inn is home to the world-famous Saddleworth Morris Men and several events take place here including the Rush Cart Festival on the August bank holiday weekend. A friendly place loved by all ages.

directions	Saddleworth signed from Oldham. From Uppermill go up New St for 1 mile. Pub on left, next to church.
meals	12pm-2.30pm; 5:30pm-9pm.12pm-9pm Sun. Main courses £5.95-£11.75.
closed	Open all day.

Julian & Christine Taylor
The Church Inn,
Church Lane,
Uppermill,
Saddleworth OL3 6LW
tel 01457 820902

map: 12 entry: 277

Leicestershire — Pub with rooms

The Queen's Head
Belton

Take a village pub by the scruff of its neck and renovate it from top to toe. The result: a cool, relaxed drinkers' bar, all leather sofas and low-slung tables, a bistro with an open fire and dining room of wood, suede and leather. Add bedrooms that have a similarly stylish feel and you have a well-nigh perfect coaching inn. The Weldons deserve applause for not losing sight of tradition: the Queen's Head serves its own beer from the local Wicked Hathern brewery, plus outstanding wines. Printed menus and blackboard dishes point to diverse ideas, from burgers and relish in the bar to roasted scallops with langoustine risotto, beef fillet with morel mushroom sauce, and a good value set menu in the restaurant. Watch out for the summer Real Ale and Gourmet Barbecue weekend, and the Champagne and Lobster night. Great staff, too.

directions	In Belton, just off B5234, 6 miles west of Loughborough.
meals	12pm-2.30pm (4pm Sun); 7pm-9.30pm (10pm Fri & Sat). Main courses £13.50-£19.50; bar meals £4-£9.50; set menu £12-£16; Sunday lunch £13 & £16.
rooms	6: 4 doubles, 2 twins £70-£100. Singles £65.
closed	3pm-7pm; Sun from 5pm.

See pp 30-57 for full list of pubs with rooms

Henry & Ali Weldon
The Queen's Head,
2 Long Street,
Belton LE12 9TP
tel 01530 222359
web www.thequeenshead.org

map: 8 entry: 278

The Cow & Plough
Oadby

A pub-restaurant housed in the former milking sheds of a working farm just outside Leicester. The Lounts founded it in 1989 and filled it with good beer and a hoard of brewery memorabilia: the two back bars are stuffed with period signs, mirrors and bottles. It later became an outlet for their range of Steamin' Billy ales (named after Elizabeth's Jack Russell who 'steamed' after energetic country pursuits). When the foot and mouth epidemic closed the farm's visitor centre, they established a restaurant there instead. Most of their dishes are made with local produce such as rib-eye steak with red wine, chestnut and thyme sauce and honey-glazed Tamworth ham. The pub has built up a great reputation, winning awards and becoming a place for shooting lunches; it's also popular with the Leicester rugby team supporters. And there's a conservatory with piano and plants and beams decked with dried hops.

The Baker's Arms
Thorpe Langton

A sleepy-village treasure with oodles of atmosphere beneath 16th-century thatch. A series of intimate little areas have been kitted out with cottagey scrubbed pine tables, antique pews and settles, paintings and prints on warm terracotta walls. The Baker's is more foodie than boozey though the pubbiness remains and if you're looking for a pint of Baker's Dozen you won't be disappointed. But most come for Kate Hubbard's first-rate cooking (do book) and use of impeccable produce. Chalked up daily on the boards are pan fried scallops with a honey, mustard and lemon dressing, confit of duck leg and breast with parsnip and apple compote, baked sea bass with spinach, mushrooms and prawn jus, white chocolate and raspberry trifle. Wines, too, are good, and may come mulled in winter. Great staff make the Baker's Arms close to perfect.

directions	On B667 north of town centre & A6.
meals	12pm-3pm (5pm Sun); 6pm-9pm. No food Sun & Mon eves. Main courses £7.75-£16.95; Sunday lunch £14.95 & £16.95; bar meals £4.95-£10.95.
closed	3pm-5pm. Open all day Sat & Sun.

Barry Lount
The Cow & Plough,
Stoughton Farm Park, Oadby,
Leicester LE2 2FB
tel   0116 272 0852
web   www.steamin-billy.co.uk

map: 8 entry: 279

directions	On A6, 10 miles south of Leicester.
meals	12pm-2.30pm Sat & Sun; 6.30pm-9.30pm (6pm-9.30pm Sat). Main courses £11.50-£18.50.
closed	All day Mon, Tues-Fri lunch, Sat 2.30pm-6pm & Sun eve.

Kate Hubbard
The Baker's Arms,
Thorpe Langton,
Market Harborough LE16 7TS
tel   01858 545201
web   www.thebakersarms.co.uk

map: 9 entry: 280

Leicestershire

The Old Barn
Glooston

This is in prime hunting country and delightfully tranquil – old stone cottages opposite; church and rectory next door. The lane itself, a dead-end, is variously named Andrew Lane, Cow Lane, Main Street, Gartree Road and Adelphi Row. And the Old Barn comes into sight. No hint of what lies inside. Gnarled oak timbers, a blackened range, walls in contemporary pastels and creams: enter a front bar where light lunches, old world wines and a pint of Greene King Abbot are served. A step down is the cellar restaurant, crisp with white linen, fresh flowers and real fire. Your chef is a well-travelled Australian who has brought his striking fusion and European cooking to Glooston. Only the freshest produce will do, be it tomato, mozzarella and basil bruschetta, or fillet of beef with celeriac and thyme confit, whisky and basil sauce. It's a concise menu prepared to order, and served by a friendly French staff.

directions	From B6047 at Tur Langton follow signs to Cranoe, then fork left after 1.5 miles to Glooston.
meals	12pm-2pm (4pm Sun); 6pm-9.30pm. No food Tues. Main courses £13.95-22.95; bar meals £5.95-£9.95.
closed	3pm-6pm.

Guy Oliver
The Old Barn,
Main Street,
Glooston,
Market Harborough LE16 7ST
tel   01858 545215

map: 9 entry: 281

Leicestershire

Fox & Hounds
Knossington

Open all day for Adnams and Marston's Pedigree (rare hours for such a rural spot) and with quiz nights and cards for the regulars, this is one lively local. Brian Baker and his sister Clare Ellis are instrumental in having created a mood of warmth at this stylishly remodelled 17th-century boozer in upmarket Knossington. Two fires are lit in winter, ceiling spots sparkle, there are soft contemporary colours and simple scrubbed pine tables (four in the bar, five in the dining room). Chef Brian's background includes a stint as personal chef to Sir Elton John, and his philosophy demands good quality ingredients and precision: there's rack of lamb (for two) with dauphinoise potatoes, mint and onion sauce, roast belly pork with braised red cabbage, hot chocolate pudding with crème fraîche, and traditional roasts on Sundays. And don't forget the Colston Bassett stilton.

directions	Through Oakham on A606, take Cold Overton Road after r'way crossing; on for 4 miles, pub on the left.
meals	12pm-2.30pm; 7pm-9.30pm. No food Mon or Sun eve. Main courses £9.95-£31; bar meals £4.95-£6.95.
closed	Open all day.

Claire Ellis & Brian Baker
Fox & Hounds,
6 Somerby Road, Knossington,
Melton Mowbray LE15 8LY
tel   01664 454676
web   www.foxandhounds.biz

map: 9 entry: 282

Tollemache Arms
Buckminster

There is cross-pollination in this neck of the woods and it emanates from Hambleton Hall. Mark Gough went from there to Hart's in Nottingham and so to chef-patron at this imposing Victorian inn in a country estate village on the Lincolnshire border. Awards have been won for the food but make no mistake, the Tollemache is an inn. As Mark says in his book of recipes, 'If we have a dozen ladies lunching, it's a restaurant; if the locals are filling the bar on a Friday night it's a pub. Often it's both.' Real ales are from Grainstore in Oakham and much of what appears on the menu arrives via local shoots, like seared hare loin with figs steeped in mulled wine. Or their take on fast food: pigeon breast on toast with onion marmalade and a sauce of port, red wine and stock. This is served in a restaurant/brasserie atmosphere with modern works of art, hide sofas, polished floorboards and tables set well apart.

Red Lion Inn
Stathern

Quirky stylishness and cheerful service. The rambling Red Lion feels like a home, with its books and papers, deep sofas and open fires; gamekeepers frequent the flagstoned bar. A trusted network of growers and suppliers fills the kitchen with game from the Belvoir estate, cheeses from the local dairy, fruits and vegetables from nearby farms. Menus are on blackboards dotted around, with a choice that leaps between fashion and tradition: potted prawns and melba toast; village-made sausages with mustard mash and onion rings; pan-fried halibut with squid ink linguine, olives, pine nuts and saffron dressing; warm chocolate and pecan pie with apple and cinnamon ice cream. The set Sunday lunch is fantastic value. The wine list is imaginative; beers include village-brewed Brewsters Bonnie and children have homemade lemonade. The outdoor play area will please them, too.

directions	Off A607 north east of Melton Mowbray; through Stathern; past Plough; pub signed on left.
meals	12pm-2pm (4pm Sun); 7pm-9.30pm (6pm Sat). Main courses £10.50-£17.50; Sunday lunch £16.50.
closed	3pm-6pm & Sun from 6.30pm. Open all day Fri & Sat.

directions	4 miles west of A1 on B676 towards Melton Mowbray.
meals	12pm-2pm; 6.30pm-9pm Main courses £9.50-£14; set menu, 2-3 courses, £10-£14.
closed	3pm-6pm, Sun eve & Mon all day.

Mark Gough
Tollemache Arms,
48 Main Street, Buckminster,
Melton Mowbray NG33 5SA
tel   01476 860007
web   www.thetollemachearms.com

map: 9 entry: 283

Ben Jones & Sean Hope
Red Lion Inn,
Red Lion Street,
Stathern LE14 4HS
tel   01949 860868
web   www.theredlioninn.co.uk

map: 9 entry: 284

Lincolnshire

Wig & Mitre
Lincoln

When army life ended, Michael and Valerie decided to open a pub in Lincoln. Here they still are, some three decades on, sandwiched between the cathedral and the courts. (They could have called it the Mitre & Wig: though lawyers dine here, the first pint was drawn by the Bishop of Lincoln.) Downstairs has a French café feel: old oak boards, exposed stone, sofas to the side; a civilised place for late breakfast and the papers. Upstairs, a cosy series of dining rooms and an open fire. In the Seventies it was hard to find decent food in a pub, let alone one in Lincoln. Valerie's kitchen became one of the most exciting in the area, serving a mix of dishes – braised blade of beef with mustard mash, pan-fried pork fillet with black pudding and celeriac purée – strongly influenced by French and Mediterranean cooking. Was this the first gastropub? The regular visits of visiting Crown Court judges have, of course, nothing to do with the late supper licence.

directions	On Steep Hill leading down from Castle.
meals	8am–11pm. Main courses £9.95–£21.95.
closed	Open all day.

Michael & Valerie Hope
Wig & Mitre,
30-32 Steep Hill,
Lincoln LN2 1TL
tel   01522 535190
web   www.wigandmitre.com

map: 9 entry: 285

Lincolnshire   Pub with rooms

Brownlow Arms
Hough-on-the-Hill

Standing proudly in the centre of a hilltop village, this magnificent building is said to have been the servants' quarters to the Manor. Inside, winged Queen Anne chairs in autumnal hues invite you to settle in by the open fire amid deep rich oak beams and polished panelling. Regulars sup Marstons Burton ale as chatter flows around the central bar. In the intimate restaurant, the food, revealing a French classical influence, is accomplished as befits such a setting – soufflés, foie gras, duck confit. It's blowy up here with idyllic open countryside all around but there is a sheltered, landscaped terrace for a quiet pint and an early supper. The mood of baronial elegance continues into four truly superb bedrooms above. Note that this is a pub for grown-ups only – and that when using the car park you don't park in the neighbours' drive!

directions	On A607 6 miles north of Grantham.
meals	6.30pm–9.30pm Tues-Sat; Sun lunch 12pm-2pm. Main courses £10.50–£21.
rooms	4 doubles £96. Singles £65.
closed	Tues-Sat lunch, Sun eve & Mon all day.

See pp 30–57 for full list of pubs with rooms

Paul & Lorraine Willoughby
Brownlow Arms,
High Road, Hough-on-the-Hill,
Grantham NG32 2AZ
tel   01400 250234
web   www.thebrownlowarms.com

map: 9 entry: 286

Lincolnshire Pub with rooms

Houblon Inn
Oasby

The word 'civilised' springs to mind, as befits the pedigree of the place; the pub is named after John Houblon, first governor of the Bank of England and honoured on the back of the £50 note. Hollyhocks round the door and pretty sash windows greet you; low beams, stone walls and cosy bar await. 'Houblon' also means 'hop' in Flemish; ale-lovers will not be disappointed. Belly Dance, Oldershaw Old Boy and Surrender may take your fancy as you perch at the bar and scan the simple yet stylish menu – moules marinières; lamb rump with roast shallots; apple and pear crumble. Owners Eddie and Hazel make this pub – passionate, gentle people who left 'the smoke' years ago and thrive on the business. Cosy, well-equipped rooms await in a converted barn across the courtyard. In the heart of a conservation village, the Houblon Inn is honest, unaffected and intelligently run.

directions	From A1, B6703 to Ancaster; right to Welby, follow road to Oasby.
meals	12-2pm; 6.30-9.30. No food Sun eve. Main courses £6.95-£16.95; bar meals £4.50-£9.95.
rooms	4: 3 doubles, 1 twin £60-£70. Singles £40-£45.
closed	2pm-6.30pm (3pm-7pm Sun) & Mon (open bank hol lunch).

See pp 30–57 for full list of pubs with rooms

Eddie Simmonds & Hazel Purvis
Houblon Inn,
Oasby,
Grantham NG32 3NB
tel   01529 455215
web   www.houblon-inn.co.uk

map: 9 entry: 287

Lincolnshire

The Chequers Inn
Woolsthorpe-by-Belvoir

A coaching inn for 200 years, the Chequers has built a reputation as a top dining pub in recent years. There's contemporary luxury and deep comfort, a flurry of open fireplaces, three dining areas and two bars, rug-strewn floors, heavy oak tables, leather sofas, linen drapes and Farrow & Ball colours. You have four ales on handpump, 24 wines by the glass, 50 whiskies, several fruit pressés and a humidor on the bar. Robust dishes – clam, squid and salmon risotto, calves' liver with mash, bacon and onion marmalade, chocolate tart with bitter orange sorbet – taste as good as they look, the weekday evening menu is a steal (three courses, £15) and small helpings are available. In summer the pub hosts the village cricket team on what must be one of the slopiest pitches in England. The Vale of Belvoir and its grand castle are as beautiful as they sound.

directions	Off A52, west of Grantham.
meals	12pm-2.30pm (4pm Sun); 7pm-9.30pm (6pm-8.30pm Sun in summer). Main courses £8.95-£15; bar meals £4.95-£8.95; Sunday lunch £10.95; set lunch £11.50 & £15.
closed	3pm-5.30pm; Sun eve in winter. Open all day Sat (& Sun in summer).

Justin & Joanne Chad
The Chequers Inn,
Main St, Woolsthorpe-by-Belvoir,
Grantham NG32 1LU
tel   01476 870701
web   www.chequers-inn.net

map: 9 entry: 288

The Manners Arms
Knipton

The Duke and Duchess of Rutland are the landlords of this village inn, a pint's throw from the family seat at Belvoir Castle; it's their local too. The pub was originally built as a hunting lodge and so is no stranger to playing host to an array of guests. The bar is rustic rural with Windsor chairs, log fire and polished boards; the restaurant is more intimate with swagged floral fabrics and deep red walls; and the pristine bedrooms, each with its own décor, are smartly feminine. Menus are seasonal, the produce sourced locally, much of it from the estate, and children get half portions at half price: brilliant. Fancy an Irish jig? There's often live music in the bar on Thursday evenings, and the Duke and Duchess may lead the dancing. The conservatory and sun terrace make delightful spots for afternoon tea.

directions	From A607 Grantham to Leicester road, follow Knipton signs from Croxton Kerrial.
meals	12pm-3pm; 6pm-9pm; 12pm-9pm Sat (8pm Sun). Main courses £11.95-£19.50; bar meals £7.50-£12.50; lunch, 2 courses, £10; Sunday lunch £12.50
rooms	10: 8 doubles, 2 singles £55-£80.
closed	Open all day.

See pp 30–57 for full list of pubs with rooms

Alex Grainger
The Manners Arms,
Croxton Road, Knipton,
Grantham NG32 1RH
tel   01476 879222
web   www.mannersarms.com

map: 9 entry: 289

Collyweston Slater
Stamford

Richard Graham and Nikki Musson have added the Collyweston Slater to their growing portfolio (see the Old Pheasant and the Jackson Stops). With a spacious, open-plan and uncluttered interior and fresh tasteful bedrooms above, the transformation from rundown village boozer into relaxed country inn is a resounding success. At heart it's a local, keeping its log fires, wooden tables, stone and planked floors, and excellent beers from Everard. But food is a major draw, and Richard's tried-and-tested formula of locally sourced produce and simplicity of style works a treat. On a short menu backed up by chalkboard specials, the repertoire runs from homebaked ham with egg and chips to pan-fried scallops with rocket, parmesan and sauce vièrge. If you want to eat in more sedate surroundings, book a table in the restaurant; if the weather's fine, head for the terrace — and round it all off with a game of pétanque.

directions	On A43 5 miles SW of Stamford.
meals	12pm-2pm (3pm Sun); 6.30pm-9pm. Main courses £9-£20.
rooms	5: 3 doubles, 1 family, 1 single £60-£120.
closed	3pm-5.30pm & Sun from 4pm.

See pp 30–57 for full list of pubs with rooms

Richard Graham
Collyweston Slater,
87-89 Main Road, Collyweston,
Stamford PE9 3PQ
tel   01780 444288
web   www.collywestonslater.co.uk

map: 9 entry: 290

London

The Seven Stars
Holborn

Nudging the backdoor of the Royal Courts of Justice, the Seven Stars is something of a barristers' den. Here since 1602, it was originally the haunt of Dutch sailors, and named after the seven provinces of the Netherlands; having survived the Great Fire it's been here longer even than the Courts. The pub's crumbling antiquity was put in order a few years ago by Roxy Beaujolais – proprietor, head cook and *Full On Food* television presenter. The glorious narrow bar has hung on to its boarded floors, low beams, old mirrors and narrow wood settles; framed vintage legal film posters bedeck red walls. The menu is short and bistro-like with original flourishes – chargrilled boned quail with polenta, dill-cured herring and potato salad, baked sea bream, an elegant club sandwich – plus two house beers, and a very decent selection of wines. Now a tiny former legal-wig shop has become the pub's new 'west wing' – but get here early if you want a seat!

directions	Nearest tubes: Temple; Chancery Lane.
meals	12pm-3pm; 5pm-10pm. 12pm-9pm Sat & Sun. Main courses £8-£10.50.
closed	Open all day.

Roxy Beaujolais
The Seven Stars,
53 Carey Street,
Holborn WC2A 2JB
tel   020 7242 8521

map: 4 entry: 291

London

The Westbourne
Notting Hill

Come to see and be seen! Sebastian Boyle and Olly Daniaud took the place some years ago and gave it a thorough going over. Westbourne Park Villas promptly became the trendiest place in England and it's worth arriving early… 11am perhaps. London's beau monde amasses throughout the day at this shabby-chic gastropub, keen to dish out for Belgian beers and scrummy food. In the main bars is a collection of old tables and chairs, with some lush sofas at the back; walls spill over with posters, photos and original art. The terrace at the front with its gas heaters is an all-year drinking spot – and just about handles the overflow. Cooking is robust modern British and the ingredients used are the freshest: oysters, game terrine with onion marmalade, pot-roasted pheasant, Old Spot pork chop with butter beans, chorizo, black cabbage and red wine sauce. All sorts love it here – including those who've been coming for 30 years.

directions	Nearest tube: Westbourne Park.
meals	12.30pm-3pm (12pm-3.30pm Sat); 7pm-10pm. Sun 12pm-9pm. Main courses £8-£14.
closed	Open all day.

Robert Proni
The Westbourne,
101 Westbourne Park Villas,
Notting Hill W2 5ED
tel   020 7221 1332
web www.thewestbourne.com

map: 4 entry: 292

London — Pub with rooms

Portobello Gold
Notting Hill

A gastro-hotel off Ladbroke Grove – bar, restaurant, internet café and fun place to stay. Sit out on the pavement in wicker chairs and watch the trendies stroll by. Or hole up at the bar with an organic lager and a plate of Cajun jumbo prawns. In the bar are tiled floors, an open fire, monthly exhibitions of photography and live music on Sunday evenings until ten. At the back, the restaurant with its retractable glass roof feels like a comfortable jungle. Dine to the sweet song of canaries on Aberdeen Angus steaks, delicate seafood dishes and four styles of oysters. There's a large bar menu and all-day Sunday lunch. Linda writes about wine, so you'll drink well too. Redecorated bedrooms have good beds, 'wet' rooms and flat-screen TVs, and the roof terrace apartment comes with a foldaway four-poster and small putting green! Broadband is free to hotel guests.

directions	Nearest tube: Notting Hill Gate. Follow signs for Portobello Market.
meals	10am-10pm (from 12pm Sun). Main courses £5-£12.95; set menu £20.50.
rooms	8: 6 twin/doubles, 1 suite, 1 apartment £60-£180.
closed	Open all day.

See pp 30–57 for full list of pubs with rooms

	Michael Bell & Linda Johnson-Bell Portobello Gold, 95-97 Portobello Road, Notting Hill W11 2QB
tel	020 7460 4910
web	www.portobellogold.com

map: 4 entry: 293

London

Ladbroke Arms
Holland Park

The warm glow emanating from the sage sash windows is enough to tempt anyone into the Ladbroke Arms. Cream-painted and ginger hessian walls, benches plump with autumnal-hued cushions, long shiny tables, paintings, books, good wines and beers to please enthusiasts: Fuller's London Pride, Greene King IPA and Abbot Ale, Adnams Bitter. The intimate Ladbroke takes its food seriously, too, the chef buying cheese twice weekly from a touring supplier and placing orders with a fishing fleet every day. The bar sparkles with olive oils, vinegars and bottled fruit; in the raised restaurant area, stylish diners savour richly flavoured dishes such as chorizo and chickpea broth, warm salad of pork confit with salsa verde and rib-eye steak with green peppercorn, garlic and herb butter. Sunday roasts are a favourite among those who live close by; the hot chocolate fondant pudding is legendary. Sup under the parasols in summer as Notting Hillbillies smooch by.

directions	Nearest tubes: Notting Hill Gate; Holland Park.
meals	12pm-2.30pm (3pm Sat & Sun); 7pm-9.45pm. Main courses £9.50-£15.50.
closed	Open all day.

	J Shubrati Ladbroke Arms, 54 Ladbroke Road, Holland Park W11 3NW
tel	020 7727 6648
web	www.capitalpubcompany.com

map: 4 entry: 294

Havelock Tavern
Shepherds Bush

It burnt down in 2005, reopened in 2006 and now it's better than ever. Jamie Oliver's favourite pub is special on two counts: it's a proper boozer and a great food pub. So passionate is Jonny Haughton about food that the menu changes twice daily and the cookbooks (signed copies) are displayed by the bar. No music, no fuss, just plain floorboards and tables squeezed around the main bar, luscious smells from the hatch and a happy, noisy, friendly crowd. When pubs are this popular service can be slow but waiting is no hardship here. Settle in with a pint of fragrant Flowers or an aromatic Côtes du Tarn, order from the board, start on the crusty homemade bread and prepare for some of the freshest, most flavoursome food in London. They do pancetta, potato and rosemary soup, Thai green tiger prawn curry with coriander and greens, chocolate brownies, English cheeses. It's as cheap as chips (rather good ones) and the only downside is it's cash or cheque only.

Paradise by Way of Kensal Green
Kensal Rise

The name was poached from G K Chesterton. Locals may have been taken aback when the arty bar first opened; now the area is full of trendies who little realise that The Paradise – all fairy lights and candles, background jazz and blues – stands on the site of the oldest pub in Brent. A statue of a fallen angel on the wall stares down in surprise on the battered reproduction Regency sofas, wrought-iron garden tables and chairs, and vast palm fronds growing in even vaster planters. The bar itself is small and not the most comfortable but there's still a pubby feel. The place doesn't take itself too seriously in spite of attracting the odd C-list celebrity; pop in for a pint of real ale and to look at the papers, or stay for a meal (must book). The menu is modern European with an oriental twist and the food extremely good: Thai green curry, penne with grilled aubergine, artichoke hearts, tomatoes and black olives, beef fillet with peppercorn sauce. A great place to spend a Sunday.

directions	Nearest tubes: Shepherds Bush; Hammersmith.
meals	12.30pm-2.30pm (3pm Sun); 7pm-10pm (9.30pm Sun). Main courses £6.50-£12.
closed	Open all day.

directions	Nearest tube: Kensal Green.
meals	12pm-4pm; 7pm-11pm; 12pm-9pm Sun. Main courses £9-£15.
closed	Open all day.

	Jonny Haughton Havelock Tavern, 57 Masbro Road, Shepherds Bush,
tel	020 7603 5374
web	www.thehavelocktavern.co.uk

	Paul & Sarah Halpin Paradise by Way of Kensal Green, 19 Kilburn Lane, Kensal Rise W10 4AE
tel	020 8969 0098

map: 4 entry: 295

map: 4 entry: 296

The Scarsdale
Kensington

We can be grateful to the French builder who believed Napoleon would invade and built The Scarsdale as living quarters for the French army. The immaculate Edwardes Square could only have been built by the French. This is a delightful little pub with a summer terrace of hanging baskets and bags of Victorian character. The old stained glass, dark panelling and burgundy walls provide a distinguished foil for old paintings in heavily gilded frames and various empty magnums of champagne, while the happy hum of drinkers flows from cosy corners as easily as the ales. Fabulous smells emanate from the kitchen hatch heralding the arrival of Aberdeen Angus rib-eye steak with sauce béarnaise, expertly followed by hot chocolate pudding. Eat in the busy bar or in the swagged dining room; sit in the garden and feel you're in the country. You could happily go on a first date here, or bring the parents.

directions	Nearest tube: High Street Kensington.
meals	12pm-10pm (9.30pm Sun). Main courses £8.95-£15.95; bar meals £3.95-£7.95.
closed	Open all day.

Ray & Sarah Dodgson
The Scarsdale,
23a Edwardes Square,
Kensington W8 6HE
tel   020 7937 1811

map: 4 entry: 297

Churchill Arms
Kensington

It's hard to say which comes first in the popularity stakes, the publican or the pub: Gerry O'Brien is an influential figure and this is a terrific pub. The Churchill is not only a shrine to the great prime minster but to Gerry's collection of memorabilia and his irrepressible Irish humour. To the left of the counter in the bar – cosy with open fire – is Chamber Lane (115 chamber pots suspended from the ceiling) while the walls of the leafy, glass-roofed Thai restaurant – once, unbelievably, a garage – display his prized butterflies. Never mind the tourists; come for great Guinness and beers, oriental feasts that don't break the bank, bags of atmosphere and a big dollop of tradition. On the annual celebration of Sir Winston's birthday unsuspecting drinkers are amazed to see everyone dressed in 40s style; sausage and mash can be bought for a shilling and the evening's takings go to the Cabinet War Office Museum. You have been warned!

directions	Nearest tube: High Street Kensington.
meals	11am-10pm (12pm-9.30pm Sun). Main courses £6.
closed	Open all day.

Gerry O'Brien
Churchill Arms,
119 Kensington Church Street,
Kensington W8 7LN
tel   020 7727 4242

map: 4 entry: 298

The Anglesea Arms
South Kensington

The raised heated terrace, historic lamp posts, wooden benches and hanging baskets are a temptation for any passer-by. And one can't help wondering whether Dickens, who lived at No 11, and Lawrence, at No 9, were similarly drawn. Original panelling, etched glass, dark floral wallpaper, heavy velvet curtains and scrubbed wooden tables – it's wonderfully, traditionally cosy. Settle down to a pint of Adnams or browse the Sunday papers over creamy hot chocolate. The little restaurant downstairs, away from the lively main bar, is a quiet snug in which to savour traditional English cooking. Daily lunch and dinner menus, built around fresh and local supplies, list crab, chilli, parsley and garlic linguine, aged club steak with garlic and rosemary butter, battered haddock with homemade chips and pea purée, and hearty roasts on Sundays. Puddings are equally down-to-earth – apple and plum crumble, bread and sticky toffee pudding with caramel sauce. Deeply, comfortingly English.

Swag & Tails
Knightsbridge

Hidden down a pretty mews in one of the smartest parts of town, the little whitewashed pub with black shutters and well-clipped topiary is an easy walk – even in your Manolos – from the Harvey Nichols-Harrods drag. Escape the crowds and rest weary feet in the warm, yellow-and-blue interior where wooden floors and swagged curtains make a fresh and glamorous alternative to the heavy trimmings of your usual Knightsbridge pub. The attractive tiled conservatory at the back – less noisy than the main bar – is a delightful spot in which to tuck into seared king scallops with lemon dill sauce or roast venison with crushed sweet potatoes. The food is stylish, modern and very good. Staff are full of smiles and, if it takes an explorer to find this little place, the wonderful photograph of Nare's Arctic expedition of 1875 – a present from landlady Annemaria to her husband – is a fitting first reward for your perseverance.

directions	Nearest tube: South Kensington.
meals	12pm-3pm (5pm Sat & Sun); 6.30pm-10pm (6pm-10pm Sat, 6pm-9.30pm Sun). Main courses £7.95-£15.95.
closed	Open all day.

Jenny Podmore
The Anglesea Arms,
15 Selwood Terrace,
South Kensington SW7 3QG
tel   020 7373 7960
web   www.capitalpubcompany.com

map: 4 entry: 299

directions	Nearest tube: Knightsbridge.
meals	12pm-3pm; 6pm-10pm. Main courses £10.95-£15.95; bar meals £5.25-£9.95.
closed	Open all day. Closed Sat & Sun.

Annemaria Boomer-Davies
Swag & Tails,
10-11 Fairholt Street,
Knightsbridge SW7 1EG
tel   020 7584 6926
web   www.swagandtails.com

map: 4 entry: 300

The Grenadier
Knightsbridge

Down a cobbled alley on the Grosvenor estate, the tiny Grenadier is unmissable with its fanfare of patriotic paintwork, tumbling flowers and sentry box — a magnet for tourists and cameras. Uneven steps lead to a charismatic interior with a military theme, a reflection of this little watering hole's past. Originally the Duke of Wellington's officers' mess, it later became a popular place for King George IV to enjoy a pint; later it was frequented by Madonna. The dimly-lit Mess Bar, with smouldering coal fire, is stuffed with memorabilia: gleaming breast plates, swords and bugles. Behind, in the restaurant, squeeze in and settle down to beef Wellington or fish and chips at battle-themed bench seats and tables dressed in starched linen. In September, the ghost of an officer — accidentally flogged to death after cheating at cards — returns to haunt the place, while the infamous Bloody Marys are best sampled on Sundays, from a specially erected bar. A small place with a big heart.

The Thomas Cubitt
Belgravia

This pub could be a metaphor for Belgravia itself: tasteful and well-upholstered. The handsome ground-floor bar has high ceilings, oak-block floors and polished tables, a bit of panelling thrown in for good measure, and floor-to-ceiling windows opening onto tables in the street. A well-heeled crowd is drawn by the classic, sophisticated, country-house feel, the real ales, the fine wines, and the kitchen, which puts more thought into what it produces than many a full-blown restaurant. In the bar is a reassuring selection of pub favourites — all-organic beef burgers, grilled sausages with roasted red onion gravy and buttery mash — while the food in the very elegant, white-clad dining room upstairs is fiercely modern: roasted wood pigeon with smoked puy lentils; sea bass fillet with creamed wild mushrooms, bacon and chicory. It's always full, and the friendliness of the staff, even under pressure, is a pleasure.

directions	Nearest tube: Hyde Park Corner.
meals	12pm-2.30pm. 12pm-9.30pm Sat & Sun. No food Mon-Fri eve. Main courses £7.95-£16.95; bar meals £4.95-£9.95.
closed	Open all day.

Cynthia Weston
The Grenadier,
18 Wilton Row,
Knightsbridge SW1X 7NR
tel   020 7235 3074

map: 4 entry: 301

directions	Nearest tubes: Victoria; Sloane Square.
meals	12pm-10pm (Sun 9.30pm). Main courses £8.50-£13.50; bar meal from £6.
closed	Open all day.

Reservations
The Thomas Cubitt,
44 Elizabeth St,
Belgravia SW1W 9PA
tel   020 7730 6060
web   www.thethomascubitt.co.uk

map: 4 entry: 302

The Builders Arms
Chelsea

You wouldn't expect such an exquisite little pub in the back streets off the King's Road. Enter and be seduced: the country-living-room feel is so enticing you'd happily move in. Settle down to a sauvignon or a pint of London Pride to a background of large puffy armchairs, low table lamps, walls in soft greens and creams and a ruby-red snug behind the bar. 'Never trust a builder without a tattoo' reads the sign on the wall, but the people here (and their pooches) are as immaculate as the interior. The Builders is a stylish pub, even if labelling the loos 'Builders' and 'Ballerinas' is a touch twee, and the food is delicious modern British well presented: pea and ham soup, roast salmon and basil risotto, and peppered sirloin steak with wilted spinach, mash and pepper sauce. The area is a shoppers' dream – but avoid the Builders on Friday lunchtimes: it's packed!

Chelsea Ram
Chelsea

A quiet residential street off the Lots Road seems an unlikely place to find a corner pub bursting with bonhomie. It used to be a junk shop; now the fine arched shop windows with etched glass are complemented by soft and subtle sage green and terracottas, tongue-and-groove cladding, a dark green wooden bar and colourful local art. A carpeted area to the back has small alcoves, soft lighting and shelves of thumbed books – an intimate spot in which to be treated to some enticing food. Salmon fishcakes with crab and citrus bisque, perhaps, or confit duck leg on roasted garlic mash and braised red cabbage, followed by sticky toffee and banana pudding with butterscotch sauce. The scrubbed wooden tables are a great place for lively card games (please bring your own) over coffee. Close to the large storage depot of Bonhams the auctioneers, this popular pub is well worth the few minutes' walk from the end of the King's Road.

directions	Nearest tubes: Sloane Square; South Kensington. Behind King's Road, between Sydney Street & Chelsea Green.
meals	12pm-2.30pm (3pm Sat, 4pm Sun); 7.15pm-10.15pm (11pm Sat). Main courses £7.50-£13.95.
closed	Open all day.

Rupert Clevely
The Builders Arms,
13 Britten Street,
Chelsea SW3 3TY

tel   020 7349 9040
web www.geronimo-inns.co.uk

map: 4 entry: 303

directions	Nearest tubes: Fulham Broadway; Sloane Square.
meals	12pm-3pm; 6.30pm-10pm (9.30pm Sun). Main courses £8.50-£13.90.
closed	Open all day.

James Symington
Chelsea Ram,
32 Burnaby Street,
Chelsea SW10 0PL

tel   020 7351 4008

map: 4 entry: 304

The Atlas
Fulham

Up high, golden letters on wooden panelling proclaim London Stout, Burton Bitter and mild ales. The Atlas is a great little place in which to delve into more modern brews: Fuller's London Pride, Caledonian Deuchars IPA, Adnams Broadside. A glazed wooden partition – a prop for the 'Wine of the Moment' blackboard – divides the bar in two. Other Thirties' features remain: floorboards, attractive black and white tiling around the foot of the bar and three brick fireplaces, two of which add a glow in winter. The third, its mantelpiece piled high with lemons and limes, has been converted into a serving hatch for fabulous dishes that change twice a day – grilled sardines and Tuscan sausages, pot-roast poussin; the wine list trumpets 24 wines by the glass. Doors lead to a walled garden where puffa-jacketed folk flock under the rain cover. In spite of its modest frontage on a residential street, the pub is next to a big Pay & Display; not hard to find.

The White Horse
Fulham

The pub on the green is reputed to have the best-kept beers in Europe: Mark Dorber's knowledge of real ale is the fruit of years working with the best tasters. The ever-changing list of guest ales above the log fire is within reading distance of some deeply comfortable sofas, while bar food is of the best sort, from ploughman's with unusual cheeses to fried bass with garlic mash. Even better, the menu suggests the best accompanying liquor; how about a crisp Bavarian wheat beer with your smoked salmon and scrambled eggs… a delicious alternative to a macon chardonnay. Inside, terracotta walls, slatted wooden blinds, lovingly polished pumps and beer memorabilia; outside, a big terrace overlooking the green and a Sunday barbecue. 'The Sloany Pony' may be a hotbed of Fulhamites but it's also a shrine to beer; come for the glorious two-day festival in November when enthusiasts gather from all over the globe.

directions	Nearest tube: West Brompton.
meals	12.30pm-3pm;
	7pm-10.30pm (10pm Sun).
	Main courses £9.50-£14;
	bar meals £4.50-£8.
closed	Open all day.

directions	Nearest tube: Parsons Green.
meals	Mon-Fri 12pm-3pm;
	6pm-10.30pm;
	snacks also available 3pm-6pm.
	Sat & Sun 11am-10.30pm.
	Main courses £9.75-£14.95;
	bar meals £4.50-£10.25.
closed	Open all day.

	George & Richard Manners
	& Toby Ellis
	The Atlas,
	16 Seagrave Road, Fulham SW6 1RX
tel	020 7385 9129
web	www.theatlaspub.co.uk

map: 4 entry: 305

	Mark Dorber
	The White Horse,
	1-3 Parson's Green,
	Fulham SW6 4UL
tel	020 7736 2115
web	www.whitehorsesw6.com

map: 4 entry: 306

The Idle Hour
Barnes

'The trouble with the Rat Race is, even if you win you're still a rat'. Thus reads the sign outside. The Idle Hour is a small haven – tucked away down a dark, secret alley – where rats don't race and time stands still. The hour can all too easily be idled away over a cocktail or Grolsch as you sit stylishly amid fat dripping candles and a bizarre mix of clocks set at different times. Stephen Thorp (relaxed owner/designer/barman/chef) has put as much thought and effort into the fresh, contemporary décor as the predominantly organic menu. Sundays at the Idle Hour are legendary; a delightful place to laze by the fire with a Bloody Mary before tucking into whole roast organic lamb served in the roasting pan and accompanied by utensils for a 'carve-it-yourself' meal. Just like home but without the washing up... with sticky toffee pudding to follow who knows what time you'll leave? A gentle, unpretentious and civilised place.

directions	Nearest rail: Barnes; Barnes Bridge.
meals	7pm-10.30pm (11.30pm Fri & Sat); 1pm-9pm Sun. Main courses £8.95-£12.95; bar meals £4.95-£8.95.
closed	Lunch. Open all day Sun.

Stephen Thorp
The Idle Hour,
62 Railway Side,
Barnes SW13 0PQ
tel   020 8878 5555
web   www.theidlehour.co.uk

map: 4 entry: 307

Cat's Back
Putney

Down a hidden backstreet, surrounded by new waterside development, an unexpected gem. You'll sense an appealing eccentricity here, as you sit among cosy-red walls, mismatched tables, African masks, a disco glitter ball, a portrait of Audrey Hepburn and all manner of flotsam and jetsam – presents from regulars and treasures picked up on the family's travels. It's mellow and fun and everyone and his hound pops by – locals, builders, business people. At night, moody candlelight and chilled music – Bob Marley perhaps. In this part of town you may expect good food and no shortage of delicious organic meats and vegetables; try shrimp tempura with oyster sauce, roast shoulder of pork, tiramisu. Red, yellow and green lights in the stairwell lead to a lovely sash-windowed restaurant and a small but lavish private dining room beyond. Extraordinary.

directions	Nearest tube: Putney.
meals	12pm-3pm; 6.30pm-10.30pm. No food Sun eves. Main courses £8.50-£11.50; bar meals from £3.75.
closed	Open all day.

Roger Martin
Cat's Back,
86 Point Pleasant,
Putney,
tel   020 8877 0818
web   www.thecatsback.com

map: 4 entry: 308

Spencer Arms
Putney

They're flying the Slow Food flag here – with guts and passion. And it's all so delicious: the whole roast rainbow trout, the rib-eye steak, the ham hock risotto, the 'British tapas' (smoked duck with beetroot pickle, venison carpaccio, potted shrimps). The lamb is from Cornwall because it tastes nicer and they love their chutneys – take some home. The stage for all this good humour is a pretty Victorian tavern with a big open dining room of sturdy tables and painted boards, a blackboard of wines and a sofa by the fire. Throw in bookshelves and games chest, chilled music for quieter moments, tailor-made orders for unfaddy children and cider punch with calvados and you have one fabulous place. The staff are brilliant and chef Adrian Jones (ex Shibden Mill) cycles 20 miles along the river to work each day, such is his enthusiasm. May God bless the Spencer Arms and all who sail in her.

directions	Nearest rail: Putney; Barnes.
meals	12pm-2.30pm (3pm Sat & Sun); 6.30pm-10pm (9.45 Sun). Main courses £7.50-£17.50; bar meals & tapas from £3.50.
closed	Open all day.

Jamie Sherriff
Spencer Arms,
237 Lower Richmond Road,
Putney SW15 1HJ
tel 020 8788 0640
web www.thespencerarms.co.uk

map: 4 entry: 309

The Earl Spencer
Southfields

Its spit 'n' sawdust days are over, its Edwardian interior restored. Now, to a clean backdrop of deep cream and dark blue, gilded ceiling mouldings and a winter fire, you can discover some of the best pub food in south London. Mark Robinson and his team bake bread twice a day, have a smokery on the premises and a bunch of cookery books on the bar. Above the central fireplace the blackboard is chalked up with a seasonal menu and inventive dishes pop up every day: chargrilled squid with chorizo, tomato and garlic; duck rillette with gherkins and chutney; daube of beef with green beans and horseradish; shoulder of lamb to be shared among four; poached pear, honey and brandy parfait. Proprietor Jonathan Cox has not forgotton the drinkers, so there are good wines by the glass and Hook Norton, Shepherd Neame and Hoegaarden on tap. Fresh flowers and papers, laid-back staff, happy drinkers, contented dogs – a place to unwind.

directions	Nearest tube: Southfields.
meals	12.30pm-2.30pm (3pm Sun); 7pm-10pm (9.30pm Sun). Main courses £7.50-£13.50.
closed	Open all day.

Jonathan Cox
The Earl Spencer,
260-262 Merton Road,
Southfields SW18 5JL
tel 020 8870 9244
web www.theearlspencer.co.uk

map: 4 entry: 310

The Ship
Wandsworth

Drinking a pint of Young's Special next to a concrete works doesn't sound enticing, but the riverside terrace by Wandsworth Bridge is a dreamy spot. Chilly evenings still draw the crowds to this super old pub, cosy inside with its warm-red and sage-green walls, and its conservatory with central chopping-board table and wood-burning stove. No music, just happy chat, newspapers, tall blackboards and fresh flowers. Chef Rob Clarson has a good pedigree and sources ingredients from specialist suppliers to create his beef and thyme stew (served with crusty bread), pan-fried cod with sautéed spinach and garlic mash, and chargrilled beefburgers. Summer barbecues find grilled swordfish and lobsters alongside Angus rib-eye steaks. At peak times expect 'who can be the loudest' Fulhamites to pack out the front bar – but don't be put off. The Ship opens its arms to all, and families merrily gather in summer.

The Fox & Hounds
Battersea

As you pass beneath yet another dripping railway bridge you might wonder if the trek from Chelsea was worth it. But the moment the bright little corner pub comes into view you'll feel spirits rise. With its excellent beers and its photos of pints on cream walls, the place appears to be a shrine to the golden brew. No longer the old boozer it once was, it's still a popular hangout for the locals – and, along with its sister pub, The Atlas, a foodie destination. As Mediterranean-style dishes flow from the open-to-view kitchen, food-loving train-spotters will think they've gone to heaven and back as they watch the Connex South Central trains whizz by. Try hake and fennel tagine, smoked haddock and saffron risotto, and rib-eye steak with sweet potato mash and salsa verde. There's a great atmosphere here, and a good little garden for summer.

directions	Nearest rail: Clapham Junction. Left towards lights; up Lavender Hill. At Police Station, left onto Latchmere Rd.
meals	12.30pm-3pm (4pm Sun); 7pm-10.30pm (10pm Sun). No food Mon-Thurs lunch. Main courses £8-£14.
closed	3pm-5pm & Mon lunch. Open all day Fri-Sun.

directions	Nearest rail: Wandsworth.
meals	12pm-10.30pm. Main courses £10.55-£14.95.
closed	Open all day.

	Oisin Rogers
	The Ship,
	Jews Row,
	Wandsworth SW18 1TB
tel	020 8870 9667
web	www.theship.co.uk

map: 4 entry: 311

	George & Richard Manners
	The Fox & Hounds,
	66 Latchmere Road,
	Battersea SW11 2JU
tel	020 7924 5483
web	www.thefoxandhoundspub.co.uk

map: 4 entry: 312

The Fentiman Arms
Kennington

Toffee-coloured walls, a relaxed mood, well-thumbed books and games – a perfect place in which to "nurse your hangover on Saturday morning with the Fentiman brunch menu". This happy pub, designed by proprietor Rupert Clevely's wife Jo, echoes the cosmopolitan themes and earthy colours of their beloved South Africa. Come rain or shine, smart regulars gather over pints of Bombardier and a menu that stretches way beyond the confines of brunch. Chicken liver parfait with red onion marmalade, braised pork belly with apricot and thyme potato rösti, and date and walnut slice with rum ice cream can be devoured in cosy corners against fat velvet cushions and suede bolsters. The upstairs function room, the Fentiroom, with high ceilings and large windows, is a popular place for big gatherings; so too is the trendy outdoor terrace, brilliant for summer drinking and dining. Get there early on Sundays!

The Garrison Public House
Bermondsey

Do dinner and a movie – there's a cinema downstairs for private hire, and a great little restaurant up. Gastropub veterans Clive Watson and Adam White have taken on an old boozer, kept the engraved glass windows and remodelled the rest into a light, airy, bare-boarded space. The furniture is silver-sprayed, lamps and objects fill every cranny. Fresh food, from apricots to Orkney mussels, arrives daily from the market down the road, and is incorporated into dishes that are elaborate but not overly so. A glass of rioja or a bottle of St Peter's goes down well with rib-eye steak with watercress and roquefort butter, or roast cod with shrimp and chive sauce. And the pub is open daily for breakfast. The kitchen is open, staff are attractively laid-back, decibels are high, tables are crammed. Forget hushed conversation: the place bounces with bonhomie.

directions	Nearest tubes: Oval; Vauxhall.
meals	12pm-3pm (4pm Sat & Sun); 6.30pm-10pm (10.30 Fri & Sat; 12.30pm-9pm Sun). Main courses £7.95-£13.95.
closed	Open all day.

Rupert Clevely
The Fentiman Arms,
64 Fentiman Road,
Kennington SW8 1LA
tel   020 7793 9796
web   www.geronimo-inns.co.uk

map: 4 entry: 313

directions	Nearest tube: London Bridge.
meals	Mon-Fri 8am-11.30am; 12pm-3.30pm; 6pm-10pm. Sat & Sun 9am-11.30am; 12.30pm-4pm; 6.30pm-10pm. Main courses £9.80-£14.90.
closed	Open all day.

Clive Watson & Adam White
The Garrison Public House,
99 Bermondsey Street,
Bermondsey SE1 3XB
tel   020 7089 9355
web   www.thegarrison.co.uk

map: 4 entry: 314

Anchor & Hope
Southwark

One of the first bistropubs to champion below stairs food. Come for some of the plainest yet gutsiest cooking in London; chefs Jonathan Jones and Harry Lester are names to watch. They describe the food as 'English bistro', and give or take the odd foreign exception (a chorizo broth, a melting pommes dauphinoise), it is just that. The menu is striking in its simplicity: pigeon terrine, smoked sprats with horseradish and lemon, slip soles with anchovy butter, rabbit with pearl barley and sherry, almond and nectarine tart. The beer comes from the Charles Wells brewery, the wine list has 18 by the glass. Staff are youthful – and may be rushed. Décor is 1930s sober and the restaurant area glows by candlelight. At the far corner of the rambling bar is the tiny theatre kitchen where you can watch the stars at work. No bookings, massively popular, but arrive at 6pm and you should get a table.

Greenwich Union
Greenwich

Master brewer Alastair Hook has turned this Greenwich boozer into a shrine to his lagers and beers. The golds and browns of the interior reflect the hues of the glorious ales he painstakingly creates at the nearby Meantime Brewery; his Red, White, Golden, Amber and Chocolate beers slip down so easily that Sainsbury's has made them part of their range. (If you're not sure which pairs with which food, helpful staff behind the bar will give you a taster.) And this quirky little pub is a great place to eat, the French chef willing to concoct tapas at short notice. He is also a dab hand at sauté of mussels with saffron, chives and orange zest, roasted chicken breast with sweet shallots, and chestnut gnocchi with porcini mushrooms. Sandwiches include homemade 'piadina' (flat bread from Romagna) served with brie and rocket salad. All are welcome including families and dogs.

directions	Nearest tubes: Southwark; Waterloo.
meals	12pm-2.30pm; 6pm-10.30pm. Sun 2pm, bookings only. Main courses £10-£20. Sunday lunch £30.
closed	Mon lunch & Sun eve. Open all day Tues-Sat.

directions	Exit Greenwich station, left & 2nd right into Royal Hill; on right.
meals	12pm-10pm (9pm Sat & Sun). Main courses £6.90-£12.90; bar meals £3.95-£12.90.
closed	Open all day.

	Robert Shaw
	Anchor & Hope,
	36 The Cut,
	Southwark SE1 8LP
tel	020 7928 9898

	Alastair Hook
	Greenwich Union,
	56 Royal Hill,
	Greenwich SE10 8RT
tel	020 8692 6258
web	www.meantimebrewing.com

map: 4 entry: 315

map: 4 entry: 316

The Gun
Docklands

It's fiendishly difficult to find, but persevere. The front room, dominated by a dark panelled bar, is hugely atmospheric – a planked floor, settles and battered leather sofas, the smell of truffles in the air; the restaurant area is pristine. A loose nautical theme runs through the prints and paintings (Lady Hamilton stayed in an upstairs room). Bag a table by the fire; settle in till the sun sets over the river, on a stunningly candlelit terrace. In the bar, a reassuring selection of pub favourites – rare-breed pork sausages with Old Spot bacon and apple and onion gravy, fish pie with sauce Mornay – while the restaurant menu is fiercely modern: braised hare and foie gras terrine with pickled beetroot, plaice with tomato and onion salsa and pea sauce. Weekend brunch from 10.30am to 1pm is hugely popular – do book; Portuguese barbecues trumpet Billingsgate fish. Superb. *Ask about transport by rickshaw.*

directions	Just off A1206 (Prestons Road); turn into Managers Street; right turn at the end.
meals	12pm–3pm (10.30–4pm Sat & Sun); 6pm–10.30 (9.30 Sun). Main courses £8.95–£17; bar meals £5–£13.30.
closed	Open all day.

Tom & Ed Martin
The Gun,
27 Coldharbour,
Docklands E14 9NS
tel   020 7515 5222
web   www.thegundocklands.com

map: 4 entry: 317

The Princess
Clerkenwell

Bare boards, bare tables, modern art and modern walls – another Clerkenwell boozer turned gastropub. This one is cool and charismatic, romantically candlelit at night, and its simple, honest cooking is hard to beat. In downstairs' one-room-serves-all bar, British classics nudge Mediterranean dishes on the menu: choose fish 'n' chips or risotto. Or book a big table for a long, lazy, entirely British Sunday lunch. If you're after slightly more formal surroundings and more adventurous cooking, trip up that spiral staircase in the corner to the restaurant above. Some daring and accomplished dishes – pan-fried queen scallops with piri piri butter and rocket; duck breast with roast pumpkin pilau, harissa and mint yogurt – are served by attentive and likeable staff. Timothy Taylor and Fuller's London Pride are on handpump if you're popping in for a drink, and they make the best Bloody Marys in town.

directions	Nearest tube: Farringdon.
meals	12.30pm–3pm (1pm–4pm Sun); 6.30pm–10.30pm. No food Sun eve. Main courses £11.95–£14.95; bar meals £5–£10.50.
closed	Open all day.

Zim Sutton
The Princess,
76 Paul Street,
Clerkenwell,
tel   020 7729 9270

map: 4 entry: 318

The Easton
Clerkenwell

Home from home for the Amnesty International set (their headquarters are down the street), this corner pub may look like the classic London tavern but inside it is airy and modern. Bare boards, plain windows, a long bar topped with fresh flowers, funky wallpaper at the far end… here drinkers and diners mingle over pints of Timothy Taylor or a glass of global house-white and wonder what to pick from the ever-changing board of Anglo-Med dishes. The kitchen goes in for rustic portions of chargrilled lemon and thyme pork chops; roast tomato and chorizo stew; Springbok sausages with spring onion champ, braised red cabbage and pancetta gravy. It's still a pub, and a godsend for the area, with pub tables spilling onto the pavement and a genuinely local feel. Staff are charming, even on Friday evenings when the drinking crowds descend, and the hearty dishes are replaced with tapas.

Coach & Horses
Clerkenwell

Gone are the days when the Coach & Horses was a corner boozer; now the Edwardian pub fills with a mod-media crowd. Savour a pint of London Pride in the small panelled bar – or al fresco in summer – as you check out a blackboard that lists some of the most scrumptious gastropub food in London. British dishes are devised with youthful enthusiasm and ingredients burst with flavour: venison and partridge terrine with chutney; rabbit rillettes; sea bream with lentils, fennel and salsa verde; quince and almond tart with clotted cream. Rare-breed meats are traditionally reared at Long Ghyll farms in Lancashire, fish is delivered daily. The bar specialises in malt whiskies and attentive staff lay on nibbles of toasted pumpkin seeds in keeping with the pub's logo, a pumpkin pulled by four mice. Note: most tables have a reserved sign on them on busy nights, so drinkers may be confined to the bar.

directions	Nearest tube: Farringdon.
meals	12.30pm-3pm (1pm-4pm Sun); 6.30pm-10pm (9.30pm Sun). Main courses £7.95-£12.95.
closed	Open all day.

Jeremy Sutton & Andrew Veevers
The Easton,
22 Easton Street,
Clerkenwell WC1X 0DS
tel   020 7278 7608

map: 4 entry: 319

directions	Nearest tube: Farringdon.
meals	12pm-3pm; 6pm-10pm. Main courses £10.75-£14; bar meals £3-£6.
closed	Open all day. Closed Sat lunch & Sun eve.

Giles Webster
Coach & Horses,
26-28 Ray Street,
Clerkenwell EC1R 3DJ
tel   020 7278 8990
web   www.thecoachandhorses.com

map: 4 entry: 320

The Well
Clerkenwell

Tom and Ed Martin's pub empire has grown. But this bright, breezy little local has not let its younger siblings – the White Swan, Holborn and the Gun, Isle of Dogs – overshadow it. Step under the deep blue awnings on this dull stretch of St John Street and enter a light-filled room of bare brick and chunky wooden furniture. It's primarily an eating venue and all is homemade, from the bread to the raspberry and almond tart. The brunch menu draws the weekend locals for excellent renditions of eggs Benedict and smoked salmon with scrambled eggs, alongside such fashionable staples as venison pie with root vegetables. During the week expect crisp pork belly with black pudding, haddock with tartare sauce, and rib-eye steak with wild mushroom and tarragon butter. The private basement bar is all contemporary fittings and dark, moody lighting – more classy Clerkenwell than plain gastropub.

Jerusalem Tavern
Clerkenwell

There's so much atmosphere here you could bottle it up and take it home – along with one of the beers. Old Clerkenwell has reinvented itself; the quaint little 1720 tavern, a former coffee house, epitomizes all that is best about the place. Its name is new, acquired nine years ago when the St Peter's Brewery of Suffolk took it over and stocked it with their ales and fruit beers. Step in to a reincarnation of a nooked and crannied interior, all bare boards and plain tables, candlelit at night with a winter fire; arrive early to bag the table on the 'gallery'. Lunchtime food is simple and English – bangers and mash, a roast, a fine platter of cheese – with ingredients coming daily from Smithfield Market down the road. There's a good selection of wines by the glass but this is a drinker's pub: staff are friendly and know their beer, and the full, irresistible range of St Peter's ales is all there, from the cask or the specially designed bottle.

directions	Nearest tube: Farringdon.
meals	12pm-3pm (10.30am-4pm Sat & Sun); 6pm-10.30pm. Main courses £13.50-£16.
closed	Open all day.

Tom & Ed Martin
The Well,
180 St John Street,
Clerkenwell EC1V 4JY

tel	020 7251 9363
web	www.downthewell.com

map: 4 entry: 321

directions	Nearest tube/rail: Farringdon.
meals	12pm-2.30pm. Main courses £5-£18.
closed	Open all day. Closed Sat & Sun.

Colin Cordy
Jerusalem Tavern,
55 Britton Street,
Clerkenwell EC1M 5UQ

tel	020 7490 4281
web	www.stpetersbrewery.co.uk

map: 4 entry: 322

London

The White Swan
Holborn

It had spent the previous ten years as the Mucky Duck. In 2003, brothers Tom and Ed Martin transformed the bird and restored the original name. The bar, with a vast mirror on one wall, evokes a classic, city pub feel. At plain tables on fashionably unpolished boards, City traders savour real ales (of which three) and fine wines (20 by the glass). Upstairs is a smart restaurant with some unusually good modern European cooking ranging from the robust (rump of lamb with crushed olive-oil potatoes and salad niçoise) to the subtle (fricassée of monkfish with fennel, chervil and truffle oil). Cheese and wine lists are encyclopaedic and regulars get lockers to store their unfinished spirits. The daily bar menu takes in classics and favourites, perhaps Denham Estate pork sausages with mash and onion gravy, open steak sandwich with fries, and brilliant fish and chips .

directions	Nearest tube: Chancery Lane.
meals	12pm-3pm; 6pm-9.45pm. Main courses £15-£18; bar meals from £8-£18.
closed	Open all day Mon-Fri. Private parties only Sat & Sun.

Tom & Ed Martin
The White Swan,
108 Fetter Lane,
Holborn EC4A 1ES

| tel | 020 7242 9696 |
| web | www.thewhiteswanlondon.com |

map: 4 entry: 323

London

The Eagle
Clerkenwell

Still mighty, after all these years – though recent reports tell of uppity service and some resting on laurels. No tablecloths, no reservations – just delicious food ordered from the bar. With its real ales and decent choice of wines, the appeal is as much for drinkers as for diners and at peak times it heaves. The atmosphere is media-bohemian and the offices of the *Guardian* lie next door. In spite of the laid-back appeal of scuffed floors, worn leather chairs, mix-and-match crockery, background Latin music and art gallery upstairs, the Eagle's reputation rests on its edible, seasonal bounty. The long bar counter is dominated by a stainless steel area at which Mediterranean vegetables, cuttlefish and pancetta are prepared. Pasta, risotto, peasant soups, spicy steak sandwiches... still worth the trek to get here.

directions	Nearest tube: Farringdon.
meals	12.30pm-3pm (3.30pm Sat & Sun); 6.30pm-10.30pm. Main courses £7.50-£14.50.
closed	Open all day. Closed Sun eve.

Michael Belben
The Eagle,
159 Farringdon Road,
Farringdon EC1R 3AL

| tel | 020 7837 1353 |

map: 4 entry: 324

Charles Lamb Public House
Islington

Everyone's welcome at Camille and Hobby's small pub, hidden down a tangle of Georgian streets behind Camden Passage. It's a dear little place that keeps its pubby feel, with two unshowy bar rooms and well-kept ales on handpump. But it's the blackboard menu – fresh, short, ever-changing – that's the main attraction (Mascha, the family dog, is the third.) Eat informally at plainly set tables in either bar – something simple like Serrano ham with celeriac remoulade, or Lancashire hot pot. Camille is French so there may be a crispy duck confit too. Best of all, perhaps, is Sunday's all-day roast beef and Yorkshire pudding with all the trimmings. It's brilliant homecooked food, but you need to get here early as tables can't be booked. Walk it all off with a stroll along the bosky banks of the Regent's Canal, and seek out the house where essayist and poet Charles Lamb lived, two streets away.

directions	Nearest tube: Angel.
meals	12pm-4pm (6pm Sun); 6pm-9pm. No food Sun eve & Mon-Wed lunch. Main courses £8-£12. Sunday roast £10.50-£12.
closed	Open all day.

Hobby & Camille Limon
Charles Lamb Public House,
16 Elia Street,
Islington N1 8DE
tel 020 7837 5040
web www.thecharleslambpub.com

map: 4 entry: 325

The Peasant
Islington

An impressive, Victorian gin palace with the original horseshoe bar, a blazing fire in the corner and acres of ceiling. Over five years the Wright brothers built up a reputation for splendid food, wines, beers and cocktails; now they have improved what was already a slick and sophisticated operation, and brought in new blood to spice up the menus. Expect the freshest ingredients and a few surprises: grilled kangaroo with globe artichoke stuffed with shiitake mushrooms and peanuts; roast cod on fennel; a fabulous South American brunch (must book). Tapas and mezze are served downstairs alongside the daily papers – chickpea salad, marinated olives, good cold meats, decent bread. The restaurant, too, has had a shake-up: a light, very pretty first-floor room with a painted corner bar and a conservatory with a balcony attached. Brilliantly positioned for antique shops, markets and visiting the Design Centre or Sadler's Wells.

directions	Nearest tubes: Angel; Farringdon.
meals	12pm-11pm (9.30pm Sun). Main courses £9-£17; bar meals £6-£11.
closed	Open all day.

Gregory & Patrick Wright
The Peasant,
240 St John Street,
Islington EC1V 4PH
tel 020 7336 7726
web www.thepeasant.co.uk

map: 4 entry: 326

Drapers Arms
Islington

The Islington Labour Party was founded in the meeting room upstairs. Islington, the Labour Party and The Drapers have come a long way in the 100-odd years since but today's Labour group would be just as happy here as their forebears. In the old days, there was probably only beer, sandwiches and Clause 4 on the menu; today's deliberations are more likely to be accompanied by grilled scallops with Montpelier butter or warm leek tart with smoked salmon, poached egg & hollandaise, washed down with an Amarone della Valpolicella at £70 a bottle. There are, of course, less pricey vintages on offer... and delicious roasts on Sundays. In a quiet side street off Upper Street, the once ramshackle Drapers has rejoiced in its renaissance ever since Paul McElhinney took over. It has won a hatful of awards for its food and is friendly, airy and scrupulously clean. A nice place in which to settle down on a comfy leather sofa with a jug of Bloody Mary. Outside is a lovely little garden.

The House
Islington

The old Belinda Castle has become The House. Robert Arnott is a Marco Pierre White protegé; people come for the character and the cooking. Mirrors gleam on pale lemon walls, one slice of the wedge-shaped building is given over to white-clothed tables, candles and twinkly lights, the other is a chic and charming bar, with a real fire and squidgy sofas. The wine menu is wide-ranging and user-friendly, and the food is simple, gutsy, characterful, be it omelette Arnold Bennett; roast salmon with cannelloni of scallop; risotto of herbs with deep-fried onion rings; corn-fed chicken with chestnuts, wild mushrooms and pancetta – or shepherds pie. And save space for Valrhona hot chocolate pudding with espresso ice cream. It's Islington-cool and far from hushed, but you could relax with anyone here – and pop in for a pint of handpumped ale. Zappy service, too.

directions	Nearest tubes: Highbury & Islington; Angel.
meals	12pm-3pm; 7pm-10pm (6.30pm-9.30pm Sun). Main courses £11.50-£15.50; Sunday roast £13.50-£15.50.
closed	Open all day.

Paul McElhinney
Drapers Arms,
44 Barnsbury Street,
Islington N1 1ER
tel   020 7619 0348
web   www.thedrapersarms.co.uk

map: 4 entry: 327

directions	Nearest tube: Highbury & Islington.
meals	12pm-2.30pm (3.30pm Sat & Sun); 6pm-10.30pm (6.30pm-9.30 Sun). Main courses £11-£23; bar meals £5.95-£10.
closed	Open all day. Closed Mon lunch.

Barnaby Meredith
The House,
63-69 Canonbury Road,
Islington N1 2DG
. tel   020 7704 7410
web   www.inthehouse.biz

map: 4 entry: 328

The Duke of Cambridge
Islington

Geetie Singh is on a mission to raise people's awareness of food and where it comes from. At the Duke, the first all-organic London pub, 'organic' and 'sustainable' are the watchwords and British rustic the style. Wines, beers, spirits are certified organic and they buy as locally as they can to cut down on food miles. Most of the beers are brewed in nearby Shoreditch, meat comes from two farms, fish is purchased from sustainable sources. Impeccable produce, not a whiff of self-righteousness and menus that change twice a day. It's a sprawling, airy space with a comfortable, easy, shoestring minimalism; take your fill of lentil and pancetta soup, mussels with chorizo, fennel and chives, game pie with braised red cabbage, venison steak with redcurrant jus, crusty bread, fruity olive oil, quince crumble and cream – in here, or in the large restaurant. Side salads and sweet potato chips are extra.

The Crown & Goose
Camden

You might wonder where the border lies between bohemian and unkempt and some would argue that this popular little pub lies on the wrong side. However, the laid-back inhabitants of Camden Town don't mind one bit... and the staff here appear as happy as the punters. There's one big room with an elaborate wooden bar and a vaguely Georgian mishmash of tables, sofas and chairs, bare boards, open fire, flickering candles and music in the background. Walls are largely bare but carry the odd piece of art; look out for an unusual bronze. Service is exuberant and warm, the beer plentiful and well-priced, the food modern British. Tuck in, upstairs (must book) or down, to delicious renditions of wild-boar sausages with roasted vegetables and beetroot and apple relish, or Cuban burgers with jalapeno salad. Some say the fish and chips are the best in town, and the Sunday roasts draw many.

directions	Nearest tube: Angel.
meals	12.30pm-3pm (3.30pm Sat); 6.30pm-10.30pm (6pm-10.30pm Sat). 12.30pm-10pm Sun. Main courses £9-£14.50.
closed	Open all day.

Geetie Singh
The Duke of Cambridge,
30 St Peter's Street,
Islington N1 8JT
tel   020 7359 3066
web   www.dukeorganic.co.uk

map: 4 entry: 329

directions	Nearest tube: Camden Town.
meals	12pm-3pm; 6pm-10pm. 12pm-10pm Sat (9pm Sun). Main courses £8.50-£12.95; Sunday roast £10.95.
closed	Open all day.

Joe Lowry
The Crown & Goose,
100 Arlington Road,
Camden NW1 7HP
tel   020 7485 8008
web   www.crownandgoose.com

map: 4 entry: 330

London

The Lansdowne
Primrose Hill

The buzzy Lansdowne is worth crossing postcodes for. Amanda Pritchett was one of the founders of the trail-blazing Eagle; later she set up the Lansdowne and followed a similar gastropub route. It's laid-back, open-plan and atmospherically lit, with big wooden tables and dark blue décor – and manages, downstairs, to keep its pubby feel, in spite of the emphasis on dining. Upstairs is an elegant and charming 60-seat restaurant where a trendy crowd is treated to adventurous food – homemade pasta dishes, sea bass en papillotte, belly of pork with mash and shallots, rib-eye steak with chips and béarnaise. Though the serious dining goes on up here, you can also eat down where the decibels are high, the atmosphere shambolic and everyone loves the pizzas (kids included). There are two draught ales and one real cider, but really this is a wine, lager and olives place. Outside in summer is a little oasis to which you can retreat and leave the city behind.

London

The Engineer
Primrose Hill

Victorian superstar Isambard Kingdom Brunel, whose silhouette decks the sign, once had an office here. Today the place is run by a painter and an actress. Behind the half-stuccoed 1850 edifice lies a cheerful, friendly gastropub with a smart bohemian feel and an outstanding reputation for food. It is particularly strong on fish cooked with a touch of the Mediterranean – sea bass with minted couscous and aubergine relish, say – but there are organic rib-eye with béarnaise, fat homemade chips and creamy and chocolately desserts to swoon over too. Wines look to the New World and beer is excellent. Eat up or down: the front bar is relaxed, bright and buzzing, the restaurant upstairs has white plates on white cloths, mirrors in gilt frames and art for sale. In summer, the large lush garden catches the sun. There's a good mixed crowd here though the majority are hip and young. The service is often praised, and the parking is easy.

directions	Nearest tube: Chalk Farm.
meals	12pm-3pm (9.30-3.30 Sat & Sun); 7pm-10pm (9.30 Sun). Pizzas all day. Main courses £10-£16.50; bar meals £5-£16.50.
closed	Open all day.

Amanda Pritchett
The Lansdowne,
90 Gloucester Avenue,
Primrose Hill NW1 8HX
tel   020 7483 0409

directions	Nearest tube: Camden Town.
meals	All day (9am-12am). Main courses £12.50-£16.50.
closed	Open all day.

Karen Northcote
The Engineer,
65 Gloucester Avenue,
Primrose Hill NW1 8JH
tel   020 7722 0950
web   www.the-engineer.com

map: 4 entry: 331

map: 4 entry: 332

The Salt House
St John's Wood

A mere scuttle from the Beatles' zebra crossing, the Salt House brings a taste of sleepy Suffolk to the metropolis. The meats are rare breed, the day-boat fish is caught by Andy in Looe and practically everything is homemade. Head chef Lucio Palagi and his team are Italian, so the occasional swearing from the kitchen feels almost exotic. The homemade pastas, bread and seafood dishes are genuinely superb, the ale is by Greene King, the wine list is excellent value and wide-ranging, and the building is 18th century, quaintly listing and utterly beautiful. Lofty, intricate, 200-year-old windows, scrubbed wooden tables and leather sofas make the bar a cosy, stylish space. The function room has a roaring open fire; so has the restaurant at the back, secluded and elegant. Add the outside tables with awnings, heaters and space and you have one special gastropub.

directions	Nearest tube: Maida Vale.
meals	10am–10pm (9.30pm Sun). Main courses £9.95–£18.95.
closed	Open all day.

Ryder Butler & Charles Leatham
The Salt House,
63 Abbey Road,
St John's Wood NW8 0AE

tel	020 7328 6626

map: 4 entry: 333

Dartmouth Arms
Dartmouth Park

The pub has style *and* a sense of humour. Sitting unobtrusively in a Highgate side street, the Dartmouth Arms may look smartly unexceptional but inside is another story. In the front bar where bare boards clatter there's huge personality; wooden tables are junk-shop simple and the wall-mounted, flat-screen TV attracts fans for the footie. The back room, where champagne bottles hang from a chandelier and half-panelled walls are painted a vibrant red, is a more peaceful space. You get three perfectly kept cask ales, loads of small-producer ciders, several wines by the glass and a modern British menu displayed on boards – landlord Nick is passionate about food and beer. Expect something for everyone here: wild mushroom soup, sausages with tomato sauce and mash, steaks, Sunday roasts, croque monsieur, generous salads. The background music is noisy at times, there are tapas on Monday, quizzes on Tuesday, and the pub attracts a lively crowd.

directions	Nearest tube: Tufnell Park.
meals	11am–3pm; 6pm–10pm (10am–10pm Sat & Sun). Main courses from £7.50.
closed	Open all day.

Nick May
Dartmouth Arms,
35 York Rise,
Dartmouth Park NW5 1SP

tel	020 7485 3267
web	www.dartmoutharms.co.uk

map: 4 entry: 334

London

The Junction Tavern
Kentish Town

From the stainless-steel, open-to-view kitchen flows food that is modern European and wide ranging – from roast belly pork with bacon, black pudding and prune and brandy jus to Spanish-style seafood stew with aïoli. The daily menu is market-based and well-priced, particularly at weekday lunchtimes when main courses are pleasingly affordable. Word has spread and at weekends you book; the place heaves. Young staff are friendly and attitude-free. The interior is high-ceilinged, corniced, wood-panelled, and there's an open fire. While half the pub is restaurant, the rest is old-fashioned bar, serving over ten real ales a week (note the August beer festival) and good wines. Enjoy a fresh glass of manzanilla in the garden in summer (or in winter, thanks to the heaters), or in the conservatory in spring. Jacky Kitching and partner Chris Leech have a background in restaurants and their experience shows.

directions	Nearest tubes: Kentish Town; Tufnell Park.
meals	12pm-3pm (4pm Sat & Sun); 6.30pm-10.30pm (9.30pm Sun). Main courses £10.50-£15.
closed	Open all day.

	Jacky Kitching & Chris Leech The Junction Tavern, 101 Fortess Road, Kentish Town NW5 1AG
tel	020 7485 9400
web	www.junctiontavern.co.uk

map: 4 entry: 335

London

Holly Bush
Hampstead

Down a Hampstead cul-de-sac the faithful flock. The stables once owned by painter George Romney have become a hugely loved pub. A labyrinth of corridors leads to cosy corners, painted settles and big tables set with board games and pints of Harvey's Sussex. Ale rules at the Holly Bush, where the chef cooks not with wine but with beer. The open-hatched kitchen is centre-stage, the aromas of beef and Harvey's pie proving a sore temptation for drinkers to become diners. Adnams rarebit or a pint of prawns, followed – why not? – by hot chocolate, marmalade and malt whisky fondant – is set to educate the beer lover's palate. Dishes are seasonal and fresh, with game and organic meats from Winchelsea and a superb selection of English cheeses. Upstairs in the dining room, elegant with pistachio walls, wooden floors and fresh lilies, the celebration of all things British continues – in style.

directions	Nearest tube: Hampstead.
meals	12-10pm (9pm Sun). Main courses £7.50-£15; bar meals from £5.
closed	Open all day.

	Jesus Anorve Holly Bush, 22 Holly Mount, Hampstead NW3 6SG
tel	020 7435 2892
web	www.hollybushpub.com

map: 4 entry: 336

London

London

The Flask
Highgate

The Flask's lights gleam so invitingly you can see why Dick Turpin stopped off with his horse. (He's also supposed to have hidden in the cellars.) Thirsty travellers now enjoy Fuller's Jack Frost from an array of real ales, where beer pulls are marked with handwritten labels and you choose between tankard and glass. The warren of little rooms may be 350 years old but its candlelit nooks and crannies have a modern feel. A vaulted sitting area with high chopping board tables and handmade paper lamps makes for a friendly place in which to indulge in stylish takes on old pub favourites: a pint jug of Atlantic shell-on prawns, homemade sausages with parsnip mash, handmade pies and sticky toffee pudding with toffee sauce. In summer, locals and walkers from Hampstead Heath come for outdoor barbecues, while 'doggie treats' invigorate pets from behind the bar. Much loved, mobbed in summer, it can be hard to find a free table.

The Bull
Highgate

A meeting place for friends, colleagues, families; something for everyone here. The plain listed Georgian façade gives way to an inspired interior – coffee-coloured leather banquettes, cream walls, painted bullfights – and the menu unveils yet more surprises. The knowledgeable staff will be happy to advise on wine and food; head chef Jeremy Hollingsworth – ex Quo Vadis – transforms fresh, seasonal and high quality ingredients into rustic-simple dishes that have huge depth of flavour. Leave the aromas behind and ascend the twisting stair, its walls strikingly embellished with animal silhouettes, to the first-floor cherry wood bar – sleek yet pub-cosy. Fall into a fat luxurious sofa and melt into the fire, try your hand at a vintage American pool table. Barnaby Meredith's latest venture (his first was The House in Islington) is a vibrant and chic retreat.

directions	Nearest tubes: Archway; Highgate.
meals	12pm-3pm; 5pm-10pm. 12pm-10pm Sat (9pm Sun). Main courses £6.90-£12; bar meals £3-£6.
closed	Open all day.

Nick Clitheroe
The Flask,
77 Highgate West Hill,
Highgate N6 6BU
tel 020 8348 7346

map: 4 entry: 337

directions	Nearest tube: Highgate.
meals	12pm-2.30pm (12pm-3.30pm Sat & Sun); 6pm-10.30pm (6.30pm-10.30pm Sat, 6.30pm-9.30pm Sun). No food Mon lunch. Main courses £9.50-£23.
closed	Open all day. Closed Mon lunch.

Barnaby Meredith
The Bull,
13 North Hill,
Highgate,
tel 0845 456 5033
web www.inthebull.biz

map: 4 entry: 338

The Baltic Fleet
Liverpool

Alone on a dockland corner, this landlocked Fleet's Victorian fabric remains unchanged with no concessions to poshness – and people like it that way. The small marble-topped bar counter is crammed with handpumps (most ferrying beers brewed in the engine room below) and furnishings are engagingly timeworn: settles, plain chairs, marble-topped tables. Two rooms beyond offer more comfort. The first has its walls lined with pictures of Liverpool's past, traders and shipowners from when the Baltic was built. The second is a snug in the 'bows' with that Liver Building view; hole up here in front of the fire and imagine sailors swapping tales. An honest outpost with cheerful, hard-working staff and a welcoming new father and son management team, the more engaging the longer you stay.

The Philharmonic
Liverpool

The Phil was built by Liverpool brewers Robert Cain & Co in the style of a gentlemen's club: a place for bodily refreshment after the aesthetic excitements of the Philharmonic Hall opposite. There's ornate Victorian extravagance at every turn, impossibly high ceilings, elaborate embellishment, etched glass; the gents is decked in marble and mosaic, its porcelain fittings of historical importance. Sweep through the columned entrance into the imposing, mosaic-tiled central bar, gawp at the scale. Beyond, a succession of small rooms and snugs separated by mahogany partitions, then a Grand Lounge with a stately frieze and table service for lunch: settle down to baked potatoes or fish and chips. In spite of the remarkable surroundings the Philharmonic is very popular with students. It is a great pub serving excellent beers, wines and whiskies and a huge dose of cheer.

directions	Liverpool city centre, opposite Albert Dock.
meals	12pm-2pm (11am-4pm Sat, 12pm-4pm Sun). Bar snacks £1.45.
closed	Open all day.

Mark Yates & Kevin Yates
The Baltic Fleet,
33a Wapping,
Liverpool L1 8DQ
tel 0151 7093116
web www.wappingbeers.co.uk

map: 11 entry: 339

directions	City centre; between the cathedrals at corner of Hardman St.
meals	12pm-9pm. Main courses £5-£15.
closed	Open all day.

Marie-Louise Wong
The Philharmonic,
36 Hope Street,
Liverpool L1 9BX
tel 0151 7072837

map: 11 entry: 340

The Wildebeest Arms
Stoke Holy Cross

In the 1990s Henry Watt decided to introduce good food to this country inn – a rarity then. Now the Wildebeest is one of the most popular dining pubs in Norfolk. The 19th-century building may look no great shakes, but the atmosphere is special. Sympathetically modernised to create one long room split by a central bar, there are rich yellow walls, dark oak beams, fresh flowers on polished tables, a winter fire and an African theme to match the pub's name. Ales include Adnams, there's a choice of wines by the glass alongside an interesting list, and the menu is up-to-the-minute with everything freshly made. Tuck into the rich delights of pot-roast duck breast with cocotte potatoes, crispy Alsace lardon and sautéed cabbage with redcurrant jus. Chef Daniel Smith may enjoy a bit of leonine bravura, but he is equally at home with old English favourites like sausage and mash and sticky toffee pudding.

directions	Off A140, 3 miles south of Norwich.
meals	12pm-2pm; 7pm-10pm. Main courses £7.50-£16.50; set menu, 2 courses, £15.
closed	2pm-6pm.

	Henry Watt
	The Wildebeest Arms,
	82-86 Norwich Road,
	Stoke Holy Cross,
	Norwich NR14 8QJ
tel	01508 492497

map: 10 entry: 341

The Walpole Arms
Itteringham

The pursuit of fine food and wine is an adventure – so says Richard Bryan, ex-producer of *Masterchef*, co-owner of this famous Norfolk pub. Exploration, one assumes, carries less guilt than indulgence. Sweating over a hot stove is Andy Parle, once head chef to Alastair Little. His daily menus are utterly seasonal and brim over with local produce – Cromer crab, Morston mussels, venison from the Gunton estate, farm-fresh fruits and vegetables; there may be pigeon, prune and pork terrine with chutney, roast cod with chorizo and lemon risotto, corn-fed chicken with dauphinoise, and baked white chocolate cheesecake. You can eat in the bar, with rough brick walls, beamed ceilings, standing timbers and big open fire, or in the stylish dining room. There are fine East Anglian ales from Adnams and Woodforde's, a first-class list of wines, and a glorious vine-covered terrace for summer eating.

directions	From Aylsham towards Blickling, then 1st right to Itteringham.
meals	12pm-2pm (2.30pm Sun); 7pm-9pm. No food Sun eve. Main courses £9-£16; bar meals £6-£10.
closed	3pm-6pm (7pm Sun).

	Richard Bryan
	The Walpole Arms,
	The Common, Itteringham,
	Norwich NR11 7AR
tel	01263 587258
web	www.thewalpolearms.co.uk

map: 10 entry: 342

Norfolk

Pub with rooms

Saracens Head

Wolterton

Real ale, fine food, good wines, a delightful courtyard and walled garden, Norfolk's bleakly lovely coast – this is why people come. But the food is the deepest seduction. Starters could be Morston mussels with cider and cream, or fricassée of wild mushrooms. Expect baked Cromer crab with apple and sherry; Gunton venison with red fruit jus and local game; baked avocado with pear and mozzarella. Then Robert works his magic on old favourites such as treacle tart. In this 1806 coaching inn modelled on a Tuscan farmhouse, the bar is as convivial as can be. There's a parlour room for residents, with a big open-brick fireplace, deep red walls, colourful tablecloths and glowing candles. Bedrooms have bold colours, sisal floors and linen curtains – top stuff. The whole mood is of quirky, committed individuality, in the middle of nowhere.

directions	From A140, signs for Erpingham. Pass church; follow road to Carthorpe & Wolterton.
meals	12.15pm–2pm; 7.15pm–9.30pm. Main courses £10.50–£15; bar meals £5–£8; set lunch, 2 courses, £8 (Mon–Fri).
rooms	6: 5 doubles, 1 twin £90. Singles £50.
closed	3pm–6pm (7pm Sun).

See pp 30–57 for full list of pubs with rooms

Robert & Rachel Dawson-Smith
Saracens Head,
Wolterton,
Erpingham NR11 7LX
tel   01263 768909
web   www.saracenshead-norfolk.co.uk

map: 10 entry: 343

Norfolk

The Anchor

Morston

Taste the salty sea – Morston mussels, Thornham oysters, Blakeney crab – and wash it down with Norwich's Winter Brewery Golden ale… or just a nice cup of Royal tea. All a village pub should be, this flintwork and whitewashed building has re-opened following a serious fire. It's a warren of intimate, loved and lived-in rooms, each with its own story to tell: cheery jade green walls, a random collection of tables and chairs, old fishing pics and faded newspaper clippings. There's even a cosy old 'front room' resplendent with stuffed birds and armchairs. Around every corner are enthusiastic birders, chattering locals and relaxed tourists lapping it up. Honest pub cooking with fine local ingredients matches the decent beers and inexpensive wines. On a sunny day stretch out in the secluded beer garden, drawing deeply on the bracing air. Book a seal trip while you sup.

directions	In the centre of Morston on the A149, 2 miles west of Blakeney.
meals	12pm–2.30pm; 6pm–9.30pm; 12pm–8pm Sun. Main courses £8.95–£18.95.
closed	Open all day.

Nick Handley
The Anchor,
The Street,
Morston,
Holt NR25 7AA
tel   01263 741392

map: 10 entry: 344

White Horse Hotel
Blakeney

The smart hub of this small coastal village attracts its share of switched-on custom; Blakeney is the jewel in north Norfolk's crown. The lamp-lit windows of the bar beckon; Adnams Bitter and Woodforde's Wherry are served to those in search of a pint. But stay for more: dressed local crab, filled ciabattas, sea bass with crayfish butter and rocket salad are all served in the polished bar, while local Cley Smokehouse smoked salmon, Morston mussels and seasonal ingredients are given a decidedly contemporary treatment in the sunny-coloured restaurant. With its airy conservatory and sheltered courtyard, Dan Goff's friendly inn is a pleasant place to rest weary limbs following a bracing coast path walk. At the bottom of the steep, narrow high street are marshes of sea lavender, mudflats with samphire and natural mussel beds; there are skylarks and redshanks, and seals a ferry ride away.

directions	Just up from quay, in village; off A149 10 miles west of Sheringham.
meals	12pm-2.15pm (bar meals only); 6pm-9pm. Main courses £10.95-£18.95; bar meals £7.95-£12.95.
closed	One week in Jan. Open all day.

Dan Goff
White Horse Hotel,
4 High Street,
Blakeney NR25 7AL
tel 01263 740574
web www.blakeneywhitehorse.co.uk

map: 10 entry: 345

Red Lion
Stiffkey

Tucked into the side of a hill, overlooking the meadows where beef cattle graze, is a cosy inn that is a pleasure to step into. Enter a warren of three small rooms with bare floorboards and 17th-century quarry tiles, 'clotted cream' walls, open log fires and an unpretentious mix of stripped wooden settles, old pews and scrubbed tables. And there's a raised garden for additional seating in busy summer. The pub attracts a loyal crowd for its fresh fish from King's Lynn (the grilled dab was delicious) and its first-rate ales from East Anglican brewers: Woodforde's Wherry, Nelsons Revenge. Locals rub shoulders with booted walkers and birdwatchers recovering from the rigours of the Peddars Way path and Stiffkey's famous marshes. After a day on the beach the large and airy conservatory is popular with families; dogs, too, are welcomed. Add friendly, easy-going staff and you have a little gem.

directions	From Wells, 2 miles along coast road towards Cromer.
meals	12pm-2.30pm; 6.30pm-9pm; 12pm-9pm Sunday. Main courses £6.95-£12.95
closed	Open all day.

Andrew Waddison
Red Lion,
44 Wells Road, Stiffkey,
Wells-next-the-Sea NR23 1AJ
tel 01328 830552
web www.stiffkey.com

map: 11 entry: 346

Carpenter's Arms
Wighton

Locals and visitors love this pub for all the right reasons: good beer, good food and a popular landlord. It looks modest enough from the outside – three knocked-together cottages in traditional knicker-pink render. But a courageous hand with the paint pot has transformed the interior: a jolly blue in the hallway, tables and chairs painted terracotta, navy and duck-egg blue, and luscious walls in a dining room that would make Barbie blink. Kelims, leather-style sofas and a pyrex bowl of grapefruit create a happy mish-mash of textures; a huge, double-sided woodburner heats the bar and dining room (in summer there's a grassy sun-trap round the back, with picnic tables). A pint of well-kept Nelson's Revenge slips down a treat with chicken liver parfait and red onion marmalade, and the cream of tomato soup is properly homemade. 'Frankie' the landlord, well-known from the Hoste Arms in Burnham Market, is a delight to meet.

directions	Village signed off A149 at Wells-next-the-Sea.
meals	12pm-2.30pm (6pm Sun); 7pm-9pm. No food Sun eve. Main courses £7.95-£12.95.
closed	Open all day.

Stephen Franklin
Carpenter's Arms,
High Street,
Wighton,
Wells-next-the-Sea NR23 1PF
tel 01328 820752

map: 10 entry: 347

The Globe Inn
Wells-next-the-Sea

The renovation of the Globe on pretty, leafy Buttlands Green has been masterminded by the owners of the Victoria at Holkham. Now the old coaching inn has two bars and a restaurant that serves unstuffy modern food: spring lamb with fresh asparagus, grilled lemon sole, venison and (rare treat) wild partridge from the Holkham estate. On sunny days you can take your plates and your pints (Adnams and Woodforde's) out into the large and sunny courtyard; in winter, settle in to the atmospheric 'new' bar – a warm mish-mash of old furniture, big woodburner and antique lighting. Children and dogs like it here too, what with child-size pies and walkies on the hugest beach ever. Sunday brunch is fun and the bedrooms are as fresh and as un-traditional as can be, gleaming with oak floors, powerful showers and digital TVs.

directions	In the centre of Wells-next-the-Sea.
meals	12pm-2.30pm; 7pm-9pm. Main courses £8.50-£14.
rooms	7: 5 doubles, 2 twins £65-£130.
closed	Open all day.

See pp 30-57 for full list of pubs with rooms

Peter Hudson
The Globe Inn,
The Buttlands,
Wells-next-the-Sea NR23 1EU
tel 01328 710206
web www.globeatwells.co.uk

map: 10 entry: 348

The Crown
Wells-next-the-Sea

The interior of this handsome 16th-century coaching inn has been neatly rationalised yet is still atmospheric with its open fires, bare boards and easy chairs. And it's run by an enterprising landlord who knows how to cook. Order pub food at the bar and eat it in the lounges, the lovely modern conservatory or the Sun Deck: a hearty serving of Brancaster mussels, grilled squid and pancetta with guacamole, or confit duck leg, perhaps, with locally brewed Adnams Bitter. Bold colours, modern art and attractively laid tables give life to the restaurant too, where local ingredients are translated into global ideas: sea bass on braised fennel with chorizo oil, aubergine ravioli and basil; lamb chump on sweet potato fondant with red onion tarte tatin. A happy, relaxed place, with a welcome for dogs and families too. Beaches and bracing salt marsh walks are only minutes away.

directions	On B1105, 10 miles north of Fakenham.
meals	12pm-2.30pm; 6pm-9.30pm. Main courses £8.50-£14; set menus £24.95 & £29.95.
closed	Open all day.

Chris Coubrough
The Crown,
The Buttlands,
Wells-next-the-Sea NR23 1EX
tel 01328 710209
web www.thecrownhotelwells.co.uk

map: 10 entry: 349

The Victoria at Holkham
Holkham

Tom and Polly (Viscount and Viscountess) Coke took on the pub on the family's estate a few years ago. The building is early 19th century and the interior is exotic. Stone flags and polished floors, velvet sofas and leather armchairs, huge bowls of fruit, a buzzing bar, a feel of anticipation… In summer, walkers come straight off Holkham beach and into the courtyard or garden for barbecues and a pint of Woodforde's Wherry. In a dining room redolent with lilies, unobtrusive young staff ferry in crabs from Cromer, game from the estate and great steaming nursery puddings; children get their own two-course menu. There are serene bedrooms upstairs, some with views to marsh and sea, and three luscious lodges in the grounds. Sands and skylarks are a stroll away — at their finest out of season.

directions	On A149, 2 miles west of Wells-next-the-Sea.
meals	12pm-2.30 (3pm Sat & Sun); 7pm-9.30 (10pm Fri & Sat). Main courses £12-£18; bar meals £4-£14.
rooms	10 + 3: 9 doubles, 1 suite £120-£225. Singles £100-£130. 3 lodges £120-£275 (max. 4). Min. stay 2 nights weekend.
closed	Open all day.

See pp 30–57 for full list of pubs with rooms

Tom Coke
The Victoria at Holkham,
Park Road,
Wells-next-the-Sea NR23 1RG
tel 01328 711008
web www.victoriaatholkham.co.uk

map: 10 entry: 350

The White Horse
Brancaster Staithe

Enter the dapper white pub, pass the lively front bar and head for the conservatory restaurant with its astonishing views. The White Horse is chic with muted tones, driftwood finds, contemporary paintings and fresh flowers. Local oysters, crabs, mussels and fish – maybe grilled red mullet with warm potato and cucumber salad and herb oil – are matched by exemplary steaks, lamb and pork, and great bar meals. Bedrooms in a wavy extension facing the tidal marshes and North Norfolk Coastal Path have generous proportions and a patio each; the roof is grassed over so that the fine-weather sun deck, dining room and some of the main house bedrooms (ask for the split-level room at the top, with telescope) have a clean view all the way to Scolt Head Island. Huge sunsets, fine food, big breakfasts, and a welcome for children and dogs.

directions	On A149 midway between Hunstanton & Wells-next-the-Sea.
meals	12pm-2pm; 6.30pm-9pm. Bar food 2.30pm-4pm Sat & Sun; 6.30pm-9pm Sun-Thurs. Main courses £9.75-£16.95; bar meals £5.25-£13.95.
rooms	15: 9 doubles, 6 twins £100-£120.
closed	Open all day.

See pp 30-57 for full list of pubs with rooms

Cliff Nye
The White Horse,
Main Road,
Brancaster Staithe PE31 8BY
tel   01485 210262
web   www.whitehorsebrancaster.co.uk

map: 10 entry: 351

The Lord Nelson
Burnham Thorpe

Once The Plough, the pub changed its name in 1798 after the Battle of The Nile to commemorate Burnham Thorpe's most famous son. It hasn't changed a great deal in 400 years: ancient benches and settles, worn brick, tile floors, a serving hatch instead of a bar, distinguish this marvellous place. If a tot of Nelson's Blood (a devilish concoction of 100 percent proof rum and spices) doesn't tempt, order a pint of Woodforde's or Greene King tapped from the cask. Nelson memorabilia reaches into every corner of the small, characterful rooms – and into the Victory Barn restaurant where the annual Nelson's Birthday Dinner (29th September) and the Trafalgar Night Dinner (21st October) are held before an open fire. All in all, a unique local asset, with a family-friendly garden, imaginative food, and a past that is well respected by licensees David and Penny Thorley.

directions	Off A149, B1155 & B1355; 2 miles south of Burnham Market.
meals	12pm-2pm (2.30pm Sat, 3pm Sun); 7pm-9pm. No food Sun eve. Main courses £9.95-£19.95; bar meals £4.50-£12.95.
closed	2.30-6pm (3pm-6pm Sat, 4pm-6.30 Sun) & Mon all day in winter (except bank & school hols).

David & Penny Thorley
The Lord Nelson,
Walsingham Rd, Burnham Thorpe,
Kings Lynn PE31 8HN
tel   01328 738241
web   www.nelsonslocal.co.uk

map: 10 entry: 352

Norfolk

The Hoste Arms
Burnham Market

As the brochure says, pub and owner are made for each other (that's Paul they are talking about): "both have struggled to avoid being popular country attractions". Brilliantly too – The Hoste has won almost every prize going. It's a luxurious place that has a genius of its own – successful mixtures of bold colour, sofas to sink into, panelled walls, an art gallery, log fires, a real buzz. And food to delight, anywhere and anytime. The 'modern British with Pacific Rim influences' menu changes every five weeks – local oysters with orange and rice wine vinegar, oriental beef broth, seafood, cockle and horseradish chowder, Arthur Howell's 21-day aged rib steak with handcut chips, Bakewell tart. The Burnhams comprise seven villages on the north Norfolk coast of which Burnham Market is the loveliest. And it is perfectly placed for some of the most unspoilt coastline in north Norfolk.

directions	By green & church in village centre.
meals	12pm-2pm; 7pm-9pm. Main courses £9.75-£23.50; sandwiches (lunch only) from £3.95; Sunday roast £10.50.
closed	Open all day.

Paul & Jeanne Whittome
The Hoste Arms,
The Green,
Burnham Market PE31 8HD
tel   01328 738777
web   www.hostearms.co.uk

map: 10 entry: 353

Norfolk   Pub with rooms

The Kings Head Hotel
Great Bircham

If you fancy urban sleek in the wilds of Norfolk, come to this grand, white-fronted Victorian pub with a snazzy makeover. The reception area is über-modern Soho: spotlighting, suede sofas, iconic flower art. The bar has a sleek satin metal counter, dark wood, green tweed, designer logs. But it's a friendly place for a simple pint of Woodforde's Wherry, or a glass of rosé accompanied by smoked haddock kedgeree. The restaurant is all striped banquettes and dark wood tables – and summer dining in the smart courtyard – with chef Ben Handley serving modern British food with a cosmopolitan flourish: Thornham oysters or marinated venison, seared Szechuan tuna with a sushi roll and pickled Vietnamese coleslaw. If you're staying, the bedrooms are swish – enormous beds, flat-screen TVs, a decanter of port as well as a mini-bar, and a welcome-you-in plate of home-baked biscuits.

directions	Village centre, on B1153 between A148 at Hillington & Brancaster.
meals	12pm-2pm (3pm Sun); 7pm-9pm. Main courses £7.75-£22.50; bar meals £4.95-£14.95.
rooms	12 doubles £125-£225. Singles from £69.50.
closed	Open all day.

See pp 30–57 for full list of pubs with rooms

Caroline Harvey
The Kings Head Hotel,
Great Bircham PE31 6RJ
tel   01485 578265
web   www.the-kings-head-bircham.co.uk

map: 10 entry: 354

The Rose and Crown
Snettisham

Roses round the door and twisting passages within, it is gloriously English. Homemade burgers with red onion relish and fish and chips with minted mushy peas (delicious) should please the traditionalists, but the menu soon spirals into the dizzy realms of pressed wild salmon with caviar cream, or seared calves' liver with fried polenta, baby gem lettuce and fig vinaigrette. It's great value. In spite of 30 wines on the list, half available by the glass, the Rose & Crown is still proud to be a pub; fine beers on handpump and a hands-on feel. The walled garden was once the village bowling green and children will like the wooden play fort and the weeping willows. Inside, a warren of rooms filled with old beams and log fires, a family-friendly garden room, and a flurry of delightfully stylish bedrooms. Brilliant.

directions	Village signed off A149 10 miles north of King's Lynn. Turn right at r'bout into village & then 1st left, pub 100yds on left.
meals	12pm-2pm (2.30pm Sat & Sun); 6.30pm-9pm (9.30pm Fri & Sat). Main courses £8.50-£14.50.
rooms	16 twins/doubles £85-£95. Singles £50-£65.
closed	Open all day.

See pp 30-57 for full list of pubs with rooms

Anthony & Jeanette Goodrich
The Rose and Crown,
Old Church Road,
Snettisham PE31 7LX
tel   01485 541382
web   www.roseandcrownsnettisham.co.uk

map: 9 entry: 355

Gin Trap Inn
Ringstead

Locate the champion conker tree and spot the plough shares above the door. Deep in lazy lavender country, the 17th century coaching house is a trendy, touristy place popular with all: visitors, families and ladies that lunch. You may sit out at the front on a fine day and watch the world go by, or relax in the sunny walled garden. Inside is a bold décor: gin-trap light fittings, dark green carpets, low black beams and a crackling log fire in winter; in the restaurant, softer coffee and cream hues, church candles and linen napkins. Local oysters grab your eye on the menu, along with seafood chowder, rabbit leg confit and poached saddle with balsamic glazed vegetables, and chilled rice pudding with mulled figs and fig ice cream. The wines are pleasing, as are the real ales – Adnams, Woodforde's Wherry, guest ales. New owners Cindy and Steve were just settling in when we visited in November.

directions	Ringstead signed off A149 at Heacham, north of King's Lynn; pub on right along High Street.
meals	12pm-2pm (2.30pm Sat & Sun); 6pm-9pm (9.30pm Fri & Sat). Main courses £8-£15.95; sandwiches (lunch) from £5.
closed	2.30pm-6pm. Open all day in summer.

Steve Knowles & Cindy Cook
Gin Trap Inn,
High Street, Ringstead,
Hunstanton PE36 5JU
tel   01485 525264
web   www.gintrapinn.co.uk

map: 9 entry: 356

Norfolk

The Orange Tree
Thornham

Up a notch or three from your average watering hole, this place knows what a contemporary foodie pub should be. From funky wicker fencing fronting the garden to sage-splashed walls, the approach from the village green says it all. Step inside – to chunky seagrass floors, light wood, bright walls and log-stuffed fireplaces. Snuggle up at a cheeky *table à deux* at the bar, or retire to one of two relaxed dining rooms. There's a faint waft of Norfolk 'money' on the air, but something for everyone on the Ivy-esque menu – from crisp confit pork belly to a perfect cheeseburger. This is a fabulous area for food, and the pub sources locally and well. Spitfire, Tiger and IPA Greene King are on handpump, and the wine list does a decent job, mostly mid-market and New World. Children have an up-market play area... come for urban chic, a particularly happy feel and great food.

directions	On A149 in village centre; from Hunstanton, pub on left-hand side.
meals	9am–2pm; 6.30pm–9pm (9.30pm Fri & Sat); 12pm–6pm Sun. Main courses £8.50–£25.
closed	Open all day.

Richard Golding
The Orange Tree,
High Street, Thornham,
Hunstanton PE36 6LY
tel 01485 512213
web www.theorangetreethornham.co.uk

map: 9 entry: 357

Northamptonshire

The Falcon
Oundle

The Falcon is a smashing place serving wonderful Italian food. Discreetly, stylishly modernised, it keeps its pubby feel – darts in the tap bar, an open fire in the main bar and well-kept Adnams on handpump. The extras are undoubtedly spoiling: high-back tapestry-covered chairs, candlelight and fresh flowers. Richard III was born in Fotheringhay Castle and Mary Queen of Scots was executed here; now the castle is a mound, but the medieval church is worth a visit and the Falcon picks up on the history in the prints in the bar. For a change of mood, head for the elegant, double conservatory with its impressive church views; it has the same daily menu and a more contemporary feel: light and open, with Lloyd Loom chairs. Cooking is stylishly simple, whether it's carpaccio of Denham Estate venison, roast breast of chicken stuffed with gorgonzola and sage, or linguine with poached salmon, dill, chilli and crème fràiche. Wines are as good, with a tempting 18 by the glass.

directions	Off A605 4 miles NE of Oundle.
meals	12pm–2pm (2.40pm Sun); 6.15pm–9.30pm (9pm Sun). Main courses £13.95–£19.95; bar meals £4.95–£10.95.
closed	3pm–6pm. Open Sat/Sun all day.

David Sims, Chris Kipping & Rachel Kipping
The Falcon,
Oundle, Peterborough PE8 5HZ
tel 01832 226254
web www.huntsbridge.com

map: 9 entry: 358

The Chequered Skipper
Oundle

Ashton is a glorious, rural, stone-and-thatch village, its houses casually arranged around an ample village green. The mellow pub blends in nicely yet is just a hundred years old (and has burnt down twice to boot). This explains the generous open-plan interior – a modern fireplace in the bistro area, striking wooden pillars and honey-coloured beams in the bar. Whether choosing from the blackboard or the printed à la carte, you'll find food that is utterly contemporary and adopts a best-bits-from-everywhere approach. So try Thai spiced fishcake with sweet chilli sauce or whole lemon sole with lemon butter, whole partridge pot-roasted in port with root vegetables and herbs, and spotted dick and hot custard. Wash it all down with any one of a regularly changing slate of local and regional ales, say Old Tosspot, or Oliver's Army, or an excellent wine, and you might find yourself checking out the house prices.

directions	Off A605, 1 mile from Oundle.
meals	12pm-2pm; 7pm-9.30pm. Main courses £10.95-£15.50; bar meals from £7.20.
closed	2-6pm. Open all day Sun.

Ian Campbell
The Chequered Skipper,
Ashton,
Oundle,
Peterborough PE8 5LD
tel   01832 273494

map: 9 entry: 359

The Queen's Head
Bulwick

A mellow old stone pub in a lovely village – you'll wish this was your local. The simple beamed and flagstoned bar rambles into several country-styled dining rooms, all nooks and crannies, bright walls and fresh flowers. This may be the owners' first pub venture, but their natural friendliness and instinct to keep things simple has worked in their favour. Bar food features the very good Grassmere Farm ham with local free range eggs, or try a steak and stilton toasted sandwich with hand-cut chips washed down with Rockingham Ales from the village microbrewery. The short à la carte menu is full of more extravagant enticements: whole roasted teal wrapped in prosciutto ham with spiced red cabbage and apple, honey-glazed turnips and celeriac crisps; roast monkfish with mussel, cockle and potato chowder; roast haunch of local wild venison rubbed in rosemary, garlic, lemon and juniper.

directions	Just off A43, between Stamford & Corby.
meals	12pm-2.30pm; 6pm-9.30pm. No food Sun eve. Main courses £8.50-£19.95; bar snacks from £4.95.
closed	3pm-6pm (7pm Sun) & Mon all day.

Geoff Smith & Angela Partridge
The Queen's Head,
Main Street,
Bulwick,
Corby NN17 3DY
tel   01780 450272

map: 9 entry: 360

Northamptonshire

Snooty Fox
Lowick

If it weren't for the sign, the pub could be mistaken for a manor house. Which it was, four centuries ago. Nowadays it's patronised by locals as both pub (Greene King IPA, Fuller's London Pride) and restaurant. The bar, with polished dining tables, caramel leather sofas and open fire, is separate from the dining room proper; both are a good size, beamed, flagged and open-stone-walled. And it's notably family friendly, with a toy box for children. But what really sets the Snooty Fox apart is chef-patron Clive Dixon. A slate of pub favourites such as cottage pie, homemade pork pie with chutney and bangers and mash are served in the bar, while in the restaurant there's a more upmarket rotisserie-grill menu – superb dry-aged steaks are cut to order – as well as other good things like braised belly pork with parmesan polenta, and fresh crab tagliatelle. Foodie heaven.

directions	A14 junc.12; follow A6116 for 2 miles.
meals	12pm-2pm; 6pm-9.30pm (7pm-9.30pm Sun). Main courses £10.50-£13.95.
closed	Open all day.

Clive Dixon & David Hennigan
Snooty Fox,
Main Street,
Lowick NN14 3BH
tel 01832 733434
web www.snootyinns.com/snootyfox/

map: 9 entry: 361

Northamptonshire

The Wollaston Inn
Wollaston

Hard to believe that back in the 60s and 70s this was the legendary Nag's Head music venue: U2 played here and John Peel DJ'd. But then the local Doc Martens factory closed, and when the boots walked, so did the pub's rockin' clientele. When Chris Spencer and Andrew Parton took it on a few years ago it was a real dive. Their aim was to clean up its act, and the result is as far from spit-and-sawdust as you can get – the walls are too creamy, the ceilings too high, the leather sofas too comfy. The beer garden is now a courtyard patio with bay trees in terracotta pots. Chef Chris is serious about his food, especially seafood, which changes daily. That doesn't mean pretentious: he won't have any truck with "drizzling", or "beds" of this or that. Instead, he does a Mediterranean saffron fish stew and hake steak – as well partridge, venison, ploughman's and steamed syrup pudding. The wine list is one to wade around in.

directions	Village signed off A509 south of Wellingborough.
meals	11am-9.30pm (10.30pn Sat & Sun). Main courses £8.50-£25; bar meals from £6.50.
closed	Open all day.

Andrew Parton & Chris Spencer
The Wollaston Inn,
87 London Road, Wollaston,
Northampton NN29 7QS
tel 01933 663161
web www.wollaston-inn.co.uk

map: 9 entry: 362

Fox and Hounds
Great Brington

It's also known as the Althorp Coaching Inn: decked with flowers inside and out, nestling under its neat hat of thatch, it rests in the heart of this ironstone estate village. For summer there's an enclosed courtyard within earshot of the cricket green, a nice spot for a pint of Langton Bowler – or one of several wonderful ales. When the nights draw in, the fires burn brightly in the restaurant and bar, glowingly traditional with floorboards, flagstones and plentiful bric-a-brac. This is a popular pub whose regulars appreciate good-value meals and baguettes from the bar. In the restaurant you can have local game and beef from their farm, cooked in an unfussy manner. Major sporting events – Silverstone is up the road – are shown discreetly in the bar, while Tuesday evenings see live music. Althorp House, home to the Spencers, is a mile away.

Royal Oak
Eydon

Everyone's welcome at the small and unpretentious Royal Oak. Walkers drop by to refuel, children are welcome in the games room (skittles, darts), dogs amble freely. No music, just the hum of happy eaters. The menu – fresh, short, regularly changing – is the big attraction and you'll find not only the best of British – rich tomato soup, Gloucester Old Spot belly pork stuffed with black pudding, Cornish hake supreme – but also a touch of the exotic (eg. spicy vegetable tagine). The pretty, 17th-century honey-stone pub has old flagstones, exposed stone walls, a woodburner in the inglenook and a Sunday-papers-and-a pint feel. The long bar is propped up by ale-quaffing regulars, the rest is made over to the games room and three small eating areas. There are picnic seats out in front and Eydon, though only seven miles from the motorway, feels as remote as can be.

directions	From Northampton, A428; 1st left after Althorp; pub near Althorp Hall.
meals	12pm-2.30pm; 6.30pm-9.30pm. Main courses £9.25-£16.75.
closed	Open all day.

Jacqui Ellard
Fox and Hounds,
Main Street,
Great Brington,
Northampton NN7 4JA

tel   01604 770651

map: 8 entry: 363

directions	Off A361 midway between Banbury & Daventry.
meals	12pm-2pm; 7pm-9pm. No food Mon. Main courses £10.95-£16.
closed	2.30-6pm (3pm-7pm Sun).

Justin Lefevre
Royal Oak,
6 Lime Avenue,
Eydon,
Banbury NN11 3PG

tel   01327 263167

map: 8 entry: 364

Northamptonshire

George & Dragon
Chacombe

It's an old pub — the building dates from 1640 and has been added to over the centuries — but a relative newcomer given that Chacombe appears in the Domesday Book. One wonders what they did for a drink until 1640. There's a great atmosphere at the George & Dragon, with its flagstones, low beams, simple furnishings, crackling log fire and mellow front festooned with flowers in summer. Like so many successful country pubs, it's reputation has been built on its food. Roast beef sandwiches, game terrine with plum compote, Norfolk crab calad, lamb Wellington, bread and butter pudding — this is good, comforting, English food. Almost all the ingredients are local, and there are real ales from Everards and seven wines by the glass. Chacombe is a delightful conservation village and a world away from the M40 just over the hill.

directions	M40 junc. 11; A361 for Daventry; Chacombe signed in 1 mile.
meals	12pm-2.30pm (3pm Sun); 6pm-9.30pm. No food Sun eve. Main Courses £7.50-£15.
closed	Open all day.

Richard Phillips
George & Dragon,
Silver Street,
Chacombe,
Banbury OX17 2JR

tel   01295 711500

map: 8 entry: 365

Northumberland

The Olde Ship
Seahouses

The Glen dynasty has been at the helm of this nautical gem for close on a century. The inn sparkles with maritime memorabilia to remind you of Seahouses' fine heritage and the days when Grace Darling rowed through huge seas to rescue stricken souls. Settle into the cosy and atmospheric main bar by the glowing fire with a decent pint — there are eight ales to choose from — and gaze across the harbour to the Farne Islands and the Longstone Light (later, take the ferry). In the smaller 'cabin' bar you can get stuck into some hearty food — lentil and tomato and sandwiches, wild boar terrine with Cumberland sauce, beef stroganoff, fish chowder, lamb curry, bread and butter pudding. Dinner in the restaurant is a set four-course affair. The place positively creaks with history — retreat here after a bracing coastal walk to Bamburgh Castle.

directions	B1340 off A1 8 miles north of Alnwick; inn above harbour.
meals	12pm-2.30pm; 7pm-8.30pm Main courses £7.50-£10.75; bar meals £4.25-£10.75.
closed	Open all day.

A & J Glen, D Swan & J Glen
The Olde Ship,
Main Street,
Seahouses NE68 7RD

tel   01665 720200
web   www.seahouses.co.uk

map: 14 entry: 366

Northumberland

The Ship Inn
Low Newton-by-the-Sea

A deeply authentic coastal inn with tongue and groove boarding and flooring, old settles, scrubbed tables and a solid-fuel stove. Step in and you step back 100 years: landlady Christine Forsyth fell in love with the simplicity of the place and gives you provender to match. Good local beers (Wylam Gold Tankard and Landlord's Choice) and fair trade coffee and chocolate go well with a menu built around the best local produce – simple, fresh, satisfying. Local hand-picked-crab rolls (stotties), lobster from yards away, Craster kippers from two miles down the coast, ploughman's with local unpasteurised cheddar or New Barns free-range ham. In the evenings there's often a choice (venison, grilled red mullet) but book first. Park on a compulsory plot back from the beach and take the short walk to the sand, green and pub – worth every step.

directions	From Alnwick B1340 for Seahouses for 8 miles to crossroads; straight over, follow signs.
meals	12pm-2:30pm; phone for evening opening & food times. Main courses £7-£22; bar meals £2-£6.95.
closed	4pm-6pm Mon-Thurs. Open all day Sat, Sun & school hols.

Christine Forsyth
The Ship Inn, The Square,
Low Newton-by-the-Sea,
Alnwick NE66 3EL
tel 01665 576262
web www.theshipinnnewtonbythesea.co.uk

map: 14 entry: 367

Northumberland

The Tankerville Arms
Eglingham

Exploring the rolling acres between Northumberland's dramatic coastline and the wild Cheviot Hills? Charming Eglingham has the best pub for miles. The long, stone-built tavern, a boon for ramblers and cyclists, cheerfully mixes traditional and new. In the lounge and bar are carpeted and stone-flagged floors, blackened beams, coal fires, plush seating and old-fashioned dominoes; in the kitchen, a modern approach. John Blackmore, owner and cook, chalks up blackboard menus featuring fresh, local, seasonal ingredients – ham and duck confit terrine with toasted brioche; black pudding tart with goat's cheese, roasted vegetables and garlic sauce. Food goes traditional in good sandwiches and Sunday lunchtime roasts, served in one of the cosy bars or in the converted barn restaurant. Children are welcome and drinkers kept happy with a range of thoroughly respectable ales, including the local Hadrian and Border brews, and a well-balanced list of wines.

directions	On B6346 towards Charlton & Wooler, 7 miles from Alnwick.
meals	12pm-2pm; 6.30pm-9pm. Main courses £10-£15.95.
closed	2pm-6.60pm Mon-Thurs, 2pm-6.30pm Fri & Sat (3pm-6.30pm Sun).

John Blackmore
The Tankerville Arms,
15 The Village,
Eglingham,
Alnwick NE66 2TX
tel 01665 578444

map: 14 entry: 368

The Pheasant Inn 🛏
Stannersburn

Everything shines inside this little stone inn. Walls carry old photos of the local community: from colliery to smithy, a vital record of their past heritage. The bars are wonderful — brass beer taps glow, anything wooden has been polished to perfection, the clock above the fire keeps perfect time and the Timothy Taylor's and Theakston's Black Sheep Bitter are expertly kept. Robin and Irene offer homemade soups and steak and kidney pies for lunch while in the evening things step up a gear: steaks cooked to your liking, fish simply grilled and served with herb butter, roast Northumbrian lamb. Bedrooms next door in the hay barn are fresh, simple, compact and cosy. You are in the glorious Northumberland National Park, so no traffic jams, no rush; hire bikes and cycle round the lake, sail or ride.

directions	From Bellingham to Kielder Water 8 miles. On left, before K. Water.
meals	12pm-2pm (2.30pm Sun); 7pm-9pm. Main courses £9.50-£14.50; bar meals £7.50-£8.50.
rooms	8: 4 doubles, 3 twins, 1 family £80-£85. Singles £45-£50.
closed	3pm-6.30pm (7pm Sun); Mon & Tues Nov-Mar.

See pp 30–57 for full list of pubs with rooms

	Walter, Irene & Robin Kershaw The Pheasant Inn, Stannersburn, Kielder Water NE48 1DD
tel	01434 240382
web	www.thepheasantinn.com

map: 14 entry: 369

Battlesteads Hotel 🛏
Wark

Battlesteads has been given a fresh lease of life by energetic new owners. Enter a large, cosy, low-beamed and panelled bar with a fire in the brick hearth and local beers on handpump. Seating is comfortable if showing its age. A step further and you find two relaxed areas for more formal dining: leather chairs at dark wood tables, blue drapes at tall windows, a sweep of new floor. A blackboard lists dishes that show a commitment to sourcing locally, and that includes lamb, beef and fish landed at North Shields. The food is flavoursome, one (meltingly tender) speciality being home-cured Aberdeen Angus beef with juniper berries, peppercorns and herbs. All the bedrooms are carpeted, well-equipped — toiletries, TVs, broadband — and a good size. The newest, with wheelchair access, are on the ground floor, and the housekeeping is exemplary.

directions	From A69 at Hexham, A6079 to Chollerford, then A6320 for Bellingham; Wark is halfway.
meals	Bar meals available all day. Dinner 6.30pm-9.30pm. Main courses £8.50-£17.95; bar snacks from £3.25.
rooms	17 twins/doubles £80. Singles £45.
closed	Open all day.

See pp 30–57 for full list of pubs with rooms

	Richard & Dee Slade Battlesteads Hotel, Wark, Hexham NE48 3LS
tel	01434 230209
web	www.battlesteads.com

map: 14 entry: 370

Dipton Mill
Hexham

Less than a ten-minute drive out of town along a rollercoaster road, Geoff Brooker's old inn squats in a deep hollow next to a stone bridge and a babbling brook. Formerly a mill house built around 1750, it's been updated but has hung on to much of its old character. Within the tiny interior is a single warm and intimate bar with panelled walls, low ceilings, small leaded windows and blazing winter log fires – comfortingly traditional. Food is home-cooked: warming soups and steak and kidney pie, or ploughman's with a rare choice of British and local cheeses. Real-ale fans will know that the Dipton Mill is the brewery tap for Hexhamshire Brewery ales, Geoff being both landlord and head brewer. Outside: a big walled garden with a wooden bridge over the mill stream. A wintery word of warning: if there's ice or snow, although you may get down the hill you may not get up again!

The Angel
Corbridge

Even older than Hadrian's Wall, quaint Corbridge is a pretty place with the 17th-century Angel, full of history and character, at its hub. You walk straight into the splendid panelled lounge, cosy with its leather armchairs, heavy drapes, big open fire and newspapers to browse through. Off to the left, a plush dining room – deep carpeting, polished tables, sparkling glassware – and to the right, the bar. This is a big room, simply decorated in brasserie style with a bright, contemporary feel. Cask beers are available and the menu, chalked on a blackboard over the fire, reveals sunblush tomato soufflé as well as more traditional dishes – and the Angel's fabulous Yorkshire pudding. There's a beer garden at the back, more places to sit at the front. A comfortable stopover on the long journey from north to south.

directions	From Hexham B6306 for Blanchland; 2nd right onto Dipton Mill Road to Whitley Chapel & Racecourse; pub 2 miles on.
meals	12pm-2pm; 6.30pm-8.30pm. Main courses £5.25-£7.30.
closed	2.30pm-6pm & Sun eve.

Geoff Brooker
Dipton Mill,
Dipton Mill Road,
Hexham NE46 1YA
tel   01434 606577

map: 12 entry: 371

directions	In Corbridge, 2 miles off A69.
meals	12pm-9pm (12pm-3pm Sun). No food Sun eve. Main courses £8.95-£16.95 (dinner); £7.95-£12.50 (lunch); sandwiches from £4.25.
closed	Open all day.

John Gibson
The Angel,
Main Street,
Corbridge,
Hexham NE45 5LA
tel   01434 632119

map: 12 entry: 372

The Feathers Inn
Hedley on the Hill

Marina Atkinson has seen a few changes to the British pub scene in her 25 years – yet has not lost sight of The Feathers' old-fashioned pubby feel. It is a rare treat west of Newcastle to find such an authentic little place. In the two bars are old beams, exposed stonework, Turkey rugs, open fires and a cottagey feel. Furnishings are simple but comfortable: red benches and settles, ornaments and soft lights. So restful – you'd feel as much at home browsing the papers here as enjoying a fireside chat. Beer is excellent, with four cask beers from local or microbreweries; wines are taken as seriously. The food – Greek beef casserole, tortillas and croustades, ginger pudding – is home-cooked and vegetarian- and vegan-friendly. Menus change twice a week, and dishes are deliberately unfussy: Marina puts the focus on freshness and flavour. Hedley on the Hill is as charming as its name.

The Manor House Inn
Carterway Heads

No wonder it's a popular place. Cheerful young staff, tasty food, a good bar with four cask ales and a cask cider, eight wines by the glass, a raft of malts. The large, light lounge bar, with wood-burning stove and blackboard menu, is a great spot for meals, though there's a dining room if you prefer. Chicken liver pâté comes with onion marmalade, scallops with chilli jam, pigeon breast with mushroom and juniper sauce. In the smallish public bar, modestly furnished with oak settles and old pine tables, is a big open fire; owners Chris and Moira Brown add a further warm touch. Take your pint of Theakstons Best into the garden in summer where the eye sweeps over the Derwent valley to the Durham moors. There's a shop/delicatessen selling a wide range of goodies – puddings, chutneys, ice cream – much of it home-produced.

directions	From Consett, B6309 north to New Ridley; follow signs to Hedley on the Hill.
meals	12pm-2.30pm Sat & Sun; 7pm-9pm. Main courses £7.95-£11.75; bar meals £4.50-£11.75.
closed	Mon-Fri lunch; 3pm-6pm Sat; 3pm-7pm Sun.

	Marina Atkinson
	The Feathers Inn,
	Hedley on the Hill,
	Stocksfield NE43 7SW
tel	01661 843607

directions	Beside A68 at junction with B6278; 3 miles west of Consett.
meals	12pm-9.30pm. Main courses £6.75-£15; sandwiches from £3.95.
closed	Open all day.

	Moira & Chris Brown
	The Manor House Inn,
	Carterway Heads,
	Shotley Bridge DH8 9LX
tel	01207 255268

map: 12 entry: 373

map: 12 entry: 374

Ye Olde Trip to Jerusalem
Nottingham

Another that's the oldest in England! The building dates from the 1600s and certainly there has been brewing on the site since the 1170s (to supply the needs of the castle above), while the crusaders probably met here en route to Jerusalem. An amazing place carved into solid rock on which the castle sits; drinking here is like drinking in a cave, only warmer. There are rickety staircases, ancient chimneys that were cut up through the rock to assist medieval brewing, a cursed galleon, hairy with dust because the last three people who cleaned it died, and Ring the Bull, a pub game which involves swinging a ring on a string over a bull's horn. The Rock Lounge, with its sandstone ceiling and chimney, is aptly named, the cellars stretch more than 100 feet beneath the castle, and there's a small courtyard for those who choose daylight. The Trip (meaning 'resting place') serves Hardys & Hansons to a mixed crowd – locals, tourists, students – and the food is standard pub stuff.

directions	From inner ring road follow A6005 'The North' to Castle Boulevard; right into Castle Road.
meals	12pm-7pm (12pm-6pm Sun). Main courses £5.10.
closed	Open all day.

Allen Watson
Ye Olde Trip to Jerusalem,
1 Brewhouse Yard,
Nottingham NG1 6AD
tel   0115 947 3171
web   www.triptojerusalem.com

map: 8 entry: 375

Cock & Hoop
Nottingham

The 'Lace Market' is undergoing a revival – and it's a treat to find a fine free house in the city centre. Opposite the law courts – now an award-winning museum – the old ale house gave sanctuary to judges preparing for the hangings that took place outside. The pub is a cheerier place today, shoppers, beer-lovers and city workers making a bee-line for the cosiest spot in town. There are two rooms, one at ground level, one below. Below is larger and softly lit; ground-level has an open fire and a tiny bar. Both have wooden panelling and bare-brick walls, plush furnishings, armchairs, benches and club chairs. Friendly staff know all about the whiskies and wines and there's an unexpectedly good selection of both. Beers include Black Sheep and London Pride; food includes club sandwiches, homemade soups, roast salmon, sticky toffee pudding, all courtesy of the stylishly informal hotel next door.

directions	From city centre, follow brown signs for Lace Market; next to Lace Market Hotel.
meals	12pm-10pm (12pm-9pm Sun). Main courses £7.95-£9.95; bar meals £4.75-£4.95.
closed	Open all day.

Katherine Abbiss
Cock & Hoop,
25 High Pavement,
Nottingham NG1 1HE
tel   0115 852 3231
web   www.cockandhoop.co.uk

map: 8 entry: 376

The Victoria
Beeston

A large picture of Queen Victoria rules the main bar of this unpretentious and bustling city-suburb pub. It's an ex-Victorian railway hotel with bags of character, and its awesome raft of ales, wines by the glass and malt whiskies pulls in a crowd. The food's good, too, with a menu strong on vegetarian options. The civilised main bar, with fire, newspapers on racks and etched windows, sets the tone for the other rooms, all plainly painted in magnolia with woodblock flooring and scrubbed dark-wood or brass-topped tables. Blackboards give the food and booze headlines. You get roast pork Catalan, braised beef in ale and veggie dishes to delight even non-vegetarians (winter vegetable bourguignon, pasta with goat's cheese and rocket pesto). At the back, there's a heated marquee area for cooler summer nights; dine as the trains go by. Service is efficient and friendly. Try to catch the summer festival of ale, food and music.

Martin's Arms
Colston Bassett

An Elizabethan farmhouse morphed into an ale house around 1700, and an inn 100 years later. Today it is a deeply civilised pub. The front room exudes so much country-house charm — scatter cushions on sofas and settles, crackling logs in Jacobean fireplaces, 18th-century prints — that the bar seems almost an intrusion. Fresh, seasonal menus change daily. Bar snacks include special sandwiches, warm salads and splendid ploughman's lunches with Colston Bassett stilton from the dairy up the road (do visit). In the restaurant, the highlight of the winter menu is Park Farm Estate game shot by Salvatore the chef. Polish it all off with raspberry and mascarpone shortbread with stem ginger. Behind the bar is an impressive range of well-kept real ales, cognacs, wines and malts from Adnams. The staff are hugely welcoming, the garden backs onto the Colston Bassett Estate and you can play croquet on the lawn in summer. Superb.

directions	Off A6005 at the bottom of Dovecote Lane. Follow signs to station.
meals	12pm-8.45pm (7.45pm Sun). Main courses £6.95-£11.95.
closed	Open all day.

Neil Kelso
The Victoria,
Dovecote Lane,
Beeston NG9 1JG
tel 0115 925 4049
web www.victoriabeeston.co.uk

map: 8 entry: 377

directions	Off A46, east of Nottingham. Take Owthorpe turning.
meals	12pm-2pm; 6pm-10pm. No food Sun eve. Main courses £12.50-£21.95; bar meals £9.95-£21.95.
closed	3pm-6pm (7pm Sun).

Lynne Strafford Bryan &
Salvatore Inguanta
Martin's Arms,
School Lane,
Colston Bassett NG12 3FD
tel 01949 81361

map: 9 entry: 378

Waggon & Horses
Halam

The Whites have built up a fantastic reputation for food. You can tell how keen they are just by looking at the menu with its exhortations to try each dish. Go for pressed trout, salmon and mackerel terrine, venison loin with cranberry and sweet potato hotpot, pork fillet with cider fondant potato or baked cod with caper and dill crust; even lunchtime's rolls are worth travelling for. Members of the Campaign for Real Food, William and Rebecca get almost everything locally; fish comes daily from Cornwall. The pub is small, beamed and softly lit with low ceilings and bold walls. In the cosy but open-plan bar, rush-seated chairs pull up to sturdy tables; there's the odd settle and masses of cricket memorabilia, and an exotic metal grill separating the dining area. It's a Thwaites' tied house, friendly and expertly run – they even do catering for parties.

Caunton Beck
Caunton

Having hatched the hugely successful Wig & Mitre in Lincoln, Michael and Valerie looked for a rural equivalent and found one in pretty little Caunton. The pub was lovingly reconstructed from the skeleton of the 16th-century Hole Arms and then renamed. A decade on and it is a hugely popular pub-restaurant, opening at 8am for breakfast – start your day with freshly squeezed orange juice, espresso coffee, smoked salmon and scrambled eggs. Later, there are sandwiches, mussels with pickled ginger and coriander laksa and pot-roasted guinea fowl. The puddings (make space for lemon and thyme posset) are fabulous. It's all very relaxed and civilised, the sort of place where newspapers and magazines take precedence over piped music and electronic wizardry. Come for country chairs at scrubbed pine tables, rag-rolled walls and a fire in winter, or parasols on the terrace in summer. Well-managed ales are on handpump.

directions	Off B6386 in Southwell for Oxton.
meals	12pm-2.30pm (3pm Sun); 6pm-9.30pm. No food Sun eve. Main courses £9-£16; set menu (lunch & early eve) £11.50 & £14.50.
closed	3pm-5.30pm. Open all day Sat & Sun.

directions	6 miles NW of Newark past sugar factory on A616.
meals	8am-11pm. Main courses £9.50-£19.95.
closed	Open all day.

William & Rebecca White & Roy Wood
Waggon & Horses,
Mansfield Road, Halam, NG22 8AE
tel 01636 813109
web www.thewaggonathalam.co.uk

Michael & Valerie Hope
Caunton Beck,
Main Street,
Caunton,
Newark NG23 6AB
tel 01636 636793

map: 9 entry: 379

map: 9 entry: 380

Miller of Mansfield
Goring-on-Thames

The Miller, once a sedate red-brick coaching inn, has lavished a small fortune on rejuvenating itself and the results are decidedly groovy. You'll find leather armchairs, sand-blasted beams, silver-leaf mirrors, shiny wooden floors, black suede bar stools, fairy-light chandeliers and candles flickering above open fires.. Bedrooms, too, pack a punch. The chrome four-poster has a leather bedhead, there are cow-hide rugs on white wooden floors and colours come in pink, orange and electric green. Bathrooms tend towards the extravagant (though two have no door from the bedroom), with monsoon showers or claw-foot baths. And there's seriously good food – so walk by the Thames, take to the hills, then return to the Miller for a night of carousing. Bells peel at the Norman church. One for the young at heart.

directions	At Streatley, on A329 between Pangbourne & Wallingford, take B4009 to Goring, Cross Thames & pub//hotel is on left.
meals	12pm-9.30pm. Main courses £15-£23.95 (restaurant), £7.95-£15.25 (bar); set lunch £13.95 & £16.95.
rooms	10: 7 doubles, 1 twin, 2 suites £90-£175. Singles £90-£110.

See pp 30-57 for full list of pubs with rooms

Sara Bates
Miller of Mansfield,
High Street, Goring-on-
Thames RG8 9AW
tel　　01491 872829
web　　www.millerofmansfield.com

map: 4 entry: 381

The White Lion
Crays Pond

A thriving pub-restaurant under the same ownership as the swishly revamped Miller of Mansfield in nearby Goring. A well-heeled Henley and Goring crowd is drawn by the imaginative and daily-changing menus that mix old favourites like steak and ale pudding with new ones such as brill with saffron potato, mussels and tarragon mustard sauce, and truffle risotto with crispy parmesan. Everything is made freshly and in-house, from the pasta to the ice cream. Simple tables are topped with fat white candles in a dining room where walls are lined with unusual prints and the floor is jauntily strewn with rugs. There's also a light and airy conservatory extension. Relax over the papers in the small bar with a pint of Greene King and tuck into a thick steak sandwich or a real burger at lunchtime. Call by for breakfast in Tuesday and Friday mornings from 8.30am.

directions	3 miles N of Pangbourne on B471.
meals	12pm-3pm (3.30pm Sun); 6pm-9.30pm. Main courses £10.95-£19.95; set lunch £13.95 & £15.95; set dinner £16.95 & £18.95; Sunday lunch £16.95 & £19.95.
closed	Sun from 5pm & Mon all day. Open all day.

Nick Lanckester
& Sophie Aghdami
The White Lion, Crays Pond,
Goring Heath RG8 7SH
tel　　01491 680471
web　　www.thewhitelioncrayspond.com

map: 4 entry: 382

The Lamb
Satwell

'Real ale, real food and real people,' reads the sign by the door. Close to riverside Henley-on-Thames, the 16th-century beamed cottage is owned by TV chef Anthony Worrall Thompson – and the words on the sign ring true. Enter a gorgeously low-beamed bar: scrubbed pine tables on tiled floors, logs crackling in the grate, local ales on handpump. Arrive early to bag a seat by the fire (no bookings) or settle into the cosy dining room next door; be treated to steaming plates of home-cooked pies, casseroles and stews very fairly priced. There's classic fish pie, Irish stew, steak and kidney pie and Wozza'a own Middlewhite pork sausages with mash and onion gravy. So start with half a pint of prawns, finish with rhubarb crumble; it's all scrumptiously English and don't miss the Sunday roasts. There's a secluded garden, too.

Rising Sun
Witheridge Hill

Much-loved landlady Judith Bishop, away from the business for two long years, is back with Brakspear and loving every minute of it. In this creamy cottage-pub, tucked up a gravel track on the edge of the Chilterns, her magic touch is clearly to be seen… in the rambling dining area and in the cosy bar, with its bare boards, terracotta walls, scrubbed pine tables, deep sofa by the crackling fire and no end of lovely touches – books, magazines, quirky objets and huge vases of flowers. Eager to do something different on the food front, Judith has introduced tapas dishes and 'grazing' plates (Indian or mezze) to share – as well as chilli, chicken and pumpkin soup, potted shrimps with crusty bread, confit roasted duck, Toulouse sausages and beans, and a classic fish, saffron and potato stew. Great ales, a secluded garden and a dell corner selling homemade and local goodies add to the pleasure.

directions	A4130 north from Henley; 5 miles; 1st exit at r'bout near Nettlebed onto B481 to Highmoor; thro' village; 1 mile to Satwell.
meals	12pm-2.30pm (4pm Sat); 6pm-9.30pm (10.30pm Fri & Sat); 12pm-9pm Sun. Main courses £7.95-£9.95. Sunday roast £9.95.
closed	3pm-6pm. Open all day Sat & Sun.

William McCord
The Lamb,
Satwell, Shepherd's Green,
Henley-on-Thames RG9 4QZ
tel   01491 628482
web   www.awtonline.co.uk

directions	Witheridge Hill is signed off B481 east of Stoke Row.
meals	12pm-2.30pm (3pm Sun); 7pm-9.30pm. No food Sun eve in winter. Main courses £8.95-£15.50; £5 lunch dish Mon-Thur.
closed	3pm-6pm. Open all day Sat & Sun.

Judith Bishop
Rising Sun,
Witheridge Hill,
Henley-on-Thames RG9 1AH
tel   01491 640856

map: 4 entry: 383

map: 4 entry: 384

The Five Horseshoes
Henley-on-Thames

This vine-strewn pub-cottage sits up high in a remote spot in the Chilterns, on a tiny lane that winds its way past Russell's Water near Stonor House. Arrive early in summer for the best seat in garden and the finest view in Oxfordshire. As you gaze on rolling hills, pint of Brakspears to hand, red kites wheel overhead (bring the binoculars) and steaks sizzle on the weekend barbecue. Picture windows in the conservatory dining room also get the view, so you can relish it all year round – or head into the rambling, low-ceilinged bar where a wood-burning stove warms the cockles. Cosy and carpeted, with cushioned settles, scrubbed tables and candles, it's a perfect place for tucking into Jamie Polito's comforting pub food. There's ham hock terrine with lamb hotpot, roast cod on garlic mash with red wine sauce, and roast beef on Sundays. Then head off into the hills.

The Crooked Billet
Henley-on-Thames

Dick Turpin apparently courted the landlord's daughter and Kate Winslet had her wedding breakfast here. Pints are drawn direct from the cask (there is no bar!) and the rusticity of the pub charms all who manage to find it: beams, flags and inglenooks, old pine, walls lined with bottles and baskets of spent corks. In the larger room, red walls display old photographs and mirrors; shelves are stacked with books... by candlelight it's irresistible. You come here to eat and the menu is Italian/French provincial, and long: bouillabaisse, beef fillet with seared foie gras and red wine jus, venison with roast figs and port and juniper sauce, dark chocolate tart with mint ice cream. It's founded on well-sourced raw materials and bolstered by a satisfying wine list. Occasional jazz, and a big garden bordering the beech woods where children can roam. Talking of children, the pub cooks the village school meals.

directions	Maidensgrove signed off B481 north of Nettlebed, & B480 4 miles north of Henley.
meals	12pm-2.30pm (3pm Sat, 4pm Sun); 6.30pm-9.30pm. Main courses £8.50-£14.75; bar meals £8-£9.75; Sunday roast £13.50.
closed	3.30-6pm & Sun from 6pm. Open all day Sat.

directions	5 miles W of Henley, off B481 Reading to Nettlebed road.
meals	12pm-2.30pm; 7pm-10.30pm (12pm-10.30pm Sat & Sun). Main courses £12.50-£20.
closed	2.30pm-7pm. Open all day Sat & Sun.

	Nataliina Langlands-Pearse The Five Horseshoes, Maidensgrove, Henley-on-Thames RG9 6EX
tel	01491 641282
web	www.thefivehorseshoes.co.uk

	Paul Clerehugh The Crooked Billet, Newlands Lane, Stoke Row, Henley-on-Thames RG9 5PU
tel	01491 681048
web	www.thecrookedbillet.co.uk

map: 4 entry: 385

map: 4 entry: 386

Oxfordshire   Pub with rooms

The Cherry Tree Inn
Stoke Row

This pub exudes 17th-century charm and 21st-century luxury. From the bar's minimalist good looks — low beams and brick walls, bare boards and flags, chunky wooden tables and muted earth tones — to gorgeous bedrooms in the barn, it's first class. And the blackboard listing imaginative dishes reinforces that impression. Come for roast belly pork with black pudding, caramelised apples and mash; salmon and basil fishcakes with lime hollandaise; sea bass with roast vegetable couscous and tomato and chilli dressing. Puddings are classics (treacle tart, chocolate and raspberry pudding), cheeses are local, beers are from Brakspear, there's a very decent selection of wines by the glass and the big lawn and terrace are great for summer. Bedrooms are contemporary and stylish, with flat-screen TVs, king-size beds and feather pillows.

directions	Off B481 Reading to Nettlebed road, 5 miles west of Henley.
meals	12pm-3pm (4pm Sat & Sun); 7pm-10.30pm. Main courses £7.50-£13.50 (lunch), £10.50-£14.95 (dinner).
rooms	4 doubles £95.
closed	Open all day. Closed Sun from 4pm

See pp 30–57 for full list of pubs with rooms

	Richard Coates & Paul Gilchrist The Cherry Tree Inn, Stoke Row, Henley-on-Thames RG9 5QA
tel	01491 680430
web	www.thecherrytreeinn.com

map: 4 entry: 387

Oxfordshire

The Bull & Butcher
Turville

Landlady Lydia Botha ensures this little pub quenches the thirsts of all who come to visit one of the most bucolic film locations in Britain — it sits beneath the Chitty Chitty Bang Bang windmill, the village is the setting for *The Vicar of Dibley* and suspects from *Midsomer Murders* have propped up the bar. Bags of atmosphere, and style, in cream walls, latched doors, a glass-topped 50-foot well, fresh flowers. Busy with Londoners at weekends, it's a jolly place in which to down a pint of Brakspear's finest or take a tipple of homemade sloe gin. Food is good modern British: fresh crayfish tails, dry-cured venison with olives and parmesan, mutton stew and dumplings, and great Sunday roasts. No piped music, no games, no pubby paraphernalia, just fine 17th-century beams, working log fires, a unique function room, and friendly people. There's a garden for fine days and great walks through the Chiltern beech woods.

directions	M40 junc. 5; through Ibstone; for Turville at T-junction.
meals	12pm-2.30pm (4pm Sun); 6.30pm-9.30pm (7pm-9pm Sun). Main courses £10-£14; bar meals £6-£10; Sunday roast £12.95.
closed	Open all day.

	Lydia Botha The Bull & Butcher, Turville, Henley-on-Thames RG9 6QU
tel	01491 638283
web	www.thebullandbutcher.com

map: 4 entry: 388

Fox and Hounds
Christmas Common

In a hamlet in the hills – a few grand houses and this 15th-century brick and flint cottage: the civilised Fox and Hounds. Once it was a rustic rural ale house, but Brakspears have transformed it into a thriving food pub under the guidance of chef-landlord Kieron Daniels. Despite the changes, it has lost none of its charm and character. Enter a beamy bar full of simple benches, cosy corners, logs glowing in a vast inglenook always lit, cribbage and cards and pints of Brakspear tapped direct from the cask. The foodie action takes place in the restaurant, with its wooden floors, open-to-view kitchen, quirky rustic décor and French windows to the garden. Farm-reared meats and local fruit and vegetables result in such dishes as mussel and brown shrimp risotto, roast partridge with cranberry gravy, John Dory with shallots and fennel, and lemon zerbena, pannacotta and candy ginger. Make time for walks through the beech woods, look up for soaring red kites.

The Lord Nelson
Brightwell Baldwin

The sleepy back-lane setting of Brightwell Baldwin lives up to expectations; cottages tumbling down the hill, a church perched on a bank, a rambling old inn festooned with flowers – and flags on Trafalgar Day. The creamy yellow façade and front veranda catch the eye, enticing you into a civilised 16th-century interior, all wooden floors, wonky beams, logs fires, cosy corners and charm. Antiques, fine old prints and Nelson memorabilia keep the eye entertained. Most come to eat and eat well you can; there's chicken liver parfait with homemade chutney, monkfish with mustard beurre blanc, lemon tart with raspberry coulis. Retire to the womb-like snug (deep sofas, table lamps, a country-house feel) for coffee and a little doze. And there's more – Brakspear on tap, 20 wines by the glass, friendly, smiley service and a wonderful rear terrace for summer sipping.

directions	From M40 junc. 5 follow old A40.
meals	12pm-2.30pm (3pm Sat & Sun); 7pm-9.30pm. Main courses £10-£18.
closed	3pm-5pm in winter. Open all day Sat & Sun.

Kieron Daniels
Fox and Hounds,
Christmas Common,
Watlington OX49 5HL

tel   01491 612599

map: 4 entry: 389

directions	Village signed off B4009 between Benson & Watlington.
meals	12pm-2.30pm; 6.30pm-10pm (7pm-9.30pm Sun). Main courses £12.95-£18.95; set lunch £10.95.
closed	3pm-6pm.

Roger & Carole Shippey
The Lord Nelson,
Brightwell Baldwin,
Watlington OX49 5NP

tel   01491 612497
web   www.lordnelson-inn.co.uk

map: 4 entry: 390

The Boar's Head 🛏
Ardington

If it's not the sweet smell of lilies, it's the aroma of fresh bread. With daily baking to tempt them, villagers arrive for a pint of the best then put in their orders – sun-dried tomato, granary, with or without olives. Here are good ales, fine wines and a welcome for kids. In a bar cosy with low beams, scrubbed wooden tables, checked curtains and log fires, sit down to a first-class seasonal menu created by a chef-patron who knows what's what. Bruce Buchan is inventive with fish from Newlyn and market-fresh produce from Newbury and Wantage – assiette of Cornish scallops, duck breast with chorizo, rösti and port sauce, hot pistachio soufflé. Even the local black pudding has won prizes. Rooms upstairs are unmistakably smart, with good beds, crisp linen and piles of cushions. The small double has a beamed ceiling, the big double comes with a claw-foot bath, the suite has a sofa for kids and views over the neat, estate village.

directions	On A417, 2 miles east of Wantage.
meals	12pm–2pm; 7pm–9.30pm. Main courses £17–£20; bar meals £7.95–£14.95.
rooms	3: 2 doubles, 1 suite £85–£130. Singles £75–£95.
closed	3pm–6.30pm Sat (7pm Sun).

See pp 30–57 for full list of pubs with rooms

Bruce & Kay Buchan
The Boar's Head,
Church Street, Ardington,
Wantage OX12 8QA

tel	01235 833254
web	www.boarsheadardington.co.uk

♿ 🏃 📖 🍺 🍷 🛏

map: 3 entry: 391

The Mole Inn
Toot Baldon

The Mole has proved a hit with Oxford foodies who have flocked to experience the pub's renaissance… it is packed most days. Now there are an impeccable stone exterior, a landscaped garden and a ravishing bar. Be delighted by stripped beams and chunky walls, black leather sofas, logs in the grate and a dresser that groans with breads and olive jars. Chic rusticity proceeds into three dining areas: fat candles on blond wooden tables, thick terracotta floors and the sun angling in on a fresh plateful of roast Oxfordshire lamb with garlic mash and rosemary jus. Daily specials point to a menu that trawls the globe 'for inspiration, and whether you go for light salad and pasta bowl lunches or rib-eye steak, sauté potatoes and dressed salad, you'll eat well. Scrumptious ice creams, British cheeses, good wines, local Hook Norton ale and polite staff complete the picture.

directions	From A4074, 5 miles south of Oxford; turn at Nuneham Courtenay for Marsh Baldon & Toot Baldon.
meals	12pm–2.30pm (4pm Sun); 7pm–9.30pm (6pm–9pm Sun). Main courses £10.95–£19.50; bar meals £4.95–£9.95.
closed	Open all day.

Gary Witchalls
The Mole Inn,
Toot Baldon,
Oxford OX44 9NG

tel	01865 340001
web	www.themoleinn.com

♿ 🏃 📖

map: 8 entry: 392

The Fishes
Oxford

Location, location, location – The Fishes has it all. Three acres of glorious gardens, minutes from the A34, walking distance from the dreaming spires. It's run by Peach Pubs, the most innovative small pub group in the land – where else can you borrow a rug for the garden, order a jug of Pimms and a picnic basket for two (ploughman's, vegetarian, deli) and spread out by a river? Just be sure to arrive early on fine days. The roasts are fabulous: order (by midweek) a family roast beef platter for the weekend, on Sunday sit down to it on the veranda. The successful Peach food formula is reproduced here: the deli board selection, the starters of pumpkin and sage risotto and Caesar salad, the main dishes of fish stew, salmon Wellington and braised blade of beef with baby onion jus. Greene King ales, decent wines by the glass and a passion for locally sourced produce complete this very rosy picture.

directions	North on A34; left junction after Botley Interchange, signed to Rugby Club. From south, exit A34 at Botley & return to A34 south; then as above.
meals	12pm-10pm (9.30pm Sun). Main courses £8.75-£14.50; Sunday roast £10.50.
closed	Open all day.

Victoria Moon
The Fishes,
North Hinksey,
Oxford OX2 0NA
tel   01865 249796
web   www.fishesoxford.co.uk

map: 8 entry: 393

White Hart
Wytham

Who says the traditional and the contemporary don't mix? At the White Hart – once a rural, Thames-side drinkers' den, now practically in Oxford – bold colours and modern art mingle with flagged floors and stone fireplaces. And the different areas have distinctive characters: the 'Parlour' room has a French feel with painted floors and furniture and a central bread block laid with fresh loaves; the cosy bar has exotic coloured walls and velvet cushions. The upstairs bar is quite different, all open brickwork, plain floorboards, log fire and walls bearing framed tomatoes. The rustic terrace has Greek terracotta woodburners and a 15th-century dovecote. There are real ales and a raft of wines by the glass in the bar and modern cooking from the kitchen. Monthly specials, described as "divine", might include local wild venison with black cherry jus, and roast halibut on saffron and herb risotto with tomato confit and green chilli salsa.

directions	A34 to Oxford, off at Botley interchange.
meals	12pm-3pm (3.30pm Sat, 5pm Sun), 6.30pm-10pm, 7pm-9pm Sun). Main courses £12-£19.50; set lunch, 2 courses, £10.
closed	3.30pm-6pm.

David Peevers
White Hart,
Wytham,
Oxford OX2 8QA
tel   01865 244372
web   www.thewhitehartoxford.co.uk

map: 8 entry: 394

The Boot Inn
Barnard Gate

It's not often you can down a pint of Hook Norton in a cosy Cotswold pub while pondering David Beckham's shoe size, Jasmin Le Bon's ankle and the flexibility of Roger Bannister's soles. The Boot's walls are covered with a rare collection of celebrity footwear, and the list is long: Stirling Moss, Henry Cooper, Prue Leith, Rick Stein. Expect standing timbers, bare board floors, good country tables, candlelight at night and a huge log fire… a deliciously traditional atmosphere in which to settle back and enjoy some fresh, flavourful cooking: monkfish with lime and ginger butter and polenta chips, bouillabaisse with aïoli, fillet steak with garlic butter. After a slice of dark chocolate cheesecake there is an overwhelming temptation to don a pair of Ranulph Fiennes's record-breaking Polar bootliners and turn into an armchair explorer by the fire.

directions	Off A40; 4 miles from Oxford.
meals	12pm-2.30pm (4pm Sat & Sun); 7pm-9pm (10pm Fri). Main courses £9.95-£16.95.
closed	Open all day Sat & Sun.

Craig Foster
The Boot Inn,
Barnard Gate,
Eynsham OX29 6XE
tel   01865 881231
web   www.theboot-inn.com

map: 8 entry: 395

The Trout at Tadpole Bridge
Buckland Marsh

Down here by the river, Ratty and Toad could be toasting their toes in front of the wood-burning stove. The Trout is a drinking fisherman's paradise. Walls are busy with bendy rods, children are liked and your dog can join you in the flagstoned bars. Experienced hoteliers Gareth and Helen Pugh took over in 2006 but chef Robbie Ellis remains at the stove, sourcing top local ingredients, namely lamb from the Blenheim estate and seasonal game from nearby shoots. Expect a treat — perhaps roast rump of lamb with lentils and red wine jus or venison fillet with spiced pear chutney. In summer, the riverside garden comes alive as drinkers in search of real ale arrive by boat. Stay the night to catch a glimpse of more *Wind in the Willows* magic: sleep tight in one of six redecorated rooms, neatly kitted out with Farrow & Ball paints, flat-screen TVs, bateau or brass beds, tasteful antiques and views across fields. Bliss!

directions	Off A420 between Oxford & Swindon.
meals	12pm-2pm; 7pm-9pm. Main courses £11.25-£17.95; bar snacks from £5.95.
rooms	6: 4 doubles, 1 twin, 1 suite £100-130. Min. 2 nights w'ends May-Sep.
closed	3pm-6pm & Sun eve.

See pp 30-57 for full list of pubs with rooms

Gareth & Helen Pugh
The Trout at Tadpole Bridge,
Buckland Marsh,
Faringdon SN7 8RF
tel   01367 870382
web   www.troutinn.co.uk

map: 8 entry: 396

Masons Arms
South Leigh

A quintessentially English inn – with attitude – in somnolent South Leigh. Who would guess there's a gentlemen's club here? This is 'Gerry Stonhill's Individual Masons Arms'; dogs, children and mobile phones are unwelcome, vegetarians visit 'by appointment only', and some folk chopper in (ask about the nearest helipad). There are 15th-century flagstone floors, crackling log fires, dark hessian walls clad with paintings, old oak tables, spent wine bottles and scattered cigar boxes on shelves. Plus three Dickensian rooms to explore and be charmed by, and a cosily clubby whisky and cognac-stocked bar. If you fancy a Cuban cigar to round off your meal, make sure you arrive before July 2007. Food is proper English, and expertly cooked: potted shrimps, wild smoked salmon, casseroles, roast duck with armagnac and orange sauce, Angus steaks and the juiciest fish from the market, perhaps Dover sole and whole sea bass.

directions	3 miles south east of Witney off A40 towards Oxford.
meals	12pm-2.30pm; 6.30pm-10.30pm. Main courses £10-£25.
closed	3pm-6.30pm; Sun eve & Mon all day.

Gerry Stonhill
Masons Arms,
South Leigh,
Witney OX29 6XN
tel   01993 702485

map: 8 entry: 397

Fleece on the Green
Witney

Lee Cash and Victoria Moon dug deep into their pockets to buy the lease on the Fleece – a Georgian building overlooking the green in genteel Witney – to establish the now hugely successful Peach Pub Company. Expect wooden floors, plum walls, squashy sofas around low tables and a continental opening time of 8.30am for coffee and bacon sarnies. Moving the bar to the front has worked wonders, drawing in casual drinkers for pints of Greene King and bucket-sized glasses of wine. Thumbs-up from locals for the all-day sandwiches, salads and deli-board menu: starters of cheese, charcuterie, fish, olive tapenade and marinated chillies. There are, too, stone-baked pizzas and modern brasserie-style dishes like braised neck of lamb with roasted winter roots and Thai curry mussels. Delightful bedrooms are big enough to hold an armchair or two.

directions	M40 junc. 15 or M6 junc. 4. On green, near church.
meals	8.30am-11.30am; 12pm-2.30pm; 6.30pm-10pm (9.30pm Sun). Snacks served 2.30pm-6.30pm. Main courses £7.50-£14.
rooms	10: 1 twin/double, 8 doubles, 1 single, £80-£90.
closed	Open all day.

See pp 30–57 for full list of pubs with rooms

Victoria Moon
Fleece on the Green,
11 Church Green,
Witney OX28 4AZ
tel   01993 892270
web   www.fleecewitney.co.uk

map: 9 entry: 398

Oxfordshire

Oxfordshire

The Swan
Swinbrook

No pool tables, no juke boxes, no fruit machines, no soggy dogs – though "dry and on a lead" will do. This old water mill going back to the 15th century, in a lovely village on the Devonshire Estate, has been charmingly restored by the Duchess and Archie and Nicola Orr-Ewing – owners of the King's Head at Bledington. In the three interconnecting rooms of this listed building you may expect well-nurtured pints of Hook Norton and modern pub food. Local ingredients dominate an enticing menu – pheasant with celeriac and parsnip mash, lamb hotpot, lunchtime salt beef sandwiches – while open fires will warm the cockles of anyone's heart, even on the coldest Cotswold day. In summer, the new, oak-beamed, high-raftered conservatory comes into its own. Flagstones and settles, fresh flowers and cheerful chatter, and the idly-flowing river Windrush across the road – a nigh-on perfect place.

Royal Oak
Ramsden

From opening time on, the jolly banter of regulars can be heard from the doorstep outside. Blazing winter fires, piles of magazines and well-thumbed books by the inglenook make this a fine place for a pint of real ale; tuck into a corner filled with plump scatter cushions. Some brilliant food can be had in the pubby bar – open-stone walls, cream and soft-green windows – as well as in the extension beyond, where glass doors open onto a pretty terrace with wrought-iron chairs in summer and outdoor heaters to keep you snug. Dishes such as roast half shoulder of Westwell lamb with rosemary and garlic sauce, roast cod with tapenade crust and sweet pepper sauce, lovely Sunday roasts and chocolate and brandy ice cream will put a smile on your face. Well-behaved children and dogs are welcome, and the village is a stunner.

directions	From Oxford A40, through Witney. Village signed right, off A40.
meals	12pm–2pm (2.30pm Sun); 7pm–9pm (9.30 Fri & Sat). Main courses £10.95–£17.50; sandwiches (lunch) from £5.25; Sunday roast £11.95.
closed	3pm–6pm. Open all day Sat & Sun.

directions	On B4022, 3 miles north of Witney.
meals	12pm–2pm; 7pm–10pm. Main courses £7.50–£18; Sunday lunch £16.95.
closed	3pm–6.30pm.

Archie & Nicola Orr-Ewing
The Swan,
Swinbrook,
Burford OX18 4DY
tel 01993 823339

Jon Oldham
Royal Oak,
Ramsden,
Chipping Norton OX7 3AU
tel 01993 868213

map: 8 entry: 399

map: 8 entry: 400

The Chequers
Chipping Norton

Eye-catching with an immaculate stone frontage, green paintwork and stylish stone urns, the 18th-century Chequers stands smartly on the village lane. The Goldings took it on in 2003 – it had been closed for five years – and months of refurbishment followed before the reincarnation was unveiled. Prepare for a dramatic, airy and open-plan interior: bare boards and pine tables, cleverly partitioned dining areas, stone walls, roaring woodburner and stacked logs, chunky tables topped with candles and flowers. Soaring rafters, modern oak tables and a vast dresser racked with wine bottles are the wow factors in the dining extension. No music, just a buzz when busy, and excellent food – smoked haddock kedgeree, fisherman's pie, rib-eye steak with red wine sauce, stewed plums in armagnac. Book for the crispy duck night (Thursday) and roast Sunday lunches. Upstairs are a lounge and private dining area.

directions	Churchill on B4450 between Chipping Norton & Stow-on-the-Wold.
meals	12pm-2pm (3pm Sun); 7pm-9.30pm (9pm Sun). Main courses £4-£16.50.
closed	Open all day.

Peter & Asumpta Golding
The Chequers,
Church Road,
Churchill,
Chipping Norton OX7 6NJ
tel   01608 659393

map: 8 entry: 401

The Kings Head Inn
Bledington

Achingly pretty Cotswold stone cottages around a green with quacking ducks, a pond and a perfect pub with a cobbled courtyard. Archie is young, affable and charming with locals and guests, but Nic is his greatest asset – she has done up the bedrooms and they look fabulous. All are different, most have a stunning view, some family furniture mixed in with 'bits' she's picked up, painted wood, great colours and lush fabrics. The bar is lively – not with music but with talk – so choose rooms over the courtyard if you prefer a quiet evening. The flagstoned dining room with pale wood tables is inviting, and there are lovely unpompous touches like jugs of cow parsley in the loo. Expect potted shrimps, crayfish and rocket linguine, steak, ale and root vegetable pie, Angus beef fillet from the family farm, and roasts on Sundays. Or just tuck into a toasted panini and a homemade pud.

directions	Burford-Stow A424; right to Idbury; Bledington, signed.
meals	12pm-2pm; 7pm-9pm (9.30pm Fri & Sat). Main courses £9.50-£17.50; bar meals from £4.50.
rooms	12: 10 doubles, 2 twins £70-£125. Singles £55.
closed	3pm-6pm. Open all day Sat & Sun.

See pp 30-57 for full list of pubs with rooms

Archie & Nic Orr-Ewing
The Kings Head Inn,
The Green,
Bledington OX7 6XQ
tel   01608 658365
web   www.kingsheadinn.net

map: 8 entry: 402

Mason's Arms
Swerford

At one time the village of Swerford was owned by a hilariously-named henchman of William the Conqueror, one Robert D'Oily, but there's not a glimpse of a crocheted doily or a Toby jug in today's pub. It may be low on roadside appeal, but inside's chic-cottage décor would knock the clips off a makeover show designer's cue-board: duck-egg blue beams, clotted-cream walls and olive checked curtains, with rugs and seagrass matting across the floor. A wardrobe is stacked with wine bottles, background music plays, the central bar stacks up locals nursing their Brakspear's Special. And the food? It's locally-sourced best-of-British, including the old-fashioned bits. Chef-patron Bill Leadbeater, who has worked for Gordon Ramsay, delivers braised shin of beef, user-friendly steaks and roast shoulder of Oxford Down lamb. Children are not pandered to with nuggets'n'chips but offered mini-portions – and a garden to romp in.

The Crown Inn
Church Enstone

With six years as head chef at the Three Choirs Vineyard behind him, Tony decided to seek out his own place. With his wife Caroline, he headed for the Cotswolds and this striking 17th-century inn. It's a mellow local-stone dream, festooned in creepers and off the beaten track in a sleepy village close to the river Glyme. Walk in to a cosy, cottagey bar, smartly comfortable with old pine tables on a seagrass floor, rough stone walls, and a log fire crackling in the inglenook. At lunchtime, walkers and weekenders come for pints of Hook Norton and generous plates of home-cooked pub grub; warming soups, Dexter beef and Hooky pie, fish and chips and the like are listed on the blackboard. Cooking moves up a gear in the evening. Fish is Tony's speciality, so look out for sea bass with scallops, chilli and garlic dressing. Food is fresh and locally sourced and Sunday lunch is deservedly popular.

directions	On A361 north-east of C. Norton.
meals	12pm-2.15pm (2.30pm Sun); 7pm-9.15pm (9pm Sun). Main courses £10.95-£13.95; bar meals £6.50-9.95; set menus £9.95 & £10.95.
closed	3pm-6pm (7pm Sun). Open all day in summer.

Bill & Charmaine Leadbeater
Mason's Arms,
Banbury Road, Swerford,
Chipping Norton OX7 4AP
tel   01608 683212
web   www.masons-arms.com

map: 8 entry: 403

directions	3.5 miles south east of Chipping Norton.
meals	12pm-2pm; 7pm-9pm. No food Mon. Main courses £7.95-£16.95; bar meals £4.75-£12.95; Sunday lunch £13.95 & £16.95.
closed	3pm-6pm, Mon lunch & Sun from 4pm.

Tony & Caroline Warburton
The Crown Inn,
Mill Lane, Church Enstone,
Chipping Norton OX7 4NN
tel   01608 677262
web   www.crowninnenstone.co.uk

map: 8 entry: 404

Oxfordshire
Pub with rooms

Falkland Arms
Great Tew

In a perfect Cotswold village, the perfect English inn. Five hundred years on and the fire still roars in the stone-flagged bar under a low timbered ceiling slung with jugs, mugs and tankards. Here, the hop is treated with reverence: ales change weekly and old pump clips hang from the bar. In summer, Morris Men jingle in the lane outside and life spills out onto the terrace at the front and the big garden behind. This lively pub is utterly down-to-earth and in very good hands. The dining room is tiny and intimate with beams and stone walls, and every traditional dish is home-cooked. Bedrooms are cosy, some verging on snug; the attic room is wonderfully private. Brass beds and four-posters, old oak and an uneven floor; you'll sleep well. It's all blissfully free of modern trappings.

directions	Off A361 between Banbury & Chipping Norton.
meals	12pm-2pm (bar meals only); 7pm-8pm. No food Sun eve. Main courses £11.50-£16.95; bar meals £7.25-£11.95.
rooms	5 doubles £80-£120.
closed	2.30pm-6pm (from 3pm Sat; 3pm-7pm Sun). Open all day weekends in summer.

See pp 30–57 for full list of pubs with rooms

Paul Barlow–Heal &
Sarah–Jane Courage
Falkland Arms,
Great Tew, Chipping Norton OX7 4DB
tel   01608 683653
web   www.falklandarms.org.uk

map: 8 entry: 405

Oxfordshire

Olde Reindeer Inn
Banbury

Oliver Cromwell held court in the heavily wood-panelled Globe Room during the Civil War. The panelling was dismantled in 1909, almost sold to America, then returned in 1964… it is a magnificent feature in Banbury's oldest pub. Owned by Hook Norton and run by Tony and Dot Puddifoot, the backstreet local has a reputation for very decently priced, home-cooked lunches, simply but perfectly done. Specialities include steak and ale pie, bubble-and-squeak in a Yorkshire pudding and delicious pies. The bar is cosy polished oak boards, solid furniture and a magnificent, carved, 17th-century fireplace, log-fuelled in winter. Hook Norton ales are served as well as country wines, including apricot and damson, that rival the beer in popularity. Parsons Street is tiny and runs off the Market Square yet the Reindeer is unmissably signed.

directions	In town centre, just off Market Square.
meals	11am-3pm. No food Sun. Main courses £4.50-£7.25.
closed	Open all day. Closed Sun from 3.30pm.

Tony Puddifoot
Olde Reindeer Inn,
47 Parsons Street,
Banbury OX16 5NA
tel   01295 264031

map: 8 entry: 406

Oxfordshire

Wykham Arms
Sibford Gower

Gordon Ramsay landed his first job here. Later, under the name The Moody Cow, it lost some of its popularity; now the listed 1700s free house is a thoroughly modern country inn. Having seen the pretty Cotswold village, you'd be forgiven for expecting cushions and chintz; in fact you get creams and deep reds, flagged floors and farmhouse furnishings. The menu, served through a warren of connected rooms, spills over with local seasonal produce, while flavours are strong, clean and uncomplicated. Try salmon with beetroot and marinated artichoke salad, or wild boar and apple sausages with a beer mustard mash and caramelised onion gravy. And there are plenty of wines by the glass, from a wine list that is excellent *and* affordable. A big welcome for children and dogs too, who, in summer, will appreciate the big patio and the wooded garden.

directions	Between Brailes & Swalcliffe; on B4035, follow signs to Sibford Gower.
meals	12pm-3pm; 7pm-9.30pm. No food Sun eve. Main courses £15-£18. Bar meals £7.50-£10.
closed	3pm-6pm & Mon all day.

Damian & Deborah Bradley
Wykham Arms,
Colony Lane, Sibford Gower,
Banbury OX15 5RX

tel 01295 788808
web www.thewykhamarms.co.uk

map: 8 entry: 407

Rutland

The Jackson Stops Inn
Stretton

Local pub entrepreneur Richard Graham – proprietor of the Old Pheasant, Glaston and the Collweston Slater strikes just the right balance between the familiar and the novel in this exemplary village pub. Everything runs smoothly in a bare-bones bar and quirky-rustic dining rooms. Imaginative short menus span roast belly pork with apple mash and cider sauce, and venison with celeriac dumplings and port wine sauce, while first-rate puddings include bitter chocolate marquise with pistachio custard; set lunch menus and bar snacks are also available. Open fires, evening candles, fresh flowers and a rambling corridor linking rooms add to the charm, while in the tiny bar (two scrubbed tables and a bench or two) two guest ales are on tap. The old thatched building was formerly known as the White Horse, but the estate agent's sign remained outside the pub for so long that the name stuck.

directions	From A1 take B668 for Oakham & Stretton. Pub 0.5 miles on.
meals	12pm-2:30pm; 6.30pm-9pm. Main courses £9.95-£18.50; bar meals £6.95-£9.95; set lunch, 2-courses, £10.
closed	2.30pm-6pm, Sun eve & Mon all day.

Gary Marshall
The Jackson Stops Inn,
Rookery Lane, Stretton,
Oakham LE15 7RA

tel 01780 410237
web www.thejacksonstops.co.uk

map: 9 entry: 408

The Olive Branch
Clipsham

There are so many blackboards here you might think that Sean Hope and Ben Jones were school teachers unable to let go. But it's the simplest way to list the speciality wines, the bar snacks and the daily lunch menu. This is not your usual chi-chi ex-boozer; a relaxed pub personality is pinned here to a Michelin star. The casual mood is created by closely arranged tables and a medley of books, furniture and roaring log fire, the adjoining barn is a small party-and-breakfast room, and there's a sheltered patio that squeezes in Saturday barbecues. The menu roams through pork and stilton pie with piccalilli to roast turbot, confit duck leg, chocolate brownies and local cheeses; British cooking and local produce hold sway. Fish 'n' chips and roast rib of beef are given a delectable modern edge, real ales are taken seriously and the wines are a joy. You can take away from the 'pub shop' list, or stay the night in Beech House across the lane. Stylish, individual rooms ooze comfort – goose down duvets, flat-screen TVs, Roberts radios, lavish bathrooms, real coffee. Superb.

directions	2 miles off A1 at Stretton (B668 junc).
meals	12pm-2pm (3pm Sun); 7pm-9.30pm (9pm Sun).
	Main courses £10.50-£22.50; set lunch £19.50; Sunday roast £14.50.
rooms	6: 5 doubles, 1 family £80-£160. Singles from £65.
closed	3pm-6pm. Open all day Sat & Sun.

SPECIAL AWARD
see pages 28-29

Ben Jones & Sean Hope
The Olive Branch,
Main Street,
Clipsham LE15 7SH
tel   01780 410355
web   www.theolivebranchpub.com

map: 9 entry: 409

Rutland

Finch's Arms
Upper Hambleton

Alone on its peninsula surrounded by Rutland Water, the Finch's has the greatest of rural views. Colin Crawford, who took over a decade ago, could have sat back and twiddled his thumbs and people would still have poured in. But he has not been idle, and has created a terrific team in the kitchen led by David Bailey. Décor in the Garden Room is ultra-elegant, with food to match; choose from lamb confit with crispy pancetta and mash, turbot with salmon mousse, mussels and asparagus in a spicy lemon sauce, and rib-eye steak with horseradish. Or sausages with mash and onion... the bar and restaurant menus change frequently. There's a small, bustling bar with log fires, a fine selection of ales, a great wine list, and a garden and a hillside terrace for summer with wonderful watery views. Staff are friendly and efficient.

directions	Off A606, east of Oakham.
meals	12pm-2.30pm; 6pm-9.30pm. 12pm-9.30pm Sun. Main courses £8.50-£25.
closed	Open all day.

Colin & Celia Crawford
Finch's Arms,
Oakham Road, Upper Hambleton,
Oakham LE15 8TL

| tel | 01572 756575 |
| web | www.finchsarms.co.uk |

map: 9 entry: 410

Rutland
Pub with rooms

The Old Pheasant
Uppingham

Richard and Nikki have introduced a clean, simple décor and a neutral colour scheme to complement an earlier renovation; expect bare brick, heavy beams, open fire and polished tables. It's still a pubby pub, with local Grainstore Brewery ales served alongside Timothy Taylor and Jennings, and friendly too, but the emphasis is on food. The menu is short, refreshingly to-the-point and changes continually, with a welcome number of old-English dishes such Lincolnshire sausages with bubble and squeak. There's a swish streak too – seared tuna loin comes with roasted peppers and coriander – and fish is a strong point. Choose to eat in the restaurant, in the bar or in the pretty courtyard in summer. The bedroom extension has been done up with a good eye: attractive wallpapers, a restful feel, and bathrooms sporting Gilchrist & Soames.

directions	On A47 between Leicester & Peterborough, east of Uppingham.
meals	12pm-2pm; 6.30pm-9pm. Main courses £9-£20.
rooms	9 twins/doubles £75-£100. Singles £50-£60.
closed	3pm-6pm & Sun from 4pm. Open all day Sat.

See pp 30-57 for full list of pubs with rooms

Richard Graham
The Old Pheasant,
Main Road, Glaston,
Uppingham LE15 9BP

| tel | 01572 822326 |
| web | www.theoldpheasant.co.uk |

map: 9 entry: 411

The Inn at Grinshill
Grinshill

A ridge of pine soars high above the village, so bring the boots and take to Shropshire's hills. Down at the inn, nothing but good things; this is a wonderfully welcoming bolthole, a top-to-toe renovation that now shines. Wander at will and you will find an 18th-century panelled family room with rugs and games, a 19th-century bar with quarry-tiled floors and a crackling fire, and a 21st-century dining room, serene in cream and flooded with light courtesy of glazed coach-house arches. Bedrooms are just as good; understatedly elegant, they come with piles of pillows, crisp white linen, wispy mohair blankets or shiny quilted eiderdowns, and technology hidden behind mirrors. Back downstairs, ambrosial delights pour from the kitchen — the breast of duck served with an orange and lemon marmalade was faultless. A grand piano gets played on Friday nights and life spills out into the garden in summer. Church bells peel, roses ramble, there's cricket in the village at the weekend and the Shropshire Way passes by outside.

directions	A49 north from Shrewsbury. Grinshill signed left after 5 miles.
meals	12pm-2.30pm; 6.30pm-9.30pm. Main courses £10-£16; sandwiches £5; Sunday roast £9.95.
rooms	6: 3 doubles, 2 twins, 1 single £50-£120.
closed	3pm-6pm, Sun from 4pm & Mon Jan-Easter. Open all day Sat.

SPECIAL AWARD
see pages 28-29

Kevin & Victoria Brazier
The Inn at Grinshill,
High Street, Grinshill,
Shrewsbury SY4 3BL

tel   01939 220410
web   www.theinnatgrinshill.co.uk

map: 7 entry: 412

New Inn
Baschurch

Outside, jolly hanging baskets and a plain, whitewashed frontage. Inside, a sensitive stripping back to old brick and beams, and a bright and open space. There are comfortable sofas at one end, light-oak dining chairs and tables at the other, and a big traditional bar in between. In spite of the 48 covers, a well-placed wall and brick fireplace lend the dining areas an air of intimacy. Out at the back, tables with sun shades and decking invite summer drinkers and diners. Archers, Abbot and Banks ales on the pump and good house wines are served by Jenny Bean and her charming staff, while Marcus prepares starters of warm black pudding salad with quails eggs, or baby beets deep-fried in batter served with horseradish sauce. We also loved the look of the bacon chop topped with apple slices and crumbled Cheshire cheese, and the homemade citrus cheesecake. All villages should have a pub like this.

directions	Pub just off B5067 in Baschurch, 5 miles north west of Shrewsbury.
meals	12pm-2pm (3pm Sun); 6.30pm-9.30pm (7pm-9pm Sun). Main courses £8.75-£17.50; bar meals £4.95-£7.25.
closed	3pm-6pm (4pm-7pm Sun).

	Marcus & Jenny Bean New Inn, Church Road, Baschurch, Shrewsbury SY4 2EF
tel	01939 260335
web	www.thenewinnbaschurch.co.uk

map: 7 entry: 413

Riverside Inn
Cressage

There's a great buzz in this large, comfortable huntin', shootin' and fishin' inn – standing on a magnificent bend of the Severn, looking gloriously out towards the Wrekin and beyond. It's worth seeking out for its crackling woodburner in winter and its dining conservatory with views all year round. In summer there's a pretty garden smartly furnished, and you can fish from the bank for salmon and trout. Seasonal monthly menus might include a starter of steamed leek and cheddar pudding – a tasty modern take on an old country dish – and a main course of creamy tarragon chicken. There's port to accompany your cheese, and make the most of the Salopian beers and the homemade sorbets and ice creams; it's all good value. Upstairs, well-proportioned Georgian bedrooms are in excellent order, and the service, as in every good pub, is both relaxed and efficient.

directions	South from Shrewsbury on A458, through Cross Houses to Cressage; pub on left.
meals	12pm-2.30pm; 6.30pm-9.30pm. Main courses £6.95-£18.55.
rooms	7: 6 doubles, 1 twin £60-£70. Singles £45.
closed	3pm-6pm. Open all day Sat & Sun May-Sep.

See pp 30-57 for full list of pubs with rooms

	Peter Stanford Davis Riverside Inn, Cressage, Shrewsbury SY5 6AF
tel	01952 510900
web	www.theriversideinn.net

map: 7 entry: 414

Feathers Inn
Brockton

Once two Elizabethan cottages built from ship-salvaged timber, the Feathers stands in prime walking country. And the rambling, characterful, individual interior comes as a surprise. Walk in to tiled and wooden floors, whitewashed stone walls, painted beams, a vast inglenook with crackling logs, big mirrors, stone busts, grand swagged curtains, chunky church candles and colourful art for sale – a feast for the eyes! Focus on the handpumps and order a pint of Hobson's or an excellent wine to accompany to some great pub food: chef-patron Paul Kayiatou comes from London's top kitchens, so sit back and enjoy roast belly pork with black pudding and apple and cinnamon chutney, grilled sole with lemon and parsley butter, and warm chocolate fondant. There's a good value early evening supper menu and local roast beef on Sundays. Mellow, warm and satisfying after a long hike along Wenlock Edge.

directions	On B4378 Much Wenlock to Craven Arms road, 5 miles south-west of Much Wenlock.
meals	12pm-2.30pm; 6.30pm-9.30pm. Main courses £8.95-£15.95; set menu (Tues-Fri before 8pm) £12.95 & £14.95; Sunday lunch £10.95 & £13.95.
closed	3pm-6.30pm & Mon all day.

	Paul & Anna Kayiatou Feathers Inn, Brockton, Much Wenlock TF13 6JR
tel	01746 785202

map: 7 entry: 415

Bottle & Glass
Picklescott

Come via All Stretton – it's worth it for the views. High in the wilds of Shropshire, in a village of under 200 souls, stands this archetypal English country inn. Cross the front terrace and enter a beamed, oak-corsetted lounge bar, warm and inviting with log fires, fresh flowers, chunky candles and merry landlord. There's an eating area with dark pink walls, a second bar with cushioned bar stools and wooden settles and, for the literary-minded, a bookcase full of novels. Classical music plays gently in the background as walkers and locals take their fill of Hobson's Bitter and Shropshire Lad. The menu is extensive and helpings are hearty, so tuck into lunchtime rolls and ploughman's and good, simple, homemade soups, dumpling stews and steak and Guinness pies. Bow-tied, jolly-jumpered Paul Stretton-Downes U.A.A. (Unencumbered by Academic Achievement) makes this place special.

directions	Village signed off A49 north of Church Stretton.
meals	12pm-2pm; 7pm-9pm. Main courses £9.50-£16; bar meals £7.50-£16.
closed	3pm-6pm, Sun eve & Mon all day.

	Paul & Jo Stretton-Downes Bottle & Glass, Picklescott, Church Stretton SY6 6NR
tel	01694 751345

map: 7 entry: 416

Crown Country Inn
Munslow

The thistles that grew around The Crown's front door have long gone. Richard and Jane Arnold bought this listed Tudor inn (variously a courtroom, doctor's surgery and jail in previous lives) in a parlous state. Now it's a happier place, where locals gather for a chat and a pint of Cleric's Cure at dark polished tables in a winter-cosy, log-stoved bar. The upstairs function room and outside terrace are also well-used. The secret of the inn's success is revealed on the rustic walls of the bar, adorned with food awards and a map of suppliers: proprietor and chef Richard is passionate about local produce and the menu is stuffed with it. Try crostini ('little toasts') of local black pudding with Wenlock Edge Farm bacon, or griddled local sirloin steak with organic smoked butter. And the cheeseboard is a treat of lesser-known British cheeses – including Hereford Hop, rolled in hops.

directions	On B4368 to Bridgnorth, at extreme western end of Munslow.
meals	12pm-1.45pm; 6.45pm-8.45pm (6.30pm-7.30pm Sun). Main courses £11.50-£16.50; bar meals £4-£15.95.
closed	3pm-6.45pm (6.30pm Sun) & Mon all day.

Richard & Jane Arnold
Crown Country Inn,
Munslow,
Craven Arms SY7 9ET
tel 01584 841205
web www.crowncountryinn.co.uk

map: 7 entry: 417

Shropshire

Fighting Cocks
Stottesdon

As you negotiate tractors and horses on the lane to get here, you pass the farm that supplies the kitchen with its excellent meat. Sandra Jeffries wears multiple hats: jolly landlady, enthusiastic chef, manager of the great little shop next door. Step into the bar and choose a velour-topped perch – or a settle or a sofa by the fire. The décor is haphazard, the carpet red-patterned, the piano strewn with newspapers and guides (the ancient hills of Shropshire beckon) and the copper-topped bar hung with pewter tankards. Up steps is a room for darts, dominoes and TV. The dining room is as unpretentious as can be and a proper match for the cooking; make the most of gamey (or spicy) casseroles, organic salmon, scrummy pies and lovely nursery puddings. There's a new function room and the ramshackle 'garden' at the back is due to be extended. A true community pub.

directions	Village signed off A4117 & B4363 east of Ludlow at Cleobury Mortimer.
meals	7pm-9pm (12pm-2.30pm; 7pm-9pm Sat). No food Mon & Sun. Main courses £6-£13.
closed	Mon-Fri lunch. Open all day Sat & Sun.

Sandra Jeffries
Fighting Cocks,
1 High Street,
Stottesdon, Bridgnorth DY14 8TZ
tel 01746 718270

map: 7 entry: 418

The Unicorn Inn
Ludlow

With its Michelin-starred restaurants, Ludlow deserves at least one pub serving proper pub tucker. The Unicorn hides at the bottom end of town on the east bank of the river Corve as ou approach the Shrewsbury road and, unlike its more distinguished neighbours, does not have to be booked weeks in advance. Along with well-priced bar snacks there's proper food and plenty of it (braised steak with mushroom risotto and red wine sauce, seafood medley for two, syrup sponge and custard). You eat before a log fire in a panelled, ancient-beamed bar where floor and ceiling slope drastically, at scrubbed tables in the dining rooms, or in the beer garden by the stream in summer. Ceremony here is about as out-of-place as Formula One tyres on a family Ford: no wonder it remains popular. And the beer is expertly kept.

The Fox
Chetwynd Aston

As you wander from room to room – each sunny space radiating off the central bar – you realise just how vast this 1920s pub is. Yet there are plenty of nooks to be private in. Fires crackle in magnificent fireplaces, heavy cast-iron radiators add warmth, Turkey rugs are scattered on stained-wood floors and summer promises a great big garden with rolling views. Pews, solid oak tables and chairs – there's a happy mix of furniture and a bistro feel here. It's a grown-ups' pub and attracts urban rather than country folk, appreciative of a good selection of wines by the glass and six regularly changing guest ales. Staff are charming, customers happy and the food looks great. Choose a table, then browse the daily-changing menu: there are ploughman's with local cheeses, salted duck breast with orange, watercress and fennel salad, venison steak with roasted vegetables, warm chocolate brownies and very good coffee.

directions	From A49, B4361 to Ludlow. After lights & bridge, bear right; bear left up hill. Next right after lights at bottom of hill. 50 yds on left.
meals	12pm-2.15pm; 6pm-9.15pm. Main courses £8.75-£21.95; Sunday roast from £7.95; sandwiches from £4.25.
closed	Open all day.

directions	Just off A41 south of Newport,
meals	12pm-10pm (9.30pm Sun). Main courses £7.95-£14.45.
closed	Open all day.

	Graham Moore
	The Unicorn Inn,
	Lower Corve Street,
	Ludlow SY8 1DU
tel	01584 873555
web	www.unicorninnludlow.co.uk

	Sam Cornwall
	The Fox,
	Pave Lane, Chetwynd Aston,
	Newport TF10 9LQ
tel	01952 815940
web	www.brunningandprice.co.uk

map: 7 entry: 419

map: 8 entry: 420

All Nations
Madeley

The old Victorian pub could be an extension of the Industrial Open Air Museum on the other side of the bridge. Once smothered with ivy, now spruce and white, it looks more family home than pub. But step across the threshold and you're into timeworn-tavern territory – cast-iron tables, leatherette benches, coal fire at one end, log fire at the other. Old photographs of Ironbridge strew the walls, secondhand paperbacks ask to be taken home (donations to charity accepted), dogs doze and spotless loos await – outside. It's a chatty, friendly ex-miners' ale house and some of the locals could have been here forever: an old boy by the fire clutching a pewter tankard; a chap in yellow waders. Drink is own-brew, well-kept, low-cost Dabley from the hatch plus three others and a cider, while the menu encompasses several sorts of roll – black pudding perhaps, or cheese and onion, with tomato on request. Catch it before it's gone.

The Hundred House Hotel
Norton

Henry is an innkeeper of the old school, with a sense of humour – he once kept chickens, but they didn't keep him. Having begun its life in the 14th century, the place rambles charmingly inside as well as out. Enter a world of blazing log fires, soft brick walls, oak panelling and quarry-tiled floors. Dried flowers hang from beams, herbs sit in vases, blackboard menus trumpet prime Shropshire sirloin, venison casserole with herb dumplings, salmon fishcakes with lobster bisque... and Hereford duck with orange sauce, confit duck and black pudding. In the restaurant, Sylvia's wild and wonderful collage art hangs on wild and wonderful walls, and there's live music in the barn. Wander out with a pint of Heritage Mild and share a quiet moment with a few stone lions in the beautiful garden, full of unusual roses, herbaceous plants and a working herb garden with over 50 varieties – a real summer treat.

directions	Off Legges Way, near entrance to Blists Hill Museum.
meals	Filled rolls £1.50-£2.20.
closed	3pm-5pm in winter. Open all day Fri-Sun.

Jim Birtwistle
All Nations,
20 Coalport Road,
Madeley,
Telford TF7 5DP
tel 01952 585747

map: 8 entry: 421

directions	Midway between Bridgnorth & Telford on A422.
meals	12pm-2.30pm; 6pm-9.30pm (7pm-9pm Sun). Main courses £7.95-£18.95.
closed	3pm-5.30pm.

The Phillips Family
The Hundred House Hotel,
Norton,
Shifnal TF11 9EE
tel 01952 730353
web www.hundredhouse.co.uk

map: 8 entry: 422

Pheasant Inn
Linley Brook

The only traffic you're likely to encounter on the way here are a couple of horses clip-clopping along – or, if things hot up a bit, a tractor. The Pheasant has been here for centuries and is wondrously unspoilt. Expect a wood-burning stove and an open fire, wooden benches, pub tables and a carpeted floor... and fox masks, fox brushes and polished horse brasses on low beams. In a second room, past the hatch, are bar billiards. Simon and Liz Reed are landlord and landlady and run the Pheasant single-handedly; they cook, clean, serve, stoke the fire *and* find time to chat to customers. There's no piped music and everything shines. Walkers and locals pop in for a quiet pint and simple, very good pub food: toasted sandwiches, local gammon and steaks, sticky toffee pudding. Even the beers have names that belong to another age: Wye Valley Butty Bach, Salopian Heaven Sent, Cannon Muzzle Loader and Shropshire Gold.

directions	Just off B4373 Bridgnorth-Broseley road, 4 miles north of Bridgnorth.
meals	12pm-2pm; 6.30pm-9pm. Bar meals £5.25-£8.50.
closed	2.30-6.30 (from 3pm Sat & Sun), from 10pm Mon, Tues & Sun.

Simon & Liz Reed
Pheasant Inn,
Linley Brook,
Bridgnorth WV16 4TA
tel   01746 762260
web   www.the-pheasant-inn.co.uk

map: 8 entry: 423

The Crown Inn
Hopton Wafers

Bring with you an appetite after your hike on the moors. In a Pickwickian dining room with inglenook and sofas, the portions are generous and the food is tasty. Antipodean staff serve Hobsons' real ales with charm as guests settle down to confit duck with stir-fry, ham hock terrine with apple and calvados chutney, and game dishes in season... moving on to that Midlands delicacy, faggots with mushy peas – or seabass fillets baked Thai-style. Wines are from the old and new worlds. A stairwell and reception lead on to an atmospheric bar: dim light from ancient windows, beams, beer pumps and bar stools, patterned carpets and 16th-century brick. Lavish bedrooms are divided between the inn and three new cottages, all with drinks trays and excellent power showers.

directions	On A4117 between Cleobury Mortimer & Ludlow, 2 miles west of Cleobury.
meals	12pm-2.30; 6.30-9.30 (12-9 Sun). Main courses £9.95-£17.50; bar meals £5.95-£17.50; Sunday lunch £13.95 & £17.95.
rooms	18: 15 doubles, 3 twins £95-£115. Singles £59.50.
closed	Open all day.

See pp 30-57 for full list of pubs with rooms

Terry Robertson
The Crown Inn,
Hopton Wafers,
Cleobury Mortimer DY14 0NB
tel   01299 270372
web   www.crownathopton.co.uk

map: 8 entry: 424

Somerset

Woods Bar & Dining Room
Dulverton

It hasn't been a pub for ever – indeed, it used to specialise in tea and cakes – but it is in the centre of a lively little village, and wine buffs and foodies have much to be grateful for. Landlords Sally and Paddy are helpful, friendly and welcome families and dogs. A stable-like partition divides the space up into two intimate seating areas, beyond which is a smart, soft-lit, deeply cosy bar: two woodburners, lots of pine, a few barrel tables and stags' heads on exposed stone walls. Outside, a small paved area and a couple of cast-iron tables. Ales include Exmoor Gold, Otter and St Austell – but the wines are the thing here, with many by the glass. Expect some fine modern British dishes, with the emphasis on food in season. Hard to resist breast of pheasant with chestnut purée and port sauce – or a slab of Montgomery's cheddar with homemade chutney.

directions	From Tiverton, A396 N; left on B3222 for Dulverton; near church & bank.
meals	12pm-2pm; 7pm-9.30pm (9pm Sun). Main courses £6.95-£14.95.
closed	3pm-6pm (7pm Sun).

Sally & Paddy Groves
Woods Bar & Dining Room,
4 Bank Square,
Dulverton TA22 9BU

| tel | 01398 324007 |

map: 2 entry: 425

Somerset

Tarr Farm Inn
Dulverton

Come for rare peace – no traffic lights, no mobile signals, not for miles. Tucked into the river Barle valley, a short hop from the ancient clapper bridge at Tarr Steps, this well-established 16th-century inn is surrounded by beautiful woodland above the hauntingly high spaces of Exmoor National Park. The blue-carpeted, low-beamed main bar has plenty of comfy window and bench seats and gleaming black leather sofas; Exmoor Ale and Mayner's cider flow as easily as the conversation. To fill the gap after a bracing walk the menu draws heavily on local game – hunting and shooting are popular sports here – so you get venison and rabbit casserole, pan-roasted partridge and a hundred French and New World wines. The garden views are sublime; where better to try the best West Country cheeses followed by perfect coffee? A great pub, whatever the weather.

directions	From Dulverton, take B3223 north, left to Tarr Steps & Inn is signed.
meals	12pm-3pm; 6.30pm-9.30pm (cream teas 3pm-5pm). Main courses £12.95-£17.50; bar meals £6.95-£12.50.
closed	Open all day.

Judy Carless & Richard Benn
Tarr Farm Inn ,
Tarr Steps,
Dulverton TA22 9PY

| tel | 01643851507 |
| web | www.tarrfarm.co.uk |

map: 2 entry: 426

Somerset — Pub with rooms

Royal Oak at Luxborough
Luxborough

Five miles south of Minehead, as the pheasant flies, is Luxborough, tucked under the lip of the Exmoor's Brendon hills. This is hunting country and from September to February beaters and loaders traditionally lunch at The Oak. Two low-beamed, log-fired, dog-dozed bars (with locals' table) lead to a warren of dining rooms kitted out with polished dining tables and hunting prints on deep green walls. (In spate, the river Washford has been known to take a detour!). A shelf heaves with walking books and maps; the owners lend them freely, all are returned. Expect first-class food: potted ham hock for starters, fish from St Mawes, vegetables from local growers, Exmoor lamb and game aplenty. For those lucky enough to stay, bedrooms ramble around the first floor (one below has a private terrace) and are individual, peaceful, homely and great value.

directions	Luxborough signed off A396 from Dunster.
meals	12pm-2pm; 7pm-9pm. Main courses £11.95-£15.95; bar meals £4.95-£10.95.
rooms	11: 8 doubles, 2 twins, 1 single £55-£85.
closed	2.30pm-6pm.

See pp 30–57 for full list of pubs with rooms

James & Siân Waller, Sue Hinds
Royal Oak at Luxborough,
Luxborough,
Dunster TA23 0SH
tel 01984 640319
web www.theroyaloakinnluxborough.co.uk

map: 2 entry: 427

Somerset

Three Horseshoes
Langley Marsh

A proper, traditional local and proud of it. Come for good beer and good food, kept and cooked by Mark and Julia. Otter Bitter, Young's and Palmers IPA are tapped from the cask and there's farm cider on tap. Lunches and dinners have been described as "home-cooked food from heaven". Pies, soup and sandwiches, daily specials – lamb steak in mint and yogurt, pork tenderloin in port and stilton – all freshly made, no chips, and veg from the garden. Just so you see how seriously they take it, they list their suppliers on the back of the menu. In the bustling front room, a timeless atmosphere prevails with polished tables, table skittles, dominoes, darts and a piano; in the dining room, old settles; in the garden, tables and sloping lawns.

directions	Off B3227 Wiveliscombe; turn in front of White Hart towards Huish Champflower; 1 mile on right.
meals	12pm-1.45pm (2pm Sun); 7pm-9pm. Main courses £5.50-£11.95.
closed	2.30pm-7pm, Sun from 3pm & all day Mon.

Mark & Julia Fewless
Three Horseshoes,
Langley Marsh,
Wiveliscombe TA4 2UL
tel 01984 623763

map: 2 entry: 428

Carew Arms
Crowcombe

Reg Ambrose has successfully revived this pub in the shadow of the Quantock Hills. It was, and still is, a mammoth task. But the outside loos have been spruced up and the old skittle alley transformed; now it's a bar-dining room whose French windows lead to a sunny back terrace and a garden with tables and gentle woodland views. The front room, with its hatch bar, flagstones, plain settles, pine tables with benches and vast inglenook remains unspoilt. Down pints of Exmoor Ale, engage in lively conversation and enjoy excellent seared scallops with garlic butter, confit belly pork with mustard mash and red wine gravy, locally farmed beef steaks and dark chocolate tart. Recently decorated bedrooms are upstairs: new pine, good linen, creaking floorboards. There's Sunday jazz once a month in summer and children and dogs get a proper welcome

directions	Off A358 between Taunton & Minehead.
meals	12pm-2pm; 7pm-9pm (10pm Sat; 8.30pm Sun). Main courses £9-£16.
rooms	6: 3 doubles, 3 twins £65-£84.
closed	3.30pm-5pm. Open all day Sat & Sun.

See pp 30-57 for full list of pubs with rooms

	Reg Ambrose Carew Arms, Crowcombe, Taunton TA4 4AD
tel	01984 618631
web	www.thecarewarms.co.uk

map: 2 entry: 429

Blue Ball Inn
Triscombe

Not so long ago the Blue Ball was 'rolled' down the hill a few yards; now the old thatched buildings join the ancient stables below. Thanks to craftsmen's skills and plenty of vision, it has metamorphosed into a rather smart pub. Climb the fabulous beech stairs to a swishly-carpeted central bar that leads to two inviting dining areas, each with open fires, country furnishings and fabrics and high-raftered ceilings. Menus are imaginative, produce local. Treat yourself to canon of salt marsh lamb with turnip gratin and red wine sauce, whole roasted Dunster plaice with potted shrimps or corn-fed duck with onion jam and orange butter sauce. At the bar, lunchtime crusty rolls and excellent cheese ploughman's make this a popular walkers' pit-stop. There are four ales, wines by the glass and local farm ciders – in summer taken out in the decked garden with views across Taunton's vale.

directions	From Taunton A358 for Minehead; past B. Lydeard, right to Triscombe.
meals	12pm-1.45pm; 7pm-8.45pm. Main courses £7.95-£16.95.
closed	4pm-6pm.

	Gerald & Sue Rogers Blue Ball Inn, Triscombe, Bishops Lydeard, Taunton TA4 3HE
tel	01984 618242
web	www.blueballinn.co.uk

map: 2 entry: 430

The Rising Sun Inn
West Bagborough

In 2002 the Sun rose from the ashes of a fire, and once again shines brightly. It sits in the heart of sleepy West Bagborough on the flanks of the Quantock Hills. Constructed around the original 16th-century cob walls and magnificent door, its reincarnation is bold and craftsman-led, with 80 tons of solid oak timbers and windows and a slate-floored bar. Add Art Nouveau features, spotlighting and swagged drapery and you have a very smart pub indeed. There's Exmoor Fox and Cotleigh Tawny to savour, modern art to buy, and, high in the rafters, a dining room with views that unfurl to Exmoor and the Blackdown Hills. It's an impressive setting for very impressive food: braised Exmoor lamb shank on mustard mash with rosemary jus, game casserole, beer battered cod with mushy peas, white chocolate cheesecake with fruit coulis.

The Blagdon Inn
Blagdon Hill

The Rushtons have a knack of finding the right pub in the right location. Now the old cider house on the edge of the Blackdown Hills — handy access for the M5 — is a stylish gastropub flourishing a modern menu and fresh, local produce. Step inside to thick stone walls, flagged and polished wooden floors, a blazing log fire fronted by leather tub chairs, and old dining tables in cosy eating areas. Fresh flowers and daily papers are further welcome touches. West Country produce, organic if available, is the mainstay of the productive kitchen: fish comes from Brixham and Looe, eggs and meat are free-range, the Ruby Red rib-eye, hung for 21 days, is served with hand-cut chips and the steak and kidney pie has a delicious shortcrust topping. Add great local beers and organic soft drinks and you have one perfect pub.

directions	Off A358 Taunton-Minehead road, 8 miles north-west of Taunton.
meals	12pm-2pm; 7pm-9pm. No food Sun eve. Main courses £5.95-£9 (lunch), £12.50-£15.50 (dinner).
closed	3pm-6.30pm & all day Mon (except bank hols).

Rob & Chris Rainey
The Rising Sun Inn,
West Bagborough,
Taunton TA4 3EF

tel	01823 432575
web	www.theriser.co.uk

map: 2 entry: 431

directions	M5 junc. 25 into Taunton; Trull road out of town, then Honiton Road for 3 miles; pub on right.
meals	12pm-2pm; 6pm-9.30pm (12pm-9.30pm Sat & Sun). Main courses £8.35-£15.50.
closed	3pm-6pm. Open all day Sat & Sun.

Steve Rushton
The Blagdon Inn,
Blagdon Hill,
Taunton TA3 7SG

tel	01823 421296
web	www.blagdoninn.co.uk

map: 2 entry: 432

Farmer's Inn

West Hatch

Country-cosy with class. Debbie and Tom have revived this old inn; the wine list is lovingly compiled, cask ales are on tap and guest beers increase with demand. There's an open rambling feel and a generous bar, small and large tables with wheelback chairs, leather sofas around the woodburner, a mass of stacked logs, the odd bench or pew. Food is imaginative and beautifully presented, be it Welsh rarebit with crispy bacon, local lamb and rosemary sausages or baked white chocolate and kahlua cheesecake. Homemade bread and olives come as a complimentary nibble. Stay the night in off-beat but elegant and big rooms with distinctive beds (all antique) and expansive, gleaming wooden floors. Bathrooms are shiny and chic, with power showers or claw-foot baths. And the grounds have great views.

directions	Exit A358 S of Taunton at Nag's Head pub, follow brown 'inn' sign for 2 miles.
meals	12pm-2pm (2.30 Sat & Sun); 7pm-9pm (9.30 Fri & Sat). Main courses £10-£16; bar meals £4.75-£9.50.
rooms	5 doubles £80-£110. Singles £60-£90.
closed	2.30-6pm (3pm-7pm Sat & Sun).

See pp 30-57 for full list of pubs with rooms

	Debbie Lush Farmer's Inn, Slough Green, West Hatch, Taunton TA3 5RS
tel	01823 480480
web	www.farmersinnwesthatch.co.uk

map: 2 entry: 433

Canal Inn

Wrantage

Blink and you could miss the pub by the A378 – closed for years until Pedro and Clare picked up on its potential in 2003. It's much more than the no-frills ale house it appears to be. Enjoy the best local ales for miles – foaming pints of Blackdown Ditch Water – in the bare-boarded bar, or choose from Somerset scrumpy-style ciders and a host of Belgian beers. Yet the key to its success in winning favour with the community is its passion for local produce. Menus proudly list the small suppliers, all within a five-mile radius – eggs and veg from Mr and Mrs Titman, vintage local cheeses, allotment veg. A farmers' market in the bar on the last Saturday of the month brings customers and suppliers together, so food miles are kept to a minimum and trade receives a boost. Regular fish nights, Monday fish and chips (eat-in or take-away), music nights and an annual beer festival complete the picture.

directions	Beside A378 towards Langport, 2 miles east of A378 Taunton-Ilminster road
meals	12pm-2pm; 7pm-9pm (7pm-8pm Mon). Main courses £10-£14; bar meals £5-£8.
closed	2pm-5pm (7pm Sat), Mon lunch & Sun eve.

	Clare Paul & Pedro Aparicio Canal Inn, Wrantage, Taunton TA3 6DF
tel	01823 480210
web	www.thecanalinn.com

map: 2 entry: 434

Lord Poulett Arms
Hinton St George

There's an upbeat yet elegant feel to this wonderful 400-year-old inn. And it sits in a ravishing village. Traditional trappings – hops, pewter tankards, country antiques – rub shoulders with quirky bits: *Carry On* posters on the wall, a hammock in the divine summer garden, a chess set laid out to play. Floors are bare flags or age-worn boards, the bar is simple and uncluttered, there's space and intimacy at the same time, a huge old fireplace crackling with logs, cider from the jug. The chef trained in Japan so the Dorsetshire fish and the Exmoor game might come with an oriental touch. Try spinach and pea soup, wild sea bass with exotic mushrooms in a sake and teriyaki sauce, Lovington's ice creams and west country cheeses. Contemporary wallpapers set the tone for super bedrooms upstairs – along with open-stone walls, brass bedsteads and seagrass floors; Roberts radios add a fun touch. Good value, friendly to dogs.

directions	Village signed off A30, west of Crewkerne.
meals	12pm-2pm; 7pm-9pm. Main courses £9-£17; bar meals from £6.
rooms	4 twins/doubles £88. Singles £59.
closed	3pm-6.30pm.

Steve & Michelle Hill
Lord Poulett Arms,
High Street, Hinton St George,
Crewekerne TA17 8SE
tel   01460 73149
web   www.lordpoulettarms.com

map: 3 entry: 435

Rose & Crown Inn (Eli's)
Huish Episcopi

Quirky, unspoilt and in the family for 140 years. The layout has evolved, gradually taking over the family home. There's no bar as such – you choose from the casks – but who cares when the locals are so lovely, the cider so rough and the beer so tasty. Walk in and you step back to the Fifties. There are worn flagstones and aged panelling, cottagey doors and coal fires in five low parlours radiating off a central tap room. The 'gentleman's kitchen' is the oldest and cosiest, the pool, darts and juke box room the largest and newest. They do crib nights and occasional quiz nights and Morris dancers drop by in summer. The food is brilliant value: creamy winter vegetable soup, a tasty pork, apple and cider cobbler, chicken breast with tarragon, chocolate and rum torte. Everyone's happy and children like the little play area outside.

directions	300 yards from St Mary's Church. On left-hand side towards Wincanton on leaving Huish.
meals	12pm-2pm, 5.30pm-7.30pm. No food Sun eve. Main courses £6.75-£6.75. Bar meals from £3.
closed	2.30pm-5.30pm Mon-Thurs. Open all day Fri-Sun.

Eileen Pittard
Rose & Crown Inn (Eli's),
Huish Episcopi,
Langport TA10 9QT
tel   01458 250494

map: 3 entry: 436

Somerset — Pub with rooms

Devonshire Arms Hotel
Long Sutton

Behind the country hotel façade, a striking modernity. Step off the village green and into an open-plan space of chunky blond-wood tables, brown leather sofas, west country photographs and stylish twiggery. The Devonshire Arms is three-quarters restaurant, one-quarter pub, there are Belgian beers on draught, four guest ales and a good wine list. The hosts are engaging and the food's a joy; choose from ploughman's with homemade chutney or grilled sardines with truffle mayonnaise, linger over a pot-roasted venison with parsnip dumplings, or baked feta cheese and parsnips with beetroot confit and spiced lentils. Puddings include ginger sticky toffee pudding, sorbets include cassis… not a glimmer left of the old pub's previous existence. Outside are a new patio and sunny walled garden; upstairs, a flurry of large, light and absolutely fabulous bedrooms.

directions	A303, then north on B3165, through Martock, to Long Sutton. Pub by village green.
meals	12-2.30pm; 7-9.30pm (9pm Sun). Main courses £12.95-£18.50; bar meals £4.20-£12.50.
rooms	9: 8 doubles, 1 family room £70-£130. Singles from £60.
closed	3pm-6pm.

Philip & Sheila Mepham
Devonshire Arms Hotel,
Long Sutton,
Langport TA10 9LP
tel 01458 241271
web www.thedevonshirearms.com

map: 3 entry: 437

Somerset

Red Lion
Babcary

A lattice of hot white bread with unsalted butter arrives unannounced and with a cheery smile – and the girls will keep an eye out for you right through from starters to coffee. Best to book at weekends, though. This is a Somerset revival that combines the best of pub tradition with excellent food. There is a single central bar with a locals' snug behind dispensing real ale, local cider and house wines from France and Oz. To one side, hair-cord carpets, sofas and the cast-iron stove give a welcome to the bright bar/lounge, while to the far right a dozen well-spaced country dining tables plainly set out on original flagstone flooring are part of an immaculate reconstruction. Daily menus offer as little or as much as you'd like, from fishcakes with buttered leeks and hollandaise to homemade burger with tomato relish, game pie, and whole sea bass on oriental rice with honey and soy dressing.

directions	Off A37 & A303 7 miles north of Yeovil.
meals	12pm-2.30pm; 7pm-9pm (9.30pm Fri & Sat). Main courses £6.95-£16.
closed	2.30pm-6pm & Sun eve.

Clare & Charles Garrard
Red Lion,
Babcary,
Somerton TA11 7ED
tel 01458 223230

map: 3 entry: 438

The Montague Inn
Shepton Montague

The O'Callaghans' 17th-century public house has been a stables, livery, grocery; now it is an inn in the true sense of the word. Small remains beautiful, with regional guest ales from Butcombe, Bath Ales and Blindman's Brewery, a wood-burner in the bar, candles on stripped pine tables and organic produce from neighbouring farms. Master Chef John McKeever's food is simple yet imaginative. There are lunchtime ploughman's of local cheeses, while daily specials could mean a hot pot on Tuesday, fresh fish in beer batter and chips on Friday. And then there's grilled local goat's cheese in a celery, apple and walnut salad, and chargrilled fillet of local beef with garlic cream mash, bacon and lentil jus, all put together from scratch. The restaurant and rear terrace have bosky views to Redlynch and Alfred's Tower; with scarcely another building in view, you could be miles from anywhere. A small place with a huge heart.

directions	Off A359 2 miles east of Castle Cary, towards Bruton.
meals	12pm-2.30pm; 7pm-9pm. Main courses £13.50-£19.50; bar meals £5.95-£8.50.
closed	3pm-6pm (3.30pm Sun), Mon all day & Sun eve.

Sean & Suzy O'Callaghan
The Montague Inn,
Shepton Montague,
Wincanton BA9 8JW

| tel | 01749 813213 |

map: 3 entry: 439

The Manor House Inn
Ditcheat

The focus of Ditcheat life has a just-renovated feel – the landlord swept in with a youthful broom in 2004 – but authenticity will follow. In the bar – big, unscuffed and open plan – there's a good fire blazing. Settle back with something tasty from Bath Ales and tune in to chatter of weather, sump oil and stock. Skittles clatter in the background – the skittle alley has had a makeover too – as enticing aromas demand you check out the chalked boards. There are baked avocados filled with Mediterranean vegetables and topped with a parmesan crust, and chargrilled steaks with stilton sauce or peppercorn and brandy. After, totter out to the single-storey building where smart and generous bedrooms await; beds are hugely comfortable, shower rooms a treat. In the morning, discover a picture-perfect village amid gently rolling hills.

directions	Between A37 & A371, in Ditcheat next to church.
meals	12pm-2pm; 7pm-9.30pm. No food Sun eve. Main courses £7.95-£16.95; bar meals £5.25-£11.95.
rooms	3: 2 doubles, 1 twin £90. Singles £50.
closed	3pm-5.30pm. Open all day Fri-Sun.

See pp 30-57 for full list of pubs with rooms

Giles Pushman
The Manor House Inn,
Ditcheat,
Shepton Mallet BA4 6RB

| tel | 01749 860276 |
| web | www.manorhouseinn.co.uk |

map: 3 entry: 440

The Three Horseshoes
Batcombe

Down a web of country lanes, the Woods' honey-stoned coaching inn sits in a lovely village. Step into a long, low bar, its beams cream, its pine scrubbed, its pink-sponged walls hung with local views. There are cushioned window seats, an inglenook with a wood-burning stove, pretty courtyards and grassed areas, even a play area. It's a treat for locals, walkers and families. The modern British menu uses local organic produce, much from the vegetable garden, and is full of promise: start with homemade pâté de campagne, move on to local lamb with red wine jus or sea bass fillet with tomato and herb salsa, finish with a trio of English puds. Plus regular wine tastings, and Bats in the Belfry made specially for the pub by Blindmans Brewery. There's a super bedroom in the eaves with church views, and two more on the same level, equally good. *Children welcome at lunchtime.*

directions	Off A359 between Frome & Bruton, 7 miles SW of Frome.
meals	12pm-2pm; 7pm-9pm. No food Sun eve. Main courses £10.50-£18.50; bar meals from £6.75.
rooms	3 doubles £75. Singles £50.
closed	3pm-6.30pm (7pm Sun) & Mon (except bank hols).

See pp 30–57 for full list of pubs with rooms

Bob & Shirley Wood
The Three Horseshoes,
Batcombe,
Shepton Mallet BA4 6HE
| tel | 01749 850359 |
| web | www.three-horseshoes.co.uk |

map: 3 entry: 441

The Talbot Inn at Mells
Mells

Even in thick fog the village is lovely. Huge oak doors open to a cobbled courtyard and rough-boarded tithe barn bar on one side, and dining rooms and bedrooms on the other. Inside, a warren of passageways, low doorways, nooks, crannies, beams and blazing log fires – all you'd hope for from a 15th-century inn. Butcombe Bitter flows from the cask and there are wines galore including five by the glass; it's a great drinking pub and, with a garden with views, a magnet for tourists in summer. Soak up any excess with Brixham crab soup, confit duck leg with braised red cabbage and peppercorn sauce, or local ham, eggs and chips. Dinner under the hop-strewn rafters highlights fresh Brixham fish such as brill fillets in nut-brown butter. Roger Elliott's effortless hospitality and easy charm is a further plus.

directions	From Frome A362 for Radstock; left signed Mells.
meals	12pm-2.30pm; 6.45pm-11pm. Main courses £6.50-£14.50.
closed	2.30pm-6.30pm (3pm-7pm Sun).

Roger Elliott
The Talbot Inn at Mells,
Selwood Street, Mells,
Frome BA11 3PN
| tel | 01373 812254 |
| web | www.talbotinn.com |

map: 3 entry: 442

The Hunters' Lodge
Priddy

Pulling up at the windswept Priddy crossroads high on the Mendip Hills, you'd be mad to ignore this starkly rendered old building. A little treasure lies within. It's been in the same family since 1840 and Mr Dors is its proudest fixture, administering ale to cavers, pot-holers, hikers and the odd local for over 30 years. Lively chatter drowns the ticking clock and the crackling fire. The pristine main bar is delightfully devoid of a modern make-up – just simple wooden benches and tables, a shove-ha'penny board, old photographs on the walls, Butcombe bitter, Blindman's Mine Beer and a varying Third Choice fresh from the barrel. There's a lounge bar and a rear room for families, equally plain. Food is straightforward, homemade, tasty, great value. Folk in muddy boots come for just-made bowls of chilli, cauliflower cheese, faggots and peas and chunks of bread and cheese. An unpretentious treat.

Wookey Hole Inn
Wookey Hole

On the edge of the Mendip hills: a traditional façade, a funky décor, excellent food and no end of choice behind the kitsch-with-style bar. The whole place throngs, particularly on summer weekends when the big garden comes into its own. It's also relaxed and properly child-friendly with toys and wax crayons for doodling on (paper) tablecloths. Terracotta tiles, open fires, stripped wood and wooden panelling, splashes of strong colour, arty lamps, photos and interesting *objets*. The atmosphere is laid-back, the cool levels boosted by live jazz at Sunday lunch times, and the food, which has good local credentials, is seriously tasty and imaginative: onion jam and goat's cheese bruschetta, fillet of beef with foie gras and a rich flageolet bean, bacon and red wine jus, spiced lamb burgers with smoked cheddar. The puddings are seductive, too.

directions	1.5 miles up Priddy-Wells road; look out for the TV mast.
meals	11.30am-2.30pm (12.30pm-2pm Sun); 6.30pm (7pm Sun)-11pm. Dishes from £3.
closed	2.30-6.30 (2pm-7pm Sun).

Mr Dors
The Hunters' Lodge,
Priddy,
Wells BA5 3AR
tel 01749 672275

map: 3 entry: 443

directions	Follow brown tourist signs for Wookey Hole off A371 or A39 in Wells.
meals	12pm-2.30pm (3pm Sun); 7pm-9pm. Main courses from £8.50 (lunch), £12.75-£19.50 (dinner).
closed	3pm-6pm; Sun eve.

Michael & Richard Davy
Wookey Hole Inn,
Wookey Hole,
Wells BA5 1BP
tel 01749 676677
web www.wookeyholeinn.com

map: 3 entry: 444

Tucker's Grave Inn
Faulkland

If only the essence of Tucker's could be bottled and preserved; 'to be used as emergency tonic for the despairing' the label would read. In an unassuming, almost-unsigned 17th-century stone building, Tucker's is defiantly informal. An unprecedentedly narrow, extremely wiggly corridor leads in from the garden door; it's like walking into someone's living room as you stoop to enter the warmth. No bar, no fridge, just four beer casks and containers of local cider sitting in their jackets in the bay (no draught) and a stack of crisp boxes against the wall. You could pour your own beer… but that privilege is reserved for real regulars. A small open fire lends cosiness to the no-frills room next to the tiny wooden serving room. The interiors are as basic as they come but the atmosphere is roaring at weekends. In the words of one regular: "you can't come here without chatting to someone". And now there's a skittles room in the big back garden.

directions	A366 Radstock-Frome; left onto A362; through Faulkland, pub near next junction.
meals	Sandwiches from £1.50.
closed	3pm-6pm (7pm Sun).

Glenda & Ivan Swift
Tucker's Grave Inn,
Faulkland,
Radstock BA3 5XF
tel 01373 834230

map: 3 entry: 445

Bear & Swan
Chew Magna

It is a four-square Victorian pub in the middle of Chew Magna – a desirable village in fine walking country. Inside, the Pushmans have created a roomy and airy bar and a damned good restaurant. Reclaimed floorboards, nestling tables, wooden pews, big log fires create a simple, sophisticated feel; in the restaurant are oriental rugs and ladderback chairs, candlelight and flowers, and bottles racked on the wall. Beers (Butcombe and Bath Ales), 40 wines and an irresistible menu draw people from near and far. Black pudding with caramelised apples and beetroot sauce; rack of lamb; tuna with fondant sweet potato, wilted spinach and star anis dressing; perfect summer pudding. The menu changes daily, much is organic and the staff are delightful. Retire to airy and spacious bedrooms; there are charming antiques, stylish bathroom suites and an open-plan living area, with a kitchen, to share.

directions	On B3130 between A37 & A38.
meals	12pm-2pm (3pm Sun); 7pm-9.45pm. No food Sun eve. Main courses £9.50-£18.50; bar meals £4.50-£12.
rooms	2 doubles £80. Singles £50.
closed	Open all day.

Nigel & Caroline Pushman
Bear & Swan,
13 South Parade,
Chew Magna BS40 8SL
tel 01275 331100
web www.bearandswan.co.uk

map: 3 entry: 446

The Black Horse
Clapton-in-Gordano

A cracking pub. The Snug Bar once doubled as the village lock-up and, if it weren't for the electric lights and motors in the car park, you'd be hard pushed to remember you were in the 21st century. All flagstone and dark moody wood, the main room bears the scuffs of centuries of drinking. Settles and old tables sit around the walls, and cottage windows with dark, wobbly shutters let a little of the outside in. The fire – a focus – roars in its vast hearth beneath a fine set of antique guns, just the sort of place to pull off muddy boots. Sepia prints of parish cricket teams and steam tractors clutter the walls and cask ales pour from the stone ledge behind the wide hatch bar. The food is unfancy bar fodder, with the odd traditional special. Ale is what's important and that's what takes pride of place; beneath a chalkboard six jacketed casks squat above drip pans; there are fine wines too. There's plenty of garden; well worth leaving the motorway for.

directions	M5 junc. 19 for Portbury & Clapton. Left into Clevedon Lane.
meals	12pm-2.30pm. No food Sun. Main courses £3.50-£5.
closed	Open all day.

Nicholas Evans
The Black Horse,
Clevedon Lane,
Clapton-in-Gordano,
Portishead BS20 7RH
tel   01275 842105

map: 3 entry: 447

The Crown
Churchill

Once a coaching stop between Bristol and Exeter, then the village grocer's, now an unspoilt pub. Modern makeovers have passed this gem by and beer reigns supreme, with up to ten ales tapped from the barrel. For years landlord Tim Rogers has resisted piped music and electronic games; who needs them in these beamed and flagstoned bars? A wooden window seat here, a settle there... the rustic surroundings and the jolly atmosphere draw both locals and walkers treading the Mendips hills. Bag a seat by the log fire, cradle a pint of Butcombe or RCH PG Steam Bitter, be lulled by the hum of regulars at the bar. If you're here at lunchtime you'll find a short, traditional, blackboard menu: warming bowls of soup, thick-cut rare roast beef sandwiches, baked potatoes, winter casseroles, treacle pud. Evenings are reserved for the serious art of ale drinking, and it's packed at weekends, especially in summer.

directions	From Bristol A38 to Churchill, right for Weston S.M. Immed left in front of Nelson Pub, up Skinners Lane, pub on bend.
meals	12pm-2.30pm. Main courses £3.40-£7.50.
closed	Open all day.

Tim Rogers
The Crown,
The Batch,
Churchill,
Congresbury BS25 5PP
tel   01934 852995

map: 3 entry: 448

Queen's Arms
Bleadon

A curious spot, for the ineffable Weston-super-Mare is just round the corner. But just behind the village begin the Mendip Hills, whose bleak winter walks challenge the most hardy, and whose wild and beautiful woodland and fields sing in summer. The Queen's Arms, like many, is not especially seductive from the outside, but cheerfully sweeps you in to four terracotta rooms, much chat and laughter and some jolly good food. There are hunting prints on the walls, wood in the burners, candles in bottles and a menu that covers pub grub to delicious calves' liver and bacon with leek mash and port gravy, and a scrumptious Bailey's bread and butter pudding. Ales come from the barrel (Butcombe Bitter, Blonde & Gold and Bath Gem), cider is Thatchers, staff are swift and Daniel and Jess run the place with good humour — not least on Sunday quiz nights.

directions	A370 from Weston-super-Mare; left towards Bleadon; 50 yds from church.
meals	12pm-2pm (2.30pm Sun); 6.30pm-9.30pm. Main courses £8.95-£14.95; bar meals from £3.50.
closed	2.30pm-5.30pm. Open all day Fri-Sun.

Daniel Pardoe & Jess Perry
Queen's Arms,
Celtic Way, Bleadon,
Weston-super-Mare BS24 0NF
tel 01934 812080
web www.queensarms.co.uk

map: 2 entry: 449

Halfway House
Pitney Hill

Somerset's mecca for beer and cider aficionados. No music or electronic wizardry to distract you from the serious business of sampling up to eight ales tapped straight from the drum, heady Hecks' ciders, and bottled beers from around the globe. Local clubs gather for chess, music, hockey; real-pub-lovers return again and again. In the two simple and homely rooms is a friendly, happy buzz: there are old benches and pews, scrubbed tables, stone-slabbed floors, three crackling log fires and the daily papers to nod off over. A quick lunchtime pint can swiftly turn into two hours of beer-fuelled bliss — so blot up the alcohol with spicy bean and tomato soup, a ploughman's lunch served with huge slabs of crusty bread and ham, a beef and beer casserole or a salmon steak straight from the pub's smokery. In the evenings the Halfway's revered homemade curries are gorgeous and go down extremely well with pints of Butcombe, Branscombe and Hop Back ales.

directions	Beside B3153, midway between Langport & Somerton.
meals	12pm-2.30pm; 6.30pm-9.30pm. No food Sun. Main courses £3.95-£9.95.
closed	3pm-5.30pm (7pm Sun).

Julian Litchfield
Halfway House,
Pitney Hill,
Langport TA10 9AB
tel 01458 252513
web www.thehalfwayhouse.co.uk

map: 3 entry: 450

Somerset
Pub with rooms

The Queen's Arms
Corton Denham

Stride across rolling fields with Dorsetshire views, feast on Corton Denham lamb, retire to a perfect room. Buried down twisting border lanes, this elegant 18th-century pub is also great for a pint and a homemade pie; Londoners Rupert and Victoria Reeves have not let it lose its countrified feel. The bar is delightful with rug-strewn flagstones and bare boards, pew benches, deep sofas and crackling fire. In the warm dining room – big mirrors on terracotta walls, new china on old tables – guests dine on imaginative dishes distinguished by ingredients from local suppliers. Try stinging nettle risotto with a glass of shiraz, or gin and juniper marinated salmon followed by gooseberry pavlova. Bedrooms are stunning with fresh checks or sumptuous silks, perfect bath and shower rooms, posh smellies and breathtaking views – book the French room! A friendly labrador, Butcombe on tap, comfort and authenticity.

directions	From A303 for Chapel Cross, thro' South Cadbury; signs to Corton Denham; pub at end on right.
meals	12pm-3pm, 6pm-10pm (9.30 Sun). Main courses £7.80-£12.70; bar meals £4.70-£11.90.
rooms	5 twins/doubles £75-£120.
closed	3pm-6pm. Open all day Sat & Sun.

Rupert & Victoria Reeves
The Queen's Arms,
Corton Denham DT9 4LR
tel   01963 220317
web   www.thequeensarms.com

map: 3 entry: 451

Staffordshire

The George
Alstonefield

Green sward ripples endlessly in this remote limestone village with its old church perched on a plateau between the remarkable gorges of the rivers Dove and Manifold. Set amidst this verdant Eden, the George is an ultra-reliable local, maturing gently these past 40 years under the guidance of Richard Grandjean and is now run by his daughter and son-in-law. Small, timeless rooms of beams, quarry tile and log fire carry benches and Britannia tables, fascinating old photos and polished plate. It's an unhurried place, where everyone knows everyone else (or soon will), ramblers cram the benches and tables out front and time passes slowly. Complement this vision with homemade chow to savour – nothing fancy, just fine filling pub food – and a couple of real ales from regional breweries. The dining room, all scrubbed pine tables, piano, antiques, watercolours and stuffed fish, is ideal for families, as is the peaceful rear courtyard shaded by an immense ash.

directions	Village signed off A515, 7 miles north of Ashbourne.
meals	12pm-2pm; 7pm-9pm. No food Sun eve. Main courses £7.50-£15; bar meals £3.50-£7.50.
closed	3pm-6pm. Open all day Sat & Sun.

Ben & Emily Hammond
The George,
Alstonefield,
Ashbourne DE6 2FX
tel   01335 310205
web   www.thegeorgeatalstonefield.com

map: 8 entry: 452

Staffordshire

Yew Tree
Cauldon

The Old Curiosity Shop meets *The Antiques Road Show*. For over 40 years, landlord Alan East has squirreled away enough artefacts to make Michael Aspel weep. Behind the tiny leaded windows of this unassuming, 300-year-old pub every space is filled: longcase clocks and flintlocks, penny-farthings and valve radios, synphonions and polyphons (insert 2p and retire), old pews and marvellously carved benches. Pianolas lie half-buried in their paper-scroll programs (there's one playing most of the time). Josiah Wedgwood would find ceramics he may have handled (and his four-poster bed), and Queen Victoria her hosiery. Look for the Serpent (a medieval church instrument); wince at the ACME dog carrier. A floor-to-ceiling treasure trove – plus local pork pies, hot baps and sandwiches, Bass, Burton Bridge Bitter and Grays Mild.

directions	Off A523 Leek to Ashbourne road at Waterhouses.
meals	Bar snacks 70p-£3.50.
closed	2.30pm-6pm (3pm-6pm Sat, 3pm-7pm Sun).

	Alan East
	Yew Tree,
	Cauldon,
	Waterhouses,
	Stoke-on-Trent ST10 3EJ
tel	01538 308348

map: 8 entry: 453

Staffordshire

The Holly Bush Inn
Stafford

Geoffrey Holland came to the Holly Bush some years ago and has turned it into a thriving local. Indeed, all the emphasis is local, especially where food is concerned. Cheeses, vegetables, meat and game (hear the shoot from the pub garden) are local and almost exclusively organic; herbs are fresh from the garden. Even a few of the recipes, such as the 'oatcakes' (that's pancakes not biscuits), are strictly Staffs. Only the fish and some of the beers (eg. Boddingtons from Manchester) are from further afield. But people travel miles for the home-smoked salmon with hollandaise sauce and the steak and ale pie. The 'second oldest licensed pub in the country' is a characterful little place, quirky even, with separate cosy areas, open fires and the odd carved beam and settle. There are picnic tables on the big back lawn, where a wood oven bakes pizzas in summer, and the village, listed in the Domesday Book, should charm you.

directions	Off A51 south of Stone & A518 north east of Stafford.
meals	12pm-9.30pm (9pm Sun). Main courses £7.25-£13.95; bar snacks £2.25-£3.25.
closed	Open all day.

	Geoffrey Holland
	The Holly Bush Inn,
	Salt,
	Stafford ST18 0BX
tel	01889 508234
web	www.hollybushinn.co.uk

map: 8 entry: 454

Staffordshire

Crooked House
Coppice Mill

Local big-wigs found coal here in about 1800 and started mining; shortly thereafter the pretty, 18th-century red-brick farmhouse fell into a hole. It has been buttressed ever since, but it is the most crooked building you are ever likely to experience and makes falling over a distinct possibility the moment you walk through the door. Inside are two wonky little bars: take your pick, both are a challenge. The grandfather clock, although upright, looks as if it is about to fall over, the red-tiled floors swim as you cross them, the bottled beers roll uphill. The whole place is faintly surreal and brings *Alice in Wonderland* to mind. The pub serves real ales such as Banks Bitter, farm cider and standard pub grub in a large (uncrooked) dining room, and sits in its own big garden near Himley Court.

directions	Off B4176 between Gornalwood & Himley.
meals	12pm-2.30pm; 5.30pm-9pm (9.30pm Fri & Sat; 8pm Sun). All day in summer. Main courses £6-£9.
closed	3pm-5pm. Open all day in summer.

Brett Harrison
Crooked House,
Coppice Mill,
Himley DY3 4DA

tel   01384 238583

map: 8 entry: 455

Suffolk

Star Inn
Lidgate

The garden is glorious on a summer's day. For winter there are two blazing fires – and two snugs, each the centrepiece of an ancient-beamed bar. Indeed, the pretty Star, built in 1588, is one of the oldest buildings in the village – two cottages knocked into one. It is also as English as can be, yet landlady Maria Teresa Axon comes from Catalonia in Spain. The rich aromas that greet you may just as well come from boeuf en daube or venison in port as from Spanish-style roast lamb, fabada asturiana (Asturian pork and bean stew) or parillada of fish. Bring a good appetite as portions will be generous, and do book; proximity to Newmarket brings racing types in droves. There are darts and dominoes to get stuck into, Greene King beers on handpump – ask about the unusual handles – and Spain is deliciously represented in brandies and wines.

directions	On B1063, 7 miles south east of Newmarket.
meals	12pm-2.30pm; 7pm-10pm. No food Sun eve. Main courses £14.50-£18.50; bar meals £5.50-£9.50.
closed	3pm-7pm.

Maria Teresa Axon
Star Inn,
The Street,
Lidgate,
Bury St Edmunds CB8 9PP

tel   01638 500275

map: 9 entry: 456

Suffolk   Pub with rooms

Old Cannon Brewery
Bury St Edmunds

Brewing is a slow process, says Richard Eyton-Jones, and he should know; for the past seven years he has been brewer-in-chief of this admirable revitalisation of a Victorian brewhouse-pub. Bare boards clatter, wooden tables are plain, a huge mirror vies with two gleaming stainless steel brewing kettles for decoration. The atmosphere is young, friendly and enlivened by pints of own-brew Gunner's Daughter and Old Cannon Best. On the menu: local sausages with onion gravy, grilled wing of skate with lemon grass and caper butter, and roast duck with sloe gin. A cobbled courtyard beyond the old coach arch has swish tables and chairs for summer sipping; in the former brewery building are five light, cheerful and airy bedrooms. And you are a five-minute walk from the town and its treasures.

directions	From A14, Bury exit, for centre, left at r'bout to Northgate St; right at Cadney Lane & into Cannon St.
meals	12pm-2pm; 6.30pm-9.30pm. No food Sun eve & Mon. Main courses £11.50-£16.95; bar meals £4.50-£7.95.
rooms	5: 4 doubles, 1 twin £69. Singles £55.
closed	3pm-5pm (7pm Sun) & Mon lunch.

See pp 30-57 for full list of pubs with rooms

Michael & Judith Shallow
Old Cannon Brewery,
86 Cannon Street,
Bury St Edmunds IP33 1JR
tel   01284 768769
web   www.oldcannonbrewery.co.uk

map: 10 entry: 457

Suffolk

The Beehive
Horringer

Look out for the beehive at the front! Housed within these converted 19th-century cottages is a local of the very best kind. It's well modernised yet the higgledy-piggledy feel remains, along with low beams and beautifully worn flagstone floors. Several country-smart rooms interlink – expect soft lighting, old prints, candlelight, linen napkins, a woodburning stove. Greene King ales are on handpump but people come for more than the beer. Blackboards announce the daily menu, perhaps a lunchtime plate of cured meats with capers and chutney, braised oxtail with Suffolk ale gravy, or shoulder of lamb with tomatoes, garlic and olives; desserts and wines are equally good. The place can fill up quickly so do book, especially at weekends – the pub's popularity is proof of Gary and Diane Kingshott's hospitality. Ickworth House, in the same pretty village and owned by the National Trust, awaits discovery.

directions	3 miles south west of Bury St Edmunds on A143.
meals	12pm-2pm; 7pm-9.30pm. Main courses £8.95-£15.95; bar meals £5.95-£9.95.
closed	3pm-7pm & Sun eve.

Gary & Diane Kingshott
The Beehive,
The Street,
Horringer,
Bury St Edmunds IP29 5SN
tel   01284 735260

map: 10 entry: 458

The Bildeston Crown
Bildeston

There are flagstones in the locals' bar, warm reds on the walls and sweet-smelling logs smouldering in open fires. The inn dates from 1529, the interior design from 2005. Not that the feel is overly contemporary; ancient beams have been reclaimed from under a thick coat of black paint and varnished wood floors shine like honey. There are gilded mirrors and oils on the walls, candles in the fireplace, happy locals at the bar. An airy open-plan feel runs throughout, with lots of space in the dining room and smart leather chairs tucked under hand-made oak tables. They're proud of their food here and it ranges from roast Suffolk beef sandwiches with mustard mayo to a sensational seven-course tasting menu in the evening. There are flowers in the courtyard and Suffolk beers to quench your thirst. Hire bikes from the shop next door and dive into the country, or come for the beer festival in May.

The Swan
Monks Eleigh

The polished, wooden floored interior is not unlike that of a bistro, but Nigel and Carol's 16th-century thatched Swan is still a pub at heart. There's a large bar, Adnams on handpump and a good line in wines by the glass. The modernised interior is invitingly open with recessed ceiling lights, soft sage tones and a winter log fire. Yet most folk come to eat. Nigel, in the kitchen, has created a menu to please both the traditionalist and the adventurer, so wintry offerings off the blackboard may include potted pork rilettes with apple and sultana chutney, whole roast partridge with braised lentils, bacon and onions, Hamish Johnson's British and Irish cheeses, and a fabulously sticky toffee pudding with butterscotch and mascarpone. Fish can be relied upon to be beautifully fresh, say Lowestoft skate wing with lemon and butter. Service, by Carol, is a lesson in how these things should be done: efficient, knowledgeable, cheerful and charming.

directions	A12 junc. 31, then B1070 to Hadleigh. A1141 north, then B1115 into village. Pub on right.
meals	12pm-3pm; 7pm-10pm (9.30pm Sun). Main course £9-£20; sandwiches from £4.50.
closed	Open all day.

Hayley Robertson
The Bildeston Crown,
Bildeston IP7 7ED

tel	01449 740510
web	www.thecrownbildeston.com

map: 10 entry: 459

directions	On B1115 between Lavenham & Hadleigh.
meals	12pm-2pm; 7pm-9pm. Main courses £10-£16.75; bar meals £4.25-£7.
closed	3pm-7pm, Mon & Tues all day.

Nigel & Carol Ramsbottom
The Swan,
The Street, Monks Eleigh,
Lavenham IP7 7AU

tel	01449 741391
web	www.monkseleigh.com

map: 10 entry: 460

Suffolk

The Crown
Stoke-by-Nayland

Several low-ceilinged but rambling rooms, one with a view of the kitchen, are decked in muted colours; the mood is warm, appealing and refreshingly music-free. There's space to prop up the bar and down a pint from Suffolk brewers Adnams, while the seasonal menu is a sympathetic combination of traditional and contemporary. Several chefs dispatch exuberant renditions of salt and pepper squid with garlic and lemon mayonnaise, crispy pork belly with creamed leek mash, pan-fried calves' liver with bubble-and-squeak potato cake, crisy bacon and red wine sauce, Adnams battered haddock with tartare sauce. Polish it all off with prune and armagnac tart with clotted cream or a platter of five British cheeses. The food is fairly priced and there's an outstanding wine list, with wines matched to the food and bottles to take home from the shop. And a glorious terrace with stunning views.

directions	Just off B1087 in Stoke-by-Nayland.
meals	12pm-2.30pm; 6pm-9.30pm (10pm Fri & Sat); 12pm- 9pm Sun. Main courses £8.95-£15.95.
closed	Open all day.

Richard Sunderland
The Crown,
Stoke-by-Nayland,
Colchester CO6 4SE

| tel | 01206 262001 |
| web | www.eoinns.co.uk |

map: 10 entry: 461

Suffolk

The Ship
Levington

The Levington Ship is a 14th-century thatched beauty overlooking the River Orwell. This alone makes it a popular watering hole, the low-ceilinged bar and flower-festooned rear terrace filling quickly with yachting types, locals and townies escaping to the country for lunch. Naturally, the bar emphasises a nautical theme, with pictures of barges, lifebuoys and a ship's wheel on the walls. Over the past few years chef-patron Mark Johnson's imaginative cooking has made its successful mark, his chalkboard menus, changed twice a day, listing fresh fish and locally reared meats – notably venison from the Suffolk Estate – as well as seasonal salads and local vegetables. Exemplary French cheeses come from the Rungis Market in Paris and superior real ales from East Anglian brewers Adnams and Greene King. Wonderful riverside walks await those who have had one glass too many – and those who haven't.

directions	A12/A14 junction to Woodbridge; follow signs for Levington.
meals	12pm-2pm (3pm Sun); 6.30pm-9.30pm (9pm Sun). Main courses from £7.75-£14.95.
closed	2.30pm-6pm. Open all day Sat & Sun.

Stella & Mark Johnson
The Ship,
Levington,
Ipswich IP10 0LQ

| tel | 01473 659573 |

map: 10 entry: 462

White Hart
Otley

Deep in Suffolk, the quintessence of community spirit. Lynda saved the pub five days before it was to be sold off as a house; a year on, it is the hub of the village. She, Sarah and chef Sam have made the White Hart their own: free-spirited, utterly individual, a place to expect the unexpected – and that includes the food. Scout leaders pop in for the warmth and the beer, Knitting and Crochet meet every other Monday, the piano may be commandeered for a singsong at any time. At weekends children sprawl on the sofa or play battleships under the tables and anything goes; a dining room is tucked around the end of the very long bar but you can eat wherever you like. So kick off your shoes, pull up a chair and order a meal – it's brilliant value. There's pâté de campagne à la Elizabeth David, Sri Lankan fishcakes and red Thai fish curry, half a pint of prawns and sirloin steak with chips. They are even founder members of the Slow Food movement so the food bursts with flavour and the sourcing is impeccable.

directions	B1079 from Otley, 0.5 miles north towards Helmingham, on left.
meals	12pm-2.30pm; 6pm-9pm. Main courses £7.45-£12; Sunday roasts £3.95 (child-size), £6.95 & £8.95.
closed	3pm-5pm, Mon lunch & Sun from 5pm.

SPECIAL AWARD
see pages 28-29

Lynda Saint
White Hart,
Helmingham Road,
Ipswich IP6 9NS
tel   01473 890312
web   www.thewhitehartotley.co.uk

map: 10 entry: 463

The Crown and Castle
Orford

Ruth's sense of style has created a distinctive bistro inn out of this late-Victorian building. Certainly not a village local but the welcome is friendly to all, the atmosphere relaxed, the food sublime. The fire in the hall lures you in, deep sofas urge you to stay. Floorboards clatter, quirky paintings amuse and the bar is as convivial as any to nibble on tapas and quaff a pint of Adnams. Cromer crab, Orford skate and lobster, local game and Gloucester Old Spot pork are splendidly taken care of: the cooking is robust and it's impossible to resist hot bitter chocolate soufflé with local Jersey cream. In summer a casual lunch on the terrace is heaven. Rooms in the main house come in pastels, those at the back have long river views, and garden rooms are big and airy, with crisp white linen and seagrass matting. You are minutes on foot from the wild river marshes so pull on a pair of the hotel's wellies and discover Suffolk.

directions	Leave A12 at Woodbridge; A1152 & B1084 to Orford.
meals	12pm-2pm; 7pm-9pm. Main courses £14.50-£19.50; bar lunch £10.50-£16.50.
rooms	18: 16 doubles, 2 twins £90-£145; family £110-£160.
closed	3pm-7pm.

See pp 30–57 for full list of pubs with rooms

David & Ruth Watson
The Crown and Castle,
Orford IP12 2LJ
tel   01394 450205
web   www.crownandcastle.co.uk

map: 10 entry: 464

The Crown Inn
Snape

A Suffolk gem. A well-preserved 15th-century inn with beams and brick floors only a stroll from the Maltings concert hall and a short drive from the Minsmere bird sanctuary. It claims to have the finest example anywhere of a double Suffolk settle, known as the 'old codgers'; for this it is worth the trip alone. But the real old codgers have long gone: this popular food pub now attracts the Aldeburgh set, who come for Diane Maylott's modern brasserie-style food – seared scallop and bacon salad, pork belly with chorizo and cider sauce, Thai salmon fishcakes. Key to The Crown's success is an insistence on fresh, local produce, particularly fish, game and organic vegetables. But despite the foodie emphasis, there is still a deliciously pubby atmosphere here, in among the dark beams, old brick floors and roaring log fires. And both the real ales and the wines (11 by the glass) are supplied by Suffolk's most respected brewery, Adnams, who own the place.

directions	Off A12, A1094 following Aldeburgh, right turn signed Snape. Pub at bottom of the hill.
meals	12pm-2pm; 7pm-9pm Main courses £9.90-£15.95.
closed	3pm-6pm.

Diane Maylott
The Crown Inn,
Bridge Road,
Snape,
Saxmundham IP17 1SL
tel   01728 688324

map: 10 entry: 465

The Westleton Crown
Westleton

Watch the world go by from this ancient coaching inn in the heart of the village. It's had a smart renovation but there's still bags of character – in flagstones and stripped floors, beams, pews, spindle-back chairs, log fires in winter and a large terraced garden for when the sun shines. As for eating, the classic English menu is executed with flair. So tuck in to warm smoked salmon with dressed rocket and sauce vièrge, stuffed Suffolk chicken with sage-crushed potatoes, pear tart tatin with cinnamon ice cream… after such indulgence, you'll be glad you've booked a room for the night. Bedrooms vary in size and are hugely stylish, some with four-posters, all with goose down duvets and flat-screen TVs, and those in the stables and the cottage have umbrellas so you'll arrive at breakfast exquisitely dry. Chic bathrooms are a further (huge) treat, and trendy Walberswick is close by.

directions	Off A12 onto Westleton road to village of Westleton.
meals	12pm-2pm; 7pm-9.30pm. Main courses £9.50-£19.50; bar meals £4.25-£9.95.
rooms	25 twins/doubles £110-£170. Singles £85-£95.
closed	Open all day.

See pp 30–57 for full list of pubs with rooms

	Matt Goodwin The Westleton Crown, The Street, Westleton, Southwold IP17 3AD
tel	01728 648777
web	www.westletoncrown.co.uk

map: 10 entry: 466

The Anchor
Walberswick

Seeking sea air, beer guru Mark Dorber (landlord of the White Horse, Parsons Green) and wife Sophie are doing wonders at this Adnams boozer. To the sound of the sea crashing on the beach beyond, the vast lawn hosts summer barbecues – and the homemade burgers draw an appreciative crowd. Inside, sand, stone and aqua tones add a contemporary touch, while Sophie's menus overflow with produce sourced from a rich vein of organic farms and top local butchers. Menus match beer with food; try Adnams Broadside with a melting Irish stew. A summer treat would be fruits de mer with a draught wheat beer, out on the new sun terrace overlooking allotments, beach huts and distant sea. A pity not to stay; there's one big bedroom above the pub, and more in the annexe chalets, set around a charming pebble and sea plant garden.

directions	From A12 south of Southwold; B3187 to Walberswick.
meals	12pm-3pm; 6pm-9pm (all day Sat & July & Aug). Main courses £10.75-£17.75.
rooms	7: 4 doubles, 3 twins, 1 family room £90. Singles £75.
closed	4pm-6pm. Open all day Sat & July & Aug.

See pp 30–57 for full list of pubs with rooms

	Mark & Sophie Dorber The Anchor, Main Street, Walberswick, Southwold IP18 6UA
tel	01502 722112
web	www.anchoratwalberswick.com

map: 10 entry: 467

The Crown
Southwold

The Crown has an eye for metropolitan sophistication. Ceilings are elegantly beamed, the walls of the big, laid-back bar are colourwashed and uncluttered – fitting for a town known as Kensington-on-Sea. The food comes as bar snacks in full modern-brasserie mode: tempura Brancaster oysters, tapas, confit duck leg, roast pumpkin and parmesan risotto. Fresh flowers sit on kitchen-style tables, there are newspapers to read, Adnams ales on handpump and fine wines to try. There's no pretentiousness and a fascinating mix of customers – suits, locals, trendies, grannies, families. A smaller, pubbier panelled back bar keeps hard-core traditionalists happy, and there's a smart, sunny, slightly more self-conscious restaurant. All in all, The Crown has succeeded in being simultaneously a simple pub, a brasserie wine bar and a restaurant with serious aspirations.

The Queens Head
Bramfield

Another chef-landlord with an interest in provenance – and Mark Corcoran's menus make reassuring reading. Recent dishes include wild rabbit braised in local cider with mustard and prunes, and Wakelyns organic farm Little Gem squash with curried nut filling and sweet and sour beetroot. Rest assured that half the ingredients will be organic and locally sourced. Lighter bites may include red onion tarte tatin with roasted cherry tomatoes and homemade soups; accompanying salads are simple and delicious. All this plenty is served in a high-raftered bar with dark timbered walls, scrubbed pine tables and a fireplace ablaze with logs in winter. A rustically cosy room lies next door. There are small portions for children and the drinks are exemplary: Adnams ales, ciders and wines and local elderflower pressé. Make time for the lovely terraced courtyard and garden with bantams and bower – and Bramfield's thatched church with its unusual bell tower.

directions	In centre of Southwold.
meals	12pm-2pm; 6.30pm-9pm. Main courses £10-£15.
closed	Open all day.

Francis Guildea
The Crown,
High Street,
Southwold IP18 6DP
tel   01502 722275
web   www.adnamshotels.co.uk

map: 10 entry: 468

directions	2 miles north of A12 on A144 Halesworth road.
meals	12pm-2pm; 6.30pm-10pm; 7pm-9pm Sun. Main courses £3.95-£13.95.
closed	2.30pm-6.30pm (3pm-7pm Sun).

Mark & Amanda Corcoran
The Queens Head,
The Street, Bramfield,
Halesworth IP19 9HT
tel   01986 784214
web   www.queensheadbramfield.co.uk

map: 10 entry: 469

Station Hotel
Framlingham

The railway disappeared long ago, the old buildings are now business units, but the 'hotel' continues to thrive. Esoteric cask ales (a classic Victorian Bitter, a sweet, wintry porter) are perfect accompaniments for gusty, earthy cooking. Who would imagine, chalked up on the board on the edge of a market town somewhere in Suffolk, creamy baked Vacherin cheese or grilled partridge with creamed Savoy cabbage and junipers? It's simple and good: the pumpkin and chilli soup a smooth spicy purée with a herb leaf garnish, the warm almond and orange polenta cake as light as a cloud. Lunch tends to be quiet but it bustles at night, helped along by the man in the kitchen, Mike Jones, and his friendly, laid-back team. The building is pretty in a shabby-boho way, the interior is charming. Expect blackened stripped boards, cream papered walls, a huge mirror, a stuffed head, and bone-handled knives partnering paper serviettes – a characterful mix.

directions	From Wickham Market, 10 min off the A12.
meals	12pm-2pm; 7pm-9pm (9.30pm Fri & Sat). Main courses £4-£14.75; bar meals £3.25-£11.
closed	2.30pm-5pm (7pm Sun).

	Mike Jones Station Hotel, Station Road, Framlingham, Woodbridge IP13 9EE
tel	01728 723455
web	www.thestationhotel.net

map: 10 entry: 470

King's Head
Laxfield

Known locally as the Low House because it lies in a dip below the churchyard, the 600-year-old thatched pub is one of Suffolk's treasures. Little has changed in the last 100 years and its four rooms creak with character – all narrow passageways and low ceilings. The simple parlour is dominated by a three-sided, high-backed settle in front of an open fire and there's no bar – far too new-fangled a concept for this place; instead, impeccable Adnams ales are served from barrels in the tap room – buy a jug. In keeping with the timeless atmosphere, food is rustic, hearty and homemade, the short, daily-changing blackboard menu listing soup, sandwiches, hot dishes and puddings. It's the sort of place where traditional folk music often starts up spontaneously, while summer brings Morris men. At the back, the secluded garden has been created from a former bowling green.

directions	From Laxfield church, left down hill for 50 yards. Left; pub on right.
meals	12pm-2pm; 7pm-9pm. Main courses £7.95-£15.95; bar meals £3.95-£7.
closed	3pm-6pm.

	Geoff Puffett King's Head, Gorams Mill Lane, Laxfield IP13 8DW
tel	01986 798395

map: 10 entry: 471

Suffolk

St Peter's Hall
St Peter South Elmham

John Murphy bought the 13th-century moated manor in 1996 to brew beer using water from the site's 60-metre bore. Now St Peter's thrives, brewing and bottling its exemplary range of bitters, fruit ales and porters. Take the weekend brewery tour or venture into the medieval hall to eat and drink like kings. The lofty stone-flagged dining hall is filled with original Brussels tapestries, fine stone fireplaces and 17th- and 18th-century furnishings: sup at candlelit tables from French choir stalls or a bishop's chair. The Library bar is more homely. It's a intriguing setting in which to show off some intriguing beers, with food to match. The bar menu reveal simple enticement: St Peter's steak and ale pie, Suffolk ham, egg and chips, steak au poivre and sausages with mustard mash and red wine gravy. Don't miss the brewery shop and take some of their bottled beers home.

directions	Follow brown amenity signs from Flixton or A144, between Bungay & Halesworth.
meals	12pm-2.30pm; 7pm-9pm. Restaurant Sat night & Sun lunch only. Main courses £7.95-£10.
closed	3pm-6pm. Open all day Sun & bank hols.

Peter & Valerie Hindle
St Peter's Hall,
St Peter South Elmham,
Bungay NR35 1NQ
tel   01986 782288
web   www.stpetersbrewery.co.uk

map: 10 entry: 472

Surrey

The Inn at West End
West End

Wine importer Gerry Price draws them in from all over Surrey. Stylishly revamped dining areas are light and modern with classy yellow walls, wooden floors and fine fabrics. The feeling is relaxed and friendly – quiz nights, film club, boules, barbecues; the homely bar has a wood-burning stove; handpumped ale comes from Fuller's and Young's and the list of wines is long, with a nod to Portuguese shores. Monthly menus have modern British choices ranging from salmon and dill fishcakes with tartare sauce to pot-roasted pork with cabbage and dauphinoise potatoes – and partridge, pheasant, woodcock and teal in winter. A pastry chef masterminds a select choice of desserts; cheeses are farmhouse best. Add great lunchtime sandwiches, good value set lunches, Saturday lunchtime wine-tasting sessions and popular wine dinners and you have a superbly run pub.

directions	M3 junc. 3; A322 towards Guildford for 2 miles.
meals	12pm-2.30pm (3pm Sun); 6pm-9.30pm (9pm Sun). Set menus from £10.75; sandwiches from £5.25; Sunday lunch £21.95.
closed	3pm-5pm Mon-Sat (4pm-7pm Sun).

Gerry & Ann Price
The Inn at West End,
42 Guildford Road,
West End GU24 9PW
tel   01276 858652
web   www.the-inn.co.uk

map: 4 entry: 473

Black Swan
Ockham

Geronimo Inns' boss Rupert Clevely must have jumped for joy when he completed the deal on the Black Swan, his first pub outside London. He couldn't have picked a better location – minutes from the A3 yet deep in leafy Surrey. A grand and expensive makeover has seen the rough old bikers' boozer transformed into swish gastropub, the brick façade of the original building dwarfed by an amazing pavilion extension. Clever design pulls informal and open-plan drinking and dining areas together around a big curving bar, with a classic bar for pints and an airy, high-ceilinged eating area that buzzes with merry diners. Décor may be eclectic and ultra-modern but, with up to six ales on tap and a flurry of non-bookable tables, it is still a pub. Good modern food ranges from all day potted salmon with pickled cucumber or cider-battered cod and chips, to shepherd's pie and herb-crusted rack of lamb. The Black Swan is thriving.

The King William IV
Mickleham

Open fires, fresh flowers, slab sandwiches and amazing views are a few of the reasons people make the steep stepped climb – unless you can park in the lane. The old alehouse was built for Lord Beaverbrook's estate staff – a hilltop eyrie that has long been a popular little pub in summer, when all and sundry spill into the terraced garden. There's a serving hatch to outside, handy for walkers with muddy boots. In winter it's super-snug and squeezes in two carpeted bars. The real badgers have gone (see the photos on the walls) but their namesake ale remains on tap as well as those from The Hogs Back Brewery. Equal attention is paid to food. Chips are banned but who cares, when homemade pies, lamb shank with red wine sauce, Thai-style sea bass and steaming puddings are brought to the table? New owners plan a conservatory for 2007.

directions	Ockham is signed off A3 just south of M25 junct 10. Pub just north of village at crossroads.
meals	12pm-10pm. Main courses £8-£17.50; bar snacks £5-£9.50.
closed	Open all day.

directions	From junc. 9 M25, A24 for Dorking. Just before Mickleham, pub on hill above Frascati restaurant.
meals	12pm-2pm; 7pm-9.30pm (12pm-5pm Sun). Main courses £6.75-£16.75; sandwiches £4.25-£5.25; Sunday roast £11.75.
closed	3pm-6pm. Open all day Sun.

	Kevin Ward Black Swan, Old Lane, Ockham, Guildford KT11 1NG
tel	01932 862364
web	www.geronimo-inns.co.uk

	Ian & Liz Duke The King William IV, Byttom Hill, Mickleham, Dorking RH5 6EL
tel	01372 372590
web	www.king-williamiv.com

map: 4 entry: 474

map: 4 entry: 475

The Parrot
Forest Green

Charles and Linda Gotto finally gave up their mini-empire of London pubs in 2006, after 25 hugely successful years, to concentrate on running a livestock farm in the Surrey hills. But, not content with just being farmers, they bought this rambling, 17th-century, tile-hung pub that overlooks the village green and cricket pitch in nearby Forest Green. The Gottos are passionate about food, its provenance and quality, and the Parrot pub showcases meats reared on their farm — Shorthorn cattle, Middlewhite pigs, mutton — both on the short, imaginative menu and in the unique farm shop inside. Surely one of few pubs where you can tuck into game pie, lamb rump with minted pea purée or roast belly pork with mash and braised cabbage, and then buy the produce to take home (farm meats and free-range eggs,

locally produced sausages, pies, pickles, cheeses). Elsewhere, beams, flagstones and bits and bobs, old settles and blazing fires, Young's on tap and 16 wines by the glass. Brilliant value.

directions	Opposite the village green, off B2127 just west of junction with B2126, 5 miles SW of Dorking.
meals	12pm-3pm (4pm Sun); 6pm-9pm (10pm Fri & Sat). No food Sun eve. Main courses £9.25-£13.50; Sunday roast £11.
closed	Open all day.

SPECIAL
AWARD
see pages 28-29

Charles & Linda Gotto
The Parrot,
Forest Green,
Dorking RH5 5RZ
tel   01306 621339
web   www.theparrot.co.uk

map: 4 entry: 476

The Hare & Hounds
Lingfield

The exterior may not look particularly beguiling but step inside and you know you've come to a special place. With proprietor-chef Fergus's collection of quirky collectables filling every corner, the place has an idiosyncratic air. Bar bustle can be surveyed from old cinema seats or one of a pair of throne-like chairs, while the cushion-laden banquettes are an ideal spot for viewing a menu studded with the names of the farms that supply much of the produce. Blackboard specialities may include pan-fried wild pheasant breast with braised leg and roast vegetables; on the printed menu, slow roast belly of pork with apple tart, leeks and cauliflower, or crab ravioli with bisque. Diners are as happy among the clutter, the hop garlands and the greenery of the main bar as beneath the bold paintings of Fergus's artist wife in the lovely dining room. Nurse a summer pint of Abbot Ale in the partly decked garden.

The Swan Inn and Restaurant
Chiddingfold

Here are a sparkling dining room and a cool bar – wood floors, chunky tables – but the old pub's origins have not been forgotten. Hogs Back TEA and Fuller's London Pride for those in for a pint; ham, egg and chips for a quick bite. And there are snails, carpaccio of beef, goat's cheese soufflé and fishcakes with smoked salmon sauce – a successful juggling of popular and modern. In the dining room a well-presented menu lists a superb choice, from seared salmon with flageolet beans and a green peppercorn sauce to confit duck leg with dauphinoise potatoes and red wine sauce. Contemporary rooms have a minimalist feel, with muted earthy colours, flat-screen TVs and trendy bathrooms with power showers and posh toiletries. All in all, this is a happy, relaxed revival of an old inn. And a prettily landscaped terraced garden tempts you outdoors on a warm day.

directions	From A22 towards Lingfield Racecourse into Common Road.
meals	12pm-2.30pm; 7pm-9.30pm (9pm Mon & Tues). Main courses £12.50-£17.50.
closed	Open all day (closed Sun from 8pm).

directions	South of village green beside the A283 between Guildford & Petworth.
meals	12pm-2.30pm; 6.30pm-10pm. Main courses £9.45-£19.95; bar meals £4.25-£7.95; Sunday roast £11.95.
rooms	11: 9 doubles, 2 suites £70-£140.
closed	Open all day.

See pp 30–57 for full list of pubs with rooms

Fergus Greer
The Hare & Hounds,
Common Road,
Lingfield RH7 6BZ
tel   01342 832351

Daniel Hall & Darren Tidd
The Swan Inn and Restaurant,
Petworth Road, Chiddingfold,
Guildford GU8 4TY
tel   01428 682073
web   www.theswaninn.biz

map: 4 entry: 477

map: 4 entry: 478

The Stag
Balls Cross

The quintessential Sussex pub – some might say (and often do) it's the best pub in the world. Under 16th-century beams by a crackling log fire, or in the big garden in summer, riders, walkers and locals enjoy a natter over well-kept Badger and Sussex Bitter. Wholesome home-cooked food is another draw, the traditional recipe pies, pastries and casseroles being the greatest temptation. A sweet shop in a former life, this little inn still welcomes children: in a set-aside room youngsters may play undisturbed. There is also plenty for adults: the Stag has its own darts team, jazz nights outdoors in summer, carol singing and visits from the travelling Mummers at Christmas. There's a 17th-century stone-floored bar and a dining room that's carpeted and cosy. And a useful tethering post for those who come by horse.

The Lickfold Inn
Lickfold

The glorious 15th-century bricks bulge in a riot of herringbone, there's a sofa plump with tweed cushions beside the huge central inglenook: it's gorgeously atmospheric. The Hickeys have settled in well and provide a popular menu and daily specials built around fresh local produce that changes with the seasons – pheasant wrapped in pancetta with wild mushroom, port and redcurrant jus, wild sea bass with chilli herb crust, smoked salmon and scrambled egg, roast pork open sandwich. Diners can relax downstairs in a cosy setting where fat cream candles reflected in the latticed windows give comfort and cheer; a more formal private dining area upstairs with sumptuous silk curtains brings a contemporary twist to the medieval framework. There's a super heated terrace at the back that leads to lushly rambling gardens.

directions	2 miles from Petworth on Kirdford road.
meals	12pm-2pm; 7pm-9pm. No food Sun eve. Main courses £7.50-£18; bar meals £4-£18.
closed	3pm-6pm (7pm Sun).

Hamish Hiddleston
The Stag,
Balls Cross,
Petworth GU28 9JP

tel   01403 820241

map: 4 entry: 479

directions	Off A272, thro' Lodsworth; cont. to bottom of road; on left.
meals	12pm-2.30pm; 7pm-9.30pm. Main courses £9.95-£19.95; bar meals £5.95-£9.95.
closed	3.30pm-6pm. Sun eve & Mon (except bank hols).

Andrea & James Hickey
The Lickfold Inn,
Lickfold,
Petworth GU28 9EY

tel   01798 861285
web   www.thelickfoldinn.co.uk

map: 4 entry: 480

Hollist Arms
Lodsworth

Villager and proprietor George Bristow rescued this lovely pub a few years ago, injected fresh enthusiasm among the staff and stuffed the menu with local and seasonal ingredients. Prawn and crayfish knickerbockers, duck breast in soy sauce with ginger and a melt-in-the-mouth cottage pie – all are first-class. Villagers prop up the very long bar for a good pint of King's Horsham Best, while civilised sofas by a huge inglenook encourage others to stay. The smaller, more intimate rooms of this former smithy have been kept: one, a cosy claret-coloured private dining room, another a sweet snug with soft green armchairs, blazing fire and tables piled high with magazines and games. Children are liked and there's a garden for summer. From the hand-cut, local-farm potato chips to the colourwashed walls, pretty feather-patterned curtains and soothing classical sounds, this Hollist oozes magic.

Welldiggers Arms
Petworth

Once occupied by well-diggers, as the name suggests, this rustic 300-year-old roadside cottage has little immediate appeal. But enter and you are greeted by Ted Whitcomb, landlord and larger-than-life persona, pulling pints of Young's and cracking jokes behind the bar for 50-odd years. Surprisingly, this is a dining-orientated pub, its low-ceilinged bar and snug packed with happy eaters at long settles and huge oak tables. Come for classic British food: delicious fish soup, king prawns in garlic, fresh mussels, whole Dover sole, Selsey crab and properly hung T-bone steaks. Alternatives may include braised oxtail and dumplings, calves' liver, black pudding and mash and seasonal game – and magnificent Sunday roasts. Popular with enthusiasts of racing (Goodwood), shooting and polo (Cowdray Park), so be sure to book. At the back is a patio with views over the South Downs.

directions	Halfway between Midhurst & Petworth; signed off A272.
meals	12pm-2pm (2.30pm Sat, 3pm Sun); 7pm-9pm (9.30pm Fri & Sat, 6.30pm-8pm Sun). Main courses £10-£16; bar meals £5-£10.
closed	3pm-6pm (4pm-6pm Sun).

directions	Beside A283 Pulborough road, 1 mile east of Petworth.
meals	12pm-3pm; 6pm-10pm. No food Sun eve. Main courses £7.50-£19.50; bar meals from £4.25.
closed	3.30pm-6pm, Sun eve, Tues & Wed eve & Mon all day.

George Bristow
Hollist Arms,
The Street,
Lodsworth,
Petworth GU28 9BZ
tel   01798 861310

Ted Whitcomb
Welldiggers Arms,
Pulborough Road,
Petworth GU28 0HG
tel   01798 342287

map: 4 entry: 481

map: 4 entry: 482

Halfway Bridge Inn

Halfway Bridge

Paul and Sue Carter bought the lease to this mellow old coaching inn in 2006. Keeping the classic three-room layout and the warren of cosy corners and split levels, they have introduced a stylish feel – scrubbed tables, cushioned benches, big lilies and fat candles. The food is good, too. Find a seat by the open fire and dive into a menu that promises first-rate fish from Billingsgate alongside game suet pudding and canon of lamb. Thirsts are quenched by Sussex beers; outside is a sheltered patio with posh tables and brollies. This is a lovely spot so stay a night or two – the old stables have been converted into excellent rooms where deep beds, leather chairs, plasma screens and PlayStations "for the boys" sit beautifully with old beams and rustic brickwork. Bath and shower rooms – big mirrors, top lotions and potions – are an equal treat.

directions	On A272 halfway between Midhurst & Petworth.
meals	12pm-2.30pm; 6.30pm-9.15pm (8.30pm Sun). Main courses £9.95-£15.95; bar meals £4.95-£8.95.
rooms	6: 2 doubles £90-£110, 4 suites £120-£150. Singles from £65.
closed	Open all day.

See pp 30-57 for full list of pubs with rooms

Paul & Sue Carter
Halfway Bridge Inn,
Halfway Bridge,
Midhurst GU28 9BP
tel   01798 861281
web   www.thesussexpub.co.uk

map: 4 entry: 483

Duke of Cumberland Arms

Henley

In spring the Duke looks divine, its brick and stone cottage walls engulfed by flowering wisteria – and beyond is the terraced garden, with its babbling trout pools and huge Weald views. Latch doors lead to two tiny bars that creak with character – painted tongue-and-groove walls, low ceilings, ancient scrubbed tables and benches, and log fires in the grate. Gas lamps, old indentures and the odd stuffed bird add to the atmosphere. Choose a pint of Adnams, Young's, Broadside or Brakspear, to name but a few, drawn straight from the cask, or a glass of farmhouse cider. Landlords Christina and Gaston Duval's popular daily menu relies on fresh local produce, including trout from their spring-fed pools and delectable roasts, notably from Sussex lamb and organic beef – brought as a joint to the table.

directions	From Fernhurst towards Midhurst; pass pub on right; next left to Henley; follow road, on right.
meals	12pm-2.30pm; 7pm-9.30pm. No food Sun eve or Mon all day. Main courses £9.95-£15.95; bar meals £5.75-£9.
closed	Open all day.

Gaston & Christina Duval
Duke of Cumberland Arms,
Henley,
Midhurst GU27 3HQ
tel   01428 652280

map: 4 entry: 484

The Keepers Arms
Trotton

Nick Troth and his fledgling Weybourne Inns has expanded to two pubs (the Hawkley near Liss being the other) with the purchase of this 17th-century inn. It backs onto Terwick Common and has a front terrace with views. Changes are afoot, but you may expect a lively bar area with changing ales from local breweries and huge fireside sofas: a refuge for lounge lizards during the long Sunday lunches that are planned. Chef Matt Appleton, is taking the food seriously, so it'll be above average for a pub… confit duck and foie gras terrine with pickled mushrooms; herb-crusted cod with baby spinach and chive velouté; calves' liver, mash, and foie gras puree; fettucine of wild mushrooms with parmesan cream and truffle oil; hot chocolate fondant and pistachio ice cream. All served at candlelit tables in the beamed and oak-floored dining area next to the bar. Plans extend to four swish bedroom suites upstairs — watch this space!

directions	On A272 between Midhurst & Petersfield.
meals	12pm-2pm; 7pm-10pm (11.30am-4.30pm Sun). Main courses £10-£16.
closed	3pm-6pm (5pm-7pm Sun).

Nick Troth
The Keepers Arms,
Trotton,
Petersfield GU31 5ER
tel 01730 813724
web www.keepersarms.co.uk

map: 4 entry: 485

The Three Horseshoes
Elsted

Low beams, latched doors, high settles, deep-cream bowed walls, fresh flowers, cottage windows, big log fires and home-cooked food: all that you'd hope for, and more. Built in 1540 as a drovers' ale house, it has no cellar, so staff pull ales from the barrel instead; the line of metal casks is visible in the lower open-timbered bar, formerly a butcher's shop and still with the ceiling hooks. Local seafood, meat and game appear on a tempting country menu — summer lobster and crab, pheasant in cider with shallots and prunes, steak and kidney in Guinness pie — and are served in snug little rooms. In the main dining room with its wood-burning stove you can't miss the flock of chickens in china, pottery and wood. Landlady Sue has a passion for poultry and in summer her feathered friends cluck cheerily outside among the drinkers with their golden pints. The South Downs views are fabulous.

directions	From Midhurst A272 for Petersfield; Elsted signed left in 2 miles.
meals	12pm-2pm; 6.30pm-9pm (7pm-8.30pm Sun). Main courses £7.95-£14.95; bar meals £6.95-£9.95.
closed	2.30pm-6pm (3pm-7pm Sun).

Sue Beavis & Michael Newton
The Three Horseshoes,
Elsted,
Midhurst GU29 0JY
tel 01730 825746

map: 4 entry: 486

The White Horse
Chichester

A lovely whitewashed 18th-century coaching inn, lying at the foot of the South Downs. Drinks are only served with food, so enjoy a pint of Ballards and a baguette overlooking the rejuvenated pond in summer. But the celebrated cellar is the biggest draw: more than 600 wines on the list, 14 by the glass. The bar is clad in old wine boxes. And the food stands up to comparison; simple fish soup, or something more substantial in the crisp-linened restaurant: hand-picked Selsey crab, organic rack of lamb, roast whole grouse with bread sauce and game chips. Good, fresh bedrooms are in a detached annexe, the best with sofas and DVDs. All have snowy bathrobes and continental hamper breakfasts, which you may take into the pretty garden in summer. What's more, this is a Green Tourism gold award-winner, committed to sourcing local and organic wherever possible. An excellent stopover for visitors to Goodwood.

directions	On B2141 towards Petersfield; 6 miles north of Chichester.
meals	12pm-2pm; 7pm-10pm. Main courses £14.95-£26.95; bar meals £5.95-£7.95.
rooms	9 twins/doubles £95-£160. Singles £65-£120.
closed	3pm-6pm, Sun eve & Mon all day.

See pp 30–57 for full list of pubs with rooms

Charles & Carin Burton
The White Horse,
Chilgrove,
Chichester PO18 9HX
tel   01243 535219
web   www.whitehorsechilgrove.co.uk

map: 4 entry: 487

The Royal Oak Inn
Chichester

There's a comfortable, cheery, wine-bar feel to the Royal Oak. Inside is a modern rustic look with: stripped floors, brickwork, leather sofas, fires, racing pictures on the walls. Pop in for a glass of wine at a scrubbed pine table, or a pint of Sussex Best. The dining area is light and airy, with a conservatory, and you can overflow onto the front terrace, warmed by outdoor heaters on summer nights; you face a road but this one goes nowhere. Six chefs deliver satisfying food: Scottish rump beefburgers, monkfish an scallops with pak choi and coconut sauce, wild mushroom risotto. Bedrooms are divided between three cottages, a nearby barn and upstairs at the back; all have DVD and CD players and plasma screens, brown leather chairs and big comfy beds. You are brilliantly placed for Chichester's theatre, and the boats at pretty Bosham.

directions	From Chichester, A286 for Midhurst. After 2 miles right for East Lavant. Over bridge; on left.
meals	12pm-2.30pm; 6.30pm-9pm. Main courses £11.50-£18; bar meals £5.25-£10.50.
rooms	8: 4 doubles, 1 twin, 3 cottages £80-£160. Singles £60-£70.
closed	Open all day.

See pp 30–57 for full list of pubs with rooms

Nick & Lisa Sutherland
The Royal Oak Inn,
Pook Lane, East Lavant,
Chichester PO18 0AX
tel   01243 527434
web   www.thesussexpub.co.uk

map: 4 entry: 488

Anglesey Arms at Halnaker
Halnaker

Laid back, relaxed, refreshingly free of airs and graces, a Georgian brick pub in an affluent part of West Sussex. It's not a pie-and-a-pint pub or a chips-with-everything roadside diner – just a cracking good local run by Roger and Jools Jackson, genuinely committed to keeping it charming and old-fashioned. Expect varnished and stripped pine, flagstones, beams and panelling, crackling log fires, locals downing pints at the bar – in short, a lovely lived-in feel. Food may not be fancy but it's fresh and home-cooked using great local produce – crab and lobster from Selsey, traceable meats (organic South Downs lamb and pork; organic, well-hung beef) from Goodwood Estate, venison and game birds from local shoots. Even the ciders, wines and spirits are organic. A great little local, with inter-pub cricket, golf and quizzes and regular 'moules and boules' events in the two-acre garden.

The Fox Goes Free
Charlton

King William III may have stopped off at The Fox Goes Free to refresh his royal hunting parties; this little pub, hidden in the South Downs, is now home to some of the best real ales from local microbreweries. In winter, visitors settle down by the big blazing fire under beamed ceilings for a pint of Ballards Best and the pub's own beer, Fox Goes Free; in summer there's a garden with sweeping views of sheep-grazed farmland. Traditional bar food includes homemade steak and kidney pie; in the restaurant – once a stable for Goodwood race horses – fresh local produce includes smoked salmon, roast rack of venison with local wild mushrooms, and homemade puddings such as banoffee pie. Goodwood racecourse and the Festival of Speed venue are just up the hill and there are miles of downland walks from the front door.

directions	On A285, 4 miles north east of Chichester.
meals	12pm-2.30pm; 6.30pm-9.30pm. No food Sun eve. Main courses £10.95-£17.95; bar meals £4.95-£12.95.
closed	3pm-5.30pm. Open all day Sun.

Roger & Jools Jackson
Anglesey Arms at Halnaker,
Halnaker,
Chichester PO18 0NQ
tel 01243 773474
web www.angleseyarms.co.uk

map: 4 entry: 489

directions	From Chichester follow A286 towards Midhurst. At Singleton right to Charlton.
meals	12pm-2.30pm; 6.30pm-10pm; 12pm-10pm Sat (9.30pm Sun). Main courses from £11.95; bar meals from £7.
closed	Open all day.

David Coxon
The Fox Goes Free,
Charlton,
Goodwood PO18 0HU
tel 01243 811461
web www.thefoxgoesfree.com

map: 4 entry: 490

The Star & Garter
Goodwood

If fresh fish and seafood appeal then take a trip down winding Sussex lanes to this 18th-century brick-and-flint pub. Hidden in the folds of the South Downs, with miles of breezy walks from the front door, the old ale house now draws the well-heeled from Goodwood and Midhurst. Seafood platters groan with whole Selsey lobster and crabs, scallops, wild salmon, crevettes and prawns. There are big bowls of mussels, whole baked bass, venison pie and, in season, a mouthwatering game grill, with partridge from West Dean, pigeon from East Dean and local wild boar sausages. Drink fine Sussex ales straight from the cellar in the single, wooden floored room, where hops adorn stripped beams, old village photographs line bare-brick walls and daily papers fill the rack by the door. In summer, spill onto the sun-trap patio, then check out the summer Shellfish Bar for fresh crab and lobster to take home.

The Foresters
Graffham

Nick is a cook, one with a history. Did he see fit to mention this when we popped in? Not for a second. But we have contacts to spill the beans... and all the other fabulous ingredients that are whisked up for your plate. Duck-liver parfait and a pear chutney, shepherd's pie with buttered cabbage, bread and butter pudding: everything is homemade and none of it costs a bomb. Nick and Serena are happy to be out of the city doing their own thing. The pub dates from the 17th century, has open fires, beamed ceilings, an exposed stone wall and cider flagons in a fireplace. Bedrooms are small and simple with good linen, trim carpets and chunky beds. There are wine tastings, curry nights, quiz nights... and dogs (pub only) and children are liked. As for Graffham, it's a cul-de-sac village, wonderfully English and an hour from London.

directions	Village signed off A286 between Midhurst & Chichester at Singleton.
meals	12pm-2.30pm; 6.30pm-10pm (12pm-10pm Sat; 9.30pm Sun). Main courses £10.50-£16.50; bar meals £5.50-£8.50.
closed	Open all day Sat & Sun.

directions	Midhurst 2 miles south on A286, left for Heyshott & Graffham; left at T-junc. in village; on right.
meals	12pm-2pm (2.30pm Sat & Sun); 7pm-9pm (9.30pm Sat). Main courses £8.95-£12.95; sandwiches from £3.75; Sunday roast £10-£11.50.
rooms	2 doubles £70-£80. Singles £45-£55.
closed	3pm-6pm; Sun eve & Mon all day.

See pp 30-57 for full list of pubs with rooms

Oliver Ligertwood
The Star & Garter,
East Dean, Goodwood,
Chichester PO18 0JG

tel	01243 811318
web	www.thestarandgarter.co.uk

Nick Bell & Serena Aykroyd
The Foresters,
The Street,
Graffham GU28 0QA

tel	01798 867202
web	www.foresters-arms.com

map: 4 entry: 491

map: 4 entry: 492

Sussex

The Cat
West Hoathly

Father and son Nick and Mark White used to have the Fountain at Ashurst; now they have The Cat. And they're slowly upgrading the 16th-century building without losing the character – a medieval hall house with a Victorian extension. They've uncovered a well in one of the bars, and carved out a semi-walled garden at the back, furnished with teak and umbrellas. Inside, wooden panelling, beamed ceilings, planked floors and splendid inglenooks. Traditional pub food – with the odd southern dish thrown in – attracts a solid, old-fashioned crowd: retired locals and walkers on the High Weald Way. Our rare roast beef and horseradish salad came with hunks of bread fresh from the oven, and the pancakes with proper maple syrup. The owners are delightful, the setting is idyllic: in a pretty village opposite a 12th-century church and up the road from a 15th-century priest's house, now a museum.

directions	Village signed off B2028 6 miles north of Haywards Heath.
meals	12pm-2pm (2.30 Sun); 6pm-9.30. 12pm-9.30 Sat. No food Sun eve. Main courses £8.95-£16.95; bar meals £5.50-£8.95.
closed	2.30-6pm (3.30-7pm Sun) & all day Mon. Open all day Sat.

Mark & Nick White
The Cat,
Queens Square, West Hoathly,
East Grinstead RH19 4PP
tel 01342 810369
web www.catinn.co.uk

map: 4 entry: 493

Sussex

The Coach & Horses
Danehill

With ale on tap from Harveys in Lewes, fresh fish from Seaford and lamb from the fields opposite, this is a very fine pub. The central bar is its throbbing hub, original wooden panelling and open fires accompanying the gentle pleasure of mulled wine in winter-cosy rooms. During the rest of the year the big raised garden (with hedged-off play area) comes into its own; spread yourselves on the new terrace under the boughs of a spreading maple. Whatever the weather, the food attracts folk from far and wide. In the stable block restaurant a changing seasonal menu from chef Jason Tidy places the emphasis on quality rather than quantity – in pheasant rillettes, grilled scallops with coriander butter, Toulouse sausages on a haricot, tomato and sweet basil ragout, sea bass with braised fennel and lobster bisque. A rural pub that is a true local.

directions	From Danehill (A275) take School Lane towards Chelwood Common.
meals	12pm-2pm (2.30 Sat & Sun); 7pm-9pm (9.30pm Sat). No food Sun eve. Main courses £9.95-£15.50; bar meals £4.50-£5.50.
closed	3pm-6pm (4pm-6pm Sat, 5pm-7pm Sun).

Ian Philpots
The Coach & Horses,
Coach & Horses Lane,
Danehill RH17 7JF
tel 01825 740369
web www.coachandhorses.danehill.biz

map: 4 entry: 494

Sussex — Pub with rooms

The Griffin Inn
Fletching

The Pullan family run the Griffin with gentle passion. There are delicious open fires, 500-year-old beams, oak panelling, settles, red carpets, photos on the walls... the inn has been allowed to age. There's a small club room for racing on Saturdays and two cricket teams play in summer. Bedrooms have an uncluttered country-inn elegance: uneven floors, country furniture, soft coloured walls, free-standing baths, huge shower heads, crisp linen. Those in the coach house are quieter; swish new rooms in next-door Griffin House are quieter still. The seasonal menu changes daily: roast Romney Marsh lamb with butternut squash and sweet and sour onions, or wild sea bass with olives, chorizo and sautéed potatoes. In summer, there's a fine terrace for al fresco eating, a smart garden with a ten-mile view, and they lay on a spit-roast barbecue every Sunday.

directions	From East Grinstead, A22 south; right at Nutley for Fletching. Straight on for 3 miles into village.
meals	12pm-2.30; 7pm-9.30 (9pm Sun). Main courses £10-£18.50; bar meals £6.50-£14.50.
rooms	13: 1 twin, 12 doubles £80-£130. Singles £60-£80 (not weekends).
closed	3pm-6pm. Open all day Sat & Sun.

See pp 30-57 for full list of pubs with rooms

Bridget, Nigel & James Pullan
The Griffin Inn,
Fletching,
Uckfield TN22 3SS
tel 01825 722890
web www.thegriffininn.co.uk

map: 4 entry: 495

Sussex

The Peacock
Piltdown

This is a pub of character – full of drunken beams and not a right angle in sight. Travellers have sought out its gracious rooms in search of sustenance for 450 years; now it's filled with locals and families. Piltdown Man aficionados might also wish to drop by: the greatest archaeological hoax of all time took place down the road in 1912. The menu looks promising and all is homemade, from smoked salmon and crayfish salad to their (much-loved) Marilyn Monroe steak, and banoffee pie. Beams are low, furniture a mix of settles and repro, and peacocks feature among the knick-knacks, most strikingly in a piece of needlepoint dated 1889. The often-lit inglenook, its uneven lintel hung with horse brasses and horse tack, is worth the trip alone. The back garden is safe for children, with a slide; picnic tables at the front survey gentle Sussex countryside.

directions	Just south of Piltdown, 0.75 miles south of A272.
meals	12pm-2pm; 6pm-9.30pm. Main courses £7.95-£18.
closed	3pm-6pm.

Matthew Arnold
The Peacock,
Shortbridge, Piltdown,
Uckfield TN22 3XA
tel 01825 762463
web www.peacock-inn.co.uk

map: 4 entry: 496

Royal Oak
Wineham

A rural survivor, the part-tiled, black-and-white-timbered cottage almost lost down a country road is six centuries old and has been refreshing locals for the last two. It is unspoilt in every way. In the charming bar and tiny rear room are brick and bare-boarded floors, a huge inglenook with winter log fires and sturdy, rustic furniture. Antique corkscrews, pottery jugs and aged artefacts hang from low-slung beams and walls; Jack the tabby lives on the bar counter – an immovable fixture. Tim Peacock, who has been in charge for 35 years, draws Harveys Best and guest beers straight from the cask (no pumps) and, in keeping with ale house tradition, limits the menu to good, freshly-made sandwiches, generous ploughman's, and hearty soups on chilly days. No music or electronic hubbub, just traditional pub games. Picnic tables on the grass at the front overlook the peaceful road.

The Fountain Inn
Ashurst

The 16th-century Inglenook Bar is a snug place to be on a cold and rainy night, as Paul McCartney and Wings thought when they made their Christmas video here. When the fireplace decides 'to blow' you're transported back centuries. In the flagstoned and candlelit bar, aromatic with woodsmoke from that wafting fire, be treated to wholesome food (steak, mushroom and ale pie, ham, egg and chips, wild boar, apple and Calvados sausages, nursery puds), along with a great selection of wines and four real ales. No need to bother with the wine list – just wander into the corridor where, on an ancient wonky wall, the bottles themselves are on display. In summer sup a pint of local Harvey's Sussex ale on the raised decking overlooking the pond. Although the annual classic car and motorbike meeting attracts those from afar, the Fountain firmly remains a local.

directions	Off A272 between Cowfold & Bolney.
meals	11am-2.30pm (12pm-3pm Sun); 5.30pm-11pm (6pm-11pm Sat, 7pm-10.30pm Sun). Sandwiches £2.50-£3.50.
closed	2.30pm-5.30pm (6pm Sat, 3pm-7pm Sun).

Tim Peacock
Royal Oak,
Wineham,
Henfield BN5 9AY

tel 01444 881252

map: 4 entry: 497

directions	On B2135, 4 miles north of Steyning.
meals	Mon-Fri 11.30am-2.30pm; 6pm-9.30pm. Sat 11.30am-9.30pm. Sun 12pm-3pm; 6pm-8.30pm. Main courses £7.50-£18.95; bar meals from £4.50.
closed	Open all day.

Craig Gillet
The Fountain Inn,
Ashurst,
Steyning BN44 3AP

tel 01403 710219

map: 4 entry: 498

The Chimney House
Brighton

The Victorian red-brick corner boozer has become a gastropub of note. It's the first pub venture of Jackie Nairn and Lia Vittone, and Jackie's background as a restaurant operations manager for the Tate's galleries has made its mark. The Chimney House takes its stylish lead from the bistro pubs of London but has not lost its community feel; expect leather armchairs, scrubbed tables and an open kitchen from which classic British dishes flow. The produce is well-sourced, often organic, and includes lamb from Jackie's family farm in the West Highlands. Tuck into smoked haddock rarebit and roasted tomatoes with a blackfaced-lamb burger and mint yoghurt, or a pork chop with garlic new potatoes, rainbow chard and apple compote. Or just pop in for a bowl of hand-cut chips and homemade ketchup to soak up the excellent Harveys ales; it's that sort of place.

The Bull
Ditchling

Inside: a dark, cosy space warmed by cheery fires and candlelight. The rambling and atmospheric bar hasn't changed for years; the other areas have been stylishly transformed: pine, parquet and modern prints on mellow walls. And there's food to match: pot-roasted rabbit with cider, rosemary and crème fraîche; fresh ciabatta filled with oaked smoked salmon and horseradish cream. Game comes from the Balcombe estate, lamb from Ditchling farms and most dishes (including sensational Sussex pond pudding!) come in half portions for children. You can eat – or drink – wherever you like, including the snug at the back. Bring bikes and try out the high-level trails on the South Downs, return to white bed linen in gorgeous rooms where new and old blend as beautifully as below. Expect bold silks, walk-in rain showers and fresh lilies.

	The Chimney House
directions	In the Seven Dials area, on the corner of Upper Hamilton Rd & Exeter St.
meals	12pm-2.30pm (3.30pm Sun); 6pm-9.30pm. Main course £8.95-£14.95.
closed	3pm-5pm; Mon all day; Sun from 7pm.

Jackie Nairn
The Chimney House,
28 Upper Hamilton Road,
Brighton BN1 5DF
tel   01273 556708
web   www.chimneyhouse.co.uk

map: 4 entry: 499

	The Bull
directions	In centre of village, by mini-r'bout at central crossroads.
meals	12pm-2.30pm (3pm Sat; 6pm Sun); 7pm-9.30pm. No food Sun eve. Main courses £9.50-£16; sandwiches £6.50.
rooms	4 doubles £80-£100.
closed	Open all day.

See pp 30-57 for full list of pubs with rooms

Dominic Worrall
The Bull,
2 High Street, Ditchling,
Burgess Hill BN6 8SY
tel   01273 843147
web   www.thebullditchling.com

map: 4 entry: 500

Sussex

The Jolly Sportsman
East Chiltington

Deep in Sussex, a little place with a passion for beers, food and wine. Brewery mats pinned above the bar demonstrate chef-proprietor Bruce Wass's support of the microbreweries, while his food has been described as "robust, savoury, skilled and unpretentious." In the stylish restaurant, where oak tables are decorated with flowers and candles, visitors natter over plates piled high and irresistibly: Jerusalem artichoke and celeriac soup, confit shoulder of local lamb, Mediterranean fish soup, ripe French cheeses. Pull up a chic chair in front of the bar's open fire and enjoy winter snifters from Bruce's impressive whisky collection (including rarities bought at auction). Outside, ancient trees give shade to rustic tables and the idyllic garden has a play area for children. A team of talented enthusiasts run this pub; the Moroccan-tiled patio tables were even made by the pub's own 'washer-upper'.

directions	From Lewes A275; B2166 for East Chiltington.
meals	12pm-2.15pm (3pm Sun); 7pm-9.15pm (10pm Fri & Sat). Main courses £11.75-£16.95; set lunch £12.50 & £15.95; bar meals £4.90-£10.45.
closed	2.30pm-6pm, Sun from 4pm & Mon all day. Open all day Sat.

Bruce Wass
The Jolly Sportsman,
Chapel Lane, East Chiltington,
Lewes BN7 3BA

tel	01273 890400
web	www.thejollysportsman.com

map: 4 entry: 501

Sussex

Ram Inn
Firle

The road runs out once it reaches Firle village... hard to believe now, but this quiet backwater was once an important staging post. Built of brick and flint and partly tile-hung, the inn reveals a fascinating history – the Georgian part was once a courthouse and the kitchen goes back 500 years. Owned by Firle Estate and rescued from closure in 2006, the Ram Inn is once again thriving. Shaun Filsell has redecorated its three rambling rooms in rustic-chic style – warm green walls, bare boards and parquet, coal fires in old brick fireplaces, chunky candles on darkwood tables. Walkers stomp in from the Downs for pints of Harvey's Sussex and hot steak sandwiches; foodies flock after dark for great fresh food, perhaps honey-glazed belly pork with roasted sweet potato and honey and thyme sauce, and dark chocolate truffle torte. You're on the foot of the Downs and there's a splendid flint-walled garden for peaceful summer supping.

directions	Pub & village signed off A27 east of Lewes.
meals	12pm-3pm; 6.30pm-9.30pm (12-9.30pm Sat; 12pm-6pm Sun). Main courses £7.95-£9.95 (lunch); £9.25-£14.95 (dinner).
closed	Open all day.

Shaun Filsell
Ram Inn,
Firle,
Lewes BN8 6NS

tel	01273 858222
web	www.theram-inn.com

map: 4 entry: 502

The Tiger Inn
East Dean

In the flickering candlelight of the old pub, where records go back nine centuries, landlord Nicholas Denyer explains why he sometimes has to say 'no': no mobile phones, no bookings, no piped music. It's the size of the main bar – all low beams, ancient settles and open fire – that dictates the 'no's', and makes it such an unusual and delightful place to be, particularly after a walk up on Beachy Head. Beside a cottage-lined green in a fold of the South Downs, the Tiger Inn is a great supporter of the community: Harveys ales come from nearby Lewes, lamb and beef for casseroles and stews from the farm up the hill. Fresh whole lobster and dressed crab are local too, the latter delectably served with lime-dressed leaves and buttery new potatoes. The ever-changing blackboard offers home-cooked dishes and 20 varieties of the famous ploughman's lunch, including local sheep's cheeses and smoked meats from the Weald smokery. *No under 14s please.*

The Cricketers Arms
Berwick

Walkers seek refuge from the breezy South Downs; so do visitors to Berwick Church and Charleston. The 500-year-old, brick and flint, creeper-clad pub is utterly unspoilt outside and in. An ale house for the past 200 years, it has three delightfully unpretentious rooms with beams and half-panelled walls dotted with cricket bats. Blazing log fires, scrubbed tables and wall benches on worn, quarry-tiled floors add to the pleasure of being here; all feels friendly and unhurried. Harveys ales are tapped from the cask in a back room and the food is perfectly straightforward pub grub, perhaps gammon steak and egg, battered cod and chips or fresh local crab. Try your luck at playing the Sussex coin game, Toad-In-Ye-Hole. Surrounded by a cottage garden resplendent with foxgloves and roses, the Cricketers is equally charming in summer.

directions	0.5 miles from A259 at East Dean, in village centre.
meals	12pm-2pm; 6.30pm-9pm (6pm-8pm Sun). Main courses £6.95-£14.95.
closed	3pm-6pm. Open all day Sat & Sun.

Nicholas Denyer
The Tiger Inn,
The Green,
East Dean,
Eastbourne BN20 0DA
tel   01323 423209

map: 5 entry: 503

directions	Just off A27 Lewes to Polegate road near Berwick church.
meals	12pm-2.15pm; 6.15pm-9pm (12pm-9pm Fri-Sun). Main courses £6.95-£15.95; bar meals £4.50-£15.95.
closed	3pm-6pm. Open all day Sat & Sun.

Peter Brown
The Cricketers Arms,
Berwick,
Polegate BN26 6SP
tel   01323 870469
web   www.cricketersberwick.co.uk

map: 5 entry: 504

Giants Rest
Wilmington

Most East Sussex pubs are supporters of Harveys brewery in Lewes and this is no exception; local produce is on the menu, too. Adrian's wife Rebecca is chef, and her wild rabbit and bacon pie, home-cooked ham with bubble-and-squeak and fruit crumbles are popular. It's hardly old by rural standards, but the high ceilings, the black and cream Hedges & Butler wallpaper, the pine dressers, the ferns and the candlelight seem the perfect backdrop for a plate of Victorian trifle. Menus for Burns Night or New Year are offered at normal prices as a 'thank you' to the regulars and served in front of a log fire. Furnishings include pews and pine tables at the long bar, and there are puzzles or games on every table. Work up an appetite – or walk off that trifle – with an invigorating downland stroll to view the impressive Long Man figure carved into the South Downs.

The Lamb Inn
Wartling

In next to no time, landlord Rob and his chef wife Alison have transformed this little pub into a place known for great ales, excellent food and good cheer. There's a bar with a woodburner, a beamy snug with chunky candles and fresh flowers, a dining room with enough space for comfy sofas around a log fire and no music just chatter. Specialising in fresh fish and local produce, the menu includes fillet of local Limousin beef, local farm sausages and cod loin on wild mushrooms with rocket mash and white wine sauce. A good selection of cheeses should follow, along with desserts like chocolate and praline bread and butter pudding. Make a mental note of this secluded pub if you are planning a visit to nearby Herstmonceux Castle: the drive across the Pevensey Levels, the largest track of wetland in East Sussex, is worth it.

directions	On A27 just past Drusilla's roundabout.
meals	12pm-2pm; 6.30pm-9pm. Main courses £8.50-£15; bar meals £3.50-£6.50.
closed	3pm-6pm. Open all day Sat & Sun.

directions	A259 to Polegate & Pevensey; 1st exit for Wartling; on right after 3 miles.
meals	11.45am-2.15pm (12pm-2.30pm Sun); 6.45pm-9pm. Main courses £7.95-£19.95; bar meals £4.50-£9.50.
closed	3pm-6pm & Sun eve.

Adrian & Rebecca Hillman
Giants Rest,
Wilmington,
Eastbourne BN26 5SQ

tel	01323 870207
web	www.giantsrest.co.uk

Robert & Alison Farncombe
The Lamb Inn,
Wartling,
Hailsham BN27 1RY

tel	01323 832116
web	www.lambinnwartling.co.uk

map: 5 entry: 505

map: 5 entry: 506

Merrie Harriers
Cowbeech

Roger Cotton changed little on his arrival at this listed clapboarded building in any way- but he did upgrade the food. Foodies travel that extra mile for the chef's delicious "new British dishes" – fillet of Sussex beef rolled in cracked black pepper, rack of lamb with lavender mash and cassis jus – and the odd, colourful, southern dish, like as parma ham with roasted figs. Sandwiches are a cut above the average, the menus change monthly, the produce is as local as can be, and the award-winning Sunday lunches have a family following. In the peaceful heart of the Weald, the Merrie Harriers is an unpretentious, unshowy pub, quietly friendly and welcoming to dogs (in the bar) and children. The simple, part-panelled bar has a huge brick inglenook with logs at the ready, the red-carpeted restaurant extension has countryside views, and there's a nice garden at the back.

The Star Inn
Old Heathfield

Head for the church and the Star is next door. Built as an inn for pilgrims in the 14th century, with a rough, honey-stone façade, it has gained a few creepers over the centuries and its atmospheric interior has mellowed nicely. Low-beamed ceilings, wall settles and panelling, huge log-fuelled inglenook, rustic tables and chairs – it's cosy, candlelit and winter inviting. The appeal in summer is the peaceful, award-winning garden, bright with flowers and characterful with hand-crafted furniture; the gorgeous view across the High Weald towards the South Downs was once painted by Turner. Popular bar food focuses on fresh fish from Hastings and Pevensey. A chalkboard lists the daily-changing choice, perhaps lightly curried crayfish risotto, smoked haddock topped with Welsh rarebit or slow-cooked lamb shoulder. To drink, try Harveys Sussex Bitter from Lewes. Allow time to visit the impressive church with its fine early-English tower.

directions	Cowbeech signed off A271; in village centre, 2 miles from Herstmonceux.
meals	12pm-2pm (12.30pm-2.30pm Sun); 7pm-9pm. No food Sun eves in winter. Main courses £9.95-£17.95; bar meals £4.75-£9.95.
closed	3pm-6pm (4pm-6pm Sat & Sun).

Roger Cotton
Merrie Harriers,
Cowbeech,
Hailsham BN27 4JQ

| tel | 01323 833108 |
| web | www.merrieharriers.co.uk |

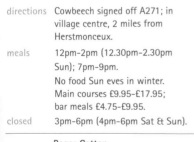

map: 5 entry: 507

directions	From A265 east of Heathfield, left onto B2096, then 2nd right.
meals	12pm-2.15pm (2.30pm Sat & Sun); 7pm-9.30pm. Main courses £9-£18.
closed	3pm-5.30pm (7pm Sun).

Greg Palmer
The Star Inn,
Church Street,
Old Heathfield TN21 9AH

| tel | 01435 863570 |
| web | www.thebestpubsinsussex.co.uk |

map: 5 entry: 508

Sussex

The Curlew
Bodiam

You could do a lot worse than round off a visit to Bodium Castle with lunch at the old hop-pickers' ale house. In 2004 this weatherboarded pub was swept clean of its hop garlands, the interior was de-cluttered, and the existing brigade in the kitchen wisely retained. In the smart homely bar the woodburner glows, Badger Bitter is on handpump and the wine list flies the flag for Britain (wines from Lamberhurst vineyard join the global list). Various menus highlight lunchtime baguettes (stuffed, perhaps, with locally smoked salmon), sausages with creamy mash and caramelised onion gravy, and extra-mature fillet steak with red onion rösti. There may be pear and apple crumble with honeycomb ice cream for dessert – or a mini selection of all the desserts for the undecisive (or just plain greedy). Colour spills from tubs and borders in summer.

directions	On B2244 Hawkhurst-Sedlescombe road; on the Bodiam crossroads.
meals	12pm-2pm (3pm Sun); 7pm-9pm (9.30pm Fri & Sat). Main courses £14.95-£19.95; bar meals £7.75-£14.95.
closed	Open all day. Closed Sun from 5pm.

Bob Leeper
The Curlew,
Junction Road, Bodiam,
Robertsbridge TN32 5UY

| tel | 01580 861394 |
| web | www.thecurlewatbodiam.co.uk |

map: 5 entry: 509

Warwickshire

The Inn at Farnborough
Farnborough

Turning a neglected inn into a pub-restaurant was an exciting prospect for chef Anthony and his wife Joanna. Their vision and dedication led to a change of name, a stylish revival and menus created daily from the best local suppliers. It's not just the food that is irresistible but the warm yellow walls, subtle lighting, open fires, rustic floors and fresh flowers. The food is gorgeous: local Dexter beef with red wine and shallots, lamb confit with pea and mint purée and rosemary jus, salmon fishcakes with hollandaise… Or there's a good value lunchtime and early evening menu. Add fine wines by the glass, posh bar nibbles, smiley staff and a fabulous landscaped garden… not everyone will be enamoured of the background music but it would be hard to find a more civilised pub. There's even a private dining room, with jaunty red walls, zebra-print chairs and a juke box.

directions	From junction 11 on M40 follow signs for Banbury. At 3rd r'bout right onto A423 for Southam.
meals	12pm-3pm; 6pm-10pm. Main courses £8.95-£19.95; bar meals £5-£12.
closed	3pm-6pm. Open all day Fri-Sun.

Anthony Robinson
The Inn at Farnborough,
Farnborough,
Banbury OX17 1DZ

| tel | 01295 690615 |
| web | www.innatfarnborough.co.uk |

map: 8 entry: 510

The Castle Inn
Edgehill

A splendid site! Charles I raised his battle standard here, before the battle of Edge Hill, and the pub sits inside the octagonal tower, built to commemorate the 100th anniversary of the battle. Unique and unusual, it opened as a pub in 1822, and later was bought by the Hook Norton Brewery. From the viewing balcony or the great big garden, spectacular views sweep over the steep scarp to the plain below and away to the Malvern Hills, some 40 miles away. In the public bar are darts, pool and a fruit machine; the octagonal walls of the lounge bar are decorated with all the Civil War maps and memorabilia you could wish for. Food is traditional English – sandwiches, steaks, home made beef and ale pie – washed down with perfect pints of Old Hooky, real cider and country wines. Malts are taken seriously, too.

The Fox & Hounds Inn
Great Wolford

The gorgeous, honey-coloured pub has been trading since 1540 and dozes contentedly in a tiny community on the edge of the Cotswold hills. On entering the bar through a low oak door the pub opens out, captivatingly, before you. Bunches of dried hops are tucked into ancient beams, there are candlelit tables on flagstoned floors, polished oak settles and a huge stone fireplace that crackles with logs in winter. Flames flicker in the copper bar counter as you order a pint of Hook Norton and study the blackboard menu announcing such treats as Gressingham duck with parsnip mousse and caramelised apple, and halibut with herb crust on chive and leek risotto. The menu is kept short and fresh and changes each day, just as it should in a small country inn. It couldn't be cosier, or more welcoming – a perfect country pub. And there's also a good terrace for summer.

directions	Off A422, 6 miles NW of Banbury.
meals	12pm-2pm (2.30pm Sat & Sun); 6.30pm-9pm. Main courses £5-£14; bar meals £3-£8.
closed	2.30pm-6pm (3pm-6pm Sat & Sun). Open all day in summer.

Tony, Sue & Rory Sheen
The Castle Inn,
Edgehill,
Banbury OX15 6DJ
tel 01295 670255
web www.thecastle-edgehill.com

map: 8 entry: 511

directions	Off A3400 between Shipston-on-Stour & Long Compton.
meals	12pm-2pm (2.30pm Sat & Sun); 6.30pm-9pm. No food Sun eve. Main courses £12-£16.
closed	2.30pm-6pm & Mon.

Gill & Jamie Tarbox
& Sioned Rowland
The Fox & Hounds Inn,
Moreton-in-Marsh CV36 5NQ
tel 01608 674220
web www.thefoxandhoundsinn.com

map: 8 entry: 512

The Fox and Goose
Armscote

A really lovely little pub, with bags of atmosphere and rather good food. Regulars gladly gather here, nursing pints of Hook Norton by the bar, and tucking into sausages. Imagine the nicest sort of country pub décor – wooden floors, warm colours, scrubbed pine tables and a woodburner that glows from two sides. To expectant diners in a separate room, jolly staff ferry delicious platefuls of confit duck terrine with onion marmalade, local Lighthorne lamb chops with bubble and squeak, beer battered cod with pea purée and chips, and apple pie with clotted cream. There's a wine list to match, and the fun spills over into the bedrooms upstairs, eccentrically dressed à la Cluedo – Plum, Scarlet, Peacock, Mustard. Bathrooms have luxurious claw-foot tubs with candleholders and Lady Godiva lotions. And there's a big elegant garden.

directions	Off A3400, 7 miles south of Stratford-upon-Avon.
meals	12pm-2.30pm; 7pm-9.30pm. Main courses £9.95–£15.95; Sunday roast £11.95.
rooms	4 doubles £85–£120.
closed	3pm-6pm.

See pp 30–57 for full list of pubs with rooms

Elizabeth Hauxwell
The Fox and Goose,
Armscote,
Stratford-upon-Avon CV37 8DD
tel   01608 682293
web   www.foxandgoose.co.uk

map: 8 entry: 513

Warwickshire   Pub with rooms

The Howard Arms
Ilmington

The place buzzes with good-humoured babble as well-kept beer flows from the flagstoned bar. Logs crackle in a vast open fire; a blackboard menu scales the wall above; a dining room at the far end has great swathes of bold colour and fresh flowers. Gorgeous bedrooms are set discreetly apart, mixing period style and modern luxury; the double oozes old world charm, the twin is more folksy, the half-tester is almost a suite. The long, lawned garden has a stream, and the village, tucked under a lone hill, an unusual church and two greens. Round off an idyllic walk with a warm chickpea and spiced mushroom salad, chargrilled chicken supreme with grilled courgettes and fresh tomato sauce, and little blackcurrant and cream cheese tarts; the menu changes weekly. Fabulous food, good people, handsome surroundings.

directions	Off A3400 between Stratford & Shipston-on-Stour; 2 miles NW of Shipston.
meals	12pm-2pm (2.30 Sun); 7pm-9pm (9.30 Sat). Main courses £10–£15.50. Bar meals from £3.75.
rooms	3: 2 doubles, 1 twin £120–£138. Singles £85.
closed	3pm-6pm.

See pp 30–57 for full list of pubs with rooms

Robert & Gill Greenstock
The Howard Arms,
Lower Green, Ilmington,
Stratford-upon-Avon CV36 4LT
tel   01608 682226
web   www.howardarms.com

map: 8 entry: 514

College Arms
Lower Quinton

Standing proud on a green opposite a church, this fabulous building was once owned by Henry VIII. For centuries after that, it was owned by Magdalen College, Oxford. Claire and husband Steve, a Roux scholar turned chef, took on the pub in 2005. Peerless technique and fair prices have foodies flocking to the cool contemporary restaurant, bewitched by ham hock and parsley terrine with piccalilli, seared sea bream with sauté potatoes and fish cream, and dark chocolate and banana mousse. Bar menus trumpet pub classics, steaks are prime-aged Aberdeen Angus and there's a mouthwatering selection of antipasti. The small flagstoned snug to the left of Henry's Bar (named after the king *and* the Loves' dog) is a cosy spot for a pint of Hook Norton, and bedrooms are cosy and comfortable, one with a romantic sleigh bed.

directions	Off B4632, S of Stratford.
meals	12pm-2pm (4pm Sun); 7pm-9pm). Restaurant: Thurs-Sat eve. Main courses £11-£19 (bar); set menu £52 (restaurant).
rooms	4 twins/doubles £65-£75.
closed	3pm-6pm, Tues lunch & Mon (except bank hols). Open all day Sat & Sun.

See pp 30-57 for full list of pubs with rooms

Steve & Claire Love
College Arms,
Lower Quinton,
Stratford-upon-Avon CV37 8SG
tel   01789 720342
web   www.collegearms.co.uk

map: 8 entry: 515

The One Elm
Stratford-upon-Avon

Stratford has a reputation for great pubs and drama, and was the birthplace of the first ever Slug and Lettuce. In the narrow building that The Slug once occupied stands The One Elm. Owned by Peach Pubs (of Warwick's Rose & Crown), it, too, is a cracker. The bar is light, airy and wooden-floored, and the décor modern and stylish, with leather sofas and bar stools reminiscent of Giacometti sculptures. In the bar downstairs there are good beers and great wines; outside, an attractive, sheltered terrace; at the back, the restaurant, with a private, secluded mezzanine and a short but mouthwatering menu. There's a chargrill section, a risotto of the week, skate with mash and a deli board that's available all day. The One Elm has a chic cosmopolitan feel and, being slightly off the tourist trail, is used by a local crowd. The staff are friendly and serve you from breakfast through until closing time.

directions	In town centre on corner of Guild Street & Shakespeare Street.
meals	12pm-10pm (9.30pm Sun). Main courses £8.50-£15.
closed	Open all day.

Victoria Moon
The One Elm,
1 Guild Street,
Stratford-upon-Avon CV37 6QZ
tel   01865 249796
web   www.peachpubs.com

map: 8 entry: 516

The King's Head
Aston Cantlow

It is said that Shakespeare's parents had their wedding reception at the King's Head. One can imagine the scene at this long, low, rambling country inn with its small leaded windows, flagged floors and inglenook crackling with logs; perhaps they even tucked into the famous Duck Supper, a house speciality. More up-to-date delicacies join the menu today, and all is tasty, from the rare roast beef sandwiches with celeriac and horseradish to salmon, lemongrass and chive fishcakes, roast venison with calvados sauce, and the lemon cheesecake. Elderly ladies chat over pots of tea and diners come from miles around, notably well-heeled Brummies. In the bar, stylish with lime-washed beams, scrubbed pine and painted brick walls hung with boozy cartoons, are real ale and good wines. There's a small garden for summer, the village creaks with history and the walks start from the door. Hugely atmospheric – and loved by American visitors.

directions	Off A46 at Aston Cantlow.
meals	12-2.30pm (12.30pm-3pm Sun); 6.30pm-9.30pm. No food Sun eve. Main courses £10-£15; bar meals £5-£8.
closed	3pm-5.30pm. Open all day Sat & Sun.

Peter & Louise Sadler
The King's Head,
21 Bearley Road, Aston Cantlow,
Stratford-upon-Avon B95 6HY

tel	01789 488242
web	www.thekh.co.uk

map: 8 entry: 517

Bell Inn
Stratford upon Avon

If things Elizabethan and Shakespearian entrance and inspire you, then the Bell will not disappoint, running alongside the village high street, set amongst the black and white timbered houses. There is a richness about the natural oak beams and settles, the stone floors partially covered with Persian rugs and the dog-grates cradling glowing embers. This is very much a historic village inn serving top-quality, locally sourced food, whether it be a simple pub favourite such as scrumpy beef and tomato casserole or, for the slightly more adventurous, roast cod on pumpkin and green bean salad with a sweet pepper coulis. If you're into food provenance, every supplier is listed on the back of the menu and they are almost all small independents – bakers, butchers, brewers. Just like this thriving free house.

directions	Leave A3400 south west of Stratford on B439; continue to Welford in 4 miles; Bell on right through village.
meals	11.45-2.30 (3pm Sat); 6.30-9.30 (6pm-10pm Sat); 12pm-9.30 Sun. Main courses £9.95-£15.95; bar meals from £5; Sunday roast £10.95-£11.95.
closed	3pm-6pm. Open all day Sun (& Sat in summer).

Colin & Teresa Ombler
Bell Inn,
Binton Road,
Welford-on-Avon CV37 8EB

tel	01789 750353
web	www.thebellwelford.co.uk

map: 8 entry: 518

Warwickshire

The Bell
Tanworth-in-Arden

First it was a row of cottages, then a hotel. In the 1930s it was taken on by Jack Hood the boxer — now the pub on the green is post office, delicatessan, restaurant and B&B rolled into one. The main bar is contemporary and sleek: furniture from Italy, textured cushions, soft lighting, modish taupes and creams. The dining room has a boudoir glow, all silvery papered walls, vast chandelier and chocolate fountain (!)... the deli is at the end of the bar, the conference room doubles up as a Sunday school. It may be swish but it's flamboyant too, and fun — just like its owner, Ashley Bent. The menu trumpets smoked fish platter and seared monkfish with pea and mint risotto alongside game casserole, rump of lamb with herb mash and red pepper and olive jus, and apple pie and custard. And they do a great Sunday roast.

directions	A435 for Evesham, 2 miles; B4101 for Hockley Heath; 3rd turning on right signed Tanworth; opp. village green.
meals	12pm-2pm (3pm Sun); 6.30pm-9pm. Main courses £6.95-£8.95 (lunch) £9.95-£15.95 (dinner); Sunday lunch, 2 courses, £13.95.
closed	3pm-6pm & Sun eve. Open all day Sat in summer.

Ashley Bent
The Bell,
The Green, Tamworth-in-Arden,
Henley-in-Arden B94 5AL
tel   01564 742212
web www.thebellattanworthinarden.co.uk

map: 8 entry: 519

Warwickshire

The Crabmill
Preston Bagot

The lovely, rambling, A-frame building, all tiny leaded windows and wonderfully wonky beams, once contained a cider press. A pub for the following two centuries, today it's a busy gastro haven with a dining room for every mood — one, fresh and pistachio-green, scented with lilies, another deep red, its walls hung with plump nudes, another a candlelit mushroom-cream. There's a steely bar with sand-blasted glass panels, great flagstones and a winter fire and, at the back, a split-level lounge with wooden floors, deep leather sofas and a landscaped garden that heads off into open countryside. And a stylish decked area for summer drinking. The food is justifiably popular, the menu imaginative and colourful, from croque monsieur and Cornish pasty to roast halibut with parsley and shallot rösti, steamed greens and lobster sauce. Fresh herbs are imported from France.

directions	From Henley-in-Arden on A4189 towards Claverdon.
meals	12pm-2.30pm (to 3.30 Sun; sandwiches only 2pm-2.30 Sat); 6.30pm-9.30pm. Main courses £9.95-14.95.
closed	Open all day. Closed Sun eve.

Sally Coll
The Crabmill,
Preston Bagot,
Claverdon B95 5DR
tel   01926 843342
web www.thecrabmill.biz

map: 8 entry: 520

The Rose and Crown
Warwick

Peach Pubs' flagship Rose & Crown opens with bacon sarnies for breakfast and stays open all day. Enter a cheery, airy, wooden-floored front bar with red and white walls, big leather sofas, low tables and a crackling winter fire. To the back is the big and bustling eating area, and a private room that can be booked for parties. Almost all of the staff trained at Raymond Blanc's Petit Blanc restaurants; the food is good. Served all day, the tapas-style portions of cheeses, hams, marinated anchovies, mixed olives and rustic breads slip down easily with a pint of Fuller's London Pride or a glass of wine, while hot dishes are modern British with a Mediterranean slant, as in baked sea trout, lemon and thyme couscous and chilli oil and pork loin with rhubarb confit, apple and cider jus. Lovely contemporary bedrooms upstairs have large bath and shower rooms and overlook the square. It's young and fun and Warwick has history in spades.

The Case is Altered
Hatton

No food, no musak, no mobiles and a Sopwith Camel propeller suspended from the ceiling. This is a Warwickshire treasure. There's even a vintage bar billiards machine, operated by sixpences from behind the bar. In the main room are stone floors, leather-covered settles and walls covered in yellowing posters offering beverages at a penny a pint. Jackie does not open her arms to children or dogs; this is a place for adult conversation and liquid refreshment. Devotees travel some distance for the pork scratchings and the expertly-kept beer, and the bar is so small you can't help but join in the chat. The sign used to show lawyers arguing but the name has nothing to do with the law; it used to be called, simply, 'The Case' and was so small that it was not eligible for a licence. It was made larger, whisky was introduced, the name was changed, and everyone was happy. They've been that way ever since.

directions	In Warwick centre, on market place.
meals	8am–10pm (9.30pm Sun). Main courses £8.75–£17.50; bar meals £4–£10.50.
rooms	5: 2 doubles, 3 triples £65–£75.
closed	Open all day from 8am.

See pp 30–57 for full list of pubs with rooms

Victoria Moon
The Rose and Crown,
30 Market Place,
Warwick CV34 4SH

tel	01865 249796
web	www.roseandcrownwarwick.co.uk

map: 8 entry: 521

directions	Follow Rowington off A4177 & A4141 junction, north of Warwick.
meals	No food served.
closed	2.30pm–6pm (2pm–7pm Sun).

Jackie & Charlie Willacy
The Case is Altered,
Case Lane,
Five Ways,
Hatton CV35 7JD

tel	01926 484206

map: 8 entry: 522

Warwickshire

West Midlands

The Boot Inn
Lapworth

The Boot was here long before the canal that runs past the back garden. With its exposed timbers, rug-strewn quarry floors, open fires and papers to peruse it marries old-fashioned charm with rustic chic. Under the guidance of Paul Salisbury and James Elliot, the down-at-heel boozer underwent a transformation and became one of the first gastropubs of the Midlands nearly a decade ago; it has been pulling foodies in ever since. People come from miles around for the buzz – the feel is still very much 'friendly local' – and to sample the fabulous food. Menus have a distinct touch of Mediterranean and Pacific rim: crispy oriental duck salad, Moroccan lamb with red onion and coriander couscous, seared sea bass with peppers, crab and lemon aïoli. Ingredients are as fresh as can be and seafood dishes are a speciality. Eat in the bars or in the stylishly revamped dining room upstairs, and in summer go al fresco: there's a lovely terrace to the side.

The Malt Shovel at Barston
Barston

There's a touch of the Mediterranean here. Never mind that the nearest expanse of water is the Stratford upon Avon canal: the pub is painted in sunshiny yellows with green windows and shutters and it serves fish – lots of it. Eat in the bar, stylish and modern with mirrors and light wood, the airy barn-restaurant or the flowery garden in summer; wherever you sit, you're in for a treat. Try red onion and goat's cheese tart with tomato chutney; Devon crab with linguine; salmon fishcakes with chive hollandaise; duck breast with braised red cabbage and juniper jus. Sunday lunches are particularly popular, when, again, you will be served with something different – venison with black pudding, maybe. The ales are good and so are the wines. Christopher Benbrook's inn continues to pull the crowds.

directions	Off M42 junc. 4 for Hockley Heath; Lapworth signed.
meals	12pm-2.30pm; 6.30pm-9.30pm (12pm-9pm Sun). Main courses £9-£18.
closed	3pm-5.30pm. Open all day Sat & Sun.

	Paul Salisbury & James Elliot
	The Boot Inn,
	Old Warwick Road,
	Lapworth B94 6JU
tel	01564 782464
web	www.thebootatlapworth.co.uk

map: 8 entry: 523

directions	Off A452; 1 mile beyond village.
meals	12pm-2.30pm (4pm Sun); 6.30pm-9.30pm. No food Sun eve. Main courses £9.95-£16.95. Set menus £21 &£25.
closed	3.30pm-5.30pm. Open all day Sat & Sun.

	Helen Somerfield
	The Malt Shovel at Barston,
	Barston Lane, Barston,
	Solihull B92 0JP
tel	01675 443223
web	www.themaltshovelatbarston.com

map: 8 entry: 524

The Wheatsheaf
Oaksey

Ancient on the outside, dark-beamed and inglenooked inside, and down a narrow lane – the archetypal English country pub. Local drinkers are welcome, but, with cooking like this, it would be silly to come merely to booze. Peep around the corner from the bar and tradition ends – the dining room has pale wood and sisal floors, cream walls and modern prints, and good-looking food served on big white plates. Chef-patron Tony Robson-Burrell and head chef Guy Opie's imaginative country dishes reflect current trends, so whether you choose a pub classic like Old Spot pork sausages with mash and mustard sauce, or pan-fried sea trout with chorizo and herb risotto and augergine cavier, you'll eat well (while pudding-lovers will relish the wild elderberry panna cotta). Real ales include Old Hooky and Ruddles, children and dogs are welcome and there's a lovely, friendly feel.

directions	Oaksey signed off A429 at Crudwell, 5 miles north of Malmesbury.
meals	12pm-2pm (12pm-2.30pm Sun); 6.30pm-9pm (6.30pm-9.30pm Fri & Sat). No food Mon. Main courses £5-£14.95; bar meals £5-£10.25.
closed	2.30pm-6pm. Open all day Sun.

Tony Robson-Burrell
The Wheatsheaf,
Oaksey,
Malmesbury SN16 9TB
tel   01666 577348

map: 3 entry: 525

The Horse & Groom
Charlton

The solidly elegant Cotswold stone house fronted by a tree-sheltered lawn stands well back from the road. Its long history as a coaching inn is documented in the framed prints that hang in the main bar, rustically atmospheric with its exposed stone, woodblock flooring and assorted scrubbed tables and chairs. Newish owners (the dynamic Merchant Inns group) are due to give bar, lounge and dining areas an overhaul in January 2007, so expect a stylish contemporary makeover. Michelin-star chef Rob Clayton may oversee the menus here but at the moment the bar champions classic pub dishes such as homemade beefburger with chips and tomato relish, and Wiltshire ham, eggs and chips. Look to the carte for innovation, perhaps pan-roasted scallops with pea purée and black pudding, honey roast duck with port sauce and bubble-and-squeak, and dark chocolate tart with raspberry compote. One to watch!

directions	Beside B4040 Malmesbury to Wootton Bassett road, 3 miles east of Malmesbury.
meals	12pm-9pm (9.30pm Fri & Sat). Main courses £8.95-£15.95; bar meals £4.95-£9.95.
closed	Open all day.

Simon Haggan
The Horse & Groom,
The Street, Charlton,
Malmesbury SN16 9DL
tel   01666 823904
web   www.horseandgroominn.com

map: 3 entry: 526

The Vine Tree
Norton

With a fine store of ales and over 30 wines by the glass the old watermill is a watering hole in every sense. It may be hidden away but the faithful, and their dogs, return. We would too, for the food and the beer. On Sundays, memorable roast sirloin of beef from the neighbour's farm is served with all the trimmings. There's plenty of fresh fish, too, and local game in season, whole crab served with saffron, lemon and herb mayonnaise, and mixed seafood paella. Service is young and friendly and surroundings are inviting: deep red walls, candlelight and beams, a wood-burning stove; meals in the miniscule upstairs room are super-cosy. In summer, relax and gaze at the immaculate Cotswolds from the terrace — a delicious spot with urns of flowers and a fountain. There's a nice garden, too. This vine tree has a rich harvest for guests to reap — no wonder Clementine looks so content.

The Castle Inn
Castle Combe

After a few thrilling laps on the local racing circuit, slip into a slower gear and head for food and good cheer at the Castle Inn. Sitting centre stage in the old market place, in what is surely one of England's prettiest villages, this famous hostelry has been here since the 12th century. Order a pint of Butcombe out at the front and contemplate the history — the village has barely changed in 400 years. Or retreat to the low-beamed bar with its log fire, stonework and period colours. The food is as civilised as the surroundings: pigeon breast with mixed salad, crispy Parma ham and pine nuts, breast of chicken stuffed with brie and basil, wrapped in bacon with a whole grain mustard sauce. For further celebration there are ten champagnes, over 30 bins of wine and heart-warming selections of brandy, cognac and armagnac. *Ask about parking in summer.*

directions	A429 for Cirencester; 1.5 miles, left for Norton. There, right; for Foxley. Follow road; on left.
meals	12pm-2pm (2.30pm Sat & Sun); 6pm-9.30pm (10pm Fri & Sat). Main courses £12.95-£19.95; bar meals £5.95-£12.95; Sunday roast £12.95.
closed	3pm-6pm (flexible Sat). Open all day Sun.

directions	M4 junc. 17; A350 towards Bath, turning right onto A420. Right for Yatton Keynell & continue to Castle Combe.
meals	12pm-3pm; 6pm-9.30pm Restaurant closed lunch & Sun eve. Main courses £10.50-£17.95; bar meals £7.75-£9.95.
closed	Open all day.

Charles Walker & Tiggi Wood
The Vine Tree,
Foxley Road, Norton,
Malmesbury SN16 0JP
tel 01666 837654
web www.thevinetree.co.uk

map: 3 entry: 527

Ann Cross
The Castle Inn,
Castle Combe,
Chippenham SN14 7HN
tel 01249 783030
web www.castle-inn.info/index.html

map: 3 entry: 528

Wiltshire

Quarrymans Arms
Box

Though once a row of simple cottage dwellings, this has been a pub since the 18th century – a friendly, quirky little place. As the name suggests, it once served the stone miners from the local quarry. The mines may be long-gone, but history lingers in the shape of fascinating maps, photos and some lethal-looking stonecutting equipment hanging on the walls. In pride of place near the bar: a framed front page Box quarry story from a 1934 edition of the *Daily Sketch* asks: 'Is this the world's toughest job?'. Food on the changing blackboard menus is more traditional than gastropub, but is straightforward and tasty. Good Wiltshire home-cured ham, steak and ale pie, calves' liver with mustard mash and other staples are perfect fuel for walkers, cyclists and pot-holers intent on visiting the disused mines. And the landscaped garden has fantastic views.

directions	Just off A4, on hillside to right of village; phone for directions.
meals	12pm-3pm; 6pm-9pm. Main courses £7.50-£14.50; bar meals £2.50-£7.25.
closed	3pm-6pm. Open all day Fri-Sun.

John & Ginny Arundel
Quarrymans Arms,
Box Hill, Box,
Corsham SN13 8HN
tel   01225 743569
web   www.quarrymans.plus.com

map: 3 entry: 529

Wiltshire

The Flemish Weaver
Corsham

Until their arrival in 2003, Nathalie and Jeremy had not run a pub before. You'd never know! The couple have turned the listed old building in the busy market town into a friendly local with a kitchen worth seeking out. And so proud are they of their food suppliers that a roll-call of them is framed near the counter. The slate-floored bar is stylish, its darkwood tables topped with fresh flowers, local artists' work on cream walls and glowing logs in the grate. Food is modern and unshowy – free-range pork steaks (from a local farm, naturally) in a cider sauce, local venison, wild rabbit, pheasant in season, Somerset smoked salmon – while well-kept Bath Ales, Banks's and a weekend guest ale come straight from the barrel. In a county with few good market-town pubs, the Flemish Weaver is a great addition.

directions	In town centre, close to entrance to Corsham Court.
meals	12pm-2.30pm; 7pm-9.30pm. No food Sun eves. Main courses £6.75-£13; baguettes £4.50; Sunday roast from £12.
closed	Open all day.

Jeremy Edwards & Nathalie Bellamy
The Flemish Weaver,
63 High Street,
Corsham SN13 0EZ
tel   01249 701929

map: 3 entry: 530

The Pear Tree Inn
Whitley

A cool rustic chic flows effortlessly through the Pear Tree – a dreamy blend of French inspiration and English whimsy. Step in under the beams, step across flagged floors, sink into an armchair and roast away in front of the fire. Keep going and you come to lofty dining rooms, where stripped floors are dressed in smart old rugs and French windows flood the place with light, opening up in summer for al fresco suppers. Menus announce stylish modern dishes based around well-sourced ingredients – braised neck of lamb with polenta, parmesan and puy lentils, warm pear and almond tart with rosemary ice cream – all served by polite and charming staff. Exquisite bedrooms, up in the eaves or out in the old barn, are painted Lime White and have suede bedheads, Bang & Olufsen TVs and funky rugs for colour. Fabulous.

directions	Onto B3353 & immed. right to Whitley; right again into Top Lane.
meals	12pm-2.30pm (3pm Sun); 6.30pm-9.30pm (10pm Fri & Sat, 7pm-9.30pm Sun). Main courses £11.95-£18.50.
rooms	8: 6 doubles, 2 family £105-£140. Singles £75.
closed	Open all day.

See pp 30–57 for full list of pubs with rooms

Martin & Debbie Still
The Pear Tree Inn,
Top Lane, Whitley,
Melksham SN12 8QX
tel   01225 709131
web   www.thepeartreeinn.com

map: 3 entry: 531

The Tollgate Inn
Bradford-on-Avon

All would pay the toll – were there one – to sample the delights of the Tollgate Inn. In a warm and convivial bar and lounge, comfy sofas, a log-burning stove, planked pine tables, newspapers and magazines encourage you to linger over a handpumped pint of Exmoor or a glass of sauvignon. The smaller dining area off the bar has a traditional appeal, the upper, in the former chapel of the weavers who worked below, is smart with high black rafters, open fire and an eclectic décor. Chef Alexander Venables' pedigree shines through in dishes that make the most of local produce and daily fish from Brixham. Light bites include omelette Arnold Bennett and set lunch is a snip at £11.95; try whole sea bass baked with ginger and fennel or Church Farm rib-eye steak. Bedrooms are in excellent order: oak beams, good antiques, smart linen, pretty views.

directions	On B3107 between Bradford-on-Avon & Melksham.
meals	12pm-2pm; 7pm-9pm (9.30pm Fri & Sat). Main courses £13.50-£19.50; bar meals £6.95-£8.50; set lunch £11.95 & £13.95.
rooms	4 doubles from £75. Singles £50.
closed	3pm-5.30pm; Sun eve & Mon.

See pp 30–57 for full list of pubs with rooms

Alison Ward-Baptiste
& Alexander Venables
The Tollgate Inn, Ham Green,
Holt, Bradford on Avon BA14 6PX
tel   01225 782326
web   www.tollgateholt.co.uk

map: 3 entry: 532

The George & Dragon
Rowde

Behind the unpromising exterior hides a low-ceilinged bar, its stone fireplace ablaze in winter, its half-panelled walls lined with old paintings, its antique clock ticking away the hours. Furnishings are authentically period, there are wooden boards in the dining room, plum-painted walls and plenty of dark timber. The kitchen's chutneys and preserves are for sale, international bottled beers and organic ciders line the shelves and handpumped Butcombe Bitter announces itself on the bar. Experienced owners are maintaining the pub's reputation for fish delivered fresh from Cornwall – with the odd concession to meat eaters. Blackboards list the day's specials like steamed black bream with spinach and garlic – and puddings to diet for. Relax in the pleasant garden in summer, or wander along the Kennet & Avon Canal.

The Three Tuns
Great Bedwyn

Life-size models of the Blues Brothers sit at either end of the bar and set the tone. This is a cracking village pub a stone's throw from the Kennet & Avon Canal. Old buildings – one the village bakery, the other the morgue – were knocked through to create an alehouse in 1756. Get here early to bag a table in the wonderful bar where original floorboards, hefty oak beams and brick inglenook (ablaze in winter) blend beautifully with more contemporary clutter; every inch of wall and ceiling space is covered. Peruse the old farming implements, tools, jugs and teapots over a pint; chuckle at the chalkboards listing funny quotes and 'Bush Telegraph' newspaper cuttings. Locals, walkers and gamekeepers come for homemade food in whopping portions: wonderful meat pies, Irish stew, pigeon and quail, and rare roast beef on Sundays, all from fresh, local produce.

directions	On A342, 2 miles west of Devizes.
meals	12pm-3pm (4pm Sat & Sun), 7pm-10pm (6.30pm-10pm Sat). No food Mon. Main courses £9-£17.50; Sunday lunch, 3 courses, 15.50.
closed	3pm-7pm (4pm Sat & Sun), Sun eve & Mon lunch.

Chris Day, Michelle & Philip Hale
The George & Dragon,
High Street,
Rowde,
Devizes SN10 2PN
tel   01380 723053

map: 3 entry: 533

directions	Great Bedwyn signed off A4 between Hungerford & Marlborough.
meals	12pm-2pm (2.30pm Sun); 7pm-9pm. Main courses £9-£16; bar meals £6-£11.
closed	3pm-6pm & Sun from 5pm.

Alan & Jan Carr
The Three Tuns,
High Street,
Great Bedwyn,
Marlborough SN8 3NU
tel   01672 870280

map: 3 entry: 534

The Millstream
Marden

A pub-restaurant that opens all day and serves champagne by the glass: not what you'd expect in the Vale of Pewsey? The Millstream has bags of character, a welcome for all and a range of handpumped ales. Pale beams, crisp colours, log-burners and open fires give a fresh appeal to the open-plan space; there's a snug with a comfy leather sofa at one end, and a dining area at the other. This picks up the vibe from the bar, but is a gentler place to be, with its upholstered chairs and serene views over the lawn to the river. The chef's modern menu changes daily and the food is divine; much produce is organic, fish comes from Looe and the wine list is long. There's mille feuille of wild mushrooms; pork loin with roast apples; cod with crushed potatoes, spinach and saffron beurre blanc; chocolate brownie with vanilla ice cream. Nicola's staff serve with smiles and on warm days you may sup on the terrace. We love this place.

The Lamb on the Strand
Semington

Keep a light foot on the accelerator between Trowbridge and Devizes or you will pass this ivy-clad red brick pub and miss a wonderfully friendly place where staff and locals rub along with easy chat and laughter. Philip and Sue (Cordon Bleu trained) are committed foodies who place an emphasis on honest well-cooked 'cuisine de campagne.' Start with grilled fig and chorizo salad with shaved parmesan before moving on to the heavenly slow-roast belly of pork with braised vegetables. With a wine list "reluctantly sampled" by Philip that covers the entire world you are spoilt for choice. There are several dining areas, log fires and some good local artwork on terracotta walls. On fine days, step out to the pretty garden and admire the sweeping views, accompanied by a pint of Ringwood, Butcombe or Keystone. Unpretentious with genuine charm is a fair summing up of both pub and landlord.

directions	Off A302 5 miles from Devizes.
meals	12-3pm; 7pm-9.30 (12-4pm, 6.30-9pm Sun). All day bank hols. Main courses £4-£15.
closed	Open all day. Closed Mon (except bank hols).

Nicola Notton
The Millstream,
Marden,
Devizes SN10 3RH
tel   01380 848308
web   www.the-millstream.net

map: 3 entry: 535

directions	On A361, 3 miles north east of Trowbridge.
meals	12pm-2pm; 6.45pm-9pm. Main courses £8.50-£11.50.
closed	3pm-6pm & Sun eve.

Philip Roose-Francis
The Lamb on the Strand,
99 The Strand,
Semington,
Trowbridge BA14 6LL
tel   01380 870263

map: 3 entry: 536

The Angel Inn
Upton Scudamore

A blaze of summer colour on the smart, sheltered decked area; beams and a huge log burner in the terracotta-coloured bar; contemporary art and sofas in the split-level restaurant. It's a comfortable and sophisticated environment for Tony and Carol Coates' menu and specials' board that delivers straightforward modern food. Informality and decent sized portions are among the attractions, the menu changes frequently and the produce is sourced locally. Fish dishes star, in the form of seared Brixham scallops, whole plaice on the bone, grilled sardines. An exemplary cherry bakewell makes a satisfying finish. There are Wadworth 6X and Butcombe on tap and several wines of the month chalked up on the board by the bar.

George Hotel
Codford

By George! The old roadside inn has been given a new lease of life. Boyd McIntosh and Joanne and Robert Fryer used to practise their art at the revered Howard's House in Teffont Evias. Here, Boyd delivers dishes from a compact modern menu: wild sea bass with black olive potato and red pepper fondant, steamed turbot with watercress risotto, corn-fed chicken with mushroom risotto. Joanne is a dab hand at front of house – and her influence is stamped over the understatedly contemporary interiors. Floors are parquet, tiled or pale-carpeted, walls are warmly hued and the furniture is stylishly simple. The bar has a blond-wood counter, there are lush plants, mirrors and a sitting room full of deep sofas. The vase of lilies on the bar adds a civilised touch, as do candles on tables; the winter fires are the icing on the cake.

directions	Village signed off A350 Warminster to Westbury road & off A36.
meals	12pm-3pm; 5pm-10pm. Main courses £12-£20.
closed	3pm-6pm.

	Tony & Carol Coates The Angel Inn, Upton Scudamore, Warminster BA12 0AG
tel	01985 213225
web	www.theangelinn.co.uk

map: 3 entry: 537

directions	Off A36 between Salisbury & Warminster.
meals	12pm-2pm; 7pm-9.30pm. Main courses £8.95-£16.95.
closed	Tues & Sun eves in winter.

	Boyd McIntosh, Joanne Fryer & Robert Fryer George Hotel, High Street, Codford St Peter BA12 0NG
tel	01985 850270
web	www.thegeorgecodford.co.uk

map: 3 entry: 538

Spread Eagle Inn 🛏
Stourhead

Mellow and 18th century it may appear but peep inside and you see slate or coir floors, Farrow & Ball colours and understated jugs of garden flowers on old pine tables. You can eat in the bar next to a wood-burning stove or in the restaurant that doubles as a sitting room. Red walls, large modern paintings and old prints create a mood that is cosy and warm. The higgledy-piggledy stairs are great if you're nimble and the bedrooms peaceful – muted colours, white linen, original fireplaces, delightful views. Bathrooms are spotless. Food is delicious: pork terrine with beetroot relish, braised venison in red wine, liver and smoked bacon. The village is charming, and you can pretend that enchanting Stourhead with its lake and follies is yours when the hoards have gone home.

directions	Off B3092 signed Stourhead Gardens. Pub below main car park on left at entrance to garden.
meals	12pm-9.30pm. Main courses £8.50-£16; bar meals £5.50-£15.
rooms	5 twins/doubles £70-£90. Singles £50-£60.
closed	Open all day.

See pp 30–57 for full list of pubs with rooms

Tom Bridgeman
Spread Eagle Inn,
Stourton,
Warminster BA12 6QE
tel   01747 840587
web   www.spreadeagleinn.com

🧗 📧 👞 🛏

map: 3 entry: 539

The Bath Arms 🛏
Horningsham

A 17th-century coaching inn on the Longleat estate in a village lost in the country. At the front, a dozen pollarded lime trees shade a gravelled garden; at the back, two stone terraces soak up the sun. Inside are the best of old and new: flagstones and boarded floors, a stainless steel bar and Farrow & Ball colours. The skittle alley doubles as a sitting room (they show movies here). Stop for caramelised onion tart, bavette steak with Lyonnaise potatoes, Pimms granita. Bedrooms are a treat, some in the main house, others in the converted barn, and there's a romantic two-bedroom lodge overlooking Longleat House and Park. Expect lots of colour, big wallpapers, beds dressed in Eygyptian cotton; bathrooms come in black slate, some with baths, others with deluge showers. The walk down to Longleat is majestic.

directions	A303, then A350 dir. Longbridge Deverill; left for Maiden Bradley, right for Horningsham. On right.
meals	12pm-2.30 (3pm Sat & Sun); 7pm-9pm (9.30 Fri & Sat); children 6pm-7pm. Main courses £12-£18.
rooms	14: 10 doubles, 2 twins, 2 singles £70-£130.
closed	Open all day.

See pp 30–57 for full list of pubs with rooms

Christoper Brooke
The Bath Arms,
Longleat Estate, Horninghsam,
Warminster BA12 7LY
tel   01985 844308
web   www.batharms.co.uk

♿ 🧗 📧 🐕 🍷 🍴 🛏

map: 3 entry: 540

The Cross Keys
Lyes Green

Two crackling log fires in winter, a landscaped beer garden in summer and ales from Wadworth all year round. The convivial bar is tailor-made for quiet drinking, the front dining room, with its wooden floors and fresh flowers on pine tables, is somewhat posher. This is primarily a dining pub, so there's an intimate restaurant too, inviting with log fire, green dresser, scrubbed oak tables, gleaming glasses and chunky candles. Three huge blackboards list the oft-changing menus. Find Wiltshire ham and apple chutney baguettes, baked potatoes with posh fillings, pork, bacon and cider pie and local sausages with onion gravy at lunchtime; on Sundays, fine roasts. Dinner promises asparagus in season, calves' liver with madeira jus and rump steak with peppercorn sauce. There's also a refurbished skittle alley and a private dining room.

The Forester Inn
Donhead St Andrew

Tiny lanes frothing with cowparsley twist down to this fine little pub in Donhead St Andrew. The revitalised 600-year-old inn sports rustic walls, black beams, a log fire in the inglenook and planked floors; colours are muted, there's not an ounce of flounce and locals still prop up the bar of a late weekday lunchtime. Foodies come from far for chef-owner Chris Matthews's cooking – rib-eye steak with béarnaise, 'a trio of lamb chops' with bubble-and-squeak, goat's cheese omelette, tomato tarte tatin – and fine puddings cooked to order, slowly. Chris uses local Rushmore venison, Old Spot pork and specialises in fresh Cornish seafood – brill with shellfish bisque and mussels, skate wing with brown butter and capers, seared monkfish with cockles and rocket pesto. There's a pretty garden and terrace with views, three ales on tap, cider from Ashton Press and ten gorgeous wines by the glass.

directions	From Frome follow A362 towards Longleat & turn left & the White Hart for Lyes Green.
meals	12pm-2pm; 7pm-9.30pm. No food Sun eve. Main courses £8.50-£20; bar meals £7.95-£15.95; Sunday roast £9.75-£14.95.
closed	3pm-6.30pm (7pm Sun).

Fraser Carruth & Wayne Carnegie
The Cross Keys,
Lye's Green,
Corsley BA12 7PB
tel   01373 832406
web   www.crosskeyscorsley.co.uk

map: 3 entry: 541

directions	A30 between Shaftesbury & Salisbury. Through Ludwell turning for Donhead on left after 2 miles.
meals	12pm-2pm (4pm Sun); 6.30pm-9.30pm. Main courses £10-£25; bar meals £5-£12.
closed	3pm-6.30pm & Sun from 4pm.

Chris & Lizzie Matthews
The Forester Inn,
Lower St,
Donhead St Andrew,
Shaftesbury SP7 9EE
tel   01747 828038

map: 3 entry: 542

Wiltshire — Pub with rooms

The Compasses Inn
Lower Chicksgrove

In the middle of a village of thatched cottages, the old inn's roof is like a sombrero, shielding the upper-floor windows that peer sleepily over the lawn. Duck into the sudden darkness of the flagstoned bar and be prepared for a wave of nostalgia as your eyes adjust to a long wooden room, its cosy booths divided by farmyard salvage: a cartwheel here, some horse tack there. At one end is a piano, at the other a brick hearth. The pub crackles with Alan's enthusiasm – he's a great host. People come for the food, too: scallops on crab risotto with saffron sauce; lamb fillet with pancetta, wild mushroom mash and basil jus. Bedrooms are at the top of stone stairs outside the front door and have the same effortless charm: walls are thick, windows are wonky, bathrooms are new. And the serenity of Wiltshire lies just down the lane.

directions	From Salisbury, A30; 3rd right after Fovant for L. Chicksgrove; 1st left down track lane to village.
meals	12pm-2.30pm; 6.30pm-9pm (9.30pm Sat; 7pm-9pm Sun). Main courses £9-£17; bar meals from £5
rooms	4 + 1: 2 doubles, 2 twins/doubles. Cottage for 3, £75-£90.
closed	3pm-6pm (7pm Sun).

See pp 30-57 for full list of pubs with rooms

Alan & Susie Stoneham
The Compasses Inn,
Lower Chicksgrove,
Tisbury SP3 6NB
tel 01722 714318
web www.thecompassesinn.com

map: 3 entry: 543

Wiltshire

The Angel Inn
Hindon

The fortunes of this 1750 coaching inn in beautiful Hindon have been restored, thanks to experienced chef-landlord John Harrington who took over in 2005. Behind the Georgian exterior is a stylish bar area in earthy tones with wooden floors, chunky tables, deep sofas and log fire. The more formal restaurant is softened by candles and fresh flowers. Good British cooking draws folk from afar: watch the team at work in the glass-fronted kitchen. At lunch: basil and garlic marinated smoked sprats with potato salad, posh shepherd's pie, home-cooked ham ploughman's. Cooking moves up a gear in the evenings, the daily menu listing, say, king scallops and crispy pancetta salad, rack of lamb with minted kumquats and port and redcurrant sauce, and lemon and lime cheesecake. A teak-tabled courtyard and a gorgeous village at the door entice you out.

directions	From A303, left 7 miles after main A36 Salisbury junction. Inn at crossroads in village.
meals	12pm-2.30pm; 7pm-9.30pm. No food Sun eve. Main courses £6.95-£12.50 (lunch), £8.95-£15.95 (dinner).
closed	3.30pm-5pm. Open all day Fri & Sat.

John & Lyn Harrington
The Angel Inn,
High Street, Hindon,
Salisbury SP3 6DJ
tel 01747 820696
web www.theangelathindon.com/

map: 3 entry: 544

The Horseshoe Inn
Ebbesbourne Wake

The Ebble valley and Ebbesbourne Wake have escaped the intrusions of modern-day life, dozing down tiny lanes close to the Dorset border. A bucolic charm pervades the village inn that has been run as a "proper country pub" by the Bath family for over 30 years. Climbing roses and honeysuckle cling to the 17th-century brick façade, while the traditional layout of two bars around a central servery still survives. Old farming implements and country bygones fill every available cranny and a mix of rustic furniture is arranged around the crackling winter fire. Beer is tapped straight from the cask and food is hearty and wholesome, prepared by Pat Bath using local meat and vegetables and game from local shoots. Tuck into steak and kidney pie, fresh fish bake, faggots in onion gravy, nursery puddings and three roasts on Sundays (do book). Rustic benches and flowers fill the garden.

Haunch of Venison
Salisbury

A tiny, ancient, city-centre pub of great character; it dates from 1320 when it was built as a church house for nearby St Thomas's. A trio of rooms, jammed with shoppers, businessmen and tourists in a bare-boarded, music-free atmosphere. The rooms are affectionately known as the Horsebox (tiny), the House of Commons (chequered stone floor, beams, carved benches and minuscule, pewter-topped bar) and, lording it on the first floor, the sloping-floored House of Lords – the restaurant. The fireplace is ancient (and not always lit) but the food is modern British; warm up with wild haunch of venison with creamed potatoes, parsnips and juniper jus. Note the small side window displaying a mummified hand and a pack of 18th-century playing cards, spookily discovered in 1903. There's an amazing collection of malt whiskies crammed behind the bar, and a rare set of antique taps for gravity-fed spirits.

directions	A354 south of Salisbury, right at Coombe Bissett; follow valley road for 8 miles.
meals	12pm-2pm (2.30pm Sun); 7pm-9pm. No food Sun eve or Mon all day. Main courses £7.25-£15; bar meals £4.50-£9.95; Sunday roast £8.25.
closed	3pm-6.30pm, Mon until 7pm & Sun from 4pm.

directions	Opposite Poultry Cross, off Market Square.
meals	12pm-3pm (2.30pn Thurs-Sat); 6pm-9pm (10pm Thurs-Sat). Main courses £6.90-£15.90.
closed	Open all day.

	Anthony & Patricia Bath The Horseshoe Inn, Ebbesbourne Wake, Salisbury SP5 5JF
tel	01722 780474

	Anthony & Victoria Leroy Haunch of Venison, 1-5 Minster Street, Salisbury SP1 1TB
tel	01722 411313
web	www.haunchofvenison.uk.com

map: 3 entry: 545

map: 3 entry: 546

Wiltshire

Worcestershire

The Malet Arms
Newton Tony

Formerly a bakehouse for a long-lost manor, the old flintstone pub draws walkers and cyclists from miles around. Expect cracking ales, robust country cooking and a cheerful welcome from Noel and Annie Cardew. In the low-beamed bar, cosy with rustic furnishings, blazing winter logs, old pictures and interesting bits and pieces, sit back and sup a pint of Wadworth 6X drawn from the cask (a modern rarity!) or local Stonehenge Heelstone. Hearty food, listed above the fireplaces, reflects the rural setting, with locally-shot game a winter favourite. Fill your boots with a rich stew of pheasant and pigeon in Guinness, or a local beef burger; follow with Annie's speciality – old English puddings (Cumbrian tart, Canterbury pie). In summer, knock a few boules about with the locals in the usually dry bed of the 'bourne' rivulet outside the door, or watch the pub cricket team on the playing field opposite.

The Chequers
Cutnall Green

On the site of an ancient coaching inn, the Chequers was rebuilt 70 years ago. You'd never know: its open fires, comfy sofas and snug little booths have evolved as smoothly as its menu. While the thirsty gather round the church-panel bar with foaming pints of Timothy Taylor's, the hungry head for the dining room – cosy and candlelit with deep red walls, pale exposed beams and a huge display of wines. Make the most of a vibrant 'mod Brit' menu from award-winning chef Roger Narbett: the food bursts with flavour. There's roasted pumpkin and sweet potato soup, spiced lamb with Brinjal pickle potatoes, banana daiquiri crème brûlée, and a classy light bites menu. And if the liqueur coffees catch your fancy, slip off and savour one in the Garden Room, whose sleek, striped, coffee-coloured curtains resemble an upside-down cappuccino. New this year: a heated patio for al fresco dining.

directions	3 miles north of Droitwich Spa on A442 towards Kidderminster. M5 exit 5.
meals	12pm-2pm; 6.30pm-9.15pm (9.30pm Fri & Sat). Sun 12pm-2.30pm; 7pm-9pm. Main courses £10.25-£13.50; bar meals £4.25-£8.75.
closed	3pm-6pm (4pm-7pm Sun).

directions	Off A338; 6 miles north of Salisbury.
meals	12pm-2.30pm; 6.30pm-10pm (7pm-9.30pm Sun). Main courses £8.50-£15.
closed	3pm-6pm (7pm Sun).

	Noel & Annie Cardew
	The Malet Arms,
	Newton Tony,
	Salisbury SP4 0HF
tel	01980 629279

	Roger & Jo Narbett
	The Chequers,
	Kidderminster Road, Cutnall Green,
	Droitwich WO9 0PJ
tel	01299 851292
web	www.chequerscutnallgreen.co.uk

map: 3 entry: 547

map: 8 entry: 548

The Talbot
Knightwick

It's run by two sisters, Annie and Wiz, chef-owners with a dedication to all things self-sufficient. Hops for their micro-brewed beers are grown right here and organic produce comes from the farmers' market they host the second Sunday of every month. Their genuine commitment to using fresh local food pulls a crowd; the fresh crab bisque, raised pies and spotted dick are legendary. Fresh fish comes from Cornwall and scallop beignets are wrapped in nori seaweed (hardly local, but delicious). The pot-roast lamb recipe comes from Alnwick Castle in Northumberland, and the wild duck – drizzled with the meat juices, a little grand marnier and served over mashed potato – suggests a touch of genius in the kitchen. Out of the way, but no matter; make a night of it and enjoy black pudding for breakfast!

directions	From Worcester A44 for Leominster; 8 miles on, through Cotheridge & Broadwas; right on B4197; on left.
meals	12pm-2pm; 6.30-9pm (7pm-9pm Sun). Main courses £10-£19; bar meals £4.50-£14.
closed	Open all day.

Annie Clift
The Talbot,
Knightwick,
Worcester WR6 5PH
tel   01886 821235
web   www.the-talbot.co.uk

map: 8 entry: 549

The Fleece
Bretforton

'No potato crisps to be sold in the bar.' So ordered Lola Taplin when The Fleece was bequeathed to the National Trust after 500 years in her family. It's the sort of tradition that thrives in the Pewter Room where you pitch up for fresh local food, ales from Uley and Weston's Old Rosie cider. Steak and ale casserole with dumplings and locally-culled rhubarb in pies and crumbles may tempt you but there is so much more: summer festivals twirl with Morris dancers and asparagus auctions, and the original farmyard is a gorgeous setting for hog roasts and musical events. The black-and-white timbered building is as stuffed as a museum with historical artefacts, stone flagged floors, big log fires, ancient beams and a wonderful collection of pewter. The timbered bedroom is small but perfectly formed, with seagrass flooring and antique mahogany bed. Leave the 21st century behind – by about half a millenium.

directions	B4035 from Evesham for Chipping Campden. In Bretforton bear right into village. Opp. church in square.
meals	12pm-2.30pm (4pm Sun); 6.30pm-9pm. No food Sun eve. Main courses £6.95-£13.
rooms	1 double £85.
closed	3pm-6pm. Open all day Sat & Sun & every day June-Sep.

Nigel Smith
The Fleece,
The Cross, Bretforton,
Evesham WR11 7JE
tel   01386 831173
web   www.thefleeceinn.co.uk

map: 8 entry: 550

Yorkshire

Ye Olde Mustard Pot
Midhopestones

Bilberry- and bracken-clad slopes rise above the wooded valley of the Little Don. In a peaceful hamlet amid a latticework of stone walls, the Pot is a beacon for the pub-goer in search of fine fodder in this corner of Yorkshire. Rejuvenated some five years ago, a tangle of heavily-beamed, slab-floored rooms ramble between dressed stone walls – from secluded alcoves to traditional restaurant. Look out for Roland tinkling the ivories! Settle into settles beside huge log fires or slump into comfy sofas with a pre-prandial cocktail, eyeing up the discrete fishing ephemera or the collection of mustard pots. The first-class ingredients may have been grazing local pastures or filling local allotments just a day or two previously; for the beer buff are beers from the Wentworth brewery. Outside, sun-kissed patios and lawns encourage one to linger.

directions	Off A616, 13 miles north-west of Sheffield.
meals	12pm-9pm (8pm Sun). Main courses £8.50-£14.95.
closed	Open all day. Closed Mon (except bank hols).

Andrew & Alison Hodgkiss
Ye Olde Mustard Pot,
Mortimer Road, Midhopestones,
Sheffield S36 4GW
tel 01226 761155
web www.yeoldemustardpot.co.uk

map: 12 entry: 551

Yorkshire

Kings Arms
Heath

Enter Heath and step back years. A string of wool merchants' houses, 100 acres of heathland, a couple of tethered ponies… who would guess that Wakefield was down the road? In the heart of Yorkshire's most unspoilt village is the equally unspoiled King's Arms. In a dark, rich network of tap rooms and snugs, softly hissing gas lamps cast an amber glow on oak-panelled walls, yellowed ceilings and low beams, while a magnificent Yorkshire range is the best of several open coal fires. It's no museum – just a superbly old-fashioned pub that serves Clarks Classic Blond, and Stella for non-believers. Pub grub includes omelettes, curries and beef ale pie; there's no music but a quiz night on Tuesdays. Attached is a serviceable restaurant, at the back is a conservatory that breaks the spell. The gardens, enclosed by high hedges and safe for children, have gentle moorland views.

directions	Heath signed off A655.
meals	12pm-2pm; 7pm-9pm (8.30pm Sun). Main courses £9.85-£13.50; bar meals £5.25-£8.50.
closed	3pm-5.30pm in winter. Open all day in summer.

Alan Tate
Kings Arms,
Heath Common,
Heath,
Wakefield WF1 5SL
tel 01924 377527

map: 12 entry: 552

Three Acres
Shelley, Huddersfield

A dining pub par excellence: everything ticks over beautifully. The bar is a work of art, brimful of bottles, pumps, flowers, with old fishing reels and tackle hanging picturesquely above. Seating is comfy pub style, the smart polished tables are craftsmen-made, and there's a large solid fuel stove to warm the central space. Separate areas around the bar have a sea of tables set for dining (white linen, shining glasses); one area specialises in seafood. The overall feel is roomy yet intimate and hugely inviting, with plants, flowers, mirrors, old prints, a baby grand. A sizeable team prepares all the food on site, from potted shrimps to assiette of moorland lamb (rack, stuffed breast, shepherd's pie), runs the on-site deli and serves the new private dining room. Well-kept beers on pump, scores of fine wines, over 50 whiskies and great sandwiches.

The Sair Inn
Linthwaite

Clinging to the side of the Colne Valley, the Sair Inn oozes character, timelessness and a warren of small coal-fired rooms. Floors of rippling flagstone or scuffed boards carry tables, pews and chairs from The Ark. Massive winter fires ensure that Vulcan would feel at home; Pandora would be delighted by the artefacts and oddments. It is a Yorkshire treasure, enhanced by welcoming locals and traditional pub games; the old pub Joanna allows impromptu entertainment, side rooms allow escape from the hubbub and the front paved terrace is a fine place on a summer weekend. Beers? – to die for, created in the brewhouse near the pub; any or all of a dozen and more. Fodder? Patrons flock from leagues around to savour the atmosphere of this iconic idyll, so concerns about catering are the last thing on anyone's mind. It's uncompromising, not one for shrinking violets, and 'grand' – in the Wallace and Grommit sense.

directions	5 miles SE of Huddersfield & off A629; signs for Kirburton on B6116; signs for Emley Moor Mast; 0.5 miles south of mast, on minor road above Shelley.
meals	12pm-2pm; 6.30pm-9.30pm. Main courses £13.95-£25.95; bar meals from £5.95.
closed	3pm-6pm.

directions	Off A62 in Linthwaite; up Hoyle Ing (opp. bus shelter by box junc.); 400 yds up steep hill.
meals	Sandwiches available at weekends. Sandwiches £1.50.
closed	Mon-Fri lunch. Open all day Sat & Sun.

	Neil Truelove & Brian Orme Three Acres, Roydhouse, Shelley, Huddersfield HD8 8LR
tel	01484 602606
web	www.3acres.com

	Ron Crabtree The Sair Inn, Hoyle Ing, Linthwaite, Huddersfield HD7 5SG
tel	01484 842370

map: 12 entry: 553

map: 12 entry: 554

Yorkshire

The Old Bridge Inn
Ripponden

A Christmas-card image of a cobbled lane, an ancient packhorse bridge and a little low inn… this is the setting of The Old Bridge Inn. Family involvement over several decades has resulted in a thoroughly civilised, unspoilt little local; a friendly one, too. Three carpeted, oak-panelled, split-level rooms – suitably dimly lit – are furnished with a mix of old oak settles and rush-seated chairs. The small, green-walled snug at the top is atmospheric; the bar has a lofty ceiling with exposed timbers and a huge fireplace with log-burning stove; the lower room is good for dining. The buffet lunches are as popular as ever, while the evening menu announces sound English cooking using local produce (Hubberton rib-eye steak with port and shallot sauce, duck with quince and rosemary sauce) with a modern slant. The bar is well-used by local folk who come for Timothy Taylor's Best and Black Sheep beers, and wines are good too.

directions	4 miles from junc. 22 M62 in Ripponden.
meals	12pm-2pm; 6.30pm-9.30pm. No food Sat or Sun eves. Main courses £7.50-£10.95.
closed	3pm-5.30pm (5pm Fri). Open all day Sat & Sun.

Tim & Lindsay Eaton Walker
The Old Bridge Inn,
Priest Lane, Ripponden,
Sowerby Bridge HX6 4DF
tel 01422 822595
web www.porkpieclub.com

map: 12 entry: 555

Yorkshire

The Millbank
Mill Bank

Savour a pint and a rolling moorland view. The Millbank, clinging to the side of a steep hill, has a stripped-down, architect-scripted interior that combines flagstones and log fires with modern paintings and bold colours. Its friendly, cosmopolitan style is echoed in the food, prepared by Chez Nico-trained Glenn Futter, who creates daily wonders with fresh local produce. There might be roast scallops or parsnip and parmesan soup for starters, beef braised in Guinness with horseradish mash or sea bass with lobster and spinach linguine. And then there are the spoiling puddings, the fine Yorkshire cheeses, the guest beers and the Yorkshire ales (Timothy Taylor's Landlord for one), the excellent wines, the malt whiskies and the first-class snacks in the bar. The steeply terraced garden has lead planters fashionably stuffed with box topiary and bamboo and those views.

directions	Off A58 between Sowerby Bridge & Ripponden.
meals	12-2.30pm (12pm-4.30pm Sun); 6pm-9.30pm (10pm Fri & Sat, 8pm Sun). Main courses £9.95-£18.95; set menu, 2 courses, £11.95; sandwiches from £4.95.
closed	3pm-5.30pm & Mon lunch. Open all day Sun.

Glenn Futter & Joe McNally
The Millbank,
Mill Bank Road, Mill Bank,
Sowerby Bridge HX6 3DY
tel 01422 825588
web www.themillbank.com

map: 12 entry: 556

The Old Bore
Rishworth

The Pennines may seem bleak in winter – but drop down to Rishworth and there's a treat in store. Scott Hessel, who has cooked his way from London to West Yorkshire, has warmed a 200-year-old pub, renamed it The Old Bore and claims it is anything but. The carved oak bar is flanked by two softly-lit dining rooms brimming with antlers, stuffed birds, old prints, Victorian screens, gilt mirrors, wine boxes and champagne bottles. The monthly carte has been refined and shows flair – local game and foie gras terrine with spiced damson chutney; monkfish and clam casserole with saffron, tomato and basil; confit of Ryburn lamb shoulder with roast garlic mash, lentils, roast peppers and rosemary – and the two-course menu is a steal. Add a raft of English wines, homemade gins and vodkas and a dining terrace outside and you have a pub that's worth a detour.

directions	M62 junc. 22; A672 for Halifax; 3 miles, then left after reservoir.
meals	12pm-2.15; 6pm-9pm (10pm Sat); 12pm-4pm; 5.30-8pm Sun. Main courses £6.95-£19.95; set menu, 2 courses, £11.95; Sunday lunch £14.95 &£17.95.
closed	3pm-6pm & Mon all day. Open all day Sun.

Scott Hessell
The Old Bore,
Oldham Road, Rishworth,
Halifax HX6 4QU
tel   01422 822291
web   www.oldbore.co.uk

☖ ☖ ☖ ☖ ☖ ☖

map: 12 entry: 557

Travellers Rest
Sowerby

Caroline Lumley took over this old pub on the moors and started from scratch: she has worked wonders. The inn has kept its big fireplaces and cast-iron stoves, flagged bar, exposed stone and ancient beams, now sanded; Caroline has added atmospheric lighting, background sound, sofas, cushions and throws – and a helipad! It's a great mix of old and new and the result is a pub that appeals both to locals and those from further afield. The pleasant dining room is two archways from the bar, with well-dressed tables and fine valley views. The blackboard menu highlights scrumptious English dishes – belly pork with sweet mustard sauce, lamb shank with redcurrant gravy – while in the stylish bar you can choose between Timothy Taylor's on tap and a champagne cocktail. From the terrace, stunning views over the Calderdale and the desolate moors.

directions	West of Sowerby Bridge on A672; 5 miles west of Halifax. Signed.
meals	Wed-Fri 5pm-9.30pm. Sat 12pm-2pm; 5.30pm-10pm. Sun 12pm-3.30pm; 5.30pm-8.30pm. Main courses £9.95-£19.50; bar meals £7.95-£12.95.
closed	Mon & Tues all day, Wed-Fri lunch & 2.30pm-5.30pm Sat. Open all day Sun.

Caroline Lumley
Travellers Rest,
Steep Lane,
Sowerby,
Halifax HX6 1PE
tel   01422 832124

☖ ☖ ☖ ☖ ☖ ☖

map: 12 entry: 558

Shibden Mill Inn
Shibden Mill

There's still a pubby feel to this rambling old inn – although it's known for its restaurant. John Smiths, Theakstons and two rotating guests drinkers happy in front of several open fires, and the wine list wins awards. The deep green valley setting within sound of the mill stream makes for an idyllic summer drinking spot. Unstuffy integrity lies behind this venture, from the front-of-house warmth to the modern British kitchen. Inventive menus promise roast pigeon and beetroot risotto; wild turbot with blue cheese soufflé and mussel broth; toffee parfait. Fruit and veg come from local Hill Top Farm. Cosy gate-leg tables and sofas in the bars, crisp napery in the dining room, and jams and chutneys for sale make this a high-class act, while bedrooms, some to be renovated this year, are carpeted, comfortable and individual; the suite is huge fun.

directions	Off A58 Halifax-Leeds, near A6036 junction.
meals	12pm-2pm; 6pm-9.30pm (12pm-7.30pm Sun). Main courses £9.95-£17.95; bar meals from £8.95.
rooms	11 doubles/singles/suites £90-£136.
closed	2.30pm-5.30pm. Open all day Sat & Sun.

See pp 30-57 for full list of pubs with rooms

Glen Pearson
Shibden Mill Inn,
Shibden,
Halifax HX3 7UL
tel   01422 365840
web   www.shibdenmillinn.com

map: 12 entry: 559

Yorkshire

The Chequers Inn
Ledsham

Fires glow, horse brasses gleam... this honey-stone-village inn could be in the Dales. In fact, you're a couple of miles from the A1: a great lunchtime stopover. A warren of panelled, carpeted rooms radiating off a central bar is cosy with log fires and plush red upholstery; faded sepia photographs are a reminder of an earlier age. Rare handpumped ales from the Brown Cow Brewery at Selby do justice to good English food of Yorkshire proportions: steaming platefuls of lamb shank, steak and mushroom pie, guinea fowl... and just when you think you're replete, along comes a treacle sponge pudding. The pub is old, deeply traditional, welcoming travellers since the 18th century. And it's closed on Sundays, a tradition that goes back to 1832 when the lady of Ledsham Hall was so incensed by a drunken farmer on her way to church that she insisted the pub close on the Sabbath.

directions	From A1(M) at junct 42, follow A63 Leeds to Selby road. Turn left & follow signs for Ledsham, 1 mile.
meals	12pm-9pm. Main courses £4.95-£16.95.
closed	Sun. Open all day Mon-Sat.

Chris Wraith
The Chequers Inn,
Claypit Lane, Ledsham,
South Milford LS25 5LP
tel   01977 683135
web   www.thechequersinn.f9.co.uk

map: 12 entry: 560

Whitelocks
Leeds

A little gem. Fixtures and fittings have changed little since Victorian times – a remarkable achievement for a pub off bustling Briggate. The long narrow bar is dominated by a tile-fronted counter with its original, marble-topped Luncheon Bar. Fine old button-backed leather banquettes come with panelled, mirrored dividers, while copper-topped tables, stained glass and several grand mirrors add to the Victorian-Edwardian mood. There is no piped music and the place is surprisingly quiet given its city centre position, though it does fill up fast at peak times. Well-kept Deuchars, good wines and a mix of traditional and up-to-date dishes make this a bit of a find. There's also a carpeted dining room with dark banquettes and upholstered chairs at linen-covered tables, and an open fire to add to the atmosphere. Be comforted by sandwiches, steak and ale pie and roast lunches, and avoid busy times – this pub is small!

The Pack Horse
Widdop

This old whitewashed inn sags beneath weathered gritstone tiles in a gloriously remote spot. Once, water engineers had a whale of a time constructing reservoirs to slake the thirst of the local textile industry – the pub's stone walls sport old plans and photos of their endeavours. Today's thirsts are those of ramblers on the Pennine Way and riders on the new Pennine Bridleway, which briefly meet right behind the pub. Four or five real ales to enjoy alongside whopping portions of crispy roast duck, rack of lamb and a whole side of grilled plaice ensure this is a popular spot. Two thickly beamed rooms off a passageway bar, with cavernous log fires, horsey ephemera and a comfy rag-tag of furnishings, invite you to unwind over a drink; this is a great pub with grand food, not a dining pub with good beer.

directions	From A646 in Hebden Bridge take the road at the Fox & Goose, signed for Heptonstall & Slack. In Slack fork right for Widdop.
meals	12pm-2pm (2.30pm Sun); 7pm-9pm (9.30pm Sat & Sun). Main courses £5.95-£10.95.
closed	3pm-7pm; Mon all day (except bank hols) & weekday lunch Oct-Easter. Open all day Sun.

directions	Next to Marks & Spencer in Central Leeds shopping area.
meals	11am-7pm; 12pm-4pm Sun. Main courses £5.47-£7.45.
closed	Open all day.

Charlie Hudson
Whitelocks,
Turks Head Yard,
Briggate,
Leeds LS1 6HB
tel 0113 245 3950

Andrew Hollinrake
The Pack Horse,
Widdop,
Hebden Bridge HX7 7AT
tel 01422 842803

map: 12 entry: 561

map: 12 entry: 562

The Fleece
Addingham

A gorgeous old place run with flair and passion. The surroundings provide atmosphere, the friendly licensees add something special, and the food's good, too. Bags of character comes from big open fires, solid tables and old settles on flagged floors, beamed and boarded ceilings, exposed stone, white walls. It's a big space that at peak times gets busy, but in summer you can spill out onto tables on the paved terrace at the front and watch the world go by. Chris Monkman has brought a refreshing enthusiasm for local, seasonal food with him: Wharfedale lamb, braised oxtail, ocean-fresh fish. Even the children's menu is brilliant: home-battered fish, omelettes, one-minute steak, moules marinieres, grilled goat's cheese salad. Plenty of choice and it's all good value, with local cheeses playing a major role. Four of Yorkshire's best beers are always available, there's a thoughtful selection of wines, and a number of whiskies, too.

directions	2 miles north of Ilkley on A65-A650.
meals	12pm-2.15pm; 6pm-9.15pm (12pm-8.15pm Sun). Main courses £7-£17.
closed	Open all day.

Chris Monkman
The Fleece,
Main Street,
Addingham,
Ilkley LS29 0LY
tel   01943 830491

map: 12 entry: 563

The Tempest Arms
Elslack

A rambling 18th-century stone inn in rolling countryside, mid-way between Skipton and Colne. In the various areas of bar and lounge are exposed stone, old timbers and a stylish feel: settles, plump cushions, Annie Tempest cartoons, three log fires and Molly the lab. Drinkers may choose from up to four Yorkshire cask ales and several good wines by big or small glass. There's a fair mix of customers here: locals, walkers and business folk. Have a light meal in the bar or fancier dishes in the dining room; they do red Thai fish soup, crispy pork with thyme-roasted potatoes, sumptuous puddings, fine local cheeses. Staff are friendly and professional. Rooms include swish new suites with private terraces and hot tubs or balconies overlooking a babbling stream; all have hand-crafted furniture and bathrooms sporting Molton Brown toiletries; a dozen are on the ground floor.

directions	Off A56 between Skipton & Colne.
meals	12pm-2.30pm; 6pm-9pm (9.30pm Sat); 12pm-7.30pm Sun. Main courses £8.95-£15.95; bar meals from £5.95.
rooms	21: 9 twins/doubles, 12 suites £74.95-£99. Singles £59.95-£74.95.
closed	Open all day.

See pp 30-57 for full list of pubs with rooms

Veronica Clarkson
The Tempest Arms,
Elslack,
Skipton BD23 3AY
tel   01282 842450
web   www.tempestarms.co.uk

map: 12 entry: 564

Yorkshire — Pub with rooms

The Lister Arms Hotel
Malham

Another jewel in the glorious Dales, this one going back to the 1600s and standing on the village green. The Pennine Way cuts through – so come to walk, ride, bike, paraglide. Return at night to a friendly bar for Trappist ales, Belgian beers, Yorkshire ales and malt whiskies, and hearty home-cooked pub grub. In summer, life spills onto the cobbled terrace at the front; in winter, you hole up in the bar warmed by woodburners. Super bedrooms are a steal: some are small and newly decorated (exposed stone walls, cast-iron beds, pretty fabrics); other big but not as up-to-date (flock wallpaper, wicker chairs, good showers). Guided walks can be arranged, you can hire mountain bikes and there's free internet in the bar. Stay a week and you can take their gorgeous cottage next door.

directions	A65 west from Skipton, then north for Malham. In village, over bridge & on left.
meals	12pm-2pm; 6.30pm-9pm. Main courses £7.95-£10.
rooms	9 + 1: 5 doubles, 3 family, 1 twin £60-£70. Singles £50-£55. Cottage for 8, £275-£1,200 p.w.
closed	3pm-6.30pm. Open all day Fri-Sun & in summer.

See pp 30-57 for full list of pubs with rooms

	Andrew & Johnothan Ditchfield The Lister Arms Hotel, Malham, Skipton BD23 4DB
tel	01729 830330
web	www.listerarms.co.uk

map: 12 entry: 565

Yorkshire

Craven Arms
Appletreewick

Recently and authentically restored by enthusiastic licensees, this rustic, creeper-clad pub dating back to 1548 stands among georgous hills overlooking Wharfedale. It's a favourite with walkers so you may end up chin-wagging with them alongside the glowing cast-iron range in the classic stone-flagged bar. Just plain settles, panelled walls, thick beams, nothing more; beyond, a snug with simple benches and valley views, and a homely dining room. The final treat are the Wharfedale Ales – Folly, Executioner, Oat Stout. Head out back to the loo to take a peek at the amazing function room housed in a replica medieval barn – the first cruck barn to be have been built in 500 years; back in the bar, free of music and flashing games, tuck into hot sandwiches and homemade steak and mushroom pie. Just the ticket after a blustery hike or cycle ride across the moors.

directions	Village signed off B6160 between Bolton Abbey & Grassington.
meals	12pm-2pm; 6.30pm-9pm (8.30pm Sun). Main courses £8.95-£14.50; bar meals £7.50-£10.50.
closed	3pm-6.30pm Mon & Tues.

	Ashley & Hayley Crampton Craven Arms, Appletreewick, Skipton BD23 6DA
tel	01756 720270

map: 12 entry: 566

The Angel Inn
Hetton

The old drovers' inn remains staunchly, reassuringly traditional – but with a stylish restaurant and wines that have come, over the years, to rival the handpumped Yorkshire ales. There's even a 'cave' for private-party tastings. There are nooks, crannies, beams and crackling fires, and thought has gone into every detail, from the antique furniture in the timbered rooms (one with a magnificent oak-panelled bar) to the fabrics and the colours. Enjoyable food ranges from filo 'moneybags' of seafood in lobster sauce – the fish comes fresh from Fleetwood – to Yorkshire lamb and rosemary sausage with juniper-scented red wine sauce. Or Goosnargh duck breast with braised red cabbage. The glorious up-hill-and-down-dale drive to get here is part of the charm, and it is best to book. It's a much-loved place, yet the owners have not rested on their laurels.

The Falcon Inn
Arncliffe

Tucked into the top corner of Littondale, one of the most remote and unspoilt of Yorkshire's dales. Several generations of Millers have been licensees here and they have preserved an inn and a way of life almost lost. The fine bay-windowed and ivy-clad building looks more like a private house than a village local… expect few frills and old-fashioned hospitality. The entrance passageway leads to a small hallway at the foot of the stairs – there's a tiny bar counter facing you, a small, simple lounge, a log fire and sporting prints on the walls. A sunny back room looks out across the garden to open fells. Beer is served, as ever, straight from the cask in a large jug, then dispensed into pint glasses at the bar. At lunchtime, call in for pie and peas, sandwiches and ploughman's lunches.

directions	Off B6265, 6 miles N of Skipton.
meals	12pm-2.15pm (2.30pm Sun);
	6pm-9.30pm
	(10pm Sat, 9pm in winter).
	Main courses £9.50-£17;
	bar meals £8.95-£16;
	Sunday lunch, 3 courses, £22.50.
	Early Bird menus £13.20-£16.50.
closed	3pm-6pm.

directions	Off B6160 16 miles N of Skipton.
meals	12pm-2pm.
	Snacks £2.50-£4.50.
closed	3pm-7pm. Reduced winter opening times, phone to check.

Juliet Watkins
The Angel Inn,
Hetton,
Skipton BD23 6LT
tel 01756 730263
web www.angelhetton.co.uk

map: 12 entry: 567

Robert Miller
The Falcon Inn,
Arncliffe,
Skipton BD23 5QE
tel 01756 770205
web www.thefalconinn.com

map: 12 entry: 568

The White Lion Inn
Cray

For centuries the White Lion has stood surrounded by moorland high in the Pennines, serving local farmers and cattle drovers. It still does, though walkers have replaced the drovers. In the main bar are deep, upholstered settles and dark, plain tables – the ideal setting for straightforward hearty soups (broccoli and stilton) ploughman's lunches, pork casseroles, homemade lasagne and steak and mushroom pies – best washed down with a well-kept pint of Taylor's Landlord, Moorhouses Bitter or Copper Dragon Golden Pippin. At quiet times the crackle of the logs on the fire and the ticking of the clock are all you hear and the owners' relaxed style permeates the whole place. There are plenty of spots for summer eating outside by the tumbling stream. Some of Wharfedale's footpaths pass by the door, and the views are all you'd hope for, and more.

The Old Hill Inn
Chapel-le-Dale

A proper, wild-country tavern – with terrific beer and food. It used to be a farmhouse, then a doss-house for walkers and potholers; now it's a comfortable old inn, a warm, safe haven in a countryside of crags, waterfalls, moors and an occasional stone dwelling. Via the porch enter the bar – a large room with open-stone walls, bare boards, old pine tables and big log fire. Six pumps deliver ales in top condition – Black Sheep Bitter, Dent Bitter, Aviator – while blackboards announce food that is well above average pub grub, served in the candlelit intimacy of the diminutive dining rooms. From Sabena come parsnip and apple soup, pheasant casserole in season and homemade bread; from master confectioner Colin, warm chocolate pudding and lemon tart. His sugar sculptures alone are worth the trip.

directions	20 miles north of Skipton on B6160.
meals	12pm-2pm; 5.45pm-8.30pm. Main courses £8.50-£13.95.
closed	Open all day.

Kevin & Debbie Roe
The White Lion Inn,
Cray, Buckden,
Skipton BD23 5JB
tel 01756 760262
web www.whitelioncray.com

map: 12 entry: 569

directions	On the B6255 between Ingleton & Ribblehead.
meals	12pm-2.30pm Sat & Sun; 6.30pm-9pm (6pm-9pm Sat). Main courses £9.95-£12.95; bar meals £4.95-£8.95.
closed	Mon all day & Tues-Fri lunch. Open all day Sat & Sun.

Sabena Martin
The Old Hill Inn,
Chapel-le-Dale,
Ingleton LA6 3AR
tel 015242 41256

map: 12 entry: 570

Foresters Arms 🛏
Carlton in Coverdale

A few miles past Middleham with its castle and racing stables, Coverdale is not exactly the forgotten Dale but is probably the least touted. And the Forester's is the quintessential Dales inn. Not just because of its log fires, low ceilings and flagstone floors; its drinking rooms are friendly and there's a darts team in the snug. The pub has young, keen and well-travelled landlords in Mike and Claire Chambers, who serve food as flavoursome as the ales; a lively kitchen delivers treats such as cod with brown shrimp butter, roe deer steak with brandy pepper sauce and steamed nursery puddings. Everyone feels happy here: locals, walkers, families, dogs. The bedrooms are either sweet and old-fashioned or the best of contemporary; two are ensuite and there's homemade marmalade for breakfast. Characterful and worth a detour.

directions	A1 exit A684 for Leyburn. Through Leyburn on A684. Left for Carlton.
meals	12pm-1.45pm; 6.30pm-8.30pm. Main courses £8.95-£14.50.
rooms	3: 2 doubles, 1 twin £79.
closed	2pm-6.30pm (4pm-7pm Sun), Tues lunch & Mon all day.

See pp 30-57 for full list of pubs with rooms

Mike & Claire Chambers
Foresters Arms,
Carlton-in-Coverdale,
Leyburn DL8 4BB
tel　01969 640272
web　www.forestersarms-carlton.co.uk

♿ 🚶 📖 🐕 🍺 🍷 🛏

map: 12 entry: 571

The Blue Lion
East Witton

The Blue Lion has a big reputation locally; so big it followed our inspector round Yorkshire. Paul and Helen came here a decade ago, and have mixed the traditions of a country pub with the elegance of a country house. This is a bustling, happy place that serves superlative food and no one seems in a hurry to leave. Aproned staff, polished beer taps dispensing Yorkshire ale, stone-flagged floors, open fires, newspapers on poles, big settles, huge bunches of dried flowers hanging from beams, splashes of fresh ones. The two restaurants have boarded floors and shuttered Georgian windows, two coal fires, gilt mirrors and candles everywhere. Food is robust and heart warming; local game, chargrilled beef fillet with shiraz sauce; braised masala mutton with cumin sweet potato. East Witton has an interesting plague tale, Jervaulx Abbey is a mile away, there's tennis next door and a lush, enclosed garden at the back.

directions	From Leyburn, A6108 for 3 miles to East Witton.
meals	12pm-2pm; 7pm-9.15pm. Main courses £9.80-£21.50.
closed	Open all day.

Paul & Helen Klein
The Blue Lion,
East Witton,
Leyburn DL8 4SN
tel　01969 624273
web　www.thebluelion.co.uk

♿ 🚶 🐕 🍺

map: 12 entry: 572

The Wensleydale Heifer Inn
Leyburn

Everything about this place is off the wall – in the best way! Be lulled into a false sense of 'leather armchair by the fire' and 'mine's a pint of Theakstons' security as you step off the street. Enter the Fish Bar and you're met with wall-to-wall seagrass and modish-naff touches. But the welcome is warm, the food is sensational, and it's brilliant value. Choose dressed crab with potato, capers and chive salad, a classic 70s prawn cocktail, Cornish fish stew with new potatoes, parsley and olive oil – all delicious. As for the Whitby cod in crispy Black Sheep Bitter batter with peas and fat chips – it's the best fish and chips this side of Whitby's Magpie Café. Chef David Moss, ex-Crab & Lobster at Asenby, has achieved the impossible: a great fish restaurant as far from the sea as you can get. And there's a shiny, slightly more formal but still kitted-out-with-joke-crockery dining room – guaranteed to put a smile on your face.

Sandpiper Inn
Leyburn

In 1999 former Roux scholar Jonathan Harrison swapped a slick city kitchen for an old stone pub in the Yorkshire Dales. In cosy alcoves beneath low black beams, locals and walkers put the world to rights over pints of Black Sheep and Theakston ale opposite chalkboards listing Jonathan's daily menus: fishcakes with herb sauce, club sandwiches, fish and chips in beer batter, braised beef in Guinness. Cooking moves up a gear in the simple stylish dining room as in-season game, Wensleydale heifer beef and home-grown herbs and veg come into play. Loosen belts before delving into ham hock, chicken and mushroom terrine, local lamb with garlic sauce, and sticky toffee pudding with butterscotch sauce. Malt whisky lovers will eye the 100 bottles behind the bar appreciatively.

directions	On A684 between Leyburn & Hawes.
meals	12pm-2.30pm; 6pm-9.30pm (12pm-9.30pm Sat & Sun) Main courses £11.50-£20.50; bar meals (lunch) £4.50-£11; set lunch/early dinner £14.50 & £16.50.
closed	Open all day.

David Moss
The Wensleydale Heifer Inn,
West Witton,
Leyburn DL8 4LS
tel 01969 622322
web www.wensleydaleheifer.co.uk

map: 12 entry: 573

directions	From A1, A684 for Bedale; on for 12 miles.
meals	12pm-2.30pm; 6pm-9pm (9.30pm Fri & Sat). Main courses £8.95-£13.95 (lunch), £9.95-£18 (dinner); bar meals £4-£6.95.
closed	3pm-6.30pm (7pm Sun) & Mon all day.

Jonathan & Michael Harrison
Sandpiper Inn,
Market Place,
Leyburn DL8 5AT
tel 01969 622206
web www.sandpiperinn.co.uk

map: 12 entry: 574

The Red Lion Inn
Arkengarthdale

Here is Langthwaite, a cluster of stone dwellings so perfectly huddled that film companies flock. Over the humpback bridge the Red Lion looks as if it has been here for ever – give or take the odd shutter. Outside are picnic tables, inside, a mix of traditional front room and shop (postcards, ice cream). All is carpeted and cosy with upholstered wall seats around cast-iron tables, a fire sometimes lit, and a small snug where children are welcome at lunchtime. Fascinating to look at all the maps and books on the area, and the film photos and darts and quoits trophies that line the bar shelves, almost obscuring the pumps. Black Sheep Best Bitter and Riggwelter are served in admirable condition – after 40 years, Rowena Hutchinson knows what makes a good pint. Sandwiches, pies and sausage rolls are on tap throughout pub hours – swiftly devoured after a morning out on the unspoilt moors.

The Oak Tree Inn
Hutton Magna

A tiny cottage at the end of a row, masquerading as a pub, the Oak Tree was snapped up four years ago by Alastair and Claire Ross – happy to swap London for the Dales. Alastair trained at the Savoy and he and Claire have created a gem. The front bar has old wooden panelling and whitewashed stone, an attractive medley of tables, chairs and pews, newspapers, fresh flowers and an open fire. The dark green dining area at the back is softly lit, its tables separated by pews. All is delightful and informal. Locally shot game appears regularly on the menu in season and the produce is as fresh as can be, much of it from within a mile of the village. Expect best end of lamb with gratin potatoes and provencal vegetables; sea bream with crab and ginger cannelloni and shellfish sauce; blueberry cheesecake with fromage frais sorbet. Booking is recommended, especially at weekends.

directions	From Reeth in Swaledale towards Arkengarthdale; right over bridge to Langthwaite; on left.
meals	11am-3pm (10.30am-3pm Sun); 7pm-11pm (10.30pm Sun). Bar snacks £1.40-£2.50.
closed	3pm-7pm.

Rowena Hutchinson
The Red Lion Inn,
Langthwaite, Arkengarthdale,
Richmond DL11 6RE
tel   01748 884218
web   www.redlionlangthwaite.co.uk

map: 12 entry: 575

directions	Off A66, 6.5 miles west of Scotch Corner.
meals	6pm-11pm (5.30pm-10.30pm), booking only. Main courses £14.50-£17.50.
closed	Lunch & Mon all day.

Alastair & Claire Ross
The Oak Tree Inn,
Hutton Magna,
Richmond DL11 7HH
tel   01833 627371
web   www.elevation-it.co.uk/oaktree

map: 12 entry: 576

Golden Lion
Osmotherley

There's never a dull moment at the old stone inn overlooking the village green and market cross, run by these young, thoughtful, hands-on owners and their friendly staff. It bustles with booted walkers on the famous Coast to Coast walk in the day, and hums with well-dressed diners at night. Arrive early to bag a seat in the brown-wood bar with pew bench seating, raised open fire and flickering evening candlelight. Nurse a pint of Timothy Taylor's Landlord or a first-class wine by the glass as you choose from a refreshingly simple menu. Nothing is over-ambitious; the chef simply gives you fresh ingredients well put together. Start with fish soup or pâté with apricot relish, move on to chicken Kiev or calves' liver with onions and mash, finish with a wicked pudding... and retire to fresh new bedrooms with appealing colours, good materials and super slate-floored showers.

directions	Off A19 10 miles north of Thirsk & Northallerton.
meals	12pm-3pm; 6pm-9pm. Main courses £6.50-£14.50.
rooms	3 twins/doubles £80. Singles £60.
closed	3pm-6pm. Open all day Sat & Sun.

See pp 30-57 for full list of pubs with rooms

Christie Connelly & Belal Radwan
Golden Lion,
6 West End,
Osmotherley DL6 3AA
tel　01609 883526
web　www.goldenlionosmotherley.co.uk

map: 12 entry: 577

Carpenter's Arms
Felixkirk

It's warm, cheerful, attractive and fun. Oriental fans by the fire and other oddities are dotted around the heavily beamed interior, along with pictures, books and antique carpentry tools. The long, panelled, barrel-fronted bar has three sections and bar stools, while rustic tables are cheerful with gingham. Beyond is the dining room, more formal with its white cloths, shining glassware and comfortable period dining chairs. A couple of Yorkshire beers are accompanied by some especially good wines by the glass and the menu is long: smoked salmon and spinach filo parcel, baked Queen scallops, fillet of pork stuffed with homemade black pudding wrapped in parma ham – and simple baguettes at lunchtime. This mother and daughter team and their young staff add a bit of spice that makes a visit huge fun. The village on the edge of the moors has a floodlit church.

directions	From Thirsk A170 to Sutton Bank; 1st left for Felixkirk. Pub 2 miles.
meals	12pm-2pm; 6.30pm-9pm. Main courses £8.95-£17.95; bar meals £8.95.
closed	3pm-6.30pm, Sun eve & Mon all day.

Karen & Linda Bumby
Carpenter's Arms,
Felixkirk,
Thirsk YO7 2DP
tel　01845 537369
web　www.carpentersarmsfelixkirk.co.uk

map: 12 entry: 578

The Nags Head
Pickhill

Three racecourses within a 15-minute drive, golf and shooting nearby — sporting guests from all walks of life predominate at this popular country inn. Behind, a manicured lawn; inside, a delightful surprise. Dark beams, snug fires and polished brass distinguish the tap room, where Black Sheep is on handpump; head for the lounge bar or mellow, picture-lined dining room if you wish to eat. If the formula holds few surprises it's because that's what customers have come to expect, and the Boynton family have been here over 30 years. That's not to damn with faint praise, only to acknowledge that generous and unaffected cooking using fresh local produce can be better than high-risk experimentation under the guise of innovation. Tuck into braised squid salad with smoked paprika and chilli, confit pork belly with roasted garlic juice, iced clementine parfait. Staff, courteous and beavering, add to the general sense of well-being.

directions	4 miles north of A1/A16 junc; 1 mile east of A1.
meals	12pm-2pm (2.30 Sun); 6pm-9.30pm (9pm Sun). Main courses £8.95-£17.95.
closed	Open all day.

Edward & Janet Boynton
The Nags Head,
Pickhill,
Thirsk YO7 4JG
tel   01845 567391
web   www.nagsheadpickhill.co.uk

map: 12 entry: 579

Freemason's Arms
Nosterfield

The Freemason's whitewashed exterior may suggest an ordinary village pub but over the years an unusual assemblage of items has been added to the traditional décor: 1900s enamel advertisements, veteran agricultural implements, Union flags, miners' lamps, a piano, and beams littered with calling cards and old bank notes. It's a low-beamed place with inter-connecting rooms, some flagged floors, two open fires, pew seating, soft lighting, candlelight — traditional, unspoilt, cosy and intriguing. It's also a darn good pub, with four local cask ales on offer and a blackboard to tantalise the hungry: partridge in rowan berry sauce, pink liver and onions with bacon. Kris Stephenson enjoys buying locally and delivers with flair. Eat in the bar, or at one of the bigger tables in the far room, perfect for dining. Just the spot after a day at the Ripon races.

directions	On B6267 for Masham, 2 miles off A1.
meals	12pm-2pm; 7pm-9pm. Main courses £8-£15.
closed	3pm-6pm & Mon all day. Open all day Sun.

Kristian Stephenson
Freemason's Arms,
Nosterfield,
Ripon DL8 2QP
tel   01677 470548

map: 12 entry: 580

Fountaine Inn
Linton in Craven

Imagine a village green with a stone bridge and a babbling stream – such is the setting for this 17th-century inn. In spite of some serious sprucing up last year, the Fountaine remains a classic Yorkshire village pub with glowing coal fires, slate floors, curved settles, old beams and cosy corners spread between interconnecting rooms. Weekend walkers arrive in droves for Black Sheep and local Litton ales, all day thick-cut sandwiches (roast beef with watercress and mustard) and traditional burgers with tomato mayonnaise, relish and pickles. Wish to linger longer? Then settle into the dining room for a plateful of Kilnsey smoked trout, brisket beef cooked in port wine gravy or slow-cooked duck with orange and marmalade sauce. The green is well used in summer; for a seat and shade bag one of the posh benches and brollies out front. Note that the Tempest Arms, Elslack and the Mason Arms in Cumbria are under the same ownership.

directions	Village signed off B6265 south of Grassington.
meals	12pm-9pm Main courses £7.50-£13.99; sandwiches from £4.95.
closed	Open all day.

	Chris Gregson Fountaine Inn, Linton in Craven, Grassington BD23 5HJ
tel	01756 752210
web	www.fountaineinnatlinton.co.uk

map: 12 entry: 581

The Boar's Head Hotel
Ripley

The Boar's Head sits four-square in this peaceful, pretty Model Estate village. Its sitting rooms are carpeted and draped: pink and green sofas, button-back armchairs, glass-topped tables, ancestor oils with brass lights over, an evening fire. There are games to play, newspapers, and a parasoled garden where you are served long summer drinks by delightful staff. The restaurant is candlelit at night and the food rich and generous: lamb noisettes with rosemary jus, red mullet with saffron mash and tapenade. Simpler fare in the bistro: sausages with parsnip and thyme purée, mixed vegetable risotto. Up the pretty staircase to very comfy bedrooms, with sherry and truffles in the best. (Twenty more rooms lie in outbuildings across the street.) Visit the castle gardens and the National Hyacinth Collection as a guest of the hotel; umbrellas and wellies are put out on rainy days.

directions	From Harrogate, A61 north for 3 miles; left at r'bout for Ripley.
meals	12pm-2.30pm (2pm winter); 6.30pm-9.30pm. Main courses £9.95-£16.50. Set dinner, 3 courses, £30-£39.50.
rooms	25 twins/doubles £125-£150. Singles £105-£125.
closed	Open all day.

See pp 30-57 for full list of pubs with rooms

	Sir Thomas & Lady Emma Ingilby The Boar's Head Hotel, Ripley Castle Estate, Ripley, Harrogate HG3 3AY
tel	01423 771888
web	www.boarsheadripley.co.uk

map: 12 entry: 582

The General Tarleton
Ferrensby

Chef-patron John Topham and wife Claire run the old coaching inn with an easy charm. The rambling, low-beamed, nooked and crannied brasserie-bar mixes rough stone walls with red ones, there are shiny oak tables and a roaring fire. You have Black Sheep Bitter on handpump, well-chosen wines by the glass and unfussy dishes of local produce. Here the menu ranges from classic fish soup and ham shank terrine with cumberland sauce to chargrilled venison with buffalo blue cheese polenta, seafood thermidor and fish and chips. The cosy-chic dining room, formerly a stables, displays white napery and a menu to match. Retire to comfortable rooms in a purpose-built extension, the newest flaunting the best of contemporary. And breakfasts are delicious.

directions	From A1 junc. 48; A6055 for Knaresborough; by road in Ferensby.
meals	12pm-2pm; 6pm-9.15pm (9.30pm Sat). Main courses £8.50-£17.50; set dinner menu £29.50.
rooms	14 doubles £97-£120. Singles £85-£108.
closed	3pm-6pm.

See pp 30-57 for full list of pubs with rooms

John Topham
The General Tarleton,
Boroughbridge Road, Ferrensby,
Knaresborough HG5 0QB
tel   01423 340284
web   www.generaltarleton.co.uk

map: 12 entry: 583

Blackwell Ox Inn
Sutton-on-the-Forest

On the main road that runs through the trim Georgian village of Sutton on the Forest, the Blackwell Ox Inn has, in the last two years, doubled in stature and size. The interior now is more country hotel than village pub, the walls bedecked with hunting prints and the odd sampler, the dining rooms spruce with cushioned window seats, stiff napery and soft lights at night. Steven Holding, an enthusiastic young chef of some pedigree, changes the menu daily and is passionate about the rustic flavours of south-western France. Salt cod fritters in beer batter come with aïoli and smoked paprika; monkfish with braised oxtail bourguignon; warm chocolate pudding with clotted cream and salted caramel. The North Yorkshire cheeses are delicious, the bread crusty and homemade, the wines fashionably listed by style. Handsome bedrooms, two with pretty views, sport generous bathrooms and every hotel comfort.

directions	Off B1363 7 miles north of York.
meals	12pm-2pm (2.30pm Sun); 6pm-9.30pm (9pm Sun). Main courses £8.95-£16.75; bar meals £3.95-£12.95; set dinner, 2-3 courses £10.50-£13.50.
rooms	5 twins/doubles £95-£110.
closed	3pm-6pm.

See pp 30-57 for full list of pubs with rooms

Marie Stothart & Steven Holding
Blackwell Ox Inn,
Huby Road, Sutton-on-the-Forest,
York YO61 1DT
tel   01347 810328
web   www.blackwelloxinn.co.uk

map: 12 entry: 584

The Durham Ox
Crayke

It stands at the picturesque top of the Grand Old Duke of York's hill. In the immaculate L-shaped bar: flagstones and deep rose walls, worn leather armchairs and settles, carved panelling and big fires. There are two more bars to either side, where well-heeled punters enjoy a pint of Theakston, and a dapper, yellow-walled and wine-themed restaurant that draws all and sundry, including Ampleforth parents out for lunch. Chalkboards above the stone fireplace and monthly menus may list game terrine with date and squash chutney, fish and shellfish pie, braised lamb shank with red wine and rosemary, and sticky toffee pudding with toffee sauce. The Bar Bites menu and the Sunday roasts are inevitably popular. Priced bin-end bottles line the old dresser in the bar, there's a deli selling homemade goodies, a garden with a marquee for summer functions, and jazz on Thursdays.

directions	Exit right off A19 York-Thirsk. Through Easingwold to Crayke.
meals	12pm-2.30pm; 6pm-9.30pm (10pm Sat, 8.30pm Sun). Main courses £9.95-£18.95; bar meals from £6.95; Sunday roast from £11.95.
closed	3pm-6pm. Open all day Sat & Sun.

Michael Ibbotson
The Durham Ox,
Crayke,
York YO61 4TE
tel   01347 821506
web   www.thedurhamox.com

map: 12 entry: 585

The Abbey Inn
Byland Abbey

The monks of Ampleforth who built this farmhouse would surely approve of its current devotion to good food; whether they'd be as accepting of its devotion to luxury is another matter. To enter the restaurant is a delight — a glorious flagstoned space lit by a skylight and full of Jacobean-style chairs and antique tables. Rambling, characterful bars have big fireplaces, oak and stripped deal tables, carved oak seats on polished boards. Food is British-based and interesting: venison with winter berry sauce or griddled, peppered rib-eye steak. Bedrooms are spacious and special with bathrobes, aromatherapy oils, fruit, homemade biscuits and a 'treasure chest' of wine. The delightful inn is owned by English Heritage and overlooks the hauntingly beautiful ruins of a 12th-century abbey.

directions	A1 junc. 49; A168 for Thirsk for 10 miles; A19. Left after 2 miles to Coxwold; left to Byland Abbey.
meals	12pm-2pm (3pm Sun); 6.30pm-9pm. Main courses £9-£15 (lunch); £11-£17 (dinner); Sun lunch 2-3 course, £16.50 & £21.
rooms	3 doubles £95-£155.
closed	3pm-6.30pm, Sun eve & Mon lunch.

See pp 30-57 for full list of pubs with rooms

Deborah Whitwell
& Richard Mason
The Abbey Inn,
Byland Abbey, Coxwold YO61 4BD
tel   01347 868204
web   www.bylandabbeyinn.com

map: 12 entry: 586

St Vincent Arms
Sutton-upon-Derwent

Humming with happy chat, the public bar is the heart of the place, sporting panelled walls lined with brass plates, warm red curtains and tartan carpet. There are up to eight cask beers to choose from and no background music or electronic gadgetry – just an old radiogram. To the left of the lobby is a smaller, snugger bar decorated in pale green with matching tartan carpet; this leads into several attractive small eating areas. Food ranges from sandwiches or smoked haddock risotto to scallops in garlic butter, mussels (recommended), steak au poivre, John Dory with pesto mash and fish sauce, roast belly pork with pak choi, soy and ginger dressing, and sticky toffee pudding. If you're not into ale there are several wines by the glass. The St Vincent Arms is a great little local and the staff seem to enjoy themselves as much as the customers – you can't ask for more.

The Blue Bell
York

Unlike most city pubs, the Blue Bell is exactly as it's always been. Its narrow brick frontage on Fossgate, not far from The Shambles and open-air market, is quite easy to miss; once you've found the old pub, you step into a long corridor that runs through to the back. On the right, a little bar with red-tiled floor and high ceilings, wooden panelling, Edwardian stained glass, a cast-iron, tiled fireplace, settle seating on two sides and iron-legged tables: one round, covered in copper, the other long, dressed in red formica, more Fifties than Edwardian. 'Ladies only' used to be allowed into the narrow back lounge; now its cosy red carpet can be trod on by all. Original fireplaces, polished panelling dotted with interesting old pictures... the place is a delight, and there's a terrific range of cask beers and wines to boot, as well as hearty sandwiches at lunchtime. Don't miss the annual beer festival in November.

directions	On B1228, 8 miles SE of York.
meals	12pm-2pm; 7pm-9.30pm. Main courses £7.50-£15.45.
closed	3pm-6pm (7pm Sun).

Simon Hopwood
St Vincent Arms,
Main Street, Sutton-upon-Derwent,
York YO41 4BN

tel	01904 608349
web	www.stvincentarms.co.uk

map: 13 entry: 587

directions	In York city centre.
meals	11am-3pm. No food Sun. Sandwiches £1.90.
closed	Open all day.

Jim Hardie
The Blue Bell,
53 Fossgate,
York YO1 9TF

tel	01904 654904

map: 13 entry: 588

The Stone Trough Inn
Kirkham Abbey

A great find: traditionally pubby and welcoming, with very good food. The bar has low beams, stone walls, two log fires, fresh flowers, and separate areas for privacy. Much care goes into running this place; it shows. Although the range of beers and wines is excellent, and the staff delightful, it's the food that people travel for. Adam Richardson is a talented chef, dispatching dishes of pressed game, foie gras and parsnip terrine, halibut on smoked salmon risotto with lemon butter sauce, roast Flaxton lamb with tomato and puy lentil sauce, and hot chocolate brownies. You choose from two menus, one for the bar, one for the restaurant. There's also a games room with pool, fruit machine, dominoes and TV. On warm days take your pint of Malton Golden Chance onto the front terrace that overlooks the gentle Derwent valley, then stroll down to Kirkham Abbey.

directions	Between York & Scarborough, 1.5 miles off A64 near Castle Howard.
meals	12pm-2pm; 6.30-8.30. Restaurant: 6.45-9.30 Tues-Sat, 12pm-2.15 Sun. Main courses £10.95-£18.95; bar meals £7.95-£14.50.
closed	2.30-6pm & Mon all day. Open all day Sun.

Adam & Sarah Richardson
The Stone Trough Inn,
Kirkham Abbey,
Whitwell on the Hill, York YO60 7JS
tel   01653 618713
web   www.stonetroughinn.co.uk

map: 13 entry: 589

The White Horse Inn (Nellie's)
Beverley

You could pass the White Horse by: its brick front and old pub sign do not stand out on busy Hengate. Inside is more beguiling – be transported back 200 years. (The building itself is even older.) Known as 'Nellie's', it's a wonderfully atmospheric little place; your eyes will take a while to become accustomed, so dim are the gas-lit passages. Little has changed in these small rooms with their old quarry tiles, bare boards, smoke-stained walls and open fires. Furniture is a mix of high-backed settles, padded benches, simple chairs, marble-topped cast-iron tables, old pictures and a gas-lit, pulley-controlled chandelier. Locals love the place, and its prices. Food is straightforward and good value: sandwiches, bangers and mash, steak and ale pie, spotted dick with custard. Charles Wesley preached in the back yard in the 18th century and the only concession to the modern age is the games room at the back with a pool table and darts.

directions	Off North Bar, close to St Mary's Church.
meals	10.30am-2.45pm. No food Sun. Main courses £4.50-£5.50.
closed	Open all day.

Anna
The White Horse Inn (Nellie's),
22 Hengate,
Beverley HU17 8BN
tel   01482 861973
web   www.e-hq.co.uk/nellies

map: 13 entry: 590

Yorkshire

Pipe & Glass Inn
South Dalton

In the elegant estate village of Dalton, rejoicing in one of the highest church spires in the Wolds, is this pan-tiled, 16th-century inn. The front garden has classic parkland vistas, the back is lushly lawned, the interiors glow with well-being. Turn right for a pubby pint; left to collapse into a manly leather sofa and plot a meal. Eating and lounging areas are woody, stylish and charming. Sofas are grouped around a woodburning fire, window seats sport chocolate cushions, a sturdy refectory table gleams with white china, and customers cluck with pleasure as they head to their tables. Kate, front of house, and James, chef, cut their teeth at the Star at Harome – so food is tuned to the best of local, seasonal, free-range, the breads are homemade and the combinations are adventurous – terrine of hare, ham hock and foie gras with pear and Juniper chutney, 'coq au vin' of guinea fowl with wild garlic mash and St George mushrooms – and the wines are listed by style.

directions	Village signed off A164 & B1248, 5 miles north west of Beverley.
meals	12pm–2pm (4pm Sun); 6.30pm–9.30pm. No food Sun eve. Main courses £8.95–£16.95; Sunday roast £10.95.
closed	3–6.30pm & Mon. Open all day Sun.

James Mackenzie
& Kate Boroughs
Pipe & Glass Inn,
West End, South Dalton HU17 7PN
tel 01430 810246
web www.pipeandglass.co.uk

map: 13 entry: 591

Yorkshire

Bay Horse Inn
Burythorpe

Long, low and inviting, built as a pub in 1836, the old Bay Horse is the flagship of Real Yorkshire Pubs. With 18 months spent running a French chalet behind them, Daniel and Claire have swapped a skiing clientele for a horsy one, and visitors and locals come for the food. Simple, flavoursome English dishes unlavishly presented are the order of the day, so expect oak-smoked salmon with brown bread, lemon and capers, fillet of beef with creamed leeks, mash and red wine sauce, and bread and butter pudding with roast plums. Meats and cheese are local, fish is from Hartlepool, wines are Chilean and French. Warm colours are Farrow & Ball, 'scrubbed' pine tables are matched with comfortable leather dining chairs, and smart light oak floors merge into fine stone flags. A small fire burns in the alcove by the door and there are books and newspapers to browse. It's friendly, young and civilised.

directions	Kirkham Priory on right, sharp left towards Langton; 3 miles; signs for Burythorpe for 1.25 miles.
meals	12pm–2pm (3.30pm Sun); 6.30pm–9.30pm. No food Sun eve. Main courses £7.95–£14.95; sandwiches from £3.95.
closed	3pm–6pm, Tues lunch & all day Mon. Open all day Sun.

Daniel Farrall & Claire Biggs
Bay Horse Inn,
Burythorpe,
Malton YO17 9LJ
tel 01653 658302
web www.bayhorseburythorpe.co.uk

map: 13 entry: 592

The Blacksmiths Inn
Westow

All sorts come here: smart young farmers, ladies who lunch, merry families and folk in tweeds. It's on the restaurant side of pub, attractive, understated and buzzy. There's a long, L-shaped bar with the short leg used by local drinkers. The other bit is spacious, flagged to the side, set with big old pine tables, candles and fresh flowers, and a well-fed log burner. The linked dining rooms are modern Yorkshire-flagged with splashes of red tartan carpet. The Marshalls are dedicated to serving fresh seasonal food: cream of butternut and lemon thyme soup with homemade bread, steamed oxtail and shin beef pudding with horseradish mash and beer gravy, posh fish pie (salmon, prawns, crayfish and parsley mash) and 21-day aged steaks with triple-cooked chips and béarnaise sauce. And the British cheeses are superb.

directions	A64 for Malton; right for Kirkham Abbey, then Westow; on main street.
meals	12pm-2pm Sat (3.30pm Sun); 6pm-9.30pm (Wed-Sat). Main courses £8-£17.95; Early Bird weekday menus £10.95 & £12.95; Sunday roast £9.95.
closed	Mon all day, Tues-Fri lunch, 2pm-6pm Sat & Sun from 3.30pm.

Gary & Sarah Marshall
The Blacksmiths Inn,
Westow,
Malton YO60 7NE
tel   01653 618365
web www.blacksmithsinn.co.uk

map: 13 entry: 593

Fairfax Arms
Gilling East

On a corner site set back from the road is a solid, heart-of-village pub supported by young and old. Farmers, families, shooting parties, even the odd parent and child from Ampleforth school — all feel at home. It's a sanctuary in winter with a blazing fire, and a pretty place in summer with a grassed and parasoled garden and a little stream. Under calm management the Fairfax has recovered from its wasteland years. Food is safe, traditional and good: fillet steak Normandy, haddock Florentine, Whitby scampi, vegetable curry, two roasts on Sundays and Yorkshire pud. Floors are coir or stripped wood, multi-paned sash windows pull in the light, curtains are plaid, the light oak bar links the two rooms, and the Ladies is *immaculate*! Upstairs are seven simple, sunny bedrooms, some overlooking the village street, with modern bathrooms and snowy towels. The suites are very good value.

directions	Gilling East on B1363 York to Helmsley, 5 miles S of Helmsley.
meals	12-2pm; 6.30-9pm (8.30pm Sun). Main courses £8.95-£18.95; Sunday lunch £11.95 & £14.95.
rooms	10: 8 twins/doubles, 2 family suites £70-£100. Singles £50.
closed	3pm-6pm.

See pp 30-57 for full list of pubs with rooms

Ray & Jayne Doyle
Fairfax Arms,
Main Street, Gilling East,
Malton YO62 4JH
tel   01439 788212
web www.fairfaxarms.co.uk

map: 13 entry: 594

Yorkshire

The Star Inn
Harome

You know you've hit the jackpot as soon as you walk into The Star – low ceilings, flagged floors, gleaming oak, flickering fire, irresistible aromas, a fat cat patrolling the bar. Andrew and Jacquie arrived in 1996 and the Michelin star in 2002. It's been a formidable turnaround for the 14th-century inn yet the brochure simply says: "He cooks, and she looks after you"... and how! Andrew's food is rooted in Yorkshire tradition, refined with French flair and written in plain English on ever-changing menus that brim with local produce. Risotto of partridge with braised chestnuts, shank of lamb with rosemary juices, gutsy puddings, a 'cheeseboard of the week' – and you're as welcome to have one course as three. There's a bar with a Sunday papers-and-pint feel (drinks range from homemade schnapps to Copper Dragon ales), a coffee loft in the eaves, and their own deli across the road. Exceptional.

directions	From Thirsk, A170 for Scarborough. Through Helmsley; right, for Harome.
meals	11.30pm-2pm; 6.30pm-9.30pm (12pm-6pm Sun). Main courses £12.95-£22.50.
closed	Mon lunch. Open all day Tue-Sun.

	Andrew & Jacquie Pern
	The Star Inn,
	Harome,
	Helmsley YO62 5JE
tel	01439 770397
web	www.thestaratharome.co.uk

map: 13 entry: 595

Yorkshire

The Appletree
Marton

She chooses the wines and he cooks: Melanie and TJ are an unstoppable team. Locals pile in for lunchtime sandwiches and a pint of locally brewed Suddaby's, while the food-conscious seek out the deli counter for its breads, chutneys, chocolates and terrines. TJ's menus reflect the seasons and change every day. Perhaps bruléed goat's cheese with tomato salad and rocket, smoked haddock, lemon and pea risotto, treacle tart with clotted cream and orange syrup – and a legendary chocolate pyramid. Herbs from the garden, fruits from the orchard, farm-reared meats... here are intense flavours with modern British eclecticism thrown in. Bliss in summer to relax on the orchard patio with a jug of Pimms; in the winter, it's cosy and comforting indoors: a beamed bar with ruby walls, flickering candles and log fires, and a farmhouse-style dining room. At busy times you'd be wise to book.

directions	2 miles from A170 between Kirkbymoorside & Pickering.
meals	12pm-2pm; 6pm-9.30pm (6.30pm-9pm Sun). Main courses £8.50-£17; snacks (in summer)£3.50-£6.
closed	2.30pm-6pm (3pm-6.30pm Sun), Mon & Tues all day.

	Trajan & Melanie Drew
	The Appletree,
	Marton,
	Kirkbymoorside YO62 6RD
tel	01751 431457
web	www.appletreeinn.co.uk

map: 13 entry: 596

The White Swan Inn
Pickering

This old coaching inn is more hotel than pub, but still full of surprises. Duck in through the front door to find a cosy panelled tap room serving real Yorkshire ales (Black Sheep, local Cropton brews), and a lounge with deep burgundy walls and log fire. The restaurant and private meeting room are handsomely furnished, the bedrooms are luxurious (antique beds, smart magazines, Penhaligon smellies). But the food is the draw. The meat comes from seven miles away, from über-butchers Ginger Pig; go to heaven on slow-roasted belly pork with mustard mash, braised red cabbage and apple sauce. Try, for a light lunch, a wild mushroom and thyme risotto, or a sandwich filled with Longhorn beef, pesto and rocket. There's a fantastic wine list and 50 clarets from St Emilion. Stay awhile – for beach walks, the moors and a ride on the steam railway.

directions	From York, A64 to Malton, then A169 to Pickering. Left at roundabout; at lights turn right; 1st right up Market Place. On left.
meals	12pm-2pm; 6.45pm-9pm. Main courses £9.95-£16.95; Sunday lunch £17.95.
rooms	21 doubles/twins/suites £129-£229. Singles from £89.
closed	Open all day.

See pp 30–57 for full list of pubs with rooms

Victor & Marion Buchanan
The White Swan Inn,
Market Place,
Pickering YO18 7AA
tel   01751 472288
web   www.white-swan.co.uk

map: 13 entry: 597

Schoolhouse Inn
Low Marishes

You walk into the School House, it puts its arms around you and gives you a squeeze. Maggie Perkins and son Sandy gutted this handsome old drinking pub and opened for Christmas in 2005. Polished stone floors and smooth cream walls, Singer sewing machine tables and Sheffield cutlery with ivory handles; Maggie has made it inviting and Sandy's in charge of the food. Seared beef salad with beetroot and horseradish is perfectly put together; fish pie with minted peas is smooth and luxurious, with a scallop in every mouthful. Fresh, locally sourced ingredients are used with flair and all is made from scratch – the olive bread like fluffy clouds, the gooey chunks of fudge with after-dinner coffee. No parsimony here; Yorkshire portions ensure everyone goes home happy. There's plenty of space outside too; sit back in the garden with a pint of Black Sheep and watch the farm traffic trundle by.

directions	Off A169 Malton to Pickering road.
meals	12pm-3pm (3.30pm Sun); 6pm-9pm. Main courses £9-£15.95; bar meals £4.50-£9.50.
closed	3pm-6pm, Sun eve & Tues all day.

Maggie Perkins
Schoolhouse Inn,
Low Marishes,
Malton YP17 6RJ
tel   01653 668247
web   www.schoolhouseinn.co.uk

map: 13 entry: 598

The Plough Inn
Fadmoor

It's been a welcoming refuge from the wintry moors for years. Catch sight of it from up high, smoke curling from the stack, and you feel irresistibly drawn. Inside the Plough all is as warm and reassuring as could be; the onetime row of cottage dwellings feels rambling but contained, the several small rooms immaculate with gleaming wood, rosy upholstery and rugs on seagrass floors. The food is a major draw and there are six dining areas in all, the nicest being half-panelled. All have open fires. Dishes range from cod and pancetta fishcakes with sweet chilli and ginger dressing to a mouthwatering steak, kidney and Guinness suet pudding; the soups are very good, and we liked the look of the chocolate and hazelnut terrine. Spill outside to bikes, boots, dogs and a pretty view of the village green in summer.

Moors Inn
Appleton le Moors

An ancient sign hangs from a long bracket. That's all there is to identify this unassuming inn but it is unexpectedly fresh and modern inside: white walls are unadorned, a few pictures and brasses on beams add colour, there's a charcoal-grey carpet, a stripped settle, little clutter. Warmth and cosiness emanate from the big old Yorkshire range with open fire and built-in ovens at one end of the main room; there's a wood-fronted bar at the other, a number of well-designed seating areas and two small dining rooms. Expect well-kept beer and good food – lamb shoulder stuffed with apricots with a honey and mint glaze, lemon and saffron chicken – largely made from their own or locally sourced organic produce. At the back, a large walled garden with dreamy vale views. The village, with its wide main street and solid stone buildings, has a timeless feel; glorious walks start from the door.

directions	From A170 Helmsley to Kirkbymoorside, left towards Fadmoor.
meals	12pm-1.45pm; 6.30pm-8.45pm (7pm-8.45pm Sun). Main courses £8.95-£14.95.
closed	2.30pm-6.30pm (7pm Sun).

Neil & Rachael Nicholson
The Plough Inn,
Main Street,
Fadmoor,
Kirkbymoorside YO62 7HY
tel 01751 431515

map: 13 entry: 599

directions	Off A170, 5 miles west of Pickering.
meals	12pm-2pm (Sat & Sun); 7pm-9pm. Main courses £8.25-£12.95.
closed	Tue-Fri lunch & Mon all day.

Janet Frank
Moors Inn,
Appleton le Moors,
Kirkbymoorside YO62 6TF
tel 01751 417435
web www.moorsinn.co.uk

map: 13 entry: 600

The Blacksmith's Arms
Lastingham

Rows of tankards suspended from low black beams, glowing fires, timeworn saddles, a ghost called Ella and a pint of Daleside Blond. It's a rural dream. You almost slide down to the lovely little village, so deep is it sunk into the valley. The low, rambling, dimly-lit pub has provided shelter and comfort to monks, shepherds and travellers since 1693; now it is visited by gamekeepers, walkers and church enthusiasts; St Mary's (1030) sits next door and, rumour has it, a secret tunnel runs between the two. Once an impoverished priest with 13 children ran both pub and church, to the dismay of his bishop; the current landlord is approved of by all. The little dining rooms are not quite as atmospheric as the bar with its lit range, but this is a great place for a gossip, a pint and hearty traditional food – lamb casserole, Yorkshire hotpot, cod in lager batter.

The Birch Hall
Beck Hole

Two small bars with a shop in between, unaltered for 70 years. Steep wooded hillsides and a stone bridge straddling the rushing river and, inside, a fascinating glimpse of life before World War II. The Big Bar has been beautifully repapered and has a little open fire, dominoes, darts and service from a hatch; the benches and tables come from the station waiting room at Beck Hole. The shop (proclaiming postcards, traditional sweets, ice creams) has its original fittings, as does the Little Bar with its handpumps for three cask ales. The original 19th-century enamel sign hangs above the door. Food is simple and authentic: local pies, specially baked stotties or baps, homemade scones and delicious beer cake. Steep steps take you to the terraced garden that looks over the inn and across the valley. Parking is scarce so show patience and courtesy in this old-fashioned place.

directions	Left off A170 Kirkbymoorside to Pickering road.
meals	12pm-2pm; 7pm-9pm. Main courses £7.95-£12.95; bar meals £4.95-£12.95.
closed	In winter, Mon-Thu 2.30pm-6pm & Tues lunch.

Peter & Hilary Trafford
The Blacksmith's Arms,
Front Street,
Lastingham,
Pickering YO62 6TL
tel   01751 417247

map: 13 entry: 601

directions	9 miles from Whitby towards Pickering.
meals	11am-3pm; 7.30pm-11pm. All day in summer. Sandwiches & pies from £2.
closed	3pm-7.30pm, Mon eve & Tues in winter. Open all day in summer.

Glenys & Neil Crampton
The Birch Hall,
Beck Hole,
Goathland YO22 5LE
tel   01947 896245
web   www.beckhole.info/

map: 13 entry: 602

Wheatsheaf Inn
Egton

Unlike many pubs in this area, the friendly, family-run Wheatsheaf has shirked expansion and held on to its character. It sits so modestly back from the wide main street you could pass it by; you would miss a good deal. The first entrance brings you into the main room with bar, a restful room with dark green walls, low beams and comfy old settles, but the main treat is the locals' bar, dominated by its Yorkshire range. This drinkers' den takes 16 at a push and is hugely popular with walkers and fishermen and dogs. A range of cask ales ensures plenty of chatter, while hearty food is a big draw, perhaps potted shrimps, fish stew, local partridge in season, and sirloin steaks from local farmers. The river Esk at the foot of the steep hill is famous for fly-fishing so there's fishing memorabilia on the walls, and a few angling pictures. Egton is lovely – and worth a linger.

Fox & Hounds
Goldsborough

Don't be fooled by the swirly carpets and artex walls of this small stone inn in the middle of nowhere. The food served is as delicious as you will find anywhere. Jason Davies brings London expertise, Sue Wren adds local charm and together they are producing some of the best pub meals in Yorkshire. Eat cosily by the winter fire or out in the summer garden. Wisely, the daily-changing menu restrains itself to half a dozen starters and mains, one pudding and a cheeseboard. Loving care is applied to spanking fresh fish from the Whitby inshore fleet, game from the North York Moors, local meat and organic vegetables. Star turns include pea and mint risotto; slow-roast belly pork and mash; halibut with fennel, new potatoes and lemon oil. Pudding might be a chocolate terrine; cheese is served with Ampleforth apples and oatcakes. Small being so beautiful, it's wise to book.

directions	Off A171; 6 miles west of Whitby.
meals	12pm-2pm (2.30pm Sun); 6pm-9pm. No food Sun eve or all day Mon. Main courses £8-£16.95; bar meals £8-£12.50.
closed	2.30pm-5.30pm & Mon lunch. Open all day Sat & Sun.

Nigel & Elaine Pulling
Wheatsheaf Inn,
Egton,
Whitby YO21 1TZ
tel 01947 895271

map: 13 entry: 603

directions	Village signed off A174 north of Whitby.
meals	12pm-2pm; 6.30pm-9pm. No food Sun eves. Main courses £9-£16.
closed	2.30pm-6pm, Mon & Tues all day & Sun eve.

Jason Davies & Sue Wren
Fox & Hounds,
Goldsborough,
Whitby YO21 3RX
tel 01947 893372

map: 13 entry: 604

Wales

Ship Inn
Red Wharf Bay

The boatmen still walk across from the estuary with their catch. Inside The Ship, fires roar in several fireplaces and bars share nautical bits and bobs. There are pews and benches and bare stone walls, and huge blackboards where the daily specials change almost by the hour. At night, the menu proffers Welsh seafood based on the best the boats have brought in: grilled turbot served with lemon and seasonal vegetables; dressed crab. But the old Ship is so much more – a family-friendly public house where, for 30 years, regulars and visitors have been enjoying great ales and freshly prepared food, from 'brechdanau' – sandwiches – to 'pwdin'. Fine Welsh cheeses, too. These lovely people are as proud of their hospitality as they are of their language – and the vast sea and sand views from the front terraces are inspiring. Bag a table if you can.

Ye Olde Bulls Head
Beaumaris

This was a favourite haunt of Samuel Johnson and Charles Dickens and now attracts drinkers and foodies like bees to clover. In the rambling, snug-alcoved bar there's draught Bass on offer, while in the contemporary brasserie in the stables you have a choice of ten wines by the glass to match your sarnies or Indian-spiced spatchcock poussin. Spot the ancient weaponry and old ducking stool, which contrasts with the sophisticated remodelling of the restaurant upstairs under hammer-beamed eaves. Here, Welsh dishes are designed around seafood from the Menai Strait, and as much beef, lamb and game as the chefs can find on the island. The results: sticky short rib of Welsh black beef, breast of duck with purple figs, and fillets of local brill, seasoned as required with Anglesey sea salt. Service comes with warmth and charm.

directions	Off B5025, north of Pentraeth.
meals	12pm-2.30pm; 6pm-9pm (5.30-9.30pm Sat; 12-9pm Sun). Main courses £7.95-£17.95; bar meals £4.75-£12.95.
closed	Open all day.

directions	Castle Street is main street in Beaumaris.
meals	12pm-2pm; 6pm-9pm. Main courses £7.95-£14.80.
closed	Open all day.

	Neil Kenneally
	Ship Inn,
	Red Wharf Bay LL75 8RJ
tel	01248 852568
web	www.shipinnredwharfbay.co.uk

	David Robertson
	Ye Olde Bulls Head,
	Castle Street,
	Beaumaris LL58 8AP
tel	01248 810329
web	www.bullsheadinn.co.uk

♿ 🏃 🐕 🍺

♿ 🏃 🐕 🍺

map: 6 entry: 605

map: 6 entry: 606

Carmarthenshire

The Brunant Arms
Caio

Miles from anywhere, the Vale of Cothi is a place of mystery and legend – the final resting place of John Harries, one of Wales's last wizards. In this lovely, secluded, time-warp village, the pub feels warm, cared-for, cosy and at the community's heart. New owners David and Micheal say, modestly, they do "good pub food", but what you get is succulent Welsh black rump steak marinated in red wine and locally sourced rabbit, pheasant and venison in season – enhanced by delightful service and candlelight. They also do proper meals for children, while walkers drop by for ploughman's and baked potato with chilli. In the lounge bar are traditional tables and chairs, a couple of high-backed settles, logs in the grate, books and bagatelle and five ales on tap – it's a snug, carpeted corner away from the public bar. No garden, but a lovely, flower-bedecked wooden patio.

directions	Signed from A482 midway between Lampeter & Llanwrda.
meals	12pm-2pm; 6pm-9pm. Main courses £7.95-£12.25.
closed	3pm-6pm. Open all day Fri-Sun.

David Waterhouse
& Micheal Edwards
The Brunant Arms,
Caio, Llanwrda SA19 8RD
tel   01558 650483

map: 7 entry: 607

Carmarthenshire

Angel Inn
Salem

A warm, candlelit, unselfconsciously styled grotto of a place – run by special people doing their own thing. Former Welsh chef of the year Rod Peterson rules the kitchen, but this isn't one of those restaurants masquerading as a pub – you'd feel equally happy just sinking into the comfy sofa with a malty pint of Rev James. The bar, one of the cosiest in Wales, has a quirky, homely charm – squishy sofas covered in throws, fairylights on corkscrew branches, the odd pot plant or Art Deco mirror – while the dining room is a revelation, its dark glossy floors broken up by lovely antique dressers and carved gothic arches. Staff are smart and attentive and the food divine; in the bar, find quiche of duck and lovage with apricot chutney; in the restaurant, braised shoulder of Welsh lamb with pulse ragout and Paloise sauce. No designer vegetables here: portions are hearty and satisfying. Enchanting in every way.

directions	Off the A40 towards Talley, 3 miles north of Llandeilo.
meals	12.15pm-2pm; 7pm-9pm. Restaurant evenings only. Main courses £9.95-£18.50; bar meals £3.95-£12.95.
closed	Tues lunch, Mon & Sun all day & 2 weeks early Jan.

Liz Smith
Angel Inn,
Salem,
Llandeilo SA19 7LY
tel   01558 823394

map: 7 entry: 608

Carmarthenshire

Y Polyn
Nantgaredig

Mark and Susan Manson, together with Simon and Maryann Wright, have stepped happily into this pub that sits by a fork in the roads, one leading to Aberglasney, the other to the National Botanic Garden of Wales. They know their onions – Susan was head chef at the Worshipful Company of Innholders, Maryann chef-patron at the Four Seasons in Nantgaredig – and have smartened up the interior with bold colours, herringbone matting, local art, fresh flowers and candles. A leather sofa and armchairs by the fire encourage the easy feel, while the restaurant has a happy mish-mash of tables and chairs. The short menu is pleasingly simple: fresh ingredients well put together and presented. Start with chicken liver parfait with rhubarb chutney, move onto roast rump of Gower saltmarsh lamb with onion, garlic and thyme purée, finish with nectarine and frangipane tart. The emphasis is on food, but you are equally welcome to pop in for a drink.

directions	Off junction of B4300 & B4310 between A48 & A40 east of Carmarthen.
meals	12pm-2pm; 7pm-9pm. Main courses £14.50-£18.50.
closed	4pm-7pm, Sat lunch, Sun eve & Mon all day.

Mark & Susan Manson,
Simon & Maryann Wright
Y Polyn,
Nantgaredig, Carmarthen SA32
tel   01267 290000
web   www.ypolyn.com

map: 6 entry: 609

Carmarthenshire

New Three Mariners
Laugharne

In one of Wales's most romantic, beautiful, weatherworn towns (Dylan Thomas haunt and inspiration behind Llareggub in *Under Milk Wood*) is one of Wales's finest community pubs. In the largest part of the old boozer, dark panelling has been painted white while further spaces are blinkingly bright as coastal light pours through big old windows onto stylishly low tables, slate floors and wicker loungers. Pot plants add to the greenhouse feel and there are boaty pictures on the walls. If all this sounds too New England to be true, then turn right into the cosy pubby part for dartboard, jukebox, (stylish) leather sofas, woodburning stove and weathered locals. Food is pub traditional – local faggots, local fish and chips, paninis for trendies.

directions	Laugharne is on A4066, south of A40 at St Clears.
meals	12pm-3pm; 5pm-9pm; 12pm-9pm summer. No food Sun & Mon in winter. Main courses £5.50-£9.95; bar meals £3.95-£4.50.
closed	Open all day.

Richard Pearce
New Three Mariners,
Victoria Street,
Laugharne SA33 4SE
tel   01994 427426
web   www.newthreemariners.co.uk

map: 6 entry: 610

Ceredigion — Pub with rooms

Harbourmaster Hotel
Aberaeron

The old whalers' inn has become decidedly chic with an inspirational restaurant and bar. Inside is a space that's cosy but cool: soft shades, a curving bar, blocked-oak tables, an open fire. In the celebrated bistro, daily menus are studded with the best local produce: Carlingford oysters, Loughor mussels, cheeses from Llandysul. And dishes delight: skate wing poached with lime and coriander, chargrilled Welsh Black beef with square-cut chips, iced chocolate mocca parfait. Lobster boats at lunch, twinkling harbour lights at dinner, real ale, well-chosen wines, dazzling service. The Ceredigion Coastal Path runs past the hotel, the beaches of New Quay lie just five miles south, and the bedrooms – cosy, characterful, contemporary – are a pleasure to return to. The Heulyns' dedication to all that is best about Wales shines forth.

directions	Between Aberystwyth & Cardigan off A487.
meals	12pm-2pm; 6pm-9pm. No food Sun eve. Main courses £10.50-£18.50; bar food £4-£11.50; set lunch & Sunday lunch, £14.50 & £16.50.
rooms	9: 7 doubles, 2 singles £55-£140.
closed	Mon lunch. Open all day.

See pp 30–57 for full list of pubs with rooms

Glyn & Menna Heulyn
Harbourmaster Hotel,
Pen Cei,
Aberaeron SA46 0BA
tel   01545 570755
web   www.harbour-master.com

map: 6 entry: 611

Conwy

The Lord Newborough
Dolgarrog

On the quiet side of the valley, yards from the river, this wayside inn was a shooting lodge. Step in to dark purple and claret hues, a multitude of candles and a whiff of incense – an exotic, almost louche mood. It's the sort of place where people drink, gather and set the world to rights… before settling down to the serious business of food. James's unshowy modern British dishes employ the very best of local or organic: seafood from the north Wales coast, pork from Rhug farm, herbs from the woods. Start with seared wood pigeon salad, follow with roasted sea bass with lemon and garlic, finish with lemon posset. There's service to match the food, some rare white Rhones hide among the more usual new world wines, Great Orme Brewery ales flow from the barrel in summer, and in winter there's a stunning array of bottled British and continental. The young owners have big plans for The Lord Newborough – but it's pretty good now.

directions	On B5106 between Conwy & Llanrwst.
meals	12pm-3pm; 6pm-9pm. Main courses £8.95- £15.95.
closed	3pm-6pm & Mon all day. Lunch & Tues all day Nov-Feb.

James & Carlin Sampson-Brunt
The Lord Newborough,
Dolgarrog,
Nant Conwy LL32 8JX
tel   01492 660549
web   www.thelordnewborough.co.uk

map: 7 entry: 612

The Queen's Head

Llandudno Junction

The old wheelwright's cottage has gone up in the world. It now has low beams, polished tables, walls strewn with old maps and a roaring fire in the bar. The food is good, the portions generous and you can see the cooks at work through the open hatch. This is home-cooked pub food with a modern twist that in summer might well include fresh Conwy crab and Great Orme lobster. Starters of foie gras and black pudding or squash and chestnut risotto are served by friendly, smartly dressed staff. Follow with Jamaican Jerk Chicken or sautéed lambs liver with smoked bacon; finish with bara brith and butter pudding. Robert and Sally Cureton have been here for years, nurturing a country local that puts those of Llandudno to shame. Complete the treat by booking a night in the sweet parish storehouse across the road, recently converted into a charming self-catering cottage for two.

Pen-y-Bryn

Colwyn Bay

Do not be put off by the exterior. Inside shines like a Hollywood film set: oak floors and bookcases, open fires and polished furniture – the make-believe world of Brunning & Price. No wonder the locals have taken to Pen-y-Bryn like ducks to water. Staff are young, well-informed and never too busy to share their knowledge of the food and its provenance. Menus are enticing and generously priced. Great Orme crab cakes are served with pickled fennel and carrot; warming leek and potato soup comes with crusty bread. Pork and lamb is local, cheeses fly the Principality's flag and luscious mussels come from down the coast. You're high up on Colwyn Heights here but a few glasses of Orme Brewery's Three Feathers or Puritan Porter will soon warm your toes. Sturdy wooden furniture in the garden fits in well with the neighbourhood's residential air… but inside is best.

directions	From A55; A470; right at 3rd r'bout for Penrhyn Bay; 2nd right to Glanwydden after 1.5 miles.
meals	12-2pm; 6-9pm; 12-9pm Sun. Main courses £8.50-£16.50; Sunday roast £9.25.
rooms	Cottage for 2, £100-£125.
closed	3pm-6pm. Open all day Sun.

See pp 30-57 for full list of pubs with rooms

directions	Follow B5113 south west of Colwyn Bay for 1 mile.
meals	12pm-9.30pm (9pm Sun). Main courses £7.45-£14.75; bar meals £4.25-£8.95.
closed	Open all day.

Robert & Sally Cureton
The Queen's Head,
Glanwydden,
Llandudno Junction LL31 9JP

tel   01492 546570
web   www.queensheadglanwydden.co.uk

map: 7 entry: 613

Graham Arathoon
Pen-y-Bryn,
Pen-y-Bryn Rd, Upper Colwyn Bay,
Colwyn Bay LL29 6DD

tel   01492 533360
web   www.penybryn-colwynbay.co.uk

map: 7 entry: 614

Conwy — Pub with rooms

Denbighshire

The Kinmel Arms
St George

In St George – just a handful of cottages – a sparkling pub-restaurant with rooms. Enter a light, open-plan space of cool, neutral colours, hard wood floors and a central bar, then a conservatory restaurant with marble-topped tables and Tim's photographs of glorious North Wales. Tim and Lynn take pride in what goes on the plate – Conwy Bay seafood and top quality local meats. Weekly changing guest ales and wines by the glass are an added bonus when dining on wild mushroom tart with Welsh blue cheese and guinea fowl supreme. You're a hop from Snowdonia and that stunning coast – walks start from the door – so treat yourself to one of the four dreamy suites, each with French windows to a decked seating area and a fabulous bathroom with vast towels. *No children or dogs overnight.*

directions	A55 for Conwy. After Bodelwyddan exit, take next exit, for St George. Left at junc 24a.; up for 200yds.
meals	12pm-2pm (3pm Sun); 7pm-9.30pm (6.30pm Fri & Sat). Main courses £9.95-£19.95.
rooms	4 suites £135-£175.
closed	3pm-6.30pm (6pm Fri & Sat), Sun from 5pm & Mon all day (except bank hols).

See pp 30-57 for full list of pubs with rooms

Tim Watson & Lynn Cunnah-Watson
The Kinmel Arms,
The Village, St George,
Abergele LL22 9BP

tel	01745 832207
web	www.thekinmelarms.co.uk

map: 7 entry: 615

Pant-yr-Ochain
Gresford

A long drive snakes through landscaped parkland to this magnificent old country house sheltered by trees. It's multi-gabled with colourwashed walls pierced both by tiny, stone-mullioned and orangery-style windows. To one side a huge conservatory opens up views across terraces to the estate lake; within, a jigsaw of richly panelled rooms and drinking areas lures those who come to dine and those in search of the hop. Intimate corners, they're here, as are huge refectory tables, comfy alcoves and private snugs, with open fires, quarry tiles and bare boards below an eccentric ceiling-line. Everywhere, a cornucopia of bric-a-brac: penny slots and cases of clay pipes, bills and flyers, caricatures and prints. It sounds OTT but it fits comfortably here, and the reliable Brunning & Price menus of home-cooked, locally sourced food are available. Beer aficionados revel in nine real ales.

directions	Gresford signed off A483 Wrexham bypass.
meals	12pm-9.30pm (9pm Sun). Main courses £8.25-£14.95.
closed	Open all day.

Lindsey Douglas
Pant-yr-Ochain,
Old Wrexham Road, Gresford,
Wrexham LL12 8TY

tel	01978 853525
web	www.pantyrochain-gresford.co.uk

map: 7 entry: 616

The Boat
Erbistock

An old riverside favourite that draws crowds in summer. Spruced up but not without charm, this 17th-century pub has open fires, stone floors, heavy oak beams and squishy sofas. You eat in a conservatory extension of marble-topped tables and metal-and-wicker chairs, before the fast-flowing Dee and a bank lined with picnic benches. The setting is unquestionably special. Open and closed sandwiches and cod and chips in beer batter by day yield to sautéed pigeon breast on mixed leaves with berry and balsamic glaze in the evening, and rump of lamb with cream and cognac sauce ; the kitchen employs "the best of everything Welsh". Wine choices, though limited, are global; there is a regularly changing choice of real ales from Black Sheep, Weetwood and Jennings. Cheery, youthful staff whizz around at quite a pace.

directions	A483 exit LLangollen/Whitchurch; left at slip road, right onto A539 to Whitchurch; 2 miles to Erbistock; right to pub.
meals	12pm-2.30; 6.30-9pm. Sun, 12pm-9pm summer, 12pm-5pm winter. Main courses £10.95-£19.95; bar meals £4.95-£9.95.
closed	Open all day.

Paul Rothery
The Boat,
Erbistock,
Wrexham LL13 0DL
tel   01978 780666
web   www.theboatinn.co.uk

map: 7 entry: 617

The Corn Mill
Llangollen

The 18th century has been left far behind in this renovated corn mill beside the swiftly flowing Dee. Not only is the interior light, airy and well-designed but the busy menu is laced with contemporary ingredients and ideas. There are also gorgeous views onto the river whether you're quaffing your Boddingtons in the fabulous bar, or settling down to eat in one of the comfortable upper-floor dining areas. The decked veranda-cum-walkway is stunning, built out over the cascading rapids with a gangway overhanging one end beyond the revolving water wheel. Watch dippers and wagtails as you tuck into bacon, brie and tomato toasted ciabatta, fish stew, lamb hotpot with pickled red cabbage, and scrumptious bread and butter pudding. The Brunning & Price formula is known for its 'something-for-everyone' appeal, and the setting is supreme.

directions	Off Castle Street, (A539) just south of the river bridge.
meals	12pm-9.30pm (9pm Sun). Main courses £6-£15; bar meals £5-£15.
closed	Open all day.

Andrew Barker
The Corn Mill,
Dee Lane,
Llangollen LL20 8PN
tel   01978 869555
web   www.cornmill-llangollen.co.uk

map: 7 entry: 618

Denbighshire

White Horse Inn
Hendrerwydd

An old drover's inn with bags of character. There's a tremendous little Poacher's Bar, all quarry-tiled floors, huntin' shootin' and fishin' ephemera, open fire, timeworn benches and chairs and a hatch dispensing three real ales and grand bar meals to ramblers and locals. In contrast: a classy dining room, created by the absorption of next door's cottages into the 400-year-old building, and a new bistro/family room. There's a chic feel to the web of polished, floorboarded rooms, ready-set for dining, the tables and reclaimed chairs contrasting with striking sculptures, textile prints, frescoes and fresh cream-washed and brick walls. Diners lounge in comfy sofas at the bar-side fireplace, and consider a choice of game and venison pâté, roast shoulder of local lamb, and wonderful Welsh cheeses. The setting is sublime, the pub huddled beneath the Clwydian Mountains, and you can savour stunning views from the newly landscaped garden.

directions	3 miles north of Ruthin just off B5429 between Llandyrnog & Llanbedr-Dyffryn-Clwyd.
meals	12pm-2.30pm; 6pm-9.15pm. Main courses £9.95-£19; bar meals £5.50-£8.95.
closed	3.30pm-6pm, Sun eve & Mon all day. Open all day Sat.

	Ruth & Vit Vintr
	White Horse Inn,
	Hendrerwydd,
	Denbigh LL16 4LL
tel	01824 790218
web	www.white-horse-inn.co.uk

map: 7 entry: 619

Flintshire

Stables Bar
Northop

In a vast landscaped parkland – a grand space for weddings – is the former Bishop's Palace, Soughton Hall. The old stable, itself listed, is somewhat smaller. Inside – a dazzling transformation: the cobbled floors have been varnished and the blacksmith's bellows recycled (now a table among old pews, chairs and benches). Metal bar stools – once seed-drill seats – front a bar dispensing beers from local breweries, huge wrought-iron light-holders hang from rough-hewn beams over tables, and a rear room still guards its saddles and tack. Upstairs, through the impressive on-site wine shop, is a relaxing restaurant in a huge-raftered roof, all colourwash and candlelight. Treat yourself to posh pub grub, or push out the boat and order roast brace of quail from a long menu. Outside, estate cattle munch contentedly as punters relax with a drink in the peaceful beer garden.

directions	Follow Northop sign from A55; A5119 through village; brown signs for Soughton Hall.
meals	12pm-9.30pm. (1pm-3pm; 7pm-9.30pm Sun). Main courses £12.95-£20.95; bar meals £5.95-£11.95.
closed	Open all day.

	John & Rosemary Rodenhurst
	Stables Bar,
	Soughton Hall, Northop,
	Mold CH7 6AB
tel	01352 840577
web	www.soughtonhall.co.uk

map: 7 entry: 620

Glamorgan

Plough & Harrow
Monknash

Originally part of a monastic grange, today's Plough & Harrow is hugely convivial. Ancient, low white walls draw you to the front door, there are low ceilings and low lights in the rooms to either side, each with a big fireplace filled with churchy candles or crackling winter logs, and the bar heaves with an impressive array of handpumps – up to 11 ales are served. Happy yellow walls, original floors, a well-loved assortment of furniture – and a trombone used to play 'Happy Birthday' the other day. Traditionalists will appreciate gammon and chips on the lunch menu; for the more adventurous there are dishes such as summer crab salad and more restauranty but fantastic value food in the evenings (moules marinière, a roasted duck breast on potato fritters). A brilliant atmosphere, a great find, the kind of pub you wish was your local – and it is as welcoming to single drinkers as it is to groups.

directions	Village signed off B4265, between St Brides Major & Llantwit Major, 6 miles SW of Cowbridge.
meals	12pm-2.30pm; 6pm-9pm. No food Sun eve. Main courses £7.95-£14.95; bar meals £3.50-£7.95.
closed	Open all day.

David & Debbie Woodman
Plough & Harrow,
Monknash,
Cowbridge CF71 7QQ
tel   01656 890209
web   www.theploughmonknash.com

map: 2 entry: 621

Glamorgan

The Blue Anchor
East Aberthaw

Inglenooks and open log fires, stories of smugglers and derring-do – it's rich in atmosphere. Inside is a warm warren of little rooms and doorways less than five feet high. The Colemans have cheerfully nurtured this 700-year-old place for 65 years and restored the pub to its former glory following a fire in 2004. Dine in winter on pheasant from their local shoot, in summer on sewin from Swansea Bay and salads from the vegetable garden. You can pop in for a roast ham baguette and a pint of well-kept Wye Valley – or dip into the chef's selection of regional cheeses. Under the eaves of a classic thatched roof, the restaurant delivers spinach and cream cheese mousse, roast monkfish with sauce vièrge and crispy seaweed, shank of lamb with roasted shallot sauce, Sunday roasts (do book). It's pubby, good looking and wonderful at doing what it knows best.

directions	2 miles west of Cardiff Airport just off B4265.
meals	12pm-2pm (12.30pm-2.30pm Sun); 6pm-9.30pm (7pm-9.30pm Sat, 6pm-9pm Sun). Main courses £9.75-£15; bar meals £4.75-£8.95.
closed	Open all day.

Jeremy Coleman
The Blue Anchor,
East Aberthaw CF62 3DD
tel   01446 750329
web   www.blueanchoraberthaw.com

map: 2 entry: 622

Glamorgan

Pen-y-Cae Inn
Pen-y-Cae

Everything about the Pen y Cae is pristine, from the multi-levelled garden at the back (the swings discreetly out of view) to the claret leather sofas and woodburner of the bar. They've even created a new upper floor, reached by a wooden staircase, supported by chunky beams. It's an exceptionally lovely interior, the best of old and new, and you feast under rafters. French windows open to the Brecon Beacons in summer, informed staff are delightful and there's food to match, from classic pub grub at lunch to liver with crispy pancetta on creamed potatoes at dinner. And cod fillet on a puy lentil and herb mash, rib-eye steaks with Lyonnaise potatoes (fabulous), and Welsh crumpety laverbread pikelets with leeks, cockles, Carmarthen ham and white wine sauce. Wash it all down with a bottled beer from Tomos Watkin, Wales's fastest growing brewery, and trundle off home – charmed, well-fed and happy.

directions	On A4067 north of Abercraf, midway between Brecon & Swansea.
meals	12pm-2.30; 6.30-9.30. Main courses £6.95-£16.95; bar meals £4.50-£5.95; Sunday roast £8.95.
closed	3pm-6pm, Sun eve & Mon all day. Open all day Sat.

	Anthony Christopher
	Pen-y-Cae Inn,
	Brecon Road, Pen-y-Cae,
	Swansea SA9 1FA
tel	01639 730100
web	www.penycaeinn.com

map: 7 entry: 623

Gwynedd

Penhelig Arms
Aberdyfi

The Dyfi estuary can inspire awe in the fiercest storm or lie like a millpond under the full moon. It's a place to share with someone special, such is the hospitality shown by the Hughes family and their staff. In front is the tiniest harbour, while along the quay come the fishermen, butchers, bakers and smallholders who deliver their daily produce to the kitchen. The seemingly inexhaustible menus are up-dated at every session to reflect what's wettest and freshest that day. At white-clothed tables sample Mediterranean fish soup, plaice with a buttery prawn velouté sauce, chargrilled leg of Welsh lamb steak with roast vegetables, panna cotta with fresh fruit. Soup and sandwiches are the staples of the pub bar, smartly cosy with a central log fire; on sunnier days they'll serve you at your chosen spot astride the harbour wall. Robert is in charge "of the ales and wines only" but all are well chosen and in the right spirit.

directions	From Dolgellau, A470 for Porthmadog; A493 to Aberdyfi.
meals	12pm-2pm; 7pm-9pm (bar meals from 6pm). Main courses £8.95-£13.95; set dinner £28; bar snacks from £3.50; Sunday lunch £17 (restaurant only).
closed	3pm-5.30pm (5pm Sat & Sun).

	Robert & Sally Hughes
	Penhelig Arms,
	Aberdyfi LL35 0LT
tel	01654 767215
web	www.penheligarms.com

map: 6 entry: 624

Gwynedd

Bryn Tyrch
Capel Curig

Bang in the heart of Snowdonia National Park, a simple roadside hostelry tailored for walkers and climbers. Its interior is well-worn, its style laid-back and in winter there's a great big fire. The lunchtime menu strays no further than sandwiches (ham and local Welsh cheese), jacket potatoes with sausage and onion, and Welsh rarebit made with Caerphilly and local ale. Evening blackboards suggest a breezy and generous approach to vegetarian and vegan dishes (wild mushroom lasagne) alongside Hungarian goulash and locally-made sausages with cheese and chive mash. Puddings will keep you going all day. Picture windows run the length of the main bar with strategically placed tables making the most of the view, there are comfy sofas to sink into by the fire, and a pool table in the bare-bones hikers' bar. Friendly staff will advise you on the best hikes and climbs.

directions	On A5, 5 miles west of Betws-y-Coed.
meals	12pm-2pm; 6pm-9pm. Main courses £7.95-£14.95.
closed	Mon-Thurs lunch Nov-Mar. Open all day Fri-Sun.

Rachel Roberts
Bryn Tyrch,
Capel Curig,
Betws-y-Coed LL24 0EL

tel	01690 720223
web	www.bryntyrch-hotel.co.uk

map: 7 entry: 625

Monmouthshire

The Bell at Skenfrith
Skenfrith

Indulge the senses at this classy 17th-century coaching inn in a lovely village on the banks of the Monnow. Inside is immaculate but informal, and the place is run with warmth — Janet treats young staff like members of the family. Expect the best of everything: proper coffee, mostly organic food and superb wine and cognacs — there's even an organic menu for children (planet spaghetti and holy macaroni etc). Bedrooms are country smart with Farrow & Ball colours and beds dressed in cotton piqué and Welsh wool; plus homemade biscuits, Cath Collins toiletries and a hi-tech console by the bed so you can listen to music in your bath. Descend for Usk Valley lamb and iced mango parfait in the restaurant overlooking the terrace, toast the occasion with local cider or champagne, then flop into a sofa by the fire.

directions	From Monmouth B4233 to Rockfield; B4347 for 5 miles; right on B4521 for Ross. 1 mile on right.
meals	12-2.30pm; 7-9.30pm (9pm Sun). Main courses £14-£18.50.
rooms	8: 5 doubles, 3 suites £100-£180. Singles £70-£110 (not weekends).
closed	Open all day. Closed Mon Nov-Mar.

See pp 30-57 for full list of pubs with rooms

William & Janet Hutchings
The Bell at Skenfrith,
Skenfrith NP7 8UH

tel	01600 750235
web	www.skenfrith.co.uk

map: 7 entry: 626

Llanthony Priory
Llanthony

Reached by a winding country road is this
a secret cluster of buildings; once upon a
time only walkers and pony-trekkers
knew Llanthony was here. What was the
abbot's cellar is now an ivy-tumbled
house with tower cradled by lush and
vertiginous hills. No mobile reception,
no cars, just beauty and birdsong. The
pub is the cellar, a white vaulted room
with an atmospheric hotchpotch of
wooden tables and high-backed pews; in
summer people wander through the
ruins, then rest, pint of Felinfoel in hand,
on the grass. The restaurant has an old
range, grandfather clock and carved
antique sideboard; its leaded windows
overlook the gracious ruins. Ian the
barman is friendly and knowledgeable, so
are the locals. Food is simple: homemade
beefburgers, spicy lamb casserole, proper
espresso, no corners cut. It is romantic,
otherworldly, special.

Hunter's Moon Inn
Llangattock Lingoed

Haydn Jones runs this deep-country inn
just off Offa's Dyke with enthusiasm and
passion. The original building, with its
low ceilings and 1217-flagged floors, was
constructed by stonemasons establishing
a place to stay before building the
neighbouring church. Book ahead; the
'table for the evening' policy ensures
much care is taken with the locally-
sourced food. Specials include 28-day
aged beef, shank of lamb, pork cooked in
Old Rosie cider and pheasant wrapped in
smoked bacon, and puddings are
homemade. Haydn looks after the wet
side of things; the local and guest ales are
well-kept, the wine list well chosen,
there's Leffe on draught and a raft of
foreign bottled beers. In summer you sit
out - under parasols overlooking the
churchyard or in the beer garden. There's
a drying room for walkers, too.

directions	Village signed off A465 north of Abergavenny & south of B4350 at Hay-on-Wye.
meals	12pm-3pm; 7pm-9pm. Main courses £6..95-£10 (dinner); £3-£6.50 (lunch).
closed	Mon (except bank hols), Tues-Fri lunch, Sun eve Nov-Feb. Open all day Sat & Jul-Aug in winter.

directions	A465 Abergavenny-Hereford; for Skenfrith on B4521 thro' Llanvetherine. Signed left to Llangattock Lingoed.
meals	12pm-2.30pm; 6.30pm-9pm in summer; 12pm-3pm Sun; 7pm-9pm Wed-Sat in winter. Main courses £10-£16.
closed	Mon-Fri lunch in winter Open all day in summer (occ. closed 4pm-6pm).

Geoff Neil
Llanthony Priory,
Llanthony,
Abergavenny NP7 7NN

| tel | 01873 890487 |
| web | www.llanthonyprioryhotel.co.uk |

Haydn Jones
Hunter's Moon Inn,
Llangattock Lingoed,
Abergavenny NP7 8RR

| tel | 01873 821499 |
| web | www.hunters-moon-inn.co.uk |

The Hardwick
Hardwick

After working in Marco Pierre White's legendary kitchens in the 1980s, Stephen Terry must be delighted to be running his own show. In the shadows of the Black Mountains, the pub's proximity to the Walnut Tree – where Stephen also worked – has helped put this modest roadside inn on the gastropub map. And the stripped-back-to-basics interior is a modest background for some astonishingly good food. While some of the ingredients are imported from Italy, most originate from closer to home, and that includes the meat, the fish and the vast range of Welsh beers on draught and in bottle. The lengthy menu incorporates the best-ever bar 'snacks' – such as grilled sandwiches with salad and triple-cooked chips – and comforting classics like Longhorn beef pie with oxtail, kidney and ale. Walk off your indulgence among some of the most stunning landscapes of Wales. Worth a detour.

directions	Two miles south-east from Abergavenny via A40 & B4598. Call for directions first.
meals	12pm-3pm; 6pm-10pm. Main courses £9.50-£16.50; Sunday lunch £15.50-£18.50; bar meals from £4.95.
closed	3pm-6pm, Sun eve & Mon all day.

Stephen Terry
The Hardwick,
Raglan Road,
Hardwick,
Abergavenny NP7 9AA
tel   01873 854220

Clytha Arms
Clytha

The inn stands on the old coaching route into border country, in gorgeous surroundings. You may sit outside in fine weather and enjoy cockles, crab sandwiches, tapas dishes or a ploughman's that promises three local cheeses. Inside, two bars: one high-ceilinged, with a button-back sofa, the other more rustic, with stripped floors and bar games; both have cheery fires. The restaurant is smart with marbled walls and white linen tablecloths. In the kitchen is Andrew Canning, the local genius who rustles up monkfish with crab and laverbread, and rack of lamb with garlic mash and rosemary sauce. The monthly set menu will tempt you with steak and oyster pudding, and iced tequila and citrus soufflé. Wines, local beers and Herefordshire ciders are excellent, and there's homemade perry for the bibulously curious.

directions	6 miles east of Abergavenny off old Abergavenny to Raglan road.
meals	12.30pm-2.15pm (2.30pm Sun); 7pm-9.30pm (9pm Mon). No food Sun eve. Main courses £11.95-£20; bar meals £5.25-£10.
closed	3pm-6pm & Mon lunch. Open all day Fri-Sun.

Andrew & Sarah Canning
Clytha Arms,
Clytha,
Abergavenny NP7 9BW
tel   01873 840206
web   www.clytha-arms.com

Beaufort Arms
Raglan

There's no missing this gracious old coaching inn. Inside, a big welcoming entrance hall, immaculate leather and wicker chairs, open fires, slate floors and cosy corners; outside, a sun-trap terrace. The place is big enough to get lost in, has a brilliant buzz, just about everybody comes here and Eliot and Jana head a dedicated team. The good-looking and contemporary restaurant has a menu to match, and the menu frequently changes. There are Beaufort beef burgers with chargrilled veg, minted pea and asparagus risotto, creamy fish pie. Wines range from classic to modern, real ales include a changing guest. Bedrooms – the best in the main house – are as pleasing as all the rest: fresh, spotless and new. Try to get one with a church view and you'll feel like the cat who got the cream.

directions	Raglan is 0.5 miles from A449/A40 junction between Monmouth & Abergavenny.
meals	12pm-5pm; 6pm-9pm (9.30 Fri & Sat; 8.30pm Sun). Main courses £8.95-£16; bar meals £4.50-£10.95.
rooms	15: 7 doubles, 7 twins, 1 single £55-£95.
closed	Open all day.

See pp 30-57 for full list of pubs with rooms

Eliot & Jana Lewis
Beaufort Arms,
High Street, Raglan,
Usk NP15 2DY

| tel | 01291 690412 |
| web | www.beaufortraglan.co.uk |

map: 7 entry: 631

Raglan Arms
Llandenny

Two reasons to stop here – the castle and the pub. The Raglan Arms effortlessly combines its function of village local and excellent place to eat. In a bright, spacious bar with slate underfoot, a sense of anticipation mounts as you peruse the menu from leather sofas arranged around a log fire. These new Anglo-French co-owners prepare fairly priced dishes showcasing produce from the area, served by helpful Scandinavian staff. Tuck into Cornish herring with good homemade bread, local black pudding, subtly flavoured imam bayaldi with crème fraîche – or a superior open sandwich of slow-roasted shoulder of Gloucester Old Spot with rocket salad and local apple sauce. To finish: banoffi tart, Bailey's creme brulée and a bravura cheese selection from McBlain's of Usk. There's a conservatory restaurant, too, but only 12 tables in all – do book. Butty Bach is the only real ale; if this doesn't appeal, console yourself with the well-chosen modern wine list. Worth the small detour to get here.

directions	In the centre of Llandenny.
meals	12pm-3pm; 7pm-10pm. Main courses £6.50-£10 (lunch); £10-£16 (dinner).
closed	3pm-6pm, Sun eve & Mon all day(except bank hols).

Giles Cunliffe & Sebastien Jalle
Raglan Arms,
Llandenny,
Usk NP15 1DL

| tel | 01291 690800 |
| web | www.raglanarms.com |

map: 7 entry: 632

Monmouthshire   Pub with rooms

Black Bear
Bettws Newydd

No hint of gastropubbery here! Beyond the glowing fire is a dining room whose dark pink walls are a shrine to British horse racing. At the lower end are more dining tables in what looks like a 1930s tea room… but the Black Bear dates from the 16th-century and the lovely old character remains. Stephen Molyneux uses produce in season, Usk salmon, pheasant, venison and duck. And you may taste turbot with avocado, wine and cream, beef fillet with stilton, Welsh rack of lamb, and – heaven on a plate – Baileys Irish Cream cheesecake. "Whatever comes out of the kitchen" will be unusual, unpredictable and rather good. Recover from your over-indulgence in one the two basic but comfortable bedrooms in the converted stables. In deepest Monmouthshire, the Black Bear is worth negotiating the several country lanes it takes to get here.

directions	On B4595 2 miles north of Usk.
meals	12pm-2pm; 6pm-9.30pm (from 7pm Sun). Main courses £13.50-£16; bar meals £6-£8.50.
rooms	2 twins/doubles £60-£75. Singles £30-£35.
closed	2pm-6pm (7pm Sun) & Mon lunch.

See pp 30–57 for full list of pubs with rooms

	Stephen Molyneux Black Bear, Bettws Newydd, Usk NP15 1JN
tel	01873 880701

map: 7 entry: 633

Monmouthshire

The Greyhound Inn
Usk

Nick is enthusiastically committed to running this unpretentious country inn; it takes a little finding on the back roads out of Usk but anyone local will point you in the right direction. Outside, the 17th-century Welsh longhouse brims with summer flower baskets. Inside, a warren of eating areas and bars cosy with open fires, hanging hops and a contented hubbub; there are darts and dominoes in one room, armchairs in another, and a long menu. Food is pub-style, nothing fancy; venison and ale pie, homemade soups and apple pie and cream are just the sort of thing to set you up for a windswept day on the Brecon Beacons. Choose from several real ales, classic bottled ciders and wines of the month at competitive prices. Staff couldn't be friendlier, and families and dogs are welcomed.

directions	From Usk centre, signs to Llantrissant for 2.5 miles.
meals	12pm-2.15pm; 6pm-10pm (10.30pm Fri & Sat). No food Sun eve. Main courses £7.50-£14.50.
closed	Open all day. Closed 4pm-7pm Sun.

	Nick Davies The Greyhound Inn, Llantrissant, Usk NP15 1LE
tel	01291 672505
web	www.greyhound-inn.com

map: 7 entry: 634

Monmouthshire   Pub with rooms

The Newbridge Inn
Usk

As darkness falls, the old stone bridge is floodlit, its arches reflected in the waters of the Usk. The setting is seductive, the garden runs down to the river and the trellises are decked with flowers. This is what a gastropub should be: warm, inviting and beautifully turned out. In several rooms on several levels, willow twigs emerge from aluminium buckets, church candles squat in cast-iron candelabras, and the interior reveals the naked beauty of floorboards and beams. You don't have to eat here, but it's a treat if you do and set lunch is a steal. Chatty, classically-trained chef Iain sources ingredients carefully – like the Cornish-landed fish and the Gloucestershire Old Spot pork from Abergavenny. If you can stay over, do. Comfortable bedrooms are purpose-built, just across the car park and rustically styled with solid oak furniture and lovely bathrooms. Go up a level for a four-poster and a view.

directions	From Usk A449 towards Caerleon; 2 miles after Llangibby, left for Tredunnock; thro' village, down hill; inn beside river.
meals	12pm-2.30pm; 6.30pm-9.30pm. Main courses £12-£18; set lunch, 2 courses, £10.
rooms	6: 4 doubles, 2 twins/doubles £95-£120. Singles from £80.
closed	Open all day.

Iain Sampson
The Newbridge Inn,
Tredunnock,
Usk NP15 1LY
tel   01633 451000
web   www.thenewbridge.co.uk

map: 2 entry: 635

Pembrokeshire   Pub with rooms

The Old Point House Inn
Angle

Lonely, windswept, so close to the sea they're cut off at spring tide. Weary fishermen have beaten a path to the old inn's door for centuries; part-built with shipwreck timbers, it started life as a bakehouse for ships' biscuits. The tiny bar, its bare walls papered with old navigation charts, is utterly authentic, the restaurant is cosy by night, and in fine weather you may sit out and devour vast prawn sandwiches. Doug, ex-fisherman, welcomes everyone, from weathered regulars meeting over pints of Felinfoel to families in for Sunday lunch. Son Lee is a good cook and the specials board is full of fish: haddock with Welsh cheeses, halibut with lemon butter, red snapper with chilli pepper sauce, Milford cod fishcakes with piles of chips. No need to rush home. Three simple white and blue bedrooms await upstairs; ask for the quiet twin with the stunning bay view.

directions	From Pembroke follow signs for Angle. There, from Lifeboat Trust, cross beach to pub.
meals	12pm-2.30pm; 6pm-9pm. Main courses £7.95-£23; bar meals from £3.50.
rooms	3 twins/doubles £60. Singles £30.
closed	3pm-6pm & Tues all day Nov-Mar.

Doug, Carol & Lee Smith
The Old Point House Inn,
Angle,
Pembroke SA71 5AS
tel   01646 641205

map: 6 entry: 636

Cresselly Arms
Cresswell Quay

The day we called, trainer Peter Bowen's Cresswell Quay had just won its fourth race of the season and there was an air of euphoria. We were treated to beer that was far better than we had any right to ask – and the horse was paying! The walls of this old pub are hung with wisteria; pick an outside table and gaze onto the estuary and the tranquil woods. Inside, ale is poured from a jug; there's no truck with modern innovation here. Well-kept pints are downed by all and sundry and you are surrounded by memorabilia of a past age: shiny brown paintwork, red-and-black tiling, a coal-fired Aga in the parlour. And, of course, pictures ancient and new of famous nags. The local talk (and occasionally TV) will be of horses and history. When the tide is up, you can get here by boat... and you won't be late for lunch, there isn't any. Take home instead a jar of the famous lemon curd. Very authentic.

directions	Off A4075 between A40 & A477.
meals	No food served.
closed	2.30pm–6pm.

Maurice & Janet Cole
Cresselly Arms,
Cresswell Quay,
Tenby SA68 0TE
tel 01646 651210

map: 6 entry: 637

The George's
Haverfordwest

Nothing in Pembrokeshire can hold a candle to John and Lesley's café-pub and restaurant. Up on the hillside, overlooking castle and town, its walled, driftwood-furnished garden has stupendous views. The old brewhouse is much as it always was, only funkier, and now you can buy all sorts of eco-friendly items – hemp bags, leather sandals, candles. There is an inexhaustible supply of coffee, too, along with real ales and splendid wines. Home-cooked meals span the globe for inspiration while ingredients are closer to home, and include organic vegetables from the Lewis's own farm. You get Cardigan Bay crab cakes with toasted pine nuts; fillets of sewin in a lime and fennel butter; creamy hummus; 'raw food energy salad'. John and Lesley can claim a real food menu that stands out from the crowd – and it's very well priced.

directions	Follow signs for town centre & then St Thomas Green. Left into Hill St; left opp. cinema into Market St.
meals	10.30am–5pm; 6.30pm–9.15pm (Fri & Sat). Main courses £5.50–£9.50.
closed	From 5.30pm Mon–Thurs & all day Sun.

John Glasby & Lesley Lewis
The George's,
24 Market Street,
Haverfordwest SA61 1NH
tel 01437 766683

map: 6 entry: 638

The Sloop
Porthgain

Perfectly in keeping with its seawashed setting, the Sloop has been welcoming fisherfolk since 1743. The village remains a fishing harbour – the landlord catches his own lobster, mullet and crab – but, until the Thirties, Porthgain was more famous for bricks and granite. The tide used to come up to the Sloop's walls before the harbour was built; now there's a little seating area out front. Weatherbeaten on the outside, the pub is surprisingly cosy within. Expect bare beams, some bare boards, a happy melée of furniture, a table made from an old mill wheel, a canoe suspended from the ceiling, a board announcing 'the catch of the day'. Tuck into homemade mackerel pâté or lobster thermidor on tomato rice; breakfast too (open to all) sounds a treat. Holiday makers descend in summer but the rest of the year this is a community pub, with a proper games room and real fires. Staff are perfect all year round.

Dyffryn Arms
Pontfaen

Miss the small sign peeping out of Bessie's well-tended garden and you'll miss the pub – which would be a shame, because it's a treasure. Bessie has been here half a century and nothing has changed in that time, including the outside loos. A trooper possessed of a dry wit she shows no sign of tiring, keeps the place spotless and serves from a hatch in the wall seven days a week. The bar has the proportions of a domestic front room so you'll fall into easy conversation with the locals: farmers, hunters and the like. Old quarry tiles on the floor, an embroidered picture of the Queen on the wall, fresh flowers on the window sill, peanuts, crisps and Bass from the barrel – it's perfect. To the left of the pub is a garden with a bench under Bessie's washing line from which you may drink in the peace and the view: of the verdant little valley below, threaded by a silver river.

directions	Village signed off A487 between Fishguard & St Davids.
meals	12pm-2.30pm; 4pm-9.30pm. Main courses £6-£15; bar meals £3-£13.
closed	Open all day.

Matthew Blakiston
The Sloop,
Porthgain,
St Davids SA62 5BN
tel   01348 831449
web   www.sloop.co.uk

map: 6 entry: 639

directions	Pontfaen is on the Gwaun Valley road off the B4313 east of Fishguard,
meals	No food served.
closed	Open all day.

Bessie Davies
Dyffryn Arms,
Cwm Gwaun,
Pontfaen SA65 9SG
tel   01348 881305

map: 6 entry: 640

Pembrokeshire

Tafarn Sinc
Preseli

The highest pub in Pembrokeshire is the quirkiest pub in the world – or a close contender. It was speedily erected in 1876 as a hotel on the GWR railway; now the giant, red-painted, corrugated zinc building oversees a tiny railway platform complete with mannequin-travellers and a Victorian pram. It is beautifully tended outside and in, with a prettily trellised garden and an arresting Alpine-panelled public bar. Hams and lamps hang from the ceiling, there's sawdust on the floors and two big woodburners belch out heat. It's warm and welcoming and full of merry walkers. Hafwen, the perfect landlady, and husband Brian oversee the cosy, constant buzz and serve a solidly traditional menu (Preseli lamb burgers, faggots with onion gravy), and their own excellent beer. Tons of character, a touch of the surreal and a fabulous setting, high in the Preseli hills. No further introduction is needed – just a visit.

directions	Rosebush is on the B4329 Haverfordwest to Cardigan road.
meals	12pm-2pm; 6pm-9pm. No food Sun eve. Main courses £8.90-£14.90.
closed	Open all day. Closed Mon in winter.

Brian & Hafwen Davies
Tafarn Sinc,
Preseli,
Rosebush,
Clunderwen SA66 7QT
tel 01437 532214

map: 6 entry: 641

Pembrokeshire

Nag's Head Inn
Abercych

Behind the vibrant orange exterior is a feast of bare wood and stone. The lighting is soft and warm, there's a rustic chicken-wire sideboard crammed with old beer bottles, a glass cabinet displaying the famous 'rat' of Abercych (actually a stuffed coypu) and a photo of old Emrys, the treasured regular after whom the home-brewed beer is named. And there's Gizmo, resident fluffball cat. The Nag's Head has a simple, tasteful charm, is full of old tales and curios and quirkery and serves the best kind of hearty pub food, from cheese and onion toasties with salad to steak and Old Emrys ale pie, and local sewin in summer. Come with the family and explore the pushchair-friendly ClynFyw sculpture trail – it starts from here. There's a play area too, in the long, lovely riverside garden. By a bridge on the river bank, at the bottom of a steep hill, the setting alone is worth the trip.

directions	Off A4332 between Cenarth & Boncath.
meals	12pm-2pm; 6pm-9pm. Main courses £5-£15.
closed	3pm-6pm & Mon all day. Open all day Sun.

Sam Jamieson
Nag's Head Inn,
Abercych,
Boncath SA37 0HJ
tel 01239 841200

map: 6 entry: 642

Bear Hotel
Crickhowell

Viewed from the square of this small market town, the 15th-century frontage of the old coaching inn looks modest. Behind the cobbles and the summer flowers, it is a warren of surprises and mild eccentricity – bars and brasserie at the front, nooks and crannies carved at the back – behind which is the family- and dog-friendly garden. The beamy lounge has parquet, plush seating and a mighty fire; settle in and savour their good beers, wines, whiskies and ports. There are two dining areas where at night you can feast on Welsh Black beef, Usk salmon, Brecon venison and locally grown seasonal vegetables and regional farmhouse cheeses. Homemade ice creams, mousses and puddings are equally sumptuous. We've never seen the place empty and Mrs Hindmarsh is still firmly in charge of an operation that rarely comes off the rails.

Nantyffin Cider Mill Inn
Crickhowell

On the other side of the road, the Usk river pours down the valley. Diners pour in here for a sight of menus that feature pork, lamb, duck, guinea fowl, beef – exuberantly casseroled in Old Rosie cider – from their small hill farm at the foot of the Brecons. A network of small suppliers provides fresh produce from courgette flowers to line-caught bass, while autumn brings mushrooms from their "secret patch" and game from the Glanusk estate. It started life in the 15th century as a drovers' inn and an old cider press occupies the middle of the main dining room. You may also sit in one of two intimate bars – choosing from a fixed-price menu that is created weekly and a specials board that is chalked up daily. Expect award-winning country cooking concocted with minumum fuss and maximum flavour – plus ales and ciders on tap, delicious wines by the glass, hot punch in winter, luscious lemonade in summer and organic apple juice.

directions	On A40 between Abergavenny & Brecon.	directions	1 mile outside Crickhowell on the A40 to Brecon, at junc with A479..
meals	12pm-2pm; 6pm-10pm (7pm-9.30pm Sun). Main courses £5.95-£20.	meals	12pm-2.30; 6.30-9.30. Main courses £7.95-£16.95; set menus £12.95 & £16.95.
closed	3pm-6pm (7pm Sun).	closed	3pm-6pm (7pm Sun), Sun eve in winter & all day Mon (except bank hols).

	Judy Hindmarsh Bear Hotel, Brecon Road, Crickhowell NP8 1BW
tel	01873 810408
web	www.bearhotel.co.uk

	Glyn Bridgeman, Jess Bridgeman & Sean Gerrard Nantyffin Cider Mill Inn, Brecon Road, Crickhowell NP8 1SG
tel	01873 810775
web	www.cidermill.co.uk

The White Swan
Llanfrynach

The front resembles the row of cottages the pub once was. Its cavernous interior has been recently remodelled and its central bar is a split-level zone, making bar staff appear unnaturally tall as they serve Brains Bitter and other fine ales or wines. Make the most of the open fire, while you consider the Specials Board; it majors in fish so there could be seared scallops with spicy salsa and baked sea bass with chilli and basil – as well as haunch of Brecon venison with beetroot risotto, red wine and juniper sauce. The restaurant menu includes Hereford beef, Brecon lamb, local pheasant; the cheeses are Welsh, the digestive biscuits homemade. There are farmhouse tables, leather sofas, big woodburners, and a trellised patio at the back – gorgeous in summer. You're spoilt for walks here, so stride off into the Brecon Beacons – or potter along the towpath of the Mommouthshire & Brecon canal.

directions	Signed from A40 3 miles east of Brecon on Crickhowell road.
meals	12pm-2pm (2.30pm Sun); 7pm-9.30pm (9pm Sun). Main courses £10.45-17.50.
closed	Mon & Tues.

Byron Lloyd
The White Swan,
Llanfrynach,
Brecon LD3 7BZ

| tel | 01874 665276 |
| web | www.the-white-swan.com |

map: 7 entry: 645

The Felin Fach Griffin
Brecon

Stylish but cosy, fresh but not fussy. This bold venture mixes the buzz of a smart city bistro with the easy-going pace of Welsh country living, and it's popular. Full of bright elegance, downstairs fans out into several eating and sitting areas, with stripped pine and old oak furniture. Make for three giant leather sofas around a raised hearth, or opt for the rustic backroom bar. A Dutch chef stars in the kitchen, turning out simple but sensational dishes for smartly laid tables: Black Mountain smoked salmon, braised ox cheeks with mash, vanilla crème brûlée. And there are perfect Welsh cheeses. Breakfast is served around one table in the morning room; wallow with the papers and make your toast on the Aga. Bedrooms are fresh, warm and simple, with a few designer touches: tulips in a vase, check curtains, snowy white towels and linen. Charles, Edmund and Julie are a great team.

directions	On A470, 3.5 miles NE of Brecon.
meals	12.30pm-2.30pm; 6.30pm-9.30pm. Main courses £8.95-£10.95 (lunch); £15-£18.50 (dinner).
rooms	7 twins/doubles £97.50-£125. Singles from £67.50.
closed	3pm-6pm & Mon lunch (except bank hols).

See pp 30-57 for full list of pubs with rooms

Charles & Edmund Inkin
The Felin Fach Griffin,
Felin Fach,
Brecon LD3 0UB

| tel | 01874 620111 |
| web | www.felinfachgriffin.co.uk |

map: 7 entry: 646

The Harp
Old Radnor

David and Jenny Ellison bring bags of experience (time spent at Bristol's Hotel du Vin) to this ancient Welsh longhouse tucked down a dead-end lane near the parish church. The interior is spick-and-span: 14th-century slate flooring in the bar; tongue-and-groove in a tiny room that seats a dozen diners; crannies crammed with memorabilia; an ancient curved settle, an antique reader's chair, two fires. Enjoy a pint of Three Tons Cleric's Cure or Hobson's Town Crier with a Welsh Black rump steak, saddle of rabbit wrapped in bacon with mustard and cream sauce, lamb tagine, venison sausages on mustard mash. (There are ploughman's and baguettes, too.) From your seat under the sycamore you can overlook the spectacular Radnor Valley at will, but don't expect much action after sunset – life in this tiny village remains unchanged.

The Talkhouse
Pontdolgoch

What was once a typical pub now serves over 70 'niche boutique' wines. Stephen and Jacqueline have a winning formula in their 17th-century drovers' rest, combining attentive service with marvellous food. The first room you come into is a sitting room with comfy armchairs and sofa – just the place for pre-lunch drinks or after-dinner coffee. The bar has beams, log fire and sumptuous sofas; the claret-and-cream dining room has French windows that open to the garden in summer so you can dine outside. Classical, seasonal cooking – the lightest sweet potato and butternut soup, juicy, plump scallops with confit tomatoes and lemon dressing, delicately cooked Welsh lamb, a lavender panna cotta with raspberries – is a treat, the daily-changing menu using the finest local produce. A small, perfect find in the rolling wilderness of mid-Wales – and booking is essential.

directions	From Kington A44; after 3 miles left for Old Radnor.
meals	12pm-2pm (Sat & Sun only); 6.30pm-9pm. Main courses £7.95-£15; bar meals £4.25-£6.50.
closed	Tues-Fri lunch, 3pm-6pm Sat & Sun & Mon all day.

Jenny & David Ellison
The Harp,
Old Radnor LD8 2RH

| tel | 01544 350655 |
| web | www.harpinnradnor.co.uk |

map: 7 entry: 647

directions	On A470 1 mile west of Caersws & 5 miles from Newtown.
meals	12pm-1.30pm Sat & Sun; 6.30pm-8.45pm. Main courses £11.95-£16.95.
closed	Tues-Fri lunch, Sun eve & Mon all day.

Stephen & Jacqueline Garratt
The Talkhouse,
Pontdolgoch,
Caersws SY17 5JE

| tel | 01686 688919 |
| web | www.talkhouse.co.uk |

map: 7 entry: 648

Powys

Wynnstay Hotel
Machynlleth

Trucking through the gastronomic desert that is mid Wales, you'll be happy to discover this rambling old coaching inn in this quaint market town. It's rather more hotel than pub – but there's a cracking bar with original oak floors, low beams, scrubbed tables, and, at night, a cosy, candlelit feel. Bag a seat by the log fire in winter and peruse chef Gareth Johns's appealing menus over a pint of Reverend James. He applies his skills to fine local produce: Conwy mussels, Borth lobster, bass from Cardigan Bay, salmon and sewin from the river Dyfi, Welsh Black beef and lamb from the valley, game shot by the landlord. Bay scallops with wilted Ynyslas chard and black pepper oil may precede roast leg of saltmarsh lamb with orange and laver gravy, and excellent Welsh cheeses to finish. Thanks to family connections with Italy, there are some wonderful wines from small Italian growers and a traditional pizzeria at the back.

directions	In the centre of Machynlleth.
meals	12pm-2pm; 6.30pm-9pm. Main courses £6.95-£14.50 (lunch), £10.95-£14.95 (dinner).
closed	2.30pm-6pm.

Charles & Sheila Dark
Wynnstay Hotel,
Machynlleth,
Powys SY20 8AE
tel   01654 702941
web   www.wynnstay-hotel.com

map: 7 entry: 649

Swansea

No Sign Bar
Swansea

The name is not a marketing contrivance, but goes back to 1690s licensing laws. In contrast to the characterless drinking halls of Wind Street, the No Sign is quirky and cosy, its Dickensian interior a match for the frontage: worn flagstones, ragged walls, shelves of books and cabinets of old curios. Slump into a leather armchair with a newspaper from the rack. (Dylan Thomas drank here when he worked at the *Evening Post* – as current scribblers do.) There's a terrace to the rear, and the longest-ever back room, new and furnished in a similarly haphazard style. Three ales are well-kept but it's the wine list that deserves heritage listing (and 'Wined' Street it once was): 40 bottles, 12 by the glass. Homemade food is served by friendly staff, the tapas and hand-cut chips are a hit, and when your insides need warming there's homely lamb cawl. Avoid the weekend crowds and slip upstairs.

directions	M4 junc. 41 to Swansea. Follow signs for city centre. Right at Sainsbury's onto Wind Street.
meals	12pm-10pm (9pm Sat & Sun). Main courses £6.50-£11.75; Sunday roast £7.95; tapas & baguettes from £2.95.
closed	Open all day.

Philippa Shipley
No Sign Bar,
56 Wind Street,
tel   01792 465300

map: 2 entry: 650

This section includes pubs that have recently changed hands and foodie pubs that we believe are on the up. All are well worth seeking out.

Bath & N.E. Somerset

1 The Hop Pole, 7 Albion Buildings, Bath BA1 3AR 01225 446327
Gently sophisticated boozer with a polished feel, a verdant summer courtyard and a modern British menu. An easy pedal from the Bristol-Bath cycle path for tip-top Bath ales.

2 The Raven, 7 Queen Street, Bath BA1 1HE 01225 425045
Ordinary looking city-centre pub in wonderful cobbled street that seduces you with its cosy atmosphere and hidden depths, great beer (try the Raven Ale!), and interesting modern take on pub food.

3 White Hart, Widcombe Hill, Bath BA2 6AA 01225 338053
Five minutes from railway and bus stations, a hugely popular place with hostel-style accommodation. Well-kept ales, and generous portions of southern-influenced gastropub food.

4 City Arms, 69 High Street, Wells BA5 2AG 01749 673916
Attractive city-centre pub carved out of a 400-year-old jail and run by larger-than-life character Jim Hardy, proud of his microbrewery ales and superb Angus beef. Dine in beamed bars or cobbled courtyard.

Bedfordshire

5 The Cock, 23 High Street, Broom SG18 9NA 01767 314411
Remarkably unspoilt village boozer. Beers tapped from the cask in the orignal tap room - there's a rarity! Plain pine-panelled rooms and a proper skittles room too.

6 Hare & Hounds, Old Warden, Bedford SG18 9HQ 01767 627225
Old village pub that's been given a gastropub overhaul – loads of leather and funky colours. Excellent food on short, seasonal, produce-led menu. Reports please.

Berkshire

7 The Horns, Crazies Hill, Wargrave RG10 8LY 0118 940 1416
Inside the Tudor hunting lodge: beams and timbers, winter fires, solid scrubbed-wood tables, and a sweet little snug behind the bar to discover. Newish owner Sam McNab offers an appealing menu of freshly produced food – reports please.

8 The Red House, Marsh Benham RG20 8LY 01635 582017
Thatched gastropub in the Kennet Valley with French owner and chef. Set bistro lunch menu and an inventive carte served in the smart, book-lined restaurant. Super summer al fresco dining.

Worth a visit

England

Birmingham

9 The Beacon, Bilston Street, Sedgley DY3 1JE 01902 883380
Fine pub with its own microbrewery. Little has changed since
WWII: a fascinating period piano bar and a Victorian till
as ornate as they come. Sandwiches only.

Bristol

10 Old Duke, 45 King Street, Bristol BS1 4ER 0117 927 7137
There's a New Orleans speakeasy, British-pub feel to this shrine
to jazz and blues not far from Bristol Old Vic. Music is served
up nightly along with the occasional curry or stew.

11 The King's Head, 60 Victoria St, Bristol BS1 6DE 0117 927 7860
Classically Victorian inside, 1660 out. A charming period
narrow bar and cosier, panelled rear snug, splendid mirrored
back bar, photos of old Bristol and gallons of Smiles.

12 Hope & Anchor, 38 Jacobs Wells Rd BS8 1DR 0117 929 2987
Unpretentious and with a dedicated following – from arty
youth to well-shod Cliftonites – who come for pub grub
without the gastro-pomp and ales that change according to the
landlord's whim.

13 The Merchants Arms, 5 Merchants Rd BS8 4PZ 0117 904 0037
Honest and real, done-up without a whiff of modern pretension.
Simple, friendly, Bath Ales-owned, with excellent beers and
good snacks.

14 Robin Hood's Retreat, Gloucester Rd BS7 8BG 0117 924 7880
Victorian red-brick boozer given the gastropub makeover,
honeypot for Bristol foodies. Chef Nathan Muir (ex-Bibendum)
is cooking up a storm, offering a modern European menu and
eight ales on tap. Arrive early if you want a table.

15 Wellington Inn, Gloucester Rd, Bristol BS7 8UR 0117 951 3022
Imposing red-brick pub a drop-kick's distance from the
Memorial Stadium. Something of a flagship for Bath Ales, plus
solid pub food, a buzzing atmosphere and occasional live blues
and folk.

Buckinghamshire

16 The Swan, Salford MK17 8BD 01908 281008
Innovative pub group Peach Pubs have revamped this ordinary
village boozer with style and panache; leave the M1 for great
antipasti nibbles and enjoyable modern pub food, all day.

17 The White Hart, Preston Bissett MK18 4LX 01280 847969
Thatched, timbered and latched – a deeply cosy village pub
where locals in thick socks prop up the bar. Logs fires, daily
papers, local ale on tap and a revamp under current owners –
reports please.

18 Lions of Bledlow, Bledlow HP27 9PE 01844 343345
An ideal base for tackling one of the local walks into the Chiltern
Hills, this time-worn 16th-century pub delivers a good range of
real ales, a pleasant garden, and hearty pub food.

19 The Mole and Chicken, Easington HP18 9EY 01844 208387
Stunning views from the immaculate garden and a far from the
beaten track location are just two of the seductive charms that
await those who beat a path to the door. This is a really cosy
winter pub, so come on a damp Sunday and settle in for the day.
Quirky blackboard menus.

20 The Crown, Little Missenden HP7 0RD 01494 862571
An unspoilt brick cottage pub in a pretty village, run by the
same family for over 90 years. Excellent beers, good wines and
sandwiches, a big garden and walking all around.

21 The White Horse, Hedgerley SL2 3UY 01753 643225
Super local in easy reach of the M40 (junc. 2). Swap the
services for the flagstones, inglenook, beamed bar and perfect
ploughman's lunch. Seven real ales are tapped from the barrel.

22 Stag & Huntsmen, Hambleden RG9 6RP 01491 571227
The setting's the thing and the picture-book village is perfect
and popular with film crews. Bars are small and traditional,
carpeted and lively; the dining room modern. Hearty food,
excellent ale and invigorating local walks into the Chilterns.

Cambridge

23 Cambridge Blue, 85 Gwydir Street, Cambridge CB1 2LG
01223 361382
Away from the centre, this simple local has a warm atmosphere
and stacks of rowing paraphenalia. A wide choice of ales, among
them Adnams and Elgoods, and straightforward bar food.

24 Dyke's End, Reach CB5 0JD 01638 743816
Real community hamlet whose "splendid pub" (to quote the
Prince of Wales) is owned by the village. A lovely old place,
well worth a visit, but food can be over ambitious.

Worth a visit

England

25 White Pheasant, Fordham CB7 5LQ 01638 720414
Very welcoming dining pub with bare boards, wooden tables,
crackling logs, fresh fish and farmhouse cheeses. Handpumped
Woodforde's Wherry and a dozen wines by the glass.

Cheshire

26 Sutton Hall Hotel, Sutton Lane Ends, Macclesfield SK11 OHE
01260 253211
Authentically 16th century: big fires, stained glass and flagstones.
Decent handpumped ales, lovely grounds with duck pond, gothic
windows in the bedrooms.

27 Swettenham Arms, Swettenham CW12 2LF 01477 571284
Remotely sited hamlet and pub in the Dane Valley next to the
Quinta Arboretum. Top-notch food, locally brewed beers.
Handy for the Jodrell Bank radio telescope and science centre.

28 Dusty Miller, Wrenbury CW5 8HG 01270 780537
Hugely popular pub in a beautifully converted watermill beside
the Shropshire Union Canal. Local food is ever-present on the
imaginative menus. Super al fresco areas.

29 Nags Head, Haughton Moss CW6 9RN 01829 260265
Spic-and-span 17th-century pub with a real fire and all the
trimmings. Conservatory extension deals in views and fresh
local food, and there's a big garden and bowling green.

30 Farmers Arms, Huxley CH3 9BG 01829 781342
Food and wine are the draw at this unassuming pub in nice
countryside south of Chester. Local meats and game from
Anglesey in the rustic dining room, Jennings on tap and 21
wines by the glass. Reports please.

31 Old Harkers Arms, Chester CH1 5AL 01244 344525
A buzzy atmosphere and a great range of microbrewery ales at
this beautifully converted warehouse down by the canal. Run
by Brunning & Price pubs – good modern pub food.

32 The Old Harp, Little Neston CH64 OTB 01513 366980
Small and unassuming in a stunning spot on the edge of the
Dee Marshes. Watch marsh harriers or little egrets as you down
real ales and enjoy views across the estuary to North Wales.

Cornwall

33 Webbs Inn, Liskeard PL14 3HW 01579 343839
Part of the select Wykeham Arms group (see Dartmoor Union
and Rose & Crown entries in Devon). Rich coloured walls,
themed art and subdued lighting create the right mood for
innovative seafood dishes on daily menus.

34 The Rashleigh, Polkerris PL24 2TL 01726 813991
A pub on the beach, in a tiny cove! The old coastguard station
is cosy in winter, unbeatable in summer; down a pint of real ale
and watch the sun set across St Austell bay.

35 Rising Sun, St Mawes TR2 5DJ 01326 270233
Delightful harbour views from the sunny terrace at St Austell
Brewery's flagship inn-hotel. Smartly decorated, lively bar,
conservatory restaurant and good food. Reports, please.

36 The New Inn, Manaccan TR12 6HA 01326 231323
Unfussy thatched village local with that 'lost in the old country'
feel. Walk over from Helford for heart-warming pub grub,
pints of Doom Bar and a natter with the locals.

37 The Ship, Porthleven TR13 9JS 01326 564204
A hit with holidaymakers and locals, this harbourside pub
revels in its fun, smuggler-meets-fishing boat interior, and
offers surprisingly good food alongside Cornish ales.

38 The White Hart, Ludgvan TR20 8EY 01736 740574
Granite stone 14th-century pub with ochre-coloured walls, low
beams and real ale from the cask. Come for intimate boxed
seating areas and log-burning fires.

39 The Maltsters Arms, Chaple Amble, Polzeath PL27 6EU
01208 812473
Inland, away from the busy beaches around Rock, is this inviting
16th-century pub. Fun and funky eating areas and a good all-
round menu, with excellent fresh-fish specials. Reports please.

40 The Earl of St Vincent, Egloshayle PL27 6HI 01208 814807
Flower-decked 15th-century inn filled to the rafters with rich
furnishings and an amazing collection of clocks in perfect
working order. 'Time' is called by a cacophony of chimes,
bongs and cuckoos.

Cumbria
41 Britannia Inn, Elterwater LA22 9HP 01539 437210
With Great Langdale Beck tumbling into the tarn, a brilliant
starting point for walkers. Return for pints of foaming
Cumbrian ale, hearty food and views from the terrace.
Irresistible.

42 Old Dungeon Ghyll, Great Langdale LA22 9JY 01539 437272
To hikers ruddy from the day's exertions, full of stories of
courage in the face of adversity, the infamous Walkers' Bar
serves decent grub, mugs of tea, and God's own beer, Yates. The
atmosphere is infectious.

England

43 The Sun Inn, Dent LA10 5QL 01539 625208

Dent is an unspoilt Dales village of cobbles and cottages. After an invigorating walk, pile into the Sun for log fires and pints of Dent beers, brewed up the valley.

Derbyshire

44 The Cheshire Cheese, Edale Rd, Hope S33 6ZF 01433 620381

Unpretentious 16th-century inn beside the twisting road to Edale – favoured by walkers. Classic taproom with log fire and five micro-brewery ales; cosy, colourwashed dining rooms; traditional pub grub; terrace with glorious views.

45 The Red Lion, Litton SK17 8QU 01298 871458

Rooms hemmed in by timeworn, bare-stone walls; shuttered, small-paned windows; huge stone fireplaces warming slab-floored spaces dappled with old kitchen and dining tables – a Peak District classic but up for sale late 2006.

46 Eyre Arms, Hassop DE45 1NS 01629 640390

Traditional pub covered by Virginia creeper, close to Hassop Hall and good walks. Beams, log fires, lamplight, ancient knick-knacks and country cooking that's great value.

47 Old Crown, Shardlow DE72 2HL 01332 792392

A fine pub for beer and cider drinkers on the banks of the Trent. Three house ales, up to seven guest beers and plenty of real ciders in the summer. Reasonable pub grub.

Devon

48 Fox & Goose, Parracombe EX31 4PE 01598 763239

By a stream in a valley between Exmoor and the dramatic coastline, an unassuming pub worth seeking out for its big blackboard menus: fish from local boats, meats from surrounding farms, great local ales.

49 The London Inn, Molland EX36 3NG 01769 550269

Honest and unpretentious village local in the Exmoor foothills full of locals, dogs, hunters and shooters. Few frills in rambling flagstoned rooms, hearty food and great beer.

50 The Peter Tavy Inn, Peter Tavy PL19 9NN 01822 810348

Atmospheric 15th-century inn on the flanks of desolate Dartmoor. Masses of charm in black beams, polished slate, long pine tables and woodburners in huge hearths. Cracking beer and walking from the door.

Photos 1. The Cheshire Cheese, Hope 2. The Red Lion, Litton 3 The Peter Tavy Inn, Peter Tavy. 4 The Warren House Inn, Postbridge 5. The Puffing Billy, Exton 6. Bickley Mill, Stoneycombe

51 The Warren House Inn, Postbridge, PL20 6TA 01822 880208
Old tin miners' pub, high and alone, in a remote part of
Dartmoor – the third highest in England. No frills, just plain,
simple and honest, with Otter on tap and log fires warming
the panelled bar. Best visited on a clear day – the view extends
for 20 miles.

52 The Puffing Billy, Exton EX3 0PR 01392 877888
Old railway inn turned smart dining pub close to Exton station
and the Exe estuary. Was noted for its trendy interior, jazz
evenings and love of local produce; new owners in 2006.
Reports welcome.

53 The Turf Hotel, Exminster EX6 8EE 01392 833128
Reached only on foot (20-min walk), by bike or by boat, a
unique, rambling old pub overlooking Exe estuary mudflats.
Bareboard bar with big bay windows for winter wader-
watching and top-notch Otter Ales. Closed Dec-Feb.

54 The Anchor Inn, Cockwood EX6 8RA 01626 890203
Fine views of Cockwood's from this 460-year-old former
fisherman's cottage. Rather fitting then to find an awesome 30
mussel dishes on a long, fishy menu. Good ale but tricky parking.

55 The Manor Inn, Lower Ashton EX6 7QL 01647 252304
Small, traditional Teign Valley local overlooking field and valley.
Crackling log fires in cosy bars, honest grub, local cider and
excellent west country ales.

56 Bickley Mill, Stoneycombe TQ12 5LN 01803 873201
Escape the nearby resorts to this secluded and special
13th century flour mill, tucked into a hidden valley
between Newton Abbot and Torquay. Relax on the
verdant, decked terrace or dine on fresh fish in the swish
modern interior.

57 Steam Packet Inn, Totnes TQ9 5EW 01803 863880
Smartly redone, but keeping its intimate panelled rooms,
wooden floors and open fires. Beautifully positioned beside the
river Dart, the terrace heaves in summer.

58 Coppa Dolla Inn, Broadhempston TQ9 6BD 01803 812455
Pub carpeting, candles in wax-encrusted bottles, walls laden
with cricketing memorabilia, log fires, and Dartmoor IPA from
the barrel. Food is hearty, fresh and local.

Worth a visit

England

59 The Church House Inn, Harberton TQ9 7SF 01803 863707
Darkly atmospheric Devon longhouse with fantastic beamed
ceiling, oak panelling, medieval glass and respectable list of real
ales. Food shows ambition.

60 The Maltsters Arms, Tuckenhay TQ9 7EQ 01803 732350
More lively London brasserie than rural Devon inn, it's the
good food, local ales and a spectacular setting on Bow Creek
that make this 16th-century pub a popular spot.

61 The Cherub, Dartmouth TQ6 9RB 01803 832571
Dartmouth's oldest building (1380) creaks with age: a
magnificent timbered house with an overhanging beamed façade.
Good ales in tiny bar with inglenook; pub food in restaurant.

62 The Start Bay Inn, Torcross TQ7 2TQ 01548 580553
Packed the minute it opens (arrive late at your peril), this
modest 14th-century beachside inn serves the best
fresh fish and chips in Devon. Arrive hungry.

63 Cricket Inn, Beesands TQ7 2EN 01548 580215
Unassuming outside, open-plan within, but a real local feel. The
great seaside location is matched by a good fish menu. Expect
jazz with Sunday lunch.

64 The Mill Brook Inn, South Pool TQ7 2RW 01548 531581
Arrive by boat (high tide) at this 400-year-old village pub on
the Salcombe estuary. Cosy bars, splendid crab sandwiches,
Bass from the barrel, farm cider and a tiny streamside terrace.

65 Sloop Inn, Bantham TQ7 3AJ 01548 560489 / 560215
16th-century smuggler's pub smack on the coastal path in the
glorious South Hams and a stroll from the beach – the
perfect stop-off for fresh fish and a pint of Palmers IPA.

66 Pilchard Inn, Burgh Island TQ7 4BG 01548 810514
Walk across the sand or take the sea tractor to this hugely
atmospheric smugglers' pub on the tidal island made famous by
Agatha Christie. Beams, flagstones, roaring log fires, BBQs,
views, cliff walks. Unique!

Dorset
67 Rose & Crown, Trent DT9 4SL 01935 850776
A rural Dorset gem – thatched, unpretentious and rustic with
rug-strewn stone floors, log fires, four ales on tap and views
across open fields to rolling hills. Peaceful end-of-lane location
by the church.

68 The Fox Inn, Corscombe DT2 0NS 01935 891330
Everything about this 17th-century thatched inn is lovely: the
food, the people, the setting. Be charmed by stuffed owls in
glass cases, gingham tablecloths, paintings, flowers, flagstones,
fires and six fish dishes a day.

69 The Royal Oak, Cerne Abbas DT2 7JG 01300 341797
Crackling log fires throughout the three flagstoned
rooms add to the charm of this creeper-clad, thatched,
historic pub. Four Badger beers, wines by the glass and
seasonal menus.

70 The Greyhound, Sydling St Nicholas DT2 9PD 01300 341303
Having made a huge success of the West Bay down by the
sea, John Ford and Karen Trimby (plus chef) moved inland
to this rambling village local in a sleepy valley north
of Dorchester. The fish should be good – reports welcome.

71 Marquis of Lorne, Nettlecombe DT6 3SY 01308 485236
Isolated inn with gardens (good for kids) at the base
of Eggardon Hill. Worth the trip down tortuous lanes
for log fires, Palmers ales, lovely food and valley views
across Powerstock.

72 The Anchor Inn, Seatown DT6 6JU 01297 489215
A terrific coastal path watering hole below Golden
Cap. The big sun terrace and gardens overlook
a pebbly beach. Open fires, pints of Palmers and
crab sandwiches.

73 The Three Horseshoes, Powerstock DT6 3TF 01308 485328
Victorian stone inn in a drowsy village down twisting lanes
below Eggardon Hill. Fresh food and tip-top Palmers ale, best
savoured on a balmy evening on the terrace watching the sun
slide over the valley.

74 The Brace of Pheasants, Plush DT2 7RQ 01300 348357
In rolling downland, one of Dorset's prettiest pubs – two
thatched cottages in a hamlet. A fine summer garden and great
walkers' pitstop, good atmosphere, good food. New owners
means changes are afoot.

75 Langton Arms, Tarrant Monkton DT11 8RX 01258 830225
Five microbrewery ales and a bistro-style menu using meat
from the owners' farm draw locals and walkers to this thatched
17th-century village pub. Beautifully restored following a
serious fire.

Worth a visit

England

76 Vine Inn, Vine Hill BH21 4EE 01292 882259
Former bakehouse run by the Sweatland family for generations, now owned by the National Trust. Two timeless bars, London Pride on tap and sandwiches for sustenance. Close to Kingston Lacy House.

77 Ship in Distress, Mudeford BH23 3NA 01202 483997
Quirky and crammed with nautical clutter as befits its name, this entertaining local is a fish fancier's dream. Arrive early for fresh Mudeford crab or grilled scallops, first-class fish and chips or a tureen of Breton-style fish soup.

Essex

78 The Mole Trap, Tawney Common CM16 7PU 01992 522394
The single-track drive through miles of gloriously unspoilt countryside is the 'wow' of this very rural pub. Excellent beers (Crouch Vale, Fullers London Pride), rambling beamed bars, three glowing coal fires and straightforward food.

79 Blue Boar, Maldon CM9 4QE 01621 855888
Old coaching inn, now a hotel, with a smart but pubby bar. Its own microbrewery turns out Farmers Ale, Blue Boar Bitter and Hotel Porter stout, tapped from the cask.

80 The White Hart, Great Yeldham CO9 4HJ 01787 237250
Classic half-timbered pub that impresses inside too, with beams, panelling, open fires and bare boards galore. Big emphasis on food, with most tables laid up for dining, but good value set lunches – reports please.

81 Peldon Rose, Peldon CO5 7QJ 01206 735248
A 14th-century smugglers' inn rescued from decay. Wonky walls, head-cracking beams and huge fires – wonderful. Fine wines from Lay and Wheeler (who own the pub), scrummy food and stylish, simple bedrooms.

Gloucestershire

82 The Bull Inn, Hinton SN14 8HG 0117 937 2332
Fine 16th-century stone pub set back from a deep-cut Cotswold lane. Enticing with tiny windows, low beams, open fires and an inventive menu. Sunny south-facing terrace.

83 Priory Inn, Tetbury GL8 8JJ 01666 503534
Modern makeover for historic town centre inn. Now a gastropub with rooms, a genuine welcome for families and a passion for buying fresh produce from local farms and suppliers.

84 The Wild Duck Inn, Ewen GL7 6BY 01285 770310
Impressive, creeper-clad 15th-century stone inn close to
Cotswold Water Park. Rambling rustic interior with roaring log
fires, red walls, four real ales and decent food.

85 Red Lion, Ampney St Peter GL7 5SL 01285 851596
Well-preserved time-warp beside A417 east of Cirencester.
Hatch bar, handpumped Hook Norton, two simple flagstoned
rooms with crackling log fires, and long-serving landlord.
Closed weekday lunchtimes.

86 Twelve Bells Inn, Circencester GL7 1EA 01285 644549
Quirky backstreet pub with glowing fires, scrubbed pine tables
and rugs on old tiled floors in three lively, low-ceiling rooms.
Character landlord, decent fresh fodder and five cracking real
ales. A must for beer drinkers.

87 Mill Inn, Withington GL54 4BE 01242 890204
Ancient, mossy-roofed inn beside the babbling Coln in a secret
Cotswold valley. Low beams, flagstones and blazing log fires fill
rambling rooms delightfully untouched. Sam Smiths on tap and
great local walks.

88 The Baker's Arms, Broad Campden GL55 6UR 01386 840515
Traditional Cotswold pub that serves home-cooked food and
a good selection of well-kept beers – try a pint of local
Stanway Stanney. Good walking all around and a welcome
for children.

Greater Manchester
89 The Swan, Dobcross OL3 5AA 01457 873451
Slabbed stone floors and colourwashed ceilings pitch like a
dinghy in a storm, rooms warmed by huge log fires hive off in
all directions from a lobby bar. New landlords – reports please.

Hampshire
90 The Fleur de Lys, Pilley SO41 5QB 01590 672158
History is as much of a pull as a good pint at this thatched pub
serving classy modern food in beamed bars. Roaring fires,
lovely garden, forest walks from door. Reports on the new
regime, please.

91 The Oak Inn, Bank SO43 7FE 023 8028 2350
New Forest walks radiate from this friendly, low-beamed, 18th-
century pub. Walkers, cyclists and locals pour in. Ale tapped
from the cask, interesting mix of hearty pub dishes and great
local fish – reports please.

England

92 The Jolly Sailor, Old Bursledon SO31 8DN 023 8040 5557
Reached via 45 steps or by boat, this former shipbuilder's
house overlooks the river Hamble. Watch all things nautical
from the terrace and from big windows in the newly
refurbished bars.

93 The Mayfly, Testcombe SO20 6AX 01264 860283
Unrivalled river scenes draw summer crowds to this beamed
old farmhouse on the banks of the fast-flowing Test.
Comfortable bar, pubby food, splendid riverside terrace.
Arrive on foot (or bike) via the Test Way.

94 The Bell, Alresford SO24 9AT 01962 732429
Respected licensees Brian and Lynn O'Callaghan have worked
their magic and restored this faded Georgian inn. Stylishly
reworked bar and dining area, upgraded bedrooms and
modern pub menus – reports please.

95 The Tichborne Arms, Tichborne SO24 0NA 01962 733760
Real ales from the cask, homely pub food and a glorious
summer garden draw folk to this thatched pub in a serene hamlet.
The Wayfarer's Walk and the Itchen Way almost pass the door.

**96 Marco Pierre White's Yew Tree Inn, Highclere RG20 9SE
01635 253360**
A contemporary and sympathetic makeover stitches the
elegant dining room into the old fabric and character of this
building with its inglenooks, timbers and light uncluttered
walls. With Marco as owner, this is more restaurant than pub,
but expect the best of British food.

Herefordshire

97 Bull's Head, Craswall HR2 0PN 01981 510616
Down a small flight of steps discover stone floors, a hatch in
the wall and a real fire; the drovers' inn, 400 years old, has
barely changed since the arrival of electricity. Located down a
tangle of lanes in a remote spot below Black Hill.

98 The New Harp Inn, Hoarwithy HR2 6QH 01432 840900
Rescued by the Coopers in 2006, having been closed for a
year, the contemporary New Harp is now the hub of the
cummunity. Be cheered by fresh local food, imaginative beers,
summer barbecues and Wye Valley walks.

99 The Boot, Orleton SY8 4HN 01568 780228
Half-timbered village inn beloved of locals with orchard
garden, horse-brasses, big fire. Real ales and cider are matched
by traditional pub roasts, grills, curries and casseroles.

Photos 1. The Bricklayers Arms, Hogpits Bottom 2. britainonview.com/Martin Brent
3. Marco Pierre White's Yew Tree Inn, Highclere 4. Chris Banks 5. Bull's Head, Craswell 6.
Russell Wilkinson

Hertfordshire

100 The Bricklayers Arms, Hogpits Bottom HP3 0PH 01442 833322
A pretty, 18th-century building with low beams, a blazing
winter fire, and timbered walls tucked away in the exotically
named Hogpits Bottom. Expect excellent beers, over 50 wines
and menus listing home-smoked fish and good old steak and
kidney pie.

101 The Holly Bush, Potters Crouch AL2 3NN 01727 851792
An immaculate, 18th-century country pub elegantly furnished
with antiques and big oak tables candlelit at night. Fabulous
Fuller's ales, straightforward food, nice garden.

Isle of Wight

102 Spyglass Inn, Ventnor PO38 1JX 01983 855338
Famous and fascinating 19th-century inn on Ventnor
Esplanade overlooking the sea. Seafaring memorabilia fills
rambling rooms; come for seafood specials, local ale and seating
by the sea wall.

103 Red Lion, Freshwater PO40 9BP 01983 297171
A short stroll from the tidal river Yar and a handy stop-off for
local Goddards ale and special food. Sofas, flagstones and fires in
the open-plan bar – civilised.

Kent

104 Rock Inn, Chiddingstone Hoath TN8 7BS 01892 870296
Timeless, tile-hung brick cottage in a glorious position.
Scuffed and charmingly laid-back, the perfect walker's
stop for a pint of Larkins and a satisfyingly thick sandwich.

105 The Tiger, Stowting TN25 6DA 01303 862130
Hard-to-find, civilised country boozer with friendly locals, rugs
on bare boards, candles on scrubbed tables, roaring winter fire,
real ales (festival in summer) and splendid live jazz evenings.
Reports please.

106 The Gate Inn, Marshside CT3 4EB 01227 860498
A charming rural local, run for years by a landlord who
resists change. Two small, well-worn bars, log fires,
Shepherd Neame tapped from the cask, and simple
hearty food.

Lancashire

107 Spread Eagle, Sawley BB7 4NH 01200 441202
A 17th-century inn on the banks of the Ribble. A serious
pub-restaurant, plus soup and sandwiches in the bar.
Great for a riverside drink in summer. Reports please.

England

108 John O'Gaunt, Lancaster LA1 1JG 01524 65356
Small city-centre pub with terrific atmosphere. Décor is 1930s, enhanced by low-key trad jazz that often floats through. Good range of beers and great choice of simple food – the cullen skink is superb!

109 The Highwayman, Burrow LA6 2RJ 01524 274249
Nigel Haworth's second pub, following the huge success of the Three Fishes at Mitton. Expect fantastic fresh food that champions time-honoured recipes and the finest ingredients from local producers and growers.

Leicestershire

110 Bewicke Arms, Market Hallaton LE16 8HB 01858 555217
Fishermen love this pretty 400-year-old inn for its proximity to Eybrook Reservoir and for its traditional, scrubbed bar. Tourists descend for the setting, the annual bottle-kicking contest on Easter Monday, and hearty pub food – reports please.

111 Fox & Goose, Illston on the Hill LE7 9EG 0116 259 6340
A good old-fashioned local. The only animals in this shrine to country pursuits are stuffed or on the walls. Excellent beers (no food) in a charming rural setting.

112 The Crown, Old Dalby LE14 3LF 01664 823134
Creeper-covered inn loved for its sweeping summer lawns and warren of tiny unspoilt rooms full of ancient oak settles, glowing coal fires and quaint hatchway bar where guest beers are tapped from the cask.

Lincolnshire

113 Ship Inn, Surfleet Seas End PE11 4DH 01775 680547
Good quality new-build pub on the site of the 17th-century Ship Inn – on the banks of the Welland and Glen rivers, with panoramic views across the fens. Local Bateman's on tap and an ambitious menu using seasonal produce.

114 Chequers, Gedney Dyke PE12 0AJ 01406 362666
Popular dining pub at the mouth of The Wash specialising in fish dishes and imaginative blackboard specials dispatched by landlady/chef. Nicely redone – reports please.

London

115 Bountiful Cow, 51 Eagle Street WC1R 4AP 020 7404 0200
New venture for TV presenter Roxy Beaujolais – a modernised corner pub kitted out with kitsch Sixties' homage-to-the-cow images such as cowboy film posters. A great, intimate venue offering a practically all-beef menu.

Worth a visit

116 Viaduct Tavern, 126 Newgate St EC1A 7AA 020 7600 1863
The only unaltered gin palace in London, wonderfully lavish and
famous for its triptych oil painting of four Viaduct statues. Join
city lunchtime throng for good beer and bar food.

117 The Gunmakers, 13 Eyre Street Hill EC1R 5ET 020 7278 1022
Low ceilings, bare boards and good cheer fill this tiny, unspoilt,
backstreet pub, commemorating Hiram Maxin (who produced
the first automatoic machine gun nearby). Simple blackboard
menus and Wells Bombardier please a mixed bunch.

118 Cumberland Arms, Dartmouth Road W14 8SZ 020 7371 6806
As sister pub to the nearby Atlas and Fox & Hounds (Battersea),
the food here is of the same high calibre. A magnet for office
workers at lunchtimes but draws the locals for pints at sundown.

119 King's Head Theatre Pub, 115 Upper St N1 1QN 020 7226 0364
Don't imagine this pub plays second fiddle to the drama upstairs
– it's a vibrant, wooden-floored local with a late licence, live
music every night and food for those who watch the show.

120 Nags Head, 53 Kinnerton Street SW1X 8ED 020 7235 1135
Tiny, wooden-floored, panelled and rambling boozer with a
big personality. The bar is low enough to serve passing
gnomes, hence the sunken floor behind, and walls are
packed with memorabilia. A great little place for
Adnams ales.

121 Fox & Hounds, 29 Passmore St, SW1W 8HR 020 7730 6367
Lovely unpretentious boozer, all the cosier for being decked out
in hunting red. Be entertained by the 'Wicked Wit' blackboards
from a corner pew as you tuck into doorstep sandwiches

122 The Cow, 89 Westbourne Park Road W2 5QH 020 7221 5400
Superb fish and crustacea: eat up or down. Laid-back staff serve a
laid-back crowd – and it's friendly at Tom Conran's pub, named
after an ex-landlady.

123 The Warrington Hotel, 93 Warrington Crescent W9 1EH
020 7286 2929
Cavernous, splendid, Victorian, with a huge arched ceiling and a
magnificent staircase among the period features. Chef Gordon
Ramsay has bought the freehold, so expect big changes.

124 The Salusbury, 50-52 Salusbury Rd NW6 6NN 020 7328 3286
Lively gastropub with a deli on the side. Red walls are covered
with seminal jazz album sleeves. Delicious, mainly Italian food
and a lengthy wine list.

England

125 William IV, 786 Harrow Road NW10 5JX 020 8969 5944
There's excellent food and wine in the elegant and sedate restaurant – and a laid-back bar with sofas, fires and music. And a garden for summer at the back.

126 Ye Olde White Bear, Well Road NW3 1LJ 020 7435 3758
Backstreet pub with country looks and higgledy-piggledy interior warmed by an open fire. Good beers, a selection of wines, smashing pub grub.

127 Lord Palmerston 33 Dartmouth Park Hill NW5 1HU
020 7485 1578
Bustling gastropub stripped down to bare boards and wooden tables, with food that's quite something (Moroccan touches; great steaks) and good wine and beer. Garden for summer.

128 The Latchmere, 503 Battersea Park Rd SW11 3BW
020 7223 3549
A pub and theatre rolled into one. Spruced up high-ceilinged bar, leather sofas, warm fire, bags of smoky atmosphere and a mini-theatre to watch new comic talent.

129 The County Arms, 345 Trinity Road SW18 3SH 020 8874 8532
This pub has been very well restored – the brass shines, log fires burn in marble fireplaces, the stained glass glows and the pints of Young's Winter Warmer flow. A great weekend place for familes – sunny terrace and summer barbecues .

Manchester

130 Circus Tavern, 86 Portland Street M1 4GX 0161 236 5818
One of Britain's smallest pubs, thrice as deep as wide, with a tiny under-stairs bar and two magnificent, panelled roomettes. Twenty punters (supping Tetleys Bitter) is a crowd here.

131 Rain Bar, 80 Bridgwater Stree M1 5JG 0161 235 6500
Wrestled from the shell of an umbrella factory in 1999, an inspired mix of bistro and traditional pub beside the Rochdale Canal in the city centre. Decent fodder and J W Lee's beers.

132 Marble Arch, 73 Rochdale Road M4 4HY 0161 832 5914
Marvellous tiled interior, with mosaic friezes high up in the vaulted roof and a deceptively sloping floor. A microbrewery at the rear produces an enticing array of organic vegan beers.

133 Arden Arms, 23 Millgate, Stockport SK1 2LX 0161 480 2185
A superb tiled lobby bar, hidden snug, real fires and sublime Edwardian wood and glass bar, in the shadow of ASDA. The limited lunchtime food is of restaurant quality.

134 Cross Keys, Running Hill Gate, Uppermill OL3 6LW
01457 874626
Superlative moorland-edge setting east of Oldham high above the
Tame Valley, with stone-flagged floors, terrific fire-blacked range,
excellent food and savoury puddings. Lee's beers.

Norfolk

135 The Lifeboat Inn, Thornham PE36 6LT   01485 512236
The glowing lamps and open fires of this bags-of-character
inn beckon. It's been an ale house since the 16th century – and
they still serve a decent pint. The sea is a brisk, bracing walk
across fields.

136 The Three Horseshoes, Warham All Saints NR23 1NL
01328 710547
Plain rooms that have barely changed since the 1930s – gas
lights, rough deal tables, Victorian fireplaces and East Anglian ales
tapped from the cask. Good home cooking too.

137 The George, Cley-next-the-Sea NR25 7RN   01263 740652
The Norfolk Naturalists Trust was formed at this rambling
Edwardian inn overlooking saltmarshes. Refurbishment continues
under Dan Goff (of the White Horse in Blakeney)and improving
menus use local produce.

138 Buckinghamshire Arms, Blickling NR11 6NF 01263 732133
Handsome, NT-owned Jacobean inn close to the gates of the
grand hall. Glowing woodburners in old pine furnished bars;
locals in winter, tourists in summer. Big lawn and courtyard.
New landlords – reports please.

139 Mad Moose Arms, Norwich NR2 3LD 01508 492497
The more relaxed, less polished sister pub to the Wildebeest
Arms. Tall windows, red walls, darkwood panelling,
funky widescreen TV, good modern pub food and ale from
Wolf Brewery.

140 Fat Cat, Norwich NR2 4NA 01603 624364
Victorian corner pub and beer drinkers' heaven: 30 real
ales with some on handpump, others tapped from cask.
The owners proudly keep this a traditional and simple
drinking pub.

141 King's Head, Bawburgh NR9 3LS 01603 744977
Unprepossesing yet with a terracotta facade, Anton Wimmer's
old pub is full of charm. Delight in East Anglian ales, wines by
the glass, piped jazz and a heated terrace. Food has been hit and
miss – reports please.

England

Northamptonshire

142 The Windmill, Badby NN11 3AN 01327 702363

Thatched 17th-century inn with hotel extension close to Althorp Park and Sulgrave Manor. Warmly decorated flagstoned bar has log fires, cask ales and traditional/modern menu.

Northumberland

143 Rat Inn, Anick NE46 4LN 01434 602814

The hard-to-find old drovers' inn may not be venerable but it has an irresistible appeal — the sort of place where everyone, kids included, is made welcome. Quaff ever-changing real ales by the log fire in the charming snug.

144 Queens Head Inn, Great Whittington NE19 2HP 01434 672267

A warm refuge in a wild country of moors, sheep and vask skies. Toast your toes over a pint of Wylam by the coal fire in the bar, dominated by a hunting mural. Feedback on food welcome; new owners took over in 2006.

145 The Ship, Marygate, Holy Island TD15 2SJ 01289 389311

Rustic bare boards and beamed bars — a spotless little pub that sits in a terrace of cottages on a fascinating tidal island. Hadrian and Border ales and good seafood.

Nottinghamshire

146 Black Horse, Caythorpe NG14 7ED 0115 966 3520

A tiny, carpeted bar where Sharron Andrews sells beer brewed on the premises and the fish menu is so popular that booking is essential. Dick Turpin once hid in the gents, apparently.

147 Bottle & Glass, Harby NG23 7EB 01522 703438

They put the emphasis on fish at this deceptively spacious village gastropub — down to fish and chip takeaway suppers on a Friday night. Good selection of real ales and wines by the glass.

148 Robin Hood, Elkesley DN22 8AJ 01777 83859

A far better pitstop than the roadside 'restaurants' on offer: take the Elkesley turning off the A1 for a decent ploughman's or a lamb confit with mint pesto, garlic and thyme sauce.

Oxfordshire

149 The Bull Inn, Charlbury OX7 3RR 01608 810689

Handsome, creeper-clad 16th-century inn overlooking the main street of this charming Cotswold town. Flagstones, fires and Hook Norton ale in the rustic bar; fresh food on daily menus in the warmly decorated dining room.

150 The Shaven Crown, Shipton-under-Wychwood OX7 6BA
01993 830330

Stone-mullioned windows, ancient faded tapestries, grand
fireplaces and suits of armour; this marvellous Tudor stone inn is
not your average local. Enjoy cracking Hook Norton ales and pot
roasted pheasant in the cosy Monk's Bar.

151 The Bear, Alfred Street, Oxford OX1 4EH 01865 728164

Oxford's oldest boozer, popular with town and gown, has a low-
beamed, shambolic interior, many years' worth of framed, frayed
ties (it's a long story) and cracking ale.

152 Rose & Crown, North Parade Avenue, Oxford OX2 6LX 01865
510551

No music or mobile phones at this characterful, three-room
Victorian city pub – just conversation, great ales, traditional
lunchtime food, and a heated back yard.

153 North Star, The Causeway, Steventon OX13 6SG 01235 831677

15th-century freehouse with a narrow corridor leading to a
warren of small rooms, with open fires, old settles and creaky
latched doors with numbers. Beer from the barrel, traditional
pub food and the resident ghost await.

154 The Goose, Britwell Salome OX49 5LG 01491 612304

New owners for this thriving pub-restaurant at the base of the
Chiltern Hills. Remodelled, informal and relaxing but more
restaurant than pub and with a pump-free bar – although Hook
Norton is straight from the cellar.

155 King William IV, Hailey OX10 6AD 01491 681845

Take an OS map to locate this rural treat tucked down single-
track lanes in the Chilterns. Spick-and-span traditional interior,
the full range of Brakspear ales, grassy front garden with peaceful
views – super after a hike in the hills.

156 Chequers Inn, Aston Tirrold OX11 9DD 01235 851272

Expect more than a hint of Gallic charm at this homely village
local close to the Ridgeway Path. Cracking locals' bar with Hooky
on handpump; first-class French country cooking in the rustic,
bistro-style dining room. Reports please.

157 The Greyhound, Rotherfield Peppard RG9 5HT 0118 972 2227

Hugely attractive and ancient tiled and timbered pub north of
Reading. Impressive country venue for TV celebrity chef
Anthony Worrall Thompson and his grill-restaurant formula –
35-day aged beef steaks and his own suckling pigs.

Worth a visit

England

158 Black Horse, Checkendon RG8 0TE 01491 680418

Persevere up the rutted lane to this old-fashioned country local and escape modern-day life. Run by the same family for 100 years, with local ales from the cask, filled rolls, pickled eggs and peaceful garden.

Rutland

159 The Grainstore Brewery, Oakham LE15 6RE 01572 770065

Working brewery with a bare-bones bar delivering nine cracking ales and simple pub food. Tours can be arranged in advance.

160 Old White Hart, Lyddington LE15 9LR 01572 821703

Spick-and-span country pub with old black beams, tiled floors, roaring log fires, seasonal menus, good ales, and a walled garden with 12 floodlit pétanque pitches.

Shropshire

161 The Wenlock Edge Inn, Wenlock Edge TF13 6DJ 01746 785678

The somewhat austere look of this stone roadside pub, set high on a limestone ridge in grand walking country, belies the warmth of the welcome inside. Arrive tired and hungry from a walk or ride and refuel on pints of Hobsons and traditional pub food.

162 The Royal Oak, Cardington SY6 7JZ 01694 771266

At the foot of Caer Caradoc, a 500-year-old pub loved by muddy-booted ramblers — with a dependable range of real ales, cider and inexpensive daily specials from local suppliers.

163 White Horse Inn, Castle Pulverbatch SY5 8DS 01743 718247

A welcome pit-stop for walkers on the beautiful Shropshire Way. Terrific bar with flagstones and roaring woodburner promises great local ales and hearty cooking using meat from local farms.

164 The Miners Arms, Priest Weston SY7 8EW 01938 561352

On the wild Welsh borders a truly rustic and unspoilt pub that's the hub of hamlet life — they sell dog food, groceries and gas, put on folk nights, marrow competitions and harvest thanksgiving. Wonderful red tiled locals' bar with big inglenook and beer brewed in Bishops Castle; food on request.

165 Sun Inn, Leintwardine SY7 0LP No phone.

No airs or graces at this terraced house beside the river: just two rooms with scrubbed tables, stone floors, barrels of beer and cider stillaged in the kitchen. Unchanged since the Ark, and landlady Floss in her 80s.

Photos 1. Alan T..J Harwood 2. Llanfair Waterdine, Knightons 3.britainonview.com 4. The Wenlock Edge Inn, Wenlock Edge 5. www.paulgroomphotography.com 6. Cat Head Inn, Chiselborough

166 Clive Restaurant with Rooms, Bromfield SY8 2JR 01584 856565
Handsome building, not particularly 'pubby' but you get a decent
pint of Hobson's, a good choice of wines in the bar and some
ambitious cooking in the restaurant. Reports please.

167 The Waterdine, Llanfair Waterdine LD7 1TU 01547 528214
The old Welsh longhouse in a hamlet by the river is a fine spot
for Ken Adams's innovative modern British cooking. With
impeccable local produce and Woods ale on tap, this is more
restaurant-with-rooms than pub.

Somerset

168 Blue Flame, West End, Nailsea BS48 4DE 01275 856910
Spartan, well-worn, 19th-century rural local frequented by
farmers and real ale and cider enthusiasts. Two basic rooms, a
coal fire, barrels on stillage, filled rolls, pub games and big
garden; open all day in summer. A rarity!

169 Pilgrim's Rest, Lovington BA7 7PT 01963 240597
More of a restaurant with a 'pubby' style delivering local Cottage
Champflower on handpump and a menu of interesting modern
dishes tht make good use of local produce and fresh fish.

170 The Helyar Arms, East Coker BA22 9JR 01935 862332
Fine gastropub worth a detour – for the food that goes
from strength to strength, and for the handsome feudal village
it lives in. Real ales, Somerset cider and global wines are
well priced.

171 Cat Head Inn, Chiselborough TA14 6TT 01935 881231
Striking hamstone pub in countryside close to Montacute.
Spotless flagstoned rooms, fresh imaginative food, Otter bitter
on tap and attractive gardens with views over the village.

172 The Notley Arms Inn, Monksilver TA4 4JB 01984 656217
Isolated, pretty village pub with a welcoming intimate feel –
perfect for cold nights. Dependable range of local ales and
good food.

Staffordshire

173 Anchor Inn, Old Lea ST20 0NG 01785 284569
Largely unaltered old boatman's pub beside the Shropshire Union
Canal. Beer and cider from jugs filled in the cool cellar beside
the canal trough. Approached by boat or down grass-centred
lanes. No food.

Worth a visit

England

Suffolk

174 The Swan, Hoxne IP21 5AS 01379 668273

Still a feel of times past at this restored village local that dates back to the late 15th century. Expect acres of oak floorboards, carved timber, colourwashed walls, Adnams on tap, and big helpings of homecooked food.

175 Ivy House, Stradbroke IP21 5JW 01379 384634

Picture-book, pink thatched village pub in arable country. Décor may be dated but menus aren't: come for local produce, Greene King and Adnams ales, and local Aspall's organic cider.

176 Victoria, Earl Soham IP13 7RL 01728 685758

Inauspicious whitewashed village local by the green, famous for its home-brewed beers (Earl Soham Brewery). Few frills in the main bar but hearty pub food and a proper pint of Victoria Ale.

177 Angel Hotel, Lavenham CO10 9QZ 01787 247388

A delightful ancient inn overlooking Lavenham's market place and famous timbered guildhall. Dining area has huge inglenook fireplace. East Anglian ales and a daily-changing menu.

178 The Henny Swan, Great Henny CO10 7LS 01787 269238

Redecoration has not lost the soul and style of this middle-of-nowhere riverside pub well worth the longish drive. Lovely light lunch menu and Suffolk ales. Reports welcome.

179 Anchor Inn, Nayland CO6 4JL 01206 262313

The old country inn by the river has been thoroughly renovated – with some detriment to the atmosphere. But regulars and tourists are drawn by the fresh gastropub food.

180 The Angel Inn, Stoke-by-Nayland CO6 4SA 01206 263245

Soft lamplight draws you into this 16th-century inn in Constable country. Carved beams, log fires, fine prints, fresh flowers and candles create a cosy, lived-in feel. Dine on Denham Estate game or fresh fish in the galleried restaurant.

181 Butt & Oyster, Pin Mill IP9 1JW 01787 280245

Impossibly charming riverside pub with old settles, tiled floors, fine views across the Orwell and Adnams tapped from the cask. Arrive early if you want a window seat.

182 Kings Head, Orford IP12 2LW 01394 450205

David and Ruth Watson, owners of the chic pub-hotel across the square, plan to upgrade this charming old building and add fresh, simple bedrooms. Good honest pub food will employ local ingredients. Feedback please.

Worth a visit

183 The Ramsholt Arms, Ramsholt IP12 3AB   01394 411229
Idyllic – on the shore of the river Deben. Down a pint of
Nethergate on the terrace, listen to the calls of the curlew.
Cosy fires, game in season and great fish and chips.

184 Plough & Sail, Snape Maltings IP17 1SR   01728 688413
Set at the front of the Maltings, next to the road, this busy bustling
Adnams pub-restaurant delivers a globally inspired menu to a vast
array of tables. A tourist magnet on weekends and holidays.

185 Sibton White Horse, Sibton IP17 2JS   01728 660337
Wonderful 16th-century free house that has hung onto its
character, renowned for its simple good value home cooking: local
ingredients and a twist on the classics alongside some novel dishes.

186 Eels Foot Inn, Eastbridge IP16 4SN   01728 830154
A plain, backwater village pub delivering good honest food,
Adnams ales, a real craic on music nights. Close to Minsmere
Bird Reserve; mobbed in summer.

187 The Bell Inn, Walberswick IP18 6TN   01502 723109
A 600-year-old inn set in a tiny summer-soft, winter-bleak fishing
village. Come for good local ales and homely bar food surrounded
by ancient beams, flagstones, wooden settles and open fires.

188 The Randolph Hotel, Reydon IP18 6PZ   01502 723603
As good for a quick bite and a pint of Adnams as for a three-course
meal that takes in local fish and game. This late Victorian pub-hotel
sports sleek modern good looks within and sunny gardens without.

189 Dukes Head, Somerleyton NR32 5QR   01502 730281
Shabby chic gastropub meets real community local in an
aristocratic estate village on the edge of Lowestoft. Gutsy food
uses state grown and shot produce. Lovely simple gardens
overlook peaceful water meadows. Reports please.

Surrey
190 The Stag, Lower Eashing GU7 2QG   01483 421568
With a lease dating back to 1771, this is an attractive, atmospheric
place to stop off for very good home cooking. And a teak-furnished
terrace by the water makes a languorous spot for quaffing.

191 Stephan Langton, Abinger Common RH5 6JR   01306 730775
Isolated country pub at the bottom of leafy Leith Hill,
with a handful of cottages and a romatic hammer pond for
company. Great refuelling spot after exploring Surrey's finest
walks. Chef/landlord Jonathan Coomb has moved on – reports
on new regime please.

England

192 Old School House, Ockley RH5 5TH 01306 627430

Some of the best fish and seafood here at Bill Bryce's former boys' boarding school. Expect fresh Selsey crab and Loch Fyne oysters alongside Gales beers.

193 The Plough, Coldharbour RH5 6HD 01306 711793

The smell of woodsmoke wafting from the Plough's chimneys is impossible to resist, as are the home-brewed ales – Crooked Furrow and Tallywacker – the delicious pub food, and the leafy walks to the top of Leith Hill.

194 Punch Bowl Inn, Oakwood Hill RH5 5PU 01306 627249

15th-century charm: a roaring inglenook, scrubbed tables and uneven flagged floors. The tile-hung pub is in superb walking country. Summer BBQs and Badger beers.

195 The Albert Arms, Esher KT10 9QS 01372 465290

Lavish refurbishment of a high street corner pub has created an impressive pub-with-bedrooms. Sleek bar area offering cask ales, many wines by the glass and eclectic menus. Live weekend jazz. Reports please.

196 The White Cross, Richmond TW9 1TJ 020 8940 6844

Real fires in cosy bars and huge windows overlooking the Thames – what views! Enjoy a pint or three on the terrace, hugely popular in summer. Bar food is swiftly served.

Sussex

197 The George, Rye TN31 7JT 01797 222114

Rye's oldest inn has reopened – in style. Expect a lively tap bar with local ale and food, Spanish influenced menus in a relaxed dining room and swish bedrooms.

198 Globe Inn, Rye TN31 7NX 01797 227918

New chef-owner with Michelin star background has taken over this weather-boarded pub on the outskirts of Rye. Expect changes to the décor and a more restaurant feel; local beers and an emphasis on local foods remain.

199 Best Beech Inn, Wadhurst TN5 6JH 01892 782046

A nice little country pub – warm and glowing. New owners have redone the dining room and there are plans to upgrade the bar areas and bedrooms. New chef offers innovative pub food.

200 White Horse, Hurst Green TN19 7PU 01580 860235

Recently renovated roadside boozer with gastropub appeal – wooden floors, leather sofas, scrubbed tables and a posh outside terrace. Come for Harvey's Best on tap and a pedigree kitchen team. Reports please.

Photos 1. The King's Arms, Fernhurst 2. The Plough, Coldharbour 3 Rose Cottage Inn, Alciston 4 Globe Inn, Rye 5 Best Beech Inn, Wadhurst 6. The Punchbowl, Lapworth

Worth a visit

201 The Rainbow Inn, Cooksbridge BN8 4SS 01273 400334
Pleasing roadside pub north of Lewes that draws local foodies for
seasonal food. Cosy clubby bar for pints of Harveys, charming
private dining rooms, decked terrace with views to the Downs.

202 Six Bells, Chiddingly BN8 6HE 01825 872227
Led Zeppelin and Leo Sayer have all played in this quirky little
boozer renowned for its music. Logs fires, Harveys on handpump,
atmosphere, boules in the garden, and great value food.

203 Rose Cottage Inn, Alciston BN26 6UW 01323 870377
In walking country close to the South Downs Way, this 17th-
century, wisteria-clad cottage is on a quiet lane to nowhere. Run
by the Lewis family since 1960, it's a bolthole for ramblers in
search of a decent pint and fresh local fish.

204 Black Jug, Horsham RH12 1RJ 01403 253526
Victorian town centre pub owned and revamped by Brunning &
Price. Expect classic wooden panelling, wooden floors,
trademark bookcases and modern pub served all day.

205 Blue Ship, Billingshurst RH14 9BS 01403 822709
Lost down a web of Sussex lanes, an unassuming Victorian
exterior and charming 15th-century core. Classic main bar with
worn brick floor, low heavy beams, fire in the inglenook and
beer from the barrel.

206 The King's Arms, Fernhurst GU27 3HA 01428 652005
Early days for new owners at this distinctive, 17th-century stone
pub – big plans to extend the dining area and add rooms. Head-
cracking beams and local ales in the spick-and-span bar; cottage
garden for summer sipping.

207 Three Moles, Selham GU28 0PN 01798 861303
Built to serve Selham Station in 1872, now an unspoilt and old-
fashioned rural local with simple furnishings. Great beer, farm
cider, monthy sing-songs, long-serving landlady, no food.

208 The Crab & Lobster, Sidlesham PO20 7NB 01243 641233
Nick Sutherland's (see Royal Oak & Halfway Bridge) latest
aquisition is just yards from Pagham Harbour bird reserve.
Expect a modern makeover and menus, local ale on tap, and
amazing bedrooms. One to watch.

Warwickshire
209 The Punchbowl, Lapworth B94 6HR 01564 784564
James Feeney has created a contemporary opulence here: candelabra
on long wooden tables, modern canvasses and ornate mirrors on
bare brick. Big fires, summer patio and great food, too.

England

210 **The Holly Bush Inn, Priors Marston CV47 7RW 01327 260934**
Well hidden down a village lane, an English rose. Sofas and armchairs fill alcoves in the flagged bar, walls are vibrant terracotta or exposed stone, a log fire and woodburner bring cheer. A friendly, rambling place with well priced food and Hook Noton on tap.

211 **The Bell, Alderminster CV37 8NY 01789 450414**
Cheerful bar and bistro in converted coaching inn. Fresh food on daily chalkboards, in bar rooms or restaurant, and popular musical suppers. Conservatory and garden with valley views.

Wiltshire

212 **The Linnet, Great Hinton BA14 6BU 01380 870354**
With enthusiasm, dedication and bags of talent, chef-patron Jonathan Furby has turned the Linnet into a popular pub-restaurant. Good value lunches, unusual combinations, everything homemade.

213 **The Swan, Bradford-on-Avon BA15 1LN 01225 868686**
Second pub for former Michelin-starred chef Stephen Ross. Plans for this imposing 16th-century inn will include simple English food from local produce and the restyling of 12 bedrooms.

214 **King's Arms, Monkton Farleigh BA15 2QH 01225 858705**
Five miles from Bath, just off the A363, this listed 17th-century inn has a charming garden and beautiful courtyard. Inside, a redecorated bar with leather sofas, roaring fires, hearty food and West Country ales.

215 **The Neeld Arms, Grittleton SN14 6AP 01249 782470**
True country boozer with friendly locals, two glowing inglenooks, fresh tasty food, good beers and drinkable wines. Four-poster beds upstairs, breakfast feasts.

216 **The Red Lion, Lacock SN15 2LQ 01249 730456**
Little has changed since Jane Austen's day at this 18th-century inn — big open fires, rugs on flagstones, bare boards, timbers. Set in a lovely, time-warp NT village, with Lacock Abbey across road and fabulous walks.

217 **Rising Sun, Bewley Common SN15 2PP 01249 730363**
Unpretentious stone pub high on a hill above Lacock. Escape the crowds for the terrace and unrivalled Avon Valley views, sup a pint of Moles as hot-air balloons drift across the sky on summer evenings.

Photos 1. The Holly Bush Inn, Priors Marston 2. The Lamb at Hindon, Hindon
3. britainonview.com 4. The Tennant Arms, Kilnsey 5. The Moorcock Inn, Garsdale Head
6. www.paulgroomphotography.com

218 The Three Crowns, Brinkworth SN15 5AF 01666 510366
Intimate, old-style bars and a huge no-smoking conservatory.
Real ale, good wine, a garden with views and a large, surprising
menu – portions are huge so arrive hungry!

219 The Lamb at Hindon, Hindon SP3 6DP 01747 820573
Magnificent old coaching inn that dominates sleepy Hindon.
Rambling rooms ooze character, big bay windows look across
the street, settles front blazing log fires. Feast on hearty
English cooking.

Worcestershire

220 Bell & Cross Inn, Holy Cross DY9 9QL 01562 730319
A cosy atmosphere with open fires, good pub food (the owner
was chef to the English football squad) and a selection of real
ales. A surprisingly unspoilt little pub so close to Birmingham.
Reports please.

221 Colliers Arms, Clows Top DY14 9HA 01299 832242
Food with a view! A top quality menu and wine list and a
'gourmet evening' to tickle foodies' tastebuds.

222 The Swan, Hanley Swan WR8 0EA 01684 311870
Worth noting if heading for the Malvern Hills – a smartly
revamped local overlooking the village green and pond.
Contemporary layout and décor, three ales on tap and modern
pub food.

Yorkshire

223 The Tennant Arms, Kilnsey BD23 5PS 01756 752301
The best of Yorkshire hospitality has been dispensed here
since stage coaches first plied through the Dales. At its
heart is a capacious flagged bar with stone fireplace,
age-burnished furnishings, settles and benches.
New owners late 2006.

224 The Moorcock Inn, Garsdale Head LA10 5PU 01969 667488
Wild and remote,crouching in an isolated moorland spot at
top end of Wensleydale. There's a quirky stylishness that is
striking in such an unworldly setting; plus local ales and
homemade pub grub.

225 Queens Arms, Litton BD23 5QJ 01756 770208
Glorious walks onto the moors and along the river from homely
16th-century Dales inn. Return for warming fires, home-brewed
ales, hot food, stunning views.

England

226 The George, Hubberholme BD23 5EJ 01756 760223

Sympathetically updated but still fairly basic Dales pub with good beer and traditional pub food. J B Priestley's favourite watering hole – he's buried in the church opposite.

227 Hack & Spade, Whashton DL11 7JL 01748 823721

Good seasonal food, Black Sheep beers and bin-end wines at this soft stone pub in an off-the-beaten-track hamlet. Log fires and long views across fertile farming country.

228 Fox & Hounds, Carthorpe DL8 2LG 01845 567433

Slip off the hectic A1 for peace and nourishment at this pristine village pub. Come for traditional interiors, delicious wines and fresh food with a fishy slant. Reports please.

229 Buck Inn, Thornton Watlass HG4 4AH 01677 422461

Archetypal village pub next to the village green (and perilously close to the cricket pitch). Ever-changing range of local ales and wide ranging menu. Homely, traditional interior, summer barbecues, children's play area.

230 Black Sheep Brewery, Masham HG4 4EN 01765 689227

Follow a fascinating tour of Theakston's high-flying brewery with a perfect pint of Riggwelter or a hearty meal in the informal bar-bistro: try shank of lamb with Square Ale sauce.

231 The Fox & Hounds, Sinnington YO62 6SQ 01751 431577

Old coaching inn in a sleepy backwater below the North York Moors. Expect homely panelled bars with open fires and well-presented modern pub food.

232 The Coachman Inn, Snainton YO13 9PL 01723 859231

It's been an inn since 1776, and the bar remains charmingly old-fashioned in an Arts & Crafts way, its solid tables glowing in the firelight. New owners are improving the food and restoring its fortunes – reports please.

233 The Grapes, Great Habton YO17 6TU 01653 669166

Honest, no-nonsense, village local with young, hard-working licensees at the helm. Cosy, country plush bars draw local diners for good 'no frills' cooking using local meats and seasonal veg. Book ahead for the rib of beef Sunday lunch.

234 The Star, North Dalton YO25 9UX 01377 217688

The long, low Star appears to rise out of the village pond; come for an idyllic setting and a harmonious and understated revamp. New owners, new kitchen, new dining areas, new bedrooms – big changes, reports welcome.

235 The Three Hares, Bilbrough YO23 3PH 01937 832128

16th-century pub in an unspoilt rural setting (roaming sheep eyeball you as you sip your wine). Revamped interior and an interesting, balanced menu strong on seasonal produce.

236 The Greyhound, Saxton LS24 9PY 01937 557202

Unchanging 13th-century stone inn next to Saxton's church. Packed with ornaments, plates and brasses in three cosy rooms with blazing winter fires. Sam Smiths from the cask.

237 The Fat Cat, Sheffield S3 8SA 01142 494861

In Sheffield and desperate for a pint, follow signs to the Kelham Island Museum to locate this bustling backstreet boozer. Great home-brewed beers and six guest ales await. Good value pub grub.

Worth a visit

Wales

Cardiff

238 Waterguard, Cardiff Bay CF10 4PA 029 2049 9034

Fascinating old buildings fill the Cardiff Bay area and this half-historic customs house is full of cosy charm – plus a bold extension with floor-to-ceiling glass framing the view across the bay.

Carmarthenshire

239 White Hart Inn, Llanddarog SA32 8NT 01267 275330

An oddity for west Wales, a thatched pub whose low-beamed rooms ooze fairytale charm. Real log fires, real homemade pies and real beers (home brewed) – worth leaving the A40 for.

Conwy

240 The Groes Inn, Ty'n-y-Groes LL32 8TN 01492 650545

A 500-year-old drovers' inn notable for its fabulous views over the Conwy Valley. Cosy bars, rambling, low-beamed dining areas filled with antiques and winter fires, real ale, a conservatory and gardens, and delicious pub food. Reports please.

Denbighshire

241 The Hand at Llanarmon, Llanarmon Dyffryn Ceiriog LL20 7LD 01691 600666

All the pleasures of a country local are on tap, at this 16th-century drovers' inn found down single track lanes in the middle of nowhere. Wood fires, beams and settle, and delicious seasonal food.

Flintshire

242 Glasfryn, Sychdyn CH7 6LR 01352 750500

Former farmhouse smartly made-over by the upmarket Brunning & Price group. Big buzzy bar, impressive beers, distinctive dining areas, modern pub food all day, and great views.

Glamorgan

243 The Bush, St Hilary, Cowbridge CF71 7DP 01446 772745

Wonderfully traditional thatched pub in gentle countryside. Cul-de-sac location opposite the church makes outside benches popular in summer. In winter head for the roaring fire, pints of Old Rosie and Speckled Hen, and great food.

Gwynedd

244 George III, Penmaenpool LL40 1YD 01341 422525

One of Wales's finest views across the estuary towards Snowdonia. Family-friendly basement; beamed and flagstoned bar; tables on the water's edge and the Mawddach Trail passes the door.

245 Pen-y-Gwryd Hotel, Nantgwynant LL55 4NT 01286 870211
Snowdonia's ex-mountain rescue HQ and training base for the
1953 Everest expedition. See their boots in the bar; dine by
candlelight; stay the night. A treasure.

Neath

246 Dulais Rock, Aberdulais SA10 8EY 01639 644611
If the Rock were any closer to the Aberdulais Falls it
would be in the splash pool — you can hear the roar
from the deck at the back. Inside is modern but not
minimalist — warm wood, slate floors, retro lighting and
a vast wood-burning stove.

Pembrokeshire

247 Stackpole Inn, Stackpole SA71 5DF 01646 672324
Former village store and post office of this hamlet
on the fringe of specatacular NT coastline: wonderful
walking from the door. Great choice of fresh local
dishes in whopping portions — reports please.

248 Pendre Inn, Cilgerran SA43 2SL 01239 614223
Tiny, old and special, this village inn, dating from the 14th
century, delivers gargantuan portions of good pub grub and
decent ales in intimate, flagstoned rooms — at low prices!

Powys

249 The Farmer's Arms, Cwmdu NP8 1RU 01874 730464
New owners for this merry rustic local filled with farmers
and a popular lunch spot for pony-trekkers and walkers
in love with the Black Mountains. Local real ales and
ciders, too, but reports on the new regime and
food welcome.

250 Royal Oak, Gladestry HR5 3NR 01544 370669
Stone-built local, smack on the Offa's Dyke Path beneath
Hergest Ridge. Filled with farmers and booted walkers in for
pints of Woods, roaring fires and good value tucker.

Worth a visit

Bag o'Nails Bristol, entry 22
Bhurtpore Inn Aston, Cheshire, entry 54
The Buffet Bar Stalybridge, Cheshire, entry 65
White Hart Inn Bouth, Cumbria, entry 86
The Watermill Inn Ings, Cumbria, entry 90
Old Poets' Corner Ashover, Derbyshire, entry 112
The Bridge Inn Topsham, Devon, entry 144
Fountain Head Branscombe, Devon, entry 147
Culm Valley Inn Culmstock, Devon, entry 150
The Swan Little Totham, Essex, entry 169
Ostrich Inn Newland, Gloucestershire, entry 182
The Royal Oak Fritham, Hampshire, entry 207
The Sun Inn Bentworth, Hampshire, entry 219
The Hawkley Inn Hawkley, Hampshire, entry 222
The Swan on the Green West Peckham, Kent, entry 257
Sun Hotel & Bar Lancaster, Lancashire, entry 265
The Eagle & Child Bispham Green, Lancashire, entry 268
The Cow & Plough Oadby, Leicestershire, entry 279
The White Horse Fulham, London, entry 306
Greenwich Union Greenwich, London, entry 316
The Victoria Beeston, Nottinghamshire, entry 377
Falkland Arms Great Tew Oxfordshire, entry 405
Canal Inn Wrantage, Somerset, entry 434
The Crown Churchill, Somerset, entry 448
Halfway House Pitney Hill, Somerset, entry 450
The Sair Inn Linthwaite, Yorkshire, entry 554
Plough & Harrow Monknash, Glamorgan, entry 621

Photo The White Horse, entry 306

Best for... own breweries

Pot Kiln Frilsham, Berkshire (West Berkshire Brewery), entry 9
Driftwood Spars St Agnes, Cornwall (Driftwood Brewery), entry 77
The Watermill Ings, Cumbria (Ings Mill Brewery), entry 90
Drunken Duck Inn Barngates, Cumbria (Barngates Brewery), entry 95
Kirkstile Inn Loweswater, Cumbria (Loweswater Brewery), entry 99
Queen's Head Tirril, Cumbria (Tirril Brewery), entry 102
Old Crown Hesket Newmarket, Cumbria (Hesket Newmarket Brewery), entry 105
Old Poets' Corner Ashover, Derbyshire (Old Poets' Brewery), entry 112
Dartmoor Union Holbeton, Devon (Union Brewery), entry 137
Flower Pots Inn Cheriton, Hampshire (Cheriton Brewhouse), entry 217
Swan on the Green West Peckham, Kent (Swan Brewery), entry 257
Church Inn Uppermill, Lancashire (Saddleworth Brewery), entry 277
Greenwich Union Greenwich, London SE7 (Meantime Brewery), entry 316
Baltic Fleet Liverpool, Merseyside (Wapping Brewery), entry 339
Dipton Mill Inn Hexham, Northumberland (Hexhamshire), entry 371
All Nations Ironbridge, Shropshire (Worfield Brewery), entry 421
Old Cannon Brewery Bury St Edmunds, Suffolk (Old Cannon Brewery), entry 457
Station Hotel Framlingham, Suffolk (Earl Soham Brewery), entry 470
St Peter's Hall St Peter South Elmham, Suffolk (St Peter's Brewery), entry 472
Foresters Inn Carlton, Yorkshire (Wensleydale Brewery), entry 492
The Talbot Knightwick, Worcestershire (Teme Valley Brewery), entry 549
Sair Inn Linthwaite, Yorkshire (Linfit Brewery), entry 554
Nags Head Inn Abercych, Pembrokeshire, (Nags Head Brewery), entry 579

Photo St Peter's Hall, entry 472

King William Bath, Bath & N.E. Somerset, entry 5
The Pot Kiln Frilsham, Berkshire, entry 14
The Harris Arms Lewdown, Devon, entry 138
The Jack in the Green Rockbeare, Devon, entry 146
The Sun Inn Dedham, Essex, entry 170
The Bell at Sapperton Sapperton, Gloucestershire, entry 175
The Stagg Inn Titley, Herefordshire, entry 229
The Wellington Wellington, Herefordshire, entry 234
Three Crowns Inn Ullingswick, Herefordshire, entry 239
George & Dragon Speldhurst, Kent, entry 260
Bay Horse Inn Forton, Lancashire, entry 266
The Three Fishes Mitton, Lancashire, entry 272
The Duke of Cambridge Islington, London, entry 329
The Olive Branch Clipsham ,Rutland, entry 409
Canal Inn Wrantage, Somerset, entry 434
The Montague Inn Shepton Montague, Somerset, entry 439
The Holly Bush Inn Stafford, Staffordshire, entry 454
The Anchor Walberswick, Suffolk, entry 467
The Queens Head Bramfield, Suffolk, entry 469
The Parrot Forest Green, Surrey, entry 476
The White Horse Chichester, Sussex, entry 487
Anglesey Arms at Halnaker Halnaker,, Sussex, entry 489
The Flemish Weaver Corsham, Wiltshire, entry 530
The Tollgate Inn Bradford on Avon, Wiltshire, entry 532
The Star Inn Harome, Yorkshire, entry 595
The Appletree Marton, Yorkshire, entry 596
The Lord Newborough Dolgarrog, Conwy, entry 612
The Felin Fach Griffin Brecon, Powys, entry 646

Photo The Parrot, entry 476

Best for... cheese

The Pheasant Keyston, Cambridgeshire, entry 47
Nobody Inn Doddiscombsleigh, Devon, entry 142
The Bell at Sapperton Sapperton, Gloucestershire, entry 175
The White Hart Lydgate, Greater Manchester, entry 203
The Stagg Inn Titley, Herefordshire, entry 229
Sun Hotel & Bar Lancaster, Lancashire, entry 265
The Freemasons Arms Wiswell, Lancashire, entry 273
Dipton Mill Hexham, Northumberland, entry 371
Martin's Arms Colston Bassett, Nottinghamshire, entry 378
The Trout at Tadpole Bridge Buckland Marsh, Oxfordshire, entry 396
Crown Country Inn Munslow, Shropshire, entry 417
The Jolly Sportsman East Chiltington, Sussex, entry 501
The Blacksmiths Inn Westow, Yorkshire, entry 593
The Star Inn Harome, Yorkshire, entry 595
White Horse Inn Hendrerwydd, Denbighshire, entry 619
Raglan Arms Llandenny, Monmouthshire, entry 632
The Felin Fach Griffin Brecon, Powys, entry 646

Photo Christopher Hubbard

The Green Dragon Haddenham, Buckinghamshire, entry 29
Rose & Crown Yealmpton, Devon, entry 119
Kings Arms Strete, Devon, entry 128
The Drewe Arms Broadhembury, Devon, entry 149
Coventry Arms Corfe Mullen, Dorset, entry 155
The Mistley Thorn Mistley, Essex, entry 171
White Horse Inn Frampton Mansell, Gloucestershire, entry 178
The New Inn Shalfleet, Isle of Wight, entry 247
The Sportsman Seasalter, Kent, entry 250
The Dering Arms Pluckley, Kent, entry 256
The White Horse Brancaster Staithe, Norfolk, entry 351
The Star & Garter Goodwood, Sussex, entry 491
The George & Dragon Rowde, Wiltshire, entry 533
The Forester Inn Donhead St Andrew, Wiltshire, entry 542
The Wensleydale Heifer Inn Leyburn, Yorkshire, entry 573
Penhelig Arms Aberdyfi, Gwynedd, entry 624
The Old Point House Inn Angle, Pembrokeshire, entry 636

Best for... authentic pubs

The Bell Inn Aldworth, Berkshire, entry 12
The Queen's Head Newton, Cambridgeshire, entry 40
Harrington Arms Gawsworth, Cheshire, entry 62
Tinner's Arms Zennor, Cornwall, entry 68
Old Crown Hesket Newmarket, Cumbria, entry 105
Ye Olde Gate Inne Brassington, Derbyshire, entry 113
The Barley Mow Kirk Ireton, Derbyshire, entry 115
Rugglestone Inn Widecombe-in-the-Moor, Devon, entry 136
Duke of York Iddesleigh, Devon, entry 139
The Bridge Inn Topsham, Devon, entry 144
The Square & Compass Worth Matravers, Dorset, entry 156
Black Bull Inn Frosterley, Durham, entry 157
The Boat Inn Ashleworth, Gloucestershire, entry 185
Five Mile House Cirencester, Gloucestershire, entry 187
The Royal Oak Fritham, Hampshire, entry 207
Harrow Inn Steep, Hampshire, entry 223
The Crown Churchill, Somerset, entry 448
Halfway House Pitney Hill, Somerset, entry 450
Yew Tree Cauldon, Staffordshire, entry 453
King's Head Laxfield, Suffolk, entry 471
The Case is Altered Hatton, Warwickshire, entry 522
The Falcon Inn Arncliffe, Yorkshire, entry 568
The White Horse Inn (Nellie's) Beverley, Yorkshire, entry 590
The Birch Hall Beck Hole, Yorkshire, entry 602
Dyffryn Arms Pontfaen, Pembrokeshire, entry 640

Photo Old Crown, entry 105

Best for... real fires

Hole in the Wall Little Wilbraham, Cambridgeshire, entry 39
The White Lion Barthomley, Cheshire, entry 59
Ye Olde Gate Inne Brassington, Derbyshire, entry 113
Duke of York Iddesleigh, Devon, entry 139
Black Bull Inn Frosterley, Durham, entry 157
The Wykeham Arms Winchester, Hampshire, entry 214
Chestnut Horse Easton, Hampshire, entry 215
Harrow Inn Steep, Hampshire, entry 223
The White Horse Inn Priors Dean, Hampshire, entry 224
The Three Chimneys Biddenden, Kent, entry 263
The Rams Head Inn Denshaw, Lancashire, entry 276
Fox and Hounds Great Brington, Northamptonshire, entry 363
Martin's Arms Colston Bassett, Nottinghamshire, entry 378
Fox and Hounds Christmas Common, Oxfordshire, entry 389
The Swan Swinbrook, Oxfordshire, entry 399
Falkland Arms Great Tew, Oxfordshire, entry 405
Royal Oak at Luxborough Luxborough, Somerset, entry 427
Halfway House Pitney Hill, Somerset, entry 450
King's Head Laxfield, Suffolk, entry 471
The Lickfold Inn Lickfold, Sussex, entry 480
The Fountain Inn Ashurst, Sussex, entry 498
The Blue Lion East Witton, Yorkshire, entry 572
The White Swan Inn Pickering, Yorkshire, entry 597
The Blacksmith's Arms Lastingham, Yorkshire, entry 601

Photo Black Bull Inn, entry 157

Best for... views

Three Horseshoes Inn Radnage, Buckinghamshire, entry 31
The Pheasant Inn Chester, Cheshire, entry 51
Hanging Gate Sutton, Cheshire, entry 61
Halzephron Gunwalloe, Cornwall, entry 70
The Bay View Inn Widemouth Bay, Cornwall, entry 83
The Mason's Arms Strawberry Bank, Cumbria, entry 89
Drunken Duck Inn Barngates, Cumbria, entry 95
The Langstrath Country Inn Borrowdale, Cumbria, entry 97
Brackenrigg Inn Ullswater, Cumbria, entry 100
Kings Arms Strete, Devon, entry 128
The Harris Arms Lewdown, Devon, entry 138
Carpenter's Arms Walterstone, Herefordshire, entry 233
The Railway Hereford, Herefordshire, entry 235
The Gun Docklands, London, entry 317
The White Horse Brancaster Staithe, Norfolk, entry 351
The Five Horseshoes Henley-on-Thames, Oxfordshire, entry 385
Finch's Arms Upper Hambleton, Rutland, entry 410
The King William IV Mickleham, Surrey, entry 475
Duke of Cumberland Arms Henley, Sussex, entry 484
The Three Horseshoes Elsted, Sussex, entry 486
The Griffin Inn Fletching, Sussex, entry 495
The Castle Inn Edgehill, Warwickshire, entry 511
Quarrymans Arms Box, Wiltshire, entry 529
The Millbank Mill Bank, Yorkshire, entry 556
Craven Arms Appletreewick, Yorkshire, entry 566
The Harp Old Radnor, Powys, entry 647

Photo Bay View Inn, entry 83

The **Dundas Arms** Kintbury, Berkshire, entry 11
The **Anchor Inn** Sutton Gault, Cambridgeshire, entry 42
The **Shipwright's Arms** Helford Cornwall, entry 72
The **Pandora Inn** Mylor Bridge, Cornwall, entry 73
The **Ship Inn** Noss Mayo, Devon, entry 120
The **Ferry Boat Inn** Dittisham, Devon, entry 129
The **Boat Inn** Ashleworth, Gloucestershire, entry 185
The **Greyhound** Stockbridge, Hampshire, entry 205
The **Royal Oak** Langstone, Hampshire, entry 226
The **Saracens Head** Symonds Yat East, Herefordshire, entry 242
Shipwright's Arms Faversham, Kent, entry 249
The **Inn at Whitewell** Whitewell, Lancashire, entry 270
The **Ship** Wandsworth, London, entry 311
The **Gun** Docklands, London, entry 317
The **White Horse** Brancaster Staithe, Norfolk, entry 351
The **Trout at Tadpole Bridge** Buckland Marsh, Oxfordshire, entry 396
Riverside Inn Cressage, Shropshire, entry 414
Ship Inn Red Wharf Bay, Anglesey, entry 605
Harbourmaster Hotel Aberaeron, Ceredigion, entry 611
The **Boat** Erbistock, Denbighshire, entry 617
The **Corn Mill** Llangollen, Denbighshire, entry 618
Penhelig Arms Aberdyfi, Gwynedd, entry 624
The **Old Point House Inn** Angle, Pembrokeshire, entry 636

Photo Ferry Boat Inn, entry 129

Best for... summer gardens

Royal Oak Marlow, Buckinghamshire, entry 34
Turtley Corn Mill Avonwick, Devon, entry 132
The Shave Cross Inn Marshwood Vale, Dorset, entry 152
The Fox Inn Lower Oddington, Gloucestershire, entry 196
The Royal Oak Fritham, Hampshire, entry 207
The Riverside Inn Aymestrey, Herefordshire, entry 227
The Dove Dargate, Kent, entry 251
Martin's Arms Colston Bassett, Nottinghamshire, entry 378
The Fishes Oxford, Oxfordshire, entry 393
The Hundred House Hotel Norton, Shropshire, entry 422
Lord Poulett Arms Hinton St George, Somerset, entry 435
Devonshire Arms Hotel Long Sutton, Somerset, entry 437
The Lickfold Inn Lickfold, Sussex, entry 480
The Fox Goes Free Charlton, Sussex, entry 490
The Griffin Inn Fletching, Sussex, entry 495
The Star Inn Old Heathfield, Sussex, entry 508
The Howard Arms Ilmington, Warwickshire, entry 514
The Vine Tree Norton, Wiltshire, entry 527
The Lamb on the Strand Semington, Wiltshire, entry 536

Photo Hundred House Hotel, entry 422

Quick reference indices

Wheelchair friendly pubs
Wheelchair access to both pub and wcs.

Quick reference indices

Wales

Live music

England

Open all Day

England

Quick reference indices

Our offices

Beautiful as they were, our old offices leaked heat, used electricity to heat water and space, flooded whole rooms with light to illuminate one person, and were not ours to alter. We failed our eco-audit in spite of using recycled cooking oil in one car and gas in another, recycling everything we could and gently promoting 'greenery' in our travel books. (Our Fragile Earth series takes a harder line.)

After two eco-audits we leaped at the chance to buy some old barns closer to Bristol, to create our own eco-offices and start again. Our accountants thought we were mad and there was no time for proper budgeting. The back of every envelope bore the signs of frenzied calculations, and then I shook hands and went off on holiday.
Two years later we moved in.

As I write, swallows are nesting in our wood-pellet store, the fountain plays in the pond, the grasses bend before a gentle breeze and the solar panels heat water too hot to touch. We have, to our delight, created an inspiring and serene place.

The roof was lifted to allow us to fix thick insulation panels beneath the tiles. More panels were fitted between the rafters and as a separate wall inside the old ones, and laid under the underfloor heating pipes. We are insulated for the Arctic, and almost totally air-tight. Ventilation is natural, and we open windows. An Austrian boiler sucks wood-pellets in from an outside store and slowly consumes them, cleanly and – of course – without using any fossil fuels. Rainwater is channelled to a 6,000-litre underground tank, filtered, and then flushes loos and fills basins. Sunpipes funnel the daylight into dark corners and double-glazed Velux windows, most facing north, pour it into every office.

Photos above Quentin Craven

We built a small green oak barn between two old barns, and this has become the heart of the offices, warm, light and beautiful. Wood plays a major role: our simple oak desks were made by a local carpenter, my office floor is of oak, and there is oak panelling. Even the carpet tiles tell a story; they are made from the wool of Herdwick sheep from the Lake District.

Our electricity consumption is extraordinarily low. We set out not to flood the buildings with light, but to provide attractive, low background lighting and individual 'task' lights to be used only as needed. Materials, too, have been a focus: we used non-toxic paints and finishes.

Events blew our budgets apart, but we have a building of which we are proud and which has helped us win two national awards this year. Architects and designers are fascinated and we are all working with a renewed commitment. Best of all, we are now in a better position to encourage our owners and readers to take 'sustainability' more seriously.

I end by answering an important question: our office carbon emissions will be reduced by about 75%. We await our bills, but they will be low and, as time goes by, relatively lower – and lower. It has been worth every penny and every ounce of effort.

Alastair Sawday

Photo above Paul Groom
Photo below Tom Germain

www.special-escapes.co.uk
Self-catering from Alastair Sawday's

Cosy cottages • Sumptuous castles • City apartments
• Hilltop bothies • Tipis and more

A whole week self-catering in Britain with your friends or family is precious, and you dare not get it wrong. To whom do you turn for advice and who on earth do you trust when the web is awash with advice from strangers? We launched Special Escapes to satisfy an obvious need for impartial and trustworthy help – and that is what it provides. The criteria for inclusion are the same as for our books: we have to like the place and the owners. It has, quite simply, to be 'special'. The site, our first online-only publication, is featured on www.thegoodwebguide.com and is growing fast.

www.special-escapes.co.uk

Where on the web?

The World Wide Web is big – very big. So big, in fact, that it can be a fruitless search if you don't know where to find reliable, trustworthy, up-to-date information about fantastic places to stay in Europe, India, Morocco and beyond....

Fortunately, there's www.specialplacestostay.com, where you can dip into all of our guides, find special offers from owners, catch up on news about the series and tell us about the special places you've been to.

www.specialplacestostay.com

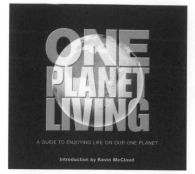

One Planet Living
Edition 1, £4.99
By Pooran Desai and Paul King

A practical guide providing us with easy, affordable and attractive alternatives for achieving a higher quality of life while using our fair share of the planet's capacity.

The Little Food Book
Edition 1, £6.99
By Craig Sams,
Chairman of the Soil Association

An explosive account of the food we eat today. Never have we been at such risk – from our food. This book will help clarify what's at stake.

The Little Money Book
Edition 1, £6.99
By David Boyle, an associate of the New Economics Foundation

This pithy, wry little guide will tell you where money comes from, what it means, what it's doing to the planet and what we might be able to do about it.

www.fragile-earth.com

Order form

All these books are available in major bookshops or you may order them direct.
Post and packaging are FREE within the UK.

British Hotels, Inns & Other Places	£14.99
British Bed & Breakfast	£14.99
British Bed & Breakfast for Garden Lovers	£14.99
Croatia	£11.99
French Bed & Breakfast	£15.99
French Holiday Homes	£12.99
French Hotels, Châteaux & Other Places	£14.99
Greece	£11.99
Green Places to Stay	£13.99
India	£11.99
Ireland	£12.99
Italy	£14.99
London	£9.99
Morocco	£11.99
Mountains of Europe	£9.99
Paris Hotels	£10.99
Portugal	£11.99
Pubs & Inns of England & Wales	£14.99
Spain	£14.99
Turkey	£11.99
One Planet Living	£4.99
The Little Food Book	£6.99
The Little Money Book	£6.99
Six Days	£12.99

Please make cheques payable to Alastair Sawday Publishing   Total £

Please send cheques to: Alastair Sawday Publishing, The Old Farmyard, Yanley
Lane, Long Ashton, Bristol BS41 9LR. For credit card orders call 01275 395431
or order directly from our web site www.specialplacestostay.com

Title   First name   Surname

Address

Postcode   Tel

PUB4

If you do not wish to receive mail from other like-minded companies, please tick here ☐
If you would prefer not to receive information about special offers on our books, please tick here ☐

Report form

If you have any comments on entries in this guide, please let us have them. If you have a favourite pub, hotel, inn, B&B or other new discovery, please let us know about it. You can return this form, email info@sawdays.co.uk, or visit www.specialplacestostay.com and click on 'contact'.

Existing entry

Property name: ____________________

Entry number: ____________ Date of visit: ___ / ___ / ___

New recommendation

Property name: ____________________

Address: ____________________

____

Tel: ____________________

Your comments

What did you like (or dislike) about this place? Were the people friendly? What was the location like? What sort of food did they serve?

____

____

____

____

____

____

____

____

Your details

Name: ____________________

Address: ____________________

Postcode: ____________ Tel: ____________

PUB4

Please send completed form to ASP, The Old Farmyard, Yanley Lane, Long Ashton, Bristol BS41 9LR

Photo The Pot Kiln, entry 14

Index by place name

Lancashire

The Church Inn
Uppermill

Next to the church on the way to the moors -- it's not easy to find. Julian Taylor brews their own Saddleworth beers and is involved in everything. At the top end of the long curved bar are a grand fire and some window tables; at the other end, a big log burner in an old fireplace, with a heavily framed mirror above. Seating is a mix of padded benches, settles, chairs and a pew named Hobson's Choice. There's a fine atmosphere: lofty beams, leaded windows, lamps on sills, nightlights on tables, brass plates, Staffordshire jugs, fresh flowers. The soft background music is entirely bearable. In the dining room with valley views the food is honest, unpretentious and good value; so are the beers. The inn is home to the world-famous Saddleworth Morris Men and several events take place here including the Rush Cart Festival on the August bank holiday weekend. A friendly place loved by all ages.

directions	Saddleworth signed from Oldham. From Uppermill go up New St for 1 mile. Pub on left, next to church.
meals	12pm-2.30pm; 5:30pm-9pm.12pm-9pm Sun. Main courses £5.95-£11.75.
closed	Open all day.

	Julian & Christine Taylor
	The Church Inn,
	Church Lane,
	Uppermill,
	Saddleworth OL3 6LW
tel	01457 820902

map: 12 entry: 277

1 Leicestershire   Pub with rooms

The Queen's Head
Belton

2 Take a village pub by the scruff of its neck and renovate it from top to toe. The result: a cool, relaxed drinkers' bar, all leather sofas and low-slung tables, a bistro with an open fire and dining room of wood, suede and leather. Add bedrooms that have a similarly stylish feel and you have a well-nigh perfect coaching inn. The Weldons deserve applause for not losing sight of tradition: the Queen's Head serves its own beer from the local Wicked Hathern brewery, plus outstanding wines. Printed menus and blackboard dishes point to diverse ideas, from burgers and relish in the bar to roasted scallops with langoustine risotto, beef fillet with morel mushroom sauce, and a good value set menu in the restaurant. Watch out for the summer Real Ale and Gourmet Barbecue weekend, and the Champagne and Lobster night. Great staff, too.

directions	In Belton, just off B5234, 6 miles west of Loughborough.	3
meals	12pm-2.30pm (4pm Sun); 7pm-9.30pm (10pm Fri & Sat). Main courses £13.50-£19.50; bar meals £4-£9.50; set menu £12-£16; Sunday lunch £13 & £16.	4
rooms	6: 4 doubles, 2 twins £70-£100. Singles £65.	5
closed	3pm-7pm; Sun from 5pm.	6

See pp 30-57 for full list of pubs with rooms

7

	Henry & Ali Weldon
	The Queen's Head,
	2 Long Street,
	Belton LE12 9TP
tel	01530 222359
web	www.thequeenshead.org

8

9

map: 8 entry: 278